Native Bush, Rainbow Springs, Rotorua

This edition of "Charming Places to Stay"
is dedicated to the marvelous hosts in
New Zealand who consistently
provide exceptional
hospitality.

For all enquiries please contact Uli or Brian at Travelwise Ltd
Ph 0064-3-476 1515.   Fax 0064-3-4761514
email: office@travelwise.co.nz
www.travelwise.co.nz

CHARMING
Places to Stay
in New Zealand

year 2008 *edition*

Another Travelwise Publication

Waterfront, Russell, Northland.

CHARMING
Places to Stay
in New Zealand

A dazzling selection of New Zealand's
finest travel accommodation.

❖ Boutique Accommodation ❖ Lodges ❖ Bed & Breakfasts
❖ Romantic Cottages ❖ Small Hotels ❖ Farmstays
❖ Seaside Escapes ❖ City Apartments ❖ Inns
❖ Homestays ❖ Guest Houses
- and much more.

ISBN 0-978-0-9582094-8-9

Published by Travelwise Ltd.,
PO Box 6226, Dunedin, New Zealand.
Production and design by Travelwise Ltd.

Printed by Printlink, Wellington, New Zealand.

Distributed by Nationwide Distributors, Christchurch.
Front Cover Photo: Photography, **Bill Nichol**.
Support photos by Brian Miller – www.phototrips.info
Furnished by '**McKenzie & Willis**' Dunedin. www.mckenzie-willis.co.nz
Accessories provided by the following Dunedin businesses:
Acquisitions, **Arthur Barnett Department Store** and with
special thanks to Judith and Sandra at '**Elizabeth Russell House**'.

Table of Contents

Introduction 9
Accommodation Categories 12

How to use this guide – "at a glance" 14
How to use this guide – guestroom details 15

General information 16
Practical travel information: Post Services 17
Practical travel information: Banking 18
Practical travel information: Telephones 19
Practical travel information: On the Road 20
Natural New Zealand 21

Map of North Island Accommodation 23
North Island Accommodation Listings 24

Map of South Island Accommodation 268
South Island Accommodation Listings 269

Introduction to translated sections 545
German language section 546
Japanese language section 552
Mandarin (Chinese) language section 558

Credits 564
Accommodation Index 565
Location Index 577

CHARMING
Places to Stay
in New Zealand

"Charming Places to Stay" presents a fabulous choice of travel accommodation. The quality, style and range of showcased properties is outstanding. As the discerning traveller knows, fine accommodation is more than fine property. Above all, the key ingredient for a truly enjoyable stay is hospitality, and this is provided by the hosts. When compiling this guide  book, where possible, we placed as much importance on the character and personality of the hosts as on the properties. Hosts are as varied as their properties – you will encounter those who simply love meeting people and sharing good times while others have taken their style of hospitality to great entrepreneurial heights. Using "Charming Places to Stay" gives you the opportunity to experience the real New Zealand – its people. You may enjoy the company of artists, high country sheep farmers, retired professionals, orchardists, musicians, vintners or writers. While styles of accommodation and hosts vary widely, they all reflect the genuine warmth and friendly hospitality that New Zealanders are known for. Wherever you stay, you will be a welcome guest and your stay a pleasant and memorable one. Enjoy the world's finest hospitality.

"Experience the real New Zealand – its People"

Enjoy unique 'Charming' places to stay.

WHAT TO EXPECT

Travel accommodation in New Zealand has a fine reputation for its standard of services. Guests can expect cleanliness, comfortable beds, a good substantial breakfast and warm, generous hospitality. In addition, your hosts can provide you with first-hand in-depth information about their area. They take pleasure in helping you with your pursuits and travel plans. Their invaluable knowledge can enrich your stay immensely.

WHAT IS EXPECTED
OF YOU

Your hosts will do everything in their power to make your stay an enjoyable and memorable one. However, it is important to remember that in most cases you are a guest in a private home. So please consider the little things, like arranging to have a house-key if returning late at night, or asking about the tariffs for toll calls prior to using the telephone. Please let your hosts know in time if you will be late. Thoughtfulness on your part will contribute to a satisfying experience for both host and guest.

WHAT TO DO – HINTS

You will avoid any disappointment by booking ahead, especially during the high summer season. It is also advisable to call your hosts one day in advance to confirm your booking and let them know about your expected time of arrival. Some hosts offer a complimentary pick-up service from coach, plane or train if guests don't have their own transport. Please give your hosts one day's notice if you would like to have an evening meal.

Most holiday memories are mere snapshots – images we treasure, but that fade with any passing year. But the people we meet – they become a part of us. They live in us. They travel with us.

PAM BROWN, b 1928

Boutique Accommodation

Within the world of travel accommodation Boutique Accommodation has been adopted by those hosts whose unique property features reflect a special ambience – period elegance, grace and charm, romance, art, etc. These features are usually enhanced by the hosts' flair for entertainment and hospitality.

Countrystay

Countrystays are often like Homestays. They offer accommodation in a private home. Being in a rural setting, they are associated with all the features and attractions of the countryside. Many Countrystays are close to popular country attractions which offer you the chance to experience rural New Zealand life.

Luxury Accommodation

Luxury Accommodation symbolizes superb facilities, excellent food and an exceptional level of service. Many properties within this category have spectacular settings and offer various additional top class attractions. They represent outstanding accommodation and hospitality.

Guesthouse/Inn

Guest Houses and Inns are usually larger establishments that cater for more guests, but still offer that personalised style of hospitality. They might have several lounge areas and a breakfast room. Guest Houses do not usually offer an evening meal.

Bed & Breakfast

Bed & Breakfast is the umbrella term for the variety of hosted accommodations that include a comfortable bed for the night and a substantial breakfast in the morning. The hosts offer warm and generous hospitality throughout your stay.

Homestay

Homestay is the popular style of accommodation that offers warm and friendly hospitality in a private home. The hosts love meeting people, they enjoy providing their guests with that "home away from home" feeling, knowing that they arrive as strangers but will leave as friends.

Self-contained Accommodation

Self-contained accommodation usually includes a separate entrance, own bathroom. Kitchen and laundry facilities may be included. It can be a self-contained part of the family home or a separate cottage. If breakfast is provided it is either served in the hosts' home, delivered to the doorstep or breakfast provisions provided on the premises.

Farmstay

Farmstays are an ideal way to experience real farm life in New Zealand. An opportunity for you to have hands-on contact with the animals and daily life on a farm. A farm tour may be included. Breakfast is usually taken with the family. Many Farmstays offer lunch and evening meals, as restaurants are often not close by.

How to use this guide – "at a glance"

"at a glance"
Easy Contact Panel
Your hosts: who they are, where they are, and how to make quick contact.

"at a glance"
Tariff Panel
*Each tariff indicates the nightly rate. **Double** indicates the cost for two people sharing one room. **Single** indicates the cost for one person occupying a room. A deposit may be required when booking. Tariffs include breakfast unless otherwise stated. **All prices quoted are in NZ$ – GST inclusive.** Please confirm details with your host.*

"at a glance"
Category Symbols
These quick-to-spot symbols are designed to make selecting your preferred accommodation easy. Particularly helpful for travellers with a limited knowledge of the English language.

"at a glance"
Category Panel
Your hosts' personal description of their category.

"at a glance"
Features & Attractions
Highlighting the main features and attractions in and around this accommodation and locality.

"at a glance"
Location Map
Your hosts' property is indicated by a red dot. Property name is displayed in white box. Maps may be accompanied by a direction panel outlining easy directions.

Clear Address Details
Clear address panel displays essential information, including property address, telephone and fax numbers, e-mail and web site.
***NOTE:** When calling from overseas dial New Zealand's international code, 0064, then drop the 0 off the area code (03), for example "Heriot House" 0064-3-477-7228.*

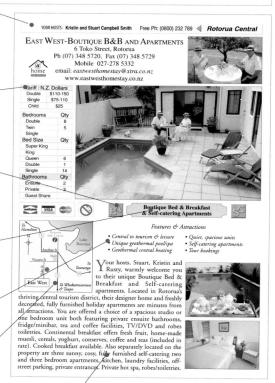

YOUR HOSTS: **Kristin and Stuart Campbell Smith** Free Ph: (0800) 232 789 ◀ **Rotorua Central**

EAST WEST-BOUTIQUE B&B AND APARTMENTS
6 Toko Street, Rotorua
Ph (07) 348 5720, Fax (07) 348 5729
Mobile 027-278 5332
email: eastwesthomestay@xtra.co.nz
www.eastwesthomestay.co.nz

Tariff : N.Z. Dollars	
Double	$110-150
Single	$75-110
Child	$25

Bedrooms	Qty
Double	8
Twin	5
Single	

Bed Size	Qty
Super King	
King	
Queen	6
Double	1
Single	14

Bathrooms	Qty
Ensuite	2
Private	3
Guest Share	

Boutique Bed & Breakfast & Self-catering Apartments

Features & Attractions
- Central to tourism & leisure
- Unique geothermal pool/spa
- Geothermal central heating
- Quiet, spacious units
- Self-catering apartments
- Tour bookings

Your hosts, Stuart, Kristin and Rusty, warmly welcome you to their unique Boutique Bed & Breakfast and Self-catering apartments. Located in Rotorua's thriving central tourism district, their designer home and freshly decorated, fully furnished holiday apartments are minutes from all attractions. You are offered a choice of a spacious studio or one bedroom unit both featuring private ensuite bathrooms, fridge/minibar, tea and coffee facilities, TV/DVD and robes toiletries. Continental breakfast offers fresh fruit, home-made muesli, cereals, yoghurt, conserves, coffee and teas (included in rate). Cooked breakfast available. Also separately located on the property are three sunny, cosy, fully furnished self-catering two and three bedroom apartments, kitchen, laundry facilities, off-street parking, private entrance. Private hot spa, robes/toiletries.

"A Personal Warm Welcome"
These words of welcome have been written personally by your hosts. They describe the features of the accommodation and portray their personality and lifestyle.

No Smoking

Abbreviations
- ♡ SH – State Highway
- h.p. – half price
- n/a – not applicable
- neg – negotiable
- Qty – Quantity
- Tce – Terrace

Book direct – Reduce costs
By booking direct with your accommodation host in New Zealand, you make the personal connection right from the start and avoid many additional costs.

www.charming-places-to-stay.co.nz

How to use this guide – Guest room details

Bedrooms

Double = Room with bed for two people
Twin = Room with two beds for two people
Single = Room with bed for one person

Bathrooms

Ensuite = Bathroom adjoining bedroom
Private = Separate bathroom for your use only
Guest Share/Family Share =Bathroom shared with other guests or host family

Bedrooms	Qty
Double	
Twin	
Single	
Bed Size	**Qty**
King	
Queen	
Double	
King/Single	
Bathrooms	**Qty**
Ensuite	
Private	
Guest Share	

Bed Size
Super King *180 x 200cm*
King *165 x 200cm*
Queen *150 x 200cm*
Double *135 x 190cm*
Single *90 x 190cm*
King Single *90 x 200cm*

How to use this guide – Category Symbols

 Bed & Breakfast

 Boutique Accommodation

 Countrystay

 Farmstay

 Guest House / Lodge / Inn

 Homestay

 Luxury Accommodation

 Self-contained Accom. & Cottages

How to use this guide – Credit Cards Accepted by Hosts

 Amex – American Express

 Japanese Credit Card

 VISA

 Diners

 Bankcard

 MasterCard

 Maestro

 Eftpos

How to use this guide – Hosts' Associations & Affiliations

 Kiwihost

 Qualmark NZ

 @home New Zealand.

 Historic Places Trust

@home New Zealand, **the Association of Farm & Home Hosts** in New Zealand, assures you of a warm welcome in a private home. Guests are treated as friends of the family and given personal care and time by the hosts. Members' homes are inspected on a regular basis.

Dairies & Supermarkets

Dairies, a long-established feature of the New Zealand landscape, are usually open 7 days a week, from early to late. Like the old general country stores, dairies stock a wide variety of goods. You can normally expect to obtain basic foods and commodities, such as bread, milk, newspapers, confectionery and grocery items.

Because of the extended trading hours, and the benefits of convenient locations, prices are normally slightly higher than those at the supermarket. Some dairies, especially in small communities, also offer Post Shop services.

Supermarkets

Nearly all New Zealand towns and cities have supermarkets.

Supermarkets provide a wider range of goods for one-stop grocery shopping, and have more competitive prices.

Free parking is normally provided, but only for genuine customers - you may be asked to show your receipt. Some supermarkets now have extended trading hours, and most are open 7 days a week.

The Corner Dairy – so much a part of New Zealand's daily life.

Petrol Stations

Also known as 'Service Stations', provide basic commodities for motor vehicles: fuel, oil, air, water, and general motoring accessories. Although petrol stations do not normally provide repair or maintenance services - these are provided by 'Garages' - those that do may have a sign saying 'Mechanic on duty' or 'Repairs carried out'.

Tourist Radio

Tourist Information FM is a service established to provide information to visitors to New Zealand 24 hours a day, and is available in most tourist areas. For English-language broadcasts, tune to 88.2 FM on your radio. For German-language broadcasts, tune to 100.4 FM, and for Japanese-language broadcasts, tune to 100.8 FM on your radio.

Visitor Information Network

Visitor Information Centres are identified by the distinctive green italic *i* logo in conjunction with the Visitor Information logo.

Over 80 of them are located throughout New Zealand. They offer a wide range of services. including travel bookings, tours and accommodation.

The staff, who have unparalleled local and national knowledge are trained and committed to providing accurate and appropriate information to visitors.

Emergency Services

If you require the police, ambulance or fire service, dial 111.
There is no charge for making a 111 call from a public phone box.

Posting a Letter

New Zealand's main postal operator is New Zealand Post with a network of 1000 Post Shops and Post Centres covering the whole country, and 5,000 post boxes where you can post letters. Some outlets combine their normal retail activities with providing New Zealand Post services, especially in smaller towns. Look for the red New Zealand Post logo displayed outside shops.

New Zealand Post Shop

Post Shops

Post Shops offer a wide range of products and services including:

- stamps
- protective packaging
- sending letters and parcels
- sending faxes and telegrams, couriering items overseas or around New Zealand
- stationery, greeting cards, phone cards, gifts (e.g. calendars) and more

Post Shop staff can help you decide which type of packaging will get your parcels delivered as cheaply as possible. A handy Parcel Packaging Guide is also available which contains advice on ways to ensure your parcel arrives safely. Post Shops accept cash, cheque, EFTPOS, MasterCard and VISA for most products and services.

If you need help and cannot get to a Post Shop, you can call New Zealand Post freephone 0800 NZPOST (0800 697 678), 8am to 7pm weekdays, or 9am to 1pm Saturdays.

Postal Costs

For Sending letters and packages within New Zealand.
A standard size letter (maximum 129mm x 235mm) costs 50 cents and takes 2-4 days to be delivered. If you want to get it there faster, FastPost costs $1.00 for a standard size letter which is then delivered by the next working day between major towns and cities. (Rural and remote areas may take a little longer.) You can send parcels from $3.80, depending on size and weight. Items can also be couriered from a Post Shop.

Packages for Japan

For sending packages to Japan, there is a special Kiwi Yu Pack for items up to 5kg, and for delivery within 2-4 working days.

For sending letters and packages overseas. You can ask at the local Post Shop about the best way to package and send items overseas. Options include first class air mail, sea post, registered post and courier. By paying an additional $8 and sending your parcel as a customs parcel, New Zealand Post extends cover for loss or damage from NZ$250 to $1,500.

The rural mailbox, a roadside feature throughout New Zealand's countryside.

Money and Banks

Currency

New Zealand has been operating on the decimal currency system with the NZ Dollar as its base since 10 July 1967. Coins in use are: 10c, 20c, 50c, $1 and $2. Bank notes are available in denominations of $5, $10, $20, $50 and $100.

**Automatic Teller Machine
24 hour access.**

Banks

All trading banks are open for business between the hours of 9:30am and 4:30pm. Monday to Friday inclusive, with the exception of public holidays. Automatic Teller Machines (ATMs), operate on a card and pin number system. Cash can be withdrawn 24 hours a day.

Changing Money

Money exchange facilities exist at all banks and at most New Zealand international airports. New Zealand banks buy and sell all major currencies and offer competitive exchange rates which are updated daily.

Travellers' Cheques

Travellers' cheques can also be cashed at Bureaux de Change and hotels or large stores in resorts and larger cities.
Import or export of foreign currency is not subject to any restrictions.
All banks are listed in the Yellow Pages at the back of the local telephone directory.

Credit cards

Payment by any of the international credit cards, including Visa, Master Card, American Express, Diners Club and JCB (Japanese credit card) is widely accepted. Most shops display the card signs in their windows. If in doubt, please check with a sales person before you commence shopping.

EFTPOS (Electronic Transfer of Funds at Point of Sale) is a highly used way of cash payments , which is being used all over New Zealand.
You will find operating EFTPOS machines in shops, museums, supermarkets, petrol stations, to name only a few. Instead of a cash payment, the cash amount is transferred directly from the customer's into the selling company's bank account. The transaction takes place at the counter or check out, where customers swipe their EFTPOS card through the machine and type in their pin number. This convenient way of cash payment can be very handy in remote places or after hours. Many stores with EFTPOS facilities also allow you to withdraw cash when making purchases.

Using the Telephone

The phone system in New Zealand is of a high technical standard and performs efficiently. There are two main service providers, **Telecom** and **Clear.** You will find public telephones throughout the entire country. The majority of public telephones in NZ operate the pre-paid phone card system. Telecom **PhoneCards** are available in NZ$5, NZ$10, NZ$20 and NZ$50 denominations. These can be purchased from many outlets including **NZ Post Shops,** supermarkets, dairies, newsagents, **Visi-** tor Information Centres and petrol stations. You may find it helpful to purchase a **PhoneCard** even if it is only for emergencies. Increasing numbers of credit card operated phones are now being established which accept major international credit cards. Some public telephones are still coin operated, using 10c, 20c, 50c, NZ$1 and NZ$2 coins. When dialling **Freephone** numbers (commencing with 0800) from public phones you will not require any cards or coins.

Typical public phone booths. Coloured for easy recognition, Yellow for Credit card, Green for PhoneCard, and Blue for Coin.

1 Lift handset, do not insert coins.

2 Dial the number you require. The price per minute or part minute will show on screen.

3 Insert coins. Usable coins:10c, 20c, 50c, NZ$1, and NZ$2.

4 Once call is finished replace handset.

5 Unused coins returned, partly used coins not returned.

Telecom PhoneCards available : NZ$5, NZ$10, NZ$20, and NZ$50. They can be easily obtained at many outlets such as Dairies, Post Offices, and Petrol Stations.

Using the PhoneCard
1. Lift handset. 2. Insert Card. 3. Dial number.
4. After call, replace handset. 5. Remove card (Don't forget!)

Coins acepted by Coin Phones:– 10c, 20c, 50c, NZ$1 and NZ$2.

e-Phone Maxi-Save Toll Card

The *e*-**Phone Toll Card** is an easy and convenient way to use almost any touch tone phone at your own expense. It can be used from a private phone, card phone, credit card phone, cellphone, **Your Yost's Phone,** etc.
Using these prepaid phone cards will make you and your host feel less apprehensive when you use their phone. *e*-**Phone Toll Cards** can be purchased in many dairies, super markets and shopping malls.
For detailed information, just call Free Phone 0800-437 4663.

EMERGENCY CALLS......111
Police, Fire, Ambulance
Useful Telephone Numbers

Operator 010
International Operator 0170
National Enquiries 018
International Enquiries 0172
International Access Code ... 00
Australia dialling code 0061
Germany dialling code 0049
Japan dialling code 008
USA dialling code 001

"Driving in New Zealand can be a pleasure,
the ever changing scenery is superb."

On the Road

Driving in New Zealand is a pleasure; the scenery is superb, the roads are generally of a high standard and New Zealanders are helpful and courteous.

However, for your safety and that of other motorists, we urge you to take a little time (New Zealand is patient, it will wait for you) and read the following before you begin driving.

The *New Zealand Road Code* is the definitive guide to correct and lawful driving in New Zealand. It is available at a small cost from the Land Transport Safety Authority. Look in the local telephone directory for the nearest office. A useful leaflet, with English, German and Japanese sections, is *Driving Safely in New Zealand*, also available free of charge from the Land Transport Safety Authority.

Driving: Some Basic Points

Keep Left: In New Zealand we drive on the **left**.
Overseas vistors may find this difficult. – We suggest you take time to adjust and plan your journeys accordingly.

Speed Limit: In general, the maximum speed limit on the open road or motorway / freeway, identifiable by this sign, is 100 kilometres per hour.

In cities and towns, it is 50km per hour. There are exceptions, so watch out for signs (positioned on the left of the road) which may indicate a lower specified speed limit.

Road Signs at Intersections:

Stop: Stop completely, then give way to all traffic.

Give way - Drive slowly. Stop if drivers are approaching from left or right, and give way to all traffic, including those opposite if you are turning left.

Seatbelts: The driver and all passengers (adults and children) - including those sitting in rear seats - must use seatbelts or approved child restraints.

The **New Zealand Automobile Association** (*AA*) offers an excellent service nationwide providing maps, guides and touring information. Freephone 0800 500 444 at any time.

"The magnificent contrasts and colourful variety are absolutely breath-taking."

New Zealand's landscapes are as colourful and diverse as its people. No other country can offer such variety of magnificent scenery in such a comparatively small area. In both islands evergreen native bush abounds. In the North Island there are also exotic forests of huge Kauri trees. A wonderland of hot springs, geysers and boiling mud pools is situated near Rotorua in the centre of the North Island. Therapeutic hot springs are located in parts of both islands, and spectacularly beautiful National Parks with their unspoiled scenery and nature will delight the traveller. The South Island offers scenery on the grand scale: mountains, glaciers, lakes and sweeping coastal beaches. Deep-water fiords slice into the south-west coast, with virgin mountain country in the background. One of the most famous fiords - Milford Sound - is accessible by road as well as by the famed Milford Track, the "most beautiful walk in the world". New Zealand has an abundance of aquatic scenery. Take your pick of spectacular waterfalls, raging torrents, broad rivers, lakes big and small, surfing beaches and rocky coast lines.

South Island West Coast - Native bush.

Waitangi Golf Course - *one of the many superb golf courses you will find in New Zealand.*

Most New Zealanders love sport and the outdoors. Their country's natural features support an abundance of outdoor activities: yachting, golf, rugby and mountaineering, to name only a few. All types of winter sports are practised in both islands and wild game and fish provide excellent hunting and fishing.

Tane Mahuta, Waipoua Forest, Northland.

North Island

24

25 - 28
26 - 29
62
Kaitaia
Kerikeri
Paihia & Russell

Whangarei

69 - 70
Dargaville

74
75 - 78
86 - 88

AUCKLAND
80 - 116

Whitianga
Thames

139 - 140

141 - 144
148 - 149
145 - 147
HAMILTON
Tauranga
Cambridge
Whakatane
Rotorua

184 - 198
199 - 203

Taupo

Taumarunui
207 - 212
213 - 215
212
204
New Plymouth
Turangi
Stratford

216 - 217
Wanganui
Taihape

234 - 236
237
238

Palmerston North
Levin

Waikanae
Masterton

WELLINGTON

30
31 - 38
39 - 61

63 - 68

71 - 73

79

121 - 123
124 - 134
121
134 - 136
117 - 120
137 - 138
150 - 154
153 - 158

158 - 159
160 - 161
204
162 - 183

205 - 206

217

Napier
Hastings
218 - 230
229 - 231
232 - 233

Dannevirke

239 - 240

Gisborne

240 - 245

246 - 248
248 - 266

HOUHORA LODGE & HOMESTAY

3994 Far North Road, RD 4, Kaitaia
Ph (09) 409 7884, Fax (09) 409 7801, Mobile 021-926 992
email: *houhora.homestay@xtra.co.nz*
www.topstay.co.nz

Tariff : N.Z. Dollars	
Double	$130-180
Single	$100-110
Child	$25

Bedrooms	Qty
Double	3
Twin	
Single	
Bed Size	**Qty**
Super King	
King	3
Queen	
Double	
Single	6
Bathrooms	**Qty**
Ensuite	2
Private	1
Guest Share	

**Your Northern Hideaway
A Fantastic Location**

Features & Attractions

- *Geographical isolation*
- *Non commercial*
- *Shell collecting*
- *Dig shellfish for dinner*
- *Spectacular, pristine beaches*
- *Organic garden and eggs*
- *Coastal wilderness hiking*
- *Internet, fax, laundry*

We who live on the slim finger of land at the top of New Zealand welcome you, and look forward to sharing its beauty and secret places with you. This is a small part of New Zealand which is different. Come share our home and the 'good life', home grown vegetables, olive oil, pure water, fresh air, eggs and fruit. Our architect designed home is set in 3½ acres. The beautiful airy pavilion opens to the east and west to fine views and amazing sunrises and sunsets with original New Zealand art adorning the walls. We are delighted to provide advice and assistance for your Far North excursions: 4x4 sightseeing, fishing, walks, trips to famous tourist spots and trips to places that few people visit or even know about (by prior arrangement). A complimentary 4x4 trip to view Ninety Mile Beach is offered. Dinner if requested. (All rooms are either double or twin)

PLANE TREE LODGE

Pamapuria, RD 2, Kaitaia
Ph (09) 408 0995, Fax (09) 408 0959
Mobile 027-433 8859
email: *reservationsplanetreelodge@xtra.co.nz*
www.plane-tree-lodge.net.nz

Tariff : N.Z. Dollars	
Double	$135-175
Single	$100-135
Cottage	$180-220

Bedrooms	Qty
Double	5
Twin	2
Single	1

Bed Size	Qty
Super King	
King	
Queen	5
King Single	2
Single	3

Bathrooms	Qty
Ensuite	3
Private	2
Guest Share	

**Great hospitality
Amazing breakfasts**

DIRECTIONS: Heading north on SH 1, through the Mangamuka Gorge, continue on SH 1 for 7.5 km. Our sign is on the left. Heading south from Kaitaia on SH 1, go past Pamapuria School. Our home is 300m on the right.

Features & Attractions

- *Cape Reinga and 90 Mile Beach*
- *Tranquil park-like gardens*
- *Peaceful, rural views from all rooms*
- *Great base to explore Far North*

- *Fishing, golf, surfing*
- *Top class restaurants*
- *Kauri heritage*
- *Spa pool at sunset*

Enjoy the difference of recieving great hospitality in a quiet, peaceful rural setting with large, romantic gardens. Come and enjoy the Cape Reinga experience, or try quad bikes, blokarts, horse riding or fishing on the beach. Visit the site of historic kauri gumfields and see the beautiful furniture and gifts crafted from ancient swamp kauri - wood buried for over 30,000 years. We are 7 minutes drive from Kaitaia, and just 20 minutes from famous 90 Mile Beach. After your days adventure, enjoy the sunset with a complimentary wine in the spa pool and wake each morning to the aroma of a delicious breakfast (our menu changes daily). At the lodge we have 3 ensuite bedrooms and a comfortable guest lounge. **Lodge Cottage** our adjoining 2 bedroom self-contained cottage is ideal for small groups. **Victoria Cottage** is a 3 bedroom house in its own private half-acre garden and is perfect for larger groups and longer stays (minimum stay: 2 nights). It would be our pleasure to help plan and book events and outings of your choice. "Hospitality of the highest kind".

BEACHFRONT

14 Kotare St, PO Box 174, Ahipara,
Ninety Mile Beach
Ph (09) 409 4007, Fax (09) 409 4007
email: *pauljenny@beachfront.net.nz*
www.beachfront.net.nz

Tariff : N.Z. Dollars	
Double	$150-300
Single	$150-300
Child	

Bedrooms	Qty
Double	4
Twin	
Single	

Bed Size	Qty
Super King	4
King	
Queen	
Double	
Single	

Bathrooms	Qty
Ensuite	4
Private	
Guest Share	

 **Upmarket Serviced Apartments
with stunning views**

Features & Attractions

- *Surf views from every pillow*
- *All bedrooms with ensuite*
- *Maximum of two client groups*
- *Privacy & separate entrances*
- *Absolute waters edge*
- *Sky television, DVD & video*
- *Sunset Magic*
- *Full kitchens & BBQs*

DIRECTIONS:
Turn right at Ahipara School toward
golf course, take left fork before the
fire station. Kotare Street is first
on the left - drive at the sea.

Beachfront

Your 5th generation New Zealand hosts Jenny and Paul continue to receive a "buzz" from the reaction of our guests. "Thank you for sharing your bit of heaven. A most wonderful stay in a beautifully appointed suite. Stunning views. We loved every minute". From BC Canada is typical. A warm Kiwi welcome awaits. Both the studio and penthouse are completely private and sleep up to six or seven people. The studio apartment is at the same level as our adjacent home, so gets the best sea level views on Ninety Mile Beach and is seven metres from the high tide mark. From the 100 square metres of luxurious space in the penthouse apartment, the view is even more dramatic. Higher than 90% of clients say "Wow" or as one travel writer described our apartments "World class". Both are serviced daily and fully self-contained. Breakfast available - Dinner by arrangement. The Penthouse is a two bedroom apartment with balconies; Studio Apartment has covered patio with additional bedroom available.

SHIPWRECK LODGE

70 Foreshore Road, Ahipara, 90 Mile Beach
Ph (09) 409 4929, Fax (09) 409 4928
email: *shipwrecklodge@xtra.co.nz*
www.shipwrecklodge.co.nz

Tariff : N.Z. Dollars	
Double	$200-350
Single	$200-350
Cottage	

Bedrooms	Qty
Double	3
Twin	1
Single	

Bed Size	Qty
Super King	1
King	1
Queen	1
King Single	
Single	

Bathrooms	Qty
Ensuite	3
Private	
Guest Share	

Absolute Beachfront
Boutique Bed & Breakfast

Features & Attractions

- *Private balconies*
- *Sounds of the surf*
- *Relaxing retreat for adults*
- *Beautifully appointed bedrooms*
- *Beachfront*
- *All ensuites*
- *Beach walks*
- *Stunning views*

Walk in and unwind in our luxurious, contemporary, informal and spacious home. Each of three guest suites opens to a private balcony overlooking 90 Mile Beach and the Tasman Sea. The soothing sound of the waves rolling in is ever present. We have direct beach access for a short stroll or long walk. Watch stunning sunsets from your private balcony with ocean views to the horizon. We offer an informal easy atmosphere and mix "leaving you alone" with "taking care of you". The guest suites are spacious and beautifully appointed in modern furnishings. Each suite has a bi-fold door opening to a private balcony, sitting area, television, fridge and large modern ensuite. Sumptuous continental or cooked breakfasts included.

90 Mile Beach is a treasure to discover! It is a mixture of safe swimming bays, world class surf bays, wild ruggedness, huge desert sand hills, wide open spaces, and stunning coastline. Remote, untouched, vast and very beautiful.

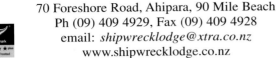

DIRECTIONS:
Take SH 1 north. From Auckland travel through Whangarei, Kawakawa to Kaitaia. As you enter the township of Kaitaia turn left at the town clock.
The road is signposted to Ahipara. Enter Ahipara and turn left just past the school. **Shipwreck Lodge** is 600m on the right.

SIESTA GUEST LODGE & APARTMENTS

Tasman Heights, PO Box 30, Ahipara, Northland
Ph/Fax (09) 409 2011, Mobile 021-260 6732
email: *ninetymile@xtra.co.nz*
www.siesta.co.nz

Tariff : N.Z. Dollars	
Double	$150-250
Single	
Child	

Bedrooms	Qty
Double	4
Twin	1
Single	
Bed Size	Qty
Super King	
King	1
Queen	3
Double	
King/Single	2
Bathrooms	Qty
Ensuite	4
Private	
Guest Share	

 **Panoramic Views and Privacy
Close to the Beach**

Features & Attractions

- *Peace, space & privacy*
- *Safe swimming*
- *Links golf course*
- *Sand-dune wilderness*
- *Cape trip from door*
- *Kauri forest close by*
- *Handy to Bay of Islands*
- *A perfect base to stay awhile*

DIRECTIONS: Take SH north
to Kaitaia, turn west to Ahipara.
Enter Ahipara and turn left just
past school. Drive 1.2 km.
Tasman Heights is 1st road up
the hill on left, just as you
reach the beach car park.

Incredible sunsets, beautiful weather year-round, a multitude of activities for young and old alike, sweeping views of Ninety Mile Beach, a wide choice of accommodation and friendly and knowledgeable hosts. This is why our guests, almost without exception, consider **Siesta Guest Lodge** a place to settle for a few days, weeks, or even months.

All the North's main attractions are within an hour's drive; including the major Kauri Forests, the Bay of Islands and Cape Reinga. If you want to be away from the tourist Mecca, this is the base for you. There are two purpose-built guest suites in the Mediterranean-style main lodge, each with panoramic views of Ninety Mile Beach. In addition, two superior self-contained apartments with dishwasher, bath, satellite TV, CD stereo, video & CD library, etc., etc. large outdoor area. Set in secluded, tropical gardens, **Siesta** is the perfect getaway spot. It is private, romantic, idyllic and popular with honeymooners, tourists and holiday-makers who love beautiful beaches, forests and the outdoors.

BEACH ABODE BEACHFRONT LODGE

11 Korora St, PO Box 134, Ahipara, 90 Mile Beach
Ph (09) 409 4070, Fax (09) 409 4070
email: *ned.susan@xtra.co.nz*
www.beachabode.co.nz

Features & Attractions

- *Remote Beachfront Setting*
- *Expansive Sea views*
- *Sounds of the Sea*
- *Brilliant Sunset*
- *Attentive Self-catering*
- *Impeccably maintained*

$	Double	$110-160
	Single	$105-155
	Child	—

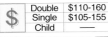

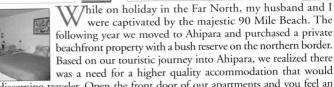

**Elegant Beachfront Retreat
South Pacific Paradise**

Bedrooms	Qty
Double	3
Twin	1
Single	
Bed Size	**Qty**
King	
Queen	3
Double	
Single	2
Bathrooms	**Qty**
Ensuite	
Private	3
Guest Share	

While on holiday in the Far North, my husband and I were captivated by the majestic 90 Mile Beach. The following year we moved to Ahipara and purchased a private beachfront property with a bush reserve on the northern border. Based on our touristic journey into Ahipara, we realized there was a need for a higher quality accommodation that would appeal to the discerning traveler. Open the front door of our apartments and you feel an immediate sense of welcome. Upon entering the apartment, the Tasman Sea draws you out to the covered deck revealing panoramic sea views and landscaped gardens. Apartments are contemporary, pristine, appointed in a warm tropical ambience. Cotton sheets, beach towels, laundry, fresh coffee, DVD, wi-fi internet. Scrumptious breakfast and dinner available with a nights notice. We hope you consider a retreat to our remote seaside village. Come by and see us. We are the house facing the sea, next door to the Korora Reserve.

TASMAN OVERLOOK

44 Tasman Heights Rd, Ahipara, Ninety Mile Beach
Ph (09) 409 2011, Fax (09) 409 2011
Mobile 021-965 085
e-mail: *carole@tasmanoverlook.co.nz*
www.tasmanoverlook.co.nz

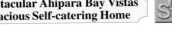

Features & Attractions

- *3 Bay bedrooms, ensuites*
- *Upscale kitchen, internet*
- *Internal garage, balcony*
- *90 Mile Beach access*
- *Sand dune rides, surfing*
- *Cape Reinga tours, golf*

$	Double
	$250-350

Bedrooms	Qty
Double	3
Twin	
Single	
Bed Size	**Qty**
King	
Queen	3
Double	
Single	
Bathrooms	**Qty**
Ensuite	3
Private	
Guest Share	

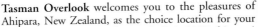

**Spectacular Ahipara Bay Vistas
Spacious Self-catering Home**

Tasman Overlook welcomes you to the pleasures of Ahipara, New Zealand, as the choice location for your self-contained accommodations. Built in 2007, this spacious home has a combined living and dining room, a master bedroom with ensuite, and a full size stainless steel kitchen on the second floor with a pair of double stackers that open to a surrounding balcony. Two additional bedrooms with ensuites are located downstairs. The arrangement of the rooms gives Ahipara Bay and the Tasman Sea visual prominence that may push adventures to the back page and make 'relaxing by the sea' the only order of the day. However, should you choose, there are many activities to serve your family's adventurous spirit. Experience a new sport or revisit a known one. Ahipara is about choices! **Tasman Overlook** allows your family to experience them from a lovely home with a spectacular view.

DIRECTIONS:
Veer left at Ahipara School, left on Tasman Heights Rd, from Foreshore, and right at the 3rd house after the Siesta sign.

29

SAILS BEACHFRONT APARTMENT

23 Kupe Road, Coopers Beach, Mangonui
Ph (09) 406 0344, Fax (09) 406 1537
email: *cliff@sails.co.nz*
www.sails.co.nz

Features & Attractions

- *Pohutukawa-fringed beach*
- *Tranquil garden setting*
- *Away from traffic noise*
- *Near Mangonui Historic Village*
- *Close to cafés & restaurants*
- *On Northland Twin-Coast-Route*

 Beachfront in Garden Setting $

Double	$90-190
Single	$90-190
Child	$10

Bedrooms	Qty
Double	1
Twin	1
Single	
Bed Size	**Qty**
King	
Queen	1
Double	
Single	2
Bathrooms	**Qty**
Ensuite	
Private	1
Guest Share	

Greetings from **Sails** in beautiful Doubtless Bay! Our beachfront apartment is perfect for your seaside holiday and also provides the peace of a sub-tropical garden. Nearby Mangonui Village and Harbour offers a range of shops and cafés as well as the famous fish shop and licensed bar built over the water.

Sailing, diving and fishing charters are available as well as the famous Cape Reinga-Ninety Mile Beach Trip.

Your hosts are the only other residents on the property, so personal assistance is available.

Sails Apartment is on its own separate level with private access to the car park. The beach has safe swimming, golden sand and, if required, shade under the Pohutukawa trees, which are a special feature of Coopers Beach. **Minimum stay 2 nights.**

A beautiful beach in Northland

114 ON WAIPAPA BED & BREAKFAST

114 Waipapa Road, RD 2, Kerikeri, Bay of Islands
Ph (09) 401 7939, Fax (09) 401 7941
Mobile 021-022 14166
e-mail: *bookings@114onwaipapa.co.nz*
www.114onwaipapa.com

Features & Attractions

- *Quality ensuite bedrooms*
- *On-site day spa/spa pool*
- *Private guest wing*
- *Close to Kerikeri airport*
- *Heritage sites, forests*
- *Wineries, cafés, galleries*

$	Double	$200-230
	Single	$120-150
	Child	

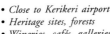
Boutique Accommodation Bed & Breakfast

Bedrooms	Qty
Double	2
Twin	
Single	1
Bed Size	**Qty**
King	
Queen	2
Double	
King/Single	1
Bathrooms	**Qty**
Ensuite	3
Private	
Guest Share	

DIRECTIONS:
From State Highway 10 turn at the round-about into Kerikeri Rd, continue through Kerikeri village, past historic Stone Store, across one-way bridge. At next round-about, turn left into Waipapa Rd. We are 1.3km on the right.

If privacy in a semi-rural Bay of Islands environment sounds like you...welcome to 114 on Waipapa. Your quality queen or king-single room – with contemporary ensuite, offers a private terrace overlooking a hectare of sweeping lawn and gardens. Your suite has the most comfortable of beds, with lovely linen. You may make refreshments in your room, watch native birdlife from your terrace, or relax in the guest sitting room with satellite television. Your delicious breakfast will feature produce from the Kerikeri Farmers Market. We respect our environment, so provide solar-heated, rain-water showers/baths. We also compost and recycle. Wishing to re-energise? Co-host Bridget is a qualified massage and beauty therapist, who welcomes you to enjoy her on-site day spa.

---

88 LODGE LUXURY BED & BREAKFAST

88 Koropewa Rd, Kerikeri, Bay of Islands, Northland
Ph (09) 407 8288, Fax (09) 407 8288
Mobile 021-0273 4693
e-mail: *stay@88lodge.co.nz*
www.88lodge.co.nz

Features & Attractions

- *Large sub-tropical gardens*
- *Tranquil luxury & privacy*
- *Swimming pool*
- *Central to Northland/B.O.I.*
- *Beach, sea, country nearby*
- *Minutes from Kerikeri*

$	Double	$180-295
	Single	$150-265
	Child	

Luxury Bed & Breakfast in Stunning Gardens

Bedrooms	Qty
Double	3
Twin	
Single	
Bed Size	**Qty**
King	2
Queen	1
Double	
Single	
Bathrooms	**Qty**
Ensuite	1
Private	1
Guest Share	1

Geoff and Chris welcome you to their homestay set in Kerikeri's beautiful countryside. Central to the Bay of Islands excursions and attractions and Northland's beautiful scenery and beaches. 6 min. to shops, restaurants and heritage sites. Botanical surprises abound in the 1.5 acres of private sub-tropical gardens with unique mature trees which surround our classical Kiwi homestead and secluded swimming pool. Refurbished to give high standards of comfort. Rooms have luxury linen and towels. Ensuite or private bathroom, TV/DVD, fridge, complimentary beverages and toiletries, hair dryer. Relax and lounge by the pool enjoying the mature park-like grounds. Memorable breakfasts created with fresh local produce. Always happy to help you plan your exploration of our surroundings.

BIRCHWOOD
11 Maraenui Drive, Kerikeri, Bay of Islands
Ph (09) 401 7961, Fax (09) 401 7962
Mobile 027-268 4848
email: *info@birchwoodbedandbreakfast.co.nz*
www.birchwoodbedandbreakfast.co.nz

VISA   MasterCard   eftpos

Features & Attractions

- *New luxurious ensuite rooms*
- *Private deck, gardens, spa pool*
- *Exclusive privacy & relaxation*
- *Walking distance to Kerikeri*
- *On art, craft and wine trails*
- *Central base for Bay of Islands*

Boutique Bed & Breakfast

Double	$150-160
Single	
Child	

Bedrooms	Qty
Double	1
Twin	1
Single	
Bed Size	Qty
King	
Queen	1
Double	
King/Single	1
Bathrooms	Qty
Ensuite	1
Private	1
Guest Share	

DIRECTIONS: From SH10 follow signs to Kerikeri. Take Kerikeri Rd for 1.3km and turn right at Maraenui Dr. **Birchwood** is 20 metres on left.

Birchwood offers the luxury of a brand new, beautifully appointed B & B in a relaxed, charming country setting. The ultimate in privacy and comfort is guaranteed with your own entrance, light and spacious ensuite bedroom with plasma screen, plunger coffee and teas, fridge and microwave, quality linen and toiletries. Open the French doors to your private, sunny deck and landscaped garden overlooking the orchards. A tranquil setting to enjoy our popular fresh breakfast, and if you can tear yourself away, a perfect base from which to explore the Bay of Islands. **Birchwood** is in walking distance to Kerikeri village and only 15 minutes drive to sandy beaches. Hosts Pamela and Ian will happily provide local knowledge and process bookings. The rooms are serviced daily and additional facilities include laundry, secure parking, beauty and massage therapy by appointment.

LANDING COTTAGE
184 Landing Road, Kerikeri
Ph (09) 401 7974
Mobile 027- 450 5850
email: *wendy@landingcottage.co.nz*
www.landingcottage.co.nz

VISA   MasterCard   eftpos

Features & Attractions

- *Single party bookings only*
- *Elegantly luxurious*
- *Artist in residence*
- *Minutes from Kerikeri village*
- *Secluded, tranquil setting*
- *Restaurants, shops, vineyards*

Bed & Breakfast Boutique Accommodation

Double	$165-225
Single	$125-155
Group(4)	$300-395

Bedrooms	Qty
Double	3
Twin	
Single	
Bed Size	Qty
King	1
Queen	2
Double	
Single	
Bathrooms	Qty
Ensuite	
Private	1
Guest Share	

DIRECTIONS: From SH10 turn into Kerikeri Rd, proceed through Kerikeri town, past the 'Stone Store' and continue along Landing Rd to Waipapa Landing.

Built 2005, **Landing Cottage** is set amongst secluded native bush and gardens yet only a hundred metres from the picturesque Waipapa Landing Boat Jetty and minutes to Kerikeri village, restaurants, vineyards, golf course, historic sites, and many other attractions. **Single-party-bookings** only guarantees privacy and relaxation in a spacious, luxurious, elegantly decorated suite for up to 4 adults with private entrance, large, private lounge, bathroom, toiletries, 3 bedrooms with quality king or queen beds, luxury linen, TV, DVD, coffee/tea making facilities and garden setting. Enjoy the resident artist's work while having a sumptuous continental or cooked breakfast chosen from the menu. (Home-made, seasonal, local, organic produce and free-range eggs are used when possible). Your hosts, Wendy and Tony, both from a professional background, will be delighted in helping you plan your exploration of the Bay of Islands and the Far North.

Matariki

14 Pa Road, Kerikeri, Bay of Islands
Ph (09) 407 7577, Fax (09) 407 7593
Mobile 027-408 0621
email: *matarikihomestay@xtra.co.nz*
www.bnbnz.com

Features & Attractions

- *Short distance to town*
- *Short walk to historic sites*
- *Handy to golfing & beaches*
- *Large garden with pool*
- *Cafés, crafts & vineyards*
- *Dinners with NZ wines*

**Homestay
Boutique Accommodation**

Double	$140-160	
Single	$100	
Child	neg	

Matariki is set in a large garden surrounded by sub tropical orchards. Just 3 km from town and an easy 15 minute walk to New Zealand's oldest buildings and church site. We have been home hosting for 17 years and have the experience and knowledge to make sure our guest's stay is informative and enjoyable. Retired sheep farmer and Kerikeri tour operator, David now has a vintage car and guests are offered a short complimentary tour. Alison, ex-nurse, now enjoys serving a three-course meal with New Zealand wines by arrangement. The bedrooms overlook the garden and are spacious and comfortable. Guests are encouraged to use all facilities. Reservations for tours can be booked by hosts. There is a lot to do in this popular area, close to northern beaches and to the top of the country. You can also just relax around the pool with clean air and birds singing. At night, when it's very quiet, a kiwi may be seen...

Bedrooms	Qty
Double	2
Twin	1
Single	
Bed Size	**Qty**
King	1
Queen	1
Double	
Single	2
Bathrooms	**Qty**
Ensuite	1
Private	1
Guest Share	

DIRECTIONS: Take turn to Kerikeri from Highway 10, turn right at roundabout onto Hobson Avenue, continue and turn left into Inlet Road. Pa Road is second on the left. Matariki is no 14.

Waitui Lodge

Yacht Drive, Opito Bay, RD 1, PO Box 256,
Kerikeri, Bay of Islands
Ph (09) 407 9033, Fax (09) 407 7176
email: *waituilodge@actrix.co.nz*
www.waituilodge.co.nz

Features & Attractions

- *Tea, coffee & TV in rooms*
- *Sea and rural views*
- *Safe swimming beaches*
- *Kiwi habitat*
- *Bush walks*
- *Great fishing*

Double	$180	
Single	$150	
Child	n/a	

**A Relaxing Homestay
In A Busy World**

Bedrooms	Qty
Double	2
Twin	
Single	
Bed Size	**Qty**
King	
Queen	2
Double	
Single	
Bathrooms	**Qty**
Ensuite	2
Private	
Guest Share	

By day the gardens are alive with native birds. By night hear the call of the morepork and kiwi. **Waitui Lodge** is nestled in a peaceful bush-clad valley, overlooking the Kerikeri Inlet and twelve minutes from Kerikeri shops, restaurants and golf course. We are close to safe swimming beaches, bush walks, boat ramps and kayak hire. Catering for a maximum of four guests, our priority is your comfort and relaxation. The spacious rooms have queen beds, luxurious ensuites with heated floors and towel rails. Tea, coffee, TV, CD player in rooms. Enjoy our spa and swimming pool, private decks and gardens. Self catering available.
Ours is a stress-free environment – relax and enjoy!

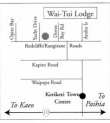

DIRECTIONS: Follow signs to Opito Bay.

PALM VIEW
8 Kotare Heights, Kerikeri, Bay of Islands
Ph (09) 407 6883
Mobile 021-0245 0615
email: *palmview@xtra.co.nz*
www.palmview.co.nz

Tariff : N.Z. Dollars	
Double	$185-300
Single	$175-290
Child	

Bedrooms	Qty
Double	
Twin	
Single	
Bed Size	**Qty**
Super King	1
King	2
Queen	
Double	
Single	
Bathrooms	**Qty**
Ensuite	3
Private	
Guest Share	

  Luxury Bed & Breakfast

Features & Attractions

- *New, luxurious ensuite rooms*
- *Historic stone store 5 min,*
- *Cafés, craft shops & wineries*
- *Bay of Islands attractions*
- *3 golf courses*
- *Short distance to town*
- *Tours & cruises*
- *Kauri forestwineries*

We are an English couple, who ran a Bed and Breakfast in Devon for 3 years, then moved to Taupo, New Zealand in 2001, where we built and then ran a lodge for 4 years before venturing north to Kerikeri in the Bay of Islands to do the same again, as we love the lifestyle and meeting people. Why not come and relax and unwind in a quiet, rural setting, where you will find **Palm View**, which is presently under construction, due to open for guests December 2007. It has been designed to a very high standard, with luxury in mind that guests can enjoy, with spectacular views of the inlet and the ocean in the distance.

All rooms have air conditioning, fridge, TV, ensuite, and many other luxuries provided. The one acre of garden will be planted with native, English and tropical plants.

Palm View is 2km from Kerikeri with its many cafés, restaurants, and other attractions.

Pau Hana Lodge

1322 State Highway 10, RD 3, Kerikeri
Ph (09) 407 9318, Fax (09) 407 6691
Mobile 021-407 931
email: *pauhanalodge@xtra.co.nz*

Tariff : N.Z. Dollars	
Double	$240-360
Single	$120-150
Child	

Bedrooms	Qty
Double	2
Twin	1
Single	

Bed Size	Qty
Super King	1
King	1
Queen	
King/Single	2
Single	

Bathrooms	Qty
Ensuite	2
Private	1
Guest Share	

**Bed & Breakfast
Luxury Accommodation**

Features & Attractions

- *The ultimate place to unwind*
- *Relaxed, friendly atmosphere*
- *Private setting, panoramic views*
- *Double spa baths/massage shower*
- *3 golf courses, incl Kauri Cliffs*
- *Award winning wineries 3 min*
- *Diving, fishing, sailing, kayaking*
- *Craft shops & galleries trail*

Welcome to **Pau Hana Lodge** which means 'Finish Work' and that's the way we want our guests to feel.

Our home is set on fifteen acres enjoying panoramic views spanning from Kerikeri to the East Coast. Indulge in your own private bush walk, natural ponds, streams and native birds. Our home offers guests an excellent standard of accommodation, use of laundry facilities, BBQ. Complimentary wine, tea or espresso on arrival, home-baking, comprehensive breakfasts and great selection of books and DVDs.

With wonderful hospitality, warmth and friendship, we are located close to all scenic and recreational activities of the Bay of Islands.

35

RAINBOW FALLS LODGE

109 Rainbow Falls Road, RD 2, Kerikeri
Ph (09) 407 4407, Fax (09) 407 4715
Mobile 027-256 3725
email: *ratkinson@xtra.co.nz*
www.rainbowfallslodge.co.nz

Tariff : N.Z. Dollars	
Double	$110-130
Single	$100-115
Child	$30

Bedrooms	Qty
Double	2
Twin	
Single	

Bed Size	Qty
Super King	
King	
Queen	2
Double	
Single	

Bathrooms	Qty
Ensuite	1
Private	1
Guest Share	

Self-contained Bed & Breakfast

Features & Attractions

- *Quiet and peaceful*
- *Sub-tropical gardens*
- *Spa pool*
- *Waterfall and bush walks*
- *In the Bay of Islands*
- *Cafés, craft shops & wineries*
- *Tours & cruises*
- *Historic sites*

DIRECTIONS: From SH 10 turn right into Kerikeri Rd, drive through Kerikeri town past the Stone Store and across bridge. At roundabout turn left into Waipapa Rd, then left into Rainbow Falls Rd. We are at the end (down Karaka Drive).

Welcome to our new self-contained Bed & Breakfast, located in sub-tropical Kerikeri. Well appointed in a quiet, tranquil setting, we are only a five minute drive from town and handy to Paihia and the Bay of Islands. The spacious self-contained unit has its own deck, where you can relax in the sun, take a relaxing spa while viewing the sub-tropical gardens, or simply just laze around in a nice quiet setting. Privacy and discretion are assured. A short stroll from your door are lovely bush walks to Rainbow Falls and scenic reserves or you could take a short drive to the splendour of Puketi Forest. We are handily based for your Northland experience including beaches, tours and cruises, swimming with dolphins, fishing trips, giant kauri trees and forest walks. Visit the historic Stone Store, Waitangi Treaty House, historic Russell township. Our interests are wildlife conservation, walking, tramping, and gardens. Our pet cat and dog will also welcome you to our home.

THE MAPLES BED & BREAKFAST

231 B Waipapa Road, R.D. 2, Kerikeri, Northland
Ph (09) 401 7323, Fax (09) 401 7023
Mobile 021-444 712
email: *the.maples@xtra.co.nz*
www.maples.co.nz

Tariff : N.Z. Dollars	
Double	$140-165
Single	
Child	

Bedrooms	Qty
Double	1
Twin	
Single	
Bed Size	**Qty**
Super King	
King	1
Queen	
Double	
Single	
Bathrooms	**Qty**
Ensuite	1
Private	
Guest Share	

 **Charming
Bed & Breakfast**

Features & Attractions

• *Quiet, secluded setting*
• *Private entry and courtyard*
• *5 min. to town centre*
• *Generous breakfast*
• *Internet, email facilities*
• *Restaurants, cafés, wineries*
• *Beaches, forests, golf courses*
• *Complimentary laundry*

Formerly a pottery studio, the **Maples B&B** has been transformed into a home full of character and charm. Our home is surrounded by colourful and fragrant gardens. Our guest room has a luxurious king-size bed, his/hers bathrobes, ensuite, walk-in wardrobe, fridge, Sky TV, library, plunger coffee and a selection of teas. Telephone, laundry, facsimile and internet facilities are available. Your separate entrance through a peaceful courtyard ensures privacy to unwind and relax. Refreshments are served on arrival in the garden. A generous continental/cooked breakfast is served with freshly baked bread, healthy cereals and seasonal fruits. Five min. from Kerikeri township we ensure a relaxed base for you to experience the local vineyards, cafés, restaurants and craft shops. Whether you stay 3, 5 or 7 days, we can assist you with an itinerary that will allow you to explore the breathtaking countryside and beaches of the Bay of Islands and Far North. Come and join Tracey and Andrew along with Rose and Jess, our lovable Jack Russell's. You will be pleased you did.

TEA TREE COTTAGE

240 Wharau Road, RD 3, Kerikeri
Ph (09) 407 8060, Fax (09) 407 8060
Mobile 021-150 9032
email: *teatreecottage@xtra.co.nz*
www.teatreecottage.co.nz

Tariff : N.Z. Dollars	
Double	$150-150
Single	$100-100
Child	

Bedrooms	Qty
Double	2
Twin	
Single	
Bed Size	**Qty**
S. King/Single	2
King	
Queen	
Double	
King Single	4
Bathrooms	**Qty**
Ensuite	2
Private	
Guest Share	

 **Bed & Breakfast
Self-contained Units**

Features & Attractions

- Stunning sea views
- Courtyard and BBQ area
- Beautifully appointed units
- Restaurants, craft shops, vineyards
- Kitchen facilities in each unit
- Safe swimming beach
- Rock fishing, golf courses
- Kauri forest & historic sites

DIRECTIONS:
From SH10 veer right into
Hobson Ave at traffic roundabout
when you reach Kerikeri town.
Turn left into Inlet Road.
Go 7.5km to Wharau Road.
The Cottage is at number 240.

Tea Tree Cottage is a modern home with two self-contained units. Each unit has tiled floors, a kitchen, ensuite and well appointed bedroom set in native landscaped surrounds. At night it is possible to hear Kiwi in the bush nearby. The main house is a huge open plan living area containing kitchen, dining and living rooms all overlooking the magnificent Bay of Islands. If you prefer, you can relax in the courtyard area especially designed for all-weather comfort. Two minutes down the road you will find a safe beach for swimming or a little rock fishing. We can help arrange your activities in the Bay of Islands: swim with the dolphins, go fishing or cruise the bay. There are several golf courses, craft shops, vineyards and historic sites, or take a leisurely walk through the Kauri forests before returning to Kerikeri to try one of the many fine restaurants or cafés. Our aim is simply to make your stay with us a memorable one.

APPLEDORE LODGE

624 Puketona Road, Paihia
Ph (09) 402 8007, Fax (09) 402 8007
email: *appledorelodge@xtra.co.nz*
www.appledorelodge.co.nz

Tariff : N.Z. Dollars	
Double	$150-190
Studio	$140-180
Cottage	$250

Bedrooms	Qty
Double	1
Twin	2
Single	

Bed Size	Qty
Super King	2
King	
Queen	1
Double	
Single	

Bathrooms	Qty
Ensuite	3
Private	
Guest Share	

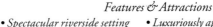
**Panoramic river views from
your pillow & deck**

Features & Attractions

- *Spectacular riverside setting*
- *Home made breakfast basket*
- *5 min from Paihia & golf*
- *Trout fishing in our river*
- *Luxuriously appointed accommodation*
- *Outdoor spa pool under the stars*
- *Bush and coastal walking*
- *Wireless internet on site*

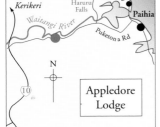

Miniature waterfalls and rapids await your discovery as the Waitangi River gently tumbles past your bedroom window. Tranquillity & peace is here to rediscover with our spellbinding riverside setting where you can fish for trout or stroll the riverbank. Set in two acres and only 25 metres from the riverbank all our accommodation have magnificent views up & down the Historic Waitangi River are self-contained with ensuite & have ranch sliders to private decks. Guests take delight in Janet's special all home made breakfast basket. Riverside Suite furnished in native rimu, with split level to lounge area & sun drenched deck. Riverside Cottage and Riverside Studio are superior & luxuriously appointed with a riverside setting. We enjoy classic cars, golf, travel and meeting new guests. With resident ducks, heron, kingfisher and the out door spa pool, Appledore Lodge offers ingredients that all holidays should contain. Appledore Lodge is unsuitable for children under 12.

CRISDON CASTLE

18 Goffe Drive, Haruru Falls, PO Box 73, Paihia
Ph/Fax (09) 402 6980, Mobile 021-206 7276
email: *info@crisdoncastle.co.nz*
www.crisdoncastle.co.nz

Tariff : N.Z. Dollars	
Double	$120-250
Single	$100-225
Child	neg

Bedrooms	Qty
Double	5
Twin	2
Single	

Bed Size	Qty
Super King	
King	1
Queen	3
King/Single	1
Single	2

Bathrooms	Qty
Ensuite	4
Private	1
Guest Share	

**Boutique B&B
and Self-contained Units**

Features & Attractions

- *Uninterrupted 180° views*
- *BBQ and fire area*
- *Tour bookings*
- *Meals available*
- *Private access to all rooms*
- *Internet access available*
- *Guest laundry*
- *Massage and sauna*

Crisdon Castle is luxury accommodation that indulges your senses. Each room has spectacular views from private balconies and, if you wander the property you can see the Haruru Falls and surrounding hinterland. Situated on the top of the highest ridge in Haruru Falls with incredible views of the Waitangi River and out to the Bay of Islands. Each suite has quality furnishings and a luxury bathroom. We have included all that you require from bubble bath to bath robes, candles to champagne, massage and meals. You can have candle lit evenings by the outdoor fireplace in winter or, relax with your favourite drink under the verandah on balmy summer nights as you watch the sunset. Enjoy lazy days in the privacy of your suite or be at the beach within 3 minutes drive.

Ask and we will let you know what's on offer in the stunning Bay of Islands. We can book you a tour, of which there is something for all ages and ability. From relaxed luxury to adventure tourism **Crisdon Castle** and the Bay of Islands has something for everyone.

We look forward to meeting you.

CHALET ROMANTICA
6 Bedggood Close, Paihia, Bay of Islands
Ph (09) 402 8270, Fax (09) 402 8278
Mobile 027-226 6400
email: *info-chalet@xtra.co.nz*
www.chaletromantica.homestead.com/accom1.html

Tariff : N.Z. Dollars	
Double	$125-235
Single	$115-225
Child	$25

Bedrooms	Qty
Double	3
Twin	
Single	

Bed Size	Qty
Super King	2
King	
Queen	1
Double	
Single	4

Bathrooms	Qty
Ensuite	2
Private	1
Guest Share	

**Quality Bed & Breakfast
& Self-contained Suites**

Features & Attractions

- *Central town location with sea views*
- *Café's & restaurants nearby*
- *Stroll to beach and water activities*
- *Heated pool, spa, mini gym*
- *TV, CD- player, DVD/video, phone in rooms*
- *Laundry facilities, internet and tour desk on site.*
- *42-foot yacht for skippered charters*
- *Francaise and German spoken*

Spoil yourself and experience the magic of **Chalet Romantica**. Nestled above Paihia Beach with unsurpassed views over the Bay and township, spectacular by day and night. Each room has its own balcony, superb sea views, quality furnishings and fittings, wireless internet, crisp linen and extra comfy beds.

A delicious breakfast with home baked breads and farm fresh eggs will await you in our conservatory overlooking the Bay. Having lived here for over 20 years we are proud of our local knowledge, passionate about where we live and love to share it all with you. Spend your days exploring or charter our luxury 42ft yacht for the day with Ed as skipper, a trip of a lifetime! You may just decide to relax on your balcony, read a book, swim in the pool, soak in the hot spa, or work out at the gym? What better way to re-charge the batteries! Bird lovers will be thrilled with lots of native birds visiting our garden and surroundings.

Excellent restaurants, shops and 'The Bay of Islands Dolphin and Cruise Departure Piers' are just a stroll from us.

DIRECTIONS:
Please phone for easy directions.

ALLEGRA HOUSE

39 Bayview Road, Paihia, Bay of Islands
Ph (09) 402 7932, Fax (09) 402 7930
email: *allegrahouse@xtra.co.nz*
www.allegra.co.nz

Tariff : N.Z. Dollars	
Double	$140-245
Single	
Child	

Bedrooms	Qty
Double	3
Twin	
Single	
Bed Size	**Qty**
Super King	2
King	
Queen	1
Double	
Single	
Bathrooms	**Qty**
Ensuite	3
Private	
Guest Share	

**Bed & Breakfast with Views
Self-contained Apartment**

Features & Attractions

- *Spectacular sea views*
- *Central Paihia*
- *Set amongst native bush*
- *Air conditioned rooms*
- *German & French spoken*
- *Peaceful location*
- *Internet access*
- *Spa pool nestled in bush*

Allegra House, our spacious, modern home is centrally located, just up the hill from Paihia's wharf, shops and restaurants. We have spectacular views from all rooms over the village to Russell and the Bay of Islands. Luxurious accommodation options are: Bed & Breakfast including continental breakfast, ensuite bathroom, your own tea/coffee making facilities, refrigerator, television and balcony; or Self-catering Apartment with super-king bedroom, large tiled bathroom, fully equipped kitchen and spacious lounge opening onto a large balcony. For your comfort each room has its own air conditioning and the whole house is smoke-free. Enjoy our spa pool nestled in the bush and make use of the barbeque, laundry facilities and internet access.

Plenty of good local information is available to help you choose the best options for your time with us. We can book activities such as sailing, dolphin watching and day trips to Cape Reinga.

BAY VIEW SUITE

19 Bayview Road, PO Box 574, Paihia
Ph (09) 402 6628, Fax (09) 427 463
Mobile 027-457 1866
email:*baysales@remax.net.nz*

Tariff : N.Z. Dollars	
Double	$150-190
Single	
Child	

Bedrooms	Qty
Double	1
Twin	
Single	

Bed Size	Qty
Super King	
King	
Queen	1
Double	
Single	

Bathrooms	Qty
Ensuite	1
Private	
Guest Share	

DIRECTIONS:
At 19 Bayview Road
proceed to top of driveway.
Bookings essential.

Self-contained
Central Paihia

Features & Attractions

- *Magic sea & village views*
- *Quality & comfort*
- *Warm hospitality*
- *Courtesy pickup*
- *Privacy*
- *Elevated site*
- *Welcome basket*
- *Quality restaurants*

Elevated setting for privacy and to capture sea view. Enjoy the sea views with twinkling lights at night and ever-changing water views by day. Accommodation is fully self-contained and serviced daily. Extra luxuries include robes, slippers, plunger coffee, iron. The tariff includes a generous continental breakfast, served in your suite so you can enjoy it at your leisure. A five minute walk takes you to all the local attractions, beaches and quality restaurants.

We offer a courtesy pickup and delivery service. A complimentary wine and welcome basket awaits you upon arrival.

Bookings essential. 2 nights minimum stay.

ABRI APARTMENTS

10 Bayview Rd, Paihia, Bay of Islands
Ph (09) 402 8003, Fax (09) 402 8035
email: *abriaccom@xtra.co.nz*
www.abri-accom.co.nz

Features & Attractions

- *Self-cont. luxury accommodation*
- *Close to all activities/restaurants*
- *Cooking facilities, dishwasher*
- *Panoramic views*
- *Double luxury spa bath*
- *Safe off-street parking*

 Self-contained Luxury Apartments

Aptmt.	$150-270
Suite	$130-240
Child	n/a

"Luxury – Privacy – Views"

Take shelter at **Abri** in Paihia, the beautiful centre of the Bay of Islands. **Abri Apartments** are nestled in beautiful gardens with all day sun and private decks that give you panoramic views of Russell and beyond.

Our air conditioned apartments are modern and individually styled using rich native timbers and tasteful furnishings with shower, hairdryer and bathrobes and double spa bath.

The beach, wharf and township are only a minute's walk away giving easy access to all facilities and excursions and to some excellent restaurants.

A warm welcome awaits you and a breakfast basket is complimentary on the first morning of your stay.

Bedrooms	Qty
Double	3
Twin	
Single	
Bed Size	**Qty**
King	
Queen	3
Double	
Single	
Bathrooms	**Qty**
Ensuite	3
Private	
Guest Share	

THE TOTARAS

6 School Road, Paihia, P O Box 586, Bay of Islands
Ph (09) 402 8238, Fax (09) 402 8238
email: *thetotaras@ihug.co.nz*
www.netnz.com/bedandbreakfast.html

Features & Attractions

- *Uninterrupted 180° sea views*
- *Breakfast on sun terrace*
- *Adjacent to reserve*
- *Insider tips*
- *Pleasant ambience*
- *Photographers dream*

 Central Hilltop Bed & Breakfast

Double	$180-220
Single	$120-165
Child	neg

For the sophisticated traveller. Luxury with charm... perched on a hill with sweeping views across Waitangi, Russell and the Bay of Islands. Wake up to the sunrise from your spacious well appointed apartment with ensuite, coffee and tea facilities, fridge and private sundeck. Enjoy the vista of ocean liners and sailing boats - or simply be mesmerized by the stunning view. Within minutes a path will lead you to the village, restaurants, wharf, beaches, bush and coastal tracks. Frank is an international photographer. His latest books, 'I Do' Classic New Zealand Weddings and 'Bay of Islands; A Paradise Found' depicts the characteristics of the bay, he and Christine fell in love with many years ago. Christine has a degree in Hotel Management. For breakfast you will be spoiled with delicious Austrian pancakes, fresh fruit and other delights. Welcome - Wilkommen! Minimum stay 2 nights.

Bedrooms	Qty
Double	1
Twin	
Single	
Bed Size	**Qty**
King	
Queen	1
Double	
Single	1
Bathrooms	**Qty**
Ensuite	1
Private	
Guest Share	

BAY OF ISLANDS BEACH HOUSE

16B Sullivans Road, PO Box 349, Paihia, Bay of Islands
Ph (09) 402 7702, Fax (09) 402 7703
Mobile 027-499 4041
email: *info@boibeachhouse.co.nz*
www.boibeachhouse.co.nz

Tariff : N.Z. Dollars	
Double	$225-295
Single	
Child	

Bedrooms	Qty
Double	3
Twin	
Single	

Bed Size	Qty
Super King	1
King	
Queen	1
Double	
Single	2

Bathrooms	Qty
Ensuite	1
Private	1
Guest Share	

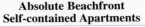
**Absolute Beachfront
Self-contained Apartments**

Features & Attractions

- *Absolute beachfront, no traffic noise*
- *Easy, short beach walk to town*
- *Golf, fishing, sailing, walking tracks*
- *Golden sands of Sullivans Beach*
- *Gated entry & secure parking*
- *Private all day sun decks*
- *Safe boat anchorage*
- *20 min airport shuttle*

The **Bay of Islands Beach House** is a short beach stroll from Paihia Township where you will find access to many activities and

more than 30 restaurants, cafés and bars. The **Penthouse Apartment** is our most luxurious with stunning views, spa bath, sauna, kitchenette and large decks. Free DVD rentals every day. The **Beach Apartment** features your own patio, barbeque and path to the safe swimming and golden sands of Sullivans Beach. It has two bedrooms, bathroom, lounge/dining, kitchen, laundry facilities plus an extra (outside) shower. Free DVD rentals every day. Be our guest... bring your boat, enjoy the sun, sea and setting. Watch the boats go by or throw out a line and catch fresh fish for lunch!

SWALLOWS NEST
14 Panorama Avenue, Binnie Street, Paihia
Ph (09) 402 8604, Fax (09) 402 6247
Mobile 021-502 860
e-mail: *stay@swallowsnest.co.nz*
www.swallowsnest.co.nz

Features & Attractions

- *Stunning sea views*
- *Air conditioning*
- *Fully equipped kitchens*
- *Heated pool (lodge only)*
- *Close to beaches, shops, restaurants*
- *Luxuriously appointed accommodation*

**Luxury
Self-contained Lodge**

Lodge	$450-750
Apart.	$175-375
Child	

This really is Bay of Islands accommodation at its best!
A million dollar setting with million dollar views, yet only 400 meters from the beach and 1 km from Paihia village centre with numerous restaurants, cafés and shops.

The **Swallows Nest** offers air conditioned, cool ambience in the long summers and warmth and comfort in the cooler winter months.

The '**Swallows Nest**' has 2 separate parts:

The Lodge: A magnificent 3 bedroom lodge sleeping up to 6, fitted to an exceptionally high standard, with a private heated and covered pool.
The Nest: A lovely 1 bedroom apartment, fitted to a very high standard and with fabulous views of the Veronica Channel. Both are fully self-contained with fully equipped kitchens.

Bedrooms	Qty
Double	2
Twin	2
Single	
Bed Size	**Qty**
Super King	1
King	1
Queen	1
Single	2
Bathrooms	**Qty**
Ensuite	1
Private	1
Family Share	1

WINDERMERE
168 Marsden Road, Paihia
Ph (09) 402 8696, Fax (09) 402 5095
Mobile 021- 115 7436
email: *windermere@igrin.co.nz*
www.windermere.co.nz

Features & Attractions

- *Great views & location*
- *Spacious sunny units*
- *Own private entrance*
- *Walk to town or golf course*
- *Spa pool & decks*
- *Sky T.V.*

**Bed & Breakfast
Self-contained Accom.**

Double	$120-220
Single	$100-180
Child	

Windermere is a large modern family home set in a bush setting and yet located right on one of the best beaches in the Bay of Islands. Superior accommodation is provided with suites having their own ensuite, kitchen facilities and Sky television. For longer stays one suite has its own laundry, dryer and fully equipped kitchen.
The other suite has microwave and refrigerator only. Each suite has its own decks (a barbeque is provided) where you can sit, relax and enjoy the view enhanced by spectacular sunsets. Jill and Richard would welcome your company to enjoy our own little part of paradise. Windermere is the jewel in the Bay of Islands.

Bedrooms	Qty
Double	2
Twin	
Single	
Bed Size	**Qty**
King	
Queen	2
Double	
Single	2
Bathrooms	**Qty**
Ensuite	2
Private	
Guest Share	

DECKS OF PAIHIA

69 School Road, Paihia
Ph (09) 402 6146, Fax (09) 402 6147
Mobile 021- 278 7558
email: *info@decksofpaihia.com*
www.decksofpaihia.com

Tariff : N.Z. Dollars	
Double	$145-220
Single	–
Child	–

Bedrooms	Qty
Double	3
Twin	
Single	

Bed Size	Qty
Super King	3
King	
Queen	
Double	
Single	

Bathrooms	Qty
Ensuite	3
Private	
Guest Share	

Luxury Bed & Breakfast

Features & Attractions

- *Quiet, central location*
- *Sun-drenched decks / pool*
- *Lovely sea views*
- *Private ensuites each room*
- *All suites air-conditioned*
- *Spacious guest lounge*
- *Broadband internet access*
- *Tea/coffee making in each room*

Contemporary designed home, completed October 2005. Three guest suites all with private ensuite bathrooms. All suites offer your own tea/coffee making facilities, TV/DVD, air conditioning, refrigerator, and open out on to sheltered, sun drenched decks overlooking swimming pool. Private garden area allows the opportunity for a lazy afternoon in the sun beside the pool. Quiet peaceful central Paihia location, with off street parking. Very comfortable interiors, stylishly furnished. Guest lounge located adjacent to suites area offers extended living space in which to relax, with a comprehensive DVD and book library. Philip and Wendy have enjoyed many years in the hospitality industry and are happy to share their home, and their extensive knowledge of the Bay of Islands and Northland with you. Philip has strong links to the area – his great grandfather Patrick McGovern was the police constable in Russell in the 1880's.

MARLIN HOUSE

15 Bayview Road, Paihia,
Bay Of Islands
Ph (09) 402 8550
email: *marlinhouse@xtra.co.nz*

Tariff : N.Z. Dollars	
$180	Double
$150	Single
	Child

Qty	Bedrooms
2	Double
1	Twin
	Single

Qty	Bed Size
	Super King
1	King
2	Queen
	Double
	Single

Qty	Bathrooms
3	Ensuite
	Private
	Guest Share

 Dutch, Greek, German and French spoken

Features & Attractions

- *Dutch-German-Greek-French spoken*
- *Refrigerator-microwave in rooms*
- *Golf tours arranged & guided*
- *TV, Dining area in all rooms*
- *Suites have private entrances*
- *Stunning views of the Bay*
- *Fishing & yacht charters*
- *20 min. airport shuttle*

Marlin House is a large, comfortable colonial-style house with ample off-street parking. It is set in a quiet tree-clad hillside cul-de-sac, yet is only a four minute easy walk to the beach and the centre of Paihia with its many shops and restaurants.

Please phone for easy directions
Advanced Booking Recommended

Marlin House offers three generous-sized suites, each with a private entrance, a sitting and dining area, a fridge, microwave and TV and has a deck with sea views over the Bay. A special breakfast with home-baking is included. Marie-Claire has a degree in hotel catering and management. George specialises in conducted golfing and fishing tours (minimum 2 nights stay).

HARBOUR HOUSE VILLA

7 English Bay Road, Opua, Bay of Islands
Ph (09) 402 8087, Fax (09) 402 8688
email: *stay@harbourhousevilla.com*
www.harbourhousevilla.com

Tariff : N.Z. Dollars	
Double	$285-480
Single	$235-430
Child	welcome

Bedrooms	Qty
Double	3
Twin	2
Single	

Bed Size	Qty
Super King	1
King	1
Queen	1
Double	
Single	4

Bathrooms	Qty
Ensuite	4
Private	
Guest Share	

    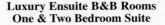

**Luxury Ensuite B&B Rooms
One & Two Bedroom Suite**

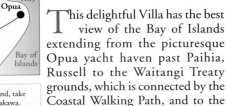

Features & Attractions

- *Sea view from every room*
- *Private and peaceful*
- *Computer / Internet*
- *Japanese spoken*
- *Courtesy transportation*
- *Deep sea fishing*
- *Sailing, cruises & tours*
- *Trip planning & information*

DIRECTIONS: From Auckland, take SH1 past Whangarei to Kawakawa. Take SH11 for 12km towards Opua. At intersection, cross into English Bay Rd. Travel 500m to **Harbour House Villa** on right.

This delightful Villa has the best view of the Bay of Islands extending from the picturesque Opua yacht haven past Paihia, Russell to the Waitangi Treaty grounds, which is connected by the Coastal Walking Path, and to the Kerikeri Inlet at the far end of the Bay's Historic Marine Park. All Villa accommodations are meticulously maintained. Each B&B ensuite room or Suite Guest can choose gourmet Kiwi, Western or Japanese breakfast, which is served on our viewing deck or in the dining room. One and two bedroom suites receive full service and may elect to have breakfast provisions provided in their kitchen. Each suite has its own private deck equipped for outdoor living including BBQ. Pleasing music played on our grand piano complements the panoramic view creating a unique ambience at the Villa. Your hosts, Robert and Masae Serge, are blue water sailors, seasoned travellers and also experienced in providing accommodation for the discerning traveller.

MAKO LODGE
18 Pt Veronica Drive, Opua, Bay of Islands
Ph (09) 402 7957
Mobile 021-256 5416
email: *info@makolodge.co.nz*
www.makolodge.co.nz

Tariff : N.Z. Dollars	
Double	$175-195
Single	–
Child	–

Bedrooms	Qty
Double	2
Twin	1
Single	

Bed Size	Qty
Super King	1
King	
Queen	1
Double	
Single	

Bathrooms	Qty
Ensuite	2
Private	
Guest Share	

 Idyllic Location with Spectacular Views of the Bay   **VISA** MasterCard

Features & Attractions
- *Panoramic sea views*
- *Spa-tub overlooking Bay*
- *North facing deck*
- *Sports fishing arranged*
- *Beach towels/umbrellas avail.*
- *Bush and coastal walks*
- *Off-road parking*
- *Generous continental breakfast*

Our Lodge at Point Veronica is in an outstanding, peaceful, coastal location of natural beauty with some of the best views of the Bay of Islands. We have stunning sea/bush views and sunsets seen from our decks. Only 5 km away is Paihia and Waitangi with its amenities and popular leisure activities for tourists. **Mako Lodge**, completed in 2003, is 5 minutes by car from Opua Marina and the car ferry taking you to Okiato, historic Russell and Long Beach. A 3 minute walk from **Mako Lodge** takes walking enthusiasts to the Coastal Path and bush walks in the area. Relax in our hot tub overlooking the Bay – you may even spot a pod of dolphins or orcas – or relax in the Bay View garden, which has commanding views over the Bay of Islands looking towards historic Russell. **Mako Lodge** is a non smoking environment. All bedrooms have sea views, fridge, complimentary tea and coffee making facilities plus TV, VCR and clock radio alarms. Regrettably **Mako Lodge** is unable to cater for animals or children under the age of 11.

PT. VERONICA LODGE

39 Pt Veronica Drive, Opua, Bay of Islands
Ph (09) 402 5579, Fax (09) 402 5579
Mobile 021-182 0697
email: *stay@ptveronicalodge.co.nz*
www.ptveronicalodge.co.nz

Tariff : N.Z. Dollars	
Double	$150-190
Single	$130-160
Child	

Bedrooms	Qty
Double	2
Twin	
Single	
Bed Size	**Qty**
Super King	1
King	
Queen	1
Double	
King/Single	2
Bathrooms	**Qty**
Ensuite	2
Private	
Guest Share	

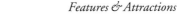

Peaceful & Enchanting

Features & Attractions

- *Overlooking the Bay*
- *Luxury cooked breakfast*
- *North facing decks*
- *6 min. to Paihia/Waitangi*
- *Bush & coastal walks*
- *Internet facilities*
- *Lovely spa on lower deck*
- *Backing onto reserve*

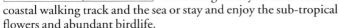

To Paihia
Veronica Channel
To Russell
Okaito
Paihia Rd
Point Veronica
Broadview
Car Ferry
Franklin
N
Pt. Veronica Lodge
Opua
To Kawakawa

Pt. **Veronica Lodge Homestay** is on a headland in the Bay of Islands. The guest bedrooms look out over an inlet. The lounge and decks have views over the water towards Paihia, Waitangi and Russell. From our garden you can access the

coastal walking track and the sea or stay and enjoy the sub-tropical flowers and abundant birdlife.

Built in 2001, our home makes wonderful use of native timbers throughout. All bedrooms are ensuite and have heatpump/air-conditioning, television and radio. Complimentary teas and coffee are available in the kitchen at any time. We hope you will try some of our home baking.

Point Veronica Lodge is ideally located for visiting Opua, Paihia, Waitangi, Russell and Kerikeri. Pick-ups at the door for swimming with the dolphins, Hole-in-the-Rock cruises and scenic flights to Cape Reinga. An ideal centre for summer and winter breaks. Audrey, John and our two lovely dogs invite you to join us in our special place.

TINAMARA

32 Puketiro Place, Te Haumi, Paihia, Bay of Islands
Ph (09) 402 8048, Fax (09) 402 8078
Mobile 027-306 4202
e-mail: *barbara.thomson@xtra.co.nz*

Features & Attractions

- *Elevated river/bay views*
- *Romantic sunsets*
- *Generous English breakfasts*
- *3 minutes drive to Paihia*
- *Sailing yacht for charter*
- *Quiet location*

 Affordable Quality Bed & Breakfast

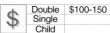

Double	$100-150
Single	
Child	

Tinamara was built for the sun and spectacular views of the Te Haumi river and the Bay of Islands. Our peaceful, secluded location with ample parking is only three minutes drive from Paihia's beaches, cafés and sporting facilities. The comfortable ensuite double room has TV, galley kitchen and private balcony.
A separate twin room with private bathroom is also available.
Full English breakfast to your specification is served on the wide, sunny deck or in the elegant conservatory.
Hosts Barbara and Alan have lived in the Far East, travelled extensively and now enjoy a relaxed lifestyle between England and New Zealand. Hobbies include sailing in the Bay and golf at Waitangi. Their 24ft yacht is available for charter. (Minimum two nights stay).

Bedrooms	Qty
Double	1
Twin	1
Single	
Bed Size	**Qty**
King	
Queen	1
Double	
Single	2
Bathrooms	**Qty**
Ensuite	1
Private	1
Guest Share	

New Zealand has a vibrant café life

WATERVIEW LODGE

14 Franklin Street, Opua, Bay of Islands
Ph (09) 402 7595, Fax (09) 402 7596
Mobile 021-102 3950
email: *info@waterviewlodge.co.nz*
www.waterviewlodge.com

Tariff : N.Z. Dollars	
Double	$150-230
Single	$90-140
Child	$20

Bedrooms	Qty
Double	7
Twin	1
Single	

Bed Size	Qty
Super King	2
King/Single	4
Queen	2
Double	2
Single	2

Bathrooms	Qty
Ensuite	3
Private	2
Guest Share	

          Quality Accommodation
Excellent Service

DIRECTIONS:
Drive to Bay of Islands.
Then towards the Opua-Russell car ferry.
Franklin St leads down to the car ferry.
Waterview is on the right,
half way down the hill.

Features & Attractions

• *Great sea views*
• *Scrumptuous breakfast*
• *Complimentary Internet*
• *Bush and coastal walks*

• *Glow-worm tour*
• *Tourist attractions 5 min.*
• *Restaurant, yacht club,*
  marina in walking distance

Overlooking the picturesque Port of Opua, **Waterview Lodge** is a quality accommodation establishment. **Waterview Lodge** has 3 private guest suites. The **Harbour** and **River Suites** have private balconies with panoramic sea views of Opua. The **River** and **Garden Suites** have a king and a single bed, the **Harbour Suite** has a king bed only. All suites have quality linen, ensuite, TV, CD, telephone, fridge and tea/coffee making facilities. Complimentary wireless internet available. Breakfasts are complimentary with the suites and consist of home-made breads and muffins, local fresh fruits, cheeses and yoghurt, a selection of cereals or a cooked breakfast. *Self-contained accommodation* (with well equipped kitchens): The 3 bedroom **Waterview Cottage** is a charming residence capturing sun and sea views. The 2 bedroom **Garden Unit** is situated downstairs next to the **Garden Suite** with a garden outlook and a great outdoor entertaining area.

Your hosts, Antionette and Jess, will offer you the very best in customer service and your stay will be an enjoyable and memorable one. **Waterview Lodge** is a smoke free environment.

ARCADIA LODGE
10 Florance Ave, Russell Village, Bay of Islands
Ph (09) 403 7756, Fax (09) 403 7721
email: *arcadia@arcadialodge.co.nz*
www.arcadialodge.co.nz

Features & Attractions

- *Landmark Historic House*
- *Bay view decks & lounge*
- *All tours arranged*
- *Healthy café style breakfasts*
- *2 swimming beaches close*
- *Short stroll to village centre*

History, Charm, Good Food and Glorious Views

	Double	$160-295
	Single	enquire
	Child	$00-00

Historic, 100 year old **Arcadia** commands a magnificent position overlooking Russell's best kept secret, tranquil Matauwhi Bay. For many of our guests one of their delights is simply to sit and drink in the views of water, bush and yachts. Downstairs we have three spacious suites with bay view decks while upstairs are two double rooms with water views and a super-king room. The house is furnished in a relaxed blend of contemporary and antique furniture on original honey-coloured kauri floorboards with western and Pasifika art helping to create a comfortable, relaxing space in which to unwind. Start your day on the deck with our generous, healthy breakfast: fresh Kerikeri orange juice, Northland fruit, home-made muesli, jams and preserves, organic coffee and teas, followed by a delicious café-style cooked special. There's no better set-up for a day out in the bay.

DIRECTIONS: On the right soon after you enter Russell. Look for signs. For our flat rear car park, drive on into village; at the church turn right up steep Robertson St. At top, right again onto Brind Rd and down hill again. Follow signs to our driveway.

Bedrooms	Qty
Double	6
Twin	1
Single	
Bed Size	**Qty**
Supe King	1
King	2
Queen	2
Double	2
Bathrooms	**Qty**
Ensuite	4
Private	1
Guest Share	1

ARAPOHUE HOUSE B & B
9 Wellington Street, Russell, Bay of Islands
Ph (09) 403 8109, Fax (09) 403 8107
Mobile 027-272 8881
email: *arapohuehouse@xtra.co.nz*
www.travelwise.co.nz

Features & Attractions

- *Close to waterfront*
- *Fine dining & cafés*
- *Beautiful beaches*
- *Boat charters*
- *Museum & crafts*
- *Nature walks*

Historic Russell Bed & Breakfast

	Double	$160-220
	Single	$140-165
	Child	

This beautiful re-designed old bungalow has been rebuilt recently with two ensuite bedrooms for guests.

Only 200 metres from Russell waterfront, it is an easy leisurely level walk to all the fine restaurants and coffee houses. Historic Russell, with its museum and craft shops, offers a natural history with nature walks and three beautiful beaches. We can organise any trips you wish. Alternatively, you are welcome to spend time in our beautiful garden relaxing with a great book.

All bedrooms have tea and coffee facilities, digital radio clocks, hair dryers, cotton dressing gowns, and colour TVs with Sky TV. A laundry is available.

Bedrooms	Qty
Double	2
Twin	
Single	
Bed Size	**Qty**
King	
Queen	2
Double	
Single	
Bathrooms	**Qty**
Ensuite	2
Private	
Guest Share	

AOMOTU LODGE

6 Ashby Street, Russell, Bay of Islands
Ph (09) 403 7693, Fax (09) 403 7683
Mobile 027 - 254 8851
email: *info@aomotulodge.com*
www.aomotulodge.com

Tariff : N.Z. Dollars	
Double	$295-395
Single	$215-345
Child	$25 u/12

Bedrooms	Qty
Double	4
Twin	2
Single	4

Bed Size	Qty
Super King	1
King	
Queen	4
Double	
Single	2

Bathrooms	Qty
Ensuite	4
Private	
Guest Share	

     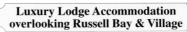

**Luxury Lodge Accommodation
overlooking Russell Bay & Village**

Features & Attractions

- *Newly renovated luxury suites*
- *Spectacular views & sunsets*
- *5 min stroll to town centre*
- *Organic toiletries, cotton & linen*
- *Island cruises & tours*
- *Dolphin & whale encounters*
- *World class restaurants*
- *Sehabla Español*

Welcome to **Aomotu Lodge**. Pronounced "our-more-too", which means "World Island", **Aomotu Lodge** is nestled in an elevated and central position overlooking the bay and village of romantic Russell. Our beautiful home has newly renovated and finely appointed luxury suites with spacious ensuites and sea views. The lodge is an architecturally unique house built with an emphasis on native woods and stained glass windows which create a warm, welcoming yet contemporary environment. The lounge and dining areas, which are available to our guests, have soaring cathedral ceilings and gorgeous vistas of the village and the picturesque bay. We serve a delicious continental and cooked breakfast on our panoramic veranda. Just a short stroll to Russell harbour and village centre, with a number of sandy beaches close by, the lodge is conveniently situated for all local attractions. We are happy to assist you in deciding what to do while in the Bay of Islands, and provide a detailed complimentary itinerary, to help make your stay memorable and relaxing.

DIRECTIONS:
Entering Russell village, turn right onto
Chapel Street. Follow road up hill,
it will become Ashby Street.
You will see **Aomotu Lodge** on your right.

BELVEDERE LODGE

James Clendon Place, Okiato, RD 1,
Russell (Old Russell), Bay of Islands
Ph/Fax (09) 403 7882
email: *jmboulter@xtra.co.nz*
www.travelwise.co.nz

Features & Attractions

- *Stunning 180° bay views*
- *Excessive tranquility*
- *Russell town 7 min*
- *Swim beach 2 min walk*
- *Beach and bush walks*
- *Initial breakfast supplies*

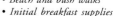

DIRECTIONS: From the Opua-
Okiato ferry, turn left after approx.
400m into Pipiroa Rd, after 50m
continue into James Clendon Place.
Belvedere Lodge is the first
residence on the right.

Self-contained Luxury Waterfront Apartment

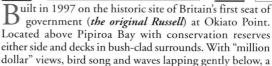

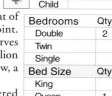

Double	$190-250
2nd Ensuite	$80-100
Child	

Built in 1997 on the historic site of Britain's first seat of government (*the original Russell*) at Okiato Point. Located above Pipiroa Bay with conservation reserves either side and decks in bush-clad surrounds. With "million dollar" views, bird song and waves lapping gently below, a good night's sleep is the norm.

The ground level apartment is accessed by covered verandah and has full kitchen, newly fitted down to the Kiwi "dish drawer"; dining, lounge and two ensuite bedrooms. Complete with own laundry, BBQ, TV, video and stereo. All in a park-like setting, it is ideal for the longer stay. Bay activities are available in Russell or, via the close-by Okiato-Opua ferry, in Paihia and Waitangi. Not suitable for small children. *Long stay rates quoted on request.*

Bedrooms	Qty
Double	2
Twin	
Single	
Bed Size	**Qty**
King	
Queen	1
Double	
King Single	1
Bathrooms	**Qty**
Ensuite	2
Private	
Guest Share	

HARDINGS' - AOTEAROA LODGE

Orongo Bay Farm, 39 Aucks Road,
RD 1, Russell, Bay of Islands
Ph/Fax (09) 403 7277, Mobile 0274-738 170
email: *info@the-lodge.co.nz*
www.the-lodge.co.nz

Features & Attractions

- *Country hospitality*
- *Farmhouse breakfast*
- *Spa and sauna*
- *Space & tranquility*
- *5 min. to Russell Village*
- *Superb cafés & restaurants*

Luxury Country Accommodation

Double	$185-285
Single	$150-250
Child	

Welcome to **Hardings' - Aotearoa Lodge**, set in seven acres overlooking Orongo Bay, just minutes from "Romantic Russell". We promise friendly hospitality, comfortable accommodation, privacy and delicious breakfasts, using eggs from our own chickens. We take pride in going 'that extra mile' to make your stay memorable. Our guest suites are well equipped. The two suites in 'Brook Barn' have their own private lounges and decks, whilst those in the main lodge have an adjoining lounge with balcony. Outside, we have decks, and a spa pool and sauna to help you relax. All suites have a refrigerator, tea/coffee facilities, hair dryer, toiletries, bath robes and ironing facilities. We will be delighted to help you with planning your excursions during your stay in the Bay, be it swimming with the dolphins, sailing, fishing or walking. Or you may simply choose to take things easy and soak up the wonderful surroundings.

DIRECTIONS:
Take the vehicle ferry from
Opua to Russell.
We are then approximately
4 km on the right hand side.

Bedrooms	Qty
Double	4
Twin	2
Single	
Bed Size	**Qty**
King	2
Queen	2
Double	
King Single	2
Bathrooms	**Qty**
Ensuite	4
Private	
Guest Share	

BAY OF ISLANDS COTTAGES

92B Te Wahapu Road, RD 1, Russell, Bay of Islands
Ph (09) 403 7757, Fax (09) 403 7758
email: *info@bayofislandscottages.co.nz*
www.bayofislandscottages.co.nz

Tariff : N.Z. Dollars	
Double	$200-250
Single	$170-220
Child	enquire

Bedrooms	Qty
Double	4
Twin	
Single	
Bed Size	Qty
Super King	
King	1
Queen	3
King/Single	1
Single	
Bathrooms	Qty
Ensuite	4
Private	
Guest Share	

**Boutique Accommodation
Bed & Breakfast**

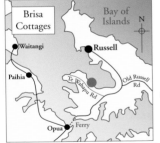

Features & Attractions

- *Delicious full breakfasts*
- *On the water's edge*
- *Peaceful garden setting*
- *Safe off-street parking*

- *Swimming with dolphins*
- *Forest/coastal walks*
- *Kiwi protection zone*
- *Dinner by arrangement*

At the end of a little road, which winds down to the water, are four charming and stylish cottages. Here you can spend time in peace and privacy enjoying the sun, fresh air and views over the bay just below. Each cottage has a wide, sunny terrace to make the most of the outdoors. The spacious interiors include a bedroom/lounge, well equipped kitchenette and ensuite. For your comfort there are top quality beds, cotton sheets, soft robes and towels. Breakfast is a special event with fine china, linen and silver, and guests gather around our big table to share good food and conversation. Where possible, the café-style fare is from our own organic garden with free-range eggs and local specialities.

Historic Russell is just seven minutes away by car and we can help you with maps and suggestions for local walks and sightseeing trips. Our dinghy is available anytime for fishing or a leisurely paddle out in the bay.

57

LA VEDUTA

11 Gould Street, Russell, Bay of Islands
Ph (09) 403 8299, Fax (09) 403 8299
email: *laveduta@xtra.co.nz*
www.laveduta.co.nz

Tariff : N.Z. Dollars	
Double	$180-250
Single	$150-180
Child	$45

Bedrooms	Qty
Double	3
Twin	1
Single	

Bed Size	Qty
Super King	
King	2
Queen	1
Double	2
Single	1

Bathrooms	Qty
Ensuite	3
Private	2
Guest Share	

**Quality Boutique Homestay
Bed & Breakfast**

Features & Attractions

- *Spectacular views of the Bay*
- *Television room*
- *5 minutes walk to town*
- *Unique stylish bedrooms*

- *Personalised service*
- *Tours & cruises arranged*
- *French & Italian spoken*
- *Excellent restaurants nearby*

DIRECTIONS:
Please phone for
easy directions.

Enjoy our mix of traditional European culture in the midst of the beautiful Bay of Islands, historic heartland of New Zealand. **La Veduta** is the perfect "pied-a-terre" for your Northland holiday. We offer our guests a warm welcome, taking care of your smallest needs.

All our bedrooms are individually styled, offering full sea views. You may be served a delicious cooked breakfast on the balcony overlooking the Bay of Russell. Enjoy complimentary afternoon tea. Relax and delight in the sunset over the Bay. **La Veduta** is only a few minutes walk from the township, wharf, sandy beaches and restaurants.

OUNUWHAO "HARDING HOUSE"
B & B HOMESTEAD

Matauwhi Bay, Russell, Bay of Islands
Ph (09) 403 7310, Fax (09) 403 8310 Mob. 027 414 1310
email: *thenicklins@xtra.co.nz*
www.travelwise.co.nz

Tariff : N.Z. Dollars	
Double	$250-350
Single	$160-200
Child	$60 (u/12)

Bedrooms	Qty
Double	4
Twin	2
Single	
Bed Size	**Qty**
Super King	1
King	1
Queen	4
Double	
Single	4
Bathrooms	**Qty**
Ensuite	5
Private	2
Guest Share	

 Boutique Accommodation & Self-contained Accommodation

Features & Attractions

- *Detached garden suite*
- *Safe, sandy swimming beaches*
- *Swimming with the dolphins*
- *Hearty, healthy gourmet breakfasts*
- *Historic Russell Village*
- *Sea and island excursions*
- *Coastal and bush walks*
- *Historic homestead*

When visiting Historic Russell take a step back into a bygone era. Spend some time with us in our delightful nostalgic, immaculately restored villa (circa 1894). Enjoy wrap-around verandahs in summer and the large guest lounge with open fire in winter. Each room has traditional wallpapers and paint work with handmade patchwork quilts and fresh flowers to create a lovingly detailed, traditional romantic interior. Breakfast is served in our farmhouse kitchen around the large kauri dining table. It is an all homemade affair, from the fresh baked bread to the yummy daily special and the jam conserves. Our 1930's self-contained cottage is set in park-like grounds for your privacy and enjoyment. With two bedrooms, two bathrooms, large lounge and sunroom and fully self-contained kitchen, it is ideal for people wanting peace and time out. Breakfast is available if required. We look forward to meeting you soon.

DIRECTIONS:
We are on the main road from
the vehicular ferry, in Matauwhi Bay
1 km from Russell Village.

EXPERIENCE OUR HISTORIC BED & BREAKFAST,
ENJOY A WORLD OF DIFFERENCE.

THE WHITE HOUSE
- Te Wharema -
7 Church Street, Russell, Bay of Islands
Ph/Fax (09) 403 7676
email: *info@thewhitehouserussell.com*
www.thewhitehouserussell.com

Features & Attractions

- *Restored & renovated Oct.'05*
- *180m to waterfront*
- *12 midday late check-out*
- *Breakfast buffet incl. until noon*
- *Complimentary port & sherry*
- *Free Broadband Internet access*

 Luxury Accommodation Bed & Breakfast

Double	$195-320
Single	$176-288
Child	

The Historic 'White House' Russell
Luxury Bed & Breakfast Accommodation

Come and have a truly unique stay with us in one of Russell's oldest houses (circa 1840). A beautifully restored villa with plenty of character. She features three well appointed rooms with super-king size beds and fresh new ensuites along with guest lounge and full kitchen.

Indulge in absolute luxury ideally situated in the heart of Russell with 12 midday check-out. Enjoy a dip in the spa pool, read a book on the shaded sundeck or wander to the waterfront.

DIRECTIONS:
Upon entering Russell, turn right into Church St, past NZ's oldest church, go straight across the next junction. We are about 20m on your right.

Bedrooms	Qty
Double/Twin	3
Twin	
Single	
Bed Size	**Qty**
Super King	3
Queen	
Double	
Single	
Bathrooms	**Qty**
Ensuite	3
Private	
Guest Share	

VILLA RUSSELL
2 Little Queen Street, Russell, Bay of Islands
Ph (09) 403 8845, Fax (09) 4038845
Mobile 027-492 8912
email: *info@kingfishercharters.co.nz*
www.kingfishercharters.co.nz

Features & Attractions

- *Spectacular views of the bay*
- *2 minutes walk to town*
- *Quiet and secluded*
- *Sail the bay with us too*
- *Close to 2 swimming beaches*
- *Delicious breakfast included*

 Luxury Accommodation with Sailing Option

Double	$165-320
Single	
Child	

DIRECTIONS: Travel through Russell village into Queen St. Little Queen St is the driveway with white picket fence at bottom of Flagstaff Hill.

Enjoy a welcoming visit to **Villa Russell**, 2 minutes from the beach and Russell's restaurants, yet totally private and secluded. Relax with magnificent views of Russell's bay and wharf from the deck of our beautifully restored 1910 villa, or from our guest cottage with spacious guest rooms, with ensuite, and large verandah, all surrounded by mature native trees and birdsong. Imagine having breakfast al fresco, while seeing nature at its best. A short walk takes you to Long Bay surf beach or historic Flagstaff Hill and native bush. Your suite is complete with tea/coffee facilities, refrigerator, microwave, TV and video, laundry facilities. Off-street parking provided. You may also be greeted by our friendly family dog. Make your stay even more special with a sailing charter on our 11.6m yacht 'Kingfisher' or 15m 'Kama Lua' to further explore the beautiful sights the Bay of Islands has to offer.

Bedrooms	Qty
Double	2
Twin	1
Single	
Bed Size	**Qty**
King	2
Queen	1
Double	
King/Single	2
Bathrooms	**Qty**
Ensuite	3
Private	
Guest Share	

60

RUSSELL BAY LODGE

71 Wellington Street, Russell
Ph/Fax (09) 403 7376, Mobile 027-417 3310
email: *info@russellbay.co.nz*
www.russellbay.co.nz

Tariff : N.Z. Dollars	
Double	$150-320
Single	
Child	

Bedrooms	Qty
Double	2
Twin	
Single	

Bed Size	Qty
Super King	
King	2
Queen	
Double	
Single	

Bathrooms	Qty
Ensuite	2
Private	
Guest Share	

Luxury
Self-contained Suites

Features & Attractions

- *Stunning sea views*
- *Short walk to village centre*
- *Warm hospitality*
- *Breakfast basket each day*
- *Modern, romantic setting*
- *Luxurious suites*
- *Superb coastal walks*
- *Pristine beaches*

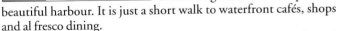

R omantic Russell, luxury accommodation, fabulous bay views... what more could you want! Our newly opened **Russell Bay Lodge** has an idyllic location on the slopes of Flagstaff Hill overlooking Russell Township and its beautiful harbour. It is just a short walk to waterfront cafés, shops and al fresco dining.

The purpose-designed accommodation offers king suites with mini kitchen, TV/DVD/Hifi, and own patio area. Our **Ocean Suite** also has a spa bath, and laundry facilities. We provide a sumptuous breakfast basket each day of your stay. Perfect for a honeymoon, or special holiday treat. If you are planning a wedding in the beautiful Bay of Islands, we would be delighted to help with any or all of your special arrangements.

Select from a wide range of local activities, then later relax on our main balcony soaking up possibly the best sea views in Russell, and reflect on another memorable day in the Bay!

TEN ON ONE COUNTRY/HOMESTAY

5 Ludbrook Road, Pakaraka, Bay of Islands
Ph (09) 405 9460, Fax (09) 405 9461
Mobile 027-227 6001
email: *ten.on.one@ihug.co.nz*
www.tenonone.co.nz

Tariff : N.Z. Dollars	
Double	$115
Single	$80
Child	half price

Bedrooms	Qty
Double	4
Twin	1
Single	

Bed Size	Qty
Super King	
King	
Queen	4
Double	1
Single	2

Bathrooms	Qty
Ensuite	4
Private	1
Guest Share	

**Affordable & Relaxing
Country - Homestay**

Features & Attractions

- *Hearty breakfast*
- *Evening meals available*
- *Complimentary tea & coffee*
- *Laundry service/iron avail*
- *Clean towels daily*
- *Courtesy airport & coach
  pick-up & return*
- *Clean swimming pool*

To all our visitors a warm and friendly greeting, the Bay of Islands awaits you. Our farmlet is situated in central Bay of Islands and is fifteen minutes from most towns and attractions including Paihia, Waitangi, Russell, Kerikeri and the Hokianga region.

Our courtesy coach meets all tours, coaches and air flights. We have exciting attractions to interest you. Would you like to visit Cape Reinga (top of New Zealand), cruise to Cape Brett (Hole in the Rock), see a 2000-year-old Kauri tree (Tane Mahuta), visit famous Waitangi and treaty house, historical Russell Town, glow worm caves, waterfalls, swimming, paragliding, tramping, horse riding, fishing, golf? Hey the list goes on.

Northland can genuinely lay claim to the most compact and diverse scenic orientated wonderland in New Zealand, come and judge for yourself. For your safety our modern home meets all fire and safety regulations. Enjoy our friendly home, feed the animals, collect the eggs, relax around the swimming pool or enjoy a barbeque.

DIRECTIONS:
At intersection of SH 10 and SH 1 travel 80 mtrs north on SH 1. We are first house on left (use Ludbrook Road entrance)

LUPTON LODGE

555 Ngunguru Road, Glenbervie, RD 3, Whangarei
Ph (09) 437 2989, Fax (09) 437 2987
email: *info@luptonlodge.co.nz*
www.luptonlodge.co.nz

Tariff : N.Z. Dollars	
Double	$115-185
Single	$99-125
Child	–

Bedrooms	Qty
Double	3
Twin	
Single	
Bed Size	**Qty**
Super King	
King	2
Queen	1
Double	
Single	
Bathrooms	**Qty**
Ensuite	3
Private	
Guest Share	

**Contemporary Luxurious
Boutique B & B Accommodation**

DIRECTIONS:
5.5 km east of the Whangarei
Falls turn-off on road
between Whangarei and the
Tutukaka Coast.

Features & Attractions

- *Tranquil, rural setting*
- *Chef-cooked breakfast/dinner*
- *Large swimming pool*
- *Young, professional hosts*
- *Tutukaka Coast beaches*
- *Poor Knights diving*
- *Whangarei art galleries*
- *1 hour to Bay of Islands*

Welcome to **Lupton Lodge** – a brand new concept in affordable luxury hosted accommodation for modern travellers. The character of an 1896 historic villa, set in picturesque dry-stone walled farmland, has been combined with contemporary uncluttered décor, superior ensuite rooms and extensive guest facilities. Luxurious beds and bathrobes, plunger coffee and DVD players come in all rooms. Indulge in a glass of NZ wine and a game of snooker in the guest lounge before a relaxed restaurant-style dinner on one of the verandas overlooking the pool and sub-tropical gardens. **Lupton Lodge** has been designed with privacy and relaxation in mind. Enjoy the abundance of activities available in the local area, or just sit back and unwind. Gourmet à la carte breakfast, wireless internet, 11am check-out and informed travel advice are complimentary. Only 10 minutes from Whangarei, but a world apart – Glenbervie is 2½ hours from Auckland and ideally located for exploring Northland. Visit Whangarei Falls, the spectacular Tutukaka Coast or the Bay of Islands. Scuba diving, Zion Wildlife Gardens tours, restaurant reservations can be arranged. **Visit our website to book online.**

PARKHILL
7d Dent Street, Whangarei
Phone (09) 438 8977, Fax (09) 438 8977
Mobile 021-074 1173
email: *parkhilltownbasin@xtra.co.nz*
www.parkhilltownbasin.co.nz

Tariff : N.Z. Dollars	
Double	$140-165
Single	$120
Child	

Bedrooms	Qty
Double	1
Twin	1
Single	

Bed Size	Qty
Super King	
King	1
Queen	
Double	
Single	2

Bathrooms	Qty
Ensuite	2
Private	
Guest Share	

Luxury Bed & Breakfast
Spectacular Harbour Views

Features & Attractions
• *1 min walk to city shopping*   • *Marina & harbour views*
• *2 min Quayside, Town Basin*   • *Laundry facilities*
• *Quality restaurants nearby*   • *Corporate guests welcome*

Discover the comforts and hospitality of our new accommodation, located in the Central Business District. Stroll to the shops and award-winning restaurants. Enjoy spectacular views of the river and the Town Basin. The yachts on their moorings by day and the lights sparkling at night make this a superb location. We have two luxuriously furnished rooms with spacious ensuites (one ensuite with spa bath). All rooms are designated smoke-free. Enjoy the luxury of in-room television, robes and extra toiletries. Exclusive guest facilities include a large lounge with kitchen, which opens onto a deck and garden with stunning views of the harbour. A scrumptious continental breakfast is included in the rates, although a cooked breakfast can be requested. Your experienced hosts, Leo and Lenore Malone, offer a 'home away from home' with kiwi hospitality.

DIRECTIONS:
From north or south follow signage to
'Town Basin & Quayside'.
We are on the corner of
Dent St./Rathbone St./Hatea Drive.

64

CHANNEL VISTA

254 Beach Road, Onerahi, Whangarei, Northland
Ph (09) 436 5529, Fax (09) 436 5529
Mobile 027-448 8507
email: *channelvista@igrin.co.nz*
www.bnbwhangarei.co.nz

Features & Attractions

- *Only 1 hour to Bay of Islands*
- *Many golf courses handy*
- *Restaurants, shopping 5 min*
- *Many interesting walks*
- *Sandy, safe beaches nearby*
- *Top diving, fishing 30 min*

$	Double	$140-170
	Single	$100
	Child	

**Harbourside
Bed & Breakfast**

Bedrooms	Qty
Double	2
Twin	
Single	
Bed Size	**Qty**
King	
Queen	2
Double	
Single	
Bathrooms	**Qty**
Ensuite	2
Private	
Guest Share	

Channel Vista is a modern purpose-built deluxe self-contained Bed & Breakfast situated on the interesting Whangarei Harbour, nine kilometres from central Whangarei and very handy to the Onerahi shopping complex and sports centres (golf, swimming, walks, pools) and only an easy five minute walk along the waterfront to a top restaurant. Bay of Islands, Kerikeri and the West Coast are only one hour away. Poor Knight's Diving and deep sea fishing at Tutukaka is thirty minutes away and lovely Whangarei Heads beaches are so handy. You can see, we are a very handy base for your Northland Holiday. Both self-contained units have lovely decks where you can sit and relax or view the garden or watch superb sunsets.

DIRECTIONS: Follow signs to Onerahi Airport, go past gates to Pah Road, go down Pah Road to roundabout and turn left into Beach Road - No 254.

TOP STOREY BED & BREAKFAST

73 Scott Road, Tamaterau, Whangarei
Ph (09) 436 2220,
Mobile 021-463 330
e-mail: *info@whangareibandb.co.nz*
www.whangareibandb.co.nz

Features & Attractions

- *Quiet and peaceful*
- *Great garden/local walks*
- *Generous breakfast*
- *Restaurants close by*
- *Email & Internet access*
- *Families welcome*

$	Double	$85-110
	Single	$55-80
	Extra pp	$20

**Quality Bed & Breakfast
Homestay**

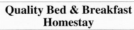

Bedrooms	Qty
Double	2
Twin	2
Single	
Bed Size	**Qty**
King	
Queen	2
King/Single	2
Single	2
Bathrooms	**Qty**
Ensuite	
Private	2
Guest Share	

Start your Northland adventure with us. Enjoy our family-friendly, spacious, character-filled colonial style home. As close to sea and city as you can get. Located on Whangarei Heads Road, east of Whangarei City, walk to the water in 2min. A short drive takes you to golf, coastal walks, beautiful ocean beaches and spectacular Mt Manaia waiting for you to climb! Water views and often glorious sunsets as you sit in the bay windows of the **Top Storey Flat** with a large lounge area with pool table. The **Garden Unit** is another story! Bright, open plan, self-contained unit opening to the garden and conservatory for your morning cuppa or evening glass of wine. A microwave, fridge and basic cooking facilities are in both, with TV, DVD, Radio/CD. Dinner by arrangement. We like to make your stay comfortable and trouble free with company and good conversation, should you wish it.

DIRECTIONS: From Onerahi follow Whangarei Heads Rd along harbour. Turn right at top of first hill, Scott Road. Go **down** hill. No.73 is 700m on left.

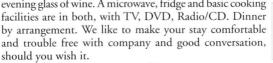

TIDE SONG

Beasley Rd, Taiharuru Estuary, Whangarei, Northland
Ph (09) 436 1959
Mobile 027 636 5888
email: *stay@tidesong.co.nz*
www.tidesong.co.nz

Features & Attractions

- *Quiet privacy*
- *Spectacular walks*
- *Bush bath*
- *Bush setting - Fishing*
- *Choice of ocean beaches*
- *Safe estuary for boating*

**Bed & Breakfast Homestay
Self-contained Accom. optional**

	Double	$100-120
	Single	$80
	Child	

From Whangarei drive east for twenty-five minutes to our eight acres on the Taiharuru Estuary. With a bush and seaside setting, there is a small jetty, and a variety of small craft to use on the estuary. Spots for fishing and shellfish are close. There is a variety of wonderful walks, with Pacific views and peaks, available to differing levels of fitness. A choice of ocean and surf beaches ten to twenty minutes away. We have a farming and teaching background and there's a small flock of sheep. We are interested in sailing, cycling, conservation, gardening, home-cooking and music. We enjoy having company and looking after guests. Our accommodation is a separate upstairs two bedroom flat with ensuite, kitchen and television. Also a downstairs bedroom with ensuite and TV. We can provide extra home-cooked meals if you wish; or cafés & restaurant are ten minutes away. Looking forward to showing you Northland hospitality.
Being members of Northland Sustainable Tourism Charter means that at Tidesong we are involved in caring for the environment.

Bedrooms	Qty
Double	3
Twin	
Single	
Bed Size	**Qty**
King	
Queen	3
Double	
Single	1
Bathrooms	**Qty**
Ensuite	1
Private	1
Guest Share	

APPIN COTTAGE

"Appin" 2432 Whangarei Heads Road,
McKenzie Bay, RD 4 Whangarei
Ph (09) 434 0819 Mobile 021-023 43114
email: *dougiechowns@orcon.net.nz*
www.aotea.co.nz/NZ_Art/Chowns

Features & Attractions

- *Peaceful setting*
- *Superb mountain seascapes*
- *Fine art & Celtic music*
- *Safe, private swimming*
- *Hot bread with breakfast*
- *Featured NZ Geographic*

**Self-contained Cottage with
Continental Breakfast**

	Double	$130
	Single	
	Child	n/a

DIRECTIONS:
From State Highway 1 follow signs to Whangarei Heads. 31 km from Town Basin yachts **Appin** McKenzie Bay is on right beyond mountain and Taurikura.

Near Whangarei, below craggy peaks of Mt Manaia, this self-contained cottage is in the subtropical garden of McKenzie Homestead, settled 1857 by Nova Scotians from St Anns, Cape Breton. Between palms, our old homestead fronts a secluded white, sandy beach and 200 metres of our pohutukawa-fringed shoreline. The cottage is fully furnished and almost new – you will sleep in comfort to the sound of the sea. Mt Manaia and other magnificent ranges offer many accessed walkways: Smugglers Bay, Peach Cove, Bream Head, Mt Aubrey and Ocean Beach. Sprats, shellfish, snapper or marlin, boats, canoes and music are part of our lifestyle and well known to visitors from the Western Isles of Scotland and Cape Breton. Gaelic and Spanish spoken. Previously resident in UK, Portugal, Spain and the Caribbean before 35 years in McKenzie Bay we live as crofters in the South Pacific. We welcome you to enjoy the sea for breakfast and share our paradise.

Bedrooms	Qty
Double	1
Twin	
Single	
Bed Size	**Qty**
King	
Queen	
Double	1
Single	
Bathrooms	**Qty**
Ensuite	
Private	1
Guest Share	

PARUA HOUSE

Parua Bay, Whangarei Heads Road, RD 4, Whangarei
Ph (09) 436 5855
Mobile 021-0250 4389
email: *paruahomestay@clear.net.nz*
www.paruahomestay.homestead.com

Tariff : N.Z. Dollars	
Double	$150-175
Single	$90-110
Child	

Bedrooms	Qty
Double	2
Twin	1
Single	1
Bed Size	**Qty**
Super King	
King	
Queen	2
Double	
Single	3
Bathrooms	**Qty**
Ensuite	2
Private	1
Guest Share	

Farmstay - Boutique Accommodation

Features & Attractions

- *Outstanding panoramic views*
- *Peaceful setting*
- *Homegrown fruit & produce*
- *Golf course nearby*
- *Superb swimming beaches*
- *Spa pool*
- *Featured on TV: "Ansett NZ-Time of Your Life" & "Corban's Taste NZ"*

Parua House is a classical colonial house built in 1883, comfortably restored and occupying an elevated site with panoramic views of Parua Bay and Whangarei harbour. The property covers 29 hectares of farmland with lush valleys leading into steep slopes of native bush. Two protected reserves on the property are rich in a variety of native trees (including kauri) and native birds abound. Guests are welcome to explore the farm, milk the Jersey house cow, track through the bush beside the Kohinui stream, explore the olive grove, sub-tropical orchard or just relax in the spa pool or on the verandah overlooking the marina. A safe swimming beach adjoins the farm with a short walk to a fishing jetty. Two marinas and an excellent golf course are nearby. We have travelled extensively and especially welcome overseas guests. Our interests are wide including travel, photography, patchwork-quilting and horticulture. The house is attractively appointed with antique furniture and a rare collection of spinning wheels. We enjoy good food, wine and conversation. Fresh home-grown produce is used where possible along with home-baked bread and freshly squeezed orange juice. Vegetarian food is provided if requested. A warm welcome awaits you.

JUNIPER HOUSE

49 Proctor Road, Maungatapere
Whangarei RD9
Ph (09) 434 6399, Fax (09) 434 6399
Mobile 027-422 4498
email: *diane.james@xtra.co.nz*

Features & Attractions

- *Art, craft, cafés*
- *Golf courses handy*
- *Fishing, sailing, charters*
- *Rural tranquility*
- *Guests tea & coffee facility*
- *Home-cooking*

Bed & Breakfast Homestay	Double	$120-135
	Single	$60-70
	Child	

Juniper House is a comfortable welcoming home, surrounded by a young avocado orchard. Relax in the extensive grounds, enjoy a game of tennis or swim in our saltwater pool. For the snooker enthusiast we have a full size billiard table, or simply relax and enjoy the peace and quiet. We are an easy fifteen-minute drive from the museum and the kiwi house, golf courses, cafés, galleries and the Whangarei yacht basin. We offer a full breakfast, dinner and drinks by arrangement.

Our interests include sailing, fishing, classic cars and decorative art. You may like to join us for happy hour and a BBQ on Friday or Saturday, or for a traditional Christmas, when the house is dressed in its best!

Bedrooms	Qty
Double	2
Twin	1
Single	
Bed Size	**Qty**
King	
Queen	1
Double	1
Single	2
Bathrooms	**Qty**
Ensuite	1
Private	
Guest Share	1

OWAITOKAMOTU

727 Otaika Valley Road, Maungatapere, Whangarei
(*Postal:* PO Box 6067, Otaika, Whangarei)
Ph (09) 434 7554, Mobile 025-806 954
email: *minniegeorge@xtra.co.nz*

Features & Attractions

- *Golf course, Kiwi House*
- *Museum & homestead*
- *Featured Whangarei garden*
- *Beaches, diving, fishing*
- *1 hour Bay of Islands*
- *1 hour Matakohe Museum*

Bed & Breakfast Homestay	Double	$85-100
	Single	$65
	Child	neg

Come and enjoy the tranquility of **Owaitokamotu**, 'Place of Water', with magnificent rocks in all shapes and sizes. Pristine native bush awaits your rambling walks. **Owaitokamotu** is set in ten acres with easy contoured and newly created gardens, featuring ponds, bridges, archways, windmill and 1850's style shanty. Our newly built home is wheelchair-friendly. All bedrooms have private access from exterior and television, tea & coffee facilities and home-baked cookies. A wide verandah offers relaxation. Join us for a three course evening meal ($25 pp). Restaurants are nearby. Our interests are travel, wood carving and creating our garden. We are smoke-free indoors. Laundry facilities are available. A very warm welcome awaits you.

Bedrooms	Qty
Double	2
Twin	1
Single	
Bed Size	**Qty**
King	
Queen	2
Double	
King Single	2
Bathrooms	**Qty**
Ensuite	
Private	1
Guest Share	1

KAURI HOUSE LODGE

Bowen Street, PO Box 382, Dargaville
Ph (09) 439 8082, Fax (09) 439 8082
Mobile 027-454 7769
email: *kaurihouselodge@ocron.net.nz*

Tariff : N.Z. Dollars	
Double	$200-275
Single	$200
Child	

Bedrooms	Qty
Double	2
Twin	1
Single	
Bed Size	**Qty**
Super King	1
King	1
Queen	
Double	
King/Single	1
Bathrooms	**Qty**
Ensuite	3
Private	
Guest Share	

**Luxury Historic
Bed & Breakfast**

Map showing Kauri House Lodge, Grey St, Bowen St, Jervois St, Route 14, Route 12, To Whangarei, To Auckland, N.

Features & Attractions

- *Kauri villa over 5000 sq ft*
- *Farm bush walk included*
- *Hearty breakfast*
- *Summer swimming pool*
- *Peaceful & tranquil location*
- *Beach, lakes & bush walks*
- *Historic homestead*
- *Close to Waipoua Forest*

Original features of this 1880s style villa include the detailed verandah balustrading, stained glass, pressed ceilings, sash windows and native Kauri panelling. Completed in 1910 by a leading bushman as a spacious family residence, **Kauri House** now

offers three private ensuite guest rooms and three lounge rooms – a billiard room, library and television lounge – furnished with antiques. Only three kilometres from the township of Dargaville, with many nice restaurants. **Kauri House** is set in three hectares of garden with abundant native birdlife including fantails, wood pigeons and seasonal tui. A swimming pool provides relaxation and exercise in summer only. Nearby is Doug's forty hectare farm on which he runs steers and donkeys. This land includes sixteen hectares of protected native bush.
"Perfect accommodation, good host, these things make holidays worthwhile" *Frank & Annie, Holland*
"Fantastic house and timber furniture, best we've seen" *Gary & Trish, Australia*

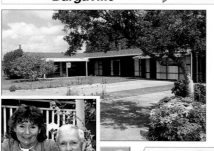

AWAKINO POINT BOUTIQUE MOTEL
SH 14 Dargaville 0340, Northland
Ph (09) 439 7870
Mobile 027-451 9474
e-mail: *awakinopoint@xtra.co.nz*
www.awakinopoint.co.nz

Features & Attractions
- *Twin Coast Discovery Route*
- *Attractive gardens*
- *Quiet country surroundings*
- *Excellent coastal golf course*
- *Good, firm beds*
- *Guest laundry & bbq area*

Boutique B&B Motel Style

Double	$125
Quad	$175
Child	–

Awakino Point Boutique Motel is located just two minutes drive (2km) from the small township of Dargaville, on State Highway 14 (The Whangarei Road). This well established, peaceful little Boutique Motel, surrounded by attractive gardens and farmland, offers you the best of both worlds: Your own spacious unit with private bathroom, a lovely, complimentary breakfast trolley delivered to your unit each morning and personal hospitality by your friendly, experienced tourism hosts, June and Mick. June does painting and pottery and has made a name for herself making "Gum Digger Boots", which she sells and is known locally as "The Boot Lady".

One bedroom S/C, Double Rate $125 – Two bedroom S/C, Four person $175
(Rates all inclusive of GST & breakfast)

Bedrooms	Qty
Double	3
Twin	2
Single	
Bed Size	**Qty**
King	
Queen	3
Double	
Single	4
Bathrooms	**Qty**
Ensuite	3
Private	
Guest Share	

TANGOWAHINE FARMSTAY
1078 Tangowahine Valley Rd, RD 2, Dargaville
Ph (09) 439 1570
Mobile 027-439 1572
email: *holiday@tangowahine.co.nz*
www.tangowahine.co.nz

Features & Attractions
- *Native forest/farm tours*
- *Giant kauri snails*
- *Bird lovers' paradise*
- *Centrally located in Northland*
- *Hot spa in bush*
- *Dinner by arrangement*

Double	$135-210
Single	$120-180
Child	

  Self-Contained Farmstay Bed & Breakfast

Bedrooms	Qty
Double	3
Twin	
Single	1
Bed Size	**Qty**
Super King	1
Queen	3
King Single	2
Single	1
Bathrooms	**Qty**
Ensuite	2
Private	1
Guest Share	1

Relax in a haven of tranquility – a new, purpose-built facility on a 250 acre farm central to Dargaville, Kaikohe and Whangarei. The ideal base for a Northland holiday, it's close to Kaiiwi Lakes, Trounson Kauri Park, Baylys Beach; ideally located for day trips to the Bay of Islands, Waipoua Forest and the Matakohe Museum. Experience bushwalks, waterfalls, streams and abundant birdlife at **Tangowahine** – literally 'place to take a woman'. Pamper yourself in the self-contained **Taraire Cottage** and enjoy a hot soak in total privacy in our wood-fired bush spa. Relax in the **Tutamoe Suite** with views to Mt Tutamoe and the private lakeside garden spa.

DIRECTIONS: Take SH 14 west from Whangarei (40 km) or east from Dargaville (10 km).
At Tangowahine turn north into Tangowahine Valley Road.
Tangowahine Farm is on the right, 10 km from the turn-off. Look for the bright red letterbox.

FLOWER HAVEN

53 St Ann Road, Waipu Cove, Northland 0582
Ph (09) 432 0421
email: *beds@flowerhaven.com*
www.flowerhaven.com

Features & Attractions

- *Panoramic ocean view*
- *Garden retreat*
- *Surf patrol in summer*
- *Extensive beach walks*
- *Walk to bird sanctuary*
- *Golf courses & fishing*

$	Double	$100-120
	Single	–
	Child	–

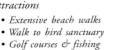 **Bed & Breakfast
Self-contained Accom.**

Bedrooms	Qty
Double	2
Twin	
Single	
Bed Size	**Qty**
King	
Queen	
Double	2
Single	
Bathrooms	**Qty**
Ensuite	
Private	1
Guest Share	

At **Flower Haven** we enjoy an elevated position, views of Bream Bay and sleeping to the sound of the surf. We are retired, with interests in genealogy, meeting people and gardening and developing the grounds as a garden retreat. Our accommodation is a self-contained downstairs two bedroom apartment with separate access, fridge/freezer, stove, microwave, washing machine, TV, radio and tiled bathroom. Linen, duvets, blankets and bath towels are provided. We are a 5 min. walk to restaurant, shop, rocks and sandy surf beach and are near many places of interest; bird sanctuaries, museums, golf courses, horse-riding treks, fishing trips, limestone caves, walking tracks, oil refinery visitors centre. Auckland is 90, Whangarei 35 min. away. Visit our website for more details.

Map: To Waipu, Cove Road, St Ann Road, Waipu Cove, Surf Club, Shop, Flower Haven, To Mangawhai

DIRECTIONS: 8 km south of Waipu on Cove Road, right into St Ann Road, **Flower Haven** is the last house on left.

ZANY'S HAVEN B & B

298/11 Cove Road, RD2, Waipu, Northland
Ph (09) 432 1517
Mobile 027-658 5217
email: *corralieb@yahoo.com*
www.zanyhaven.co.nz/www.zanyhaven.com

Features & Attractions

- *Peaceful and quiet*
- *Panoramic views*
- *Restaurants/ shops 3km*
- *Walking distance to beach, river*
- *On Twin Coast Discovery Route*
- *Close to horsetrekking, golf, caving*

$	Double	$150
	Single	$120
	Child	

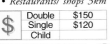 **Coastal and Scenic
Ensuite Accommodation**

Bedrooms	Qty
Double	2
Twin	1
Single	
Bed Size	**Qty**
King	1
Queen	
Double	1
Single	2
Bathrooms	**Qty**
Ensuite	3
Private	
Guest Share	

Our new Bed & Breakfast is situated on a quiet and peaceful hill overlooking beautiful Bream Bay beaches in northern New Zealand, thirty minutes south of Whangarei. Only two hours north of Auckland. On the 'Twin Coast Discovery Route' off SH1. We are located halfway between Waipu Centre and Waipu Cove with fabulous views of Bream Bay, the Waipu River Estuary, Whangarei Heads and Hen and Chicken Islands. Within easy reach of beaches, walks and tourist amenities such as golf, kayaking, horse-trekking – good for re-charging the batteries and recovering from jet-lag.

 We offer two double/twin ensuite rooms and one self-contained flat. Not suitable for children.

Map: To Whangarei, Zany's Haven, Waipu, To Auckland, Cove Rd

MANGAWHAI LODGE
"A ROOM WITH A VIEW"
4 Heather Street, Mangawhai Heads, 0505 Northland
Ph (09) 431 5311, Fax (09) 431 5312
email: *info@seaviewlodge.co.nz*
www.seaviewlodge.co.nz

Tariff : N.Z. Dollars	
Double	$155-175
Single	$135-155
Child	

Bedrooms	Qty
Double	4
Twin	
Single	

Bed Size	Qty
Super King	
King	3
Queen	1
Double	
King Single	3/6

Bathrooms	Qty
Ensuite	3
Private	1
Guest Share	

 Boutique Bed & Breakfast Inn

Features & Attractions

- Beaches & walkways
- Fishing & water activities
- Ideal for couples & groups
- Arts, crafts & wine trails
- Adjacent to championship golf course
- 2 hours to international airport
- Off-street parking
- Walk to shops & cafés

Indulge, escape to the tranquility and magic of **Mangawhai Lodge**. Midway between Auckland Airport and the Bay of Islands, **Mangawhai Lodge** offers the perfect beach retreat for rest and relaxation or base to discover the treasures of Northland. Spectacular sea and island views of the Hauraki Gulf, Bream Bay, and white sandy beaches of Mangawhai make **Mangawhai Lodge** the ultimate "room with a view". The self-contained apartment and three stylish guest rooms open onto wrap-around verandahs. Spend your days on the championship golf course, explore beaches and walkways, curl up reading or watch the boats sail by. A licensed café and championship golf course are adjacent, harbour access 400m. Sleep to the sound of the sea, awake to sumptuous cooked and continental breakfast. Having travelled extensively, we look forward to ensuring your stay is enjoyable and relaxing.

Bookings and two-day stay recommended.

ZENFORD LODGE

1034 Cove Rd, Langs Beach, RD 2, Waipu
Ph (09) 432 0757, Fax (09) 432 0757
Mobile 021-400 383
email: *enquiries@zenfordlodge.co.nz*
www.zenfordlodge.co.nz

Tariff : N.Z. Dollars	
Double	$140-240
Single	$120-190
Child	enquire

Bedrooms	Qty
Double	4
Twin	1
Single	

Bed Size	Qty
Super King	1
King	2
Queen	1
Double	
King/Single	1

Bathrooms	Qty
Ensuite	3
Private	1
Guest Share	

VISA **MasterCard** **eftpos**

**Bed & Breakfast Tranquility
Rural, Sea and Native Bush Views**

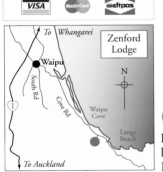

DIRECTIONS: Please phone or email for bookings and directions.

Features & Attractions

- *Warm, friendly Kiwi hospitality*
- *Multicultural décor*
- *Rural, sea and bush views*
- *Croquet and activities lawn*
- *Private native bush walk*
- *Restaurants and local arts*
- *Golf, beach, bush & water activities*
- *Midway Auckland & Bay of Islands*

Centrally located between Auckland and the Bay of Islands, **Zenford Lodge** enjoys ten acres of gardens, native bush and rural countryside with views over Bream Bay. Also centrally located between Waipu Historic Village and Mangawhai Heads, the immediate area offers two wonderful beaches, two golf courses, a variety of cafés and restaurants, art galleries, bird sanctuaries, bush walks, horse treks, water activities and much more! Your choice of accommodation offers four rooms decorated to reflect New Zealand's multicultural flavours and providing tea and coffee making facilities, complimentary snacks and refreshments, fridge, TV, hair dryer and toiletries with fine linen and bedding. All rooms have access to balconies or courtyards. Enjoy venturing out to the beaches and attractions, and after enjoying a delicious meal at one of the local restaurants, each evening returning to the serenity of **Zenford Lodge** to relax to the sound of the surf, waterfall and bird life. We look forward to meeting and sharing our home and experiences with you over a coffee or glass of wine, and helping to make your stay enjoyable and memorable.

PALM HOUSE

Pahi Road, RD 1, Paparoa
Ph (09) 431 6689, Mobile 027-688 8296
email: *palmhouse@paradise.net.nz*

Features & Attractions

- Close to Matakohe Museum
- Home cooked dinners
- Complimentary kayak
- Golf course nearby
- In house & s/c garden cottage
- Excellent restaurant nearby

On the River
Bed & Breakfast

  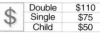

Double	$110
Single	$75
Child	$50

Bedrooms	Qty
Double	2
Twin	
Single	1
Bed Size	**Qty**
King	
Queen	2
Double	
King Single	2
Bathrooms	**Qty**
Ensuite	1
Private	
Guest Share	1

Hector and Jenny are renowned for their relaxed, friendly hospitality; delicious meals of fine local produce, accompanied by fine New Zealand wines.

Enjoy staying at peaceful Pahi. Stroll along the tideline or stand on the wharf and watch the fish jump. Just two hours from Auckland, thirteen kilometres from the famous Matakohe Museum and en route to the spectacular Kauri Forest.

Signposted on the main Highway 12, travel seven kilometres down Pahi Road and reach **Palm House.**

PETITE PROVENCE

703c Tinopai Road, RD 1, Matakohe
Ph (09) 431 7552, Fax (09) 431 7552
email: *petite-provence@clear.net.nz*
www.petiteprovence.co.nz

Features & Attractions

- Dinner by arrangement
- Complimentary tea/coffee
- Matakohe Kauri Museum 9km
- 2 hrs from Auckland
- Panoramic views
- Peace and tranquility

Quality Countrystay
Bed & Breakfast

Double	$145
Single	$100
Child	

Bedrooms	Qty
Double	2
Twin	1
Single	
Bed Size	**Qty**
Super King	1
Queen	2
Double	
King/Single	2
Bathrooms	**Qty**
Ensuite	2
Private	1
Guest Share	

Just 10 minutes from Matakohe Kauri Museum, **Petite Provence** is set on 7 hectares of rolling farmland with neighbouring bush and distant water views. All rooms (insect screens) open onto a covered deck, a very peaceful and relaxing atmosphere with stunning panoramic views. Delicious evening meals, mediterranean, vegetarian, local cuisine (home produce when possible).

Guy is French, Linda a New Zealander.

Our home in the south of France was also a Bed & Breakfast. 'Loopy' is our outside dog.

Bookings preferrred.

DIRECTIONS:
From Matakohe Museum
drive 2 km towards
Tinopai, turn left into
Tinopai Rd, drive 7 km.
Look for our roadside
sign on the left.

Welcome to
Petite Provence.

74

KAWAU ISLAND EXPERIENCE

North Cove, Kawau Island
Ph (09) 422 8831, Fax (09) 422 8832
Mobile 021-951 038
email: *mail@kawaulodge.co.nz*
www.kawaulodge.co.nz

Tariff : N.Z. Dollars	
Double	$175
Single	$150
Child	

Bedrooms	Qty
Double	2
Twin	
Single	

Bed Size	Qty
Super King	
King	
Queen	2
Double	
Single	

Bathrooms	Qty
Ensuite	2
Private	
Guest Share	

Island Retreat
Gourmet Meals

Features & Attractions

- *Only 1½ hrs. from Auckland*
- *Tranquil, peaceful location*
- *Kayaks and dinghy*
- *Superb alfresco dining*
- *Bush and coastal walks*
- *Relaxed, friendly hosts*
- *Underfloor heating in ensuites*
- *Fishing and sightseeing trips*

Kawau Island Experience

Matakana
To Whangarei
Warkworth
Snells Beach
Sandspit
Kawau Island
N
To Auckland

DIRECTIONS:
Approaching Warkworth from Auckland, follow directions to Sandspit. Contact Kawau Kat ferry service. Phone 09 425 8006 prior to arrange either a ferry crossing or water taxi out to Kawau Island.

Experience peace and tranquility only 1 hour's drive from Auckland city. **Kawau Lodge** is set in picturesque North Cove on Kawau Island. From the minute you step off the ferry or water taxi onto our private, all-tide jetty, you will be captured by the quietness of your surroundings, only interrupted by the songs of the native birds. From your tastefully appointed queen room, complete with its own coffee/tea making facilities, television and luxurious ensuite, you will enjoy magical bush and sea views. A delicious breakfast with a choice of continental or gourmet, served with fresh fruit, yoghurt, cereal and specialty muffins, can be served in your room either outside on your deck or upstairs in the dining alcove. Enjoy a fabulous hosted evening dinner, made from a fine selection of carefully prepared local produce. Our salads and vegetables are often picked fresh from our garden. Local wine list available. Great for honeymooners or that special weekend away.

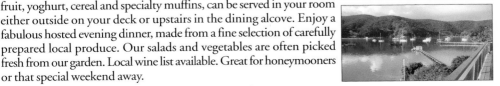

BELVEDERE HOMESTAY

38 Kanuka Road, RD 2, Sandspit, Warkworth
Ph (09) 425 7201, Mobile 027-284 4771
email: *belvederehomestay@xtra.co.nz*
www.belvederehomestay.co.nz

Tariff : N.Z. Dollars	
Double	$160
Single	$100
Dinner	$45

Bedrooms	Qty
Double	2
Twin	1
Single	

Bed Size	Qty
Super King	
King	
Queen	2
Double	
Single	2

Bathrooms	Qty
Ensuite	1
Private	2
Guest Share	

**Quality Homestay
Bed & Breakfast**

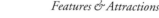

Features & Attractions

- *Panoramic sea views*
- *Air conditioned home*
- *Dinner an occasion*
- *Warm, friendly hospitality*

- *Home produce for breakfast*
- *Glassed spa pool & games room*
- *"Goat Island" marine reserve*
- *Beaches, wineries, pottery*

Warkworth Sandspit is the perfect stop going to and from the Bay of Islands. **Belvedere Homestay** is sited on top of the hill with 360° views overlooking the spit where the ferries leave for Kawau Island and Governor Grey's restored mansion. The view is awesome which you will enjoy while relaxing on our spacious decks and terraces. Stroll around our property with sunken barbeque, rose garden, orchards, lawns, native birds and bush and two lily ponds and enjoy a friendly game of pétanque (boule) or pool. Laundry facilities available. Fishing off the beach or boat, golf, tennis, swimming etc are all within seven kilometres. Our house is for your comfort and enjoyment and as Roger Hall (NZ/ English stage and televison playwright) wrote about **Belvedere Homestay**: "It is no wonder people come for one day and stay a week." Margaret's flair with cooking is a great way to relax after an adventurous day, with pre-dinner drinks and two course meal and wine ($45pp). Come and enjoy a friendly, relaxing stay with Margaret and Ron. – Good, safe parking available.

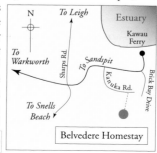

ALEGRIA BEAUTYFARM

180 Monarch Downs Way, Matakana 0983
Ph (09) 422 7211, Fax (09) 422 7833
email: *alegriabeautyfarm@xtra.co.nz*
www.beautyfarm.co.nz

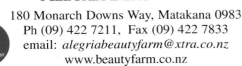

Tariff : N.Z. Dollars	
Double	$180-195
Single	on request
Child	12 yr. +

Bedrooms	Qty
Double	2
Twin	
Single	

Bed Size	Qty
Super King/Twin	1
Super King	1
King - Single	2
Queen	
Single	

Bathrooms	Qty
Ensuite	1
Private	1
Guest Share	

      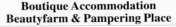

**Boutique Accommodation
Beautyfarm & Pampering Place**

Features & Attractions

- *Professional face & body treatments*
- *Mouthwatering breakfast*
- *Swimming Pool*
- *Spectacular views, peaceful*
- *Wheat-free, organic homebaking*
- *Wineries, markets, art & craft close by*
- *Golf course, beaches, regional parks*
- *Diving, snorkeling at Goat Island*

Advance booking essential.

Aperfect Mediterranean setting provides spectacular views across the vineyards to Kawau Island and Warkworth with magnificent sunrises and sunsets. "Where the wine grapes flourish, so do good times". Claudia, Alex and Julia(15) welcome you at **Alegria Beautyfarm**, which is the ideal place to experience the good living of the Matakana Coast Wine Country and offers rare tranquillity to unwind and relax. Two tastefully appointed rooms, each with its own charm and amenities like tea/coffee making facilities, TV, hair dryer and underfloor heating in the large European-style bathrooms. The ensuite room has a private entrance and patio. The other room, with private bathroom, is in the main house. Start your morning with fresh pressed juice and fresh brewed coffee or a cup of tea out of an extraordinary assortment. Claudia's home-baked German bread and homemade mueslis are famous. Be surprised by a mouth watering variety of sweet and savoury delicacies. Claudia is a German-trained beauty therapist and loves to pamper you in her cosy **Beautyfarm**. Indulge in unique face and body treatments using the best ingredients. All your senses are getting spoiled, leaving you with glowing skin, more energy and calmness. German, French and Japanese spoken.

WARKWORTH COUNTRY HOUSE

18 Wilson Road, RD 1, Warkworth, Auckland
Ph (09) 422 2485, Fax (09) 422 2485
Mobile 027-6001510
email: p-jbathgate@xtra.co.nz
www.warkworthcountryhouse.co.nz

Features & Attractions

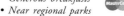
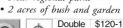

- *Private entrance and patio*
- *Each room with ensuite*
- *Television in each room*
- *Generous breakfasts*
- *Near regional parks*
- *2 acres of bush and garden*

Quality Countrystay Bed & Breakfast

Double	$120-145
Single	$95-110
Child	

Warkworth Country House is situated on the fringe of Warkworth historic township. We have sheep and cows as neighbours with views of the rolling countryside towards the Mahurangi estuary. Bird life is abundant in our 2 acres of garden and bush. Warkworth is the ideal place for a peaceful and relaxing weekend getaway. After a leisurely breakfast, enjoy a stroll through the groves of kauri and bush at the Warkworth museum and Parry Kauri Park just 500 metres up the road. Drive into Warkworth for coffee or to Matakana for lunch at the wineries and potteries in the area. Beaches, Kawau Island, Scandrett or Tawharanui Regional parks are within easy reach.
Let us make your stay enjoyable and refreshing.

DIRECTIONS: Approaching Warkworth from Auckland turn right into McKinney Rd signposted Warkworth Museum/Parry Kauri Park, then turn left into Wilson Road.

Bedrooms	Qty
Double	1
Twin	1
Single	
Bed Size	**Qty**
King	
Queen	1
King/Single	
Single	2
Bathrooms	**Qty**
Ensuite	2
Private	
Guest Share	

OUR FARM-PARK

450 Krippner Rd, Puhoi,
postal: RD 3, Kaukapakapa, Auckland 0873
Ph/Fax (09) 422 0626, Mobile 021-215 5165
email: *ofp@friends.co.nz*
www.friends.co.nz

Tariff : N.Z. Dollars	
Double	$125-225
Single	$115-175
Child - no charge	

Bedrooms	Qty
Double	1
Twin	1
Single	

Bed Size	Qty
Super King	
King	
Queen	1
Double	
Single	2+1

Bathrooms	Qty
Ensuite	
Private	1
Guest Share	

**Organic Farmstay
...the gentle way**

Features & Attractions

- *Children welcome*
- *International cuisine*
- *Gentle treatment of animals*
- *"Conversation English" courses*
- *Activities provided for children*
- *Educational courses*
- *Organic & GE free food*
- *Nobody smokes here*

Farmstay, the gentle, organic way. Your family are the only guests when you are here. We farm with kindness sheep, Belted Galloway cows with calves at foot, horses, ducks, poultry running free, providing milk, butter, yoghurt, ice-cream, cheeses.

International cuisine - taste-filled organic meals included in tariff. Includes fruit and vegetables we grow and fresh baking. Come relax (no charge for your welcomed children), sleep off 'jet-lag'. Our beds are very comfortable. Panoramic views, fresh air, clean water. Share experiences, ideas and knowledge over dinner. Walk through our 'Farm' fields and the 'Park' - trees, streams, bird life, flora and fauna, private and secluded places. Gardeners will love it here. Use our library, email, business facilities... more information at www.ustay2.com.

BAYVIEW BED & BREAKFAST

1Beach Road Manly Village, Whangaparaoa Peninsula,
Hibiscus Coast, North Auckland
Ph/Fax (09) 428 0990, Mobile 027-280 8346
email: *bayviewmanly@xtra.co.nz*
www.bayview-manly.co.nz

Tariff : N.Z. Dollars	
Double	$139 - 179
Single	$129 - 169
Child	n/a

Bedrooms	Qty
Double	3
Twin	1
Single	

Bed Size	Qty
Super King	
King/Twin	1
Queen	2
Double	
Single	

Bathrooms	Qty
Ensuite	2
Private	1
Guest Share	

  Quality Bed & Breakfast
with **Spectacular Sea Views**

Features & Attractions

- *30 min. north of Auckland*
- *2½ hours Bay of Islands*
- *3-4 hours Rotorua and Taupo*
- *Discounts for stays over 3 nights*

- *Separate guest lounge & patio*
- *TV, tea & coffee, all bedrooms*
- *Complimentary afternoon tea and pre-dinner drinks & nibbles*

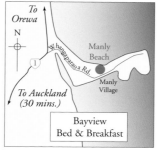

Bayview is an exceptional Bed & Breakfast on the beautiful Hibiscus Coast, just north of Auckland. Ideal for inbound and outbound travelers, perfect stopover between Rotorua, Taupo and Bay of Islands. Set above Manly Beach and adjacent to Manly Palms

Village with its variety of excellent shops and restaurants. Whangaparaoa boasts uncrowded beaches, golf courses, bush walks, ferry to world renowned bird sanctuary Tiritiri, and much more. Arrive to 'Afternoon Tea' on the patio, settle into your comfortable room. Two rooms have balcony and spectacular seaviews. Ten minute walk to restaurant of your choice. Stroll along the beach before the 'Bayview Breakfast', usually served alfresco overlooking the bay. Restauranteurs, Roger and Chris are passionate about food and hospitality. Enjoy mouthwatering home baked goodies and scrumptious breakfasts. **Bayview** has undergone a rigorous quality assessment by **Qualmark** – and proudly displays **4 stars**, giving you confidence to stay at **Bayview**. Great location, fantastic food, warm hospitality.

GULF HARBOUR VIEWS

56 Shakespear Road, Army Bay, Whangaparaoa
Ph (09) 424 4979, Fax (09) 424 4979
Mobile 027-471 8878
email: *firecal@ihug.co.nz*
www.gulfharbourviews.co.nz

Tariff : N.Z. Dollars	
Double	$140-160
Single	$120
Child	Enquire

Qty	Bedrooms
3	Double
1	Twin
	Single

Qty	Bed Size
	Super King
1	King
2	Queen
	Double
2	King/Single

Qty	Bathrooms
2	Ensuite
1	Private
1	Guest Share

**Luxury Accommodation
Exclusive & Personal Service**

DIRECTIONS:
Gulf Harbour Views is easy to find. Please phone for directions or visit our web site.

Features & Attractions

- *Privacy, Quality, Service*
- *Gourmet or home-style meals on request*
- *Selection of NZ's top wines*
- *FREE meet your hosts drink*
- *FREE burn your pics to CD*
- *Bush, farm & beach treks*
- *Tranquil garden setting*

All room rates include generous continental breakfast and available is a sensational cooked breakfast.

Dinner by sunset – Relax with breathtaking views overlooking the Pacific Ocean Islands, Shakespear Park Farm, and "Rangitoto" an 800 year old volcano.

Just 5 minutes to all of these **"Outstanding"** attractions - A 'Free to roam' Sheep and Cattle Farm, two golf courses, fishing and diving charters, ferries to the Gulf Islands and Auckland, shops and restaurants.

Within 30 min's drive, hot pools, wineries, 12 beaches, 5 golf courses. World renowned wild bird sanctuary **"Tiritiri Island"**. Just 15 minutes by ferry to view New Zealand's rarest and endangered birds, an amazing experience. Includes our **complimentary** packed lunch.

All 6 day bookings include: – Shuttle to and from the airport – a day trip with scrumptious complimentary picnic lunch to view our amazing 'Gannet Colony', a beautiful wild West Coast beach and the serene 'Cascades Waterfall' and forest walk. **Enjoy a touch of paradise with Sharon and Les.**

PEONE PLACE

35 Surf Road, Stanmore Bay, Whangaparaoa
Ph (09) 424 1455, Fax (09) 424 1455
Mobile 027-353 7745
email: *info@peone.co.nz*
www.peone.co.nz

@ home
NEW ZEALAND

Tariff : N.Z. Dollars	
Double	$110-150
Single	$30-80
Child	neg

Bedrooms	Qty
Double	3
Twin	
Single	

Bed Size	Qty
King	
Queen	1
Double	
King/Single	2
Single	3

Bathrooms	Qty
Ensuite	
Private	1
Guest Share	1

**Bed & Breakfast Homestay
& Self-contained Apartment**

Features & Attractions

- 1/2 hr Nth Auckland City
- A private, peaceful oasis
- World class golf courses
- Beautiful beach 5min. walk
- Great restaurant options
- Children welcome
- Extended stay/group rates
- Dinner by arrangement

The raison d'etre of **Peone Place** is to provide a truly unforgetable experience with genuine warm hospitality, in a beautiful gracious home and a delightful setting. Wake in the morning to birdsong and the aroma of freshly baked bread. Enjoy a balcony or indoor breakfast as you catch up on the mood of the sea – then indulge in delicious home baking with tea or coffee whenever you feel the need! Our self-contained apartment is ideal for families (sleeps 4-5). Relax in your own private garden or explore the many local attractions including thermal pools, wineries, potteries, coastal walkways, indoor snowslope, ferry trips to Auckland City or Tiritiri Matangi Bird Sanctuary (lunch pack available) and those magnificent coastal golf courses!
Please visit our website for options and seasonal specials.

DIRECTIONS:
Travelling on Northern Motorway from City, exit at Silverdale, right at traffic lights into Whangaparaoa Road. After 5km, just past 'Placemakers' turn left into Hiwi Cresc. (this runs into Surf Rd). We are number 35.

THE PALMS ON TINDALLS

75 Deluen Avenue, Tindalls Bay, Whangaparaoa
Ph (09) 424 1930, Fax (09) 424 1930
Mobile 027-293 4929
email: *davies@palmsretreat.co.nz*
www.palmsretreat.co.nz

Tariff : N.Z. Dollars	
Double	$150-280
Single	$150-280
extended stay neg	

Bedrooms	Qty
Double	2
Twin	
Single	

Bed Size	Qty
Super King	
King	
Queen	1
Double	1
Single	

Bathrooms	Qty
Ensuite	
Private	1
Guest Share	

**Beachfront
Luxury Retreat**

Features & Attractions

- *Romantic ambience*
- *Beachfront & tranquil*
- *Close Hauraki Gulf & Islands*
- *30 min north of Auckland City*
- *Superb scenery & parklands*
- *5 min restaurants & cafés*
- *Handy boat ramp & golf course*
- *Self service breakfast by request*

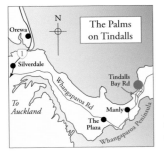

Enjoy and delight in the magic of this private, **beachfront**, luxury, cabana-style villa. **The Palms on Tindalls** beach, is one of the twelve fabulous beaches on the incredible **Whangaparaoa Peninsula**. The area is popular for water sports and many other recreational activities. It is handy to amazing regional parks, geothermal hot pools, Gulf Harbour marina and golf course, Snowplanet, shopping centres and top quality restaurants. Your fully equipped kitchen, Italian tiled bathroom, full laundry, together with spacious lounge and cosy gas fire will ensure a romantic and restful ambience. All rooms have French doors opening to the tropical garden and views over the bay. The two separated and beautifully appointed bedrooms, together with the gentle sounds of the sea will complete for you another day in paradise.

WATERS EDGE MANLY

83 Laurence Street, Manly
Whangaparaoa, Auckland
Ph (09) 428 0102, Fax (09) 428 2103
Mobile 027-492 1926
email: *watersedge@paradise.net.nz*

home
NEW ZEALAND

Tariff : N.Z. Dollars	
Double	$200-300
Single	$150
Child	

Bedrooms	Qty
Double	2
Twin	1
Single	

Bed Size	Qty
Super King	1
King	
Queen	1
Double	
King/Single	4

Bathrooms	Qty
Ensuite	1
Private	1
Guest Share	1

**Luxury
Beachfront Accommodation**

Features & Attractions

- *Absolute watersedge*
- *Spacious & comfortable*
- *Private entrance*

- *Golf courses incl international*
- *Fishing and boating available*
- *Excellent dining nearby*

DIRECTIONS:
Take northern motorway out of
Auckland, take Silverdale turn-off.
At the top of Silverdale Hill turn right
at lights, follow Whangaparaoa Rd to
Plaza Town Centre -10 min. Through
3 sets of lights take 2ʳᵈ road on left-
Ladies Mile - to the end. We are on
corner Ladies Mile/ Lawrence St.

We invite you and your friends to share our magical location right on the shores of one of North Auckland's most beautiful beaches.

Enjoy a continental or cooked breakfast on the deck to the soothing sounds of lapping waves while you contemplate a lazy day on the beach (towels provided). Or we can arrange a Tee time for you and your party at one of three golf courses nearby, including, the internationally acclaimed Gulf Harbour Course. Boating/fishing excursions on the Hauraki Gulf can also be organised. Comfort is assured.

Our spacious, sunny rooms have their own tea/coffee facilities (with home baking), microwave, fridge, TV and video. Laundry, facsimile and internet facilities are also available. Relaxing, rejuvenating, we look forward to your company at **Waters Edge** very soon.

WAIARI

85 Whangaparaoa Rd, Hadley Park,
Red Beach, Auckland
Ph (09) 427 5914, Mobile 0274-850 170
email: *waiari@xtra.co.nz*
www.waiari.co.nz

Tariff : N.Z. Dollars	
Double	$120-140
Single	$100-120
Child	n/a

Bedrooms	Qty
Double	3
Twin	
Single	

Bed Size	Qty
Super King	
King	
Queen	2
Double	1
Single	

Bathrooms	Qty
Ensuite	3
Private	
Guest Share	

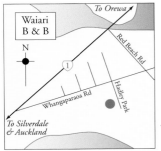

 Bed & Breakfast Homestay

Features & Attractions

- *20 min north of Harbour Bridge*
- *World class golf courses*
- *Waiwera thermal pools*
- *Close to Orewa Beach*
- *Quiet, rural hideaway*
- *Stopover for Tiri Tiri Matangi Bird Sanctuary*
- *The perfect place to relax*

Waiari is a quality purpose-built guest house, set on two acres of gardens and lifestyle block running down to the Weiti River,

which is a tidal estuary. Enjoy the ever-changing moods of the river with the seclusion and rural lifestyle that **Waiari** offers, yet be only minutes away from everything that the coast and surrounding areas has available including world-famous golf courses, marina, regional parks and fabulous beaches. An ideal stopover for a visit to the thermal pools at Waiwera, the vineyards and potteries at Matakana, historic Puhoi and fabulous Tiri Tiri Matangi Bird Sanctuary. We are only 20 minutes north of the bridge. The ideal stop-over for inbound and outbound visitors. We have three guest bedrooms. All have their own private facilities and patios. One double room with views over the estuary and two queen size with views over the gardens and surrounding farmlands. The perfect place to relax with a pre-dinner drink and watch the fabulous sunsets. Awaken to the dawn chorus of the Tuis throughout the valley.

85

THE SHEEP & SHAG
6A Roberts Road, Gulf Harbour, Whangaparaoa
Ph (09) 428 5256
Mobile 021-645 485
email: *info@sheepandshag.co.nz*
www.sheepandshag.co.nz

Features & Attractions
- *Panoramic views*
- *20m solar-heated pool*
- *Purpose-built in 2001*
- *Private entrances & patio*
- *Golf, swimming, boating*
- *Tiritiri bird sanctuary*

Superior Bed & Breakfast **Self-contained Apartment**			
Double	$108-165
Single	$100-135
Child	neg

Relax around the pool in our sunny, modern facilities on a lifestyle block on the beautiful Hibiscus Coast. Viable alternative to staying in downtown Auckland and close to shops, restaurants, beaches and golf courses, including the Gulf Harbour Country Club – venue for the NZ Open.

Guest lounge available for your convenience. Laundry, SKY TV, DVD, and assistance with transportation and onward arrangements will help make your stay a memorable experience. Plenty of parking for your boat, if required. Our single-level home was purpose-built in 2001 with a guest accommodation wing for your enjoyment.

Bedrooms	Qty
Double	3
Twin	
Single	
Bed Size	Qty
King	
Queen	3
Double	
Single	2
Bathrooms	Qty
Ensuite	3
Private	
Guest Share	

ORMOND HOUSE BED & BREAKFAST
470 Waitoki Rd, RD 1, Wainui, Silverdale, North Auckland
Ph (09) 420 3317 , Fax (09) 420 3318
Mobile 021-048 5522
e-mail: *ormondhouse@xtra.co.nz*
www.ormondhousenz.com

Features & Attractions
- *Tranquil rural setting*
- *Full breakfast, home baking*
- *Broadband internet/email*
- *Large conservatory*
- *Great restaurants 15min.*
- *Explore Hibiscus Coast*

Bed & Breakfast **Luxury Accommodation**			
Double	$130-175
Single	$90-110
Child	$40-00

Ormond House is a large American-style house set on 4 acres with a two hole 75 metre fairway in the rolling hills of the Wainui Valley. We have four large ensuite bedrooms with walk-in wardrobes, underfloor heating, a large dining room, lounge, family room and a large conservatory. Guests are welcome to use the large fitted oak kitchen, laundry, hair dryer and internet facilities. A full breakfast, tea and coffee are provided. Located close by are three golf courses, one of the largest ski slopes in the world, go-karting, horse riding, fishing, bush walks, beaches, shopping and the North Shore Aero Club. Auckland is 35 min. away. Your hosts, Bridie and Martin Butler, are Irish, well-travelled and seek to make you feel at home in our house and enjoy your stay with us. Pet free house.

Bedrooms	Qty
Double	4
Twin	
Single	
Bed Size	Qty
Super King	1
King	1
Queen	2
King/Single	1
Bathrooms	Qty
Ensuite	4
Private	
Guest Share	

WHITEHILLS

224 Whitehills Road, Wainui, RD 1, Kaukapakapa
Ph (09) 420 5666,   Fax (09) 420 5666
Mobile 027-448 9503
email: *d-m.evans@clear.net.nz*
www.bnbauckland.co.nz

Tariff : N.Z. Dollars	
Double	$120-130
Single	$75
Child	neg

Bedrooms	Qty
Double	1
Twin	2
Single	

Bed Size	Qty
Super King	
King	
Queen	1
Double	
Single	5

Bathrooms	Qty
Ensuite	
Private	2
Guest Share	

 Bed & Breakfast and Self-contained Accommodation

Features & Attractions

- *Genuine hospitality*
- *Tea, coffee & TV in rooms*
- *Native bush & bird life*
- *Peaceful surroundings*
- *Orewa 15 minutes*
- *Continental breakfast*
- *Golf courses close by*
- *Laundry facilities available*

Relax and unwind at **Whitehills** which is situated 30 minutes north of the Auckland Harbour Bridge and seven minutes from the Silverdale Motorway exit. It is convenient for shops, beaches and golf courses. If you have just arrived in New Zealand or are travelling north to the Bay of Islands, **Whitehills** would be a perfect "stopover" for you.

Enjoy quality Bed & Breakfast accommodation in the main house with a choice of twin or double room in guest wing. The comfortable separate self-contained accommodation has its own entrance and deck and breakfast provisions can be provided.

You are most welcome to wander around our garden, take a walk in the six acres of native bush or simply relax on the covered verandah. An evening meal is available by prior arrangement at $35 per person. We offer genuine hospitality and look forward to meeting you.

KAIPARA HOUSE B&B

Cnr State Highway 16 & Parkhurst Road, Helensville
Ph (09) 420 7462, Fax (09) 420 7458
Mobile 027-661 103 or 027-814 617
email: *stay@kaiparahouse.co.nz*
www.kaiparahouse.co.nz

Tariff : N.Z. Dollars	
Double	$120
Single	$65
Child	

Bedrooms	Qty
Double	3
Twin	1
Single	2
Bed Size	Qty
Super King	
King	
Queen	2
Double	1
Single	4
Bathrooms	Qty
Ensuite	3
Private	
Guest Share	1

 Bed & Breakfast and Self-contained Accommodation

Features & Attractions

- *Restored 1894 villa*
- *Surrounded by gardens*
- *3 min Helensville & Parakai*
- *Adventures & sightseeing*
- *Quality studio summerhouses*
- *Ozone spa*
- *All amenities on request*
- *Fabulous hospitality*

DIRECTIONS:
Situated at the corner of State Highway 16 and Parkhurst Rd (roundabout). 3 minutes from Helensville, 3 minutes from Parakai.

Our 112 year old villa, set in nearly an acre of seasonal gardens, has been lovingly restored and adorned with yesteryear's furniture and today's lovely rich colours which enhance the enchanting architecture of older homes. We offer you an Edwardian or Victorian room with morning sun and comfort through our home, with an open fire in winter. We also have two self-contained Studio Summerhouse units, facing north and east with your own open flame gas fireplace. With queen beds, ensuite and kitchenette you can have either a rural view or look over our picturesque garden with its gazebo and large ozone chlorine-free spa. Quality linen and furnishings.

Rate: $120.00 per night. Breakfast extra on request. We are in our 50's, young at heart, have two cats and have enjoyed travel throughout New Zealand and abroad. Being on the Northland Tourist Route we can advise you on local activities and attractions – we have them all!

WARBLERS RETREAT

8/361 Paremoremo Road, Albany, Auckland
Ph (09) 413 6553, Fax (09) 413 6554
Mobile 027-259 2624
email: *pru_young@hotmail.com*

Tariff : N.Z. Dollars	
Double	$180
Single	$125
Child	$35

Bedrooms	Qty
Double	2
Twin	
Single	
Bed Size	**Qty**
Super King	
King	
Queen	2
Double	
King/Single	1
Bathrooms	**Qty**
Ensuite	
Private	1
Guest Share	

      Peace & Tranquility
Self-contained Bed & Breakfast

Features & Attractions

- *Tranquil bush setting*
- *Bush walks on property*
- *Park at the door*
- *West Coast beaches*

- *Albany Mega Centre 6 min*
- *Free range hens and eggs*
- *Close to all major highways*
- *Local vineyards*

Welcome to paradise. Just twenty minutes north of Auckland City and two hours from Whangarei. A quiet getaway of native bush and birdlife.

Set on five acres, our self-contained accommodation offers serene ambience and tranquility. Your accommodation includes a romantic upstairs bedroom or spacious studio downstairs, cosy separate lounge with double sofa sleeper and private bathroom. Sky TV, refrigerator, hot beverage facilities. Studio contains a small kitchenette. Your breakfast hamper is delivered to your door.

With our three beautiful, happy dogs we invite you to share our hospitality.

An ideal base from which to visit the vineyards of West Auckland, wild West Coast beaches and numerous great local restaurants.

Browns Bay - Auckland ▶ YOUR HOST: Raeburn Van Lierop Ph (09) 475 5230

ST CLAIR BED & BREAKFAST

30 St Clair Place, Browns Bay, Auckland
Ph (09) 475 5230, Fax (09) 475 5303
Mobile 027-620 7704
email: *st_clair@xtra.co.nz*

Features & Attractions

- *Friendly Kiwi hospitality*
- *Exclusive cul-de-sac*
- *Beautiful views*
- *Full English breakfast*
- *Guests lounge*
- *Beaches, cafés, restaurants*

 **Luxury Bed & Breakfast
Beautiful Sea Views**

Double	$130
Single	$80
Child	

Welcome to my modern New-England style purpose-built Bed & Breakfast. Enjoy the antiques, bric-a-brac and memorabilia or maybe relax on the spacious deck with magic views of Coromandel, Rakino Island and the Noises. Minutes drive to Browns Bay shops and glorious beach with full view of Rangitoto Island, North Harbour Stadium for shows and sporting events, Albany Mega Centre for great shopping and convenient access to North and South Motorway. Queen bed, ensuite, kitchenette, TV or king bed, private spa/bathroom, TV, private balcony for both bedrooms. Off-street parking. Well behaved family dog.

DIRECTIONS: When on East Coast Rd, look for No 826a. This is the 'Northcross Community Church', which is well sign-posted. St Clair Pl is directly opposite the church. Drive to bottom of small cul-de-sac. We are 2nd to last house on left.

Bedrooms	Qty
Double	2
Twin	
Single	

Bed Size	Qty
King	1
Queen	1
Double	
Single	

Bathrooms	Qty
Ensuite	1
Private	1
Guest Share	

.... you're never far from water!

AUCKLAND NUMBER ONE HOUSE

1 Princes Street, Northcote Point, Auckland Northshore 0627
Ph (09) 480 7659, Fax (09) 480 7657
Mobile 021-143 8645
email: *briankh@xtra.co.nz*
www.nz-homestay.co.nz

Tariff : N.Z. Dollars	
Double	$185-200
Single	$120
Child	$20

Bedrooms	Qty
Double	3
Twin	
Single	

Bed Size	Qty
Super King	
King	
Queen	2
Double	1
Single	

Bathrooms	Qty
Ensuite	2
Private	1
Guest Share	

Bed & Breakfast Plus
Self-Contained Apartment

Features & Attractions

- *200° spectacular harbour view*
- *Delightful, warm, picturesque villa*
- *On water's edge*
- *Shuttle right to the door*

- *Excellent restaurants close*
- *Rental cars arranged*
- *Romantic jacuzzi,*
  looking at city lights

DIRECTIONS:
Over Harbour Bridge to North Shore.
first left is Stafford. Up the hill and
left to Queen, left at Northcote
Tavern into King, right into Princes
then under bridge as far as possible.
We are next to Stokes Park Reserve.

Their guest book says *"NZ's best B&B", "Far and away the friendliest place in NZ"*. They welcome tired travellers with a meet service at the airport and your flag at the door. **No 1 House** is only 8 minutes from the city centre by ferry – and a world away. The view of harbour and city from nearly every room is stunning – wait till you see the magical city lights at night! **No 1 House** even has its own swimming beach. Did we mention Jay's superb full cooked breakfasts? World famous in Auckland!

No 1 House features a new family friendly self-contained apartment, an enchanting Hobbit House in the garden, and a 12m sailing catamaran to take you on the water. This couple sail yachts, ride motorbikes, bush walk, travel regularly and drink champagne – even have been known to jump off the Skytower! They will share as much or as little time with you as you wish, and help you plan your holiday. Book two nights minimum and really enjoy Auckland.
Certified Kiwi Hosts with NZ Tourism Board.

BIRDWOOD HOUSE

12A Moore Street, Hillcrest, North Shore, Auckland
Ph (09) 418 1612, Fax (09) 480 0407
Mobile 027-477 7722
email: *barbie@birdwood.co.nz*
www.birdwood.co.nz

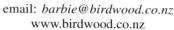

Tariff : N.Z. Dollars	
$130-150	Double
$120-140	Single
	Child

Qty	Bedrooms
3	Double
	Twin
	Single
Qty	Bed Size
	Super King
	King
2	Queen
1	Double
	Single
Qty	Bathrooms
2	Ensuite
	Private
1	Guest Share

 Elegant Bed & Breakfast Accommodation

Features & Attractions

- *Native bush and birds*
- *Breakfast our speciality*
- *Quiet, tranquil location*
- *Sunny verandas & courtyard*
- *City 10min., bus close by*
- *Elegant, well appointed bedrooms and guest lounge*
- *Bush walks, golf course, beaches*

DIRECTIONS:
From motorway just north of Harbour Bridge, take exit 421, drive to top of Onewa Rd, turn right into Birkenhead Ave. Moore St. is 1st on right after lights at Pupuke Rd. 12A is 150m down the hill on the left.

Barbie Bell, ex Birdwood House Parnell, and husband Dr David Scott, invite you to share their newly renovated **Birdwood House** in Hillcrest on Auckland's North Shore. The colonial farmhouse style villa, wrapped with verandas, and a courtyard, is set amongst native bush and birds. Guests are offered three tastefully furnished bedrooms with best quality beds and cotton bed linen, wool duvets, underlays and pillows, TV, robes and tea/coffee. The modern bathrooms are tiled, with under-floor heating and one has a claw-foot bath. Breakfast, served in our formal dining room, or on the veranda, has an emphasis on home-made cuisine, an elegant gourmet affair with linen napkins, candles and silver cutlery, described by a previous guest as "A dinner-party at breakfast time!" A three-course dinner is an option with 24 hours' notice. Enjoy a port wine while listening to music or reading a book from our library. Barbie will be delighted to acquaint herself with previous **Birdwood** guests.

CALICO LODGE

250 Matua Road, RD 1, Kumeu
Ph (09) 412 8167
Mobile 027-866064
email: *bed@calicolodge.co.nz*
www.calicolodge.co.nz

Tariff : N.Z. Dollars	
Double	$140-195
Single	$110-160
Child	

Bedrooms	Qty
Double	3
Twin	1
Single	
Bed Size	**Qty**
Super King	1
King	
Queen	2
Double	
Single	2
Bathrooms	**Qty**
Ensuite	2
Private	2
Guest Share	

Arrive as Guests – Depart as Friends

Features & Attractions

- *Friendly Kiwi hospitality*
- *Separate guest wing*
- *Guest lounge, tea/coffee*
- *Peaceful, tranquil garden*

- *Wireless Broadband*
- *Wineries & cafés*
- *Golf courses nearby*
- *Muriwai gannet colony*

Kerry and Kay, Zippy our little dog, three cats and tame sheep welcome you to **Calico Lodge**. Set amidst the wineries of Matua, Westbrook, Nobilos, Coopers, Soljans, and many more, 25 minutes northwest of Auckland, our modern home on four acres has beautiful trees and tranquil gardens. Nearby are many wedding venues – Gracehill, Markovina and Rivermill. Muriwai's black sand surf beach, golf course and renowned gannet colony are only 20 minutes away.

Hand-made teddy bears and patchwork quilting (for sale) adorn the bedrooms in separate guest wing with private entrance. Heated towel rails, heaters, hairdryers, robes, fresh flowers and amenities complete the bathrooms – ensuite, private or guest share. A guest lounge with television, refrigerator, tea and coffee making facilities opens onto a private deck, where peace and beautiful bush views complete the picture. Two minutes from SH 16 and Kumeu village we love to share our little piece of paradise.

EASTVIEW

2 Parkside Road, Hobsonville, Auckland
Ph (09) 416 9254, Mobile (027) 4373400
email: *eastview@xtra.co.nz*
www.eastview.co.nz

Tariff : N.Z. Dollars	
Double	$120-135
Single	$85-100
Child	$30

Bedrooms	Qty
Double	2
Twin	1
Single	
Bed Size	**Qty**
Super King	
King	
Queen	2
Double	
Single	2
Bathrooms	**Qty**
Ensuite	
Private	2
Guest Share	

 Bed & Breakfast/ Homestay With Panoramic Views

Features & Attractions

- *Stunning daytime views*
- *Amazing views by night*
- *Quiet and restful location*
- *Extra person discounts*
- *Delightful local restaurants*
- *Friendly cat & small dog*
- *15 min. to Auckland City*
- *Divine breakfasts*

DIRECTIONS:
From city/south take SH16. Turn right T-intersection onto Hobsonville Rd. SH18. 6th street on right Westpark Drive, 2nd left Parkside Road. **From north** take SH18 Greenhithe/Upper Harbour highway into Hobsonville Rd.

Eastview, so easy-to-find from the airport and travel routes north and south, is located ideally for exploring Auckland. Just the place to unwind at the end of a long journey or a day of sightseeing. Relax in the comfort of **The Marina Suite**, bathed in all-day sun, opening onto a colourful garden. This area has two bedrooms (one queen, one twin), a private bathroom and a comfortable lounge (with studio kitchen).

Rosie's Retreat offers a queen-size bedroom plus private bathroom. An inviting sunny lounge is available for your use and a log fire for winter evenings. From **Eastview** discover superb beaches, rainforest-clad hills, gannet colonies, golf courses, thermal pools or harbour excursions. Handy to Kumeu wineries (popular wedding venues). Marina close by… catch a ferry to the city.

PANORAMA HEIGHTS

42 Kitewaho Road, Swanson, Waitakere City
Ph (09) 832 4777, Fax (09) 833 7773
Mobile 027-272 8811
email: *nzbnb4u@clear.net.nz*
www.panoramaheights.co.nz

Tariff : N.Z. Dollars	
Double	$150
Single	$110
Child	

Bedrooms	Qty
Double	2
Twin	1
Single	

Bed Size	Qty
Super King	
King	
Queen	2
Double	
Single	2

Bathrooms	Qty
Ensuite	3
Private	
Guest Share	

Bed & Breakfast With a Little Indulgence

Features & Attractions

- *Dinner on request*
- *30 min. to Auckland City*
- *Kumeu Wineries 16km*
- *Non-smoking environment*

- *45 min to airport*
- *Train to the city*
- *Shopping centres 10 min.*
- *Two scenic golf courses*

Paul and Allison invite you to visit and enjoy their private peaceful location high in the Waitakere Ranges Native Rainforest - Gateway to the Wild West Coast of Auckland - **Panorama Heights** is a unique base to explore; west coast beaches of Karekare, Piha, Bethells & Muriwai; 250km of walking/hiking trails in 17,000 hectares of surrounding Regional Park or just perfect for taking it easy in this wonderful setting. Your hosts who reside next door encourage you to relax and be pampered with all the comforts of home. Having travelled extensively we appreciate the importance of excellent accommodation at a reasonable price and we offer you this in our guest home with magnificent views across native bush/kauri trees to Auckland City and Rangitoto Island beyond. Unwind on the deck or in the spacious lounge. If time permits, let us take you on a bush walk and show you some of the local flora & fauna. A delicious 'Panorama' breakfast is served in the dining room at your leisure. You'll love it here. Directions to bring you 'stress-free' to our place are available.

HASTINGS HALL

99 Western Springs Road, Western Springs, Auckland
Ph (09) 845 8550, Fax (09) 845 8554
Mobile 021-300 006
email: *unique@hastingshall.co.nz*
www.hastingshall.co.nz

Tariff : N.Z. Dollars	
Double	$145-375
Single	$115-325
Child	

Bedrooms	Qty
Double	8
Twin	2
Single	

Bed Size	Qty
Super King	
King	2
Queen	6
Double	2
Single	

Bathrooms	Qty
Ensuite	6
Private	1
Guest Share	3

 Unique Heritage Bed & Breakfast

Features & Attractions

- *Beautifully landscaped early New Zealand mansion*
- *Walk to parks, zoo, golf*
- *Easy access to city centre*
- *Fax, phone, email, library*
- *Beautifully appointed suites*
- *Pool, spa & guest function room*
- *Conference – seminar facility*

This magnificently restored 1878 colonial mansion, set in beautifully landscaped extensive grounds, is just five minutes by motorway from Auckland City. Within walking distance is Kingsland with its cafés and ethnic restaurants, Auckland Zoo, and the beautiful Western Springs Park, Chamberlains Golf Course, the Transport Museum and Western Springs Stadium. Hastings Hall is ideal for the tourist, businessman or as a retreat. Enjoy gourmet breakfasts in the conservatory, formal dining room, gazebo (above the pool and spa pool) or in your suite with own verandah. Seven of the nine themed guest suites have marble ensuites, one for disabled guests. Choose from the Grand Hastings Suite with private lounge to the Moulin Rouge loft suite in the Lodge. Enjoy extensive tropically landscaped grounds, formal lounge and large pool lounge with library, home theatre, computer and email and fax facilities. All rooms are furnished with antiques and early New Zealand furniture from the period, fine linen and fluffy towels. Come and experience a bygone era with today's refinements.

96

THE BIG BLUE HOUSE

103 Garnet Road, Westmere, Auckland
Ph (09) 360 6384, Mobile 021-884 662
email: *info@thebigbluehouse.co.nz*
www.thebigbluehouse.co.nz

Features & Attractions

- *Close to city centre*
- *Panoramic views*
- *Swimming pool & spa*
- *Spacious comfortable rooms*
- *Near Ponsonby cafés & restaurants*
- *Adjacent to zoo & parks*

Double	$130-160
Single	$80-140
Child	$10-20

Be 'at home' in comfort

Bedrooms	Qty
Double	2
Twin	
Single	1
Bed Size	**Qty**
King	2
Queen	
King/Single	1
Single	1
Bathrooms	**Qty**
Ensuite	1
Private	
Family Share	2

Kate and Lynne warmly invite you to share their unique Homestay B&B close to central city and harbour. Be greeted by our friendly cat and dog. Enjoy the sense of retreat in our spacious rooms – luxury of king-size beds, robes and heated towels. Relax in spa, play in pool or watch cable television. Coffee and tea making facilities, refrigerators, desks and internet connections. Generous breakfasts.

Take an easy stroll to cafés, restaurants, Auckland Zoo or Western Springs Park. Shop at nearby Ponsonby or hop on the bus to city centre (15 minutes). We have a range of rooms to suit your needs. The very large 'Seaview Room' with ensuite, king bed (extra single) suits couples or families. The 'Mountview Room', large with king bed and shared bathroom (own basin and facilities) provides a very comfortable option. The 'Hideaway Room' offers a cosy retreat for the single traveller.

-"Make yourself at home!"

CHALET CHEVRON - A GREAT LITTLE HOTEL

14 Brighton Road, Parnell, Auckland
Ph (09) 309 0290, Fax (09) 373 5754
email: *info@chaletchevron.com*
www.chaletchevron.com

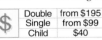

Features & Attractions

- *Historic hotel*
- *Unbeatable location*
- *Charming surroundings*
- *Stunning views*
- *Stroll to restaurants*
- *1.5kms from city centre*

Double	from $195
Single	from $99
Child	$40

**Historic Parnell
A Great Little Hotel**

Bedrooms	Qty
Double	5
Twin	3
Single	4
Bed Size	**Qty**
King	
Queen	3
Double	3
Single	12
Bathrooms	**Qty**
Ensuite	12
Private	
Guest Share	

Chalet Chevron has a rich history of providing comfortable lodging in charming surroundings to travellers for generations. This great little hotel offers personal service, comfort, informality, a sense of fun and a warm welcome in one of Auckland's premier locations - 12 guest rooms with ensuite bathrooms at prices that won't blow the budget.

To stroll down Parnell Road is to indulge your senses. It is abuzz with an amazing selection of restaurants, cafés and bars - traditional, quirky or hip. From some of the best fish and chips you will ever taste to gourmet burgers and gastronomic delights. It is all here, as is New Zealand's highest concentration of Art Galleries side by side with the best fashion designers, fine New Zealand and imported products and specialty shops - all just 1.5kms from the city centre.

PONSONBY STUDIO LOFT

9 Picton Street, Ponsonby, Auckland
Ph (09) 361 2461
Mobile 021-637 908
email: *info@ponsonbystudioloft.co.nz*
www.ponsonbystudioloft.co.nz

VISA
MasterCard
AMERICAN EXPRESS

Features & Attractions

- *4 houses from Ponsonby Road*
- *Quiet tree-lined street*
- *Shops, cafés, bars close by*
- *Central city bus every 10 min.*
- *Sky TV*
- *Separate shower/separate toilet*

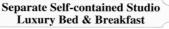
**Separate Self-contained Studio
Luxury Bed & Breakfast**

Double	$180
Single	$180
Child	$30

We are so close to the cute, historic cafés and shops of Ponsonby, yet nestled away in a tree-lined street of early 1900's wooden villas. The modern studio is completely separate and self-contained. Its elevated position and balcony provides a city outlook, yet retains a cozy and private feeling. King bed with fine linen.

Bedrooms	Qty
Double	1
Twin	
Single	
Bed Size	**Qty**
King	1
Queen	
Double	1
Single	
Bathrooms	**Qty**
Ensuite	1
Private	
Guest Share	

Ponsonby Studio Loft is very central. Up the street, the Link Bus leaves every ten minutes for central city, shopping in quaint Parnell, upmarket Newmarket, ethnic Karangahape Road, funky High Street, ferries to the gulf, Viaduct waterfront bars and restaurants and connections to wider Auckland. We offer a breakfast with local fresh fruit and cereals etc, but most of our guests opt to try out the many great cafés as part of the Ponsonby experience. Please inquire about our special bed-only, long stay and winter pricing. Free broadband connection.

The view from our balcony

AKARANA'S NAUTICAL NOOK - SAILING

23B Watene Crescent, Okahu Bay, Orakei, Auckland
Ph (09) 521 2544
email: *nauticalnook@bigfoot.com*
www.nauticalnook.com

MasterCard
VISA

Features & Attractions

- *Complimentary sailing!*
- *Free wireless internet*
- *Swimming beach 100m*
- *Perfect central location*
- *Pay cash 10% discount*
- *Early 'am' check-in available*

**Homestay Bed & Breakfast
Harbour Yacht Sailing**

Double	$110-150
Single	$90-120

Friendly, relaxed, beachside hospitality overlooking park/harbour, 4.8km from Downtown. 100m from Okahu Bay, fringed by Pohutukawa trees, for swimming and picnics. Gourmet cooked breakfast, served at Captains Table or Promenade Deck. Stroll along picturesque promenade to Kelly Tarlton's Underwater World, Mission Bay beach, cafés and bars. Bus at door to Downtown, ferry terminal, museums and Vector Stadium. Unwind for 2-3 day stopover – our home is your home (take our handsome Irish Setter Shamus for a walk). Enjoy the thrill of complimentary sailing on the sparkling harbour on our 34ft yacht. We have a wealth of local knowledge and international travel experience and can assist with sightseeing and travel planning. Take taxi or shuttle to our door. **Welcome!** Excellent website.

Bedrooms	Qty
Double	3
Twin	
Single	
Bed Size	**Qty**
King/Twin	1
Queen	2
Double	
Single	
Bathrooms	**Qty**
Ensuite	1
Private	2
Guest Share	

ART HOTEL - THE GREAT PONSONBY

30 Ponsonby Terrace, Ponsonby, Auckland
Ph (09) 376 5989, Fax (09) 376 5527
Free Phone (0800) 766 792
email: *info@greatpons.co.nz*
www.greatpons.co.nz

Tariff : N.Z. Dollars	
Double	$180-350
Single	
Child	

Bedrooms	Qty
Double	5
Twin	6
Single	
Bed Size	Qty
Super King	6
King	
Queen	5
Double	
Single	
Bathrooms	Qty
Ensuite	11
Private	
Guest Share	

 A Small Art Hotel

Features & Attractions

- *Eco friendly*
- *Winter rates*
- *Place to have fun*
- *Breakfasts a speciality*
- *Free offstreet parking*
- *Hospitality & Service*
- *Walk to the city attractions*
- *Free wireless internet access*

Ponsonby is the liveliest area of Auckland, full of restaurants, cafés, boutiques and ceramic shops. The Great Ponsonby, a large, restored villa, is tucked away in a quiet street. No traffic noises. Centrally located, close to major attractions, walk or bus to harbour and downtown. Off-street parking. Bus every ten minutes. The white exterior is deceptive. Inside is a bold profusion of colour with art from the Pacific Islands and New Zealand. Queen rooms, roomier courtyard studios, palm garden suites. All rooms have colourful, understated modern design. Private bathroom with heated mirror and towel rail, hairdryer. Tea and coffee making facilities, Sky television, DDI phones, internet access. Studios have a refrigerator, king or twin beds, leather couch, CD player, video player. Bath in suites. Leisurely breakfasts served from our extensive menu. Jason Cochrane, editor of Frommer's travel magazine, November 2002 said *"my top choice is Great Ponsonby B&B"*. English travel guide "Footprint" says *"one of the best B&Bs in the city"*. The Great Ponsonby topped accommodation chosen by NY Times 26/1/03. Resident cat and dog.

We can take pets under some conditions, so please telephone to make a booking.

SUNDERLAND HOUSE

1A Cox Street, Herne Bay, Auckland
Ph (09) 376 6336
Mobile 025-249 9025
email: *sunderlandhouse@ihug.co.nz*

Tariff : N.Z. Dollars	
Double	$200-215
Single	$185
Child	

Bedrooms	Qty
Double	2
Twin	
Single	1
Bed Size	**Qty**
Super King	
King	2
Queen	1
Double	
Single	
Bathrooms	**Qty**
Ensuite	3
Private	
Guest Share	

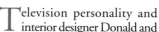

**Luxury Boutique
Accommodation**

Features & Attractions

- *Elegant sumptuous villa*
- *Great service & hospitality*
- *Walk to cafés & restaurants*
- *Walk to Ponsonby shopping*
- *Breakfast a specialty*
- *Close to central city*
- *Rooms all ensuite*
- *Beautiful library*

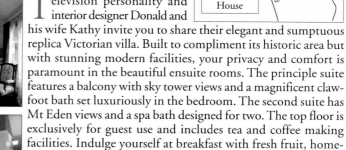

Television personality and interior designer Donald and his wife Kathy invite you to share their elegant and sumptuous replica Victorian villa. Built to compliment its historic area but with stunning modern facilities, your privacy and comfort is paramount in the beautiful ensuite rooms. The principle suite features a balcony with sky tower views and a magnificent claw-foot bath set luxuriously in the bedroom. The second suite has Mt Eden views and a spa bath designed for two. The top floor is exclusively for guest use and includes tea and coffee making facilities. Indulge yourself at breakfast with fresh fruit, home-made muffins, cereals and great espresso coffee in the French farmhouse kitchen and unwind in the evening with complimentary port in the library. Restaurants and cafés are a short stroll, trendy Ponsonby shopping is within easy walking distance and the city centre is 3km (bus every 20 min.).

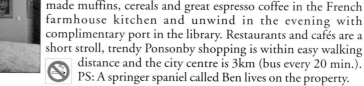

PS: A springer spaniel called Ben lives on the property.

MOANAVISTA

60 Hamilton Road, Herne Bay-Ponsonby, Auckland
Ph (09) 376 5028, Fax (09) 376 5025
Mobile 021-376 150
email: *info@moanavista.co.nz*
www.moanavista.co.nz

Tariff : N.Z. Dollars	
Double	$180-240
Single	$140-180
Child	

Bedrooms	Qty
Double	3
Twin	
Single	
Bed Size	Qty
Super King	
King	
Queen	3
Double	
Single	
Bathrooms	Qty
Ensuite	2
Private	1
Guest Share	

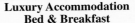

**Luxury Accommodation
Bed & Breakfast**

Features & Attractions

- *Close to city, Ponsonby restaurants*
- *Quiet and peaceful*
- *Wireless high-speed internet*
- *Sea views, beach nearby*

- *Modernised Victorian villa*
- *Continental breakfast*
- *LCD TV/DVD in all rooms*
- *Grand piano, open fire*

Stylish Boutique Accommodation

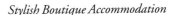

Moanavista, a stylish and comfortable boutique guest house, is situated in the quiet leafy suburb of Ponsonby, close to award winning restaurants, cafés, shops, beaches and city. Buses to Downtown Auckland are five minutes walk away. With the grace and elegance of the 1890s this modernised Victorian villa has two furnished rooms upstairs with superb sea views, verandahs and ensuite/private bathrooms. On the ground floor the Pacific Suite has an ensuite bathroom and French doors to the garden. All rooms have heated towel rails, soaps, shampoos, hair dryer and dressing robes. Enjoy a continental breakfast with fresh fruits, cereals, bakery before checking your emails on our complimentary high speed computer. Your hosts Tim and Matthew are well travelled (Tim is a gardener and Matthew runs an inner city café – 'Barretta Espresso') and enjoy sharing their knowledge on Auckland and beyond. You are welcome to join them for a complimentary cocktail. The atmosphere at **Moanavista** is casual and relaxed - a home away from home! Long term rates available. Supershuttle from the airport will bring you to our door at NZ$20 or NZ$25 /2 people.

BRAEMAR ON PARLIAMENT STREET

7 Parliament Street, Central Auckland
Ph (09) 377 5463, Fax (09) 377 3056
Mobile 021-640 688
email: *braemar@aucklandbedandbreakfast.com*
www.aucklandbedandbreakfast.com

DIRECTIONS:
Take the PORT exit from the motorway. At the traffic lights take the free left turn up Alten Rd. Turn right at lights into Anzac Ave. Parliament St. is the 1st street on the left. We are the 4th building on the right, opposite the high court and next to Middle Courtville.

Tariff : N.Z. Dollars	
Double	$180-295
Single	
Child	

Bedrooms	Qty
Double	4
Twin	
Single	
Bed Size	**Qty**
Super King	
King	
Queen	3
Double	1
Single	
Bathrooms	**Qty**
Ensuite	1
Private	1
Guest Share	1

Elegant Inner City Haven

Features & Attractions

- *In downtown Auckland*
- *Walk to city attractions*
- *Non smoking indoors*
- *Heritage building*
- *Projector Television*
- *Pet poodles*

Braemar on Parliament Street is an elegant heritage-listed home in the Auckland Central Business District. We offer a comfortable high-quality environment. Being in the heart of Auckland means that our Bed & Breakfast is a short walk from all the city amenities. Close to all public transport and the inner city's beautiful parks.

If nightlife is what you are after, you can saunter to theatres, cinemas, cafés, restaurants and bars, or if you crave the quiet life, we can provide that too.

All of our bedrooms feature posturepaedic beds, goose-down duvets and fluffy pillows. All of our bathrooms feature walk-in showers and large claw-foot baths. Toiletries are complimentary.

Savour a full cooked breakfast in our Rose Dining-Room with fine linen, silver cutlery and bone china. Relax in the guest lounge and watch wide screen TV from our projector and enjoy our collection of Kiwi movies.

102

ASCOT PARNELL

St Stephens Avenue, Parnell, Auckland 1
Ph (09) 309 9012, Fax (09) 309 3729
email: *info@ascotparnell.com*
www.AscotParnell.com

Tariff : N.Z. Dollars	
Double	$245-385
Single	$245-325
Child	$60

Bedrooms	Qty
Double	
Twin	3
Single	
Bed Size	**Qty**
Super King	1
King	
Queen	2
Double	
Single	
Bathrooms	**Qty**
Ensuite	3
Private	
Guest Share	

Bed & Breakfast in a charming atmosphere

Features & Attractions

- *Walk to all city attractions*
- *City-centre at 1 mile (1.5 km)*
- *Airport bus stops at the door*
- *Free internet access*
- *Helpful and friendly hosts*
- *Garden setting, gourmet food*
- *Free cookies, teas, coffee, juice*
- *Free parking inside building*

DIRECTIONS: From airport take road No. 20 motorway to Auckland city, exit at Queenstown Rd, follow Auckland centre. Follow Manukau Rd (Road No 12) to Parnell. Turn right at the Cathedral of the Holy Trinity into St. Stephens Ave. The **Ascot Parnell** is 300m down on your left.

A tranquil, convenient, central location, a moment's stroll from Parnell Village cafés, restaurants and city centre attractions. Built amidst the sub-tropical gardens of this historic neighbourhood, Ascot Parnell provides bright and airy guest suites with luxury bathrooms, spectacular views of Auckland's harbour and city skyline. Free car parking inside building. Guest suites are tastefully furnished and have comfortable queen or super-king beds with fine quality linen. Each room has a luxury bathroom, with shower and/or full bathtub, underfloor heating, hair dryer, television, climate control, internet connection and telephone. The spacious lounge opens up to a large sunny balcony with spectacular panoramic harbour views. A desk with Mac-PC offers free internet access. On cool nights cuddle up around the open fireplace with a hot drink or a glass of wine. Breakfast is a sumptuous affair with such choices as fresh organic fruit, yoghurt, Belgian pancakes, French toast, crêpes, gourmet omelettes etc, and is served in the morning room or alfresco on the balcony. We cater for special diets. Complimentary fresh coffee, teas and cookies are available throughout the day. Reservations essential.

AMERISSIT LUXURY ACCOMODATION

20 Buttle Street, Remuera, Auckland
Ph (09) 522 9297, Fax (09) 522 9298
Mobile 027-284 4883
email: *barbara@amerissit.co.nz*
www.amerissit.co.nz

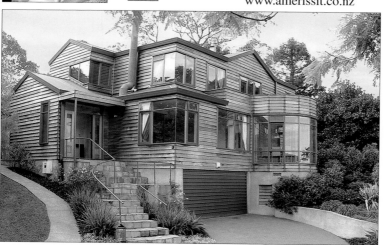

Tariff : N.Z. Dollars	
Double	$182-295
Single	$150-245
Child	neg

Bedrooms	Qty
Double	3
Twin	
Single	

Bed Size	Qty
Super King	
King	2
Queen	1
Double	
Single	

Bathrooms	Qty
Ensuite	3
Private	
Guest Share	

 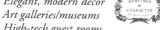 Luxury Accommodation

Features & Attractions

- *Private and peaceful*
- *Elegant, modern décor*
- *Art galleries/museums*
- *High-tech guest rooms*

- *Minutes to central city*
- *and Viaduct Harbour*
- *Stroll to cafés & restaurants*
- *Local bush & beach walks*

Amerissit is architecturally designed and close to Newmarket. Located among prestigious streets in a quiet cul-de-sac, the emphasis is on privacy, peace and tranquillity. By car it's only a few minutes to the city's popular tourist attractions, the restaurants, bars, cafés, shopping, art galleries, museums of Viaduct Harbour, Parnell and Newmarket. All motorway access is within easy reach. **Amerissit's** minimalist-style suites are designed with the executives and the discerning traveller in mind. Latest technology includes slimline TVs, Sky, DVDs, CDs, and tuner at the touch of a button, in-wall or ceiling speakers, direct-dial phone and high-speed internet access. All rooms are non-smoking with ensuite, balcony/patio and offer total privacy, the finest bed linen and facilities. Suites maximise the views of Remuera, Mt Hobson and surrounding trees and gardens. Breakfast is a sumptuous affair with a choice of continental or gourmet, served in your room, dining room or on the balcony. **Amerissit** is the perfect choice for the working week, that indulgent weekend and as a base to explore Auckland.

LAUREL COTTAGE

83 Ranfurly Road, Epsom, Auckland
Ph (09) 630 4384, Fax (09) 630 4384
Mobile 027-498 6909
email: *enquiry@laurelcottage.co.nz*
www.laurelcottage.co.nz

Tariff : N.Z. Dollars	
Double	$170-190
Single	$140-150
Child	

Bedrooms	Qty
Double	1
Twin	
Single	
Bed Size	**Qty**
Super King	
King	
Queen	1
Double	
Single	
Bathrooms	**Qty**
Ensuite	1
Private	
Guest Share	

 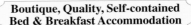

**Boutique, Quality, Self-contained
Bed & Breakfast Accommodation**

Features & Attractions

- *Perfect central location*
- *Basic grocery provisions*
- *Laundry available*
- *Antiques, arts & crafts*
- *Near tourist attractions*
- *Near beaches, tennis, golf*
- *Help with bookings*
- *Privacy & sunny courtyard*

Welcome to **Laurel Cottage**, a tastefully renovated early 1900s cottage, situated in a lovely and very central suburb. The cottage has luxurious furnishings and bed linen, stereo, television, fully equipped kitchen, and much more to make your stay with us comfortable. We are twenty minutes from the airport and a few minutes by car to the city and harbour, an ideal base for the many attractions Auckland has to offer. Laurel Cottage is within easy strolling distance of many cafés and restaurants, NZ Expo Centre, Alexandra Park Raceway, Greenlane, Brightside and Mercy Hospitals. Bus stops are also nearby. For those who enjoy a walk in the park, we are a few minutes walk from beautiful Cornwall Park or Eden Gardens. Close by is the popular shopping and entertainment centre of Newmarket. At the end of your busy day relax in our private, sun-filled courtyard. Whether you are here for leisure or business, we feel sure you will enjoy our warm hospitality and peaceful surroundings.

WOODLANDS

18 Waiatarua Road, Remuera, Auckland
Ph (09) 524 6990
email: *jude.harwood@xtra.co.nz*
www.travelwise.co.nz

home
NEW ZEALAND

Tariff : N.Z. Dollars	
Double	$135-155
Single	$105
Child	n/a

Bedrooms	Qty
Double	2
Twin	1
Single	

Bed Size	Qty
Super King	
King	1
Queen	
Double	1
Single	2

Bathrooms	Qty
Ensuite	1
Private	1
Guest Share	

 Bed & Breakfast in Native Woods

  VISA MasterCard

Features & Attractions

- *Secluded, peaceful woodland setting*
- *On bus route*
- *Divine breakfasts*
- *Handy to Auckland airport*
- *Solar heated swimming pool*
- *Close to Ericcson stadium*
- *Day trips - 1/2 day trips organised*

Our three bedrooms overlook the solar heated swimming pool and lush native greenery. The ensuite king-sized room is large with French windows opening out to a private conservatory, for your use only, and a private entrance to the pool. The 'Pool Room' with a private bathroom, steps out directly to the pool – have a swim before breakfast. The smaller 'Deck Room' opens to the pool area, suitable for two friends, as it is a twin room. Each room has a coloured TV, tea/coffee making facilities, pool towels, heated towel rails, and hairdryers. A guest refrigerator is provided. The rooms are very quiet and secluded. Safe off-street car parking provided. Breakfasts are very special – we use fresh seasonal fruit, then a cooked breakfast of your choice, home-made jams and preserves, herbal teas/teas or percolated coffee, cereals, freshly squeezed juices, muesli.

Visitors book comments 2006: "A magic stay – such a stunning place and superb hosts", "Wow, what a wonderful start to our Honeymoon – you spoilt us", "Gorgeous breakfast, great, divine hosts", "PERFECT, first class, I mean 11/10!!", "Tres Bon – Magnifique!!"

Join us for a glass of New Zealand wine by the pool. Arrive as a guest and leave as a friend.

OMAHU LODGE

33 Omahu Road, Remuera, Auckland
Ph (09) 524 5648, Fax (09) 524 5108
Mobile 021-954 333
email: *info@omahulodge.co.nz*
www.omahulodge.co.nz

Tariff : N.Z. Dollars	
Double	$175-275
Single	$160-200
Child	

Bedrooms	Qty
Double	4
Twin	1
Single	1

Bed Size	Qty
Super King	
King	1
Queen	2
Double	1
Single	2

Bathrooms	Qty
Ensuite	4
Private	1
Guest Share	

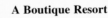 **A Boutique Resort**

Features & Attractions

- *Spacious, private setting*
- *Solar-heated pool*
- *Spa, sauna, central heating*
- *Large plasma/DVD room*
- *Minutes to central city*
- *Walk to restaurants/cafés*
- *Parnell, Newmarket 5 min*
- *Mt Hobson/Cornwall Park 5 min*

Omahu Lodge offers luxury Bed & Breakfast accommodation with total privacy in a peaceful residential setting. The Lodge is very spacious with beautifully appointed bedrooms all with ensuites, fine bed linen, heated towels, bathrobes, slippers, hair dryers, ironing and tea/coffee facilities. Rooms have views of Cornwall Park, Mt Hobson, Mt St John and the eastern suburbs. Relax in the large lounge amongst the antiques or in the separate entertainment room with a large plasma television, DVD and CD player or enjoy the solar heated pool, sauna or spa. **Omahu Lodge** is a boutique resort. The city centre and Auckland's renowned harbour are just 10 minutes away by car. Remuera, Parnell and Newmarket's exclusive shopping, restaurants and antique shops are only minutes away. Walks in Cornwall Park, Mt Hobson and Mt St John add to the peaceful ambience of the suburban setting. A full sumptuous breakfast is served in the conservatory overlooking the pool, on the patio beside the pool or room service is available. Dinner is available by arrangement.

107

MARTINI HOUSE

183 Whitford Road, PO Box 38406, Howick, Auckland
Ph (09) 534 8585
Mobile 027-496 1987
email: *martinico@xtra.co.nz*

Tariff : N.Z. Dollars	
Double	$185-215
Single	$135-165
Child	

Bedrooms	Qty
Double	3
Twin	
Single	

Bed Size	Qty
Super King	
King	1
Queen	2
Double	
Single	

Bathrooms	Qty
Ensuite	1
Private	
Guest Share	1

   Luxury Bed & Breakfast

Features & Attractions

- *Airport & city 25 min.*
- *Cafés & restaurants nearby*
- *Car ferry to Waiheke Island*
- *Ferry to Auckland City*
- *Pacific Coast Highway link*
- *Local walks & golf courses*
- *Relaxing ambience*
- *Healthy, hearty breakfast*

DIRECTIONS:
Please phone for directions.

Martini House is an architecturally designed home offering visitor accommodation with a touch of luxury.
If you are looking for a staging post for your New Zealand tour after landing in Auckland, we are located 25 minutes from the airport, 25 minutes from Auckland central, and most significantly we are also very conveniently positioned at the gateway to the Seabird Coast which leads into Coromandel. When you stay with us, you will relax and revitalise. You can unwind either outdoors, or inside with our magazine library and home theatre. We will set you up for the day with our generous breakfast and share our local knowledge to assist you to enjoy your visit.

Facilities include a guest lounge with plasma screen home theatre and private garden area, in-ground swimming pool (unheated) and off-street parking.

Local features include historic Howick Village, art galleries, Botany Shopping Complex, restaurants, cafés, brasseries and safe swimming beaches. Sylvia Park Shopping Complex and Manukau City Centre are each within 15 minutes drive.

COCKLE BAY HOMESTAY B&B

81 Pah Road, Cockle Bay, Howick, Auckland 2014
Ph (09) 535 0120 Fax (09) 535 0120
Mobile 021-244 0080
email: *cocklebay@bnbnz.co.nz*
www.bnbnz.co.nz

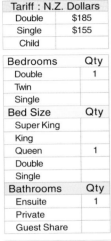

@ home
NEW ZEALAND

Tariff : N.Z. Dollars	
Double	$185
Single	$155
Child	

Bedrooms	Qty
Double	1
Twin	
Single	

Bed Size	Qty
Super King	
King	
Queen	1
Double	
Single	

Bathrooms	Qty
Ensuite	1
Private	
Guest Share	

**Luxury Accommodation
Spectacular Sea Views**

Features & Attractions

- *Ferries to city, Waiheke Is.*
- *Shuttle to / from airport*
- *Quiet & peaceful location*
- *Historical Village Museum*
- *Gateway to Pacific Coast Highway*
- *Walk to beach & historic restaurant*
- *Auckland airport / city 25 minutes*
- *Golf courses (four) within easy reach*

Welcome to our modern, comfortable home above Cockle Bay Beach. Cockle Bay is a lovely old area of Howick that has a special charm. Make a booking with us, at the same time book your rental car from our website and receive instant online confirmation for both (**Special rates for two nights or more**). The ferry runs daily to downtown Auckland (35 min.), a wonderful way to see the harbour with no parking hassles. The City bus leaves from our gate. Howick Village for shopping, cafés and restaurants, is 3km away. **The Taylor Suite** with queen-size bed is one large room with ensuite, two comfortable chairs, coffee table and private balcony. This guest room is well appointed

DIRECTIONS: Please phone for directions.

with TV, ceiling fan, tea & fresh coffee facilities, luggage racks and hairdryer. A fridge is conveniently situated in the hallway for guests' use only. Unfortunately we cannot cater for children.
We enjoy helping you plan your days whilst with us. Come and enjoy our warm Kiwi hospitality, we like to join our guests for breakfast in the dining room, or if the weather permits outside on the terrace. We have wonderful discussions on all sorts of subjects.

BROOKWOOD LODGE

33 Bell Road, Beachlands, Auckland
Ph (09) 536 6975, Fax (09) 536 6976
Mobile 027-479 6453
email: *info@brookwoodlodge.co.nz*
www.brookwoodlodge.co.nz

Tariff : N.Z. Dollars	
Double	$120-150
Single	$90
Child	

Bedrooms	Qty
Double	3
Twin	
Single	

Bed Size	Qty
Super King	
King	1
Queen	
Double	2
Single	2

Bathrooms	Qty
Ensuite	1
Private	
Guest Share	1

Bed & Breakfast
Semi-rural Homestay

Features & Attractions

- *Warm, relaxed hospitality*
- *Tranquil semi-rural setting*
- *Ferry to Auckland City*
- *Swimming pool*
- *Close to 2 golf courses*
- *Dinner by arrangement*
- *Internet & email facilities*
- *Your comfort our priority*

DIRECTIONS:
Please phone or
email for easy directions.

Brian and Heather invite you to relax and unwind at **Brookwood Lodge**, our charming 100 year old villa, set in four acres of cottage gardens, sweeping lawns and paddocks. Two double bedrooms, the **Tulip Room** with its pretty antique brass bed and the **Rose Room,** are within our main house and share a guest bathroom. The **Lavender Suite**, our beautiful garden suite, offers total privacy with its own entrance and ensuite bathroom. All rooms are well-appointed and comfortable with TV, electric blankets, bathrobes, hairdryer, tea and coffee making facilities and personal toiletries. Indulge in a sumptuous breakfast in our dining room or in summer on the patio overlooking our swimming pool. Enjoy the tranquillity of our small sea-side village, yet only 30 minutes from the centre of Auckland City via our regular ferry service. Waiheke Island, famous for its vineyards, olive groves, restaurants and beautiful beaches, is also only a few minutes away by ferry. Explore the surrounding countryside with its beautiful regional park walks, boutique wineries, safe swimming beaches and excellent restaurants. We look forward to making your stay with us a happy and memorable one.

TOTARA LODGE

327 Redoubt Road, Manukau, Auckland
Ph (09) 263 7777
Mobile 027-488 5535
email: *totara-lodge@xtra.co.nz*
www.nzaccommodation.co.nz

Tariff : N.Z. Dollars	
Double	$100-230
Single	$75-110
Child	

Bedrooms	Qty
Double	2
Twin	1
Single	1
Bed Size	**Qty**
Super King	
King	
Queen	2
King/Single	2
Single	1
Bathrooms	**Qty**
Ensuite	2
Private	1
Guest Share	1

VISA MasterCard AMERICAN EXPRESS JCB bankcard ◑

 Luxury Bed & Breakfast

Features & Attractions

- *15 minutes to Airport*
- *Peace and quiet, bush walks*
- *Wireless broadband available*
- *Auckland City 20 min*
- *5 acres of gardens around the Lodge*
- *400 acres of Totara Park and Botanical Gardens adjacent*
- *Complimentary laundry*

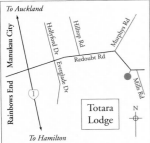

Sited adjoining Totara Park, the Lodge is set in five acres of gardens with established trees and a pond. Extensive views, overlooking the 400 acres of Park Reserve with native bush and farmland to the harbour beyond, enhance the peace and quiet of this secluded location, yet Manukau City is only five minutes drive away, Auckland City twenty minutes away. Built in 1988, **Totara Lodge** features French and old English interior style. Guests have tea and coffee facilities, refrigerator, television, hair dryer and bathrobes. Breakfast is served in the dining room or alfresco on the deck looking out on to the pastoral scene beyond the harbour. Lunch and dinner with complimentary wine are also available at an extra charge. Staying at Totara Lodge is like staying in an oasis, no traffic noise, just peace and quiet. You will think you are miles away from the hustle and bustle, yet shops and restaurants are minutes away.

HILLPARK HOMESTAY
16 Collie Street, Hillpark, Manurewa, Auckland
Ph (09) 267 6847, Fax (09) 267 8718
Mobile 021-207 2559
email: *stay@hillpark.co.nz*
www.hillpark.co.nz

Tariff : N.Z. Dollars	
Double	$100
Single	$60
Child	$20

Bedrooms	Qty
Double	1
Twin	2
Single	

Bed Size	Qty
Super King	
King	
Queen	
Double	1
Single	4

Bathrooms	Qty
Ensuite	1
Private	
Guest Share	1

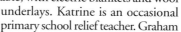

Bed & Breakfast Homestay

VISA   MasterCard

Features & Attractions
- Friendly, helpful hosts
- Near to airport –15 min.
- Ellerslie Flower Show
- Regional botanic garden
- Pacific events centre
- Tipapa events centre
- Close to motorway Nth/Sth
- Dinners available $20 pp

Welcome to our sunny, spacious home in Hill Park, a quiet, pleasant suburb of Manurewa, where our friendly Tonkinese cat will greet you. The beds are comfortable, with electric blankets and wool underlays. Katrine is an occasional primary school relief teacher. Graham has retired from working for the Red Cross. We are 15 min. from Auckland International Airport, 20 min. from Auckland city centre, on the route south and the Pacific Coast Highway. Nearby are restaurants, regional botanic garden – site of the Ellerslie Flower Show, Pacific Events Centre, Tipapa Events Centre, Nathan Homestead, Manukau City Shopping Centre, Rainbows End Adventure Park, the Manukau Superclinic and Surgery Centre and attractive bush walks. Our interests include teaching, classical music, painting, gardening, photography, Christian activities, reading and travel. We offer warm, relaxed hospitality and like conversation and sharing experiences with guests. Come and enjoy home-made bread and dinner with fresh garden vegetables in season from Graham's garden. Visit our web site for more information.

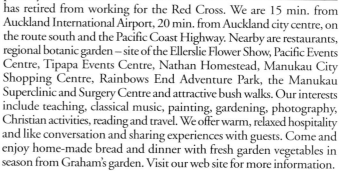

AIRPORT BED & BREAKFAST

1 Westney Road, Mangere, Auckland
Ph (09) 275 0533, Fax (09) 275 0968
Mobile 027-270 5810
email: *airportbnb@xtra.co.nz*
www.airportbnb.co.nz

Features & Attractions

- *5 min Auckland Airport*
- *Internet access & Wi-Fi*
- *Car, cycle, luggage storage*
- *Sky television lounge*
- *Central heating*
- *Buffet breakfast*

**Guest House
Bed & Breakfast**

Double	$90-120
Single	$75-105
Child	

Bedrooms	Qty
Double	8
Twin	2
Single	
Bed Size	**Qty**
King	1
Queen	2
Double	5
Single	9
Bathrooms	**Qty**
Ensuite	4
Private	
Guest Share	3

A warm Kiwi welcome awaits you at **Airport Bed & Breakfast**. Just five minutes from Auckland Airport, a courtesy transfer is available from 6.30am to 8.45pm. Dial 28 on airport freephone.
Airport Bed & Breakfast is comfortable, clean and cost effective accommodation – so convenient to Auckland International and Domestic Airports. Restaurants, takeaways, dairy, liquor store and city bus stop are all within an easy stroll. See our lovely city by bus/ferry on the $11 day pass. Rental cars, sightseeing and New Zealand-wide tours can be arranged.

Complimentary tea and coffee. Internet access Wi-Fi zone, car, cycle and luggage storage is available.

DRURY HOMESTEAD

349, Drury Hills Rd, RD‡, Drury
Ph (09) 294 9030, Fax (09) 294 9035
Mobile 021-158 5061
email: *druryhome@paradise.net.nz*
Features & Attractions

- *Quiet country setting*
- *Near local restaurants*
- *20 mins. from airport*
- *Native bush and stream*
- *35 mins. to central Auckland*
- *Character-filled colonial home*

**Country Paradise
Bed & Breakfast**

Double	$120
Single	$70-90
Child	neg

Bedrooms	Qty
Double	3
Twin	1
Single	
Bed Size	**Qty**
King	
Queen	3
Double	
King/Single	2
Bathrooms	**Qty**
Ensuite	3
Private	1
Guest Share	

DIRECTIONS:
From State Highway 1 (SH1) exit at the Pukekohe/Drury off ramp and follow the map below to 349 Drury Hills Rd.

The Drury Homestead is our wonderfully restored early colonial home, set amidst paddocks and bordered by native bush and stream. Choose from four character-filled bedrooms, lovingly refurbished with an emphasis on comfort and style. The **Lily Room** is a queen-sized studio with kitchen, ensuite and its own entrance on the ground floor. Upstairs the **River Room**, queen-size with ensuite, overlooks our stream whilst **Dunedin**, also queen-size with ensuite, has views over the country side. **Cape Reinga** has twin king/single beds and a private bathroom. We provide a warm and friendly introduction to your New Zealand experience, 20 minutes from the airport, 5 minutes off SH1 and 35 minutes from Auckland City. Children welcome. Family cat and dogs.

Ramarama - Bombay

 YOUR HOST: **Sue and Archie McPherson**   Ph (09) 238 1912

THISTLEDOWN LODGE

42 Coulston Road, Ramarama, Auckland
Ph (09) 238 1912
Mobile 027-473 6313
email: *inquiries@thistledownlodge.co.nz*
www.thistledownlodge.co.nz

Features & Attractions

- *25min from airport*
- *Country hospitality*
- *Quiet, spacious bedrooms*
- *Easy to find, secure parking*
- *Friendly farm animals*
- *Spa, guest lounge*

Quality Bed & Breakfast

	Double	$130
	Single	$80
	Child	neg

Warm hospitality in a peaceful country setting will make this the perfect start or end to your New Zealand holiday. Find out why guests remember Archie's breakfasts and keep returning for more! **Thistledown Lodge** has an idyllic setting down a peaceful country lane, just 25 minutes from Auckland International Airport and five minutes from the southern motorway. The English style country house is set among giant puriri and taraire trees with extensive rural views to Auckland city. Spacious second floor guest bathrooms are freshly decorated and have their own bathrooms. Guests can unwind in the spa, stroll through the country garden and native woodland or feed the friendly sheep. A guest lounge-games room is also available.

Bedrooms	Qty
Double	3
Twin	
Single	
Bed Size	**Qty**
King	1
Queen	2
Double	
King/Single	
Bathrooms	**Qty**
Ensuite	
Private	3
Guest Share	

Waiuku - Franklin

YOUR HOST: **Anthea and David Adams**   Ph: (09) 235 9812

NGODEVWA GARDEN AND BED & BREAKFAST

8 Whiriwhiri Road, RD 2, Waiuku
Ph (09) 235 9812, Fax (09) 235 9812
Mobile 021-397 259
email: *daadams@ps.gen.nz*

Features & Attractions

- *Peaceful & relaxing*
- *Delightful planters garden*
- *Charming 90-year-old house*
- *Rural setting near coast*
- *Arabian horse stud*
- *45 min from Airport*

Bed & Breakfast Countrystay

	Double	$125
	Single	$90
	Child	n/a

Welcome to **Ngodevwa** (Tibetan for 'Flowers of the Angels'). Set in two hectares of tree studded colourful garden and pasture, **Ngodevwa** offers peace and tranquility with intimate areas for relaxation. Let the magic of the garden relax and rejuvenate you. Guests have queen bed accommodation, private bathroom and a sunny sitting room overlooking the garden. Full cooked or continental breakfast is served in the conservatory overlooking pond and fountain in courtyard. We have arabian horses to befriend, two siamese cats to cuddle, our golden retriever, and a rare 1932 convertible Sunbeam car. Local attractions include the beautiful Awhitu Peninsula with its surf and harbour beaches and the Glenbrook Vintage Railway.

DIRECTIONS: Going south turn off Sthn Motorway at Drury direct to Waiuku, or north turn off at Bombay, through Pukekohe to Waiuku. At town centre turn left. 3 km to Ngodevwa on RH corner of Whiriwhiri Rd

Bedrooms	Qty
Double	1
Twin	
Single	
Bed Size	**Qty**
King	
Queen	1
Double	
Single	
Bathrooms	**Qty**
Ensuite	
Private	1
Guest Share	

114

HUNUA GORGE COUNTRY HOUSE

482 Hunua Road, PO Box 27, Papakura, Auckland
Ph (09) 299 9922, Fax (09) 299 9922
Mobile 021-669 922
email: *hunuagorge@xtra.co.nz*

Tariff : N.Z. Dollars	
Double	$125-250
Single	$90
Child	$40

Bedrooms	Qty
Double	3
Twin	1
Single	1

Bed Size	Qty
Super King	
King	1
Queen	1
Double	1
Single	4

Bathrooms	Qty
Ensuite	1
Private	1
Guest Share	1

Countrystay
Bed & Breakfast

Features & Attractions

- *Stunning views*
- *Sunsets*
- *Dinners a speciality*
- *Farm animals*
- *Native plants and birds in garden*
- *Parking, laundry, internet*
- *Wineries, beaches, golf close by*
- *Fishing, scenic flights, shops close by*

Hunua Gorge
Country House

Papakura

Hunua Rd

To Auckland City

Drury

Runciman

To Pukekohe

To Hamilton

DIRECTIONS: SH1 off-ramp at Papakura proceed east along Beach Rd, thru 3 sets of lights onto Settlement Rd. Hunua Rd is on right corner of Edmond Hilary School, proceed 5 km thru housing and light industrial, into Hunua Gorge. We are on left, opp. Winstones Aggregates entrance with a steep gravel drive.

Welcome to the character-filled **Hunua Gorge**, just off the beaten track, where nature abounds, yet half an hour to Auckland City, Auckland and Ardmore Airports. We are half an hour to either coast and on route to Coromandel.

Come and discover the wonders of Auckland, something for everyone on offer.

We have a choice of superior rooms and delicious breakfasts and dinners. We live in the food basket of Auckland. Vegetarians are catered for gladly, alternatively enjoy our wonderful seafood or famous lamb and beef. Prior notice is appreciated. Weather permitting dine alfresco under the southern stars.

We are 3 personable generations on 50 acres of a magic country. *Welcome!*

BROOKFIELD LODGE
2114 State Highway 1, RD, Bombay,
Auckland South
Ph (09) 236 0775
Mobile 027-292 1422
email: *brookfieldleen@xtra.co.nz*

Photo: Cheryl Fuller

Tariff : N.Z. Dollars	
Double	$130
Single	$100
Child	neg

Bedrooms	Qty
Double	2
Twin	1
Single	

Bed Size	Qty
Super King	
King	
Queen	2
Double	
Single	2
Bathrooms	Qty
Ensuite	1
Private	2
Guest Share	

Luxury Bed & Breakfast Homestay

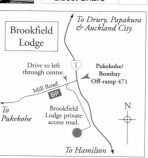

Features & Attractions

- *Main route south easy access*
- *25 minutes from airport*
- *Beautiful Auckland show garden*
- *Sub-tropical areas*
- *Relaxed, friendly hospitality*
- *Surrounded by sunny patios*
- *30 minutes from Auckland*
- *Small flock of sheep*

Easily accessed on the Main South Highway. 25mins from the Airport. A perfect and memorable place to start and finish your holiday. Also an ideal midway en route overnight between Bay of Islands - Coromandel - Taupo - Rotorua etc. **Brookfield Lodge** is set in 5 acres with lovely established trees, lawns & gardens, and with a small flock of sheep. One of Auckland's frequently visited gardens. Our spacious and attractive home is comfortable, relaxing and surrounded by sunny patios. One ensuite queen bedroom opens onto a deck in a subtropical garden. Pretend you are in Fiji! Ensuring your

comfort and pleasure will be our priority. Fresh flowers, bathrobes, hairdryers, complimentary tea, good coffee and home baking will add to your enjoyment. Delicious special breakfasts. Dinner by arrangement. There are many nearby restaurants including the renowned 'Bracu' in an olive grove setting. We have retired from farming and working with thoroughbred horses. Enjoy travelling and meeting other travelers.

WESTWIND HOMESTAY B&B

228 North Road, Mangatarata, RD 6, Thames
Ph (07) 867 3305, Fax (07) 867 3356
Mobile 021-803 293
email: *beds@westwindhomestay.co.nz*
www.westwindhomestay.co.nz

Features & Attractions

- *Bush walks and glowworms*
- *Mouth-watering breakfasts*
- *Super king size beds*
- *Alfresco dining*
- *Woodturners workshop*
- *Insect screens*

	Double	$120-150
$	Single	$90
	Child	

Country Homestay
Only 1 hour south of airport

Bedrooms	Qty
Double	2
Twin	
Single	
Bed Size	**Qty**
King	2
Queen	
Double	
Single	
Bathrooms	**Qty**
Ensuite	1
Private	
Guest Share	1

Escape the city to absolute country quiet overlooking native bush and feel exhilarated by the breathtaking views towards Coromandel. Expect to be pampered and rejuvenated from the moment you arrive. Feel the stresses melt away. Enjoy fabulous fresh New Zealand food and wine, coffee to die for and choose Ian's fluffy pancakes for breakfast. Stretch out on the king-sized bed and cuddle up with the softest feather duvets for the best night's sleep ever. Be amazed by the Miranda seabirds or unwind with a game of golf. Gateway to deserted white sandy Coromandel Beaches and Rotorua's Thermal wonderland. Only one hour south of Auckland Airport. Take time out, have heaps of fun. Your haven at **Westwind** will not disappoint.

DIRECTIONS: From north: Take exit 477, travel 35km south/east on SH 2. Take RH fork at Coromandel intersection, continue for 5km on SH 2. At Tirau/Tauranga turn-off go straight ahead 100m on SH 27. Turn right into North Road.

BONNIEBRAE FARMSTAY

556 State Highway 27, RD 1, Ngatea
Ph (07) 867 3387, Fax (07) 867 3387
Mobile 021-255 8005
e-mail: *rhyshilda@xnet.co.nz*

Features & Attractions

- *Award-winning farm*
- *Dinner by arrangement*
- *1hr from Auckland airport*
- *Private entrances & ensuites*
- *Relaxed, friendly atmosphere*
- *Many tourist attractions nearby*

	Double	$110
$	Single	$75
	Child	Neg.

Farmstay
Spectacular Views

Bedrooms	Qty
Double	1
Twin	1
Single	
Bed Size	**Qty**
King	
Queen	
Double	1
Single	2
Bathrooms	**Qty**
Ensuite	2
Private	2
Guest Share	

DIRECTIONS:
See Map: We are on SH 27 - Gate #556 (either 5.5 km south of Mangatarata, or 2 km north of Torehape).

This is a farmstay **not** to be missed. A beautiful 450 acre sheep and beef farm on rolling hills with amazing views, tree plantings and native bush. Winners of the 'Environmental Wildlife Habitat Enhancement Award'. The Judges commented: "It is a beautiful place, where few spirits would not be raised." We farm romney ewes, hereford cows and dairy grazers. We offer home-grown beef, lamb, free-range eggs and organic produce from our own orchard and vegetable garden. This farm has fenced wetland and duck ponds. All areas are beautifully planted, natural streams running through the property, that also holds some native bush. Laundry/internet/private spa bath/tea/coffee facilities available. Try **Bonniebrae Farmstay** for a very warm and welcoming Scottish/Kiwi experience.

117

WHARFEDALE FARMSTAY
Kopu, RD 1, Thames, Coromandel Peninsula
Ph (07) 868 8929, Fax (07) 868 8926
email: *wharfedale@xtra.co.nz*

Features & Attractions

- *Personal attention*
- *Healthy hearty breakfast*
- *Period English furniture*
- *Safe private swimming*
- *Quiet tranquil setting*
- *1¼ hrs Auckland Airport*

**Country Homestay
Self-contained Accomm.**

	Double	$150
	Single	$100
	Child	n/a

Bedrooms	Qty
Double	1
Twin	1
Single	

Bed Size	Qty
King	
Queen	
Double	1
Single	2

Bathrooms	Qty
Ensuite	2
Private	
Guest Share	

For fifteen years our guests have enjoyed the beauty of **Wharfedale** which has featured in Air NZ "Airwaves" and Japan's "My Country" magazines. We invite you to share our idyllic lifestyle set in nine acres of parklike paddocks and gardens surrounded by native bush. Delight in private river swimming and abundant bird life. We enjoy wholefood and organically grown produce. There are cooking facilities in the studio apartment. We have no children or indoor animals. Cool shade in summer, and cosy log fires and electric blankets in winter. Close to Thames Golf Club and restaurants. We look forward to meeting you. Unsuitable for children.

DIRECTIONS:
3 miles south of Thames to Kopu, turn left onto SH 25A to Tairua, approx 2 miles on right.

COTSWOLD COTTAGE
46 Maramarahi Road, Totara, Thames
Ph (07) 868 6306, Fax (07) 868 6202
Mobile 021-113 3463
email: *cotswoldcot@gmail.com*
gjhamlett@hotmail.co.uk
www.cotswoldcottage.co.nz

Features & Attractions

- *Hiking and walking*
- *Golf, bowls, mineral pools*
- *Hot Water Beach*
- *Goldrush towns, historic buildings*
- *Beaches, scenic flights, diving*
- *Arts, crafts, famous gardens*

**Luxury Boutique
Bed & Breakfast**

	Double	$140-185
	Single	$90
	Child	$15

Bedrooms	Qty
Double	2
Twin	1
Single	

Bed Size	Qty
King/Single	2
Queen	
Double	2
Single	

Bathrooms	Qty
Ensuite	3
Private	
Guest Share	

Relax and unwind in our lovely restored 1920's villa just one hour's drive from Auckland and five minutes from Thames, **Cotswold Cottage** is the perfect place to stay while you discover the Coromandel Peninsula. Moved from Epsom in 1990 our gracious old villa was re-sited in Totara overlooking the Firth of Thames, the race course, and the lovely Kauaeranga River and Valley. Enjoy our sunny, well appointed rooms with stunning views, quality bedding, tea and coffee making facilities and private access. The lounge, conservatory and terrace offer a choice of places to read, write or simply relax. Delicious breakfasts included, evening meals by arrangement. We look forward to welcoming you.

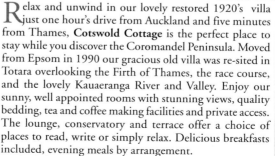

THE HEIGHTS BED & BREAKFAST

300 Grafton Rd, Thames, Coromandel Peninsula
Ph (07) 868 9925
Mobile 021-150 9642
email: *info@theheights.co.nz*
www.theheights.co.nz

Tariff : N.Z. Dollars	
Double	$195-225
Single	
Child	

Bedrooms	Qty
Double	2
Twin	
Single	
Bed Size	**Qty**
Super King	1
King	1
Queen	
Double	
Single	
Bathrooms	**Qty**
Ensuite	2
Private	
Guest Share	

The Views Go On Forever...

Features & Attractions

- *Beaches, fishing, sea*
- *Hot Water Beach*
- *Hiking, eco-tours, birds*
- *Ancient kauri groves*
- *Arts, crafts, dining*
- *Historic gold rush towns*
- *Scenic railroads*
- *Explore the Coromandel*

Sweeping views of sea, mountains and historic Thames are all yours from **The Heights**.

The short climb to Te Moana Room gives you the best views in the house, while garden view Te Koru Room has a cosy fireplace. Both let you relax in spacious luxury with a private deck or patio, private entrance, ensuite, king or super-king bed, fine linens, tea making, fridge, SKY TV/DVD, internet and guest lounge. A warm welcome from our friendly cats and special touches like home-made cookies, turndown service and full breakfast in our romantic garden help make a memorable stay.

Discover the best of Coromandel Peninsula – the spectacular coastal drive, ancient kauri groves, great hiking, historic towns, crafts, fine dining, plus every imaginable way to enjoy the sea. Then end the day in our garden spa. Only 1.5 hours from Auckland, **The Heights** is ideal for your first or last night in New Zealand or as a home base for exploring the Coromandel.

DIRECTIONS: From SH25 in Thames, at BP turn onto Bank St. which becomes Parawai. Left at Grafton Rd. **The Heights** is on the right, across from Millington Pl.

KAUAERANGA COUNTRY B&B THAMES

33 Pakaraka Lane,
446 Kauaeranga Valley Rd, RD 2, Thames
Ph/Fax (07) 868 6895, Mobile 027-426 1157
email: *kauaeranga.country@xtra.co.nz*
www.thames-info.co.nz/KauaerangaCountry

Tariff : N.Z. Dollars	
Double	$120-140
Single	$80
Child	$20-30

Bedrooms	Qty
Double	1
Twin	1
Single	

Bed Size	Qty
Super King	
King	
Queen	1
Double	
Single	2

Bathrooms	Qty
Ensuite	
Private	1
Guest Share	

**Self-contained Accommodation
Countrystay**

Features & Attractions

- *Peaceful rural hideaway*
- *Booked exclusively to you*
- *Safe private swimming*
- *Laundry facilities*
- *Kayaks for river fun*
- *Marvel at glow-worms in garden*
- *Fish for elusive Rainbow Trout*
- *Great base from Pinnacles Walk*

Kauaeranga
Country

●Thames
Bank St
Parawai
Rd
Kauaeranga Valley R
Pakaraka
Lane
Kauaeranga River
25
35
To Paeroa & Auckland

DIRECTIONS: Thames 6.2 km from
the Thames Toyota Plant. Pakaraka Lane
is No 446 Kauaeranga Valley Road,
we are first left down the lane.

At **Kauaeranga Country** a warm welcome and comfortable bed await. Fluffy duvets and electric blankets for winter warmth and crisp cotton sheets for summer. To add to your comfort, your kitchen is complete with refrigerator, microwave, tea and coffee facilities. Guests can enjoy the privacy of their own apartment, while relaxing and enjoying the scenery close enough to touch. A large comfortable lounge area with books on New Zealand and local history overlooks the rambling bush garden.

The beautiful Kauaeranga River is literally on the doorstep with its 100% pure New Zealand water, great for swimming or kayaking. The valley offers hiking both easy and strenuous and we will happily recommend the walk to suit you.

Enquire about car security if overnighting at the Pinnacles Hut. We also enjoy travelling and meeting people from other parts of the world. With only one party of guests at a time, we can ensure your stay with us is the very best it can be.

Te Puru Coast Bed & Breakfast

2a Tatahi Street, Te Puru, Thames Coast, Coromandel
Ph (07) 868 2866, Fax (07) 868 2866
Mobile 027-656 6058
email: *tepurucoastbnb@xtra.co.nz*
www.tepurucoastbnb.co.nz

Features & Attractions

- *Self-contained unit*
- *Lovely beach & bush walks*
- *Swimming*
- *Historical visits*
- *Laundry facilities*
- *Off-street parking*

**Bed & Breakfast
Plus Self-contained Unit**

Double	$110-130
Single	$80
Child	$25

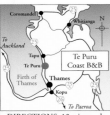

DIRECTIONS: 12 min north of Thames. Turn left off main road at Te Puru into Aputa Avenue, turn right into Tatahi Street. We are the second house on the right. Look for our sign.

Welcome to the beautiful Thames Coast. Our modern home is just twelve minutes from Thames and eighty metres off the main coast road with off-street parking. Your guest lounge has TV and tea/coffee facilities. Enjoy crisp, cool linen in summer and fluffy, warm duvets and electric blankets in winter. You may choose continental or cooked breakfast. Evening meals are on request ($35.00 pp) with complimentary wine or beer. Our large deck is your's to enjoy or take a short two minutes stroll to the beach. Our lovely, separate self-contained unit (do your own cooking) has double bedroom, laundry, kitchen/dining/lounge, BBQ area and double sofa bed in lounge. Tarriff is $125.00 for two people. Extra person $25.00.

Bedrooms	Qty
Double	3
Twin	1
Single	1
Bed Size	Qty
King	
Queen	1
Double	2
Single	2
Bathrooms	Qty
Ensuite	1
Private	1
Guest Share	

The Green House Bed & Breakfast

505 Tiki Road, Coromandel Town
Ph (07) 866 7303
email: *greenhouse@orcon.net.nz*
www.greenhousebandb.co.nz

Features & Attractions

- *Beautiful views*
- *Relaxed and friendly*
- *Generous hospitality*
- *Short walk to town*
- *Excellent eating places*
- *Many attractions, walks etc.*

Double	$140-165
Single	$120-125
Child	n/a

**Quality
Bed & Breakfast**

Bedrooms	Qty
Double	2
Twin	
Single	
Bed Size	Qty
King	1
Queen	1
Double	
Single	
Bathrooms	Qty
Ensuite	2
Private	
Guest Share	

The Green House is a modern home with beautiful views from the dedicated guest lounge, the **Seascape** (king bed) and **Upper Deck** (queen bed) rooms. The lounge has many facilities including television, videos, CDs and games and tea/coffee facilities available at all times. There is a refrigerator for guests' use. Rooms have robes, slippers, hair dryer, toiletries etc. The local attractions are many and varied, for example great day trips to Hot Water Beach and Cathedral Cove, or The Coastal Walkway. Other nearby attractions are easily organised. The coastal road from Thames to Coromandel offers some of New Zealand's most beautiful scenery. Coromandel Town is quaint, friendly and relaxed, with excellent restaurants.

DRIVING CREEK VILLAS
21A Colville Road, Coromandel Town
Ph (07) 866 7755, Fax (07) 866 7753
Mobile 021-116 6393
email: *reservations@drivingcreekvillas.com*
www.drivingcreekvillas.com

Tariff : N.Z. Dollars	
Double	$245-295
Single	$225
Child	$25

Bedrooms	Qty
Double	2
Twin	2
Single	
Bed Size	**Qty**
Super King	
King/Twin	
Queen	2
Double	
Single	4
Bathrooms	**Qty**
Ensuite	2
Private	
Guest Share	

 Boutique Self-contained Cottages

Features & Attractions

- *5 min walk to Driving Creek Railways*
- *5 min drive to the beach*
- *Fantastic fishing, native bush walks*
- *Private bush setting*
- *Handy to fine restaurants*
- *Private Japanese hot tub*
- *Fully self-contained*
- *Wireless broadband*

Set in beautiful, private bush surrounds, our spacious, fully self-contained boutique villas offer the perfect place to unwind – beside the meandering stream where gold was first discovered in New Zealand over 150 years ago.

Purpose-built to a high standard, **Driving Creek Villas** combine colourful pacific themes with modern colonial styling, providing a unique Coromandel accommodation experience.

Enjoy a breakfast in your own private sunny north facing garden and listen out for the captivating birdsong of Tui, Bellbird and Fantail, or chill out under the stars in your own Japanese hot tub. On the fringe of Coromandel Town, the popular Driving Creek Railway is only a short stroll away. There you can view some of New Zealand's finest ceramic art and enjoy the bush railway.

Breakfast basket available ($25 per person).

DRIVING CREEK COTTAGE

21a Colville Road, Coromandel Town
Ph (07) 866 7755, Fax (07) 866 7753
Mobile 021-116 6393
email: *reservations@drivingcreekcottage.com*
www.drivingcreekcottage.com

Tariff : N.Z. Dollars	
Double	$245
Extra pp	$25
Child	

Bedrooms	Qty
Double	2
Twin	
Single	

Bed Size	Qty
Super King	
King	
Queen	2
Double	
Single	

Bathrooms	Qty
Ensuite	1
Private	
Guest Share	

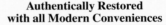
**Authentically Restored
with all Modern Conveniences**

Features & Attractions

- *Acre of gardens with stream*
- *2 living areas plus dining area*
- *Modern kitchen*
- *Egyptian cotton sheets*
- *Outdoor living/ BBQ*
- *TV, stereo and DVD player*
- *Laundry facilities*
- *2 mountain bikes*

DIRECTIONS: Drive 2 km north of Coromandel Township, where the road forks keep left and follow signs to Driving Creek Villas.

Tucked snugly into the township of Coromandel's surrounding countryside is the magical **Driving Creek Cottage**. In a stunning picturesque setting, next to a tributary stream of Driving Creek, is this fully restored, self-contained historical cottage. The lush acre of gardens consisting of exotic and native species provides a place of peace and tranquility. The cottage has two double bedrooms, two bathrooms, full kitchen and dining facilities with indoor/outdoor living. Unique yet affordable this is a wonderful private place to unwind and chill out. The Coromandel Peninsula is renowned for both its rugged environment and its natural beauty. A two hours drive from Auckland to Thames, you then drive the stunning coast road to Coromandel – a one hour journey. **Driving Creek Cottage** is 2 km north from the Coromandel townships centre. In a 5min. walk you are at Driving Creek Railway, one of the most popular attraction on the Coromandel Peninsula. The area is renowned for its beautiful beaches and in a five minute drive you can be dipping your toes in the blue waters of the Hauraki Gulf at Oamaru Bay, a safe swimming Beach.

Kuaotunu - Whitianga ▷ YOUR HOSTS: **Jill and Robert Kaeppeli**   Ph: (07) 866 2445

KAEPPELI'S BED & BREAKFAST
40 Gray Avenue, Kuaotunu, RD 2, Whitianga
Ph (07) 866 2445, Mobile 027-656 3442
email: *paradise@kaeppelis.co.nz*
www.kaeppelis.co.nz

Features & Attractions
- *Ausgezeichnetes Essen*
- *Unbeatable sea views*
- *Alfresco dining*
- *Unschlagbare Meersicht*
- *Exquisite meals*
- *Quiet, peaceful setting*

Panoramic Coastal Paradise

	Double	$120-180
	Single	$85-120
	Child	neg

DIRECTIONS: In Kuaotunu west turn off SH 25 into Bluff Road, across bridge, first left into Gray Avenue, end of Gray Avenue up hill on gravel driveway.

Country living in style and comfort, with exquisite meals, glorious views, privacy, character and simplicity. Robert is an excellent Swiss chef using top quality local produce and the wood fired oven. Jill's Swiss bread makes a pleasant change from toast. Meals served in our panoramic gazebo or guests dining room. A unique peaceful place off the main road where you can relax and enjoy the beauty and tranquility of Kuaotunu. Short walk to the beach. There's a choice of clean, safe, white sandy beaches, bush walks, fishing, tennis, kayaking, swimming, Matarangi's championship golf course and horse trekking nearby. Our daughter and pets make children welcome. Ideal for exploring the Coromandel Peninsula.

AND OUR VIEW?? SIMPLY THE BEST!

Bedrooms	Qty
Double	2
Twin	2
Single	
Bed Size	**Qty**
King	2
Queen	
Double	
Single	4
Bathrooms	**Qty**
Ensuite	4
Private	
Guest Share	

KUAOTUNU BAY LODGE

8. State Highway 25, Kuaotunu
Ph (07) 866 4396, Fax (07) 866 4396
Mobile 027-601 3665
email: *muir@kuaotunubay.co.nz*
www.kuaotunubay.co.nz

Tariff : N.Z. Dollars	
Double	$200-250
Single	$180-200
Child	

Bedrooms	Qty
Double	3
Twin	1
Single	

Bed Size	Qty
Super King	
King	
Queen	3
Double	
King/Single	2

Bathrooms	Qty
Ensuite	3
Private	1
Guest Share	

Boutique Accommodation & Self Service Accommodation

DIRECTIONS: 18 km north of
Whitianga on SH 25.
Please phone for bookings
and easy directions.

Features & Attractions

- *Affordable luxury*
- *Panoramic views*
- *Purpose-built*
- *Overlooking safe beach*
- *Golf nearby*
- *Central to all activities*
- *Decks own entrance*
- *2.5 hrs Auckland airport*

Welcome to our elegant beach house, set in four hectares of bush and pasture, offering panoramic views of the Peninsula and Mercury Island.
Savour a generous breakfast watching the waves. The safe, sandy beach is just a short walk through the garden. Central to all activities a two or three day stay allows time to explore the whole peninsula. Bush/beach walks, kayaking, horse riding all within easy reach.
A choice of fine dining in Whitianga or at the local Golf Club. Having enjoyed this property since 1972 we offer our guests affordable luxury and a true 'Kiwi' experience. A tastefully decorated self-service unit is also available.

LEIGHTON LODGE

17 Stewart Place, Opito Bay, RD 2, Whitianga
Ph (07) 866 0756, Fax (07) 866 5867
Mobile 025-230 0656
email: *leightonlodge@xtra.co.nz*
www.leightonlodge.co.nz

Tariff : N.Z. Dollars	
Double	$110-150
Single	$90-110
Child	$30

Bedrooms	Qty
Double	2
Twin	
Single	
Bed Size	**Qty**
Super King	
King	
Queen	2
Double	1
Single	
Bathrooms	**Qty**
Ensuite	1
Private	1
Guest Share	

**Bed & Breakfast
Self-contained Haven**

Features & Attractions

- *Views of Mercury Islands*
- *Safe swimming & boating*
- *Excellent diving*
- *Peace & tranquility*
- *Special dinners*
- *Great local fishing*
- *Local gourmet seafood*
- *Watch the dolphins*

Leighton Lodge

Maire and Wally welcome you to share the tranquil and peaceful environment of their Coromandel Peninsula paradise. Our spacious deck commands panoramic views of the Great Mercury Islands. You are just two minutes walk from the stunning white sands of Opito Bay beach. Enjoy a scenic walk to the historic Maori Pa site or a beach ramble (our dog will lead the way). Excellent diving, safe swimming, or fishing and boating are available. There are two golf courses in the area. Alternatively you may like to sit under a pohutukawa tree or laze in our hammock with a good book. Sometimes you can swim with the dolphins that regularly visit.

We offer either our **Pacific Room** – a large double bedroom with ensuite or the privacy of our self-contained apartment which includes a bedroom kitchen/living area and bathroom. Sample the excellent local seafood. Delicious home cooked dinners can be prepared by prior arrangement. We are a non-smoking family.

WITHIN THE BAYS

49 Tarapatiki Drive, Whitianga
Ph (07) 866 2848, Fax (07) 866 2849
Mobile 021-178 7778
e-mail: *info@withinthebays.co.nz*
www.withinthebays.co.nz

Features & Attractions

- *Remote-controlled curtain, lights & TV in Bay View Room*
- *Magnificent sea views*   • *European breakfast*
- *Accessible native bush*   • *Quiet, private road*

$	Double	$240-300
	Single	$90-110
	Child	$30-75

Contemporary Luxury Accommodation

Bedrooms	Qty
Double	2
Twin	
Single	
Bed Size	**Qty**
King	
Queen	2
Double	
Single	
Bathrooms	**Qty**
Ensuite	
Private	1
Guest Share	

Within the Bays is a purpose-built Bed & Breakfast accommodation, comprising two modern guest rooms, each with its own private balcony/patio – also catering for the less able traveller. You can look forward to a warm welcome with refreshments on arrival. Enjoy magnificent views over Mercury Bay including Cooks Beach, Shakespeare Cliff and Whitianga Harbour. **Within the Bays** offers peaceful and quiet accommodation on a private road, the ideal location to relax and explore the beautiful Coromandel Peninsula. We are looking forward to meeting our guests and help plan trips and activities. We speak English, Dutch and a fair bit of German and French.

DIRECTIONS: From Whitianga, follow the signs to Coromandel until you come to the beach. Go left at Buffalo Beach Road, then left again into Centennial Drive and drive up the hill. Turn left into Rimu Street, which will change into Tarapatiki Drive. After 1km turn right into our private road (look for our sign).

AT PARKLAND PLACE

14 Parkland Place, PO Box 59, Whitianga
Ph (07) 866 4987, Fax (07) 866 4946
Mobile (021) 404 923
email: *parklandplace@wave.co.nz*
www.atparklandplace.co.nz

Features & Attractions

- *European hospitality*   • *Spa pool and barbecue*
- *Luxurious, romantic*   • *Dinner by arrangement*
- *Sunny outdoor area*   • *Quiet and peaceful*

$	Double	$165-200
	Single	$150
	Child	Neg

Luxurious Bed & Breakfast Quiet Location

Bedrooms	Qty
Double	5
Twin	1
Single	
Bed Size	**Qty**
Super King	4
Queen	1
Double	
King Single	2
Bathrooms	**Qty**
Ensuite	5
Private	
Guest Share	

Enjoy European hospitality in Whitianga's most luxurious boutique hotel style Bed & Breakfast. Maria, a ship's chef from Poland and her New Zealand husband Guy, a Master Mariner, will make your stay a memorable experience with hospitality that has become renowned around the world. Large luxuriously appointed rooms with television, radio, writing desk and comfortable beds. Take your time over a magnificent breakfast and let Maria surprise you with a superb dinner or barbecue. Relax in the large guest lounge, watching Sky television, reading a book or listening to music. Enjoy the sunny outdoors relaxing in the spa pool or take a quiet stroll along the reserve to popular Brophy's Beach. Being situated next to farmland and reserves ensures absolute peace and quiet. You will never regret your stay! Privacy and discretion is assured.

DIRECTIONS: Take SH 25 to Whitianga. Drive through township along Buffalo Beach Road for 4 km. Turn left into Centennial Drive, then first left into Parkland Place.

CENTENNIAL HEIGHTS BED & BREAKFAST
141 Centennial Drive, Whitianga
Phone (07) 866 0279, Fax (07) 866 0276
Mobile 027-237 9086
email: *blackmanmathis@xtra.co.nz*
www.centennialheights.unitrental.com

Features & Attractions
- Spectacular sea views
- Friendly border collie
- Comfortable luxury
- Quiet peaceful enviroment
- Tennis court nearby
- Swimming beach

Luxury Boutique Accommodation with Spectacular Sea Views

Double	$150
Single	$100
Child	$20

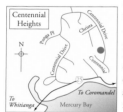

Centennial Heights Bed & Breakfast sits atop Centennial Drive, overlooking the sparkling waters of the Whitianga Harbour. Paul, Johanna and Mollie (our lovable border collie) offer warm and friendly hospitality in elegant surroundings. Buffalo and Simpsons Beaches are within easy reach and the township is a five minute drive. Over pre-dinner drinks we can assist you with information on the best of the area's attractions including fishing, kayaking, tramping, scuba diving and snorkelling, boat cruises, dining out, etc. We offer a delicious, wholesome cooked and continental breakfast which can be enjoyed along with the spectacular sea views. We look forward to welcoming you and making your stay a pleasant and memorable experience. We welcome overseas guests. Johanna is fluent in German and French.

Bedrooms	Qty
Double	3
Twin	
Single	1
Bed Size	**Qty**
Super King	1
Queen	2
Double	
Single	1
Bathrooms	**Qty**
Ensuite	3
Private	1
Guest Share	

FLAXHAVEN LODGE

995 Purangi Road, Flaxmill Bay, RD1, Whitianga
Ph (07) 866 2676, Fax (07) 866 2396
Mobile 021-286 1088
email: *welcome@flaxhavenlodge.co.nz*
www.flaxhavenlodge.co.nz

Tariff : N.Z. Dollars	
Double	$180-250
Single	$70
Child	

Bedrooms	Qty
Double	2
Twin	
Single	

Bed Size	Qty
Super King	1
King	
Queen	1
Double	
King/Single	2

Bathrooms	Qty
Ensuite	
Private	2
Guest Share	

**Luxury Coastal
Accommodation**

Features & Attractions

- *Centrally located*
- *4 safe sandy beaches
  all within a short stroll*
- *Close to cafes restaurants*
- *Historic bush walks*
- *Boating kayaking fishing*
- *Purpose-built 2005*
- *Internet wi-fi*

Flaxhaven Lodge is nestled alongside picturesque Flaxmill Bay, set in 1.5 acres of gardens surrounded by countryside and native bush. Flaxmill Bay and Eggcentric Café are a 2 min. walk. In 3 min. on the quaint passenger ferry to Whitianga town you can experience numerous cafés and retail opportunities. Famous Cathedral Cove and Hot Water Beach are a 10 minute drive. Luxury accommodation is designed for guests' relaxation, privacy and comfort, with quality linens and fittings, TVs, fridges, tea and coffee making facilities, tiled bathrooms, laundry, private entrances and patios. A separate cottage has a queen-size bedroom with ensuite, livingroom and kitchenette with microwave. A private wing of the house has a superking bedroom, private sittingroom (with sofabed), bathroom and separate toilet. Enjoy special breakfasts in the sunny kitchen or alfresco on the patio and sometimes for lunch a thermos and muffins. We will welcome you with warmth, help you unwind with refreshments, and share with you our home and the beautiful Coromandel coastline.

Cosy Cat Cottage

41 South Highway, (town end), Whitianga, Mercury Bay
Coromandel Peninsula
Ph (07) 866 4488, Fax (07) 866 4488
email: *cosycat@xtra.co.nz*
www.cosycat.co.nz

Features & Attractions

- *Picturesque cottage*
- *Amusing catty decor*
- *A-la-carte breakfast*
- *Separate self-contained cottage*
- *Comfortable guest lounge*
- *Helpful, friendly service*

 Bed & Breakfast Self-contained Cottage

	Double	$90-110
	Single	$65-75
	Child	

DIRECTIONS:
1 km south of
the town centre

Welcome to our picturesque cottage and enjoy the amusing catty décor and unique feline ambience! Cosy queen/double/twin/single bedrooms with ensuite/private bathrooms are available all year. Delicious a-la-carte breakfasts are complimentary and teas or coffees can be served when required. An easy drive may take you to Hot Water Beach, Cathedral Cove and other fascinating places. Friendly and helpful service is assured and you will probably like to meet Sylvie the Tonkinese cat and perhaps visit the "cat hotel" in the garden. A self-contained cottage is also available with two queen  bedrooms, bathrooms and kitchen.

Bedrooms	Qty
Double	2
Twin	1
Single	1
Bed Size	**Qty**
King	
Queen	2
Double	
Single	2
Bathrooms	**Qty**
Ensuite	2
Private	1
Guest Share	

Glenvin Bed & Breakfast

22 Cholmondeley Crescent, Whitianga 3510
Ph (07) 867 1487
Mobile 021-174 5177
e-mail: *glenvin@slingshot.co.nz*
www.glenvin.co.nz

Features & Attractions

- *Walk to cafés & restaurants*
- *Relaxed, friendly hosts*
- *Off-street parking*
- *Yummy breakfasts*
- *Close to beach*
- *Quiet location*

 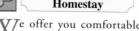 **Bed & Breakfast Homestay**

	Double	$120
	Single	$50
	Child	

We offer you comfortable, homely accommodation in a purpose-built home, situated in a quiet street with off-street parking. Use Whitianga as your base for visiting the many scenic attractions in the area. Whitianga's shops, cafés and restaurants are all just a short walk away. The beach is within easy walking distance.

Continental breakfast provided with fresh fruit. Cooked breakfast available by prior arrangement. Tea and coffee facilities available 24/7. Guests are encouraged to use the deck for drinks at the end of the day. We will help you plan local trips and enjoy your stay in this beautiful part of the Coromandel. We hope to make your stay a memorable one, where you arrive as strangers, but leave as friends .

Bedrooms	Qty
Double	2
Twin	1
Single	
Bed Size	**Qty**
King	
Queen	2
Double	
Single	2
Bathrooms	**Qty**
Ensuite	2
Private	1
Guest Share	

THE MUSSEL BED

892 Purangi Road, Cooks Beach, RD 1, Whitianga
Ph (07) 866 5786, Fax (07) 866 5706
Mobile 027-234 8747
email: *welcome@musselbed.co.nz*
www.musselbed.co.nz

Features & Attractions

- *Capt Cooks 1769 Discovery*
- *White, sandy beaches*
- *Bush & coastal walks*
- *Hot Water Beach 10min.*
- *Passenger Ferry Whitianga 5min.*
- *Famous 'Eggsentric Café' nearby*

	Double	$175-250
$	Single	$150-225
	Child	$50

**Bed & Breakfast
Luxury Accommodation**

Bedrooms	Qty
Double	4
Twin	2
Single	
Bed Size	**Qty**
King	
Queen	4
King Singles	2
Single	2
Bathrooms	**Qty**
Ensuite	3
Private	1
Guest Share	

We have the best of both worlds at The Mussel Bed, nestled amidst native bush, gardens and streams, yet only 5 minutes walk to historical Cooks Beach. A perfect base to explore nearby Cathedral Cove and Hot Water Beach! Kayak the stream from our jetty and enjoy the natural bird habitat, exploring caves and walking on gorgeous Lonely Bay! Finish your day unwinding by the fire, with a wine from our local vineyard, in the company of fellow travellers! Our guest wing has 3 luxurious suites, tiled ensuites and french doors opening onto private decks with all those special touches our guests love! We bring breakfast to you to enjoy in the garden, room or deck – try our delicious homemade muesli and bread, yoghurt drizzled with honey, fruit compote and maybe muffins to take on your picnic. We look forward to making your stay on the beautiful Coromandel a special one!

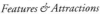

FERRY LANDING LODGE

1169 Purangi Rd, Ferry Landing, RD 1, Whitianga
Ph (07) 866 0445, Fax (07) 866 0792
Mobile 027-250 3388
email: *info@ferrylandinglodge.co.nz*
www.ferrylandinglodge.co.nz

Features & Attractions

- *Water's edge next to bush reserve, beautiful garden setting*
- *Complimentary guided walk to the Maori Pa*
- *Fresh muffins, fruit preserves, delicious home-made jams*

	Double	$180-250
$	Single	$130-200
	Extra pp	$50

**Take the ferry to Whitianga
- it's at your doorstep!**

Bedrooms	Qty
Double	4
Twin	
Single	
Bed Size	**Qty**
King	2
Queen	2
Double	
Single	2
Bathrooms	**Qty**
Ensuite	
Private	2
Guest Share	

The only Bed and Breakfast at picturesque Ferry Landing. ❖ Peaceful, coastal location across the water from Whitianga. ❖ Enjoy the convenience of a short, leisurely stroll to the ferryboat. ❖ Restaurants and café's, minutes away from the waterfront. ❖ Spacious, comfortable accommodation, en-suites, on-site parking. ❖ Guest PC with broadband. ❖ Kayak, bikes, fresh garden produce. ❖ Exceptional hospitality with friendly well travelled hosts. ❖ Cooks beach, Hahei & Hot water beaches nearby.

"Their passion for New Zealand, local knowledge and enthusiasm for guests is undeniable!"
"The location is absolutely fantastic, so convenient!"

MERCURY ORCHARD BED & BREAKFAST

141 Purangi Road, RD 1, Whitianga
Ph (07) 866 3119, Fax (07) 866 3115
email: *relax@mercuryorchard.co.nz*
www.mercuryorchard.co.nz

Tariff : N.Z. Dollars	
Double	$130-175
Single	$130
Child	

Bedrooms	Qty
Double	3
Twin	
Single	1
Bed Size	**Qty**
Super King	
King	1
Queen	2
Double	
Single	2
Bathrooms	**Qty**
Ensuite	3
Private	
Guest Share	

     Peaceful Garden Cottages

Features & Attractions

- *Outdoor bath, swimming pool*
- *Private deck with BBQ*
- *Tranquil garden setting*
- *Bush walks*

- *Golf course nearby*
- *Hot Water Beach and Cathedral Cove 8min.*
- *Delicious breakfast*

DIRECTIONS:
14 km north of Tairua turn
into Hot Water Beach Road.
Then 1.5 km left into Purangi
Road. – 1.5 km on left
is **Mercury Orchard**.

Paua Bach and Fig Tree Cottage are nestled amongst 5 acres of peaceful country gardens and orchard. Self-contained country-style luxury with French doors opening out into the orchard, crisp cotton bed linen, bath robes, fresh fruit, flowers and candles. Special to Paua Batch is an old fashioned outdoor bath (to be taken with a glass of wine and bubbles).

Watch the variety of our birdlife while enjoying a full breakfast brought out onto your private deck. Freshly squeezed orange juice, in-season fruit, home made muesli and our own free-range eggs. Quiet and relaxing, perfect for that special anniversary or as a restful stay. The area is well known for crafts and gardens. Local activities include swimming, diving, bush walking, tramping, horse riding, fishing, kayaking, scenic boat cruises and gold. Cathedral Cove, Cooks and Hot Water Beaches are 7-8 min. drive. There are several good restaurants close by, alternatively BBQ your evening meal Kiwi style.

We normally have fresh produce available from our garden. Meet our friendly sheep, kunekune pig, donkey, cat and two small dogs.

HALCYON HEIGHTS COUNTRY RETREAT

365 Mill Creek Road, RD 1, Whitianga
Ph (07) 866 0166, Fax (07) 866 0166
Mobile 021-172 0561
email: *p.park@xtra.co.nz*
www.halcyonheights.co.nz

MasterCard   *VISA*

Features & Attractions

- *Tranquil setting*
- *15 acre farmlet*
- *Bird aviaries & gardens*
- *Beaches & restaurants 10 min*
- *Comfortable, relaxed atmosphere*
- *Dinner by arrangement*

$		
Double	$120
Single	
Child	

**Country Retreat
Bed & Breakfast**

Bedrooms	Qty
Double	1
Twin	2
Single	
Bed Size	**Qty**
King/Twin	1
Queen	2
Double	
Single	4
Bathrooms	**Qty**
Ensuite	2
Private	1
Guest Share	

Halcyon Heights is set in a peaceful valley with a bush backdrop. We offer a warm welcome with nothing but peace and tranquility, set on fifteen acres. Enjoy breakfast outside on the deck, while listening to the many native birds. Later, enjoy a walk through our park-like gardens and view our bird aviaries, housing over forty species of birds and parrots. Amble along our stream walkway when you visit our friendly donkeys and farm animals. On the way back to the house, eat the fruit from a variety of vines and trees. Plan on spending more than one night while using **Halcyon Heights** as a base for exploring the Coromandel Peninsula.

DIRECTIONS:
Just 3.6 km along Mill Creek Road off State Highway 25.
Just south of Whitianga.

YOUR HOSTS: **Kay and Peter Harrison**   Ph (07) 866 3281 ◄   *Hahei - Whitianga*

HAHEI HORIZON

20 Grierson Close, Hahei, RD 1, Whitianga
Ph (07) 866 3281, Mobile 021-160 7213
email: *pkharrison@xtra.co.nz*
www.haheihorizon.co.nz

MasterCard   *VISA*   *@home NEW ZEALAND*

Features & Attractions

- *Cathedral Cove close by*
- *Cafés & restaurants*
- *Kayak, dive, boat trips*
- *Sparkling, safe beach*
- *Golf & tennis nearby*
- *Hot Water Beach 5 min.*

$		
Double	$140-220
Single	$120-200
Child	on request

**Dare to Dream
Quality Accommodation**

Bedrooms	Qty
Double	3
Twin	
Single	
Bed Size	**Qty**
King	2
Queen	1
Double	
Single	2
Bathrooms	**Qty**
Ensuite	3
Private	
Guest Share	

Peter and Kay invite you to share their little piece of this special part of New Zealand. **Hahei Horizon**, our home on the hill, is ideally suited for Bed & Breakfast. Every room has a stunning view of the coast and the native surrounding. With down to earth Kiwi hospitality, relaxation is hard to avoid. Enjoy a cooked or a continental breakfast on the deck. At the end of the day join us for refreshments before dining at one of Hahei's 3 fine restaurants. The large rooms, prepared with quality linen and electric blankets, have ensuites, tea/coffee facilities and a fridge. Internet connection is available. Rest and relaxation or fun and exhilaration! Walk or cruise to Cathedral Cove, snorkle or dive in the Marine Reserve, kayak or swim at our beautiful beach, play golf or tennis or soak in a hot self-dug thermal pool. We can arrange it all – except the weather.

DIRECTIONS:
From SH25 follow signs to Hahei. Grierson Close is 4th left along main Beach Rd between speed bumps. **Hahei Horizon** is at end of street, up the private driveway on right.

HOT WATER BEACH BED & BREAKFAST

48 Pye Place, Hot Water Beach, Coromandel Peninsula
Ph (07) 866 3991, Fax (07) 866 3291
Mobile 027 479 9620
email: *TKnight@xtra.co.nz*
www.hotwaterbedandbreakfast.co.nz

Features & Attractions

- Hot springs on beach
- Spectacular night skies
- Sun-drenched decks
- Spa pool, billiard table
- Glowworm walk
- Restaurants 5 min. drive

 **Premier Beachside Panoramic Views**

Double	$180-250
Single	$180-200
Child	

Our modern home, which is only a stone's throw from the beach, has been specifically designed for the comfort of our guests. On the beach you can swim, surf or observe the native bird life. You can use our spades to dig your own natural hot spring pool close to low tide. This can be a truly romantic experience if done in the evening with a bottle of wine under the spectacular night skies. Enjoy a generous breakfast on our extensive sun-drenched decks. Relax with a fresh coffee or cool drink and view the dolphins which often come to play in the bay. Tazz, our friendly boxer, welcomes you. Proud members of @home NZ.

VISA, MasterCard, JCB, AMERICAN EXPRESS, Diners

DIRECTIONS: Follow Hot Water Beach Rd from SH 25. Travel past Beach Shop. We are 50m on right uphill.

Bedrooms	Qty
Double	2
Twin	
Single	
Bed Size	**Qty**
King	
Queen	2
Double	
Single	
Bathrooms	**Qty**
Ensuite	2
Private	
Guest Share	

KOTUKU

422 Otahu Road, Whangamata, Coromandel
Ph (07) 865 6128, Fax (07) 865 6128
Mobile 027-358 1227
email: *lindapeter@slingshot.co.nz*
www.kotukuhomestay.co.nz

VISA, MasterCard, Diners

Features & Attractions

- New home, solar heating
- Close to estuary and surf beach
- Campervan facility
- Outdoor spa
- Bikes, kayaks
- Internet access

Double	$120	
Single	$100	
Child		

Bedrooms	Qty
Double	3
Twin	
Single	
Bed Size	**Qty**
King	
Queen	3
Double	
Single	
Bathrooms	**Qty**
Ensuite	3
Private	
Guest Share	

 Homestay Bed & Breakfast Self-contained Studio Unit

We offer you comfortable accommodation in a purpose-built home. Rosie, our friendly Huntaway cross and Elizabeth, the cat, will give you a warm welcome too. Relax in the spacious lounge or private patio. Enjoy the Coromandel sunset from our deluxe outdoor spa.

Kotuku is situated at the quieter end of Whangamata, just a two minute stroll to the lovely Otahu Estuary and Reserve; ideal for swimming, kayaking or just walk along the reserve to the beach and observe the fascinating shore birds.

Our **Studio Unit** (with queen, large single bed and a cot) at the rear of the house, is fully self-contained and suitable for a family with young children. They will love playing in the safe estuary!

COLONIAL HOMESTAY

202 Paku Drive, Tairua, Coromandel Peninsula
Ph (07) 864 7743, Fax (07) 864 7743
Mobile 027-290 9555
email: *colonialhomestay@paradise.net.nz*
www.colonialhomestay.co.nz

Tariff : N.Z. Dollars	
Double	$200-225
Single	$170-200
Child	

Bedrooms	Qty
Double	2
Twin	
Single	

Bed Size	Qty
Super King	
King	
Queen	2
Double	
Single	1

Bathrooms	Qty
Ensuite	1
Private	1
Guest Share	

Homestay
Bed & Breakfast

Features & Attractions

- *Warm & friendly hospitality*
- *Relaxed & peaceful setting*
- *Stunning views*
- *Bush walks*
- *Golf course nearby*
- *Laundry facilities*
- *Internet access*
- *Elevator to all floors*

DIRECTIONS: Follow SH 25 to Tairua, after one-way bridge turn 1st right onto Manaia Road, then right onto Paku Drive up to the top of hill.

Jenny and Bob welcome you to **Colonial Homestay** where you can make our home "your home" in a quiet and restful location. Our home is situated high on Paku Mountain with panoramic views of the ocean and offshore islands. With our extensive knowledge of the area, we can assist with sightseeing, activities and travel plans, helping you to experience the wonderful Coromandel. Why not try one of the many walks around Mount Paku including the summit where fabulous views of the ranges, harbour, coast and islands can be enjoyed? We are only a short drive to marvellous beaches including Sailor's Grave, Hot Water Beach and Cathedral Cove. There is a good choice of restaurants for evening meals. Enjoy a magnificent breakfast overlooking the views. Refreshments can be served on the surrounding decks on your arrival or at the end of the day. Stay a few nights or a few weeks; we look forward to your company.

COPSEFIELD BED & BREAKFAST

1055 SH 25, RD 1, Whangamata
Ph (07) 865 9555, Fax (07) 865 9510
Mobile 021-895 566
email: *copsefield@xtra.co.nz*
www.copsefield.co.nz

@home
NEW ZEALAND

Tariff : N.Z. Dollars	
Double	$180
Single	$130
Child	–

Bedrooms	Qty
Double	2
Twin	1
Single	

Bed Size	Qty
Super King	
King	
Queen	2
Double	
Single	2

Bathrooms	Qty
Ensuite	3
Private	
Guest Share	

 Countrystay Bed & Breakfast and Self-contained Cottage

Features & Attractions

* *Stunning country scenery*
* *Canoes & mountain bikes available*
* *Peace and tranquillity*
* *Six hole pitch'n putt*
* *Hot tub*
* *3 acres of garden*
* *River, views*
* *Close to beaches*

Copsefield Bed & Breakfast is situated in a central location on the Coromandel Peninsula. Peaceful and private, approximately one and a half hours distance to Auckland Airport. Ideal base for visiting attractions of the

Copsefield Bed & Breakfast

To Opoutere

To Whangamata

Coromandel Peninsula. Close to exquisite native fauna, magnificent beaches and walks, within easy driving distance to all Coromandel attractions including Cathedral Cove and Hot Water Beach. Designed for your comfort. Two double rooms, each with queen bed and one twin room. Each bedroom has its own ensuite and adjoining verandah. Relax on the spacious decks, with a glass of wine and a good book! Wander along the bush-clad riverbanks or stroll the green acres amongst the fruit and chestnut trees. Our full breakfasts include freshly squeezed juice, yoghurt, cereal and organic fruit from our orchard, fresh eggs, accompanied by bacon, tomatoes and mushrooms. Bikes and canoes available, beaches close by and a private stream swimming hole at our back door. Come and enjoy our piece of paradise.

WAIHI BEACH LODGE

170 Seaforth Road, Waihi Beach, Coromandel
Ph (07) 863 5818, Fax (07) 863 5815
Mobile 021-657 888
email: *waihi.beach.lodge@xtra.co.nz*
www.waihibeachlodge.co.nz

Tariff : N.Z. Dollars	
Double	$220-265
Single	$195-235
Child	n/a

Bedrooms	Qty
Double	4
Twin	
Single	

Bed Size	Qty
Super King	
King	3
Queen	1
Double	
Single	

Bathrooms	Qty
Ensuite	3
Private	1
Guest Share	

       Luxury Coastal Accommodation

Map / Directions

Waihi Beach Rd
Wilson Rd
To Waihi & SH 2
Waihi Beach
N
Seaforth Rd
Hanlen Ave
Waihi Beach Lodge
Emerton Rd
To Katikati & SH 2

DIRECTIONS:
From North: Turn off SH2 to Waihi Beach, turn right at roundabout, 1½ km on right after shopping village. Cnr Seaforth Rd and Hanlen Ave with main entrance off Hanlen Ave. From South: Turn off SH2 to Waihi Beach, turn left at roundabout, 400m on left. Proceed as above.

Features & Attractions

- *Stunning sea and rural views*
- *Short stroll to beach*
- *Full gourmet breakfasts*
- *Quality linen and décor*
- *5 local cafés*
- *Close to K'gorge walks*
- *Wireless internet connection*
- *Less than 2hrs – Auckland*

Waihi Beach is a friendly seaside resort and one of the safest surf beaches in New Zealand. Your restful escape from a bustling lifestyle or your gateway to the Coromandel. Surrounded by natural beauty **Waihi Beach** offers a whole range of leisure opportunities from beach and gorge walks to golf and fishing. Or if you prefer, relax and experience the many sea views available from the **Lodge** with a book from our library. We have 3 king bedrooms with ensuites and a modern studio apartment with a queen-size bed. 3 rooms have private entrances. All rooms are furnished with quality beds, cotton linen, bath robes, toiletries, hair dryers, televisions, DVD players and fridges. Pre-dinner drinks are offered each evening. Waihi Beach has great cafés for dining or we would be happy to provide a 3-course meal by prior arrangement. Scrumptuous full breakfasts are served in the dining room or alfresco on one of the many decks.

Trout & Chicken Boutique Accommodation

9137 State Highway 2, RD 2, Waihi
Ph (07) 8636964, Fax (07) 8636966
Mobile 027-206 4080
email: *troutandchicken@paradise.net.nz*
www.troutandchicken.co.nz

Features & Attractions

- On an organic orchard
- Peaceful, rural setting
- Excellent quality
- Full-sized double rooms
- Purpose-built/rural views
- Waitete stream on boundary

Boutique Accommodation or Self-contained

Double	$190-230
Single	$90-110
Studio	$150

We strongly recommend a minimum of two nights in this award winning town to give you time to soak up the history, see the goldmine, walk on the beach, play golf, see the art, the gardens, taste the coffee. Breakfast in our dining room or the deck, enjoy the *'oh so comfortable beds'*. In winter, a weekend in front of the open fire in a family-size lounge with a blueberry muffin. Our organic blueberries are a favourite as are eggs from our hens. Feed the trout, fish the Ohinemuri River, take a spectacular walk in the Karangahake Gorge or on the coast, guided or on your own. Restaurants, cafés, shops close by.
We look forward to welcoming you to our home.

DIRECTIONS: Less than 2km west of Waihi Town on SH2

Bedrooms	Qty
Double	2
Twin	1
Single	
Bed Size	**Qty**
King	
Queen	2
King/Single	2
Single	2
Bathrooms	**Qty**
Ensuite	2
Private	1
Guest Share	

Waihi Waterlily Gardens

441 Pukekauri Road, Waihi
Ph (07) 863 8267, Fax (07) 863 8231
Mobile 021-369 671
e-mail: *stay@waterlily.co.nz*
www.waterlily.co.nz

Features & Attractions

- Unforgettable R & R
- Special for all occasions
- Stylish, warm & inviting
- Award-winning wineries
- Captivating region
- Gold mining attractions

Luxury Accommodation Enchanting Environment

Double	$250-420
Single	
Child	P.O.A.

Self-contained architectural cottages, **Lily Pad** and **Lotus**, are situated at the Waihi Waterlily Gardens, within 15 enchanting acres of established gardens, ponds and parklike grounds. Newly completed, the luxurious cottages are offered as self-contained, Bed & Breakfast, or fully catered accommodation. Built for four seasons, spacious decks ensure summer relaxation, while cosy fires ensure a snug winter. Challenge yourselves to giant chess, relax in the gardens, watch the star-lit sky alive at night. Your hosts, Sam and Olivia, will tailor-make your stay, ensuring an unforgettable experience. The historical town of Waihi, bushwalks, golf and trout fishing are all within 6 km. You won't need to travel much further to discover beaches, bays and a fascinating region filled with creative talent, bound by history.
Make our environment your place.

DIRECTIONS: Please visit our website or phone us to get easy directions.

Bedrooms	Qty
Double	2
Twin	
Single	
Bed Size	**Qty**
King	2
Queen	
Double	1
Single	
Bathrooms	**Qty**
Ensuite	2
Private	
Guest Share	

HERB GARDEN BED & BREAKFAST

114 Plantation Road, Te Kauwhata, North Waikato
Ph (07) 826 3031, Fax (07) 826 3035
Mobile 021-251 4170
email: *info@herbhaven.co.nz*
http://www.herbhaven.co.nz

Features & Attractions

- *Renowned herb garden*
- *Golf clubs*
- *Superb meals on request*
- *Wineries*
- *Heritage attractions*
- *Peace & tranquility*

Romantic Herb Garden B&B With Rural Views

Bedrooms	Qty
Double	$150-190
Single	
Child	

Bedrooms	Qty
Double	3
Twin	
Single	

Bed Size	Qty
King	1
Queen	2
Double	
Single	

Bathrooms	Qty
Ensuite	1
Private	
Guest Share	2

DIRECTIONS: Midway Auckland – Hamilton. 1km off SH 1. On the right hand side down Plantation Road.

A 'well kept secret', 1km from State Highway 1, nestled in the heartland of the Waikato. Experience the charms of a romantic setting amidst a country lifestyle. Savour the 'famous' lavender scones on arrival and relax in the **Rose, Lily,** or **Lavender Rooms**. Enjoy the tranquility while meandering through a 'herb haven', or sit and relax on one of the large verandahs which overlook rural New Zealand and the lingering sunsets. Scrumptious meals are available with a selection of fine wines. The boutique villa is separate to owners, with large lounge and dining room for your privacy and comfort. A gift shop features specialty gourmet food and gifts. Only 40 minutes to Auckland or Hamilton International Airports.

HERONS RIDGE FARMSTAY

1131 Lake Waikare Scenic Dr, Te Kauwhata
Ph (07) 826 4646, Fax (07) 826 4171
Mobile (027)462 0253
email: *herons.ridge@xtra.co.nz*
www.huntly.net.nz/herons.html

Features & Attractions

- *Rural tranquility*
- *Horse riding*
- *Wineries*
- *River & country walks*
- *Four golf courses*
- *Hot pools nearby*

Farm Stay & Quality Garden Studio

Double	$120-140
Single	$60-80
Child	

Bedrooms	Qty
Double	1
Twin	
Single	

Bed Size	Qty
King	
Queen	1
Double	
Single	

Bathrooms	Qty
Ensuite	1
Private	
Guest Share	

W elcome to **Herons Ridge**, your home in the Waikato. One hour from Auckland and Hamilton, quality in-house suites and superb Garden Studio, overlooking both pool and garden, a perfect setting. Close to the shores of Lake Waikare and three of New Zealand's international wetlands. A selection of fine local wines can be served with a scrumptious homecooked dinner. Whilst respecting your privacy we are delighted to share our home with you. Seniors Card New Zealand is welcome here.

DIRECTIONS: From State Highway 1 travel through Te Kauwhata village, travel 6 km east along Waerenga Road turn right at Waikare Rd, **Herons Ridge** is 1 km on right

PARNASSUS FARM & GARDEN

191 Te Ohaki Road, Huntly
Ph/Fax (07) 828 8781, Mobile 021-458 525
email: *parnassus@xtra.co.nz*
www.parnassus.co.nz

Features & Attractions

- *Only minutes off SH1*
- *Working farm*
- *Auckland under 1 hour*
- *Glorious gardens*
- *Bush and farm walks*
- *Families welcome*

$	Double	$120-140
	Single	$70-100
	Child	neg

Bed & Breakfast Farmstay on "Real Working Farm"

DIRECTIONS: Leave SH 1 at traffic lights by Huntly KFC. Cross river, turn right into Harris Street 2 km, right into Te Ohaki Road, 1.9 km on left

Bedrooms	Qty
Double	2
Twin	1
Single	
Bed Size	**Qty**
Queen	
Double	2
King Single	2
Single	2
Bathrooms	**Qty**
Ensuite	
Private	3
Guest Share	

Experience farm life or simply relax on a working farm, 1hr south of Auckland and only 4km off SH 1. All our bedrooms are beautifully appointed with private facilities, we also have a small self-contained private unit. We have extensive gardens which supply produce and preserves for the 'Farm to Fork' dining experience that we are renown for and showcase a diverse range of trees and shrubs, fruits and vegetables.

We are very centrally located for day trips to the thermal wonderlands of Rotorua and Taupo and to either east or west coast beaches. Farm, bush and wetland walks are easily accessible and there is a beautiful 18 hole golf course just a few kilometres along the road.

LAS PALMAS B&B HOMESTAY

16A Acacia Crescent, Hamilton South
Ph (07) 843 3769, Fax (07) 843 3242
Mobile 027-275 5200
email: *info@laspalmas.co.nz*
www.laspalmas.co.nz

Tariff : N.Z. Dollars	
Double	$110-180
Single	$90-150
Child over 12	$20

Bedrooms	Qty
Double	2
Twin/Double	
Single	
Bed Size	**Qty**
Super King	1
King	
Queen	1
Double	
Single	
Bathrooms	**Qty**
Ensuite	1
Private	1
Guest Share	

DIRECTIONS:
Please phone for easy directions.
Same day bookings are fine with us if we have a vacancy

Bed & Breakfast Homestay
Superior Self-catering

Features & Attractions

- *Peaceful private setting*
- *Delicious full breakfasts*
- *Luxury self-contained unit*
- *Swimming pool & spa*
- *Dinner by arrangement*
- *10 min Mystery Creek*
- *5 hole golf course*
- *Family pets welcome*

Caroline and Malcolm guarantee you a warm welcome. **Las Palmas** is set on five acres of parklike gardens with a five hole 'golf course', swimming and spa pools, pétanque and garden walks. We offer either a luxury self-catering unit with a kitchenette, refrigerator, microwave and laundry facilities; or a queen size bedroom in the house with private bathroom. Both rooms have fresh flowers, fruit, bathrobes and luxury towels. Full or continental breakfast is offered which usually includes fresh fruit from the garden and home preserves. Dinner can be provided by arrangement. A complimentary beverage is offered on arrival. We are only eight minutes from central Hamilton with its celebrated public gardens, river walks, a plethora of cafés and restaurants and just ten minutes from Mystery Creek and the airport. **Las Palmas** is the ideal base from which to visit Rotorua, Taupo, Tauranga, Waitomo Caves, Raglan and the West Coast surf beaches. Rates are negotiable for longer stays. Airport transfers are available. We and the family dog Quincee and cat Hudson will endeavour to make your stay enjoyable.

MATANGI OAKS

634 Marychurch Road, Matangi, RD 4, Hamilton
Ph (07) 829 5765, Fax (07) 829 5765
Mobile 027-242 7429
email: *matangi.oaks@xtra.co.nz*
www.matangioaks.co.nz

Tariff : N.Z. Dollars	
Double	$195
Single	$120
Child	

Bedrooms	Qty
Double	2
Twin/Double	1
Single	

Bed Size	Qty
Super King	2
King	
Queen	1
Double	
Single	

Bathrooms	Qty
Ensuite	1
Private	1
Guest Share	

Boutique Countrystay Bed & Breakfast

Features & Attractions

- Midway Hamilton & Cambridge
- Stud tours available
- Maungatautari Sanctuary
- Hamilton Gardens
- 10 min. to Mystery Creek
- Peaceful and relaxing
- Waikato River Cruises
- Dinner by arrangement

DIRECTIONS: From SH 1 at Tamahere turn onto Tauwhare Road to Matangi. Cross railway line, turn 1st right, SH 1B. We are 500m on left. From Taupiri travel 33km along SH 1B towards Cambridge.

Matangi Oaks is situated midway between Hamilton and Cambridge on State Highway 1B in a delightful rural setting. Our American Colonial Home, built in 1997, offers peace and tranquillity while being only 12 minutes from the city. An ideal stopover for visits to the National Agricultural Field Days at Mystery Creek or for taking a tour of some of the famous thoroughbred horse studs in the district. Only 10 minutes from Hamilton Airport. For the golfing enthusiasts there are 12 golf courses within half an hour's drive. An hour's drive and you can be in Rotorua, Tauranga, Mt Maunganui and Waitomo Caves and only 1½ hrs to Lake Taupo and Auckland Airport. Cooked and continental breakfasts are provided and tea and coffee making facilities are available. Three-course evening meals are available with your hosts with great locally-grown vegetables. Pre-dinner drinks and dinner wines are all included at a cost of $55 pp. A separate guest lounge is available or visitors are welcome to join their hosts in the evening. Extra bedroom available upstairs for one party. Laundry facilities available.

ARBOR LODGE

126C Woodcock Rd, Tamahere, RD 3, Hamilton
Ph (07) 856 3820, Fax (07) 856 3825
Mobile 021-554 846
e-mail: *emms2003@xtra.co.nz*

Features & Attractions

- *Private country setting*
- *Golf courses nearby*
- *Waitomo Caves 1 hour*
- *Close to city & airport*
- *Rotorua 1.25 hours*
- *Hamilton gardens/river walks*

$	Double	$120-160
	Single	$120-160
	Child	

Self-contained Bed & Breakfast

Bedrooms	Qty
Double	1
Twin	
Single	
Bed Size	**Qty**
King	
Queen	1
Double	
Single	
Bathrooms	**Qty**
Ensuite	1
Private	
Guest Share	

Arbor Lodge is set in landscaped gardens on 11 acres just south of Hamilton. The property is 12 min. from both Hamilton CBD and Cambridge. The Airport and Mystery Creek, the "Fieldays" venue, are only a 6 min. drive away. Hamilton's central location makes it an ideal base for day trips to Rotorua, Waitomo Caves and beaches at Raglan and Tauranga. Guests can enjoy private, self-contained accommodation with lovely views over the property. Relax by the pool in summer, unwind with a game of tennis or wander around the peaceful gardens. The spacious air-conditioned studio has tea/coffee making facilities, fridge, microwave, TV, DVD, sofa, breakfast table for two and complimentary toiletries. Continental breakfast is provided in your room.

SAXON LODGE 'THE ORGANIC PLACE'

Rural No 266, Peacockes Road, RD 2, Hamilton
Ph (07) 843 3497, Fax (07) 843 3473
email: *saxonlodge@ihug.co.nz*
http://homepages.ihug.co.nz/~saxonlodge

Features & Attractions

- *Dawn chorus*
- *Stylish one storey home*
- *Great gardens & orchard*
- *Comfortable beds*
- *Campervan facilities*
- *Handy to city & airport*

$	Double	$150
	Single	$130
	Child	$50

Organic Homestay

Bedrooms	Qty
Double	
Twin	2
Single	
Bed Size	**Qty**
King	
Queen	
Double	
Single	4
Bathrooms	**Qty**
Ensuite	
Private	1
Guest Share	

Saxon Lodge, 'The Organic Place', is set on two acres just south of Hamilton. You wake up to the 'dawn chorus' – the birds greeting you and the morning. After a morning cup of herbal tea you can collect fresh eggs from our hens (the girls) and pick in season fruit for your breakfast. Our dog Sophie (a Pembroke corgi) and our cat Tara will help! You may have to chase the wild ducks, rabbits and pukekos (a native bird) out of your way! The house, designed by a local architect, is a stylish New Zealand single storey home with high raked timber ceilings and brick veneer. We love it and would like you to enjoy it too.

KUA MAKONA

142 Reid Road, Ngahinepouri, RD 2, Ohaupo, Waikato
Ph (07) 825 2852, Fax (07) 825 2852
Mobile: 027-496 0064
e-mail: *themarcrofts@nettel.net.nz*

Tariff : N.Z. Dollars	
Double	$135-155
Single	$100
Child	$50

Bedrooms	Qty
Double	2
Twin	1
Single	

Bed Size	Qty
Super King	
King	
Queen	2
Double	
Single	2

Bathrooms	Qty
Ensuite	1
Private	
Guest Share	1

H Countrystay **Deer Farm** **C**

Features & Attractions

- Deer Farm
- Swimming pool & spa pool
- Formal garden
- Quiet and relaxing

- Auckland & Rotorua 1½ hour
- Waitomo Caves 40 minutes
- Otorohanga Kiwi House and Aviary 20 minutes

Relax in a quiet rural setting with homestyle welcome and atmosphere. Centrally situated for tourist attractions, 1½ hours from Auckland Airport and Rotorua, Waitomo Caves 40 minutes, Tongariro National Park two hours, Otorohanga Kiwi House & Aviary 20 minutes and National Field days site and Hamilton Airport 15 minutes. We run a deer finishing unit. The surrounding district has traditional dairy and beef farms as well as a diverse range of horticulture: asparagus, nashis, apples, flowers and vegetables.

There is a superb country golf course just down the road and an award winning vineyard close by. Transfers from Hamilton or airport can be arranged. Relax by a cosy fire in the formal lounge in the winter or cool off beside the pool in the summer. There is also an outdoor spa pool and croquet. French doors open out into the garden from all the bedrooms, which are furnished in country style complete with fresh flowers, hairdryers, robes and complimentary toiletries. There's also a cot should you require one. Fax, internet and laundry facilities available. Cooked or continental breakfast is included and dinner by request $45 per person. We have one Burmese cat.

ABSEIL BREAKFAST INN

709 Waitomo Caves Road, Waitomo Caves
Ph (07) 878 7815
email: *abseilinn@xtra.co.nz*
www.abseilinn.co.nz

Tariff : N.Z. Dollars	
Double	$130-160
Single	$130
Child	

Bedrooms	Qty
Double	3
Twin	1
Single	
Bed Size	**Qty**
Super King	
King	
Queen	4
Double	
Single	1
Bathrooms	**Qty**
Ensuite	4
Private	
Guest Share	

Rural Splendour
Romantic Accommodation

Features & Attractions

DIRECTIONS:
Turn opposite the
Red Rabbit shearing shed.

- *At the Waitomo Caves*
- *Blackwater rafting*
- *Bush walks*
- *Close to restaurants*

- *Spectacular rural views*
- *Romantic themed rooms*
- *Canopied queen beds*
- *Helen rocks*

Wanted: Guests full of the joy of life for the delightfully bijou **Abseil Breakfast Inn**. Applicants must have a hearty appetite for a leisurely breakfast of local delicacies – after all breakfast is our middle name. Mingling with other guests is required (in the guest lounge, on the deck or at the communal dining table in the morning) – can your tall stories better Helen's? Enjoyment of sunsets behind stunning rural scenery an advantage; wine glass in hand optional. Having an adventurous attitude towards the bedroom aspect of the stay is an essential; these are themed to the utmost skill and imaginative reach of the hostess, including the **Farm Room** with its spectacular views out over the Waitomo Valley, the **Bush Room** with its magnificent canopy, the **Swamp Room** with its bath built for two and a range of bath oils and candle, and the hairy but cuddly **Cave Room**. You must be adventurous – overly faint of heart will not make it up the driveway. And above all you must 'Approach with Enthusiasm'.

Recommended by most good guide books and chance-met strangers.

Mt Heslington

1375 Main North Road, RD 4, Otorohanga
Ph (07) 873 1873, Fax (07) 873 7622
Mobile 027-226 1119
e-mail:*jean.phil-newman@xtra.co.nz*
www.ubd-online.co.nz/mtheslingtonfarmstay/

Features & Attractions

- *Waitomo Caves*
- *Swimming pool*
- *Pool table*
- *Kiwi House - Otorohanga*
- *Te Awamutu Golf Course*
- *Waitomo Golf Course*

Comfortable Farmstay Accommodation

Double	$90
Single	$70
Child	$35

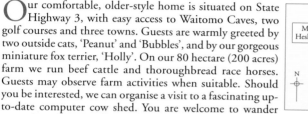

Our comfortable, older-style home is situated on State Highway 3, with easy access to Waitomo Caves, two golf courses and three towns. Guests are warmly greeted by two outside cats, 'Peanut' and 'Bubbles', and by our gorgeous miniature fox terrier, 'Holly'. On our 80 hectare (200 acres) farm we run beef cattle and thoroughbred race horses. Guests may observe farm activities when suitable. Should you be interested, we can organise a visit to a fascinating up-to-date computer cow shed. You are welcome to wander around our large garden, in summer relax by the swimming pool. Our pool table is available for your evening entertainment. All our meat, vegetables and fruit are home-grown. Children are welcome, we have a highchair and a portable cot.

Bedrooms	Qty
Double	1
Twin	1
Single	
Bed Size	**Qty**
King	
Queen	
Double	1
Single	4
Bathrooms	**Qty**
Ensuite	
Private	1
Guest Share	1

Redwood Lodge

222 Puketawai Road, RD 6, Otorohanga
Ph (07) 873 6685, Fax (07) 873 6694
Mobile (027) 541 1905
email: *welcome@redwood-lodge.co.nz*
www.redwood-lodge.co.nz

Features & Attractions

- *Explore Waitomo Caves*
- *Great bush treks*
- *Glow-worm walks*
- *Blackwater rafting*
- *Excellent fly-fishing*
- *Kiwi House native birds*

Deluxe Homestay Bed & Breakfast

Double	$140-170
Single	$110-130
Child	neg

Only ten minutes from Waitomo Caves, **Redwood Lodge** offers travellers a tranquil escape from the hustle and bustle of town, whilst being conveniently situated for explorations of Otorohanga (Kiwiana capital of NZ) and Te Kuiti (world sheep shearing capital). John and Georgina Owen welcome you into their comfortable and well-appointed home, offering a choice of four large heated/air-conditioned ensuite bedrooms. Rooms are comfortable and spacious with tea/coffee making facilities and ranch sliders opening onto the garden. Following a restful night's sleep, guests can enjoy a choice of continental or delicious full English breakfast. There is a guest lounge with sky TV and pool table; guests can relax outside on the patio or take a relaxing dip in our sparkling pool.

Bedrooms	Qty
Double	4
Twin	
Single	
Bed Size	**Qty**
King	1
Queen	3
Double	
Single	3
Bathrooms	**Qty**
Ensuite	4
Private	
Guest Share	

146

TAPANUI COUNTRY HOME

1714 Oparure Road, RD 5, Te Kuiti
Ph (07) 877 8549, Fax (07) 877 8541
Mobile 027-494 9873
email: *info@tapanui.co.nz*
www.tapanui.co.nz

Tariff : N.Z. Dollars	
Double	$195-250
Cottage	$200-370
Child	n/a

Bedrooms	Qty
Double	3
Twin	
Single	

Bed Size	Qty
Super King/Twin	2
King Single	
Queen	1
Double	
Single	

Bathrooms	Qty
Ensuite	1
Private	1
Guest Share	

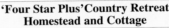

'Four Star Plus' Country Retreat Homestead and Cottage

Features & Attractions

- 4 star plus country retreat
- Near Waitomo Caves
- Delicious meals with NZ wine
- NZ rural hospitality
- Farm tours by arrangement
- Peace, seclusion and tranquillity
- Kiwi House, golf courses
- 2.5 hrs Auckland Airport

DIRECTIONS: From Te Kuiti, take SH 3 north for 3km. Turn left into Oparure Road and continue for 17 km. We are on the right – limestone entrance.

Elegant 4-star plus country retreat near the world famous Waitomo Glow-worm Caves. Magnificent homestead and self-contained cottage, farmstay, Bed & Breakfast on 1900-acre working sheep and cattle farm with 'Boots' the cat. The homestead offers the **Huntaway Suite** with spacious ensuite in the private guest wing. Relax and revitalize with super-king size bed or two singles, quality linen, mohair throws, electric blankets, central heating, toiletries, hairdryers & heated towel rails. Experience rural NZ hospitality and delicious home-cooked meals with NZ wine, peace, seclusion and tranquillity. Close by is an attractively decorated, spacious, self-contained cottage with 1 super-king/twin and 1 queen bedroom, bath/shower, 2 toilets, fully equipped kitchen (microwave, dishwasher, dining room, guest laundry, casual lounge with log fire, TV, CD/DVD stereo system). $200-$250 per night – double ($60 extra person, maximum 4 guests. Minimum 2 night stay - Cottage) Ideal for "romantic getaways"!

147

PARK HOUSE

Queen Street, Cambridge
Phone (07) 827 6368, Fax (07) 827 4094
e-mail: *park.house@xtra.co.nz*
www.parkhouse.co.nz

@home NEW ZEALAND

qualmark ★★★★ guest & hosted

Tariff : N.Z. Dollars	
$160	Double
$130	Single
	Child

Qty	Bedrooms
2	Double
	Twin
	Single
Qty	Bed Size
	Super King
	King
1	Queen
	Double
1	King/Single
Qty	Bathrooms
1	Ensuite
1	Private
	Guest Share

BA

**Warm, Gracious, Elegant
Georgian-style Manor House**

BB

VISA MasterCard AMERICAN EXPRESS

Features & Attractions

- *Overlooking village green*
- *Georgian-style manor house*
- *Warm, gracious and elegant*
- *Generous full English breakfast*
- *Cosy library*
- *Tours arranged*
- *Centrally located*
- *Antique furniture*

Welcome to Park House. Located in the heart of Cambridge and overlooking the tree-lined village green, our warm, gracious and elegant home is a 1920s Georgian-style manor house filled with handsome antique furniture, stained glass, carved fireplaces, board and batten ceilings, original patchwork, artworks and a cosy library. In the separate upstairs guest

wing choose between the charming queen room with ensuite or the super-king/twin with private bathroom (includes shower and claw foot bath). A generous full English breakfast is served at a time to suit in the formal dining room. Choose from a selection of cereals and fruit, home-made preserves, tender bacon and eggs, sauteed mushrooms or potatoes and breakfast sausages, plus piping hot tea and coffee. Let us help you arrange your day. Maybe a stroll across the village green to explore the local shopping centre, including antiques, old books, art galleries, restaurants. Or perhaps fishing, surfing, golf, bicycle hire, heritage walks, kayaking, jet boating or museums. We can also arrange half and full day personalised tours of the area including sumptuous lunch. We recommend a two-night stay. Looking forward to hosting you.

GLENELG

6 Curnow Place, Cambridge
Ph (07) 823 0084, Fax (07) 823 4279
Mobile (027) 702 8041
email: *glenelgbnb@ihug.co.nz*

Features & Attractions

- *Ensuite accommodation*
- *Warm hospitality*
- *Quiet, peaceful setting*
- *Hamilton Airport 15 min*
- *Spa and air bath*
- *5 min to Lake Karapiro*

$	Double	$95-130
	Single	$75
	Child	neg

Bedrooms	Qty
Double	3
Twin	1
Single	

Bed Size	Qty
King	
Queen	3
Double	
Single	3

Bathrooms	Qty
Ensuite	3
Private	1
Guest Share	

Quiet Rural Outlook B&B, Homestay

Cambridge, 15 km from Hamilton and 1 hour from Rotorua, is famous for its picturesque old English atmosphere and known as the "Town of Trees". If you are looking for a "Home away from Home", restful and away from the hustle, bustle and traffic noise, **Glenelg** is the place for you to be. We have a new, modern home in a quiet, peaceful setting with 200 roses in our garden. Breakfast is either cooked or continental with a menu to choose from – evening meals by prior arrangement. Guest laundry and off-street parking is available. We are in comfortable driving distance from the main tourist attractions: Mystery Creek Events Centre 10 min, Rotorua 1 hour, Waitomo Caves 45 min, Auckland or Taupo 2 hours.

RIVERSONG BED & BREAKFAST COUNTRYSTAY

213 Horahora Road, RD 1, Tirau, South Waikato
Ph (07) 883 1477, Fax (07) 883 1477
Mobile 027-642 3239
email: *riversong.bb@xtra.co.nz*

Features & Attractions

- *Relaxed rural setting*
- *Antiques, arts & crafts*
- *Water sports & golf*
- *Mystery Creek - Field days 30 min*
- *Central to Waikato, Rotorua, BOP*
- *Hobbiton tours close by*

$	Double	$95-130
	Single	$75
	Child	neg

Bed & Breakfast Countrystay Self-Contained Accommodation

Bedrooms	Qty
Double	2
Twin	2
Single	

Bed Size	Qty
King	1
Queen	
Double	1
Single	4

Bathrooms	Qty
Ensuite	1
Private	1
Guest Share	1

You are assured a warm welcome at **Riversong** situated in the heart of the beautiful South Waikato with Lake Karapiro views. We are an ideal base for touring the central North Island, only 45 mins from Rotorua, Tauranga 50 mins, Hamilton Airport 30 mins. Our new, fully equipped two bedroom unit (one queen and one twin) will ensure your comfort and privacy. Tariff $125 per night two persons, $15 each extra person. The main house has three bedrooms, one double with ensuite, one twin and one double, both with private bathrooms. Breakfast is full cooked or continental. Dinner by prior arrangement. Tea and coffee facilities in all rooms. Guest comment: Joan & David, UK have stayed several years and say *"We are their home down-under!"*

DIRECTIONS: Heading south turn right off SH 1. 500m south of Route 29 (Tauranga) **Riversong** is 2.13 km on left opposite lake. Right hand driveway.

OAKLANE LODGE

78A Horrell Road, Morrinsville
Ph (07) 889 1045, Fax (07) 889 1046
e-mail: *oaklanelodge@xtra.co.nz*
www.oaklanelodge.co.nz

Features & Attractions

- *Swimming pool, BBQ, petanque*
- *Croquet & outdoor giant chess*
- *Landscaped gardens,orchard*
- *Native bird aviary*
- *Clay target shooting*
- *Hot mineral pools nearby*

Luxury Accommodation Bed & Breakfast

  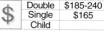

Double	$185-240
Single	$165
Child	

You are assured a warm welcome and friendly hospitality during your stay at Oaklane Lodge. Private accommodation with breakfast is offered at the homestead which is nestled among beautiful mature oak trees and landscaped gardens. The Lodge has 3 guest bedrooms featuring king, queen and twin/king single accommodation. Swim or relax by the pool, enjoy alfresco dining in summer, cosy log fires and superb homestyle meals in winter. Our Lodge is also suitable for weekend retreats, meetings/day seminars/small conferences, social functions and a range of activities, including clay target shooting, to keep everyone satisfied. We are situated just 3km from Morrinsville and a short drive to Te Aroha (hot pools), Matamata (Hobbitown) and Hamilton (Mystery Creek).

Bedrooms	Qty
Double	2
Twin	1
Single	
Bed Size	**Qty**
King	1
Queen	1
Double	
Single	2
Bathrooms	**Qty**
Ensuite	3
Private	
Guest Share	

TRANQUILITY LODGE

325 Rea Road, RD 2, Katikati, Bay of Islands
Ph (07) 549 3581, Fax (07) 549 3582
Mobile 0274-522 960
e-mail: *tranquilitylodge@xtra.co.nz*
www.tranquilitylodge.co.nz

Features & Attractions

- *Generous hospitality*
- *Warmth and comfort*
- *Supper with a wee drom*
- *Local art, craft & murals*
- *Special packages available*
- *Home-cooked, hearty breakfast*

Luxury Country B&B in our Peaceful Valley

Double	$150
Single	$120
Child	

Nestled in a peaceful valley, warm Kiwi hospitality and our friendly Maremma dogs, cats and farmyard pets await you. Relax on our large freestanding deck and indulge in birdsong, stream and view of the Kaimai Ranges, or play a game of pétanque beside our patio. Our lovely breakfasts are made from home-grown and locally sourced produce. Each king suite is sumptuously furnished and has its own private entry and deck. Bathrobes, slippers, toiletries and hair dryers are supplied. Wheelchair access and laundry facilities are available. First class 18 hole golf course, Day Spa, bird gardens, crafts, museum, art, bush walks, beaches, winery, cafés and more are located close by. Come, rest a while and enjoy with us.

Bedrooms	Qty
Double	2
Twin	
Single	
Bed Size	**Qty**
King	2
Queen	
Double	
Single	
Bathrooms	**Qty**
Ensuite	2
Private	
Guest Share	

COTSWOLD LODGE COUNTRYSTAY

183 Ongare Point Road, RD 1, Katikati
Ph (07) 549 2110, Fax (07) 549 2109
email: *cotswold@ihug.co.nz*
www.cotswold.co.nz

home
NEW ZEALAND

Tariff : N.Z. Dollars	
Double	$140-165
Single	$110
Child	

Bedrooms	Qty
Double	2
Twin	1
Single	

Bed Size	Qty
Super King	
King	
Queen	2
Double	1
Single	1

Bathrooms	Qty
Ensuite	3
Private	
Guest Share	

**Country Bed & Breakfast
- with a little Luxury**

Features & Attractions

- *Stunning country scenery*
- *Peace & tranquility*
- *Hot spa for relaxation*
- *Abundant birdlife*
- *Scenic walks from lodge*
- *Laundry available*
- *Romance package available*
- *Tours can be arranged*

To Waihi
Cotswold
Lodge
2
N
Kauri Pt. Rd
Ongare Pt Rd
Lindeman Rd
Tauranga
Harbour
Katikati

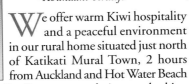

We offer warm Kiwi hospitality and a peaceful environment in our rural home situated just north of Katikati Mural Town, 2 hours from Auckland and Hot Water Beach and 1.5 hours from Rotorua. Quality accommodation overlooking the garden and orchards to the Kaimai Ranges. Expect to be pampered on arrival and rejuvenated by the time you leave. All rooms with ensuite bathroom, quality linens, hairdryers etc. Guest refrigerator, tea and coffee available. Choose a mouth-watering breakfast from our menu. Evening meals by prior arrangement. Watch the sunset while relaxing in the Spa, or over a pre-dinner drink. Petanque in the garden. Take a short stroll through the orchard and down to the harbour. Our Labrador can show the way. Short distance to restaurants, wineries, golf, walking tracks, museum, beaches, fishing, gardens, etc. Come and enjoy our piece of paradise or make us a base to explore the beautiful Bay of Plenty. We look forward to meeting you.

PANORAMA COUNTRY LODGE

901 Pacific Coast Highway (SH 2), RD 1, Katikati
Ph (07) 549 1882, Fax (07) 549 1882
Mobile 021-165 5875

email: *mckernon@xtra.co.nz*
www.panoramalodge.co.nz

Tariff : N.Z. Dollars	
Double	$170-200
Single	$120-130
Child	neg

Bedrooms	Qty
Double	2
Twin	1
Single	

Bed Size	Qty
Super King	
King	1
Queen	1
Double	
Single	2

Bathrooms	Qty
Ensuite	1
Private	1
Guest Share	

Quality Bed & Breakfast with Magnificent Sea Views

Features & Attractions

- Secluded peaceful & rural retreat
- Homecooked gourmet breakfasts
- Landscaped gardens, swimming pool
- Awesome sun & moon risings
- Relaxed hospitality
- Room service
- 5 min to Waihi Beach
- Internet access

Panorama Country Lodge is perfectly located between beautiful Waihi Beach and the mural town of Katikati. Nestling in the foothills of the Kaimai Mountain Ranges it commands outstanding views of the Pacific Ocean and outlying islands. Only minutes from wineries, cafés and restaurants, a good base for exploring the western Bay of Plenty and the Coromandel Peninsula which offer many attractions and activities (beaches, golf courses, museums, bush walks, fishing and boating etc). The spacious private guest suites are situated in the northern wing with french doors to the swimming pool and terrace, quality furnishings, television DVD and CD player, radio, fresh coffee and tea making facilities, slippers, robes, hair dryers and wonderful sea views! Let yourself be pampered a little, enjoy generous gourmet breakfasts, relax and soak up the wonderful surroundings or roam the grounds Kiwifruit and Avocado orchards and say *Hi* to our boys (the Alpacas). We love it here – so will you!

SAGEWOOD LODGE

14D Sagewood Road, Pahoia, RD 6, Tauranga
Ph (07) 548 0229, Fax (07) 548 2029
Mobile 027-609 4932
email: *sagewood@ihug.co.nz*
www.sagewoodlodge.com

Tariff : N.Z. Dollars	
Double	$220
Single	$200
Child	

Bedrooms	Qty
Double	3
Twin	1
Single	
Bed Size	Qty
Super King	3
King	
Queen	
Double	
Single	2
Bathrooms	Qty
Ensuite	4
Private	
Guest Share	

Luxury Country Accommodation

Features & Attractions

- *Tennis court*
- *Olive grove*
- *Wineries nearby*
- *French doors open to garden*
- *Swimming and spa pool*
- *2 golf courses 10 min away*
- *Laundry facilities*
- *Generous breakfast*

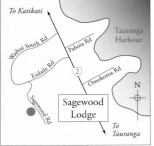

DIRECTIONS:
Please phone for easy directions

Sagewood Lodge is a fine luxurious Queensland-style home midway between Tauranga and Kati-Kati. It is set in 65 acres, including an olive grove and has breathtaking views over Mayar and Matakana Islands. Extensive gardens include a swimming and spa pool and tennis court. Ensuite bedrooms all have tea making, fridge, robes etc.

Hearty breakfasts may be taken on the terrace or in the dining room. Gourmet suppers with fine wines by arrangement.

BURR-WOOD COUNTRYSTAY

home
NEW ZEALAND

449 Lund Rd, RD 2, Katikati
Ph (07) 549 2060, Fax (07) 549 2061
email: *nzjewellery@clear.net.nz*

Tariff : N.Z. Dollars	
Double	$100
Single	$60
Child	neg

Bedrooms	Qty
Double	1
Twin	1
Single	

Bed Size	Qty
Super King	
King	
Queen	1
Double	
Single	2

Bathrooms	Qty
Ensuite	
Private	1
Guest Share	

 Peaceful and Private Country Homestay

Features & Attractions

- *Stunning coastal views*
- *Friendly hospitality*
- *One party only*
- *Native timber jewellery*
- *Beautiful garden, secluded & quiet*
- *Dinner by arrangement*
- *Complimentary pre-dinner drinks*
- *Tourist attractions & golf nearby*

Welcome! **Burr-wood** is set in a 2½ acre well known garden and surrounded by native bush. Positioned in an elevated situation, we overlook a panorama of land, sea, harbour and islands. Relax and enjoy cooked or continental breakfast including home-made bread and jams, on our verandah or indoors. Enjoy complimentary pre-dinner drinks. A delicious dinner is available by arrangement. Home produce is used where possible. We are five minutes from State Highway 2 and within easy reach of Bay of Plenty attractions, including our 'Mural Town'. Bush walks about two minutes.

You are welcome to view our unique jewellery which we make from New Zealand native timbers in our studio at home. And of course you are welcome to wander through our tranquil garden. As we only have one party at a time, your relaxation is assured. We offer home-baking, tea/coffee on arrival. Laundry available.
Look forward to seeing you.

TAU TAU LODGE

1133 Pyes Pa Road, Greerton, Tauranga
Ph (07) 543 1600, Fax (07) 543 5089
email: *tautaulodge@ihug.co.nz*
www.tautaulodge.co.nz

Tariff : N.Z. Dollars	
Double	$170-200
Single	$140-160
Child	neg

Bedrooms	Qty
Double	4
Twin	
Single	

Bed Size	Qty
Super King	
King	
Queen	3
Double	1
Single	

Bathrooms	Qty
Ensuite	3
Private	
Guest Share	

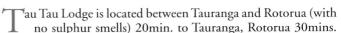

Superior Bed & Breakfast with Stunning Bay of Plenty Views

Features & Attractions

- *Tauranga 20 minutes*
- *Peace, privacy & tranquillity*
- *Rotorua 35 minutes*
- *Email, fax & laundry*
- *Romantic packages available*
- *Close to bush walks & hot pools*
- *Quilting, needlework and giftware shop on premises*

Tau Tau Lodge is located between Tauranga and Rotorua (with no sulphur smells) 20min. to Tauranga, Rotorua 30mins. Whitanga 4hrs. Whakatane 1½hrs travel time from the Lodge. The Lodge sits on 2 acres of lovely gardens and lawns, commanding stunning views over Tauranga, Mt Maunganui, Kaimai Ranges and the Coromandel. We have 4 superior bedroom, 3 with their own private bathroom. Large, private guest lounge with balcony, library, TV, stereo and antique furniture. Complimentary tea and coffee facilities, cotton robes, chocolates and flowers in each bedroom. Hairdryers in each bathroom. A fully cooked farmhouse-style or gourmet continental breakfast is included. Upon arrival, complimentary afternoon tea is served and later pre-dinner drinks and nibbles. An evening dinner serving delicious innovative entreé and desserts along with traditional NZ fare of beef, salmon, chicken, lamb is offered by prior arrangement. A select wine list is also available. Two cats live in Churchill and Clementine.

VILLA COLLINI

36 Kaiate Falls Road, RD 5, Welcome Bay, Tauranga
Ph (07) 544 8322, Fax (07) 544 8322
Mobile 021-047 8394
email: *margrit@naturetours-nz.com*
www.villacollini.co.nz

Features & Attractions

- Simply superb breakfasts
- Very quiet hilltop location
- Close to Kaiate waterfalls
- Tauranga/beach 15min.
- Gourmet cuisine
- German spoken

Quality Bed & Breakfast with Panoramic Views

Double	$130-170
Single	$105-140
Child	neg

"Paradise means different things to different people, but for us Villa Collini is as close as it gets" (guest comment).
Enjoy spectacular panoramic views of Mt. Maunganui and the sea in a quiet, relaxing atmosphere. Get spoiled with a warm welcome and great hospitality, gourmet Mediterranean dinners ($45pp), comfortable beds, generous continental breakfast with homemade breads, croissants, cereals, cheese, sliced cold meat, Italian coffee etc. Relax in our park-like garden or walk the endless beaches of Papamoa. Our location is an ideal base for Rotorua, Tauranga or White Island. We both have travelled world- and nationwide, so there is a lot to talk about. "Come as a stranger and leave as a friend".

Bedrooms	Qty
Double	2
Twin	
Single	
Bed Size	**Qty**
Super King/Twin	1
Queen	1
Double	
Single	
Bathrooms	**Qty**
Ensuite	1
Private	
Guest Share	1

SANDTOFT

83 Simpson Road, Papamoa Beach, Tauranga
Ph (07) 542 3459, Fax (07) 542 3459
email: *sandtoft@xtra.co.nz*
email: *sandtoft@excite.com*

Features & Attractions

- Short walk to ocean beach
- Off street parking
- Close to restaurants & shops
- Complimentary tea, coffee etc
- Handy to laundromat
- Dinner by arrangement

Beachstay Bed & Breakfast

Double	$100
Single	$70
Child	neg

Sandtoft is a comfortable home, just two minutes walk from the beautiful Pacific Ocean. Enjoy a stroll along the sandy beach, sunbathe, swim, surfcast. Sample our local restaurants. We offer two spacious bedrooms with double/queen and single beds. These rooms each have their own wash basin, coffee table, and comfy chairs, plus a north facing balcony. Also available is a smaller double/single bedroom at a lower rate. Bath, shower, toilet facilities are each separate. A guest refrigerator, television, tea/coffee are at your disposal. Continental only and/or cooked breakfast is offered. We are a semi-retired couple who enjoy travelling and meeting people. To meet you would be a pleasure.

Bedrooms	Qty
Double	3
Twin	2
Single	1
Bed Size	**Qty**
King/Single	2
Queen/Double	3
Double	
Single	3
Bathrooms	**Qty**
Ensuite	
Private	
Guest Share	1

BOATSHED MOTEL APARTMENTS

31 Maranui Street, Mt Maunganui, Tauranga
Ph (07) 572 1044, Fax (07) 572 2092
Mobile 027-493 7325
email: *info@boatshed-accommodation.co.nz*
www.boatshed-accommodation.co.nz

Tariff : N.Z. Dollars	
Double	$100-220
Single	$90-140
Child	neg

Bedrooms	Qty
Double	8
Twin	10
Single	8

Bed Size	Qty
Super King	8
King	
Queen	
Double	
Single	30

Bathrooms	Qty
Ensuite	6
Private	6
Family Share	2

Self-contained Accommodation and Homestay

Please telephone for bookings and easy directions.

Features & Attractions

- *Groups and corporates a speciality*
- *Jet boating, stock cars*
- *Fishing and diving*
- *Golf and driving range*
- *Kiwifruit country tour*
- *Mini farm, feed animals*
- *Vintage car display*
- *Hot salt water pools*

Boatshed Apartments are new, architect designed with brilliant interior colours with 3-piece wicker lounge suite, large bifold doors opening onto large balconies, full kitchen, dishwasher, refrigerator, deep freeze, Sky television, gas hobs. Super king beds, rollaway beds available. These units are serviced daily. Three apartments have some sea views. Two units can sleep up to seven or eight people. The Penthouse Suite (sleeps four) on the third floor has panoramic sea and city views. All units have their own  barbeque. There is also a separate private spa. We are situated one minute's walk to white sandy safe beach, one minute's walk to fish shop and pizza restaurant, 2 km to golf course, 1 km to Bay Fare Shopping Mall and BayWave Hot Pools. We are approximately 6 km to Mt Maunganui shopping centre. Walk around the Mount and then take a swim in the hot salt water pools. Also approximately 8 km to Tauranga Shopping Centre. We offer the discerning traveller a place to unwind and rediscover the simple pleasures in life with good old Kiwi hospitality. Corporate rates continental breakfast available. Mini putt, island trips, kitesurfing, adventure park, animal park, ten pin bowls, visit winery, kiwifruit guided tour, Vintage Cars Auto Barn. Groups and corporates a speciality.

HESFORD HOUSE BED & BREAKFAST
45 Gravatt Road, Royal Palm Beach,
Papamoa, Mt Maunganui
Ph (07) 572 2825
e-mail: *derek.sally@clear.net.nz*
www.hesfordhouse.co.nz

Features & Attractions
- Beach close by
- Views of hills & Mount
- Opp. cafés & restaurants
- Fashion Island shopping
- Excellent holiday base
- Close to water activities

**Boutique Bed & Breakfast
Close to Beach**

Double	$90-140
Single	$70-90
Child	neg.

We invite you to stay in our tastefully decorated character home. Enjoy panoramic views of the Papamoa Hills together with exquisite sunsets. Opposite is the fabulous CentaMax shopping complex, complete with Fashion Island, cafés, popular restaurants, internet café and English Pub. Relax in a beautiful garden setting. Complimentary tea/coffee facilities, fridge and TVs in each room. Our location offers you blokarts (land yachts), numerous water activities and a short stroll to our magnificent beach. Our B&B can be used as a base to visit Rotorua, Whakatane and Whangamata (Coromandel) – all just 50 min. drive. Courtesy pickup from public transport. We, as your hosts, will ensure you have a wonderful stay at **Hesford House**.

Bedrooms	Qty
Double	2
Twin	1
Single	
Bed Size	**Qty**
King	
Queen	2
Double	
Single	2
Bathrooms	**Qty**
Ensuite	1
Private	
Guest Share	1

FOTHERGILLS ON MIMIHA
84 Mimiha Rd (RD 4, Whakatane) Pikowai/Matata
Ph (07) 322 2224, Fax (07) 322 2224
Mobile 027-4605958
email: *beverlyf@xtra.co.nz*
www.fothergills.co.nz

Features & Attractions
- 2 bdrm self contained B&B suite
- 2 bdrm fully equipped cottage
- Covered carparks, own entrances
- Quiet location close to coast
- Easy access from main road
- Glorious large country garden

**Bed & Breakfast/Homestay
and Self Contained Cottage**

Double	$110-170
Single	$90-120
Child	$20

Do you like to be pampered or to look after yourselves? Get the best of both worlds! The stylish B&B suite offers comfort and wonderful peace. Hilton & Bev host breakfasts featuring their garden-fresh food and delicious preserves. **Mimiha Cottage** is a home-away-from-home, with everything you need for a relaxing weekend or holiday. Stroll in our idyllic garden, enjoy the lake, play petanque, go walking along the unspoilt beach, up the no-exit country road or climb the wonderful hills. Enjoy our friendly hospitality and the company of our two fox terrier dogs.

Take day trips to White Island, Rotorua, Tauranga, Ohope beach. After a busy day, soak in the outdoor spa. Come and enjoy this slice of heaven!

DIRECTIONS: Approx. halfway between Te Puke and Whakatane (25min each way) Mimiha Rd turns off Pacific Coast Highway 5 km north of Matata.

Bedrooms	Qty
Double	2
Twin	1
Single	1
Bed Size	**Qty**
King Single	1
Queen	2
Double	
Single	2
Bathrooms	**Qty**
Ensuite	1
Private	1
Guest Share	

Pohutukawa Beach B&B & Cottage

693 State Highway 2, (RD 4, Whakatane), Pikowai/Matata
Ph (07) 322 2182, Fax (07) 322 2186
email: *joe@prinztours.co.nz*
www.beachbnb.co.nz

Tariff : N.Z. Dollars	
Double	$120
Single	$100
Child	

Bedrooms	Qty
Double	3
Twin	1
Single	

Bed Size	Qty
Super King	
King	1
Queen	2
Double	1
King Single	2

Bathrooms	Qty
Ensuite	2
Private	1
Guest Share	

 Coastal Country Stay and Cottage

Features & Attractions

- *Cottage SC. from $160*
- *Outdoor pool*
- *Sauna*
- *Organic farm*
- *100 metres to the beach*
- *Dinner on request*
- *German spoken*
- *Guided tours*

DIRECTIONS:
Directly on State Highway 2. Just 8 km
west of Matata, 34 km east of Te Puke.

Pohutukawa Beach Bed & Breakfast and Cottage are set in a picturesque location on the Pacific Coast Highway offering outstanding ocean views. Glance up from the breakfast table and see active volcano White Island. Sometimes dolphins and even whales pass by.

The Farmhouse is the base of our tour company "Prinz Tours". We are specialists for guided tours and offer day tours in the area and personalised itineraries for New Zealand-wide holidays. We encourage visitors to stay several days. There is so much to see and do in the Bay of Plenty region. Or simply relax in our garden, by the pool, at the beach or have a "talk" to our many farm animals. Dinners with ingredients from our organic farm on request. We also speak German and are looking forward to meeting you. Cottage Bed & Breakfast from $200.

BEIGHTONS

124 East Bank Road, Thornton, Whakatane
Ph (07) 304 8789, Fax (07) 304 8784
Mobile 021-033 5585
email: *lyell@xtra.co.nz*
www.beightons.co.nz

Tariff : N.Z. Dollars	
Double	$135-165
Single	$100
Child	

Bedrooms	Qty
Double	2
Twin	
Single	
Bed Size	**Qty**
Super King	
King	1
Queen	1
Double	
Single	
Bathrooms	**Qty**
Ensuite	2
Private	
Guest Share	

**Quality Riverside
Rural Accommodation**

Features & Attractions

- *Whakatane 10 min.*
- *Whale & dolphin tours*
- *Deep-sea fishing*
- *Internet facilities*
- *Rotorua 60min.*
- *White Island tours*
- *Rafting & Jetboating*
- *Laundry facilities*

DIRECTIONS:
1 km off the Pacific Coast Highway,
or 7 km from Edgecumbe

Set in acres of park-like grounds alongside the Rangitaiki River, our very comfortable architecturally designed English-style home, in a very peaceful yet convenient location, is waiting to welcome you. As semi-

retired international hoteliers, we have prepared **Beightons** for the most discerning guests. Downstairs, with separate entry, is a very spacious ensuite guest room with private patio, kingsize

bed and lounge area. Upstairs, the ensuite guest room with a queen-size bed overlooks native trees and amazing bird life. Additional rooms are available if sold in conjunction with these rooms. Both ensuite guest rooms have airconditioning, security safe, TV/DVD, radio, CD, fridge, tea/coffee, electric blankets, robes, toiletries, hairdryer and to welcome you, wine and refreshments on arrival. Monty, our friendly golden retriever, will be delighted to escort you around our grounds, or to kayaks or bicycles, if you would like to explore our private jetty, river, or nearby Thornton Beach.

OCEANSPRAY HOMESTAY

283A Pohutukawa Avenue, Ohope, Bay of Plenty
Ph (07) 312 4112, Fax (07) 312 4192
Mobile 027-286 6824
email: *frances@oceanspray.co.nz*
www.oceanspray.co.nz

@home
NEW ZEALAND

Tariff : N.Z. Dollars	
Double	$150-190
Single	$80-100
Child	neg

Bedrooms	Qty
Double	3
Twin	2
Single	

Bed Size	Qty
Super King	
King	
Queen	3
Double	
Single	4

Bathrooms	Qty
Ensuite	1
Private	2
Guest Share	

    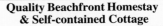

Quality Beachfront Homestay & Self-contained Cottage

Features & Attractions

- *Absolute beachfront*
- *Separate downstairs unit*
- *Self-contained cottage*
- *Views to White Island*
- *Deep-sea fishing nearby*
- *Safe swimming beach*
- *Swimming with dolphins*
- *Two golf links nearby*

We warmly welcome you to **Oceanspray Homestay** – a beachfront property 100m from the Pacific Ocean surf. Panoramic views from the upstairs decks extend to the East Cape and to White Island, an active volcano 50km offshore. **Oceanspray Homestay** has three attractively furnished bedrooms, lounge/kitchen, two bathrooms (one is ensuite) and is a downstairs, private, self-contained unit within our home.

We also offer a cosy, well furnished, two bedroom, self-contained cottage adjacent to our house. We offer an excellent standard of accommodation, use of laundry facilities, barbeque, beach gear. Complimentary wine and delicious home-baking on your arrival. Comprehensive breakfast provisions are supplied into your unit and renewed daily or when required. A great selection of books, videos, toys – children well catered for, makes this an ideal family holiday retreat. We , and our very sociable cat, Barnaby, ensure your stay is a memorable experience.

PANORAMA COUNTRY HOMESTAY

144 Fryer Rd, Hamurana, RD 2 Rotorua
Ph/Fax (07) 332 2618, Mobile 021-610949
email: *panoramahomestay@xtra.co.nz*
www.panoramahomestay.co.nz

Tariff : N.Z. Dollars	
Double	$170-240
Single	$110-150
Child	$30-50

Bedrooms	Qty
Double	2
Twin	1
Single	

Bed Size	Qty
Super King	1
King	1
Queen	1
Double	
Single	2

Bathrooms	Qty
Ensuite	2
Private	1
Guest Share	

 Peaceful Luxury Homestay

Features & Attractions

- *Private and peaceful retreat*
- *Spacious ensuite rooms*
- *Magnificent lake views*
- *Heated massage spa pool*
- *Championship sized tennis court*
- *15 min. from Rotorua*
- *Close to all major attractions*
- *Internet access*

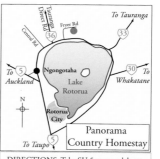

DIRECTIONS: Take SH 5 to roundabout. Travel north around lake through Ngongotaha towards Hamurana. Turn left into Fryer Rd and travel 1.5km to **Panorama** driveway on your right (No 144).

Aptly named, **Panorama** is your ideal base to stay near Rotorua's many attractions. Take in the magnificent views overlooking Lake Rotorua and legendary Mokoia Island, Mt. Tarawera and surrounding country-side. Feel the peace and tranquility as you relax under the stars in the outdoor heated massage spa pool, then curl up in front of the log fire in winter. You may prefer an energetic game of tennis or take in fantastic walks before you stretch out on the extra large beds in **Panorama's** peaceful surrounds for a perfect nights' sleep. The large house is centrally heated and wheelchair accessible. The 3 spacious luxury bedrooms have private bathrooms/ensuites containing toiletries, heated towel rails, hairdryers, shaving points and heaters. The large, comfortable inner-spring beds are warmed with electric blankets, woollen underlays, and feather quilts in winter. Only 15 min. from Rotorua, smoke free and away from sulphur smells.

KOTARE LODGE

1000J Hamurana Road, Wilsons Bay, Hamurana, Lake Rotorua
Ph (07) 332 2679, Fax (07) 332 2678
Mobile 027-622 0629
email: *pollards@kotarelodge.co.nz*
www.kotarelodge.co.nz

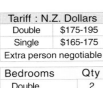

Tariff : N.Z. Dollars	
Double	$175-195
Single	$165-175
Extra person negotiable	

Bedrooms	Qty
Double	2
Twin	
Single	

Bed Size	Qty
Super King Twin	1
King	
Queen	1
Double	
Single	3

Bathrooms	Qty
Ensuite	1
Private	1
Guest Share	

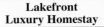

**Lakefront
Luxury Homestay**

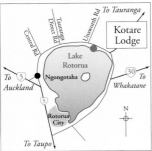

DIRECTIONS: **Kotare Lodge** is located on the northern shores of Lake Rotorua. Please ring/fax for simple directions.

Features & Attractions

- *Absolute lake edge location*
- *Secluded, tranquil beauty*
- *Delicious breakfasts*
- *Sulphur free location, trout fishing*
- *Glorious views & sunsets*
- *Luxurious private suites*
- *Helicopter/floatplane excursions*
- *High speed Internet access*

Welcome to the perfect retreat. Designed with your comfort in mind, **Kotare Lodge**, set in beautiful parklike grounds, is situated on the shores of Lake Rotorua. The lake views across to the city and surrounding hills are magnificent as are the sunsets. The

Rimu Suite, sleeps two and has a queen bedroom, private bathroom and garden lounge. The **Garden Suite** sleeps three and is separate from main house, has a super king/twin bedroom, ensuite bathroom. The lounge, with divan bed, fridge and DVD/TV, can sleep another person. Your private suites have glorious views of the lake, heated towels, robes, toiletries, hairdryers, fresh flowers and tea/coffee making facilities. Easy, level access to patios, decks, lawn and lakefront. There is also a spacious guest lounge which offers audio/visual entertainment. Relax with us at **Kotare Lodge**, enjoy a memorable stay of peaceful nights, luxury, wonderful breakfasts and warm, friendly hospitality.

SPRINGWATERS LODGE

9 Te Waerenga Rd, Hamurana, Rotorua
Ph(07) 332 2565, Fax(07) 332 2565
Mobile 021-295 3652
email: *info@springwaterslodge.co.nz*
www.springwaterslodge.co.nz

Tariff : N.Z. Dollars	
$180-200	Double
$150-180	Single
Neg.	Child

Qty	Bedrooms
4	Double
	Twin
	Single

Qty	Bed Size
3	Super King/Twin
1	King
	Queen
	Double
	Single

Qty	Bathrooms
4	Ensuite
	Private
	Guest Share

Affordable Luxury on Lake Rotorua's Doorstep

Features & Attractions

- *Relaxed, friendly hosts*
- *Extra large living areas*
- *Ensuite, TV, DVD in room*
- *Prime trout fishing spot*
- *Spa pool*
- *Dinner by arrangement*
- *500m to golf course, springs*
- *Very generous breakfasts*

Haere mai and welcome to our spacious family home. Trout fishing, golf, walks and Hamurana Springs are all within 500m of our doorstep.

Spacious dining and lounging areas overlooking the lake allow plenty of space for relaxation. Newly refurbished throughout with quality furnishings and linen, your comfort is guaranteed. **Springwaters Lodge** is one level, offering 4 guest rooms, each with ensuite, TV and DVD. Two rooms open onto their own patio, with lake views. A buffet-style continental breakfast is to be enjoyed whilst a hot

dish is being prepared. Join us for dinner and drinks or you may choose to dine at a local café. Complimentary home baking and refreshments available 24 hrs.

Our two school aged children, Nadia and Jaxon, share our passion for entertaining and are happy to share our family life with you. Located just 10 to 15 minutes drive to many of Rotorua's leading attractions makes our location central. We are happy to help you with our local knowledge and assist you with booking your activities.

TE NGAE LODGE

54 State Highway 33, RD 4, Rotorua
Ph (07) 345 4153, Fax (07) 345 4153
Mobile 027-620 9312
email: *enquire@tengae.co.nz*
www.tengae.co.nz

Tariff : N.Z. Dollars	
Double	$100-200
Single	$80-115
Child	

Bedrooms	Qty
Double	3
Twin	1
Single	
Bed Size	**Qty**
Super King	
King	
Queen	3
Double	
Single	2
Bathrooms	**Qty**
Ensuite	1
Private	2
Guest Share	

Country Homestay

Features & Attractions

- *Quiet country setting*
- *Two acres of attractive gardens*
- *Views of Lake Rotorua sunsets*
- *Elegant antique dining room*
- *Dinners with New Zealand wines*
- *Home grown vegetables*
- *Bush walks & fishing trips arranged*
- *Handy to geothermal attractions*

DIRECTIONS:
Coming from Rotorua on SH 30,
which becomes SH 33,
we are 300m past the turn-off
to Whakatane. **Te Ngae Lodge**
driveway is on the right.

Te Ngae Lodge – for the discerning guest wanting to enjoy hospitality with superior accommodation in a tranquil garden setting. Wake to bird song in the morning.

Mokoia Suite looks to Mokoia Island and Lake Rotorua, furnished with antique and modern pieces.

The Garden Room outlooks to mature trees and opens to an attractive deck.

The Library Room has a view of garden and trees.

All comfortable queen size beds, while the Mokoia Suite has a second bedroom with twin beds.

Enjoy pre-dinner drinks with your hosts, our special dinners, or a more casual meal alfresco. We are twelve minutes drive from Rotorua City and handy to all geothermal attractions.

Finish the day in the spa pool. Relax and enjoy.

ROTOKAWA LODGE
1135c Te Ngae Road, RD4, Rotorua
Ph (07) 345 5911, Fax (07) 345 5910
Mobile 027-447 6533
email: *rotokawalodge@xtra.co.nz*
www.rotokawa-lodge.co.nz

Features & Attractions

- *Relaxed Kiwi hospitality*
- *Superb restaurants close by*
- *Laundry facilities available*
- *'Japanese Spa Bathhouse'*
- *Dinner by arrangement*
- *Hearty Kiwi breakfasts*

Luxury Bed & Breakfast
Peaceful and Secluded

$	Double	$195
	Single	$160
	Child	Neg.

Bedrooms	Qty
Double	5
Twin	
Single	
Bed Size	**Qty**
Super King	3
Queen	2
Double	
Single	
Bathrooms	**Qty**
Ensuite	3
Private	
Guest Share	2

"Welcome to the highlight of your holiday".
Our Cedarwood Lodge is nestled on the shores of Lake Rotorua overlooking Mokoia Island on the fringe of the city, but central to Rotorua's finest tourist attractions ie: thermal geysers, Maori villages, trout fishing, etc. We offer sunny, spacious super king or queen ensuite rooms containing tea and coffee facilities, TV, fridge, and hairdryers. Rooms are serviced daily. Your own guest lounge with TV and DVD's available. Our 'Japanese Spa Bathhouse' is a must for weary travelling bodies. Our hearty cooked or continental breakfasts served in the dining room will sustain you for your day's adventures. Come, take delight in our lovely, rural, spacious surroundings and let us pamper you. Our cats, Benny and Ozzy, will show you all the cosy spots for a catnap. The local wildlife loves to pay a visit – as you will!

ARODEN
2 Hilton Road, Lynmore, Rotorua
Ph (07) 345 6303, Fax (07) 345 6353
Mobile 027-696 4211
email: *aroden@xtra.co.nz*

Features & Attractions

- *Central – 4km to city*
- *Luxuriant garden, patio*
- *Two lounge areas, spa*
- *Leonie parle francais*
- *Memorable breakfast*
- *Central heating, open fire*

Delightful Homestay
Bed & Breakfast

"Taupo" Paul's guide dog.

$	Double	$130-145
	Single	$90-110
	Child	neg

Bedrooms	Qty
Double	2
Twin	
Single	
Bed Size	**Qty**
King	
Queen	2
Double	
Single	
Bathrooms	**Qty**
Ensuite	1
Private	1
Guest Share	

Discover real character, warmth and comfort nestled in a secluded garden, en route to the lakes and just five minutes from the city centre. Relax in a choice of sunny, private and attractive spaces, enjoy a spa under the stars, take a tour of the native tree collection and stroll to the magnificent Redwood Grove nearby (glow-worms at night!). Enjoy well-appointed rooms, comfortable beds with quality linen, modern tiled bathrooms with excellent showers, full bath in one room.
Leonie, who has a teaching background, and Paul, scientist, are fifth generation Kiwis, who delight in their country – share in their enthusiasm and knowledge over complimentary refreshments, tea coffee etc. or a wine (New Zealand of course!).....and meet the charming 'Taupo', Paul's guide dog. Breakfast is indeed special, fresh fruit and juice, cereals, home baking, a tempting choice of cooked course – this couple enjoys food! Smoke-free inside. Laundry.

DIRECTIONS: Route 30 east 2.5 km (towards airport). Turn right at roundabout onto Tarawera/Blue Lake Road, 3rd street left Lynmore Avenue, 2nd right Hilton Road, opposite corner store. No 2 is on left.

MAPLE HOUSE

154A Tarawera Road, Lynmore, Rotorua
Ph (07) 345 8434, Fax (07) 345 8434
email: *j.nicol@actrix.co.nz*
www.maplehouse.co.nz

Tariff : N.Z. Dollars	
Double	$140
Single	$90
Child	$25

Bedrooms	Qty
Double	1
Twin	1
Single	

Bed Size	Qty
Super King	
King	
Queen	1
Double	
Single	2

Bathrooms	Qty
Ensuite	
Private	1
Guest Share	

 **Homestay
Bed & Breakfast**

Features & Attractions

- *Close to major attractions*
- *New warm comfortable home*
- *Quiet nights*
- *Delicious breakfast menu*
- *Scenic forest walks*
- *Spacious bathroom*
- *Single party bookings*
- *Free laundry facilities*

DIRECTIONS:
Route 30 East 2.5km (towards airport).
Turn right at roundabout onto
Tarawera Road. Maple House
is 154A, just past Hilton Road.

You've found it! Walk in, relax and experience genuine New Zealand hospitality in a warm, quiet, well appointed home. Choose from a comfortable queen or twin bedroom with spacious private bathroom and separate toilet. After a busy day you will enjoy the tranquillity of the sunny lounge, share refreshments on the garden patio or curl up beside a cosy fire in Winter. Across the road is Whakarewarewa Forest with scenic trails, magnificent redwoods, tree ferns and glow worms. Just five minutes to airport, town centre, restaurants, golf courses, or the luxury of thermal spa facilities. Use your hosts' wide local knowledge of scenic, thermal, adventure and cultural activities to help you plan a memorable visit. We have travelled and worked extensively overseas. Joan loves gardening, walking, museum guiding, entertaining, theatre. Barry, avid reader and rugby follower, enjoys company and a red wine! Once you've shared the wonders of Rotorua, you'll want to return again and again bringing your friends!

*"Your beautiful home and exceptional hospitality
made Rotorua a memorable stay!"* – GUEST COMMENT.

APPLEDALE COTTAGE
26 Springfield Road, Rotorua
Ph (07) 348 6630, Fax (07) 348 6065
Mobile 027-605 9949
email: *appledalecottage@clear.net.nz*

Features & Attractions
- Charming yesteryear décor
- Warm, friendly hosts
- Swimming pool
- Sumptuous cooked breakfast
- Gourmet dinners if required
- Restaurant/ golf courses close by

 Boutique Bed & Breakfast and Self-contained Cottage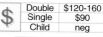

Double	$120-160
Single	$90
Child	neg

Appledale Cottage offers something with a difference for you. Appledale Cottage is an English summer house, which is nestled amongst trees and cottage gardens. We have Boutique Bed & Breakfast rooms and in addition our fully self-contained cottage with old-world, charming yesteryear furniture and romantic atmosphere for you. What we have to offer to you is your hosts, Bruce and Justine, who are well travelled and enjoy meeting new people. Your comfort and experience whilst in Rotorua is our top priority. We offer complimentarty nibbles and drinks upon arrival and serve a sumptuous, fully cooked breakfast, prepared by a gourmet cook. We are happy to assist with bookings and information for your tourist attractions and sightseeing arrangements.

Bedrooms	Qty
Double	3
Twin	
Single	

Bed Size	Qty
King	
Queen	2
Double	1
Single	2

Bathrooms	Qty
Ensuite	
Private	2
Guest Share	

FERNTREE COTTAGE
1 Tatai Street, Rotorua
Ph (07) 348 0000,
Mobile 021-049 1910
e-mail: *v.g.brannan@xtra.co.nz*
www.ferntreecottage.co.nz

Features & Attractions
- Central, quiet garden location
- Hospitality award finalists
- Almost on lake shore
- Welcoming, hospitable hosts
- Three course breakfasts
- Off-street parking

 Homestay Bed & Breakfast Self-contained Accommodation

Double	$110-130
Single	$100-120
Child	Neg.

After a busy day, come and relax in the peaceful garden of **Ferntree Cottage.** Enjoy a welcoming drink and snack, and allow Geoff or Val to describe why Rotorua is a must-visit! Thermal parks, bubbling mud, Maori cultural evenings, adventure and nature attractions, day trips to volcanic valleys and islands, pamper packs – make sure you stay an extra day. Take a short stroll to Lake Rotorua, watch black swans glide by and in summer paddle the double kayak along the shore or reflect on your day while relaxing in the fernery spa pool. The **Garden Room** has a private entrance and deck with guest BBQ, TV, DVD, CD, ensuite, toiletries, fridge, microwave, complimentary tea and coffee and in winter a cosy log-fire. The **Lavender Twin Room** is a homestay where facilities are shared with your hosts. Laundry available. Please view our website, enquire at i-site, or telephone for directions.

Bedrooms	Qty
Double	1
Twin	1
Single	

Bed Size	Qty
King	
Queen	1
Double	
Single	2

Bathrooms	Qty
Ensuite	1
Private	
Family Share	1

TRESCO CLASSICAL OASIS B&B & COTTAGE

3 Toko Street, Victoria, Rotorua
Ph (07) 348 9611, Fax (07) 348 9611
Mobile 021-355 777
email: *trescorotorua@xtra.co.nz*
www.trescorotorua.co.nz

Tariff : N.Z. Dollars	
$120-240	Double
$65-80	Single
neg	Child

Qty	Bedrooms
5	Double
1	Twin
2	Single

Qty	Bed Size
1	King
3	Queen
2	Double
2	King/Single
2	Single

Qty	Bathrooms
4	Ensuite
1	Private
2	Guest Share

**Bed & Breakfast
Boutique Accommodation**

Features & Attractions

- *2 minutes walk to city*
- *1930s NZ classic home*
- *Authentic geothermal hot pool*
- *Private lake edge cottage*
- *Glorious sunrise & views*
- *Relax, walk, canoe & fish*

Trevor and Trinka warmly welcome you to Rotorua - the geothermal wonderland of NZ. Whether sunny or wet, outstanding opportunities can be had here. Warm days give way to fun, outdoor activities such as canoeing, golf, trout fishing and forest walking. In the cold, Rotorua 'erupts' as this volcanic plateau 'explodes' into view with steam, geysers and boiling mud. **Tresco Classical Oasis** provide an authentic, geothermal hot-pool. Soak your aches and pains away. Add to this, natural central heating, four bathrooms/ensuites and quality furniture, fittings and bedding. Our art, hat and origami collection is surrounded by rare NZ Rimu wood throughout. Laptop technology and laundry facilities included. With a full cooked breakfast and relaxing gardens you truly are in an oasis. Now also a Tresco one bedroom cottage on the waters edge of Lake Rotorua. Private peninsula and jetty, canoes, BBQ, and tennis court. 2-3 people, fully self-contained, ensuite, central heating, air conditioning and more. Recommendations are our guarantee. Long rates negotiable. Tresco courtesy transport/collection. Bookings essential.

INNES COTTAGE
18A Wylie Street, Rotorua
Ph (07) 349 1839, Fax (07) 349 1890
Mobile 027-498 2100
email: *chris@clican.com*
www.innescottage.co.nz

Features & Attractions

- *Very central location*
- *Quiet tree-lined street*
- *Fishing & golf 5 min*
- *Close to thermal attractions*
- *City centre just 5 min*
- *Friendly welcome, lots of fun*

Bed & Breakfast Homestay		Double	$100-140
		Single	$95-110
		Child	neg

Enjoy the tranquil surroundings of our centrally situated home in a quiet tree-lined street, within easy walking distance to the city. Our spacious guest rooms overlook a sunny garden. An easy walk will bring you to the 'Te Puia' thermal area, with the famous Pohutu Geyser, and other major attractions are only a short distance away. We have travelled extensively and have a wealth of knowledge and many valuable contacts. Chris does private tours around the region and throughout New Zealand and can help with any arrangements you require to make your stay more memorable. We serve a generous continental breakfast, giving you a great start to the day. We assure you warm hospitality and a memorable fun-filled stay.

Bedrooms	Qty
Double	2
Twin	1
Single	
Bed Size	**Qty**
King	
Queen	2
Double	
Single	2
Bathrooms	**Qty**
Ensuite	2
Private	1
Guest Share	

MOANA ROSE LAKESIDE BED & BREAKFAST

23 Haumoana Street, Koutu, Rotorua
Ph (07) 349 2980, Fax (07) 349 2997
Mobile 027-273 2008
email: *moanarose@bktours.co.nz*
www.bktours.co.nz

Features & Attractions

- *Within minutes of:*
- *Sporting venues*
- *All major attractions*
- *Excellent Cafés*
- *Shopping/city centre*
- *Trout fishing*

$	Double	$150
	Single	$100
	Child	$40

**Lakeside Homestay
Bed & Breakfast**

Welcome to the peace and tranquility of our garden lakeside home. Enjoy our company or relax in the guests' sitting room with tea/coffee making facilities, fridge and Sky TV. As we are small and intimate, we only cater for single party bookings. From the breakfast table admire the view, then wander down to the lake edge and watch the birdlife with Lizzie, our cat, in hot pursuit.

Relaxing in our garden courtyard spa is a wonderful way to complete your day. Pauline's interests are art and crafts, and Bruce is a licenced tour operator and will gladly assist with your sightseeing or travel arrangemets. For your convenience, high speed internet and wireless services are available.

DIRECTIONS: From Lake Road turn into Bennetts Road, left into Koutu Road, right into Karenga Street, left into Haumoana Street.

Bedrooms	Qty
Double	2
Twin	
Single	
Bed Size	**Qty**
Super King	1
Queen	1
Double	
Single	2
Bathrooms	**Qty**
Ensuite	
Private	1
Guest Share	

ROBERTSON HOUSE

70 Pererika Street, Rotorua
Ph (07) 343 7559
email: *info@robertsonhouse.co.nz*
www.robertsonhouse.co.nz

Features & Attractions

- *Old world charm*
- *Perfect central location*
- *Beautiful cottage garden*
- *Warm & friendly hosts*
- *All activities easily arranged*
- *Quiet & relaxing*

$	Double	$110-170
	Single	$80-120
	Child	

**Charming Bed & Breakfast
Homestay**

Bedrooms	Qty
Double	4
Twin	1
Single	
Bed Size	
Super King	1
Queen	2
Double	2
King/Single	4
Bathrooms	**Qty**
Ensuite	3
Private	
Guest Share	1

Our historic home, only 2 minutes drive from the city centre, was built by one of Rotorua's forefathers in 1905. Under the auspices of the Historic Places Trust it has been carefully renovated, retaining its colonial charm.

Relax in its warm, comfortable atmosphere, or take time out on the veranda and enjoy our old English cottage garden resplendent with colour and fragrance, citrus trees and grape vines.

Our friendly hosts are happy to assist with information and bookings for Rotorua's many Maori cultural, and sightseeing attractions.

Robertson House – a historic colonial villa, carefully restored, is warm and inviting with a peaceful cottage garden.

EAST WEST-BOUTIQUE B&B AND APARTMENTS
6 Toko Street, Rotorua
Ph (07) 348 5720, Fax (07) 348 5729
Mobile 027-278 5332, Free Phone 0800 232 789
email: *eastwesthomestay@xtra.co.nz*
www.eastwesthomestay.co.nz

Tariff : N.Z. Dollars	
Double	$140-175
Single	$100-140
Child	$30

Bedrooms	Qty
Double	6
Twin	7
Single	1
Bed Size	**Qty**
King	
Queen	6
Double	1
King/Single	1
Single	14
Bathrooms	**Qty**
Ensuite	2
Private	5
Guest Share	

 Boutique Bed & Breakfast & Self-catering Apartments

Features & Attractions

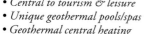

- *Central to tourism & leisure*
- *Unique geothermal pools/spas*
- *Geothermal central heating*
- *Group unit rates*
- *Quiet, spacious B&B units*
- *Self-catering apartments*
- *Self-catering cottages*
- *Tour bookings*

Your hosts, Stuart, Kristin and Rusty, warmly welcome you to their unique Boutique Bed & Breakfast and Self-catering apartments. Located in Rotorua's thriving central tourism district, their designer home and freshly decorated, fully furnished holiday apartments are minutes from all attractions. You are offered a choice of a spacious studio or one bedroom unit both featuring private ensuite bathrooms, fridge/minibar, tea and coffee facilities, TV/DVD and robes toiletries. Continental breakfast offers fresh fruit, home-made muesli, cereals, yoghurt, conserves, coffee and teas (included in rate). Cooked breakfast available. Also separately located on the property are four sunny, cosy, fully furnished self-catering two and three bedroom apartments and cottages, kitchen, laundry facilities, private parking/entrances. Private hot spas, robes/toiletries. Sky Digital TV.

KOURA LODGE ROTORUA

209 Kawaha Point Road, PO Box 1600, Rotorua
Ph (07) 348 5868, Fax (07) 348 5869
Mobile: 027-519 1000
email: *stay@kouralodge.co.nz*
www.kouralodge.co.nz

Tariff : N.Z. Dollars	
Double	$295-595
Single	–
Extra pp	$100

Bedrooms	Qty
Double	8
Twin	3
Single	–
Bed Size	**Qty**
Super King	–
King	6
Queen	3
Double	–
King Single	4
Bathrooms	**Qty**
Ensuite	All
Private	–
Guest Share	–

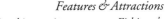 **Genuine Lawn to Lake Luxury**

DIRECTIONS: From north, take SH 5 towards Rotorua City. Turn left into Kawaha Point Road, left into Koutu and right again. Travel to Lodge at end. From city, take SH 5 north. Turn right into Kawaha Point Road. Then as above.

Features & Attractions

- *Championship tennis court*
- *Buffet breakfasts*
- *5 minutes from City centre*
- *Sauna & spa facility*
- *Fishing & hot pool trips, canoes*
- *High speed internet*
- *On-site massage*
- *Complimentary off-street parking*

Koura Lodge is situated on the tip of Kawaha Point, nestled in sub-tropical gardens, only five minutes drive from the City Centre, yet secluded from traffic noise and sulphur fumes.

The Lodge offers a range of double accommodation as well as family suites and a 2 bedroom apartment, all with private ensuites, veranda seating and spectacular lake views. Other on-site facilities and activities include lake-edge sauna/spa complex, Astro-grass tennis court, canoes, fishing and floatplane excursions.

Koura Lodge is minutes from three well-known golf courses, mountain bike trails and dozens of restaurants.

AFFORDABLE WESTMINSTER
LODGE & COTTAGE

58A Mountain Road, Rotorua
Ph (07) 348 4273, Fax (07) 348 4205
email: *westminster@slingshot.co.nz*
www.westminsterlodge.co.nz

Tariff : N.Z. Dollars	
Double	$100-150
Single	$80-100
Child	$20-25

Bedrooms	Qty
Double	4
Twin	5
Single	5
Bed Size	**Qty**
Super King	
King	
Queen	4
Double	2
Single	6
Bathrooms	**Qty**
Ensuite	3
Private	2
Guest Share	

   Affordable Quality B & B
Self-Catering Accommodation

Features & Attractions

- *Only 5 min to city centre*
- *Close to all major attractions*
- *Laundry facilities*
- *Telephone, fax and email*
- *Maori concert & hangi*
- *Spa pool*
- *Friendly animals*
- *Very generous breakfast*

Westminster Lodge and Cottage are English Tudor homes nestled into the slopes of Mt Ngongotaha overlooking the city of Rotorua. So country, yet only 5 minutes to the city centre. Panoramic views in the day and fairy land at night. We offer superior Bed & Breakfast accommodation in semi self-contained units or lodge rooms at affordable prices. Our self-catering cottage has two bedrooms with room for extra in lounge and is fully equipped. In the lodge enjoy our delicious continental breakfast with fresh fruit salad, yoghurt and cereal, hot apple muffins (baked daily) and a freshly laid egg or a scrumptious fully cooked breakfast at a small extra cost. Experience all the comforts of home in a warm and friendly atmosphere. Our semi self-contained units with ensuites, have a queen bed and a futon couch that opens out to a double bed. Each has a small equipped kitchenette with tea and coffee. The large lodge rooms are designed for families and have ensuites/ private bathrooms and access to a small shared kitchenette with tea and coffee.

TIROHANGA-NUI

21 Grand Vue Road, Kawaha Point, Rotorua
Ph (07) 349 4810, Fax (07) 349 4811
Mobile 021-170 3477
email: *a_thompson@clear.net.nz*
www.bigview.co.nz

Tariff : N.Z. Dollars	
Double	$140-160
Single	$90
Child	Neg.

Bedrooms	Qty
Double	2
Twin	
Single	

Bed Size	Qty
Super King	
King	
Queen	2
Double	
Single	

Bathrooms	Qty
Ensuite	1
Private	1
Guest Share	

Homestay - Bed & Breakfast
Self-contained Accommodation

Features & Attractions

- *Spa & swimming pool*
- *5min. from city centre*
- *Panoramic views*
- *Tour bookings organised*
- *Cooked or continental breakfast*
- *Dinner by arrangement*
- *Central heating*
- *Minimum 2 nights stay*

Your hosts, Angela and Tony, invite you to share the experience, the peace and serenity of **Tirohanga-nui** with its magnificent panoramic lake and city views, only five minutes from the city and local attractions. Accommodation is offered either self-contained with private entrance and private deck area or in the upstairs bedroom with private bathroom. Also sharing our home are two very friendly, adopted cats, who love being admired. Angela and Tony have visited all areas of New Zealand and extended their adventures in over twenty countries around the globe. Their wealth of knowledge of the Rotorua area would benefit any visitors keen to learn more about this beautiful country. Rotorua is the 'Tourist Capital' of New Zealand, where you can experience Maori culture, geothermal activity, many beautiful lake and bush walks, as well as a variety of the more adventurous attractions. We recommend a 2 night stay to allow yourself enough time to discover and enjoy this amazing area.

ARIKI LODGE

2 Manuariki Ave, Ngongotaha, PO Box 578, Rotorua
Ph (07) 357 5532, Fax (07) 357 5562
email: *info@arikilodge.co.nz*
www.arikilodge.co.nz

Tariff : N.Z. Dollars	
Double	$150-250
Single	$130-230
Child	Neg.

Bedrooms	Qty
Double	3
Twin	
Single	

Bed Size	Qty
Super King	1
King	
Queen	2
Double	
Single	

Bathrooms	Qty
Ensuite	3
Private	
Guest Share	

 Bed & Breakfast Luxury Accommodation

Features & Attractions

- *Lake edge*
- *Close to major attractions*
- *Trout fishing*
- *Quiet and relaxing*
- *Warm and friendly hosts*
- *Generous breakfasts*
- *Quality bedding and furnishings*
- *Your comfort is our business*

Set on the edge of Lake Rotorua, **Ariki Lodge** offers luxury accommodation in a tranquil garden setting, where you can relax in comfort and style. Take a short stroll along the beach to the Waiteti Stream and famous fly fishing spots. The bedrooms are beautifully appointed with quality linen, fresh flowers, toiletries and hair dryers. The suite is self-catering with provisions for a continental breakfast the first morning. It has a queen bedroom, Italian-tiled bathroom with spa bath, private sitting room, full kitchen and laundry. The super-king/twin and queen bedrooms both have tea and coffee making facilities and are on a Bed & Breakfast basis. We can help you arrange your time to experience Rotorua's many attractions, including Maori cultural performances, thermal areas, scenic flights from our beach and bush walks. Only ten minutes drive to the centre of Rotorua and many activities.

DIRECTIONS: Drive to Ngongotaha. At shops turn right into Taui Street, through "Give Way" sign towards Lake and right into Manuariki Avenue.

BAYADERE LODGE

38 Hall Road, PO Box 288, Ngongotaha
Ph (07) 357 5965, Fax (07) 357 5965
Mobile 027-292 8520
email: *c.clark@clear.net.nz*
www.bayaderelodge.com

Tariff : N.Z. Dollars	
Double	$175-195
Single	$155-175
Child	neg

Bedrooms	Qty
Double	2
Twin	1
Single	
Bed Size	**Qty**
Super King	2
King	1
Queen	
Double	
King Single	2
Bathrooms	**Qty**
Ensuite	3
Private	
Guest Share	

 Boutique B & B Accommodation

Features & Attractions

- *Lake and rural views*
- *Quiet & relaxing setting*
- *Wireless Internet*
- *Guest lounge*
- *Delightful breakfasts*
- *Dinner by arrangement*
- *Close to tourist attractions*
- *Trout streams nearby*

DIRECTIONS: From SH 5 take SH 36 into the centre of Ngongotaha village, approximately 1 km. Turn left into Hall Rd. Travel up the hill 400 metres. We are on the right.

Bayadere Lodge offers you superior accommodation in a modern, spacious home. Just 8 km from Rotorua, but far enough away to be sulphur free. It has splendid views of the lake and surrounding countryside. Walking distance to famous trout fishing streams. Quiet nights in the bedroom of your choice with superior beds, robes and other extras. Your own ensuite with hairdryer, quality toiletries and linen.

You will be amazed at our wonderful garden, which is colourful and peaceful. So sit on the deck and enjoy. Each morning you will arise to our delightful breakfast with a cooked dish of the day, local and tropical fruits, home-baking, tea or coffee. The guest lounge has a cosy fire for cool winter evenings and Sky TV. Take the opportunity to use our local knowledge as we help you plan your days visiting the local attractions. We offer a discount for multiple nights. Secure parking. Wireless connection facility for notebooks. Warm hospitality.

CLOVER DOWNS ESTATE

175 Jackson Road, Ngongotaha, Rotorua
Ph (07) 332 2366, Fax (07) 332 2367
Mobile 021-712 866
email: *reservations@cloverdowns.co.nz*
www.accommodationinrotorua.co.nz

Bedrooms	Qty
Double	4
Twin	
Single	
Bed Size	**Qty**
Super King	3
King	1
Queen	
Double	
Single	
Bathrooms	**Qty**
Ensuite	4
Private	
Guest Share	

Fine Country
Bed & Breakfast Retreat

Features & Attractions

- *Secluded, peaceful rural retreat*
- *Spacious home-like comfort*
- *Telephone & email facilities*
- *Laundry facilities available*

- *Tourist attractions nearby*
- *Trout fishing trips available*
- *Close to horse-riding*
- *Deer & ostrich farm tour*

Tariff : N.Z. Dollars	
Double	$225-335
Single	$205-310
Child	neg

DIRECTIONS:
Take SH 5 to roundabout. Travel northaround lake, through Ngongotaha on Hamurana Rd. Take 3rd left into Central Rd, then right into Jackson Rd. Travel 1.75 km to **Clover Downs** on left.

"A Unique Place to Stay"

So country yet so close to town... just fifteen minutes drive north of the city centre. For the discerning traveller, we offer a place to unwind and rediscover the simple pleasures in life whilst having the best facilities available. Experience the tranquillity and style of our character home, situated on a secluded six acre deer and ostrich farm with magnificent rural and Lake Rotorua views. We offer fine country accommodation with a choice of four beautifully appointed king-size suites, each equipped with tea and coffee making facilities, refrigerator, telephone, television and video. Enjoy the privacy of an ensuite bathroom in each bedroom complete with toiletries, hair dryer and bathrobes. After a sumptuous breakfast take a farm tour with Lloyd and the dogs, maybe try a game of pétanque or just relax and enjoy the rural vistas from your own private deck. Major tourist attractions, trout fishing, golf and horse riding are all nearby.

COUNTRY VILLA

351 Dalbeth Road, RD 2, Rotorua
Ph (07) 357 5893, Fax (07) 357 5893
email: *countryvilla@xtra.co.nz*
www.countryvilla.biz

Tariff : N.Z. Dollars	
Double	$175-245
Single	$175-225
Child	neg

Bedrooms	Qty
Double	4
Twin	1
Single	1

Bed Size	Qty
Super King	
King	
Queen	4
Double	
Single	5

Bathrooms	Qty
Ensuite	4
Private	1
Guest Share	

**Romantic Country Home B&B
and Self-contained Loft**

Features & Attractions

- *Quiet location – close to town*
- *Large gardens*
- *Close to golf course*
- *Choice of excellent restaurants*
- *Maori culture*
- *Tourist attractions 5-20 min.*
- *Forest walks*
- *White-water rafting*

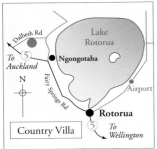

DIRECTIONS: From SH 5, turn left past the Lakeview Golf Course into Dalbeth Rd. From Rotorua, through Ngongotaha, over railway crossing, first road left.

Away from sulphur fumes and traffic noise, **Country Villa** is an elegant restored villa in an idyllic and peaceful setting on the outskirts of Rotorua. Surrounded by large gardens with many native birds, views over green fields towards Lake Rotorua and in the distance Mount Tarawera – just how you expected

New Zealand to be! **Country Villa** was originally built in Auckland in 1906 and transported in 3 parts to Rotorua, 90 years later. The turret is a lovely sitting area and part of the two bedroom suite upstairs. All rooms have ensuite or private bathroom. Enjoy a stroll through the garden or curl up with a good book in front of the log fire in the guest lounge. Breakfast is served in the conservatory with beautiful stained glass windows. New is the self-contained loft with private entrance. Continental breakfast provisions supplied for guests staying in loft. Make Rotorua your 'base' for exploring Central North Island. Taupo and Tauranga 1 hours drive.

DEER PINE LODGE
255 Jackson Road, PO Box 22,
Ngongotaha, Rotorua
Ph (07) 332 3458, Fax (07) 332 3458
Mobile 027-312 0338
email: *deerpine@clear.net.nz*

Tariff : N.Z. Dollars	
Double	$90-110
Single	$80-90
Child	Neg.

Bedrooms	Qty
Double	4
Twin	1
Single	
Bed Size	Qty
Super King	
King	3
Queen	1
Double	
Single	2
Bathrooms	Qty
Ensuite	5
Private	
Guest Share	

 **Farmstay Bed & Breakfast
Self-contained Accommodation**

Features & Attractions
- *Quiet, peaceful surroundings*
- *Beach 30 minutes away*
- *Architecturally designed units*
- *Beautiful views of lake*
- *Tourist attractions nearby*
- *Telephone & Email facilities*
- *Horse riding close by*
- *No sulphur smells*

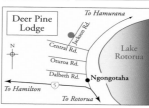

DIRECTIONS:
Please phone or write for brochure
and easy directions.

Welcome to **Deer Pine Lodge**. Come and relax in peaceful, quiet countryside surroundings with lovely views of Lake Rotorua and wake up to the singing of the birds. During your stay you are most welcome to have a look at the stags and sheep and take photographs. Our property is surrounded with trees, planted by New Zealand Forest Research. We have a cat and a Boxer (Jake), who is very gentle. The nearby city of Rotorua is fast becoming New Zealand's most popular tourist destination. Our bed/breakfast units/rooms are private with ensuite, television, radio, refrigerator, microwave, heaters, electric blankets on all beds and tea/coffee making facilities. There are heaters and hair dryers in bathrooms. Our two-bedroom fully self-contained units, designed by prominent Rotorua architect Gerald Stock, each have a private balcony, carport, sundeck, ensuite, spacious lounge, kitchen, also laundry facilities, television, radio, heaters etc (cot/highchair available). Smoke detectors fitted in all bedrooms and lounges, fire extinguishers installed in all kitchens. We hold the NZ Certificate in Food Hygiene, which ensures high standards of food preparation and service.

An evening meal with pre-dinner drinks is available by prior arrangement. Hosts John and Betty, originally from Scotland, have travelled extensively overseas and have many years experience in hosting. We look forward to your stay with us.

NGONGOTAHA LAKESIDE LODGE

41 Operiana Street, Ngongotaha, Rotorua
Ph (07) 357 4020, Fax (07) 357 4020
Mobile 027-385 2807
email: *lake.edge@xtra.co.nz*
www.rotorualakesidelodge.co.nz

Tariff : N.Z. Dollars	
Double	$170-230
Single	$150-200
Child	neg

Bedrooms	Qty
Double	2
Twin	1
Single	
Bed Size	**Qty**
Super King	
King	1
Queen	1
Double	
Single	2
Bathrooms	**Qty**
Ensuite	3
Private	
Guest Share	

**Lakeside
Quality Bed & Breakfast**

DIRECTIONS:
Drive through Ngongotaha Village,
cross over railway line, then first
right into Wikaraka Street, then left
into Okana Cresent, left again
into Operiana Street.
We are on the right.

Features & Attractions

- *Absolute lake edge*
- *Separate guest floor*
- *Generous breakfasts*
- *Activities arranged*
- *Fly fishing in lake & stream*
- *Fishing gear provided*
- *Licenses sold*
- *Sulphur free*

"Where the magic begins"

Come, stay a while and feel the peace and tranquility of your Lakeside 'home-away-from-home'. Relax in the guest conservatory or garden with a fresh coffee or wine. Unwind as you soak up the atmosphere and enjoy the many moods of Lake Rotorua. Your ensuite bedroom is all you could wish for; superior beds guarantee a restful night's sleep and a special breakfast sets you up for another exciting day. Feed the ducks, paddle the canoe, experience the thrill of fly fishing at the lake edge and have your catch pan-fried for breakfast or smoked at '**Trout Time**' with pre-dinner drinks. Sit with a book, daydream, sip a wine...**Ngongotaha Lakeside Lodge**...your perfect Bed & Breakfast choice. Ideal as a base for central island touring and for the longer stay, with multiple night discounts. Quiet, restful, great food and facilities, with warm hospitality at affordable prices. Close to all major tourist attractions, but far enough away to be '**Sulphur Free**'. Free use of fly fishing gear; licenses sold; BBQ and canoe; off-street parking.

ASHPIT PLACE
815 Ashpit Road, Rerewhakaaitu, Rotorua
Ph (07) 366 6709, Fax (07) 366 6710
Mobile 021-117 0317
email: *samarshall@clear.net.nz*
www.ashpitplace.co.nz

Features & Attractions
- *Farm, lake & mountain views*
- *Fire heating ducted through home*
- *Continental or cooked breakfast*
- *Double spa bath in ensuite*
- *Dinner by arrangement*
- *Plenty of parking spaces*

**Peaceful Rural Retreat
Bed & Breakfast**

Double	$180
Single	$160
Child	neg

Bedrooms	Qty
Double	1
Twin	
Single	
Bed Size	Qty
King	
Queen	1
Double	
Single	
Bathrooms	Qty
Ensuite	1
Private	
Guest Share	

Ashpit Place is a private home where you are hosted by Alison and Scott. A relaxing and peaceful atmosphere is preserved for those seeking to get away from the city and be enchanted by the views. The house is set in a Dairy Farm overlooking Lake Rerewhakaaitu with breathtaking sunsets and Mt Tarawera standing a kilometre away. Use our local knowledge of nearby scenic, thermal, walking, fishing, hot pools, adventure, cultural or shopping. We are a short distance to both Rotorua and Taupo and close to Whirinaki National Park for recreational walking. There is plenty of space to walk at your leisure on our property or by the lake. Tariff includes continental or cooked breakfast and 3 course dinners with wine, is available at $35 per person upon request.

DIRECTIONS:
From Rotorua take H/W 5 south, turn left at Rainbow Mountain (H/W 38) take 3rd left to Rerewhakaaitu, travel to T intersection, turn left, then take next left travel to No 815 just before seal ends. (30mins drive from Rotorua)

TE ANA FARMSTAY

Poutakataka Road, Ngakuru RD 1, Rotorua
Ph (07) 333 2720, Fax (07) 333 2720
Mobile 021-828 151
email: *teanafarmstay@xtra.co.nz*
www.teanafarmstay.co.nz

Tariff : N.Z. Dollars	
Double	$100-150
Single	$90
Child	neg

Bedrooms	Qty
Double	2
Twin	2
Single	

Bed Size	Qty
Super King	
King	
Queen	2
Double	
Single	4

Bathrooms	Qty
Ensuite	2
Private	
Family Share	1

Farmstay
Bed & Breakfast

Features & Attractions

- *Dairy Stock/cattle*
- *Proximity to Rotorua/Taupo*
- *Cottage & homestead accommodation*
- *4-wheel drive farm tour*
- *Spacious country garden*
- *Mountain/lake views*
- *Local thermals*
- *Canoe & Lake*

"Rural New Zealand at its Best"

Te Ana, in the Oberer family since 1936, offers peace and tranquillity in a spacious, rural garden setting, affording magnificent views of lake, volcanically formed hills and lush farmland.
A wonderful opportunity for the keen photographer. Cosily wrapped in the warmth of a down-filled duvet atop a woollen underlay awake to the sounds of the dawn chorus heralding another adventure-packed day Downunder. Enjoy a leisurely stroll on the farm or in the garden, before joining your host for an extremely generous country breakfast, as healthy or indulgent as you desire. Soak in the wonderful views of hills and lake over a last coffee before heading off to Waiotapu or Waimungu Thermal Reserves, Waikite Thermal Mineral Swimming Pool, or another of the many Rotorua/Taupo attractions.

A Farm Tour, by arrangement, introduces guests to local farming practises in season, and some great scenery. A three-course dinner is available – by prior arrangement only. Families welcomed by our loyal Jack Russell, Jack Russell-Oberer.

KINARA COUNTRY HOMESTAY

159 Palmer Mill Road, RD 1, Wairakei, Taupo
Ph (07) 378 8837, Fax (07) 378 8837
Mobile 027- 478 5606
email: *info@kinara.co.nz*
www.kinara.co.nz

Tariff : N.Z. Dollars	
Double	$160-185
Single	$160-185
Child	neg

Bedrooms	Qty
Double	2
Twin	
Single	1

Bed Size	Qty
Super King	
King	
Queen	2
Double	
Single	2

Bathrooms	Qty
Ensuite	2
Private	1
Guest Share	

 Country Homestay Bed & Breakfast

Features & Attractions

- *Mountain & lake views*
- *Quiet, comfortable home*
- *Safe off-street parking*
- *Huka Falls, Aratiaia Rapids*
- *Close to tourist sites*
- *Highland cattle*
- *12 min. to Lake Taupo*
- *Relaxed country setting*

"Welcome to Kinara Country Homestay!"

We have a new, large, comfortable, modern home with a touch of the Mediterranean, out in the countryside. Relax in our

beautiful, tranquil garden and natural surroundings and enjoy what **Kinara** has to offer you. Have a relaxing sleep in our comfortable, warm and cozy beds. Awaken to birdsong and the smell of breakfast cooking and freshly brewed coffee.

Would you like to be close to a lot of Taupo's tourist attractions, such as Huka Falls, Aratiatia Rapids and Wairakei Geothermal Park? If so, then come and join us, as these amenities are only five minutes away from our home.

We look forward to seeing you at **Kinara** and welcoming you as a friend.

DIRECTIONS:
Palmer Mill Road links both SH1 & 5, approx. 5km from the Wairakei intersection.
Just look for the big orange sign on Palmer Mill Road and phone us,
follow the driveway round and look for the terracotta roof.

SOUTH CLARAGH AND BIRD COTTAGE

Ph (07) 372 8848, Fax (07) 372 8047
email: *welcome@countryaccommodation.co.nz*
www.countryaccommodation.co.nz

Features & Attractions

- *Tranquil mature gardens*
- *Fine country cooking*
- *On routes to/from Waitomo to Rotorua, Tongariro*
- *Comfortable relaxed atmosphere*
- *Friendly donkeys*

$		
Double	$110-160
Single	$30-90
Child	$15-50

Countrystay and Self-contained Cottage ©

Bedrooms	Qty
Double	2
Twin	1
Single	1
Bed Size	**Qty**
King	
Queen	1
Double	1
Single	3
Bathrooms	**Qty**
Ensuite	
Private	2
Guest Share	

Turn into our leafy driveway and relax...

Both **Bird Cottage** and our comfortable, centrally heated **Farmhouse** are set in rambling gardens. Summer means picnics under the walnut tree, snoozing in a hammock, drinks on our wisteria-shaded terrace. In autumn wake to misty, russet mornings. Snuggle up by the fire in winter or share good conversation over dinner. Enjoy the wonderful spring garden. Home-grown produce and excellent cooking make dining recommended. Great fishing, trekking and golf within 20 min. Accommodation options: 1. The Farmhouse – spacious guestroom with private deck and garden access. Farmhouse tariff includes delicious breakfasts. 2. Bird Cottage – through a stand of trees, ferns and redwoods, private, with french doors to verandahs from both bedroom and living room. Self-contained and cosy, perfect for 2, but will sleep 4. Linen and firewood provided. No meals included in Cottage tariff but available by arrangement. Details and pictures on website.

DIRECTIONS: Easy to find from whichever direction you come. Contact us by phone/email/fax or check our website for map.

BRACKENHURST

801 Oruanui Road, RD 1, Taupo
Ph (07) 377 6451, Fax (07) 377 6451
Mobile 027-445 6217
email: *rgbg@xtra.co.nz*

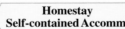

Features & Attractions

- *Dinner by arrangement*
- *14 acres of picturesque farmland*
- *Friendly highland cattle*
- *Peace and tranquility*
- *Separate cottage*
- *Tourist attractions nearby*

$		
Double	$110-150
Single	$60
Child	$30

Homestay Self-contained Accomm. H

Bedrooms	Qty
Double	3
Twin	
Single	1
Bed Size	**Qty**
King	
Queen	2
Double	1
Single	4
Bathrooms	**Qty**
Ensuite	2
Private	1
Guest Share	

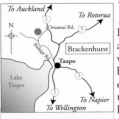

DIRECTIONS: Turn off SH 1 approx. 9km north of Wairakei- "Challenge" fertilizer-bins on Oruanui Road corner - 500m on right. Please phone first.

Brackenhurst is a warm, comfortable, modern Lockwood design home, enjoying beautiful views over 14 acres of peaceful countryside. We offer a warm welcome, wonderful food, peace and tranquility. Whilst enjoying your breakfast you may see twenty different kinds of birds and enjoy the sounds of tuis and bellbirds. A private guest wing in the house or a separate annex offer the ultimate in 'away-from-home' comforts. Breakfast to suit, either continental style or a full English. Come and enjoy **Brackenhurst** and share in our warm hospitality (dinner $45 pp). We are in reach of the famous Huka Falls, five golf courses, geothermal activity, trout fishing (river or lake), ski-fields, Rotorua and Waitomo.

MINARAPA

620 Oruanui Road, RD 1, PO Box 1310, Taupo
Ph (07) 378 1931
Mobile 027-272 2367
email: *info@minarapa.co.nz*
www.minarapa.co.nz

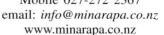

Tariff : N.Z. Dollars	
Double	$125-160
Single	$100-120
Child	POA

Bedrooms	Qty
Double	2
Twin	2
Single	
Bed Size	**Qty**
Super King	
King/Twin	1
Queen	2
Double	
Single	2
Bathrooms	**Qty**
Ensuite	2
Private	1
Guest Share	

   Countrystay Bed & Breakfast

Features & Attractions

- Tree-lined drive
- Park-like grounds
- Tennis and billiards
- Peace, privacy and space
- Tourist attractions nearby
- Dinner by arrangement
- German spoken
- Lifestyle farming

Wind your way along a wonderful tree-lined drive into rural tranquillity. **Minarapa**, our 11-acre country retreat is 12 minutes (14km) north of Taupo, 45 minutes from Rotorua and within easy reach of golf courses and major attractions, including Huka Falls, Wairakei Terraces, Orakei Korako and other thermal areas. **Minarapa** offers space and character aplenty. Downstairs relax in the large guest lounge/billiard room with television and refrigerator. Upstairs retire to one of the guestrooms – light, spacious, appointed with a view to your comfort, each with individual style. Two rooms have ensuite bathroom, balcony, TV and tea/coffee facilities. They overlook our park-like grounds where you may play tennis, wander among colourful tree-sheltered gardens, cross the pond and stream to visit our friendly farm animals or simply sit and enjoy the birdsong. In addition to continental or cooked breakfast, dinner with wine is available on request ($35-$45pp). Barbara spricht fliessend Deutsch.

KINLOCH LODGE

3 Yasmin Lane, Kinloch, Taupo
Ph (07) 378 6332, Fax (07) 378 6332
Mobile 027-481 6345

email: *relax@kinlochlodgetaupo.co.nz*
www.kinlochlodgetaupo.co.nz

Tariff : N.Z. Dollars	
Double	$145-165
Single	$100-120
Child	POA

Bedrooms	Qty
Double	3
Twin	
Single	
Bed Size	**Qty**
Super King	1
King	1
Queen	1
Double	
Single	2
Bathrooms	**Qty**
Ensuite	3
Private	
Guest Share	

**Quality Homestay
Bed & Breakfast**

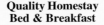

DIRECTIONS:
Take the Te Kuiti/Kinloch turn-off north
of Taupo on SH 1 (Poihipi Road). Turn
left into Whangamata Rd and follow the
signs to Kinloch. On entering Kinloch,
take the first turning left after the
roundabout (Kenrigg Road), then
next left to Yasmin Lane.

Features & Attractions

- *Only 15 minutes to Taupo*
- *Experienced & friendly hosts*
- *Comfortable beds*
- *Adjoins local golf course*
- *Close to lake edge beach & Marina*
- *Professional fishing guides available*
- *Comprehensive tourism assistance*
- *Local café & restaurant*

Nestled near the Western shores of Lake Taupo in this world-renowned trout fishing, volcanic, golfing and adventure region, **Kinloch Lodge** offers high standard accommodation in the picturesque, tranquil village of **Kinloch**. Relaxing and comfortable, the Lodge provides guests with en-suite bathrooms, a private lounge/library with tea and coffee making facilities, Sky Television, CD and email. Relax with a glass of wine on the deck overlooking the delightful garden. Step through the gate onto the golf course. Boat or fly fish with our recommended local professional guides. Stroll to the lake and marina or take a relaxing lake tour. A short drive from the hustle of Taupo, **Kinloch Lodge** is ideally located to explore our many exciting and unique area attractions, with easy access to other nearby regions. Our extensive local

knowledge enables us to provide helpful advice in planning your activities to ensure you maximise your visit. A two-day stay is highly recommended. Our scrumptious breakfasts are legendary. An evening meal and wine are available by arrangement, or enjoy our local restaurant by the lake. As totally committed "Home Hosts", we invite you to experience our warm hospitality, and look forward to welcoming you to our home. We assure you of a memorable stay.

TWYNHAM AT KINLOCH

84 Marina Terrace, Kinloch, Lake Taupo
Ph (07) 378 2862, Fax (07) 378 2868
Mobile 027-285 6001
email: *twynham.bnb@xtra.co.nz*
www.twynham.co.nz

Features & Attractions

- *Five minutes stroll to Lake*
- *Short 15 min drive to Taupo*
- *Coffee, cake and relaxation*
- *Compl. kayak/fishing tackle*
- *Hearty breakfasts & dinners*
- *Email and fax facilities*

Country Village Accommodation

Double	$145-175
Single	$110
Child	POA

Bedrooms	Qty
Double	2
Twin	1
Single	
Bed Size	**Qty**
Super King	1
King	1
Queen	1
Single	2
Bathrooms	**Qty**
Ensuite	2
Private	1
Guest Share	

Twynham at Kinloch — Poihipi Rd — Kinloch Rd — Taupo — Lake Taupo

DIRECTIONS: Driving north out of Taupo on SH 1 take the Te Kuiti/Kinloch turn-off on left (Poihipi Road). Follow Kinloch signs to village.

Nestled within large private gardens in the picturesque lakeside village of Kinloch - **Twynham** is a haven for fresh air, good coffee and relaxation and unequaled as a base for exploring the delights of the Taupo region, plus the more strenuous delights of golf (adjacent), fishing (five minutes), water sports, snow skiing, bush and mountain walks. Hearty breakfasts, wholesome dinners and warm welcomes assure guests of an enjoyable stay. Guest accommodation is a private wing with bedrooms, bathrooms and elegant lounge. Laundry service available. Elizabeth has a wide knowledge of the volcanic and geothermal history of the region. Paul is a New Zealand Kennel Club Judge and golf, music, dog sports and travel are family interests. We are owned by two friendly dogs. Pets are welcome.

www.phototrips.info

ACACIA BAY LAKEFRONT
21 Te Kopua Street, Acacia Bay, Taupo
Ph (07) 378 8449, Fax (07) 378 8449
Mobile 027-481 8829
email: *bibbys@taupohomestay.com*
www.taupohomestay.com

Tariff : N.Z. Dollars	
Double	$280-400
Single	$280-350
Child	POA

Bedrooms	Qty
Double	3
Twin	
Single	
Bed Size	Qty
Super King	1
King	1
Queen	1
Double	
Single	2
Bathrooms	Qty
Ensuite	3
Private	
Guest Share	

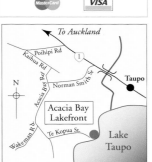

To Auckland
Poihipi Rd
Kaihua Rd
Norman Smith St.
Acacia Bay Rd
Wakeman Rd
Te Kopua St.
Acacia Bay
Lakefront
Taupo
Lake Taupo
N

**Absolute Lakefront
Luxury Accommodation**

Features & Attractions

- *Comfortable beds*
- *Private beach & jetty*
- *Generous breakfasts*
- *Quiet and relaxing*
- *Uninterrupted panoramic views*
- *Boat fishing, sightseeing trips*
- *Close to all major attractions*
- *Hot pool and golf nearby*

Paeroa Lakeside Homestay set on the lake edge with private beach, native bush and gardens, in sheltered Acacia Bay, with panoramic views of Lake Taupo and beyond. A warm, welcoming environment waits – comfort, private facilities, spacious lounge areas and outdoor living. Guest areas and beds are warm, comfortable and tastefully decorated. Television and tea/coffee facilities in rooms, email and laundry service available. Retired sheep farmers, we enjoy living in our peaceful, private home beside the beach next to a bushwalk, just minutes from the town centre.

Three golf courses, thermal areas, restaurants, boating, fishing and all major attractions, and within easy driving distance from mountains, National Park, extensive thermal areas and wineries. Amongst our interests are travel, golf, gardening, fishing, hospitality, having travelled and fished extensively overseas. Guided fishing and sightseeing experiences available from John's new 30 foot cruiser. The catch can be smoked or may be cooked for breakfast. A welcome tea or coffee on arrival. We assure you of a memorable stay. Please email, fax or phone for bookings.

FOURWINDS BED & BREAKFAST

57 Woodward Street, Taupo
Ph (07) 376 5350, Fax (07) 376 5360
Mobile 027-476 5350
email: *bnb@fourwindsbedandbreakfast.co.nz*
www.fourwindsbedandbreakfast.co.nz

Tariff : N.Z. Dollars	
Double	$110-125
Single	$85-95
Child	

Bedrooms	Qty
Double	1
Twin	1
Single	

Bed Size	Qty
Super King	
King	
Queen	
Double	1
Single	2

Bathrooms	Qty
Ensuite	
Private	
Guest Share	1

**Homestay
Bed & Breakfast**

Features & Attractions

- *Panoramic views*
- *Quiet relaxed atmosphere*
- *Warm friendly hospitality*
- *Close to all attractions*
- *Short walk to shops & restaurants*
- *Transfer airport/coach depots*
- *Email & laundry facilities*
- *Home away from home*

A warm welcome and a refreshing cup of tea await your arrival at **Fourwinds**, a charming home close to Taupo and all its main attractions, with panoramic views over Lake Taupo, the Kaimanawa Ranges and the mountains of the Central Plateau. Guests are accommodated in a double or twin room. The bathroom (shower

DIRECTIONS:
From north (SH 1) take Acacia Bay turn-off then left twice. From south (SH 1) cross Waikato River, left Norman Smith St, right Woodward St.

and bath) facilities are shared between the two rooms with a separate toilet. A maximum of only 4 guests are accommodated at any one time. Your generous cooked or continental breakfast is served in the dining room overlooking the panoramic view. Taupo's central position makes it an ideal base for day trips to Rotorua, Hawkes Bay, Tongariro National Park and Waitomo, with guests returning each night to the same warm welcome and comfortable bed. At day's end relax on the deck and watch the magnificent sunsets over the mountains or find the Southern Cross constellation in the night sky. *Your Taupo home away from home.*

HIGHLAND COTTAGE

50 Highland Drive, Acacia Bay, RD 1, Taupo
Ph (07) 377 1117, Fax (07) 377 1124
Mobile 021-956 020
email: *suzanne.mccleary@xtra.co.nz*

Tariff : N.Z. Dollars	
Double	$120-150
Single	$90
Child	$30

Bedrooms	Qty
Double	1
Twin	
Single	

Bed Size	Qty
Super King	
King	
Queen	1
Double	
Single	

Bathrooms	Qty
Ensuite	1
Private	
Guest Share	

Quiet Country Get-Away
Self-contained Bed & Breakfast

Features & Attractions

- *Fully self-contained*
- *Rural garden setting*
- *5min. to excellent restaurant*
- *5min. walk to licensed art café*
- *Sunny outdoor deck*
- *Secure parking at door*
- *23-30min. walk to lake*
- *Laundry & cooking facilities*

Highland Cottage is situated on peaceful, private five acres overlooking the Tukairangi Valley. Lake Taupo is accessible in 15 minutes by foot, for a swim or a fish. Also within a 5 minute drive are tennis courts, restaurant/bar and shop. Vineyard, golf course and boat ramps are all close by.

The Cottage includes 1 queen-sized bedroom ensuite, a fold-out double bed, a self-contained kitchen with full cooking facilities, dining area and lounge with TV and cosy fire.

Enjoy your self-help breakfast 'al-fresco'-style on your own sunny deck. It includes free-range eggs and bacon, or provisions for continental breakfast as required.

Alternatively take a short wander down the quiet road to the café for a coffee and view some local art.

Fishing trips (by arrangement), thermal attractions, beaches, ski fields (1 hour away) and mountain bike riding all easily accessible.

Te Moenga Lodge

60 Te Moenga Park, Acacia Bay, Taupo
Ph (07) 378 0437, Fax (07) 378 0438
Mobile 027-452 1459
email: *info@temoenga.com*
www.temoenga.com

Tariff : N.Z. Dollars	
Double	$150-295
Single	$120-220
Child	POA

Bedrooms	Qty
Double	2
Twin	2
Single	

Bed Size	Qty
Super King	2
King	1
Queen	1
Double	
Single	

Bathrooms	Qty
Ensuite	4
Private	
Guest Share	

**Chalet Accommodation and
Bed & Breakfast**

VISA MasterCard AMERICAN EXPRESS eftpos

Features & Attractions

- *Luxury private chalets*
- *Magnificent panoramic views*
- *Secure off-street parking*
- *Lake & river trout fishing*
- *Studio rooms with garden outlook*
- *Peace, privacy & luxury*
- *Small group options*
- *Comfortable guest lounge*

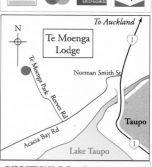

DIRECTIONS: Follow directions to Acacia Bay. Take 1st street on right, Reeves Rd and continue on to **Te Moenga** Park to end.

Te Moenga Lodge is a luxury retreat just a few minutes from the centre of Taupo providing the best view of Lake Taupo guaranteed! As you drive up the private driveway and enter the delightful Lodge, be prepared to stand back and allow a few seconds to take in the breath taking view. Two private Chalets are very spacious, well equipped with true attention to detail. King bedrooms, spacious lounge and bathroom with double spa bath. Sky TV, kitchenette and BBQ facilities. Relax on your own deck with a breakfast hamper enjoying your magnificent views. Our two Studio rooms, with garden outlook have the added benefit of an extremely comfortable guest lounge, dining room and outdoor terrace with BBQ, all with the former mentioned views. Ensuite, TV, tea and coffee making facilities. Your hosts, Brent and Jacque offer first class, friendly and efficient service, no request is too much trouble for them. A visit to **Te Moenga Lodge** is one to cherish for years to come, you'll find it hard to beat the view, quality serivce and accommodation on offer.

MAGNIFIQUE
52 Woodward Street, Taupo
Ph (07) 378 4915, Mobile 021-388 498
email: *rexandgay@magnifique.co.nz*
www.magnifique.co.nz

Tariff : N.Z. Dollars	
Double	$130-150
Single	$100-120
Child	

Bedrooms	Qty
Double	2
Twin	1
Single	
Bed Size	**Qty**
Super King	
King	
Queen	2
Double	
Single	2
Bathrooms	**Qty**
Ensuite	
Private	2
Guest Share	

**Quality Homestay
Bed & Breakfast**

DIRECTIONS: From north (SH 1)
turn off to Acacia Bay, then 1st left twice.
From south (SH 1) - just over bridge,
take 1st left, then 1st right.

Features & Attractions

• *Magnificent sweeping views*
• *Overlooking Boat Harbour*
• *Delightful garden setting*

• *Short walk to town*
• *Golf, fishing, skiing*
• *Guest laundry*

Welcome to **Magnifique** with stunning views of beautiful Lake Taupo, framed by the snow-clad Central Plateau and mountain ranges. Only seven minutes walk to Taupo's superb shops and restaurants. The accommodation includes an upstairs double bedroom with television, tea making facility and private bathroom, or downstairs self-contained double unit with living and kitchen facilities, television and bathroom. Being central, Taupo is ideal for day trips to Rotorua, Hawke's Bay art deco and wineries, Tongariro National Park or Waitomo Caves. More and more of our guests are choosing this option and returning to the same comfortable bed and welcome. Allow us to assist you with plans that will maximise your Taupo experience. Our focus in life is "people", having many friends in New Zealand and beyond with capacity for many more. Enjoy a relaxed stay in our lovely home and special attention to details.

ABOVE THE LAKE AT WINDSOR CHARTERS
46 Rokino Road, Taupo
Ph (07) 378 8738, Free Phone 0800 788 738
Mobile 027-272 9856

email: *windsor-charters@xtra.co.nz*
www.taupostay.com

Tariff : N.Z. Dollars	
Double	$150-180
Single	$140-170
Child	POA

Bedrooms	Qty
Double	3
Twin	
Single	
Bed Size	**Qty**
Super King	1
King	
Queen	2
Double	
Single	
Bathrooms	**Qty**
Ensuite	1
Private	1
Guest Share	

 Boutique Bed & Breakfast Lake Fishing/Cruising with Hosts

Features & Attractions

- *Chartered fishing with host*
- *Close to all major attractions*
- *Golf 5 minutes*
- *Activities advice*
- *Breathtaking lake views*
- *Kiwi-style breakfast*
- *Stroll to lake swimming*
- *Quality accommodation*

On arrival, relax and enjoy magical lake, mountain and Taupo town views. Your supremely comfortable accommodation is centrally located in the heart of Taupo. Easy to find, and just a stroll to the lake and Taupo's own, hot-water beach. Walking distance to award winning restaurants. Join your hosts, Bruce and Angela for coffee or a glass of wine. Make use of our extensive local knowledge to plan your Taupo experience. In the morning, wake to a leisurely, generous, Kiwi-style cooked breakfast. Accommodation is first class and tastefully decorated. The ground floor suite features a queen-size and a super/king bedroom. Lounge opening to private, sunny courtyard. On the upper floor, the **Lake View Suite** is a romantic, private haven. Queen bed, panoramic water views, sitting room. ensuite with shower box and spa bath. Suites have tea/coffee facilities, fridge, heating, electric blankets, Sky TV, iron. Toiletries, hair dryer in the bathrooms. Charter boat fishing with your hosts is optional.

THE PILLARS

7 Deborah Rise, Bonshaw Park, RD 3, Taupo
Ph (07) 378 1512, Fax (07) 378 1511
email: *info@pillars.co.nz*
www.pillarstaupo.co.nz

Tariff : N.Z. Dollars	
Double	$290-490
Single	
Child	13 yrs.+

Bedrooms	Qty
Double	4
Twin	
Single	
Bed Size	**Qty**
Super King/Twin	1
King/Twin	1
Californian King/Twin	2
Single	
Bathrooms	**Qty**
Ensuite	4
Private	
Guest Share	

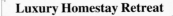

Luxury Homestay Retreat

Features & Attractions

- *Offers privacy and tranquility*
- *5 acre park-like rural grounds*
- *Lake and mountain views*
- *Tennis court & swimming pool*
- *World famous trout fishing*
- *Golf courses nearby*
- *Ski fields only 1 hour away*
- *Hot pools nearby*

Welcome to Taupo's exclusive Homestay Retreat offering privacy and tranquility amidst five acres of park-like rural grounds with views of lake and mountains. At Lake Taupo, – New Zealand's largest lake, covering 616 square kilometres – you will be amazed about how much there is to do in both summer and winter. **The Pillars**, built in Mediterranean style, is set in landscaped gardens, featuring a pond, gazebo, swimming pool and tennis court (racquets and balls provided). All rooms have underfloor heating, complimentary toiletries and quality furnishings, including television, radio-clock, refrigerator with bottled water, selection of teas and coffee, fresh fruit and a complimentary bottle of wine. Fresh flowers, home-cooked biscuits, bathrobes and hair dryers will add to the enjoyment of your stay with us. The room and winter rates includes a continental breakfast. With prior notice we will provide a three-course evening meal with aperitifs, nibbles and a night cap for $65 per person. If you wish to visit Taupo's many bars and restaurants, we will provide complimentary transport. Brochure available on request.

DIRECTIONS: 5.7 km from the lake edge up SH 5 towards Napier. Turn into Caroline Drive. Deborah Rise is the first on your left.

FAIRVIEWS

8 Fairview Terrace, Taupo 3330
Ph (07) 377 0773
email: *fairviews@reap.org.nz*
www.reap.org.nz/~fairviews

Tariff : N.Z. Dollars	
Double	$135-155
Single	$115-135
Child	n/a

Bedrooms	Qty
Double	1
Twin	1
Single	

Bed Size	Qty
Super King	
King	
Queen	1
Double	
Single	2

Bathrooms	Qty
Ensuite	1
Private	1
Guest Share	

 Homestay Boutique Accommodation

Features & Attractions

- *Email/laundry (small charge)*
- *Generous breakfasts*
- *Tea/coffee facilities*
- *Private entrance/patio*
- *Extensive local knowledge*
- *Unrivalled hospitality*
- *Off-street parking*
- *Airport pick-up*

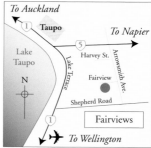

DIRECTIONS: Approaching from State Highway 1, turn onto State Highway 5. Take first turning on the right then second turning on the right. **Fairviews** is on the left.

Brenda and Mike welcome you to **Fairviews** and invite you to stay in our comfortable, modern home situated in a quiet, safe neighbourhood. Whether you desire privacy or company, we will host you in a friendly, relaxed atmosphere. **Fairviews** provides an excellent standard of accommodation and, as we are seasoned travellers, we know the importance of superior service. We take pride in going the extra mile for our visitors. **Fairviews Homestay** recently featured in the "Readers Recommend" Column of the LA Times.

Our interests include travel, cycling, computers, theatre, antiques/collectibles, gardening and tramping. **Fairviews** is situated 4.5 km from town, five minutes from the lake, botanical gardens and Taupo Hot Springs. Discover the stunning beauty of Taupo – relax and enjoy your time at **Fairviews**.

AMBLESIDE BED & BREAKFAST

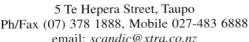

5 Te Hepera Street, Taupo
Ph/Fax (07) 378 1888, Mobile 027-483 6888
email: *scandic@xtra.co.nz*
www.ambleside.co.nz

Tariff : N.Z. Dollars	
Double	$165-180
Single	$150
Child	n/a

Bedrooms	Qty
Double	2
Twin	
Single	

Bed Size	Qty
Super King	
King	
Queen	2
Double	
Single	

Bathrooms	Qty
Ensuite	1
Private	1
Guest Share	

**Boutique Accommodation
Bed & Breakfast**

Features & Attractions

- *Quality accommodation in private and tranquil setting*
- *Panoramic lake, mountain & town views*
- *Delicious cuisine & warm hospitality*
- *Private thermal pool*
- *Fishing, sightseeing on lake*
- *Close to local attractions*
- *Ample off-street parking*

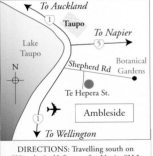

DIRECTIONS: Travelling south on SH1 take 2nd left turn after Napier SH 5 turnoff, onto Shepherd Road, then 1st right into Te Hepera Street.

Magnificent views, private geothermal plunge pool, delicious cuisine, five-star friendliness - just some of the pleasant surprises that await you when you stay at Ambleside. Built for the sun and views, our home is situated in a quiet cul-de-sac, a stroll away from the lake and restaurants.

Upstairs is exclusive to you. Two queen bedrooms offer stunning views. Both have Sky television, refrigerators (complimentary refreshments) and tea/coffee facilities, and both suites are air conditioned. One bedroom adjoins a well equipped guest lounge, and these open onto a sunny balcony. Capture one of life's better experiences when you relax in our geothermal plunge pool set in the fern garden. Robes are provided. You are welcome to use our internet facilities at no extra expense. As one guest put it "It's all about human warmth and wit". Enjoy sharing travel stories and life's adventures with us whilst you enjoy a gourmet breakfast. Take the opportunity to use our knowledge to plan your day, and experience the magic of Taupo.

YOUR HOSTS: **Anne and Grahame Velvin**   Ph (07) 377 2922

MOSELLE

3 Te Hepera St, Taupo 3330
Ph (07) 377 2922, Fax (07) 377 2290
Mobile 021-254 4511
e-mail: *ragevelvin@xtra.co.nz*
www.moselletaupo.com

Features & Attractions

- *Handy to the lake*
- *Superb lake views*
- *Quiet cul de sac*
- *Full laundry facilities*
- *Off-street parking*
- *Guests' private entrance*

Self-contained Luxury Accommodation

Double	$170
Single	$150
Child	

To Auckland — Taupo — *To Napier* — Lake Taupo — Shepherd Rd — Botanical Gardens — Te Hepera St. — Moselle — *To Wellington*

This property offers quality furnishings in a French theme. Brand new super king bed and top quality linen. New, modern ensuite and full laundry facilities. Full kitchen facilities and fresh breakfast food supplied daily to your requirements. Specialty foods are no problem.

A DVS system has been installed for warmth, comfort, and to prevent allergies. A five minute drive to the Taupo township and walking distance to the lake. Private parking outside this accommodation.

All this for $170.00 per night.

Bedrooms	Qty
Double	1
Twin	
Single	
Bed Size	**Qty**
Super King	1
Queen	
Double	
King/Single	
Bathrooms	**Qty**
Ensuite	1
Private	1
Guest Share	

DIRECTIONS: Travelling south on SH 1 take the second left turn after the Napier SH 5 turn-off, onto Shepherd Road, then first right into Te Hepera Street.

YOUR HOSTS: **Raewyn and Neil Alexander**   Ph: (07) 378 5481

PATAKA HOUSE

8 Pataka Road, Taupo
Ph (07) 378 5481, Fax (07) 378 5461
email: *pataka-homestay@xtra.co.nz*
www.patakahouse.co.nz

Features & Attractions

- *Quality hospitality in spacious home*
- *Private garden room with ensuite*
- *Central to Taupo's many attractions*
- *Quiet neighbourhood*
- *Large colourful garden*
- *Outdoor swimming pool*

Double	$120-130
Single	$90
Child	$30

Homestay and Garden Cottage

DIRECTIONS:
We are 100 metres off the Lake Taupo lakefront drive.
Please phone or fax for bookings or directions.

Bedrooms	Qty
Double	2
Twin	2
Single	
Bed Size	**Qty**
King	
Queen	2
Double	
Single	4
Bathrooms	**Qty**
Ensuite	1
Private	1
Guest Share	1

Pataka House is highly recommended for its hospitality. We assure guests that their stay lives up to New Zealand's reputation as being a home away from home. We are easily located, one turn off the lakefront and up a tree-lined driveway. Our garden room is privately situated, has an appealing décor and is extremely popular to young and old alike. Stay for one night or stay for more as Lake Taupo will truly be the highlight of your holiday.

We have a private spacious parking area. We can plan your fishing trips and, if required, help to plan your day's activities. Enjoy a relaxed stay at Pataka House and experience the magic of Taupo.

TUI LODGE

196 Taupahi Road, Turangi
Ph (07) 386 0840, Fax (07) 386 0843
Mobile 027-441 1625
email: *tui-lodge@xtra.co.nz*
www.tui-lodge.co.nz

Tariff : N.Z. Dollars	
Double	$260
Single	$150
Child	

Bedrooms	Qty
Double	4
Twin	
Single	
Bed Size	**Qty**
Super King	4
King	
Queen	
Double	
King/Single	8
Bathrooms	**Qty**
Ensuite	4
Private	
Guest Share	

**Luxury
Bed & Breakfast**

Features & Attractions

- *Personalised Maori culture tours*
- *Fly fishing*
- *Tongariro crossing and short walks*
- *Tongariro trout centre 5min. away*
- *Whakapapa ski fields*
- *Tokannu thermal area 5 min.*
- *Rafting 4x4 & horse trekking*
- *Train trip (spiral)*

Tui Lodge is located near the Tongariro River, renowned for fly fishing for Brown and Rainbow Trout. All year round fishing with the Back Country Rivers offering seasonal fishing.

Tui Lodge, purposely built as a Bed & Breakfast and opened in 2005, is a blend of classic and contemporary design. Peaceful luxury accommodation. Offering four ensuited guest bedrooms, large guest lounge, open fire, underfloor heating with views of Mt Pihanga and the Kaimanawa Ranges.

Close vicinity to wonderful bush and river walks. Apart from the skiing on the mountains, there are many beautiful short walks and several day tramps around the mountain.

Very good restaurants within walking distance. A haven for artists. Trout fishing guide Ian is a member of the professional guides association and a talented artist.

PUKATEA HOMESTAY
29 Rangimoana Avenue, Motuoapa, RD 2, Turangi
Ph (07) 386 0114, Fax (07) 386 0345
Mobile 027-227 3319
email: *spocky@xtra.co.nz*
www.lakeviewpukatea.co.nz

Features & Attractions

- *Native garden setting*
- *Friendly & relaxed atmosphere*
- *Dinner by arrangement*
- *Fantastic lake view*
- *45 min to ski fields*
- *Adventure activities area*

Homestay Bed & Breakfast		$	Double	$140
			Single	$110
			Child	

P**ukatea** offers quality accommodation in a peaceful, native garden setting with magnificent views over Lake Taupo. A warm and friendly welcome awaits you from your host Jenny, border collie Jess and our cat Mr Spock.

Relax in the sun and enjoy expansive views from the lounge and the deck, or take advantage of the many activities available in the region – Tongariro National Park is on our doorstep. We are just ten minutes north of Turangi and thirty minutes south from Taupo.

Delicious breakfasts are included. Dinner, with complimentary wine, is available upon request. Vegetarians are catered for but advance notice is always appreciated.

Bedrooms	Qty
Double	2
Twin	
Single	
Bed Size	**Qty**
King	1
Queen	1
Double	
Single	
Bathrooms	**Qty**
Ensuite	1
Private	
Family Share	1

FOUNDERS AT TURANGI
253 Taupahi Road, Turangi
Ph (07) 386 8539, Fax (07) 386 8534
Mobile 025-854 000
email: *chris@founders.co.nz*
www.founders.co.nz

Features & Attractions

- *Fly fishing guides available*
- *Rafting, kayaking, skiing*
- *Golf, horse treks, 4x4 bikes*
- *Tongariro Nat. Park tramping*
- *Lake Taupo water sports*
- *Thermal pools, historic sites*

Bed & Breakfast Homestay		$	Double	$170
			Single	$120
			Child	

P**eter** and Chris Stewart offer you a warm welcome to their home in Turangi, a small town at the southern end of Lake Taupo, where you can 'get away from it all'. **Founders at Turangi** is new and purpose built to ensure you a comfortable, relaxed base from which to visit the volcanoes of Tongariro National Park or flyfish nearby rivers. We are close to Lake Taupo, where you can sit in a quiet bay and enjoy the beauty, swim, sail, water ski or cruise. Breakfast in our sunny dining room is a good start to each morning as you set out to explore the unique magic that is the North Island's Central Plateau. Stroll to dinner at good local restaurants each evening.

Bedrooms	Qty
Double	4
Twin	
Single	
Bed Size	**Qty**
S. King/Twin	1
Queen	3
Double	
Single	
Bathrooms	**Qty**
Ensuite	4
Private	
Guest Share	

SOUTHERN COMFORT HOMESTAY

35 Taupahi Road, PO Box 312, Turangi
Ph (07) 386 7172
Mobile 027-251 2715
email: *homestaytaupo@xtra.co.nz*
www.homestaytaupo.co.nz

Tariff : N.Z. Dollars	
Double	$110-130
Single	$90
Child	n/a

Bedrooms	Qty
Double	2
Twin	
Single	

Bed Size	Qty
Super King	
King	1
Queen	1
Double	
Single	

Bathrooms	Qty
Ensuite	2
Private	
Guest Share	

    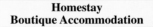

**Homestay
Boutique Accommodation**

DIRECTIONS:
From SH1 turn into Link Road, then left into Taupahi Road. No 35 is on right. **Southern Comfort** is at end of the driveway on right.

Features & Attractions

- *Quiet peaceful setting*
- *Ensuite bathrooms*
- *Dinners a speciality*
- *Swimming pool*
- *Backs onto Tongariro River*
- *Just two minutes off SH 1*

Southern Comfort Homestay welcomes you to Turangi, trout fishing and adventure paradise. Conveniently situated equal distance between Auckland and Wellington, only one minute from the Tongariro River. A good place to break your journey through the North Island. Let me offer you an oasis to rest, relax and make yourself at home. Working locally in the tourism sector, I am able to advise you on the area's exciting outdoor adventures – skiing, whitewater rafting, golfing, trout fishing, birdwatching or tramp the fabulous 'Tongariro Crossing'. The choice is yours. With a background in corporate catering, providing a special three course evening meal (with New Zealand wine) is my specialty. Together with my feline friends, Sid and Wylie, I look forward to welcoming you.

THE BIRCHES

13 Koura Street, Turangi
Ph (07) 386 5140, Fax (07) 386 5149
Mobile 021-149 6594
email: *tineke.peter@xtra.co.nz*

Features & Attractions

- *Tongariro River 2 min. stroll*
- *Fly-fishing, rafting*
- *Quiet, peaceful setting*
- *Skiing, golf, tramping*
- *Thermal pools*
- *Special breakfasts*

Bed & Breakfast Homestay

	Double	$150
	Single	$120
	Child	

Close to the world-renowned Tongariro River we welcome you to our attractive residence, set in park-like surroundings on a quiet street. This unique location is ideally situated for many outdoor pursuits such as fly fishing, skiing, tramping, golf and rafting.

We offer superior and spacious ensuite accommodation with TV and coffee/tea making facilities in a separate part of the house. Your Dutch/Canadian hosts have considerable international experience through living in Canada, the Netherlands, France, Belgium and Singapore and can speak Dutch and French.

Dinner by prior arrangement.

VISA   MasterCard

Bedrooms	Qty
Double	1
Twin	
Single	
Bed Size	**Qty**
King	
Queen	1
Double	
Single	
Bathrooms	**Qty**
Ensuite	1
Private	
Guest Share	

OMORI LAKE HOUSE

31 Omori Rd, Omori, (PO Box 334) Turangi
Ph (07) 386 0420, Fax (07) 386 0420
Mobile 021-667 092
email: *stay@omorilakehouse.co.nz*
www.omorilakehouse.co.nz

Features & Attractions

- *New specialist-built luxury lodge*
- *Kiwi hospitality at its best*
- *Kiwi cuisine with dining options*
- *Panoramic views*
- *Volcanic landscape*
- *World-class trout fishing*

Boutique Lodge

	Double	$135-150
	Single	
	Child	

We invite you to experience Kiwi hospitality at its best. We offer brand-new Boutique Accommodation, set high above Omori with stunning views looking across to Taupo. There are two luxury guest rooms with king-size beds, ensuites, tea/coffee facilities and private deck.

One room suits disabled with wide access, handrails and wet-floor shower, while the other has its own bath.

Raewyn loves to cook and eating well is part of the experience. Enjoy barbeques in summer or sit at the large rimu table for Kiwi cuisine with Kiwi classics on the menu. Omori, on the south-west of lake Taupo, is close to a variety of activities including world-renowned fly fishing, bush walks, thermal hot pools and ski slopes.

Bedrooms	Qty
Double	2
Twin	
Single	
Bed Size	**Qty**
Super King	2
Queen	
Double	
Single	
Bathrooms	**Qty**
Ensuite	2
Private	
Guest Share	

WILLSPLACE

145 Omori Road, RD 1, Omori, Turangi
Ph (07) 386 7339, Fax (07) 386 7339
Mobile 027-228 8960
email: *willsplace@wave.co.nz*
www.willsplace.co.nz

Features & Attractions

- *Private suite*
- *Bush & lakeside walks*
- *Children welcome*
- *Fabulous lake views*
- *Good fishing & boating*
- *Close to National Park*

$		
	Double	$135
	Single	$100
	Child	neg

Bedrooms	Qty
Double	2
Twin	
Single	
Bed Size	**Qty**
King	
Queen	2
Double	
Single	2
Bathrooms	**Qty**
Ensuite	
Private	1
Guest Share	

Lakeside Bed & Breakfast

DIRECTIONS:
From Turangi take SH 41.
After 14 km turn right into
Omori Rd. Drive 2.5 km
towards lake, small uphill
climb, 2nd house on right.

Our home overlooks the beautiful southwest corner of Lake Taupo. Just off the beaten track, yet only 10-15 min. to Tokaanu hot thermal pools, Turangi and Tongariro River. Forty min. to Tongariro National Park. We offer you a superior, comfortable, spacious two-bedroom suite with own entry, and safe parking. Separate living area with tea-making facilities, refrigerator, microwave, TV. Private patio overlooking the lake. A full sized bathroom with bath and shower. Laundry and internet available. Start the day with a substantial breakfast. After your day's activities sample Turangi's restaurants, or with prior arrangement, come home to a delicious home cooked dinner. Omori is a special place that we would love to share with you.

RANGIMARIE BEACHSTAY

930 Anaura Road, Anaura Bay, East Coast
Fax (06) 868 9340, Mobile 021-633 372
email: *anaurastay@xtra.co.nz*
www.anaura-stay.co.nz

Features & Attractions

- *Beach front accommodation*
- *Gisborne Airport pick-ups*
- *Special dietary needs catered for*
- *Sensational views*
- *Bush walks*
- *Peaceful retreat*

$		
	Double	$90-185
	Single	$80-155
	Child	neg

Beachstay Bed & Breakfast
Self-contained cottage

Bedrooms	Qty
Double	1
Twin	2
Single	
Bed Size	**Qty**
Super King	1
Queen	1
Double	1
Single	
Bathrooms	**Qty**
Ensuite	1
Private	2
Guest Share	

Rangimarie covers 1.5 acres, sweeping down to a white, sandy beach and is bordered on one side by a native bush reserve. All suites have private decks with sensational views of the Bay and sunrises. Guests enjoy relaxing in time-out spots such as the secluded bush sleeping platform, the outdoor bath, or swing seat with an elevated view of the surrounds. Hosting has become a focal point in our lives. We enjoy the wonderful guests we share our 'piece or paradise' with and look forward to the frequent return visits. There are no restaurants on the Bay – we are happy to prepare lunches and dinners by prior arrangement or guests are welcome to use the outdoor cooking facilities. Sky and DVD/video players in all suites. **Rangimarie Cottage** has a large, tiled bathroom with twin showers and claw foot bath, great for winter stays, and is available for self-contained rental.

CEDAR HOUSE BED & BREAKFAST

4 Clifford Street, Gisborne
Ph (06) 868 8583, Fax (06) 868 8623
email: *stay@cedarhouse.co.nz*
www.cedarhouse.co.nz

Tariff : N.Z. Dollars	
$200-250	Double
$175-200	Single
over 12yrs	Child

Qty	Bedrooms
4	Double
	Twin
	Single
Qty	Bed Size
4	Super King
	King
	Queen
	Double
	Single
Qty	Bathrooms
2	Ensuite
2	Private
	Guest Share

**Quality Select
Bed & Breakfast Accommodation**

Features & Attractions

- *Art, craft and wine trails*
- *Warm and friendly hosts*
- *Handy to beaches*
- *Central location*
- *Quality bedding and furnishings*
- *Swimming pool & spa pool*
- *Cafés & restaurants nearby*
- *Broadband internet access*

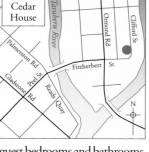

An Edwardian mansion in an established residential area, **Cedar House** is a short stroll to the CBD and shopping, cafés and restaurants, parks, rivers, museum and art galleries. The two major beaches are just a few minutes drive away. The old-world charm is enhanced with modern conveniences: Four refurbished, spacious guest bedrooms and bathrooms, sumptuous super king or twin beds, cotton robes, superior linen, artworks, fresh flowers, magazines, and nightly turn-down treat. Full breakfast provided. Sky TV, DVD player are installed in the guest lounge along with books and magazines, complimentary tea/coffee making. **Cedar House** has been lovingly restored featuring timber panelling, over three meter high ceilings and lead light windows. The ground floor guest room with ensuite is accredited 'disabled accessible'. The three 2nd floor rooms offer views and splittable super king/twin beds, one with ensuite and spa bath. The property has a salt water swimming pool and spa pool.

BEST BEACH VIEW

8 Tuahine Cres, Wainui, Gisborne
Ph (06) 868 9757
Mobile 027-356 6229
email: *bestbeachview@xtra.co.nz*

Tariff : N.Z. Dollars	
Double	$120-140
Single	$60
Child	

Bedrooms	Qty
Double	2
Twin	
Single	
Bed Size	**Qty**
Super King	
King	
Queen	2
Double	
Single	
Bathrooms	**Qty**
Ensuite	2
Private	
Guest Share	

Bed & Breakfast Homestay

Features & Attractions

- *Good parking*
- *Quiet location*
- *Stunning sea views*
- *One of NZ's nicest beaches*
- *8 minute walk to restaurant*
- *One of NZ's best golf courses*
- *Tennis courts, horse trekking*
- *Wineries*

Annabel Reynolds, your host, welcomes you to a peaceful, comfortable and memorable stay from an elevated section, with breathtaking and panoramic views of Wainui Beach. Unwind with a swim or a walk on the beach which is right on your doorstep.

Gisborne is quickly being discovered as a jewel on the East Coast. The city is beautiful with different species of palm trees lining the streets and a great selection of cuisine from excellent cafés and restaurants on the water and in the CBD.

The city has its own charm and is very beautiful with beaches and rivers running through it and surrounding it. There are wineries to visit and Eastwood Hill Arboretum is internationally recognised as having the greatest selection of oak trees in Australasia.

Gisborne is a tremendous experience and staying at Wainui Beach at Annabel's **Best Beach View B&B** will remain a special memory.

COTTAGE BY THE SEA

66 Lower Turangi Road, RD 43, Waitara, New Plymouth
Ph (06) 754 4548 or (06) 754 7915
email: *cottagebythesea@clear.net.nz*
www.cottagebythesea.co.nz

Tariff : N.Z. Dollars	
Double	$145-185
Single	$135-175
Child	

Bedrooms	Qty
Double	4
Twin	
Single	
Bed Size	**Qty**
Super King	
King	1
Queen	3
Double Sofabed	2
Single	
Bathrooms	**Qty**
Ensuite	4
Private	
Guest Share	

**Spectacular Sea Views
Quiet Garden Setting**

Features & Attractions

- *Expansive gardens and lawns*
- *20min. north of New Plymouth*
- *Breakfast optional extra*
- *Cafes, gardens, art/crafts*
- *Near golf, coastal walks*
- *BBQ, DVDs & movies*

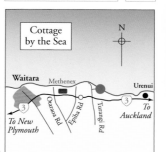

Find yourself, lose yourself - the choice is yours. Peacefulness and privacy are our specialty - a perfect atmosphere to unwind.

Lose yourself in the everchanging seaviews, or find yourself in our tranquil sunken garden. Hear the sounds of the waves and chorus of birds. Wander down 100 handcrafted steps to the secluded blacksand beach or relax with a book on your patio. Treat yourself to the magnetism that brings guests back again and again. Two cottages, nestled in their own gardens, each sleeps 4. Two boutique, open-plan suites opened in 2007, each sleeps 2. All have kitchens and ensuites. Regrettably our property is not suitable for children. Please go to our website for more photos and details.

DIRECTIONS:
Nearest Town: New Plymouth
- about 25km north,
just a 20min drive.
1/2 km off State Highway 3
between Waitara and Urenui

93 BY THE SEA

93 Buller Street, New Plymouth
Ph (06) 758 6555, Mobile 027-230 3887
email: *pat@93bythesea.co.nz*
www.93bythesea.co.nz

Tariff : N.Z. Dollars	
Double	$130-160
Single	$100-130
Child	

Bedrooms	Qty
Double	2
Twin	1
Single	

Bed Size	Qty
Super King	1
King	
Queen	1
Twin/Single	1
Single	

Bathrooms	Qty
Ensuite	1
Private	1
Guest Share	

**Boutique
Bed & Breakfast**

Features & Attractions

- *Central yet peaceful*
- *Off-street parking*
- *Ensuite or private spa bathroom*
- *Private guest entrance*
- *On the Coastal Walkway*
- *National Park nearby*
- *Dinner by prior arrangement*
- *Laundry facilities available*

DIRECTIONS:
Please phone for easy directions.

We are ideally centrally situated near the award-winning 7 kilometre Coastal Walkway, leading from the mountain-fed river mouth to sea-port, past a golf course, beaches, cliffs, city centre, amenities and parks. **93 By the Sea** is a supremely comfortable, revitalised 1930's bungalow within easy walking distance to shops, restaurants, riverways, beaches and gardens. Choose either the **Gingkho Room** with a spacious lounge, private bathroom with spa bath, or the **Rimu Room**, totally cosy with ensuite, sea outlook and gas fire. Neither will disappoint. Enjoy my especially prepared sumptuous breakfasts in the north-facing dining area (in or outside) that treats you to lovely views of Bruce's garden and surf and swimming beaches bordering the everchanging Tasman Sea. This is also a relaxingly wonderful spot to enjoy that evening moment Let us spoil you! Cheers, Pat.

"The sound of waves upon the shore,
The smell of roses by the door,
A spa to ease the muscles sore,
Who could ask for anything more?"
Dale Cameron, Auckland

GLEN ALMOND HOUSE

18C Glen Almond Street, New Plymouth
Ph (06) 758 2920, Mobile 021-054 1555
email: *sleep@glenalmondhouse.co.nz*
www.glenalmondhouse.co.nz

Tariff : N.Z. Dollars	
Double	$100-160
Single	$80-125
Child	neg

Bedrooms	Qty
Double	2
Twin	1
Single	

Bed Size	Qty
Super King	
King	2
Queen	
Double	
Single	2

Bathrooms	Qty
Ensuite	
Private	2
Guest Share	1

**Boutique
Bed & Breakfast**

Features & Attractions

- *Secluded location*
- *Wireless internet*
- *Balcony with sea views*
- *Aromatherapy massage*

- *Character house with original features*
- *10 min walk to coastal walkway*
- *Warm & friendly atmosphere*
- *Private drawing room*

DIRECTIONS:
From city follow SH 45 towards
Oakura, along Devon Street West
(1 km), turn left at Belt Road, up the
hill, 50m turn right, Glen Almond St,
driveway on right 100m.

Indulge yourself in total comfort and pleasure at **Glen Almond House**! Located minutes from the city, tucked down a private driveway with a peaceful, sunny enclosed garden and courtyard for your

enjoyment. Enjoy stunning sea and city views from this fully restored historic home. Share in the elegance of a bygone era. For your comfort the residence is centrally heated and offers two generous size double bedrooms with king-size beds and a twin bedded room, all furnished with high quality linen, with two private and one shared bathrooms. The **Balcony Room** overlooks the city and coastline, enjoys all day sun, enjoy a quiet drink on the private verandah.

The **Glyndwr Room** is on the ground floor for ease of access. We are a Kiwi/Welsh couple who are well seasoned travellers and who know what is needed to make your stay memorable. We offer you our convivial company, delicious home-made breads and muffins, a choice of hearty, healthy breakfasts and more...! Anne is a London trained beauty therapist specialising in aromatherapy massage. So for total body and mind relaxation you can be pampered with a massage of your choice. Ideal after a hard day of sightseeing!

HIDEAWAY COTTAGE
231 Henwood Road, Bell Block, New Plymouth
Ph (06) 755 1360, Fax (06) 755 1361
Mobile 027-212 7099
email: *donrobyn@xtra.co.nz*
www.hideawaycottage.co.nz

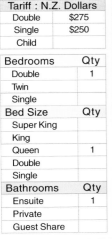

Tariff : N.Z. Dollars	
Double	$275
Single	$250
Child	

Bedrooms	Qty
Double	1
Twin	
Single	

Bed Size	Qty
Super King	
King	
Queen	1
Double	
Single	

Bathrooms	Qty
Ensuite	1
Private	
Guest Share	

DIRECTIONS:
Please telephone for
easy directions.

**Boutique Accommodation
Luxury Bed & Breakfast**

Features & Attractions

- *Peaceful and secluded*
- *Sumptous breakfast*
- *Free airport pickup*
- *BBQ available*

- *Just 3 min. from SH3*
- *5 golf courses within 10min.*
- *10 min. to city or surf*
- *20 min. to Mt Taranaki*

If privacy, tranquility and centrality are high on your list of holiday accommodation requirements, follow the tree-lined path to **Hideaway Cottage**. Just ten minutes north of New Plymouth, but a world away from the bustling city, the cottage is tucked away in an established Bell Block country garden overlooking a native forest valley. **Hideaway Cottage** is both very private and exceptionally comfortable and well appointed (complete with DVD movies available and 29-inch TV). Hosts Don and Robyn Johnson offer a free airport pick-up and spoil guests with a complimentary bottle of wine each night to be enjoyed beside the pool, or as the season dictates, tucked up in front of a roaring log fire or soaking in the outdoor spa pool. A 'Honeymooners Paradise'.

A sumptuous breakfast, often featuring the produce from the property's extensive avocado orchard, is delivered to your doorstep – fuel for a day of sightseeing, fishing, golfing, tramping or simply savouring the hideaway atmosphere.

AVOCADO ABODES
14 Arthur Rd, RD 3 Bell Block, New Plymouth
Ph (06) 755 4123, Fax (06) 755 2296
Mobile 027-277 4520
email: *avocado.abodes@xtra.co.nz*
www.avocadoabodes.co.nz

Features & Attractions

- *Peaceful, relaxing environment*
- *Free airport transfers*
- *Under 10min. city/attractions*
- *Five golf courses 10min. away*
- *Separate, modern & spacious*
- *Set amongst avocado farm*

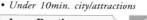

**Modern, Boutique
Self-contained Accommodation**

Double	$130-150
Single	$120-140
Child	

Avocado Abodes is lodging with a difference - so close to the city, but away from the hustle and bustle, set amongst a working avocado farm. Enjoy a new, completely separate, modern unit with two ensuited bedrooms, full kitchen, dining and lounge with laundry facilities. Being just minutes from five golf courses it's ideal as your Taranaki base. A haven to return to after the Rhodo festival or the province's many tourist attractions. Just the place for a romantic night or two retreat, away from it all with that someone special... You choose, it's your slice of luxury in Taranaki just waiting for you. Continental breakfast provided, cooked meals or provisions by arrangement. Discounts for long stays, group or corporate bookings.

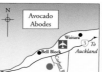

DIRECTIONS: On SH3 from airport to New Plymouth, take 1st left, Corbett Rd - 1.3km on right is Arthur Rd before railway crossing. **Avocado Abodes** is up long Row at the very end on right.

Bedrooms	Qty
Double	1
Twin	1
Single	
Bed Size	**Qty**
King	1
Queen	
Double	
King/Twin	2
Bathrooms	**Qty**
Ensuite	2
Private	
Guest Share	

DIRECTIONS:
Please phone for easy directions or download from our website for easy access from SH 3 or SH 43.

TE POPO GARDENS
636 Stanley Road, RD 24, Stratford, Taranaki
Ph (06) 762 8775, Fax (06) 762 8775
email: *tepopo@clear.net.nz*
www.tepopo.co.nz

Features & Attractions

- *Private suites in guest wing*
- *Fine food and wines*
- *Bathe under the stars*
- *Beautiful environment*
- *Famous for its birds*
- *Wonderful wood fires*

**Country Garden Retreat
Bed & Breakfast**

Double	$150-190
Single	$120-140
Child	

This natural environment is a special place – secluded, quiet and idyllic. **Te Popo Gardens** is a 'Garden of National Significance' – a large, rural woodland garden and park merging imperceptibly into old growth forest that clothes the 20m deep ravines encircling the propery. We offer you warm hospitality and every comfort to enhance your stay. The Homestead's guest wing has 4 spacious suites, each with ensuite, wood-fire, sound system, TV, superior beds/linen and private access to the garden. Luxuriate in our bath under the stars. Special breakfast is served in the sunny conservatory or beside the fire. Dinner is available by arrangement. Self-catering facilities are also provided. Wonderful dogs. Easily accessible from the 'Forgotten World Highway' (SH43) - to/from Taupo.

Bedrooms	Qty
Double	2
Twin	2
Single	
Bed Size	**Qty**
Super King	1
King	2
Queen	1
Single	2
Bathrooms	**Qty**
Ensuite	4
Private	
Guest Share	

VILLA HEIGHTS BED & BREAKFAST

333 Upland Road, RD 2, New Plymouth, Taranaki
Ph (06) 755 2273, Mobile 027-416 4131
email: *hosts@villaheights.co.nz*
www.villaheights.co.nz

Tariff : N.Z. Dollars	
Double	$130-160
Single	$110-120
Child	neg

Bedrooms	Qty
Double	2
Twin	1
Single	

Bed Size	Qty
Super King	
King	
Queen	2
Double	
Single	2

Bathrooms	Qty
Ensuite	3
Private	
Guest Share	

Quiet and Peaceful Setting
Gracious Victorian Villa

DIRECTIONS:
For easy directions please
phone 06-755 2273.

Features & Attractions

- *15 minutes to city*
- *Off-street parking*
- *Full cooked breakfast*
- *Free pick-up from airport*
- *Spacious rooms with views*
- *Dinner by arrangement*
- *Internet access*
- *30 min to Egmont National Park*

John and Rosemary warmly welcome you to their newly restored Victorian villa, set in lovely gardens with views of Mt. Egmont and the sea.
Spacious, quality, smoke-free accommodation with private entrance. Guest lounge with tea and coffee facilities and fresh home-baking. Full breakfast. Open fires in winter. Off-street parking. Evening meal by arrangement with complimentary wine. Special rates for more than one night. Free pick-up from airport and bus terminal.
We are just fifteen minutes away from New Plymouth City, beaches, golf courses, beautiful gardens, restaurants and the lovely coastal walkway. Egmont National Park is just a thirty minute drive away.

FERNLEAF B&B & FARMSTAY

58 Tunanui Road, RD 1, Owhango, Taumarunui
Ph (07) 895 4847, Fax (07) 895 4837
Free Phone 0800 FERNLEAF
email: *fernleaf.farm@xtra.co.nz*
www.travelwise.co.nz

Tariff : N.Z. Dollars	
Double	$85-120
Single	$70-90
Child	neg

Bedrooms	Qty
Double	4
Twin	
Single	
Bed Size	Qty
Super King	
King	
Queen	2
Double	2
Single	
Bathrooms	Qty
Ensuite	2
Private	1
Guest Share	1

**Bed & Breakfast
Farmstay**

Features & Attractions

- *Beautiful country setting*
- *Ruapehu skifields*
- *Midway Auckland/Wellington*
- *Pet lambs in season*
- *Dinner by arrangement*
- *Enjoy our friendly pets*
- *Log fire in winter*
- *Stroll across the farm*

Relax in the tranquil Tunanui Valley midway between Auckland and Wellington. Just 500m from SH 4, close for convenience, far enough away for peace and quiet.

We are the third generation to farm **Fernleaf** and our Romney flock has been recorded for eighty years. The views from various vantage points are awesome, taking in the mountains Ruapehu, Ngaruahoe, Tongariro and in the far distance Taranaki.

Enjoy our generous country hospitality, wonderful breakfasts, our beautiful dalmatian and friendly cats. Dinner by arrangement.

212

CAIRNBRAE HOUSE

140 Mangawhero River Road, Ohakune
Ph (06) 385 3002, Fax (06) 385 3374
Mobile 027-292 5491
email: *peterm@cairnbraehouse.co.nz*
www.cairnbraehouse.co.nz

Features & Attractions

- *Ski fields, golf, tramping*
- *Dinner by arrangement*
- *Fishing, biking, scenic flights*
- *Tongariro Crossing*
- *Views of deer park*
- *Comfort & privacy*

$	Double	$175-220
	Single	$150
	Child	

Boutique Bed & Breakfast

VISA MasterCard

Bedrooms	Qty
Double	3
Twin	2
Single	
Bed Size	**Qty**
Super King	1
King	1
Queen	1
King/Single	1
Bathrooms	**Qty**
Ensuite	3
Private	1
Guest Share	

Our purpose-built *'Guest Hosted 4 Star'* Bed & Breakfast was designed with our guest's total comfort and privacy in mind. Peace and tranquility abounds in our rural setting on the southern slopes of the Tongariro World Heritage National Park, with breath taking views of Mt Ruapehu and 30 minutes from Turoa ski field. Each guest bedroom is beautifully appointed, with quality linen, bathroom toiletries, and hairdryers. These rooms overlook our fallow deer park. The private guest lounge has a mini bar, microwave, complimentary tea and coffee, Sky TV and DVD. Our guests can relax and enjoy our English garden setting, or a stroll beside the Mangawhero River situated on our property, and also take time to feed Devon's pet deer.

TUSSOCK GROVE BOUTIQUE HOTEL

3 Karo Street, Ohakune
Ph (06) 385 8771, Fax (06) 385 8171
Mobile 027-480 5925
e-mail: *relax@tussockgrove.co.nz*
www.tussockgrove.co.nz

Features & Attractions

- *Skiing/snowboarding*
- *Mountain/river walks*
- *Golf course*
- *Tennis courts*
- *Mountain biking*
- *Horse riding*

$	Double	$140-260
	Single	$120-240
	Child	

Boutique Hotel Park-like surroundings

Bedrooms	Qty
Double	6
Twin	2
Single	
Bed Size	**Qty**
King	
Queen	4
Double	4
Single	
Bathrooms	**Qty**
Ensuite	8
Private	8
Guest Share	

The hotel offers eight well-appointed guest rooms with some having stunning mountain views. At **Tussock Grove**, we welcome you as a friend – but we'll do all the work! If you wish, we can take the time to suggest activities or driving routes. And at day's end, if you want to chat, we're always keen to hear what you've been up to.
We have a large comfortable lounge with a log fire and full bar and dining facilities with delicious breakfast menus available.
A European sauna and spa pool is available with tennis courts, adjacent. Situated in Turoa Alpine Village, we offer a park-like environment just minutes from Ohakune town centre.

MOUNTAIN HEIGHTS LODGE
State Highway 4, PO Box 43,
Tongariro National Park Village
Ph (07) 892 2833, Fax (07) 892 2850
email: *mountainheights@xtra.co.nz*
www.mountainheights.co.nz
Features & Attractions

- *Private guest wing*
- *Tongariro Crossing*
- *Hot spa*
- *15 minutes to ski fields*
- *Spacious, self contained accomm*
- *Delicious breakfasts*

**Bed & Breakfast
Self-contained Accomm.**

Double	$110-160
Single	$90-110
Child	neg

Mountain Heights is situated on the edge of Tongariro National Park, a World Heritage Area. An ideal place from which to explore the mountains and volcanoes of the Central Plateau. Activities abound for all abilities, including the world renowned **Tongariro Crossing,** classed as the best one-day walk in New Zealand. Excellent mountain bike rides, horse trekking, canoeing the Whanganui River and scenic flights across the volcanoes.

For the less strenuous, enjoy the comfort of our centrally heated lodge. Soak in the hot spa or relax in front of the log fire with a good book or a game of chess. After a good night's sleep enjoy a delicious breakfast with freshly baked bread.

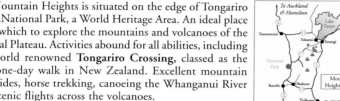

Bedrooms	Qty
Double	3
Twin	3
Single	
Bed Size	**Qty**
King	
Queen	2
Double	3
Single	4
Bathrooms	**Qty**
Ensuite	4
Private	
Guest Share	2

www.phototrips.info

SPIRAL GARDENS

Raurimu Road, RD 1, Owhango, Raurimu
Ph (07) 892 2997, Fax (07) 892 2653
Mobile 027-475 3482
email: *spiralgardens@xtra.co.nz*
www.spiralgardens.co.nz

Tariff : N.Z. Dollars	
Double	$100-165
Single	$100-140
Child	$30-50

Bedrooms	Qty
Double	4
Twin	
Single	
Bed Size	**Qty**
Super King	
King	
Queen	3
Double	4
Single	
Bathrooms	**Qty**
Ensuite	2
Private	1
Guest Share	

**Homestay - Bed & Breakfast
& Self-contained Cabin**

Features & Attractions

- *Location, Location, Location*
- *Skiing, golf, tramping*
- *Discover hidden treasures*
- *Dinner by arrangement*
- *Central to activities/attractions*
- *Fishing, hunting, biking*
- *Families welcome*
- *Vegetarians catered for*

Our home overlooks the Piopiotea Stream and a magnificent stand of native bush. We are five minutes north of National Park Village, gateway to the Tongariro and Whanganui National Parks. The Whakapapa ski area is a 25 minute drive. Transport to the world renowned Tongariro Crossing day walk is available at National Park Village. We can organise any of the adventure activities on offer in the Central Plateau area, horse treks, river rafting, guided hunting and fishing tours. Our luxury suites feature a queen bed, ensuite or private bathroom, a double bed settee, casual chairs and table, writing bureau and refrigerator.

We have central heating throughout in winter. Coffee and tea making facilities are on hand for guest use in our family kitchen and we encourage you to use the lounge and decks in casual relaxation. The cabin is small and cosy with a pot belly fire, stereo, television, private deck and carport and self-catering.

TARATA FISHAWAY

Mokai Road, Mokai Valley, RD 3, Taihape
Ph (06) 388 0354, Fax (06) 388 0954
Mobile 027-279 7037
email: *fishaway@xtra.co.nz*
www.tarata.co.nz

Tariff : N.Z. Dollars	
Double	$120-180
Single	$65-100
Child	half price

Bedrooms	Qty
Double	6
Twin	4
Single	
Bed Size	**Qty**
King	4
Queen	5
Double	1
King Single	4
Bathrooms	**Qty**
Ensuite	4
Private	1
Guest Share	1
Spa Bath	1

**Fishingstay-Farmstay- B&B
River Retreat-Honeymoon Suite**

Features & Attractions

- *Trout fishing and scenic rafting*
- *Visit LOTR, Middle Earth*
- *6km past Bungy & Flying Fox*
- *'Mini' Golf (with a difference)*
- *Swimming & spa pool*
- *Bush walks & spotlight safaris*
- *Camp outs*
- *Clay-bird shooting*

DIRECTIONS:
Central North Island –
Turn off SH 1, 6 km south
of Taihape, at the Gravity
Canyon Bungy and
Ohotu signs. Follow signs
for 14 km to the Bungy
Bridge. We are 6 km past
here on Mokai Road.

We are very lucky to have a piece of New Zealand's natural beauty. **Tarata** is nestled in bush in the remote Mokai Valley where the picturesque Rangitikei River meets the rugged Ruahine Ranges. With the wilderness and unique trout fishing right at our doorstep, it is the perfect environment to bring up our three children. Stephen offers guided fishing and rafting trips for all ages. Raft down the gentle crystal clear waters of the magnificent Rangitikei River, visit Middle Earth and a secret waterfall, stunning scenery you will never forget. Our spacious home with guest bedrooms and our large garden allow guests private space to relax and unwind. Whether it is by the pool on a hot summer's day with a book, soaking in the spa pool after a day on the river or enjoying a cosy winter's night in front of our open fire with a glass of wine. Come on a farm tour meeting our many friendly farm pets and experience our 'nightlife' on our free spotlight safari. Stay in our homestead or in **Tarata's** fully self-contained 'River Retreats' where you can enjoy a spa bath with 'million dollar views' of the river and relax on the large decking amidst native birds and trees. Peace, privacy and tranquillity at its best! We will even deliver a candle light dinner to your door. Approved pets welcome. We think **Tarata** is truly a magic place and we would love sharing it with you.

Mt Huia

906 Ruahine Road, Mangaweka
Ph (06) 382 5726, Fax (06) 382 5776
email: *info@mthuia.co.nz*
www.mthuia.co.nz

Features & Attractions

- *9 km from SH1*
- *3-course dinner*
- *Peaceful and scenic*
- *Large country garden*
- *Many local attractions*
- *Midway Rotorua – Wgtn*

$		
Double	$250
Single	$155
Child	n/a

Sheep and Cattle Farm
Dinner, Bed & Breakfast

Bedrooms	Qty
Double	1
Twin	
Single	

Bed Size	Qty
King	
Queen	
Double	1
Single	

Bathrooms	Qty
Ensuite	1
Private	
Guest Share	

A 10 minute drive from SH1 takes you to an area of unique scenery around this authentic sheep and cattle hill country farm. Enjoy refreshments on the sunny verandah or spacious deck, overlooking the attractive garden and stands of native bush.

If time allows, Neil can take you on a 4-wheel drive tour of the farm, or you may prefer to follow the marked farm walk for some fresh air and exercise. Renowned golf courses, gardens, hiking trails and adventure activities all close by. Personal attention is guaranteed in a friendly, relaxed environment, where even Jessie, the dog, will be pleased to see you! Meals are of a high standard using plenty of farm and fresh produce. Prior booking essential.

Reomoana

629 Mahanga Road, RD 8, Nuhaka, Hawke's Bay
Ph (06) 837 5898, Fax (06) 837 5990
email: *reomoana@paradise.net.nz*
www.reomoana.co.nz

Features & Attractions

- *Panoramic ocean view*
- *Morere Hot Springs*
- *Mahia Scenic Reserve*
- *Safe, white sandy beaches*
- *Fishing charters arranged*
- *Sunset Point Restaurant 6 km*

$		
Double	$120
Single	$60
Child	$20

Coastal Bed & Breakfast
Self-contained Unit

Bedrooms	Qty
Double	2
Twin	
Single	1

Bed Size	Qty
King	
Queen	2
Double	
Single	1

Bathrooms	Qty
Ensuite	1
Private	1
Guest Share	

DIRECTIONS:
Please phone for easy directions

W elcome to **Reomoana** – the voice of the sea. Pacific Oceanfront farm at beautiful Mahanga Beach on the Mahia Peninsula, the spacious, rustic home with Hungarian and New Zealand creativity makes this a home of character, with cathedral ceilings and hand-carved furniture. Breathtaking views to the Pacific Ocean. Come and relax and bring your paints - the area is a painter's paradise. Enjoy the miles of white sandy beaches. Go swimming, surfing, fishing or discover the unique rocky reefs of Mahia. Lake Waikaremoana in the Urewera National Park can be enjoyed as a day trip – or visit Mahia's Scenic Reserve. 'Sunset Point Restaurant' is 6 km away or else dinner may be served by prior arrangement. **Reomoana** is one hour south of Gisborne or 2¼ hours north of Napier. **Cottage** is available in avocado orchard – ideal for families – self-contained.

A ROOM WITH A VIEW

9 Milton Terrace, Napier
Ph (06) 835 7434, Fax (06) 835 1912
email: *roomwithview@xtra.co.nz*

Features & Attractions

- *Spectacular view*
- *Central location*
- *Fourth generation property*
- *Internet available*
- *Art deco expertise*
- *My home is your home*

 Homestay Bed & Breakfast

Double	$100
Single	$70
Child	n/a

Having home-hosted for ten years with my late wife, I'm continuing to enjoy conversation and laughter with guests from the world over. My two-storeyed home on the sunny side of the Napier Hill is set in a large 100-year-old garden. Breakfast can be served in the dining room or in the generous guest room where you can enjoy the 180° view over Hawke Bay and parts of Napier to the distant Ruahine Mountains. It's only a fifteen minute walk to our world-famous Art Deco city centre or the historic port area, at both of which there are many excellent restaurants. I'm interested in travel, gardening, the arts and especially local history, as I am Executive Director of the Art Deco Trust. Other amenities include television, tea making facilities in your room, separate bath and shower, free laundry facilities, free pick-up service and off-street parking.

DIRECTIONS: From Marine Parade take Tennyson Street, Milton Road, veer left into Milton Terrace. More detailed instructions via email.

Bedrooms	Qty
Double	1
Twin	
Single	
Bed Size	**Qty**
King	
Queen	1
Double	
Single	
Bathrooms	**Qty**
Ensuite	
Private	1
Guest Share	

COBDEN GARDEN HOMESTAY

1 Cobden Crescent, Bluff Hill, Napier
Ph (06) 834 2090, Fax (06) 834 1977
Mobile 027-695 1240
email: *info@cobden.co.nz*
www.cobden.co.nz

Features & Attractions

- *Quiet, private surroundings*
- *Extensive views*
- *Guest computer provided*
- *10 minute walk to city centre*
- *Guest laundry facilities*
- *Off-road parking & easy access*

 Boutique Homestay Bed & Breakfast

Double	$160-200
Single	$140-180
Child	$50

We invite you to stay in our quiet, sunny colonial villa on Bluff Hill. Relax in a spacious room with ensuite. Feel pampered in king or twin single beds with fine cotton linen, duvets, electric blankets, plump pillows and robes. Enjoy lounge seating, TV, heater, fan, tea/coffee making facilities and complimentary refreshments in your room. Unwind with a walk around our ½ acre garden or take in the view from our verandah, guest lounge or upstairs sunroom. Prior to indulging your taste-buds at a local restaurant join us on the verandah or in the lounge for complimentary tasting of local wine and produce. Choose your breakfast from our menu of local foods and home-made delights. We make every effort to make your stay extra special and memorable. When booking, please advise of any special dietary requirements. Two unobtrusive cats in residence.

Bedrooms	Qty
Double	3
Twin	
Single	
Bed Size	**Qty**
Super King	2
King	1
Double	
Single	5
Bathrooms	**Qty**
Ensuite	3
Private	
Guest Share	

BAY BACH
117 Rogers Rd, Bay View, Napier
Ph (06) 836 5141 , Fax (06) 836 5141
Mobile 021-105 7512
e-mail: *jill-iain@xtra.co.nz*
www.baybach.co.nz

Features & Attractions
- *Hear the sea*
- *Uniquely stylish*
- *Heart of wine country*
- *Art deco, walk/cycle tracks*
- *Architects' award 2006*
- *Friendly, relaxed, welcoming*

Double	$140
Single	$100
Child	neg

Bed & Breakfast
Homestay

Bedrooms	Qty
Double	2
Twin	1
Single	

Bed Size	Qty
Super King	1
King	1
Double	
Single	2

Bathrooms	Qty
Ensuite	2
Private	
Guest Share	

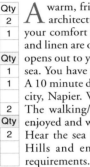

A warm, friendly welcome awaits you at **Bay Bach**. Our architectural award-winning home has been built with your comfort and relaxation as its primary goal. The beds and linen are of the highest quality and comfort. Your room opens out to your own patio with a two minute stroll to the sea. You have a private entrance and car park.

A 10 minute drive will take you into our beautiful Art Deco city, Napier. Wineries abound as do cafés and restaurants. The walking/cycling pathways around Napier are to be enjoyed and we can offer you bikes for your pleasure. Hear the sea and look down the grapes to the Bay View Hills and enjoy a delicious breakfast, made to your requirements.

DIRECTIONS:
Please phone for easy directions.

BROUGHTON HOUSE
383 Kennedy Road, Napier
Ph (06) 842 1116, Mobile 027-491 1169
email: *broughtonhouse@xtra.co.nz*
www.broughtonhouse.co.nz

Features & Attractions
- *Superb hospitality*
- *Swimming pool*
- *Off-street parking*
- *5 min from Napier's art deco city*
- *Private guest wing with separate entrance*
- *Handy to beaches & wineries*

Double	$120
Single	$80
Child	neg

Quality Bed & Breakfast
Accommodation

Bedrooms	Qty
Double	2
Twin	
Single	

Bed Size	Qty
King	
Queen	1
Double	1
Single	

Bathrooms	Qty
Ensuite	2
Private	
Guest Share	

Janet and Wayne of **Broughton House** welcome you to relax in their peaceful, friendly home. Our private guest wing is beautifully furnished with country-style décor and offers all the extra touches that you would expect to find in quality accommodation. Our two guest rooms each have an ensuite bathroom, tea and coffee making facilities, television, bath robes, hair dryer and complimentary toiletries and confectionery, along with freshly picked flowers and magazines to browse through at your leisure.

We offer both continental and cooked breakfast, including when available, home-baked muffins and fresh produce from our garden. After a day's sightseeing in the beautiful Hawke's Bay you can relax with a glass of wine by the pool or take a stroll around our cottage garden. We pride ourselves on our superior hospitality and attention to detail, which makes **Broughton House** so special.

219

MAISON BÉARNAISE BED & BREAKFAST
25 France Road, Bluff Hill, Napier
Ph (06) 835 4693, Fax (06) 835 4694
email: *chrisgraham@xtra.co.nz*
www.maisonbearnaise.co.nz

  Features & Attractions

• *Views*	• *Single level & off-street parking*
• *Colourful gardens*	• *Wineries - restaurants & tastings*
• *10 minute walk to CBD*	• *Golf, walks, trout fishing nearby*

 Quality Homestay Bed & Breakfast

	Double	$155
	Single	$110
	Child	

A warm invitation to share our charming oasis of ever changing gardens - for as long as you need - our door is open 365 days a year. Christine, Napier born, happily assists with local and national sightseeing suggestions. Both large guest rooms are privately appointed with ensuite bathrooms, have comfortable queen beds, electric blankets, hairdryers, tea/coffee making facilities and DVD television. Email access is available in the light and airy guest lounge, or you may prefer to curl up with a book, newspaper or magazine. The sunny private courtyard provides the opportunity to relax and savour the delicious breakfast choices including homemade and local produce. Napier city centre is a ten minute walk away and the historic suburb of Ahuriri, with many fine eateries, is two minutes drive away. Off-street parking, courtesy transfers and laundry service available. Welcome, unwind we want you to feel at home.

Bedrooms	Qty
Double	2
Twin	
Single	
Bed Size	**Qty**
King	
Queen	2
Double	
Single	
Bathrooms	**Qty**
Ensuite	2
Private	
Guest Share	

DIRECTIONS: North on Marine Parade. Left Coote Road. Right Thompson Road. Left France Road (first driveway on left).

MON LOGIS

415 Marine Parade, Napier
Ph (06) 835 2125, Fax (06) 835 8811
Mobile 027-472 5332
e-mail: *monlogis@xtra.co.nz*

Features & Attractions

• *Gourmet breakfast*	• *Overlooking Pacific Ocean*
• *Feather duvets, fine cotton*	• *Close to wineries & shopping*
• *Expert French Chef*	• *French and Spanish spoken*

 Boutique Accommodation Bed & Breakfast

	Double	$160-220
	Single	$120-160
	Child	

A little piece of France, nestled in the heart of the beautiful wine growing region of Hawkes Bay, built as a Private Hotel in 1915, this grand colonial building, overlooking the Pacific's breakers, is only a few minutes walk from the City Centre.

Now lovingly renovated, **Mon Logis** caters for a maximum of eight guests. Charm, personal service and French cuisine are our specialities. All upstairs bedrooms are individually furnished, and have their own private facilities. Downstairs an informal guest lounge invites you to relax, watch television or have a quiet time reading. Breakfast is served in your room or in the downstairs dining room. Should you wish to dine out, Gerard is happy to give you some recommendations. Perfectly designed for comfort and relaxation, **Mon Logis** is a non-smoking establishment and does not cater for children.

"Mon Logis – casual elegance at a price you can afford".

Bedrooms	Qty
Double	4
Twin	
Single	
Bed Size	**Qty**
Super King	2
King	1
Queen	1
Single	
Bathrooms	**Qty**
Ensuite	3
Private	1
Guest Share	

KERRY LODGE B&B AND GARDEN COTTAGE

7 Forward Street, Greenmeadows, Napier
Ph (06) 844 9630, Fax (06) 844 1450
Mobile 025-932 874
email: *kerrylodge@xtra.co.nz*
www.kerrylodge.co.nz

Tariff : N.Z. Dollars	
Double	$145-180
Single	$100-120
Child	$70

Bedrooms	Qty
Double/Twin	3
Twin	
Single	

Bed Size	Qty
Super King/Twin	2
King	1
Queen	1
Double	
Single	

Bathrooms	Qty
Ensuite	1
Private	1
Guest Share	

**Bed & Breakfast
Homestay**

Features & Attractions

- *Spacious rooms*
- *Quiet location*
- *Off-street parking*
- *Wheel chair accessible*
- *Tranquil, spacious gardens*
- *Caring, informative hosts*
- *Close to wineries, restaurants*
- *Laundry available*

To Taupo &
Gisborne
N
NAPIER
Church Rd
Prebensen Dr
Avenue Rd
Greenmeadows
Forward St
Kennedy Rd
Kerry
Lodge
Puketapu
Rd
50 Meeanee Rd
To Dannevirke & Wellington

DIRECTIONS: From Napier, travel
along Kennedy Rd & Gloucester St
until Greenmeadows, turn right into Avenue
Rd, then left into Forward St

Within walking distance to restaurants, shops and wineries. Set in spacious, tranquil gardens, we invite our guests to share the warmth and comfort of our home. From the large comfy beds, the 24 hour complimentary refreshments, television, refreshing swimming pool and patio area, to the scrumptious breakfast, which includes locally grown produce and home-made conserves, your satisfaction is our pleasure. Let us help plan your time in Napier over a coffee and share with you some of our natural treasures. We're happy to drive you to your evenings restaurant, make reservations and help make your time in Napier memorable.

The **Garden Cottage**: Our new 2-bedroom, self-contained cottage, with fully equipped kitchen, dishwasher, laundry and large spa bath, offers an alternative accommodation style for minimum 2 night stays. A continental breakfast is included.

OCEANS 63
63 Hardinge Road, Ahuriri, Napier
Phone (06) 833 6467,
Mobile 021-430 189
e-mail: *marion.smith@xtra.co.nz*

Features & Attractions
- *Stunning ocean views*
- *Close to many cafés & bars*
- *Airport/City 5min. or less*
- *Stylish, warm & comfortable*
- *Complimentary glass of wine*
- *3 nights or more 10% discount*

Bed & Breakfast Homestay		Double	$160-200
		Single	
		Child	

Welcome to my home with spectacular views of the ocean. From this home I offer the very best in genuine comfort, style and friendliness. A great location! Close to so many restaurants and cafés along the waterfront. Central city is just over the hill. It's my pleasure to help in any way possible to assist with bookings of the area. Laundry facilities available. Three good size bedrooms with comfortable beds. Relax on the deck or simply relax. Start the evening off with a complimentary glass of Hawke's Bay wine. In the morning enjoy your continental breakfast with the view that makes you know you are on holiday.

Bedrooms	Qty
Double	3
Twin	
Single	
Bed Size	**Qty**
King	1
Queen	2
Double	
Single	
Bathrooms	**Qty**
Ensuite	1
Private	
Guest Share	1

SEAVIEW LODGE
5 Seaview Terrace, Napier
Ph (06) 835 0202, Fax (06) 835 0202
Mobile 021-180 2101
email: *cvulodge@xtra.co.nz*
www.aseaviewlodge.co.nz

Features & Attractions
- *Overlooking Pacific Ocean*
- *3 min walk to city centre*
- *Across from heated pools*
- *Quiet, elevated location*
- *Off-street parking*
- *Quality bed linen*

Quality, Central City Bed & Breakfast		Double	$140-160
		Single	$100-120
		Child	n/a

Seaview Lodge is a lovingly renovated, spacious late Victorian home. This inner city, beachside Bed & Breakfast offers a warm welcome and spectacular views over the city and ocean. Enjoy your continental breakfast of fresh croissants and fruit salad on the lower verandah while watching the waves break on the shore. At the end of the day relax in the comfortable guest lounge or on the large upstairs balcony and enjoy a glass of local wine while watching the sun set.

A spacious single and a double room share the large guest lounge with TV and tea/coffee making facilities. The other double/twin room has its own lounge area including TV. All rooms are stylishly furnished and show attention to detail.

Bedrooms	Qty
Double	1
Twin/Double	1
Single	1
Bed Size	**Qty**
SuperKing/Twin	1
King	1
Queen	
King/Single	1
Bathrooms	**Qty**
Ensuite	1
Private	2
Guest Share	

SPENCE BED & BREAKFAST

17 Cobden Road, Napier
Ph (06) 835 9454, Fax (06) 835 9454
email: *ksspence@actrix.gen.nz*

home
NEW ZEALAND

Features & Attractions

- Guest suite and garden patio
- Art deco walk and museum
- Visit gannet colony
- Close to Napier City Centre
- Wineries tasting and lunch
- Visit excellent gardens

$	Double	$150
	Single	$100
	Child	

Bedrooms	Qty
Double	1
Twin	
Single	

Bed Size	Qty
King	
Queen	1
Double	
Single	1

Bathrooms	Qty
Ensuite	1
Private	
Guest Share	

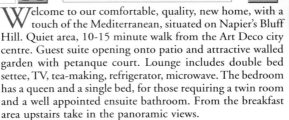

**Quality Homestay
Bed & Breakfast**

Welcome to our comfortable, quality, new home, with a touch of the Mediterranean, situated on Napier's Bluff Hill. Quiet area, 10-15 minute walk from the Art Deco city centre. Guest suite opening onto patio and attractive walled garden with petanque court. Lounge includes double bed settee, TV, tea-making, refrigerator, microwave. The bedroom has a queen and a single bed, for those requiring a twin room and a well appointed ensuite bathroom. From the breakfast area upstairs take in the panoramic views.

Napier, Hawke's Bay is a great place to be and we hope it will be for you. We have hosted for over ten years and enjoy overseas travel. Able to meet public transport.

DIRECTIONS: Port end Marine Parade, Coote Road, right into Thompson Rd, left into Cobden Rd, opposite water tower.

THE GREEN HOUSE ON THE HILL

18B Milton Oaks, Milton Road, Napier
Ph (06) 835 4475, Fax (06) 835 4475
Mobile 021-187 3827
email: *ruth@the-green-house.co.nz*
www.the-green-house.co.nz

home
NEW ZEALAND

Features & Attractions

- Friendly, relaxed atmosphere
- Central, yet peaceful location
- Art Deco Napier 5min. walk away
- Free email access
- Laundry facilities
- Off-street parking

$	Double	$110-130
	Single	$80-90
	Child	neg

**Vegetarian
Bed & Breakfast**

Bedrooms	Qty
Double	3
Twin	
Single	

Bed Size	Qty
King	
Queen	3
Double	
Single	1

Bathrooms	Qty
Ensuite	1
Private	
Guest Share	1

Our home is situated on a hillside in quiet woodland only 5 minutes walk from the heart of 'Art Deco' Napier. We offer a friendly and peaceful base for your visit to Hawkes Bay. All rooms have TV, radio, bathrobes, toiletries, hairdryer, magazines, tea/coffee and snacks. I make my own bread and preserves and use local, organic produce as much as possible. I am always happy to cater for special diets, just ask! We are originally from the south west of England, have lived in New Zealand for 14 years and are happy to share our knowledge of this scenic and interesting area. There are many things to do and see in Hawkes Bay. Highlights are: Art Deco walk; gannet colony visit; wine tours; farmers market; national aquarium; great scenery…and lots more.
A stay of at least 2 nights is recommended.

VILLA VISTA

22A France Road, Bluff Hill, Napier
Ph (06) 835 8770, Fax (06) 835 8770
Mobile 027-435 7179
email: *accommodation@villavista.net*
www.villavista.net

Tariff : N.Z. Dollars	
Double	$145-160
Single	$110-125
Child	

Bedrooms	Qty
Double	3
Twin	
Single	

Bed Size	Qty
Super King	
King	
Queen	3
Double	
Single	1

Bathrooms	Qty
Ensuite	3
Private	
Guest Share	

 Bed & Breakfast

Features & Attractions

- *Pacific Ocean views*
- *Spacious & private bedrooms*
- *Delicious continental/cooked breakfast*
- *3 minutes drive to CBD*
- *Off-street parking*
- *Art Deco attractions*
- *Winery tours*
- *Families welcomed*

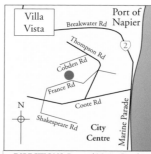

DIRECTIONS: Port end Marine Parade, Coote Road, right into Thompson Road, left into France Road, house on your right.

Villa Vista is a beautiful turn-of-the century Edwardian villa with fantastic uninterrupted views of Cape Kidnappers, Te Mata Peak and the Pacific Ocean, located 10 min. walk and 3 min. drive from the CBD. We offer 3 large, private rooms, situated on the top floor.

One double room has a balcony. Every room has delightful views, ensuite, TV, coffee/tea making facilities, air conditioning, hair dryer and bathrobes. Continental and cooked Kiwi breakfast is served in the spacious dining room. A variety of home-made delicacies will set you up for a busy or relaxing day in all that Hawke's Bay has to offer, such as wineries, Art Deco tours, gannet colonies.

~ Welcome to Napier, Hawke's Bay.

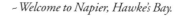

224

MISSION VISTA

359 Church Road, Greenmeadows, Napier
Ph (06) 844 5727, Fax (06) 844 5727
Mobile 027-452 0725
email: *mission.vista@xtra.co.nz*
www.missionvista.co.nz

Tariff : N.Z. Dollars	
Double	$120-150
Single	$80-100
Child	neg

Bedrooms	Qty
Double	3
Twin	1
Single	

Bed Size	Qty
Super King/Twin	1
King	
Queen	2
Double	1
Single	2

Bathrooms	Qty
Ensuite	1
Private	1
Guest Share	1

VISA   MasterCard   eftpos   AMERICAN EXPRESS   bankcard

**Homestay
Self-contained Apartment**

Features & Attractions

- *Personalized trips organised*
- *Halfway Napier/Hastings*
- *Cafés & restaurants nearby*
- *4 golf courses within 30 min.*
- *Pottery Ceramic Design Studio workshop on site*
- *Art deco attractions*
- *36 wineries within 30 min.*

We have a luxurious self-contained apartment, also spacious queen and twin accommodation with adjoining lounge and bathroom. All have tea and coffee making facilities. Enjoy a continental or fully cooked breakfast. Ideally

situated for a Hawke's Bay getaway holiday, we are 5 min. from the airport, and 10 min. from Napier/Hastings. If needed, we will pick you up from any public transport. Fine and casual dining is available within walking distance. In close proximity are shops, golf course, garden centres and the Mission and Church Road Wineries. As we are both experienced tour guides and 4th generation Napierites, we are more than happy to organise specialized tours and to share our knowledge and love of the Bay. Our Pottery Ceramic Design Studio workshop is on site. Drop in for a chat whilst we are working, we are happy to direct you to all the things to do for a relaxed or busy holiday and help make it a great time for you to remember.

Touch Th' Tide

7 Charles Street, Westshore, Napier
Ph/Fax (06) 835 7280
Mobile 027-222 9321
email: *suggy@xtra.co.nz*

Features & Attractions

- *Absolute beachfront, safe*
- *Off-street parking*
- *Email/laundry facilities*
- *Walk to village/restaurants*
- *Shuttle from airport/bus*
- *Central to tourist amenities*

Absolute Beachfront Bed & Breakfast

Double	$140
Single	$95
Child	

Welcome to our home, a quiet and gracious place with fine Kiwi hospitality and quality comfort. Watch the waves, the yachts, the distant port, people fishing or meandering along the reserve. Swim, then after a relaxed 'top of the morning' breakfast on the terrace soaking in the view, your hosts can help plan your day. Take a stroll along the walkways, visit the historic village of Ahuriri, which has excellent cafés and watersport facilities. Drive ten minutes to the world renowned Art Deco city, its Ocean Spa and beautiful shops. Visit the Gannet Colony, the wineries, or play golf. We are a well travelled, recently retired pharmacist and registered nurse who have lived locally for many years. We share our home with you. It includes lounge, dining room, and kitchen (for tea making). We endeavour to repay some of the wonderful hospitality we have experienced ourselves. We welcome you.

Bedrooms	Qty
Double	2
Twin	
Single	
Bed Size	**Qty**
King	
Queen	2
Double	
Single	2
Bathrooms	**Qty**
Ensuite	
Private	1
Guest Share	1

"279" Church Road

279 Church Road, Taradale, Napier
Ph (06) 844 7814
Mobile 021- 447 814
email: *sandy.279@homestaynapier.co.nz*
www.homestaynapier.co.nz

Features & Attractions

- *Quality accommodation*
- *Superb hospitality*
- *Dinner by arrangement*
- *Adjacent to wineries & restaurants*
- *Golf courses & Art Deco nearby*
- *Internet, fax, laundry available*

Quality Homestay Bed & Breakfast

Double	$120-150
Single	$90
Child	

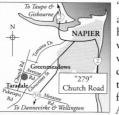

To Taupo & Gisbourne
N
NAPIER
Tamatea Dr
Church Rd
Avenue
Greenmeadows
Gloucester St
Taradale
Puketapu Rd
Meeanee Rd
"279" Church Road
To Dannevirke & Wellington

DIRECTIONS:
From Greenmeadows shops take Avenue Road to Church Road. Turn left.

"279", an elegant spacious home set in ¾ acre of gardens and trees, offers New Zealand and overseas visitors a peaceful haven to unwind from travelling or exploring the region's wineries, architecture etc. Bedrooms are located upstairs, while living areas, including lounge and games room, are downstairs. Breakfast, continental or full, is served at a time to suit you and nearby restaurants offer a variety of cuisine for evening dining.

As your host, I delight in offering relaxed and friendly hospitality, and strive to make your stay a memorable experience – my visitors book is a testament to this. I look forward to welcoming you to "279" and helping to make your stay in Hawke's Bay the highlight of your travels.

Bedrooms	Qty
Double	1
Twin	1
Single	
Bed Size	**Qty**
King	
Queen	1
Double	1
Single	1
Bathrooms	**Qty**
Ensuite	
Private	
Guest Share	1

ASHCROFT GARDEN HOMESTAY
51 Jervois Road, Taradale, Napier
Ph (06) 844 9446, Fax (06) 844 4221
Mobile 027-441 5740
email: *croft@paradise.net.nz*
www.geocities.com/ashcroft_homestay

Tariff : N.Z. Dollars	
Double	$100-130
Single	$85
Child	neg

Bedrooms	Qty
Double	3
Twin	
Single	

Bed Size	Qty
Super King	1
King	1
Queen	1
Double	
Single	2

Bathrooms	Qty
Ensuite	2
Private	
Family Share	1

Homestay
Bed & Breakfast

Features & Attractions

- *Delightful semi rural setting*
- *Halfway Napier - Hastings*
- *Restaurants, golf courses nearby*
- *Minutes from wineries & shops*
- *Friendly atmosphere*
- *Large swimming pool*
- *Two cats - Sugar & Spice*
- *Peaceful garden setting*

Our home is in a semi-rural setting. We offer our guests warm hospitality combined with relaxed and comfortable accommodation. Breakfasts at our home are prepared in a relaxed, informal atmosphere and feature fresh, local organic fruits, cereals or full cooked breakfast, if required. Our large family room, which opens onto its own patio and garden, has a king bed, two single king beds plus ensuite and coffee making facilities. The pool room with super king bed, ensuite and coffee making facilities, offers privacy and relaxation in the garden by the pool or under the trees. Sally's passion for gardening, combined with her experience in garden centres, has led to the creation of a garden retreat which features a wide variety of tropical, succulent and other plants. We have two delightful, friendly cats, Sugar and Spice, who may greet you.

Hawke Bay

Napier

Ashcroft Gardens

Expressway to Hastings

Jervois Rd

Meeanee Rd

To Hastings

Meeanee

To Hastings

N

DIRECTIONS: From Airport travel on expressway from Hastings. At Taradale/ Meeanee Rd intersection turn left then 1st left into Jervois Road. From south follow expressway north to Taradale/ Meeanee Rd intersection turn right into Meeanee Rd then 1st left into Jervois Rd.

GREENSWOOD ON THE PARK

395 Westminster Ave, Greenmeadows, Napier
Ph (06) 844 5354, Fax (06) 844 5354
Mobile 027-420 9663
email: *ejskud@xtra.co.nz*

Features & Attractions

- *Warm, friendly welcome*
- *Quality accommodation*
- *Full cooked breakfast*
- *Wineries and golf nearby*
- *Handy to Taradale shops*
- *Large heated pool*

Bed & Breakfast Homestay

Double	$100-130
Single	$75-80
Child	

We are situated only minutes from Napier's CBD, New Zealand's Art Deco City and central to the Hawke's Bay Wine Country, where wining and dining is popular. **Greenswood on the Park**, as the name suggests, is in a unique setting, opposite Anderson Park, a haven for passive recreation. Our tranquil garden offers privacy and relaxation along with our heated swimming pool to unwind in. A guest lounge is available. It is our pleasure to make your stay as happy and comfortable as possible. We offer a cooked breakfast with an informative chat to help you plan your day. We extend a warm and friendly welcome to all our guests and offer comfortable accommodation with tea-making facilities in all rooms.

DIRECTIONS: From Napier travel along Kennedy Road to Greenmeadows, at traffic lights turn right into York Avenue. Westm. Ave is 3rd road on left.

Bedrooms	Qty
Double	2
Twin	1
Single	
Bed Size	Qty
King	
Queen	2
Double	
Single	2
Bathrooms	Qty
Ensuite	1
Private	
Guest Share	1

OMARUNUI HOMESTAY

69 Omarunui Road, Waiohiki, Napier
Ph (06) 844 9396, Fax (06) 844 9396
Mobile 021-071 0159
email: *kate.ladson@slingshot.co.nz*

Features & Attractions

- *Quiet, peaceful location*
- *Private entrance & patio*
- *Laundry, email available*
- *Wineries & golf courses nearby*
- *Centrally heated in winter*
- *Tea, coffee making facilities*

Quality Bed & Breakfast With Panoramic Views

Double	$150
Single	$130
Child	

Our traditional New Zealand homestead, which we share with our two friendly cats, Sooty and Tiddles, stands in an acre of secluded gardens overlooking vineyards, the Tutaekuri River and, in the distance, the Kaweka range of mountains. We are centrally located between the lovely Art Deco city of Napier and Hastings, with Taradale shops and restaurants only 5 minutes away.

We love meeting new people and enjoy travel, golf, good food and good company. We invite you to start your day with a delicious cooked or continental breakfast before exploring the many attractions of Hawke's Bay. Come home to relax before joining us on the deck in the evening sun for a glass of wine.

A visit to one of the many fine restaurants in the area will complete your day in this lovely part of New Zealand.

Bedrooms	Qty
Double/Twin	1
Twin	
Single	
Bed Size	Qty
Super King/Twin	1
Queen	
Double	
Single	
Bathrooms	Qty
Ensuite	1
Private	
Guest Share	

WAIWHENUA FARMSTAY

808 River Road, RD 9, Hastings
Ph (06) 874 2435, Fax (06) 874 2465
Mobile 027-479 4094
email: *info@waiwhenua.co.nz*
www.waiwhenua.co.nz

Tariff : N.Z. Dollars	
Double	$120-150
Single	$60-100
Child	$50

Bedrooms	Qty
Double	2
Twin	2
Single	

Bed Size	Qty
Super King	
King	1
Queen	
Double	1
Single	3

Bathrooms	Qty
Ensuite	
Private	1
Family Share	1

Unique Farmstay

Please phone for easy directions.
Advance booking recomended

Features & Attractions

* *Extensive sheep, beef & deer farm*
* *Families & children welcome*
* *Historic homestead & cottage*
* *Relaxing swimming pool*

* *Trout fishing onsite*
* *Informative farm tours*
* *Fresh farm-style meals*
* *Bush and farm walks*

The perfect place to experience a genuine farmstay and friendly rural hospitality at our 120 year old historic homestead. Come and join us on our extensive 440 ha sheep, beef and deer farm. Enjoy guided tours and farm activities, fish in our trout-filled river, or just relax with a book on our cool verandahs or in our garden. Our home and family offer guests a friendly environment, catering for individuals or families interested in the outdoor life. (Two night stay recommended.) Enjoy specialty farm-cooked meals of homegrown beef, lamb or venison, complimented with fresh garden vegetables and fruit. Enrich your stay by including other outdoor activities at our backdoor; hunting, fishing, bush and farm walks, garden tours, jet boating and extensive mountain hikes, plus many attractions in the greater sunny Hawkes Bay area.

 "Annie's Cottage" - For those seeking total privacy and a longer stay at Waiwhenua. Our recently renovated, fully self-contained, cosy, three bedroom rural retreat awaits visitors.
Sleeps six people at $150-$200 per night.

WHINFIELD

615 Puketapu Road, RD 3, Taradale, Napier
Ph (06) 844 8623, Fax (06) 844 8623
email: *whinfield@xtra.co.nz*

Features & Attractions

- *Art, craft & wine trails*
- *Art deco attractions*
- *Gannet safari & fishing*
- *2 self-contained ensuite rooms*
- *Peaceful lifestyle*
- *Outdoor chess board*

To Taupo

Whinfield

Napier

Puketapu Rd

Taradale

N

To Wellington

DIRECTIONS: Take Puketapu Rd at roundabout in Taradale - Whinfield is 6.15 km on left.

Countrystay Bed & Breakfast

Double	$130
Single	$85
Child	

Whinfield is a comfortable country home with spectacular river views. Our new accommodation is in a separate cottage in the garden and offers two ensuite bedrooms opening onto a large sunny verandah. Enjoy breakfast on the terrace of the main house and then have a game of chess on the outdoor board or stroll down to the river to swim or fish. There are excellent shops and restaurants just 5 minutes away in Taradale, an excellent golf course, or the art deco attractions of Napier just 20 minutes away. We are retired farmers grazing a few cattle and our many visitors enjoy the peace and quiet of the countryside while being within easy reach of the attractions of Hawkes Bay.

Bedrooms	Qty
Double	1
Twin	2
Single	1
Bed Size	**Qty**
Super King	1
King Single	1
Queen	
Single	4
Bathrooms	**Qty**
Ensuite	2
Private	
Guest Share	2

THE LOFT HOMESTAY

10 Woodford Heights, Havelock North
Ph (06) 877 5938
Mobile 021-474 729
www.hawkesbayhomestay.co.nz

Features & Attractions

- *Refreshments on arrival*
- *Fax, e-mail,*
- *Tea making & TV in Queen Room*
- *Non smoking*
- *Superb views*
- *Great breakfasts*

 Premium Homestay Bed & Breakfast

Double	$120-230
Single	$120
Child	

Come and be pampered in our little piece of paradise. Enjoy your comfortable room(s) in the guest wing - Queen or King bed, TV, spa bath, sitting room with TV and own entry. Complimentary refreshments on arrival, sumptuous breakfasts; dinner by request in romantic setting. John is a full time artist, specialising in New Zealand themes, he has a house studio to visit. Use our intimate courtyard or deck at your leisure. Just minutes to the picturesque village of Havelock North with cafes, restaurants, and boutique shopping. We are central to the many world renowned local wineries - Craggy Range, Te Mata Estate, Black Barn to name but a few; Cape Kidnappers with one of the largest mainland gannet colonies in the world. There is so much to see in Hawke's Bay, which makes **The Loft Homestay Bed & Breakfast** the perfect base in which to explore. Tour bookings available.

Bedrooms	Qty
Double	2
Twin	
Single	
Bed Size	**Qty**
King	1
Queen	1
Double	
Single	
Bathrooms	**Qty**
Ensuite	1
Private	1
Guest Share	

OPTIONS

92 Simla Avenue, Havelock North, Hawke's Bay
Ph (06) 877 0257, Fax (06) 877 0257
Mobile 027-653 7270
email: *gr.duff@xtra.co.nz*

Tariff : N.Z. Dollars	
Double	$125
Single	$100
Child	neg

Bedrooms	Qty
Double	2
Twin	1
Single	

Bed Size	Qty
Super King	
King	1
Queen	1
Double	
Single	2

Bathrooms	Qty
Ensuite	1
Private	1
Guest Share	

**Bed & Breakfast
Homestay**

DIRECTIONS:
OPTIONS is easy to find.
Please ring for directions.
Advance booking recommended

Features & Attractions

- *Wine, gannets & Art Deco -*
  all within 30minutes
- *Near Te Mata Peak – views*
- *Internet with wireless connection*
- *Swimming pool & spa*
- *Laundry facilities*
- *Mini petanque court*
- *Private patios*

OPTIONS is halfway between the centre of Havelock North village and Te Mata Peak which at 399 metres is the best place to start sightseeing in Hawkes Bay. The wineries, Cape Kidnappers with the gannets, and Napier with its Art Deco buildings are all within thirty minutes of **OPTIONS**.

OPTIONS offers friendly hospitality and guests are accommodated within our home in either a large double bedroom with king-size bed and ensuite, or a suite with a double room with queen-size bed, a twin room, a private bathroom and separate lounge. The internet is available to guests and all rooms have wireless connection.

In its elevated position, **OPTIONS** has lovely views and with the private patios there is a choice of sun or shade. The pool, heated to extend the summer season, and spa offer respite after a day's sightseeing. During winter the fire is welcoming.

A delicious breakfast of your choice is served inside or outside depending on the weather. In the village there is a range of restaurants available. Sharing an evening meal with us, at an additional cost, is a great way to learn about our area.

THE BROW

190 Argyll East Road, RD 3, Waipawa, Hawkes Bay
Ph (06) 857 5117, Fax (06) 857 5117
Mobile 027-249 6175
e-mail: *thebrow@xtra.co.nz*

Features & Attractions

- *Winery and farm tours can be arranged*
- *Separate private cottage*
- *Trout fishing*
- *Peace & tranquility*
- *Delicious home-cooked meals*

Countrystay & Homestay
Dinner & Breakfast included

Double	$180
Single	$90
Child	

DIRECTIONS:
From Hastings Waipawa, right at BP station into Ruataniwha Street, onto Tikokino Rd. After approx. 11km right into Argyll East Rd. Travel 2km, go over bridge, sign on our gate on right.

Our farm, **The Brow**, is a well known Hawkes Bay property. We are handy to a great variety of the wonderful tourist attractions that Hawkes Bay has to offer. We have a private, small semi self-contained cottage with tea and coffee making facilities.

Our large menagerie of farm animals include Rosie, the cairn terrier, Annie, Abbie and Ruby the labradors, cats, hens, and pet lambs in the spring. Enjoy real farm experiences as well as trout fishing in our local river, and we can organise winery tours with our local operators. Take time to unwind in our special and peaceful part of the world and finish the day off with a delicious home-cooked evening meal, using only the freshest of Hawkes Bay produce and our home-grown beef and lamb. Please book ahead to avoid disappointment. Tariff includes an evening meal and a cooked breakfast.

Bedrooms	Qty
Double	2
Twin	
Single	
Bed Size	**Qty**
King	
Queen	2
Double	
Single	
Bathrooms	**Qty**
Ensuite	
Guest Share	1
Family share	1

OTAWA LODGE

132 Otawhao Road, Kumeroa, RD 1, Woodville
Ph (06) 376 4603
Mobile 027-230 1327
email: *rest@otawalodge.co.nz*
www.otawalodge.co.nz

Features & Attractions

- *Gourmet four course dinner*
- *Te Apiti windfarm visits*
- *Fishing & Hunting*
- *Woodville antique shopping*
- *Hill & native bush walks*
- *Gottfried Lindauer studio*

Historic Country Lodge

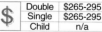

Double	$265-295
Single	$265-295
Child	n/a

DIRECTIONS:
Please phone for easy directions.

Rest, relax, rejuvenate in our magnificent 1914 historic homestead and garden, nestled in 70 acres of rolling hills a short drive from Woodville. Be enchanted by the Edwardian elegance of wood panelling, stained glass windows, unique Art Nouveau plasterwork and authentic period furniture. Take a walk in the mature gardens, or wander through the walnut grove to the stream accompanied by native birds. Unwind in the privacy of the spacious guest sitting room, or the sunny octagonal library. Dine on the award winning four course dinner, featuring fish and organic cuisine, with a selected wine list. Be warmed by the hot water radiators, which ensure comfort in all seasons. At the end of the day sleep peacefully in one of two luxurious bedrooms, each with its own private bathroom. In the morning arise refreshed to birdsong and a hearty breakfast. Above all indulge yourself in historic opulence and friendly service.

Bedrooms	Qty
Double	2
Twin	
Single	
Bed Size	**Qty**
King	1
Queen	1
Double	
King/Single	2
Bathrooms	**Qty**
Ensuite	
Private	2
Guest Share	

ABBOTSFORD OAKS

85 Abbotsford Road, PO Box 37, Waipawa, Hawke's Bay
Ph (06) 857 8960, Fax (06) 857 8961
Mobile 025-296 1160
email: *nicolette@abbotsfordoaks.co.nz*
www.abbotsfordoaks.co.nz

Tariff : N.Z. Dollars	
Double	$170-325
Single	$140-290
Child	

Bedrooms	Qty
Double	4
Twin	
Single	

Bed Size	Qty
Super King	
King	1
Queen	3
Double	
Single	

Bathrooms	Qty
Ensuite	1
Private	3
Guest Share	

 **Boutique Accommodation
Bed & Breakfast**

Features & Attractions

- *Luxurious spacious rooms*
- *Park-like grounds*
- *Golf & fishing close by*
- *Email & fax facilities*
- *Friendly hospitality*
- *Ample parking*
- *Dutch spoken*
- *Dinner available*

Nicolette and Chris warmly welcome you to **Abbotsford Oaks**. Nestled in picturesque central Hawke's Bay and surrounded by 3.5 acres of gardens, **Abbotsford Oaks** offers a relaxing and special venue for those wanting a break from their busy lifestyle. It is an ideal base to explore the many attractions Hawke's Bay has to offer. Beaches, wineries and art deco/spanish mission architecture are only thirty minutes away. Golf courses and trout fishing are close by.

Our property was purpose built as a children's home in the 1920s and has been renovated to provide quality Boutique Bed & Breakfast accommodation. It has spacious rooms most with their own sitting/sun room and private bathroom, with wonderful views of the grounds and countryside. Breakfast, either cooked or continental, can be served in the dining room, the garden or your private lounge. Dinner is available by arrangement. Visit our web site for more details.

ASHLEY PARK

SH 3, PO Box 36, Waitotara 5180, South Taranaki
Ph (06) 346 5917, Fax (06) 346 5861
email: *ashley_park@xtra.co.nz*
www.ashleypark.co.nz

Features & Attractions

- *Peaceful country setting*
- *Pet farm animals & aviaries*
- *Park, lake & farm walks*
- *Antique and tea-shop*
- *Swimming pool*
- *Tennis and mini golf*

Farmstay Bed & Breakfast and Self-contained Chalets

Double	$90-130
Single	$80
Child	

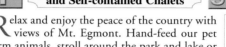
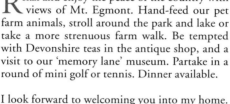

Relax and enjoy the peace of the country with views of Mt. Egmont. Hand-feed our pet farm animals, stroll around the park and lake or take a more strenuous farm walk. Be tempted with Devonshire teas in the antique shop, and a visit to our 'memory lane' museum. Partake in a round of mini golf or tennis. Dinner available.

I look forward to welcoming you into my home.

Guests comment – *"Feels like we belong here, very welcoming and friendly".*

Bedrooms	Qty
Double	1
Twin	2
Single	
Bed Size	Qty
King	
Queen	1
Double	
Single	4
Bathrooms	Qty
Ensuite	1
Private	
Guest Share	1

ARLES BED & BREAKFAST

50 Riverbank Road, SH4, Wanganui
Ph (06) 343 6557, Fax (06) 343 6557
Mobile 021-257 8257, Skype sueday1234
email: *sue@arles.co.nz*
www.arles.co.nz

Features & Attractions

- *Sumptuous full breakfast*
- *Tea/coffee in rooms*
- *Toiletries and fresh flowers*
- *Central heating*
- *Broadband/wireless/skype*
- *Salt water pool and BBQ*

Historic Bed & Breakfast and Modern Apartment

Double	$140-180
Single	$120-140
Child	$30-35

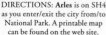

At **Arles** you will find affordable luxury. Every need is taken care of, from rooms with comfortable beds, tea/coffee facilities, toiletries and fresh flowers to complimentary internet, kitchen and laundry facilities. Breakfast features homemade breads and jams, fresh fruit and a full cooked breakfast option. **Arles**, built in the late 1880's, is the first accommodation house as you reach Wanganui from the north on SH4. It features an original kauri staircase and rimu-panelled lounge. The spacious grounds, adjacent to the Whanganui River, feature the southernmost Queensland Kauri. The guest lounge has a piano, organ, TV/CD/DVD and complimentary wine. The library is well-stocked with books, board games and jigsaw puzzles, and a computer with internet facilities. **Arles** offers spacious double rooms, a two bedroom suite, plenty of off-road parking and two acres of lawns and gardens to relax in. Stay 3 nights or more and receive a discount.

DIRECTIONS: **Arles** is on SH4 as you enter/exit the city from/to National Park. A printable map can be found on the web site.

Bedrooms	Qty
Double	4
Twin	2
Single	
Bed Size	Qty
King	1
Queen	2
Double	1
Single	4
Bathrooms	Qty
Ensuite	2
Private	2
Guest Share	

KEMBALI

26 Taranaki Street, Wanganui
Phone (06) 347 1727
Mobile 027-244 4347
email: *wespalmer@xtra.co.nz*

Features & Attractions

- *Exclusive - one party only*
- *Central, quiet and friendly*
- *Overlooks wetlands - trees*
- *Guest lounge with tea/coffee*
- *Cooked breakfast*
- *Off-street parking*

$	Double	$100-115
	Single	$70-85
	Child	n/a

Bed & Breakfast Homestay

Bedrooms	Qty
Double	1
Twin	1
Single	
Bed Size	Qty
King	
Queen	1
Double	
Single	2
Bathrooms	Qty
Ensuite	
Private	1
Guest Share	

Welcome to **Kembali**, our modern, centrally heated home. As we take only one group/party at a time, the sunny guest lounge, bedrooms and bathroom are for your exclusive use. These upstairs rooms overlook trees and wetlands, where native birds roam. The lounge has television, refrigerator, tea and coffee making facilities. We are semi-retired, our children married, and we offer a relaxing, peaceful stay. We enjoy people, gardens, books, travel and have Christian interests. Five minutes drive will take you to a variety of restaurants, shops, art and craft, and walks. Historic Wanganui with its river is a lovely place to visit. Our tariff includes a cooked/continental breakfast and laundry facilities are available. We look forward to meeting you.

MISTY VALLEY FARMSTAY

97 Parihauhau Rd, Wanganui
Ph (06) 342 5767
email: *linda.garry.wadsworth@xtra.co.nz*

Features & Attractions

- *Quiet, rural location*
- *Large country garden*
- *Families welcome*
- *Near Whanganui River Park*
- *Short drive to Wanganui*
- *Dinner by arrangement*

$	Double	$100
	Single	$60
	Child	$20-30

Farmstay Self-contained

Bedrooms	Qty
Double	2
Twin	1
Single	
Bed Size	Qty
King	
Queen	
Double	2
Single	2
Bathrooms	Qty
Ensuite	
Private	
Guest Share	1

Misty Valley is an organic farm of nine hectares, set in the picturesque Parihauhau Valley. We are twenty five kilometres north of the historic river city of Wanganui, on State Highway 4, and fifteen minutes from the Whanganui River National Park turn-off. We have people-friendly farm animals for you to meet, including our Brittany dogs and two cats. All our animals live outside year round. Children visit the farm regularly and yours will be made very welcome. We are non-smoking, but offer pleasant deck areas for those who do. Start your day with our hearty farm breakfast before exploring Wanganui, the surrounding area and famous River Park. We can help you make the best of your time with us. In the evenings we can prepare a three-course dinner for you (by arrangement), using our own produce when possible. Alternatively you can prepare your own in the kitchen facilities available.

ANNDION LODGE

143 Anzac Parade, Wanganui
Ph (06) 343 3593, Fax (06) 343 3056
email: *info@anndionlodge.co.nz*
www.anndionlodge.co.nz

Tariff : N.Z. Dollars	
Double	$80-140
Single	$65-90
Child	

Bedrooms	Qty
Double	7
Twin	3
Single	2
Bed Size	**Qty**
Super King	1
King	
Queen	2
Double	5
Single	9
Bathrooms	**Qty**
Ensuite	2
Private	
Guest Share	4

**Bed & Breakfast
Guest House/Inn**

Features & Attractions

- *Opposite river walking track*
- *Laundry facilities*
- *Licensed mini bar*
- *Scooter hire*
- *Sunny balcony overlooking river*
- *Free high speed & wireless internet*
- *Physiotherm infrared sauna*
- *Salt-water swimming pool & spa*

Stunning river views and a warm welcome await you at the **Anndion Lodge.** Located on the banks of the Whanganui River offering affordable yet superior accommodation for business or pleasure, ranging from an elegant superking with large ensuite through to a tasteful bunkroom with guest share facilities, just a short drive from the city centre with 12 rooms and able to accommodate 27 guests. Facilities including a salt-water swimming pool and steaming outdoor spa, an infrared sauna and covered BBQ courtyard, a fully equipped self-catering kitchen, 3 lounge areas, a DVD/Video library and cosy gas log fire, computers with free high speed and wireless internet, guest laundry, courtesy vehicle, secure motor cycle garaging and scooter hire are all available to guests staying at the Lodge. Hosts Anne and Dion offer genuine Kiwi hospitality in a home away from home environment. "Unusually luxurious, it feels more like a small hotel" (Rough Guides). "It's pricier than your average hostel, but thoroughly worth it" (Lonely Planet).

ROTHESAY

10 Bruce Street, Hunterville
Ph (06) 322 8122
email: *d-r.mcnie@xtra.co.nz*
www.rothesaybnb.co.nz

Tariff : N.Z. Dollars	
Double	$110-150
Single	$90
Child	neg

Bedrooms	Qty
Double	3
Twin	1
Single	

Bed Size	Qty
Super King	
King	
Queen	3
Double	1
Single	1

Bathrooms	Qty
Ensuite	2
Private	
Guest Share	1

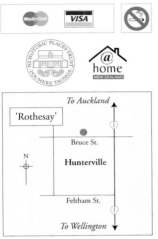

  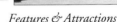

**Historic
Bed & Breakfast**

Features & Attractions

- *Golf courses*
- *Trout fishing*
- *Skiing*
- *Bungy jumping*
- *Jet boating, river rafting*
- *Antique and craft shops*
- *Historic restored Post Office*
- *Dinner by arrangement*

Rothesay, previously the Hunterville Post Office, was built in 1903. A heritage building, listed with the Historic Places Trust Category One. This lovely old building, close to State Highway One, has been tastefully renovated and converted to superior guest accommodation on the first floor with large comfortable bedrooms and separate guest lounge. Our garden with stream is a perfect place to relax in after a day of travel.

Your hosts Robyn and Duncan welcome you and invite you to experience the ambience of a bygone era. The atmosphere at **Rothesay** is friendly, relaxed and informal. A hearty breakfast is included and dinner is provided by arrangement. Hunterville is centrally located in the lower North Island, close to the ski fields and is a convenient two hour drive from Taupo and Wellington, making it an ideal stopover for the inter-island ferry. The Rangitikei district offers stunning scenery, many attractive gardens to visit as well as numerous other activities throughout the area.

@ RIVERHILLS
41 Dittmer Drive, Palmerston North
Ph (06) 356 7045, Fax (06) 356 7214
e-mail: *info@riverhills.biz*
www.riverhills.biz

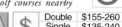

Features & Attractions

- *Quiet suburban street*
- *Located on riverbank*
- *5 minutes from City*
- *Private & peaceful*
- *Guest only office*
- *Golf courses nearby*

Boutique Accommodation Bed & Breakfast	$	Double	$155-260
		Single	$135-240
		Child	N/A

Spectacular views of the Tararua Mountain Ranges and the Manawatu River. Luxury Bed & Breakfast accommodation and traditional Manawatu hospitality. Take advantage of the diverse range of dining establishments in the city. Located close to the city centre, Massey University, International Pacific College, Dairy Research Institute, Rose Gardens, Rugby Museum and sports facilities. Riverbank Path is an easy five min. walk to the Botanical Gardens. Enjoy facilities that come standard: Free Broadband, spacious guest only lounge with welcoming open fire, hot tub, gym, 8ft TV or DVD screen. Play the piano, chess or a jigsaw puzzle. Enjoy the 8 golf courses within an hour of the city. Cycle – there is an 8 km track just outside the front door.

Bedrooms	Qty
Double	3
Twin	
Single	
Bed Size	**Qty**
King	
Queen	3
Double	
Single	
Bathrooms	**Qty**
Ensuite	2
Private	1
Guest Share	

LARKHALL
42 The Strand, Palmerston North
Ph (06) 353 3749, Fax (06) 353 3748
Mobile 0274-416 890
email: *jlwhitelock@inspire.net.nz*

Features & Attractions

- *First class accommodation*
- *Quiet, peaceful location*
- *Indoor heated pool*
- *Private luxury facilities*
- *Outstanding views*
- *Close to City and University*

Luxury Accommodation Homestay Bed & Breakfast	$	Double	$200-250
		Single	$175
		Child	

A stunning, newly created up-market home with picturesque views of Palmerston North City and the Manawatu region. Your hosts, John and Lyndall, have a wealth of local knowledge and international experience. They can assist and direct you to a wide selection of sights and activities. Palmerston North, apart from local attractions, is on the central pathway leading to Wellington. Palmerston North is a centre of major agricultural, educational (Massey University and International Pacific College), business and sporting (Adidas Rugby Academy and museum) activities and interests. Palmerston North Airport offers domestic and international services. John and Lyndall invite you to enjoy the scenery and native dell as you take in the views from the patio. A warm welcome awaits you.

Bedrooms	Qty
Double	1
Twin	1
Single	
Bed Size	**Qty**
King	1
Queen	
Double	
King Single	1
Bathrooms	**Qty**
Ensuite	2
Private	2
Guest Share	

SERENDIPITY BED & BREAKFAST

86 MacArthur St, Levin
Ph (06) 368 6766, Fax (06) 368 6764
Mobile 027-413 1504
email: *relax@serendipitynz.co.nz*
www.serendipitynz.co.nz

Tariff : N.Z. Dollars	
Double	$125
Single	$125
Extra pp	$30

Bedrooms	Qty
Double	2
Twin	
Single	

Bed Size	Qty
Super King	1
King	
Queen	1
Double	
Single	

Bathrooms	Qty
Ensuite	1
Private	1
Guest Share	

Bed & Breakfast
Homestay

Features & Attractions

- *Superb uncrowded beaches*
- *River rafting, horse riding*
- *Vintage cars, museums, gardens*
- *Birdlife and sanctuaries*
- *Public indoor swimming pool*
- *Golf courses, mountain biking*
- *Arts and crafts*
- *Great range of restaurants*

Experience Kiwi heartland hospitality on the Nature Coast – stop, relax and take your time. Chris and Barbara invite you to unwind at **Serendipity** – in a quiet corner of town. A pleasant 30-minute walk, or 5 minute drive from the centre – close to the theatre and restaurants. The Nature Coast is ideally located to explore the lower North Island. 1½ hours to Wellington, 40 minutes to Palmerston North, 3 hours to the Hawkes Bay or Taranaki. Discover the pleasures of the Nature Coast – take your time to enjoy the fine foods, produced in the 'market garden' of New Zealand, the talented local artisans and craftspeople. Historic Otaki, the Foxton Windmill and museums, the Manawatu Estuary and Lake Papaitonga for birdlife, are all within a ½ hour drive.

Visit the unspoiled beaches, enjoy the fantastic sunsets, picnic by rivers, tramp in the Tararua Ranges, go white-water rafting or take a 4X4 motorcycle excursion. With prior notice we can arrange permits and passage to Kapiti Island. A world-class vintage car museum and several golf courses are all within easy distance.

FANTAILS ACCOMMODATION
40 MacArthur Street, Levin,
Ph (06) 368 9011, Fax (06) 368 9279
email: *fantails@xtra.co.nz*

www.fantails.co.nz

Features & Attractions
- Golf courses, mountain biking
- Vintage cars, museums,
- Doll gallery, balloon rides
- 'De Molen' working mill
- Wetlands/Kapiti Is. bird tours
- River rafting, horse riding

Self-contained Cottages / Bed & Breakfast

Double	$125-150
Single	$100-125
Child	neg

'Looking for something a little different?'
Well, **Fantails** offers much more than Accommodation.
(a) Two acres of themed gardens.
(b) Bird life amazing.
(c) Organic food - specialty breakfasts (home cooking).
(d) Lovely self-contained cottages and B&B in a totally relaxing environment.
(e) Comfortable beds. Simply the best value say returning guests.
(f) Security. Plenty of parking.
(g) Golf putting area and pitching/swing nets.
(h) Internet access.
We look forward to your visit and will give you a memory to last a lifetime.

DIRECTIONS: Please phone for easy directions

Bedrooms	Qty
Double	5
Twin	1
Single	
Bed Size	**Qty**
King	2
Queen	3
Double	
Single	2
Bathrooms	**Qty**
Ensuite	3
Private	
Family Share	1

DRIFTWOOD
71 Rodney Avenue, Te Horo, Otaki RD
Ph (06) 364 2169, Fax (06) 364 2269
Mobile 027-497 8007
e-mail: *mnscott@xtra.co.nz*

Features & Attractions
- Comfortable & modern
- Views of Kapiti Island
- Absolute beach front
- Beach & bush walks, hot spa
- Outlet & markets at Otaki
- Cafés, arts & crafts

Bed & Breakfast / Homestay

Double	$160-185
Single	$150
Child	

Welcome to **Driftwood** your modern luxury Bed & Breakfast accommodation situated halfway between Wellington and Palmerston North. Built on the iconic Te Horo beachfront, **Driftwood** enjoys panoramic views of Kapiti Island, west to the Wanganui coastline and east to the Tararua Ranges. Enjoy a walk along the beach, relax in the hot spa and fall asleep to the sound of the sea – then it's time for a delicious breakfast! The house is spacious and well appointed, the guest lounge, dining and music room inviting you to relax and enjoy the company of the two resident felines, Honey and Minka. Te Horo is still a quiet community, but situated close to the cafes and shopping centres of Otaki, Waikanae and Paraparaumu. We love the place and know that you will too!

Bedrooms	Qty
Double	1
Twin	1
Single	
Bed Size	**Qty**
King	1
Queen	
Double	
King/Single	2
Bathrooms	**Qty**
Ensuite	1
Private	1
Guest Share	

COUNTRY PATCH

18 Kea Street, Waikanae
Ph (04) 293 5165, Fax (04) 293 5164
Mobile 027-296 3716
email: *stay@countrypatch.co.nz*
www.countrypatch.co.nz

Tariff : N.Z. Dollars	
Double	$150-220
Single	
Child	$20-25

Bedrooms	Qty
Double	3
Twin	1
Single	

Bed Size	Qty
Super King/Twin	2
King	
Queen	1
Double	
Single	2

Bathrooms	Qty
Ensuite	3
Private	
Guest Share	

Self-contained Bed & Breakfast

Features & Attractions

- *Delightful country style*
- *Magnificent views*
- *Cosy and comfortable*
- *Good restaurants close by*
- *2 minutes drive from SH 1*
- *Wellington commuter train 7 min*
- *Villa has large verandah and wheelchair access*

It's the little extras... that keep guests staying an extra night. Our visitor book glows with appreciative accolades. Two delightful self-contained accommodation sites...

Country Patch Studio, with its own entrance and deck, has a queen bed with ensuite and twin beds on the mezzanine floor of the kitchen-lounge.

Country Patch Villa has an open fire and large verandah with magical views. It is wheelchair accessible and the two bedrooms, each with ensuite, have super-king beds that can unzip to make twins.

Set on 2½ acres in the Waikanae foothills with breathtaking views over the Kapiti Coast and historic Kapiti Island, the property is handy to Wellington and the Manawatu. Bush walks can be enjoyed from over the back fence.

Hosts Brian and Sue display an infectious hospitality. **A treat you can't beat!**

241

AWATEA LODGE

19 Hadfield Rd, Peka Peka, RD 1, Waikanae
Ph (04) 293 2404, Mobile 027-2427572
email: *brent@awatealodge.co.nz*
www.awatealodge.co.nz

Tariff : N.Z. Dollars	
Double	$120-150
Single	$90-100
Child	

Bedrooms	Qty
Double	1
Twin	1
Single	

Bed Size	Qty
Super King	
King	
Queen	1
Double	
Single	2

Bathrooms	Qty
Ensuite	
Private	1
Guest Share	

A Relaxing Farmstay/Homestay Bed & Breakfast

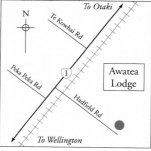

Features & Attractions

- *Restful, friendly atmosphere*
- *Panoramic views/sunsets*
- *Private spa pool*
- *Gourmet breakfast*
- *Bush or beach walks*
- *Great local restaurants*
- *Spinning/weaving studio*
- *45 min. to Wellington*

We welcome you! Take time to relax and enjoy eight acres of garden and beautiful natural surroundings. Unwind in the hammock on the deck, or walk around the farm and meet the friendly alpacas and llamas.

A spectacular way to enjoy a beautiful Kapiti Island sunset is to either stroll up the back hill or wander along the beach – or you may just prefer to "chill-out" in the spa pool.

Local eco-tourism includes coastal, river and bush walks, or a special day trip to the Kapiti Island. Other popular attractions include the 'Kapiti Arts Trail', Maori Arts gallery and golf courses.

Our specialty is "slow-food" using where possible our own fresh, organic produce. We can prepare delicious home-made dinners and hampers on request. A cooked or continental breakfast is included in the tariff.

Guests' comments:

"An extremely wonderful and relaxing setting, lovely food, comforts and company". Lower Hutt.

"Our stay here was the highlight of our trip". UK.

HELEN'S WAIKANAE BEACH B&B/HOMESTAY

115 Tutere St, Waikanae Beach, Kapiti Coast
Ph (04) 902 5829, Fax (04) 902 5840
Mobile 021-259 3396
email: *waikanaebeachbandb@paradise.net.nz*
www.waikanaebeachbandb.net

Tariff : N.Z. Dollars	
Double	$110-150
Single	
Child	neg

Bedrooms	Qty
Double	2
Twin	
Single	
Bed Size	**Qty**
Super King	
King	
Queen	2
Double	
Single	1
Bathrooms	**Qty**
Ensuite	1
Private	1
Guest Share	

A Relaxing Seaside Homestay/ Bed & Breakfast

Features & Attractions

- *Warm, friendly hospitality*
- *Dinner by arrangement*
- *Direct beach access*
- *Tea/coffee-making facilities*
- *Awesome sea views & sunsets*
- *Good local restaurants*
- *Tennis courts for hire nearby*
- *Bicycles, racquets available*

Helen's B&B is situated on a long, sandy beach, 55min. drive north of Wellington City on SH1.

With spectacular views of Kapiti Island and all the way to the South Island, this is the perfect location to relax and unwind. At night, from the comfort of your bed, marvel at the beauty of the night sky, and be lulled to sleep by the soothing sounds of the ocean. In the morning, either before or after tucking into a munificent breakfast, enjoy a leisurely walk on the beach.

Why not treat someone special to a weekend stay, dinner included – Helen's speciality! (Offer applies only between 1 June and 30 September.) Visit Helen's website for suggestions of what to do and see on the Kapiti Coast.

– **Guests' comments...** "A wonderful experience - your home truly welcomes 'Guests' that leave as 'Friends' - USA. "5 Star! A very relaxing 2 days" - UK. "Everywhere in NZ is wonderful but this is the best. Unrivalled position and hospitality." - UK. "We loved our stay, very beautiful, and a wonderful welcome." - Hamburg.

DIRECTIONS:
On SH1, travelling north from Wellington, after crossing the Waikanae Bridge, turn left into Te Moana Rd . Follow road down, keep left where road splits. Upon reaching T-intersection at end of the road, turn left into Tutere St.

Reikorangi Country Cottage

154 Akatarawa Road, R.D. Waikanae, Kapiti Coast
Ph (04) 293 5908, Fax (04) 293 5908
Mobile 021- 214 0654
email: *the.country.cottage@xtra.co.nz*

Features & Attractions

- *Peaceful country setting*
- *Veranda BBQ area*
- *Golf & beach shops 7min.*
- *5min/5km from SH1*
- *120 acres of tranquillity*
- *Cooked meals available*

Self-contained Cottage Bed & Breakfast		Double	$120-160
		Single	$90-130
		Child	neg

Bedrooms	Qty
Double	1
Twin	
Single	
Bed Size	**Qty**
King	
Queen	
Double	1
Single	
Bathrooms	**Qty**
Ensuite	
Private	1
Guest Share	

Superb, quiet Countrystay in a newly built self-contained cottage only 5 minutes/5km from Waikanae State Highway 1. The cottage comprises of a kitchen/dining/lounge and bedroom open plan area with a private bathroom and toilet. Outside is a veranda and deck BBQ area. We have 120 acres of farm with river and bush walks on the property as well as sheep, calves, pigs, chooks and a big vegie garden, orchard and berries. Cooked breakfast and evening meals are available in traditional Kiwi style with most ingredients grown on the farm.
Waikanae has many restaurants, shops, golf course and safe beach. Wellington is 50 minutes away. On arrival it's our pleasure to show you around and point out the best day tours to make your stay most enjoyable.

Riverstone

111 Ngatiawa Road, Waikanae, Kapiti Coast
Ph (04) 293 1936, Fax (04) 293 1936
email: *riverstone@paradise.net.nz*

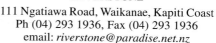

Features & Attractions

- *Rural self-contained*
- *Local dining out*
- *River and bird song*
- *Bush and local walks*
- *Shops, beach, Lindale*
- *Golf and car museum*

Rural Cottage Bed & Breakfast		Double	$100-120
		Single	$70
		Child	$45

Bedrooms	Qty
Double	1
Twin	1
Single	
Bed Size	**Qty**
King	
Queen	1
Double	
Single	2
Bathrooms	**Qty**
Ensuite	
Private	1
Guest Share	

The cottage has self-contained accommodation with bedrooms, bathroom, lounge and kitchenette. Courtyard and barbecue area with views of river and bush. Continental or full breakfast. Paul is an engineer and writer, and Eppie sketches and paints. Laundry facilities. Local café, pottery and birdpark with river walks and you can swim in the river. There are more restaurants in Waikanae village, six minutes drive, and in Paraparaumu, ten minutes towards Wellington. Craft shops and boutiques at Lindale and general shopping at Paraparaumu. Beaches and swimming pools in both centres. The capital city Wellington is forty-five minutes away and has the airport, inter-island ferries, shops, galleries and museums. Internet available.

DIRECTIONS: Turn off SH 1 across railway lines onto Akatarawa Road. At 5km turn left before small church into Ngatiawa Road. 1km to **Riverstone** on left.

OCEAN RETREAT

94 The Esplanade, Raumati South, Paraparaumu
Ph (04) 902 1210, Fax (04) 902 1210
email: *stay@oceanretreat.co.nz*
www.oceanretreat.co.nz

Tariff : N.Z. Dollars	
$150	Double
$135	Single
	Child

Qty	Bedrooms
1	Double
	Twin
	Single

Qty	Bed Size
	Super King
	King
1	Queen
	Double
	Single

Qty	Bathrooms
1	Ensuite
	Private
	Guest Share

**Absolute Beachfront
Bed & Breakfast**

Features & Attractions

- *Ocean/beach/island views*
- *Right on the beachfront*
- *Swim/kayak/bike/walk*
- *QEII Park on doorstep*
- *Lovely sunsets/nightsky*
- *Far infrared sauna*
- *Lots to see, do & enjoy!*
- *2min SH1 45min Wellington*

Take a break at **Ocean Retreat**. Whether travelling, attending a special occasion, or just needing a break away, you will be welcomed here at **Ocean Retreat**. We have a new home right on the beachfront. Sit and relax, enjoy endless ocean views, safe swimming, sandy beaches, or walk to QEII Park. Take the mountain bikes, ride the trails, try out the kayak. You have ocean views from your ensuite bedroom and patio. The comfortable bedroom has a queen bed, TV/DVD/video/CD, tea making facilities and fridge. The far infrared sauna is also available to our guests by appointment. With plenty of wonderful cafés and restaurants nearby you're spoilt for choice. Shop at local markets, Coastlands or Lindale; see a movie, play golf, enjoy Southwards Car Museum, Nga Manu Bird Sanctuary, horse riding, visit antique and craft shops, wineries and potteries. It's all here for you! Need a retreat? Come stay with us. **Ocean Retreat**. You're very welcome!

THE MARTINBOROUGH CONNECTION

80 Jellicoe Street, Martinborough, Wairarapa
Ph (06) 306 9708, Fax (06) 306 9706
Mobile 0274-381 581
email: *martinboroughconnection@xtra.co.nz*
www.martinboroughconnection.co.nz

Tariff : N.Z. Dollars	
Double	$130
Single	$110
Child	

Bedrooms	Qty
Double	4
Twin	
Single	

Bed Size	Qty
Super King	
King	
Queen	4
Double	
Single	

Bathrooms	Qty
Ensuite	4
Private	
Guest Share	

 **Historic Bed & Breakfast
Boutique Accommodation**

Features & Attractions

- *Restored heritage building*
- *Guest lounge, open fire*
- *Sky TV, wireless internet*
- *Lovely outdoor area*

- *6 minute walk to cafés*
- *Wine tours arranged*
- *Cape Palliser Lighthouse*
- *Fur seal colony 55 min*

Your visit to the wine village of Martinborough, one hour's drive "over the hill" from Wellington, will be enhanced by your stay at The Martinborough Connection. Built in 1889, originally as a boot store and home, the property has been beautifully renovated and converted to a B&B, retaining its original character and charm.

Open your bedroom door to a sunny veranda and garden. Commence your day with a scrumptious breakfast using fresh fruit and local products. Spend your day sampling Martinborough's award-winning wines or alternatively visit an olive grove, take part in the various adventure activities or a walk. Stay an extra day and ensure that you visit Cape Palliser with its spectacular coastline, lighthouse, and fur seal colony. Or relax at the property. Sip a wine in front of the open fire in the guest lounge, or outside in the lovely garden, on the deck or the garden swing under the willows. Our interests include travel, sport, bridge, art & wine. We look forward to hosting you.

THE VICARAGE

94 Jellicoe Street, Martinborough, Wairarapa
Ph (06) 306 8596, Fax (06) 306 8597
Mobile 021-472 794
email: *mike.cooper@paradise.net.nz*
www.thevicarage.co.nz

Tariff : N.Z. Dollars	
Double	$150
Single	$150
Child	

Bedrooms	Qty
Double	1
Twin	1
Single	

Bed Size	Qty
Super King	
King	
Queen	1
Double	
King Single	2

Bathrooms	Qty
Ensuite	
Private	1
Guest Share	

 BA **Boutique Cottage** SC

Features & Attractions

- *1890's restored vicarage*
- *Short walk to Town Square*
- *Close to wineries*
- *Gas barbeque*
- *Sky digital television*
- *Gas log fire*
- *Fully equipped kitchen*
- *Laundry facilities*

Historic early 1890's cottage built as the Anglican Vicarage in Wanganui. Relocated to Martinborough in 2001 and completely restored so as to preserve the original character. Renovated and appointed to the highest standards of convenience and warmth. Set in a peaceful discreet sunny location alongside similar character cottages immediately behind the First Presbyterian Church in Jellicoe Street, Martinborough.

It's just a short walk to Martinborough Square with its shops, bars, cafés and restaurants. Within easy reach of the vineyards and olive groves. Martinborough is an excellent base for wine tours, walking (hill and rugged coastline), hill country quad biking, jet boating, golfing, great meals and just plain relaxing. Tariff includes breakfast provisions.

Managed by M and Jays Homestays (021 036 1436).

MARTINBOROUGH EXPERIENCE B & B
84 Venice Street, Martinborough
Ph (06) 306 9912
Mobile 027-445 8266
email: *info@martinboroughexperience.co.nz*
www.martinboroughexperience.co.nz

Features & Attractions

- Peaceful locality
- 5 min. walk to village
- Café & vineyards
- Large rooms & ensuites
- Spa bath unit
- Family unit available

Boutique-style Bed & Breakfast Accommodation

Double	$130-150
Single	$100-120
Child	$10-20

Experience a night of luxury in one of our beautiful self-contained suites, followed by a scrumptuous breakfast. Our boutique-style Bed & Breakfast accommodation is situated on a half-acre section, five minutes walk to village square, restaurants, cafés, art and crafts. We are also close to the vineyards and olive groves that Martinborough is famous for. Our three main guest rooms have super-king size beds, their own ensuite (one with spa-bath), tea and coffee making facilities, fridge, couch and TV. The beds can convert to singles if required. Fold-away beds and a port-a-cot are available on request.
We also have available a three bedroom family unit.

Bedrooms	Qty
Double	5
Twin	1
Single	
Bed Size	**Qty**
King	3
Queen	2
Double	
Single	2
Bathrooms	**Qty**
Ensuite	3
Private	
Family Share	1

BEACH HAVEN

26 Pukerua Beach Road, Pukerua Bay, Porirua
Ph (04) 239 9384, Fax (04) 239 9553
email: *Pukerua.Glass@xtra.co.nz*

Features & Attractions

- Sea & Kapiti Island views
- Modern spacious guest wing
- Handy to SH1, ferry, public transport
- German spoken
- Beaches, coastal walks
- Off-street parking

Boutique Bed & Breakfast Stunning Sea Views

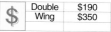

Double	$190
Wing	$350

Enjoy the best of both worlds - Pukerua Bay is a coastal village in a region that boasts a wide range of outdoor activities and yet is only a thirty minute drive from Wellington and all the attractions of the capital city. Visit wildlife sanctuaries, art and craft galleries, walk in the bush or tramp in the nearby Tararua Ranges. Local sports include golf, fishing, wind-surfing, paragliding, sailing and swimming.
Ideal for a group of one to four people, the guest wing in our large modern home has two bedrooms, which share a bathroom. Both rooms are sunny and have stunning sea views. The largest room has a balcony. We only take one group at a time, so you can be sure of privacy. Share an upstairs lounge with open fire and large deck with us, as well as our landscaped private courtyard surrounded by native bush.
We provide meals on request. Laundry facilities available.

Bedrooms	Qty
Double	2
Twin	
Single	
Bed Size	**Qty**
Super King	1
Queen	
Double	
King/Single	2
Bathrooms	**Qty**
Ensuite	1
Private	
Guest Share	

DREAMWATERS

9A Gordon Road, Karehana Bay, Plimmerton
Ph (04) 233 2042
Mobile 027-688 8371
email: *relax@dreamwaters.co.nz*
www.dreamwaters.co.nz

Tariff : N.Z. Dollars	
Double	$150-180
Single	$150
Child	$20

Bedrooms	Qty
Double	1
Twin	
Single	
Bed Size	Qty
Super King/Twin	1
King	
Queen	
Double/Sofa bed	1
Single	
Bathrooms	Qty
Ensuite	
Private	1
Guest Share	

**Self-contained
Seaside Accommodation**

Features & Attractions

- *Awesome sea views*
- *Architecturally designed*
- *Ideal for honeymooners*
- *Sky television & phone*
- *Just 25 min. to Wellington*
- *Listen to the waves*
- *Off-street parking*
- *Private and safe*

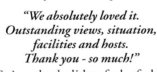

***"We absolutely loved it.
Outstanding views, situation,
facilities and hosts.
Thank you - so much!"***

Enjoy the holiday feel of this stunning Bed & Breakfast, just 20-25 minutes away from Wellington. Spectacular sea, island and coastal views from your private accommodation in our new architecturally designed home. Elevated sea front location overlooking rocks and waves only a stone's throw away. Spacious lounge, bathroom and fully equipped kitchen. Skylights, double-glazed, tinted glass and heated floor tiles for your comfort. We provide a tasty and substantial continental breakfast for you to enjoy whenever it best suits you. Listen to the sigh of the sea as you relax indoors with books, music and Sky TV. Marvel at the sunsets from your lounge or the deck. Breathe the salt air, stroll along the beach, dine in the village cafés. It's all yours. Kiwi/American hosts. Porirua City 8km. Golf courses within 10 minutes drive. *"An excellent weekend - we'd love a ten trip ticket"*.

BOATING CLUB POINT BED & BREAKFAST

Whale Cottage, 9 Gordon Road, Karehana Bay,
Plimmerton, Wellington
Ph (04) 233 9690, Mobile 027- 354 8832
email: *lizpeter@actrix.co.nz*

Features & Attractions

- Superb sea panorama
- Unique décor
- Beach, bush & coastal walks
- 1 min. walk to safe beach
- Ensuite spa bath
- No stairs, extra sofa bed

Panoramic Sea View, Privacy and a Tale to Tell

Double	$120
Single	$95
Child	Half price

Your self-contained wing of our character home, Whale Cottage, has breathtaking views of harbour and sea from every window. Rest in your comfortable rooms or fill your spa bath to unwind. The house has a unique nautical décor of NZ maritime history, ship fittings, curiosities and seagoing books. Your sitting-room has a telescope, easy chairs, double sofa, music, TV/DVD, M/W oven, fresh coffee, tea and breakfast (continental, self-service). On upper level, parking at your door. 2km from traffic lights on SH1. Wellington 25 minutes away - we can help plan your visit. Will meet commuter train. Enjoy the ever-changing blues of the sea. Relax watching the boats or go fishing from the jetty. At night a thousand pretty lights shine across the harbour. Good village cafés and takeaways.

Bedrooms	Qty
Double	1
Twin	
Single	1
Bed Size	Qty
King	
Queen	1
Double	
Single	1
Bathrooms	Qty
Ensuite	1
Private	
Guest Share	

AQUAVILLA SEASIDE BED & BREAKFAST

16 Steyne Avenue, Plimmerton
Ph (04) 233 1146
Mobile 027-231 0141
email: *aquavilla@paradise.net.nz*
www.aquavilla.co.nz

Features & Attractions

- Beach, a few steps away
- Safe off-street parking
- Gourmet full breakfasts
- Walk to cafés and shops
- Easy 20mins to Wellington
- Garden setting

Self-Contained Seaside Accommodation

Double	$150-180
Single	$150
Child	neg

Breathe deep the sea-scented air and treat yourself, mind, body and soul at our seaside haven. In the gorgeous garden of our character villa, your architecturally-designed accommodation features a delightful courtyard – and comfort plus. Guests love the little touches, crisp cotton sheets, flowers, home-made biscuits and artistic details inside and out. Best of both worlds here: explore Wellington by easy car or rail ride, or savour the serenity of this very special retreat. Forest and beach walks right at hand, as is great golfing, galleries, shopping, windsurfing and diving. You'll relish our scrumptious breakfasts: muesli, yoghurt and fruit or choose from the full cooked menu including blueberry pancakes and sweet-corn fritters. Later, watch the sun set before strolling to excellent cafés and restaurants, or use your kitchenette and barbeque. Warm, welcoming and widely-travelled, we're art and nature lovers with a patch of paradise we love to share. Off-street parking at your door.

Bedrooms	Qty
Double	1
Twin	
Single	
Bed Size	Qty
King	
Queen	1
Double	
Single	1
Bathrooms	Qty
Ensuite	
Private	1
Guest Share	

EIRENÉ RETREAT

1029 Akatarawa Road, Birchville, Upper Hutt
Ph (04) 526 3638, Fax (04) 526 3628
Mobile 021-107 6949
email: *beachen@paradise.net.nz*
www.eirene.co.nz

Tariff : N.Z. Dollars	
Double	$175-220
Single	$150-190
Child	$50

Bedrooms	Qty
Double	2
Twin	
Single	

Bed Size	Qty
Super King	
King	
Queen	1
Double	
Single	2

Bathrooms	Qty
Ensuite	
Private	1
Guest Share	

qualmark ★★★★ — home NEW ZEALAND

Advance booking recommended

Eirene Rural Retreat

Rural Retreat
Self-contained Accommodation

Features & Attractions

- *Single-party bookings*
- *Quiet, peaceful surrounds*
- *Private river access*
- *Outdoor ozone spa pool*
- *Sumptuous breakfasts*
- *Two bedrooms, sleep four*
- *Sky Television*
- *30 min. to ferry*

'Time Out' – it sounds so familiar, doesn't it? But somewhere in our busy lives it's become a distant memory. We all need time out. You simply need the space to recharge and refresh your soul. Welcome to **Eirené Retreat**. No crowds, just a gentle rural pace. Our guests say:

'Charming place, lovely hosts, an unforgettable experience'– France
'A special spot for the weary traveller' – USA
'Delightful, relaxing place' – UK
'Amazing, we have been spoilt, thank you so much' – UK
'Lovely piece of paradise' – Singapore
'Thank you for sharing your paradise with us. We could not have started the New Year better' – USA
'Delightful stay, very relaxing and sumptuous breakfasts. A lovely place to relax and explore the area' – Germany
'This place is magic' – Australia

BRENTWOOD MANOR

5 Brentwood Street, Trentham, Upper Hutt, Wellington
Ph (04) 528 6727, Fax (04) 528 6725
Mobile 027-527 0122
e-mail: *info@brentwoodmanor.co.nz*
www.brentwoodmanor.co.nz

Features & Attractions

- *Park-like setting*
- *Close to transport*
- *Open-air spa pool*
- *City centre just 30 min.*
- *Cafés/restaurants 3 min.*
- *Unique historic experience*

Heritage-style B&B and Self-contained Accommodation

Double	$125-185
Single	$110-140
Child	Neg.

R on and Misty invite you to capture the essence of early 20th century New Zealand in one of only 80 Chapman-Taylor designed and handcrafted homes. Set in private, tree-fringed grounds, **Brentwood Manor** provides a welcome sanctuary from the hustle and bustle of life. Stay in the Manor itself in Bed & Breakfast-style accommodation or spend the night in one of two unique self-contained settler-style cottages. Just minutes from Upper Hutt City Centre and around the corner from buses, trains and the well known Trentham Race Course, **Brentwood** is the ideal location to relax and unwind. Romantic Getaway Packages available on request. Airport transfers and dinner available by prior arrangement. **Accommodation with a touch of class!**

Bedrooms	Qty
Double	4
Twin	2
Single	1
Bed Size	**Qty**
King	
Queen	3
Double	1
Single	5
Bathrooms	**Qty**
Ensuite	2
Family Share	1
Guest Share	1

.... a great way to start the day!

DUNGARVIN

25 Hinau Street, Woburn, Lower Hutt, Wellington
Ph (04) 569 2125
Mobile 021-252 2933
email: *t.b.cudby@clear.net.nz*
www.bnbnz.com

Tariff : N.Z. Dollars	
Double	$105-120
Single	$80-100
Child	n/a

Bedrooms	Qty
Double	1
Twin	
Single	
Bed Size	Qty
Super King	
King	
Queen	1
Double	
Single	
Bathrooms	Qty
Ensuite	
Private	1
Guest Share	

Homestay
Bed & Breakfast

Features & Attractions

- *Bountiful breakfasts*
- *Totally relaxing environment*
- *20 min to Te Papa Museum*
- *15 min to ferries & stadium*
- *Variety of cafés/restaurants*
- *Secluded garden setting*
- *Dinner by prior arrangement*
- *Laundry and email facilities*

Our 75-year-old character cottage has been fully refurbished whilst retaining its original charm. We have a secluded property landscaped for quiet living, with ample off-street parking. Our home is centrally heated and has space for you to relax, read, listen to our CD collection or watch television. The sunny guest bedroom has windows opening over our well-established garden and pétanque court. The bed has an electric blanket and a wool duvet, and the private bathroom is equipped with a hairdryer, robes and toiletries.

Dinner is available by arrangement and vegetarians are catered for. Our main interests are travel, music, gardening, shows, entertaining and enjoying New Zealand wines. We will help you to plan local trips and enjoy your stay in this lovely area.

Paparangi Homestay

145 Helston Road, Johnsonville, Wellington
Ph (04) 478 1747
Mobile 0274-856432
email: *autry.joy@xtra.co.nz*

Features & Attractions

- *Airp/Ferry pickup by arrangement*
- *Train/shops/restaurants 2km*
- *Secluded garden setting*
- *10 min. to city/ferry*
- *20 min. to airport*
- *Off-street parking*

Secluded Garden Setting

Double	$95
Single	$60
Child	neg

Bedrooms	Qty
Queen	1
Twin	1
Single	1
Bed Size	**Qty**
King	
Queen	1
Double	
Single	2
Bathrooms	**Qty**
Ensuite	1
Private	
Family Share	1

DIRECTIONS: From the north from SH1 motorway take Johnsonville turn-off, sharp right around roundabout. Sharp right next roundabout , over bridge which brings you to Helston Road.

aparangi Homestay is a restored cottage, over 100 years old and set in over 1 acre of cottage gardens. We are situated only 2 km from Johnsonville Railway Station and shopping centre. We have a friendly dog, 2 cats, ducks and hens, so you can have free range eggs for breakfast if desired. We enjoy sharing a pre-dinner drink with our guests and you are very welcome to have dinner with us. Ample parking is available. Bedrooms have TV/Radio and Sky TV is available in the lounge. Autry is a keen hunter and golfer and can arrange a game. We also enjoy watching rugby. We can accommodate a small dog by arrangement and have a small secure kennel. Children are welcome and smoking is okay on the verandah. Autry and Joy enjoy the company of other nationalities and our home is your home while you are with us.

Devenport Estate

1 Korokoro Road, Korokoro,
Petone, Wellington
Ph (04) 586 6868. Fax (04) 586 6869
email: *devenport_estate@hotmail.com*
http://homepages.paradise.net.nz/devenpor

Features & Attractions

- *Edwardian-style charm*
- *Unrivalled sea views*
- *Close to Picton Ferry*
- *Free Internet*
- *Continental breakfast*
- *Bohemian restaurants*

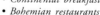

Boutique Vineyard
Private Bed & Breakfast

Double	$125-150
Single	$100-125
Child	neg.

Bedrooms	Qty
Double	1
Triple	2
Single	
Bed Size	**Qty**
King	
Queen	3
Double	
Single	2
Bathrooms	**Qty**
Ensuite	2
Private	1
Guest Share	

tay at the closest hobby vineyard to the capital. Only 15 minutes to Interisland ferry, city and stadium yet with the privacy and quietness of a country retreat. An Edwardian-styled homestead overlooking Wellington harbour, built at the turn-of-the-century (2000!) based upon the MacDonald family home in Scotland. Nestled amongst native bush we have planted 400 Pinot Gris/Pinot Noir grapevines in our hobby vineyard. Guests enjoy stunning sea, bush and garden views. Bedrooms contain queen sized bed, writing desk, chairs, television, tea-making services, hairdryer, electric blanket with either ensuite or private bathroom. Free WiFi broadband internet access and laundry service for 2 or more night stays (see Devenport's website as limits apply). Ample off-street parking. Enjoy the gardens, play pétanque or sink back into a deck chair and admire Somes Island. Alasdair, Christopher and our two cocker spaniels, welcome you to a comfortable stay in Wellington on our vineyard estate.

AT THE BAY

Marine Drive, Sorrento Bay, Eastbourne
PO Box 3717, Wellington
Ph/Fax (04) 568 4817, Mobile 027-568 4817
email: *at.the.bay@ihug.co.nz*

Tariff : N.Z. Dollars	
Double	$95-130
Single	$70-105
Child	neg.

Bedrooms	Qty
Double	1
Twin	
Single	1

Bed Size	Qty
Super King	
King	
Queen	
Double	1
Single	1

Bathrooms	Qty
Ensuite	
Private	1
Guest Share	

       **Homestay
Bed & Breakfast**

Features & Attractions

DIRECTIONS:
Please phone, fax
or email us for directions

• *Awesome harbour & city views*
• *Bush and beachfront setting*
• *Sleep to lapping waves*
• *Awaken to birdsong*

• *Relaxed peaceful atmosphere*
• *Friendly hosts and cat*
• *20 min to ferry and CBD*
• *Single party bookings*

Jennifer, Ken and our neighbour's friendly cat Ginger look forward to giving you a warm welcome to our homestay, **At The Bay**. It is nestled amongst native bush on the beachfront at Sorrento Bay. Share with us the magical views of Wellington's picturesque harbour and city, and the tranquility of lapping waves in the evening and birdsong in the morning.

We invite you to join us for a drink on a deck in summer, or in front of a cosy fire in winter.

We are on the bus route and only twenty minutes by vehicle from Wellington's CBD, close enough to enjoy the vibrancy of the city but far enough away to relax from its hustle and bustle. Cafés and shops are close by in Eastbourne Village and historic Petone.

We hope to make your stay a memorable one, where you arrive as strangers but leave as friends. No smoking inside, please.

NGAIO HOMESTAY

56 Fox Street, Ngaio,
Wellington
Ph (04) 479 5325, Fax (04) 479 4325
email: *enquiries@ngaiohomestay.co.nz*
www.ngaiohomestay.co.nz

Tariff : N.Z. Dollars	
Double	$150-180
Single	$100-140
Child	neg

Bedrooms	Qty
Double	2
Twin	1
Single	1
Bed Size	**Qty**
Super King	
King	
Queen	1
Double	1
Single	3
Bathrooms	**Qty**
Ensuite	3
Private	1
Guest Share	

**Homestay
Self-contained Accommodation**

Features & Attractions

- *Family home atmosphere*
- *Safe, quiet surroundings*
- *Off-street parking*
- *Extensive views*
- *2 min walk to local train station*
- *Ferry 5 min, city 10 min by car*
- *Internet facilities available*
- *Music salon*

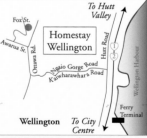

DIRECTIONS: From ferry take north exit, left at first traffic lights – Ngaio Gorge Road, at roundabout take Ottawa Road fork, at shops turn left Awarua Street – Fox Street is second on right. Use driveway at No.56.

Welcome to Wonderful Wellington! Share your visit with us and enjoy helpful personal hospitality! Our unusual multi-level open plan character home (built1960) is in the suburb of Ngaio. Guests may leave their car here and take the train to CBD (10 min). Our double room has tea/coffee facilities, quality bedding, tiled ensuite and French doors opening onto a deck and private "jungle" garden. Breakfast is continental. Evening meals an optional extra. Adjacent to our property, two self-contained apartments, one queen, one twin, are comfortable, convenient, tastefully furnished and recently redecorated. Each apartment has a couch with a fold out bed in lounge, fully equipped kitchen, shower, bath, laundry facilities, cable television, telephone and internet (small fee). There is a large garden with trees, birds and views. Jennifer plays harp at home and live piano music daily in NZ's top department store. Compliment from guest "This is a home where there is beautiful music, art and love". Please phone before 11am or after 3pm or fax or email.

HARBOUR VISTA

24 Kilsyth Street, Karori, Wellington
Ph (04) 476 2477, Fax (04) 476 2479
Mobile 021-139 0606
email: *pgsisson@xtra.co.nz*
www.harbourvista.co.nz

Features & Attractions

- *Quiet cul-de-sac*
- *City 8-10 minutes*
- *Magnificent harbour views*
- *Free pick-up and drop-off*
- *Free internet, laundry*
- *German spoken*

$		
	Double	$180-200
	Single	$140
	Child	

**Quality Homestay
Bed & Breakfast**

Bedrooms	Qty
Double	2
Twin	
Single	

Bed Size	Qty
King	1
Queen	1
Double	
Single	

Bathrooms	Qty
Ensuite	1
Private	1
Guest Share	

Welcome to our home, situated in a quiet cul-de-sac with awesome views of our suburb, hills and our beautiful harbour. We are 5-10 minutes from the Cable Car, botanical gardens, the world renowned 'Bird Sanctuary' and the city. We have travelled extensively ourselves and enjoy meeting and sharing our home with fellow travellers. Rooms have tea and coffee making facilities, electric blankets, hair dryer and bathrobes. Extremely comfortable beds and a warm welcome awaits you. We encourage you to relax and enjoy our lovely lounge with its views, books, music and a piano. A scrumptious breakfast is served in our elegant dining room. Free internet and laundry facilities, off-street parking. – 'Home-away-from-home'.

KARORI COTTAGE

11 Shirley Street, Karori, Wellington
Ph (04) 977 5104
Mobile 027-609 9003
e-mail: *kaye@karoricottage.co.nz*
www.karoricottage.co.nz

Features & Attractions

- *Cosy & self-contained*
- *Two storeys*
- *Close to bus route*
- *Sunny court yard*
- *Children welcome*
- *Outside play area*

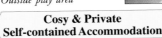
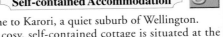

$		
	Double	$120-150
	Single	$120
	Child	$20

**Cosy & Private
Self-contained Accommodation**

Bedrooms	Qty
Double	1
Twin	1
Single	

Bed Size	Qty
King	
Queen	1
Double	
Single	2

Bathrooms	Qty
Ensuite	
Private	1
Guest Share	

Welcome to Karori, a quiet suburb of Wellington. Our cosy, self-contained cottage is situated at the rear of our section. Guests have their own, safe drive-on access. Upstairs **Karori Cottage** has a double room with queen-size bed and a twin bedroom with two single beds. Also upstairs is a private bathroom. Downstairs you will find the the lounge / dining kitchen area with an open fire and french doors opening onto a sunny court yard. Guests' children are welcome to play on the large front lawn, climb trees and share the trampoline with our three children (11, 14, and 16 years). Laundry facilities available. Close to bus route and great local deli/café.

MOUNT VICTORIA HOMESTAY

11 Lipman Street, Mount Victoria, Wellington
Ph (04) 802 4886, Fax (04) 802 4877
email: *stay@mountvictoria.co.nz*
www.mountvictoria.co.nz

Tariff : N.Z. Dollars	
Double	$280
Single	$230
Child	

Bedrooms	Qty
Double	2
Twin	
Single	

Bed Size	Qty
Super King	
King	
Queen	2
Double	
Single	

Bathrooms	Qty
Ensuite	2
Private	
Guest Share	

Bed & Breakfast Homestay

Features & Attractions

- *Walk to restaurants*
- *Close to Te Papa Museum*
- *Private court yard*
- *Complimentary refreshments*
- *Walk to café district*
- *Central city*
- *All rooms ensuite*
- *Pre-dinner wine & canapés*

Located in the heart of Wellington City we are a short walk from Wellington's cafés and a few minutes walk from Wellington's major attractions such as Te Papa Museum and the Oriental Bay beaches. We are also a short walk from some of Wellington's best restaurants and cafés. We offer two double rooms with ensuite and television in a luxuriously renovated Edwardian villa for discerning travellers who desire comfort and personal hospitality of the highest quality. Staying this close to the attractions of Wellington you will not require transport locally. Your room will have TV and complimentary tea, coffee and cookies. Full English breakfast is included.

Dinners can be provided by arrangement, but if you choose to dine out, enjoy pre-dinner refreshments with your hosts. We will be pleased to make arrangements for guided tours, theatres or other events either before you arrive or during your stay.

HARBOUR LODGE WELLINGTON

200 Barnard Street, Wadestown, Wellington
Ph (04) 976 5677, Mobile 021-032 6497
email: *lou@harbourlodgewellington.com*
www.harbourlodgewellington.com

Tariff : N.Z. Dollars	
Double	$180-260
Single	$160-240
Child	neg

Bedrooms	Qty
Double	4
Twin	
Single	

Bed Size	Qty
Super King	
King	4
Queen	
Double	
Single	

Bathrooms	Qty
Ensuite	4
Private	
Guest Share	

Luxury Bed & Breakfast

Features & Attractions

- *Fabulous harbour views*
- *Heated indoor pool*
- *Spa pool & sauna*
- *Beautiful bush setting*
- *2 km to central city*
- *Close to ferry & stadium*
- *Rooms with balconies*
- *Large lounge with woodburner*

DIRECTIONS: From north - take
Hawkestone St exit off motorway.
Turn right onto bridge, right again onto
Tinakori Rd. Follow signs to Wadestown
(3rd on left), follow Wadestown Rd up
hill for 2 min, turn right into Sefton St
(changes name to Barnard St).
Look for our sign on left.
Drive down driveway to the bottom.

Harbour Lodge is situated on a quiet hillside amongst beautiful native bush, with all day sun and sweeping harbour views, yet only three minutes drive from central Wellington, Wellington Stadium and the ferry terminal. Admire the fabulous views of Wellington Harbour from the large sunny deck. Idly watch as the ferries curve in and out of the harbour and the yachts drift by. Enjoy a dip in the heated pool, treat yourself to a sauna or spa, or on cooler evenings warm up around a crackling fire in the spacious guest lounge. The guest rooms have been refurbished to the highest quality with king size beds and snowy white linen. Each room has a private bathroom and views to the native bush-clad hills or harbour. Cable television, tea /coffee making facilities are available in each room. Let your stresses be gently lulled away in the luxurious comfort of this beautiful new lodge.

You might never want to leave.

VILLA VITTORIO
6 Hawker Street, Mt. Victoria, Wellington
Ph (04) 801 5761, Fax (04) 801 5762
Mobile 027-432 1267
email: *villa@villavittorio.co.nz*
www.villavittorio.co.nz

home
NEW ZEALAND

Tariff : N.Z. Dollars	
Double	$180-220
Single	$120-135
Child	

Bedrooms	Qty
Double	1
Twin	
Single	

Bed Size	Qty
Super King	
King	
Queen	1
Double	
Single	

Bathrooms	Qty
Ensuite	
Private	1
Guest Share	

**Boutique Bed & Breakfast
Restored 1870 Villa**

Features & Attractions

- *Historic suburb*
- *5 minute walk to cafés etc*
- *Sitting room with balcony*
- *Italian-styled courtyard*

- *Gourmet breakfasts*
- *Dinner by arrangement*
- *Good shopping nearby*
- *Close to Te Papa Museum*

Built in 1870 and recently renovated, Villa Vittorio offers a guest bedroom with television, tea and coffee making facilities and an adjoining sitting room with balcony with city views. You have your own luxurious bathroom with shower and bath. Te Papa National Museum, shopping, theatres, restaurants and the upgraded Oriental Bay Beach are all within easy walking distance. Westpac Stadium is within a thirty minute walk. The café scene at Courtenay Place is only a short stroll. We cater for special occasions and small intimate weddings. We also offer dinner by arrangement, including a complimentary bottle of New Zealand wine. Recent guests have recorded in our visitors book: "Beautiful home, wonderful breakfast, superb hospitality". Garaging, internet and laundry are available at a small charge. Parking is also available. No children or pets please. Reservations are recommended – please phone, fax, email or write. We have travelled extensively ourselves and enjoy having guests. We hope your stay with us will be memorable.

LAMBTON HEIGHTS BOUTIQUE BED & BREAKFAST

20 Talavera Terrace, Kelburn, Wellington
Ph (04) 472 4710, Fax (04) 472 4715
Mobile 027-693 1952
email: *lambtonheights@paradise.net.nz*
www.lambtonheights.co.nz

Tariff : N.Z. Dollars	
Double	$200-275
Single	$180-225
Child	

Bedrooms	Qty
Double	3
Twin	2
Single	

Bed Size	Qty
Super King	3
King	
Queen	
Double	
Single	4

Bathrooms	Qty
Ensuite	3
Private	
Guest Share	

**Luxury
Bed & Breakfast**

Features & Attractions

- *Beautiful heritage home*
- *Private and peaceful*
- *Stroll to the C.B.D.*
- *Garden spa pool*
- *Views of city and harbour*
- *Two min walk to the cable car*

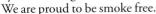

L **ambton Heights** offers Boutique Bed & Breakfast accommodation two minutes off the motorway and a short walk from the CBD. **Lambton Heights** is a heritage home in Wellington's inner suburb of Kelburn with sweeping views of city and harbour. Our guest lounge overlooks the garden. Facilities include a small library and tea/coffee making facilities with delicious home-made baking. The olde-world charm and character of **Lambton Heights** has been enhanced with new, modern bathroom facilities. Our luxurious suites include super-king beds, quality linen, bath-robes, toiletries, hair dryer and Sky TV. Internet access available if required. Enjoy the sound of New Zealand's native tui in the morning, the short stroll to the botanic gardens, historic cable car, parliament buildings, Te Papa and Victoria University. Breakfast includes fresh fruit salad, cereals, bread and preserves accompanied by a delicious gourmet-cooked course.
We are proud to be smoke free.

HOMESTAY AT EVANS BAY

4/378 Evans Bay Parade, Wellington
Ph (04) 386 1504, Fax (04) 386 1503
Mobile 021-043 5683
email: *leishas@xtra.co.nz*
www.homestayevansbay.co.nz

Tariff : N.Z. Dollars	
Double	$190-250
Single	$170-190
Extra pp	$75

Bedrooms	Qty
Double	1
Twin	1
Single	

Bed Size	Qty
Super King	
King	
Queen	1
Double	
King/Singles	2

Bathrooms	Qty
Ensuite	1
Private	1
Guest Share	

**Luxury Homestay/Bed & Breakfast
with Stunning Harbour Views**

Features & Attractions

- *Collected from airport*
- *5 min. from city & airport*
- *Drive to the door*
- *Email & internet facilities*
- *City bus in front*
- *Gourmet breakfast*
- *Dinner by arrangement*
- *Stylish & comfortable home*

Homestay at Evans Bay is a luxury Boutique Bed & Breakfast, overlooking the bay, swimming beach and restaurants. Elisabeth is a

watercolour artist, has travelled extensively and is bi-lingual. The home is luxuriously furnished and decorated, with indoor/outdoor living. The guest rooms are on the same floor, thus very private. They overlook the Bay and have coffee and tea making facilities with complimentary biscuits and chocolates. You are welcomed with drinks and hors d'oeuvres and we serve an extensive gourmet breakfast at your convenience, either in the dining room or alfresco in our private rose garden.

There are electric blankets on the beds, robes and quality toiletries, hair dryers and heated towel rails in the bathroom. SKY television and music in bedrooms.

Negotiable 'out-of-season rates'. See our web site.

Mentioned in the New York Times and Frommers.

AUSTINVILLA BED & BREAKFAST

11 Austin Street, Mt. Victoria, Wellington
Ph (04) 385 8334
email: *info@austinvilla.co.nz*
www.austinvilla.co.nz

Features & Attractions

- *Top central location*
- *Easy walk to inner city*
- *Sun and beautiful views*
- *Private entrance & courtyard*
- *Off-street parking/laundry facilities*
- *Self-contained and private*

$	Double	$140-180
	Single	
	Child	

Boutique Bed & Breakfast & Self-contained Accommodation

Bedrooms	Qty
Double	2
Twin	
Single	

Bed Size	Qty
King	
Queen	2
Double	
Single	

Bathrooms	Qty
Ensuite	2
Private	
Guest Share	

Top location: Set amongst beautiful gardens in one of Mt Victoria's elegant turn-of-the-century villas, Austinvilla is within minutes walk of theatres, restaurants, Oriental Bay and Te Papa. Close to public transport and short drive to airport, ferries and Westpac Stadium. 2 self-contained apartments with individual entrances come equipped with queen bed, ensuite (bath and shower), kitchen, living/dining area, cable TV, phone and wireless internet access. Both offer privacy, sun and city views with one having its own patio/garden. Laundry facilities and off-street parking available. Not suitable for children. Smoke-free.

TOP O' T'ILL

2 Waitoa Road, Hataitai, Wellington
Ph (04) 976 2718, Fax (04) 976 2719
Mobile 027-471 6482
email: *top.o.hill@clear.net.nz*
www.topotill-homestay.co.nz

Features & Attractions

- *Friendly and helpful hosts*
- *Attractive warm rooms*
- *Popular suburb near city*
- *Studio – short & long-term stays*
- *Continental & cooked breakfasts*
- *Wireless Internet*

$	Double	$120-140
	Single	$75-110
	Child	

Homestay / Bed & Breakfast Self-contained

Bedrooms	Qty
Double	2
Twin	1
Single	1

Bed Size	Qty
King	
Queen	2
Double	
Single	3

Bathrooms	Qty
Ensuite	2
Private	1
Guest Share	1

Hataitai, 'breath of the ocean', is midway between the Airport and City. Our comfortable character two storey home, built in 1919, has been in our family over 60 years. Upstairs there are views of Evans Bay and Mt Victoria. Our charming Studio/Apartment – Áit Siocháin (Peaceful Place), is fully self contained, and is a popular choice for relocaters and guests who prefer independent accommodation.
We enjoy the beauty of our vibrant harbour city, including its cultural life and superb restaurants. The CBD, airport, ferry, National Museum – Te Papa, and sports venues, are 5-10 minutes by car or two good bus routes. Our interests include travel, music, the arts, historical places and meeting people. Enjoy your stay in Wonderful Wellington!

BUCKLEY HOMESTAY
51 Buckley Road, Melrose, Wellington
Ph (04) 934 7151, Fax (04) 934 7152
Mobile 021-112 3445
email: *willy.muller@paradise.net.nz*
www.buckleyhomestay.co.nz

Tariff : N.Z. Dollars	
Double	$120-140
Single	$95-110
Child	neg.

Bedrooms	Qty
Double	2
Twin	2
Single	2
Bed Size	Qty
Super King	1
King Single	2
Queen	1
Double	
Single	3
Bathrooms	Qty
Private	1
Family Share	1
Guest Share	1

 Bed & Breakfast Homestay and Self-contained Suite with Views

Features & Attractions

- Private and peaceful
- Te Papa Museum 4km
- Handy to golf course
- Sleeps up to 6
- Handy to Red Rocks and seals
- Handy to airport, on bus route
- Handy to restaurants and zoo
- Private and spacious suite

Buckley Homestay is a large and sunny two storey home with spectacular scenery and beautiful views over Wellington, Cook Strait and the surrounding mountains. Sit in the award winning garden or join me in my home. I am a trained nurse, love cooking and gardening, have travelled extensively and I do speak Dutch. Alternatively you may like to stay in the modern, tastefully decorated self-contained guest suite with private entrance and balcony. I also offer a wide variety of extra facilities. Easy access to bushwalks and walkways or relax and enjoy my garden peace and views. Dinners by arrangement.

DIRECTIONS: From Newtown go straight to end of Newtown past Hospital, McDonalds. Take right hand fork at roundabout, up the hill on Russell Tce. past hockey stadium to top of hill, then right into Buckley Rd. From Island Bay up the hill through Mersey St. then Melrose Rd to Buckley Rd.

Take time out to surf or swim at our safe local beach or enjoy complimentary tea and coffee with a good book. A wide range of restaurants is available nearby. Whether you desire company or privacy – the choice is yours.

MA MAISON

9 Tamar Street, Island Bay, Wellington
Ph (04) 383 4018, Fax (04) 383 4018
Mobile 027-242 9827
email: *bedandbreakfast@paradise.net.nz*
www.nzwellingtonhomestay.co.nz

Tariff : N.Z. Dollars	
Double	$130
Single	$110
Child	

Bedrooms	Qty
Double	2
Twin	
Single	

Bed Size	Qty
Super King	
King	
Queen	2
Double	
Single	

Bathrooms	Qty
Ensuite	1
Private	1
Guest Share	

Advance booking recommended.

**Charming Romantic
Boutique Accommodation**

Features & Attractions

- *A place of style and comfort*
- *Warmth and hospitality*
- *Luxurious, romantic bedrooms and bathrooms*
- *Only 8 minutes to City Centre*
- *Really comfortable beds*
- *Plump down duvets*
- *Quiet, peaceful garden setting*

Ma Maison offers you Boutique Homestay Bed & Breakfast accommodation in our 1920's home, decorated with a French flavour, set in  a lovely garden with drive to front door. Two romantic guest rooms, both with queen posturepaedic beds, tea and coffee making facilities, television, quality white linen, featherdown duvets, electric blankets – in fact, everything to make your stay as comfortable as possible. One room has a private bathroom with shower and claw foot bath, the other room, which has an ensuite, has its own private entrance. Delicious cooked breakfast is served at a time to suit you.

Ma Maison is within easy walking distance to excellent local restaurants or eight minutes drive to swinging Courtenay Place, in the centre of Wellington, with a great variety of places to eat. Close by are a golf course and private and public hospitals. We are very handy to public transport. Island Bay has an excellent bus service into Wellington City, Te Papa, Stadium, shopping and theatres.

Owhiro Bay - Wellington ▷ YOUR HOSTS: **Natsuko and Maarten Groeneveld**   Ph (04) 383 6977

NATURE'S TOUCH GUEST HOUSE

25A Happy Valley Road, Owhiro Bay, Wellington
Ph (04) 383 6977, Fax (04) 383 6977
Mobile 027-559 0966
email: *info@naturestouchguesthouse.com*
www.naturestouchguesthouse.com

Tariff : N.Z. Dollars	
Double	$110-160
Single	$90-140
Child	$25 - 45

Bedrooms	Qty
Double	2
Twin	
Single	
Bed Size	**Qty**
Super King	
King	2
Queen	
Double	1
Single	1
Bathrooms	**Qty**
Ensuite	1
Private	
Family Share	1

Just Nature
Bed & Breakfast

Features & Attractions

- *Free seals tour May - August*
- *Private lounge & double bedroom*
- *Ever changing seaviews*
- *Peaceful stream sounds*

- *10% off after 3 nights*
- *Gourmet breakfast*
- *Free pick up / drop off*
- *Japanese meals available*

The Terrace Tunnel
End of SH ①
Webb
Wellington City
Ohiro Rd
Brooklyn Rd
N
Nature's Touch
Happy Valley Rd
Owhiro Bay PDE

"Warm welcome and delightful hospitality in beautiful craftsman-built home. Spacious, comfortable suite with stunning views. Convenient location. Superb cuisine, both Western and Japanese. A true gem."
Margaret, Australia

"Thank you again for a wonderful visit to your home. Your meal was stupendously prepared and we often

DIRECTIONS:
Feel free to give us a call for easy directions.

regret that our appetites were not up to the generous portions! We loved our seal hunt" Leslie, Mike, Zealand and Scotland from USA.
A warm welcome from us and our friendly dog, Lucky! We are just a short stroll to the beach and reserve. Only 10 min. drive to the city,

15 min. drive to ferry terminal and airport. **Upper Boat Bedroom** is for you to enjoy whole of upstairs, elevated views as well as privacy. We are building **Lower Boat Bedroom** and a laying bath with seaviews. It will be completed around Spring 2007. Enjoy tranquillity.

" . . . . and now for the South Island."

South Island

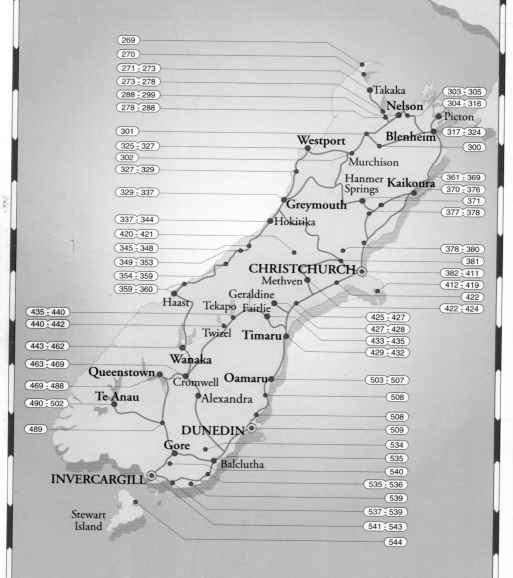

269
270
271 – 273
273 – 278
288 – 299
278 – 288

Takaka
Nelson

303 – 305
304 – 316
Picton
317 – 324
300

301
325 – 327
302
327 – 329

329 – 337

Westport
Murchison

Blenheim

Hanmer
Springs **Kaikoura**

361 – 369
370 – 376
371
377 – 378

337 – 344
420 – 421
345 – 348
349 – 353
354 – 359
359 – 360

Greymouth
Hokitika

CHRISTCHURCH
Methven

378 – 380
381
382 – 411
412 – 419
422
422 – 424

435 – 440
440 – 442

443 – 462

463 – 469

469 – 488
490 – 502

489

Haast
Tekapo
Geraldine
Fairlie

Twizel
Timaru

Wanaka
Queenstown
Cromwell **Oamaru**
Alexandra

Te Anau

DUNEDIN
Gore

425 – 427
427 – 428
433 – 435
429 – 432

503 – 507
508

508
509
534
535
540
535 – 536
539
537 – 539
541 – 543
544

INVERCARGILL
Balclutha

Stewart
Island

CLEMMIEC

1737 Collingwood-Puponga Road, Pakawau, Collingwood
Ph (03) 524 8787, Fax (03) 524 8785
Mobile 027-262 2947
email: *bookings@staygoldenbay.co.nz*
www.staygoldenbay.co.nz

Tariff : N.Z. Dollars	
Double	$150
Single	$120
Child	neg

Bedrooms	Qty
Double	2
Twin	1
Single	

Bed Size	Qty
Super King	
King	
Queen	2
Double	
King/Single	2

Bathrooms	Qty
Ensuite	
Private	2
Guest Share	

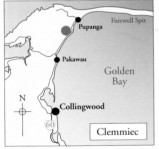

**Homestay
Bed & Breakfast**

Features & Attractions

- *Barbeque available*
- *Stunning beaches*
- *Walking tracks*
- *Comfort plus*
- *Excellent rural views*
- *Birdwatchers' dream*
- *Quiet peaceful location*
- *Evening meals by arrangement*

DIRECTIONS: From Collingwood, follow the signs north through Pakawau to Farewell Spit. **Clemmiec** is just 6 km north of Pakawau. Turn left at our sign and drive 300m up the driveway.

Clemmiec – the homestead of the children of the Matriarch Clem. As in the early 16th century **Clemmiec** is today a homestead of family and friends. Stay at **Clemmiec** and become part of that family or enjoy solitude, as you wish. Our house is your house with a choice of three large bedrooms, a lounge and reading area. Bathrooms are private and adjacent to the bedrooms. A full breakfast menu is provided with dinners by arrangement at a small additional cost. We are situated just 4 km from Farewell Spit, an internationally renowned wetland and bird sanctuary, Kahurangi National Park is literally at our back door. Use **Clemmiec** as a base to explore the many beaches and walkways in the immediate area and the greater Golden Bay, to enjoy a horse trek, go fishing or to visit some of the many craft galleries in our region. We can organise your tour of Farewell Spit with pick-ups at our gate. Evening meals by arrangement (on night of arrival).

HERON'S REST B & B

23 Gibbs Road, Collingwood, Golden Bay
Ph (03) 524 8987, Fax (03) 524 8987
Mobile 027-2471970
email: *stay@herons-rest.co.nz*
www.herons-rest.co.nz

Tariff : N.Z. Dollars	
Double	$90-110
Single	$65
Extra pp	negotiable

Bedrooms	Qty
Double	2
Twin	1
Single	2
Bed Size	Qty
Super King	
King	
Queen	1
Double	1
Single	2
Bathrooms	Qty
Ensuite	2
Private	
Guest Share	1

 Bed & Breakfast & Self-contained Accommodation

Features & Attractions

- *Panoramic views of mountains & sea*
- *Farewell Spit Eco Tours/bird-watching*
- *Pottery & Pacific Carver's Studio*
- *4 min. bush walk to eateries, beach*
- *Friendly & welcoming hosts*
- *Landscaped, private gardens*
- *Large deck with BBQ facility*
- *Spacious lounge; Sky TV*

DIRECTIONS: Just before Collingwood township, turn right up Lewis St, left into Washington Rd, then left into Gibbs Rd. Proceed to end, taking left fork of (LEVEL) gravel road - to end . We're on the headland overlooking Collingwood.

Situated in a unique, unspoilt location, your welcoming hosts enjoy making guest stays comfortable and memorable. We offer home-made and locally-produced foods and complimentary drinks. Hairdryer, laundry and internet available. A wide choice of outdoor activities caters for all fitness levels. Excellent walks. Farewell Spit, Abel Tasman and Kahurangi National Parks are nearby, as is access to the Heaphy Track. Guests can follow the trail of Golden Bay's many artisan outlets sampling, en route, our interesting cafés and restaurants (including *The Mussel Inn*), or merely relax on the deck, nearby sandy beaches or in the garden. **Heron's Rest** is a peaceful location, yet very convenient to amenities in Collingwood.

In addition, our charming, self-contained **Treetops' Cottage** (sea vistas from each bed) has a variety of options, offering a double bed, single and pullout, sleeping 3-4 persons. It has an ensuite bathroom, hairdryer, private deck, with gas BBQ giving outdoor dining options overlooking superb sea/mountain/estuary views, TV, most kitchen appliances including fridge and microwave; we provide breakfasts.

BAY VISTA HOUSE

Paradise Way, Pohara, Golden Bay
Ph (03) 525 9772, Fax (03) 525 9772
Mobile 021-378 736
email: *hosts@bayvistahouse.co.nz*
www.bayvistahouse.co.nz

Tariff : N.Z. Dollars	
Double	$230-280
Single	$200-250
Child	

Bedrooms	Qty
Double	3
Twin	
Single	

Bed Size	Qty
Super King	
King	3
Queen	
Double	
Single	

Bathrooms	Qty
Ensuite	3
Private	
Guest Share	

Luxury Accommodation with Panoramic Sea Views

Features & Attractions

- *Views across Golden Bay*
- *Spacious rooms*
- *TV, fridge, tea/coffee in rooms*
- *Spa pool*
- *Walk to 3 restaurants*
- *5 min. walk to beach*
- *Abel Tasman National Park*
- *Farewell Spit & walking tracks*

Bay Vista House sits above Pohara Beach with spectacular sea and mountain views across Golden Bay to Farewell Spit. Our spacious rooms all enjoy the panoramic views and open to the terrace. Each room has its own ensuite, lounge furniture, TV, fridge, tea and coffee making facilities. Three restaurants are within 5 minutes easy walk for a good choice of evening meals featuring local produce and seafood.

All the natural features of Golden Bay are within easy reach, including Abel Tasman National Park, Farewell Spit, Pupu Springs, forests, waterfalls and spectacular coastlines. Sea kayaking, horse trekking, fishing, birdwatching, Spit tours and coastal boat trips can be readily arranged and there are many bush and coastal walks through the national parks and conservation reserves. The northern loop of the fabled Abel Tasman National Park Coastal Walkway can be walked from **Bay Vista House** in a single day. Active local artists and potters abound and can be visited in their studios.

DIRECTIONS: From SH60 turn right on entry to Takaka (Motupipi St) and follow signs to Pohara, 8km. Turn right up Richmond Road opposite camping ground entrance (sign), and left to Paradise Way (sign).

271

BEAUTIFUL PATONS ROCK
SEA & BEACHVIEW HOMESTAY
Patons Rock, RD 2, Takaka, Golden Bay
Ph (03) 525 7230, Fax (03) 525 7231
Mobile 021-2020459
email: *kaliswj@clear.net.nz*

Tariff : N.Z. Dollars	
Double	$89
Single	$50-55
Exta pp	$15

Bedrooms	Qty
Double	3
Twin	
Single	

Bed Size	Qty
Super King	
King	1
Queen	1
Double	
Single	5/6

Bathrooms	Qty
Ensuite	
Private	2
Guest Share	

**Homestay Bed & Breakfast
& Self-contained Accommodation**

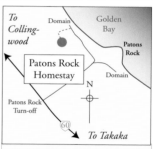

DIRECTIONS: From Takaka Post Shop drive 10 km towards Collingwood, take Patons Rock turn-off. At end of Road take private track "Byders Terrace" We are last house on left.

Features & Attractions

- *View over whole of Golden Bay*
- *Private lounge/kitchen/balcony*
- *Separate shower and bathroom*
- *Safe, clean beach 2 min*
- *Good log burner*
- *Very comfortable & cosy*

Our separate upper floor gives a beautiful view over the Bay from Farewell Spit to Separation Point. We are only two minutes from a safe, clean, good walking beach. You will enjoy our big lounge with log burner and television. Bathroom, toilet and shower are separate. A balcony on three sides gives ample room to sit and enjoy the views. Patons Rock area has about 100 houses and no shops. In Takaka or Collingwood you find facilities like restaurants, pubs and shops, only twelve kilometres away. Golden Bay has plenty to offer with its variable scenery and good walkways. We can pick you up from the Tasman or Heaphy Track or in Takaka or drop you off at Collingwood for a Farewell Spit Safari. Kayak, windsurfer and barbeque available.

 Self-contained option:
Our downstairs self-contained flat comprises of an open-plan kitchen/ living area and has one bedroom with queen-size bed and one bedroom with 3 single beds. Divan in lounge. Tariffs per night: $49 for double and $35 for single, extra person $15. Breakfast is available.

GARDEN RETREAT BED & BREAKFAST
598 State Highway 60, Puramahoi RD 2, Takaka
Ph (03) 525 6121, Fax (03) 525 6121
Mobile 027-272 4200
email: *info@gardenretreat.co.nz*
www.gardenretreat.co.nz

Features & Attractions

- *Only 8 km from Takaka*
- *Orchard and sheep farm*
- *Many arts, crafts & walks*
- *National parks vicinity*
- *Swimming and fishing*
- *Picnic lunches available*

$	Double	$115-165
	Single	$90-100
	Child	5+ neg

Take Time To Unwind

Bedrooms	Qty
Double	2
Twin	1
Single	
Bed Size	**Qty**
King	
Queen	2
Double	
Single	2
Bathrooms	**Qty**
Ensuite	1
Private	
Guest Share	1

Surrounded by lush sub-tropical gardens, **Garden Retreat** is the perfect place for the weary traveller to relax and unwind. All rooms are located upstairs, are sunny, light and have lovely garden views. The guest breakfast lounge has a self-service home-made continental breakfast available at your convenience. **Garden Retreat** is en-route to such wonderful attractions as Farewell Spit with its internationally renowned wetlands and bird sanctuary, the spectacular Wharariki Beach and the famous Heaphy Track. Patons Rock Beach, popular for swimming and fishing, is only minutes away. Diane and Alan are happy to share their knowledge of the local attractions, eateries, artists, walks and other points of interest in the glorious Golden Bay to help make your stay extra enjoyable.

SPLIT RIDGE
Toko Ngawa Drive, Split Apple Rock, RD 2, Motueka
Ph (03) 527 8487, Fax (03) 527 8497
Mobile 027-229 6729
email: *split.ridge@xtra.co.nz*

Features & Attractions

- *Set amongst native bush*
- *Use of swimming pool*
- *Quiet & peaceful*
- *Expansive sea views*
- *Spacious rooms*
- *Close to national parks*

$	Double	$130-160
	Single	$120-140
	Child	

**Expansive Sea Views
Bed & Breakfast**

Bedrooms	Qty
Double	2
Twin	
Single	
Bed Size	**Qty**
King	
Queen	2
Double	
Single	
Bathrooms	**Qty**
Ensuite	1
Private	1
Guest Share	

Split Ridge sits above the picturesque and turquoise waters of the Abel Tasman National Park, with expansive sea views to the north and mountains to the south.
Each room has its own ensuite or private bathroom, tea and coffee making facilities and outdoor terraces.
You are free to walk around our extensive gardens, enjoy the use of our swimming pool or walk to the Split Apple Rock and adjacent beaches.
Alternatively visit the local national parks or visit the many vineyards, craft outlets or local cafés and restaurants.
Dinner (including wine) is shared with hosts and is available by arrangement.

DIRECTIONS:
4 km past the well marked Kaiteriteri Beach, turn right into Toko Ngawa Drive.
Split Ridge is at the top on right (1km)

BAYVIEW B & B

2 Bayview Heights, Kaiteriteri, RD2 Motueka
Ph (03) 527 8090, Fax (03) 527 8090
Mobile 027-454 5835
email: *book@kaiteriteribandb.co.nz*
www.kaiteriteribandb.co.nz

Features & Attractions

- *Gateway to Abel Tasman*
- *Kayaking trips organised*
- *Hiking trips arranged*
- *Sea views from your room*
- *Golden sand beaches*
- *Restaurants close by*

Purpose Built B&B with Views to Die for

$	Double	$165-195
	Single	$130-160
	Child	

Bedrooms	Qty
Double	1
Twin/Double	1
Single	
Bed Size	**Qty**
King	1
Queen	
Double	
King/Single	1
Bathrooms	**Qty**
Ensuite	2
Private	
Guest Share	

DIRECTIONS: 8km north of Motueka on HW60 turn right into Kaiteriteri Rd. After 4km take 2nd right into Cederman Drive. **Bayview** is 200mtrs on right.

We welcome you to paradise. Kaiteriteri Beach, the gateway to the Abel Tasman National Park with the most beautiful coastline in New Zealand and the sunniest weather. Here we can offer you Bed & Breakfast at its best. Your rooms are large and beautifully furnished with extensive views of the bay. You have a comfortable sitting area, outside terrace, ensuite with heated towel rail and hair dryer, fridge, tea/coffee making facilities, radio and TV. Laundry, phone, fax and email are available. You are welcome to share our living area, terraces, extensive collection of books or be as private as you wish. Kayak adventures and water taxi services leave from our pristine beach. We recommend a minimum 2 night stay to explore this unique area.

FRASER HIGHLANDS

177 Riwaka - Sandy Bay Rd, (Main route to Abel Tasman Park), RD 2, Motueka
Ph (03) 528 8702
Mobile 027-3150688
email: *fraserhighlands_nz@hotmail.com*

Features & Attractions

- *Abel Tasman National Park*
- *Crafts, wineries, cafés*
- *Bordering Golden Bay*
- *Boating, biking, tramping*
- *Kaiteriteri/Motueka 14min.*
- *Transport & tours available*

Spectacular Views Tasman Bay Bed & Breakfast

	Double	$110-160
	Single	$90-140
	Child	$10

Bedrooms	Qty
Double	2
Twin	
Single	1
Bed Size	**Qty**
King	
Queen	2
Double	
Single	1
Bathrooms	**Qty**
Ensuite	2
Private	
Guest Share	1

Welcome to **Fraser Highlands**, where we offer Bed & Breakfast with a 'Scottish' atmosphere 180 metres above sea level. The peaceful native bush property offers spectacular sights of Tasman Bay and surrounding mountainous areas. A resident bagpiper and dancer could provide a wee bit of extra entertainment! Comfortable accommodation includes two queen bedrooms with ensuites, TV, tea/coffee facilities, and email access. A self-contained cottage and a family room are available. Hosts Jim and Sue would be happy for you to settle in the lounge with an open fire. Continental breakfast provided includes home baking, and evening meals can be arranged. 5-15 minutes from **Fraser Highlands**, you could be enjoying a great variety of activities – parks, rivers, beaches, aircraft, golf link, town or mountains.

DIRECTIONS: Riwaka-Sandy Bay Rd. - 2nd driveway on left up hill on main route to Marahau.

BELLBIRD LODGE

Sandy Bay Road, RD 2, Kaiteriteri, Motueka
Ph (03) 527 8555, Fax (03) 527 8556
Mobile 021-057 1470
email: *stay@bellbirdlodge.com*
www.bellbirdlodge.com

Tariff : N.Z. Dollars	
Double	$220-275
Single	$180-200
Child	

Bedrooms	Qty
Double	2
Twin	1
Single	

Bed Size	Qty
Super King	1
King	
Queen	1
Double	
Single	4

Bathrooms	Qty
Ensuite	1
Private	1
Guest Share	

**Luxury Boutique Accommodation
Panoramic Sea Views**

DIRECTIONS:
From Kaiteriteri Beach follow the road up the hill towards Marahau for approx 1.5 km. At the **Bellbird Lodge** sign, turn right into our private road. We are the 3rd house.

Features & Attractions

- *Panoramic sea views*
- *Relaxed and friendly*
- *Spacious and comfortable*
- *Lounge with TV, video, CD & piano*
- *Phone, fax, email available*
- *Laundry and barbeque*
- *Art, craft and wine trails*
- *Winter specials*

Welcome to Bellbird Lodge, where warm friendly hospitality, superb food and fine accommodation await you. Nestled on the hillside in a tranquil setting with panoramic sea views, Bellbird Lodge is close to Kaiteriteri Beach with its stunning golden sands, the gateway to Abel Tasman National Park. The tastefully furnished guest rooms are on the ground floor and have either ensuite or private bathrooms. All have tea/coffee making facilities, hairdryers, electric blankets, bathrobes and have sea or bush views and outdoor terraces. Wake to the songs of bellbird and tui and marvel at the sunrise over Tasman Bay. Enjoy a delicious buffet breakfast with fresh local produce and homemade muesli, bread and preserves and featuring a hot gourmet special of the day, served in the dining room or alfresco on the terrace. The area has much to offer all year round. Walk the coastal track, take a scenic cruise, water taxi or kayak and discover the unspoiled beauty of the Abel Tasman National Park. Excellent restaurants are a few minutes drive away. Dinner available by prior arrangement (May-October). We look forward to welcoming you soon.

KAIRURU FARMSTAY COTTAGES

1792 Takaka Hill, Highway 60,
(*or* Private Bag), Motueka
Ph/Fax (03) 528 8091, Mobile 027-433 7457
email: *kairuru@xtra.co.nz*
www.kairurufarmstay.co.nz

Tariff : N.Z. Dollars	
Double	$130-160
Single	$130-145
Child	$15-30

Bedrooms	Qty
Double	3
Twin	3
Single	
Bed Size	**Qty**
Super King	
King	
Queen	2
Double	1
Single	2
Bathrooms	**Qty**
Ensuite	
Private	3
Guest Share	

 **Farmstay
Self-contained Cottages**

Features & Attractions

- *Breakfast provisions optional*
- *Spectacular views*
- *Peaceful and private*
- *Children welcome*
- *Self-contained cottages*
- *Farm animals and - activities*
- *Abel Tasman National Park*
- *Gateway to Golden Bay*

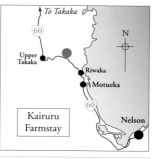

DIRECTIONS:
From Motueka travel north-west towards Takaka. We are 17 km from Motueka on the rights side of the road. **Kairuru** sign at gate.

Guests' accommodation is offered in three self-contained, comfortable, fully equipped cottages. 'Kea Cottage' has three bedrooms, sleeping up to six. 'Pipit Cottage' has two bedrooms, sleeping up to five and 'Canaan Cottage' is one bedroom, suitable for two. All cottages have full kitchens, sitting/ dining, laundry, telephone, TV, microwave, BBQ and great views. **Kairuru** is a working sheep and cattle farm of 4000 acres on the unique Takaka Hill. Perfectly situated between the Abel Tasman National Park and Golden Bay. Relax in the privacy, peace and quiet of your own cottage or enjoy the many attractions of the area. Dinners are available by prior arrangement, at $55 per adult, either in our home or delivered to your cottage.
We are 3rd generation farmers who enjoy sharing their farm with others and happy to assist you to experience the local attractions.

THE RESURGENCE

Riwaka Valley Road, RD 3, Motueka
Ph (03) 528 4664, Fax (03) 528 4605
email: *info@resurgence.co.nz*
www.resurgence.co.nz

Tariff : N.Z. Dollars	
Double	$325-495
Single	$290-445
Child	

Bedrooms	Qty
Double	6
Twin/Double	4
Single	
Bed Size	Qty
Super King/Twin	4
King	
Queen	6
Double	
Single	
Bathrooms	Qty
Ensuite	10
Private	
Guest Share	

     Five Star Nature

Features & Attractions

- *Swimming pool and spa pool*
- *Gourmet dining*
- *Wilderness with bush tracks*
- *Sorry, no children under 18*
- *Abel Tasman National Park 15 mins*
- *Nelson art and wine trails*
- *Golden Bay day trips*
- *Guided walks & eco tours*

Perfect for couples who love nature, the outdoors and good food.

The Resurgence is a tranquil haven alive with native birdsong overlooking the Kahurangi wilderness. An excellent base for three or four days exploring the Nelson-Tasman region and just fifteen minutes from the start of the Abel Tasman track.

DIRECTIONS: Follow SH 60 from Motueka, through Riwaka and past the two turnings towards Abel Tasman National Park. After 2 km, just as SH 60 starts to go uphill, turn left down Riwaka Valley Rd. Continue towards the source of the river for 5.7 km.

Your well-travelled hosts, Clare and Peter, are keen conservationists and outdoor enthusiasts; they will help you select the very best local activities to make your stay truly memorable.

The welcoming **Lodge** provides informal luxury in four well-appointed ensuite guest rooms with balconies and views. **Lodge** tariff includes full cooked breakfast with free-range eggs, home baking and espresso coffees plus cocktails and four-course dégustation dinner with fresh local produce. Licensed with fine Nelson wines.

Escape the world in our unique self-contained **Bush Lodge** and **Chalet Suites**. Luxurious and very private with BBQ, kitchen and large deck. Serviced daily, tariff includes a wholesome breakfast hamper. Ideal for honeymoons and longer stays. Dinner by reservation.

We are 50 minutes from Nelson airport and 15 minutes from Motueka.

CENTRE RIDGE FARMSTAY

Blackbird Valley 176,
RD 2, Upper Moutere, Nelson
Ph/Fax (03) 543 2882, Mobile 027-660 9369
email: *centreridge@xtra.co.nz*

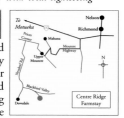

Features & Attractions

- *Spacious family home*
- *Welcoming cuppa*
- *Amazing sheep dogs*
- *Beaches & sea kayaking*
- *Excellent restaurants nearby*
- *Help with local sightseeing*

$	Double	$90-100
	Single	$90
	Child	neg

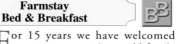
Farmstay Bed & Breakfast

Bedrooms	Qty
Double	1
Twin	
Single	
Bed Size	**Qty**
King	1
Queen	
Double	
Single	
Bathrooms	**Qty**
Ensuite	
Private	1
Guest Share	

For 15 years we have welcomed guests to our 96 year old family home where we invite you to enjoy our sunny deck, our garden, the birds and the valley views. Feel free to go walking on our sheep farm, or a farm tour can be arranged. **Centre Ridge** is halfway between Nelson City and the Abel Tasman National Park, in an area of award winning wineries. Stay a night or more. Meet Millie and Smooch, our cats, and Tim and Luke, our farm dogs. Enjoy an evening meal with us (by arrangement) $25pp. Sample farm food, home-made bread and jams with a cooked or continental breakfast. Our king room has a spa in the bathroom.

DIRECTIONS: 1.5 km south of Richmond turn right. After 6 km turn left (Moutere Highway). After 17 km turn left at Prices Corner. Travel 4.4 km to Blackbird Valley, turn left. Find us after 1.76 km.

LEMONADE FARM APARTMENT

99 Roses Road, Upper Moutere , RD2, Nelson
Ph (03) 543 2686, Mobile 021-059 0464
email: *stay@lemonadefarm.co.nz*
www.lemonadefarm.co.nz

VISA **MasterCard**

Features & Attractions

- *Outdoor Spa Pool*
- *Abel Tasman 35 min.*
- *Vineyard region*
- *Rural retreat*
- *Air conditioning*
- *You're the only guests*

Luxury Country Retreat

$	Double	$170-200
	Extra pp	$40
	Child	4-12 $20

You are the only guests in this self-contained apartment. Soak in the outdoor spa pool and watch the cows graze after a day of exploring the Abel Tasman or tasting Moutere wines. There's a substantial cook-your-own breakfast basket. Relax in modern décor with quality linens, air-conditioning, a full kitchen plus broadband internet available. Expect freshly ground coffee, flowers and a great night's sleep on a quality bed. Our philosophy is to treat you the way we'd like to be treated - a friendly welcome and then left to enjoy your space.

"What a wonderful peaceful place! We felt truly pampered with all the special touches. Hands down one of the finest B&Bs we've ever stayed in!" Stephanie and Marty, California.

Bedrooms	Qty
Double	2
Twin	
Single	
Bed Size	**Qty**
King	
Queen	2
Double	
Single	2
Bathrooms	**Qty**
Ensuite	
Private	1
Guest Share	

LARCHWOOD HOUSE

1 Dicker Road, Tasman,
RD 1, Upper Moutere 7152
Ph/Fax (03) 526 6204, Mobile 027-452 7249
email: *larchwood.house@paradise.net.nz*
www.larchwoodhousetasman.co.nz

Tariff : N.Z. Dollars	
Double	$170-230
Single	$170-230
Child	neg

Bedrooms	Qty
Double	2
Twin	
Single	

Bed Size	Qty
Super King	
King	
Queen	1
Double	1
King/Single	

Bathrooms	Qty
Ensuite	
Private	1
Guest Share	

**Stylish Country Homestay
Bed & Breakfast**

Features & Attractions

- *Genuine Kiwi hospitality*
- *Bird watchers delight*
- *World class trout fishing*
- *35 min from Abel Tasman*
- *3 golf courses nearby*
- *Superb alfresco dining*
- *Private guest entrance*
- *Beaches & sea kayaking*

To Golden Bay
Larchwood House
Motueka
Tasman Bay
Tasman
Mapua   Nelson
To Alpine National Parks

Larchwood House is a sanctuary of gardens, wonderful home grown fruit and vegetables, with BBQs and intimate dining. Your guest room is beautifully furnished, sunny, spacious with a writing desk, quality cotton bed linen, bathrobes, hair dryer your own refrigerator, tea and coffee, in-room DVDs, e-mail and TV. French doors open onto wide decks and verandahs overlooking the gardens, ornamental pond and views to the mountains beyond. The excitement of exploring the region is balanced by coming home to the tranquility of **Larchwood House** each day. Complimentary drinks are served at 6pm followed by a BBQ or quiet meal in-house or at a local award-winning restaurant. Our focus is quality. This has been reflected in some of the written guest comments: *"Heavenly accommodation... perfect hosts... 5-star hotel in a lovely country garden... we expected to stay 2 nights and stayed 5... glad we found you, perfect stay"*. Expect to find this same care and quality at Larchwood House when you stay with us.

HARAKEKE LODGE CHALETS

Cnr. Moutere Highway/Harley Road, Harakeke,
RD 2, Upper Moutere, Nelson
Ph (03) 543 2588, Fax (03) 543 2588
email: *harakekelodge@paradise.net.nz*

Features & Attractions

- *Peaceful garden setting*
- *Three National Parks*
- *Guided walks*
- *Art, craft and wine trails*
- *Excellent restaurants nearby*
- *Trout fishing, kayaking, golf*

Countrystay Bed & Breakfast

Double	$95-120
Single	$70-90
Child	neg

Harakeke Lodge offers you quiet, comfortable and very affordable accommodation in a peaceful country-garden setting with extensive rural views towards Kahurangi National Park. Our aim is to allow you to feel at home in your private well-appointed, separate lodge and to meet any special needs that you require. Each lodge is equipped with self-catering facilities, including microwave, refrigerator, television etc. Email available. A wholesome continental breakfast is provided for you to enjoy at your leisure. There are a wide variety of award winning restaurants situated locally to cater for your discerning tastes. The central location of our lodge makes **Harakeke** an ideal base from which to explore the surrounding National Parks, beaches, wine and craft trails. Be assured of a very warm welcome.

DIRECTIONS:
On SH 60 to Motueka, 26 km from Richmond (Nelson) turn left into Harley Road at Tasman. **Harakeke Lodge** is 5 km on left.

Bedrooms	Qty
Double	1
Twin	2
Single	
Bed Size	**Qty**
King	
Queen	1
Double	
Single	5
Bathrooms	**Qty**
Ensuite	2
Private	
Family Share	1

FOUR ACRE PARK ACCOMMODATION

Permin Rd, Tasman, Nelson
Ph (03) 540 2756, Mobile 021-153 9980
email: *info@fouracre.co.nz*
www.fouracre.co.nz

Features & Attractions

- *Peaceful country setting*
- *Warm, helpful hospitality*
- *New, fully equipped cottage*
- *Central to beaches, Abel Tasman*
- *Cafés, wineries, art & craft*
- *Original paintings for sale on site*

Self-contained Cottage

Double	$130-210
Single	
Extra pp	$15 each

Richard and Karyn welcome you to **Four Acre Park**. Our quality, affordable cottage is part of our peaceful rural park. Let us help you plan your stay. Relax and feed the ducks at the pond. The beach is within walking distance. We are centrally located to Nelson, Mapua, Abel Tasman. Our spacious double-glazed cottage is tastefully decorated. Facilities include well-equipped kitchen, laundry, heated towel-rails, hairdryer, heaters, electric blankets, TV and DVD player. We have a large selection of DVDs you are welcome to use. Tea, herbal tea, coffee complimentary. Continental breakfast available. Serviced. Children welcome and baby-sitting service available. Karyn, a water-colour artist has original paintings of local vistas for sale.

DIRECTIONS: From HW60, turn into Permin Rd, then 1st right. Four Acre Park signposted from Permin Rd.

Bedrooms	Qty
Double	1
Twin	1
Single	
Bed Size	**Qty**
King	1
Queen	
Double sofa bed	1
Single	2
Bathrooms	**Qty**
Ensuite	
Private	1
Guest Share	

OLIVES @ MARIRI BED & BREAKFAST

2597 Coastal Highway, Mariri, Tasman
Ph (03) 526 6775, Fax (03) 526 6775
Mobile 021-163 7610
email: *stay@olivesatmariri.co.nz*
www.olivesatmariri.co.nz

Tariff : N.Z. Dollars	
Double	$160-170
Single	$120-130
Child	$20

Bedrooms	Qty
Double	1
Twin	
Single	

Bed Size	Qty
Super King	
King	
Queen	1
Double	
Single	1

Bathrooms	Qty
Ensuite	1
Private	
Guest Share	

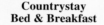
**Countrystay
Bed & Breakfast**

Features & Attractions

- *Yours Exclusively*
- *Peaceful rural setting*
- *Quality Accommodation*
- *Superb restaurants 10 min.*
- *Vineyards*
- *Day trips to Abel Tasman*
- *Local potters & artists*
- *Golf course nearby*

You will be our exclusive guests when you stay at **Olives @ Mariri,** our 90 year old farmhouse, situated among olive and fruit trees. The elegant, comfortable suite with bathroom opens through French doors to the patio and lovely garden. It includes tea/coffee making facilities, refrigerator, TV and a comfortable sofa bed for a third person. Wake to bird-song and a leisurely breakfast of home baking, fresh fruit and vegetables from the garden. Walk in the olive grove, relax with a book and a glass of wine, or use the telescope to explore the Milky Way Galaxy on those beautiful dark starlit nights. **Olives @ Mariri** is a convenient staging post for Abel Tasman and Kahurangi National Parks and close to beaches, wineries, potters and artists. We have travelled or worked in most continents and would love to share our little bit of paradise with you. You are assured of a warm welcome.

Olives @
Mariri

To Golden Bay

Motueka

Tasman Bay

Tasman

N

Mapua   Nelson

To Alpine National Parks

DIRECTIONS:
Between Tasman and Motueka,
300 metres north of Harley Road
on Highway 60, take the unsealed
loop road and follow the signs.

MAHANA ESCAPE BED & BREAKFAST

750 Old Coach Rd, Mahana, RD 1 Upper Moutere, Nelson
Ph (03) 540 3090, Fax (03) 540 3090
Mobile 027-289 0060
email: *gloria@mahanaescape.co.nz*
www.mahanaescape.co.nz

Tariff : N.Z. Dollars	
Double	$160 - 350
Single	$160 - 350
Child	

Bedrooms	Qty
Double	3
Twin	2
Single	
Bed Size	**Qty**
Super King	
King	1
Queen	2
King-Single	2
Single	2
Bathrooms	**Qty**
Ensuite	1
Private	2
Guest Share	

Luxury Accommodation in Stunning Setting

Features & Attractions

- *Alpacas on property*
- *Golf courses nearby*
- *Local potteries & art studios*
- *Dinner available on request*
- *Mapua village & restaurants 6 min*
- *Walking/kayaking in Abel Tasman & Kahaurangi National Parks*
- *Small weddings catered*

Upon arrival at your ridge top escape you will be rewarded with stunning views of the Tasman Bay. Relax and enjoy a platter of local produce and wine. With four beautiful rooms and suites your comfort is of prime importance to us at **Mahana Escape**. In all suites nothing has been spared when it comes to comfort, so each day's outing will end in a deep revitalising slumber. Sumptuous breakfast awaits you. Your day will begin with a wonderful gourmet breakfast in the dining room, on the patio or in the privacy of your suite.

Mahana Escape is in the heart of the Tasman district, where artisans are abundant. Walk the Abel Tasman and Kahurangi National Parks. Small groups and conferences are our speciality. This is also a fabulous honeymoon destination, where every luxury is provided for you in the King Suite.

Facilities include... private parking, barbecue area, petánque, new developing gardens and walkways. Families and children are welcome.

282

WHARETUTU

12B Kina Beach Road, Nelson, Tasman
Ph (03) 526 6800
Mobile 021-622 175
e-mail: *bookings@wharetutu.co.nz*
http://www.wharetutu.co.nz

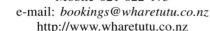

Tariff : N.Z. Dollars	
Double	$175-220
Single	$160-205
Child	Neg.

Bedrooms	Qty
Double	2
Twin	
Single	

Bed Size	Qty
Super King	
King	1
Queen	1
Double	
Single	

Bathrooms	Qty
Ensuite	2
Private	
Guest Share	

Bed & Breakfast
Boutique Accommodation

DIRECTIONS:
From Richmond, SH 60 to
Tasman. Turn right into Kina
Beach Road. Driveway
100 metres on right.
Wharetutu at top of ridge.

Features & Attractions

• *Warm, friendly hospitality*
• *Swimming pool & spa*
• *Pétanque/boules*
• *BBQ available*

• *20 min. from Abel Tasman*
• *Golf courses nearby*
• *Superb coastal walks & beaches*
• *Wine & craft trails*

Jenny and Stan welcome you to **Wharetutu** with its breathtaking views of mountains and peaceful countryside. It is perfectly located for you to explore the many attractions the Nelson region has to offer from the beautiful golden-sand beaches and stunning scenery of the Abel Tasman, to the award winning Nelson wines and succulent food available at nearby vineyards and restaurants. Our guest wing with private entrance, offers two luxurious well appointed suites with quality bed linen, robes and flat screen LCD TV's. Ranch sliding doors lead out to a courtyard with swimming pool and spa. The dining room has a fridge, microwave and bench area with a choice of coffees and teas. Complimentary internet access available. Enjoy our delicious continental and gourmet cooked breakfasts alfresco or in the dining room overlooking the pool. And of course our evening hospitality hour where you can relax with your hosts before dining out at one of our local restaurants, or cook your own BBQ. If you value the good things in life and are looking for an authentic cultural experience then come and enjoy **Wharetutu**.

NEUDORFS GINGERBREAD HOUSE

Neudorf Road, Upper Moutere, Nelson
Ph (03) 543 2472
email: *dandp@gingerbreadhousenz.com*
www.gingerbreadhousenz.com

Features & Attractions

- *Home-baked, organic bread*
- *Vineyards, cafés, beaches*
- *Abel Tasman National Park*
- *Swiss/Kiwi hosts*
- *Special diets on request*
- *Good beds, email, laundry*

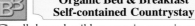
**Organic Bed & Breakfast
Self-contained Countrystay**

Double	$100-150	
Single	$75-150	
Child	neg	

DIRECTIONS:
From **Richmond** 6 km on SH 60, turn left into Moutere Highway. After 17 km turn left, then 3.4 km along Neudorf Road. From SH 61 please contact us for directions

Stroll through wild, romantic, organic gardens. Let magic colours and scents, the song of birds and thousands of stars take you into a world, where you forget daily life's rush and stress. Enjoy stunning rural views from the sunny verandas. You can choose the self-contained, private cottage with its simple beauty and natural elegance, or the character B&B, where you experience real Kiwi life and warm, welcoming hospitality. We love sharing our beautiful home and our time with you. Our central location and local knowledge help you to make the most of your holiday. We aim to offer you more than just a comfortable accommodation. Our guests shall experience a special place and atmosphere that nurtures body and soul.

Bedrooms	Qty
Double	3
Twin	1
Single	3
Bed Size	**Qty**
SuperKing/Twin	1
Queen	3
Double	
Single	2
Bathrooms	**Qty**
Ensuite	1
Private	1
Guest Share	1

MAPUA "SEAVIEW" BED & BREAKFAST

40 Langford Drive, Mapua Village, Nelson
Ph/Fax (03) 540 2006
email: *seaview@mapua.co.nz*
www.mapua.co.nz

Features & Attractions

- *Abel Tasman Park 30 min*
- *Walk to restaurants/wharf*
- *Nelson City 30 min drive*
- *Panoramic views - peaceful*
- *Quality bedding/furnishings*
- *Off-street parking*

**Bed & Breakfast
Homestay**

Double	$135-145	
Single	$135-145	
Child		

Thirty minutes from Nelson, **Mapua "Seaview" Bed & Breakfast** is nestled in the coastal village of Mapua. Our new home offers uninhibited panoramic views overlooking the Waimea Estuary and the Richmond mountain vista beyond. A five minute stroll takes you to four picturesque waterfront licensed restaurants, to Leisure Park and popular beaches. Being central within the Nelson Bay's coastal region makes us an ideal base to explore Abel Tasman National Park, Farewell Spit and many other well known attractions. We have sought to create a homely friendly atmosphere with the accent on comfort. Our cosy guest rooms offer comfortable quality queen beds with feather duvets, television and private bathrooms. Coffee/ tea and homebaking always available. Cooked/continental breakfast provided with fresh local fruit. The numerous leisure activities, sightseeing highlights and sunshine should cater for everyone's interests and tastes. The regions vineyards, arts and craft studios surround us.

Bedrooms	Qty
Double	2
Twin	
Single	
Bed Size	**Qty**
King	
Queen	2
Double	
Single	
Bathrooms	**Qty**
Ensuite	2
Private	
Guest Share	

ACCENT HOUSE

148 Aranui Road, Mapua Village, Nelson
Ph (03) 540 3442, Fax (03) 540 3442
Mobile 027-540 3442
email: *info@accentbnb.co.nz*
www.accentbnb.co.nz

Tariff : N.Z. Dollars	
Double	$185-225
Single	$165-205
Child	

Bedrooms	Qty
Double	3
Twin	1
Single	
Bed Size	**Qty**
Super King	
King	
Queen	3
Double	
Single	
Bathrooms	**Qty**
Ensuite	4
Private	
Guest Share	

Boutique Bed & Breakfast

Features & Attractions

- *Walk to nearby restaurants*
- *Outdoor giant chess*
- *Relaxed & friendly*
- *Elegant rooms & ensuites*
- *Private guest lounge & laundry*
- *Access to outdoor seating*
- *Walk to art & craft studios/beach*
- *Abel Tasman Park/Nelson 30 min.*

Welcome to our beautiful home, designed especially for your relaxation and comfort, and overlooking a private lagoon. Stay with us for a few days and check out all that our stunning region has to offer. What better way to recharge your batteries than to soak up the warm Tasman Bay sunshine, stroll to several local restaurants, Mapua Village and local original art & craft studios. Enjoy beach walks, kayaking, jet boating and much more. We have 3 spacious, elegantly appointed rooms all with stunning ensuites, warm fluffy towels, heated tile floors, TV's and access to private outdoor seating. Luxurious beds that will have you waking up refreshed and ready for a sumptuous Kiwi-style breakfast, served in the dining room or al fresco. A short drive to Nelson City or Abel Tasman National Park. We would be delighted to arrange any local tours for you. We have a beautifully appointed guest lounge with private guest entrance, tea, coffee & ice facilities where you can relax and unwind at the end of the day.
Freephone 0800 540 3442 – we look forward to hearing from you!!

CLAYRIDGE HOUSE & COTTAGES

77 Pine Hill Rd, Ruby Bay, RD 1, Upper Moutere, Nelson
Ph (03) 540 2548, Fax (03) 540 2541
Mobile 027- 447 2099
email: *enquiries@clayridge.co.nz*
www.clayridge.co.nz

Tariff : N.Z. Dollars	
Double	$180-250
Single	$150
Child	neg

Bedrooms	Qty
Double	5
Twin	3
Single	
Bed Size	**Qty**
Super King	3
King	2
Queen	
Double	
Single	
Bathrooms	**Qty**
Ensuite	1
Private	3
Guest Share	

 Quiet Country Cottages and Homestay

Features & Attractions

- 360 degree views
- Peaceful & private country stay
- Email & high speed internet
- Comfortable guest lounge
- 35 min. Abel Tasman National Park
- Minutes from restaurants, crafts, wineries
- Golf clubs for loan
- Personalised day trips organised

DIRECTIONS: On Coastal Highway (SH 60) 20 min from Richmond or 15 min from Motueka, turn into Pine Hill Road. Drive 700m up the valley to the **Clayridge House** and Cottage sign on the left. Then proceed up the drive to the top of the hill.

A stunning setting – Nestled on a ridge at Ruby Bay, in the heart of the beautiful Nelson Province, is **Clayridge House and Cottages**. Providing classic country accommodation, with panoramic views of Tasman Bay, rolling hills and the nearby mountain ranges. **Clayridge** is the ideal place to relax in peace and privacy. The Mt Arthur room in the house offers DVD, radio, robes, toiletries, broad band internet, computer, tea and coffee making facilities and local art. You will enjoy the comfortable guest lounge with an inviting open fire, and a sunny serving area for your delicious **Clayridge** breakfast. The sun-filled two bedroom cottages offer space and privacy. Choose to self-cater or enjoy a breakfast tray delivered to your cottage. Equipped with a full kitchen, TV, DVD, radio, linen, hairdryers, electric blankets, robes, towels and toiletries, heat pumps, washing machine and access to broadband internet. Take a walk through our landscaped gardens or enjoy a game of croquet or petanque. A friendly Labrador and two Llamas are our resident pets.

KIMERET PLACE

Bronte Rd East, Nr Mapua,
RD 1, Upper Moutere, Nelson
Ph (03) 540 2727, Fax (03) 540 2726
email: *stay@kimeretplace.co.nz*
www.kimeretplace.co.nz

Tariff : N.Z. Dollars	
Suites	$260-340
Apartments	$160-210
Cottage	$300-370

Bedrooms	Qty
Double	4
Twin	
Single	

Bed Size	Qty
California King	1
King	3
Queen	
Double	
Single	

Bathrooms	Qty
Ensuite	4
Private	
Guest Share	

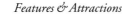

Boutique Bed & Breakfast

Features & Attractions

- *Stunning views*
- *Swimming pool & spa*
- *Self-contained cottage*
- *Craft & wine trails*
- *Space, peace, privacy*
- *Elegant rooms & suites*
- *Award winning restaurants*
- *National Parks & beaches*

At **Kimeret Place** the emphasis is on comfort and relaxation. Enjoy the peace of our secluded two acres overlooking the Waimea Inlet. Soak up the sun and the stunning views from our heated pool and terrace or escape to the hammock and the shade of mature trees. Then, in the evening, after a delicious meal at a local restaurant, immerse yourself in the spa under the star-filled southern sky. What better way to recharge the batteries?

Situated in the heart of Nelson's wine and craft area, **Kimeret Place** is an ideal base to explore the diversity of the region, from the beautiful beaches of the Abel Tasman NP to the dramatic mountains of Kahurangi NP. Our accommodation options include two luxurious suites and two adjoining apartments (which can be booked as a two bedroom cottage, ideal for families or groups). All have tea/coffee facilities, fridge, mini-bar, hair dryers, toiletries, sitting-area with TV, DVD and Hi-fi as well as views from either balcony or deck. Also available light meals, internet and laundry.

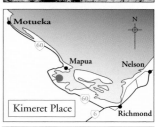

DIRECTIONS: From Richmond on SH 60 turn right after 12 km into Bronte Road East. From Mapua: 4 km on left.

TUIVALE BED & BREAKFAST

76 Higgs Road, Mapua, Nelson
Ph/Fax (03) 540 3300, Mobile 021-152 9310
email: *tuivale@actrix.co.nz*
www.tuivale.co.nz

Features & Attractions

- *Relaxed & friendly*
- *Rural views to sea*
- *Wheelchair entrance*
- *Private access to Rimu Room*
- *Quality bedding*
- *Special diets catered for*

$	Double	$85-120
	Single	$65-90
	Child	

Bed & Breakfast Homestay

Bedrooms	Qty
Double	2
Twin	
Single	
Bed Size	**Qty**
King	
Queen	1
Double	1
Single	
Bathrooms	**Qty**
Ensuite	1
Private	
Family Share	1

Relaxation starts here... **Tuivale Bed & Breakfast** offers you a real home away from home. Situated in the picturesque village of Mapua, **Tuivale** is the ideal location from which to explore the beautiful Nelson/Tasman Region. It is also the perfect place to kick back, relax and recharge. Guests are invited to enjoy the genuine southern hospitality of Vesper and Max Harrison.

The Rimu Room is large with queensize bed and ensuite with heated tile floor. The ranchslider door opens to private balcony and alternative access.

The Kowhai Room is also a double. Both have tea and coffee making facilities, televisions and hairdryers. Delicious gourmet breakfasts are a feature.

We look forward to your company.

FELBRIDGE COTTAGE & HOUSE

6 Pitfure Rd, Wakefield, 7181, Nelson
Ph (03) 541 8505
Mobile 021-022 42540
email: *dplatt33@hotmail.com*
www.felbridge.co.nz

Features & Attractions

- *Welcome basket*
- *Local attractions*
- *Relaxing spa*
- *Fishing, golf, horse riding*
- *15 min. from Nelson*
- *Pets welcome by prior arrangement*

Boutique & Self-contained Accommodation

$	Double	$150-185
	Single	
	Child	

DIRECTIONS: From Nelson SH6 Wakefield Village sign - fork left into Pitfure Rd, we are 600 metres on left. **From Christchurch** SH 6 enter Wakefield Village 1st turn right Edward St, 3rd turn left, we are on the right.

Welcome – Haere Mai. Sheryle and Dave are proud owners of historic **Felbridge House & Cottage**, a magnificent Victorian house with wrap-around verandas and the cottage a 'Dutch Barn', fully equipped self-catering accommodation. Queen and single beds and choice of breakfasts from fresh local produce. Wakefield Village is in a prime location for all that the Nelson region has to offer – fishing, golf, local wineries, arts and crafts, horse trekking. Our local beaches are just a short drive away. Steam railway, historic churches or a relaxing stroll in 'Faulkner Bush Reserve' with native trees in abundance, play area and BBQ facilities. A friendly community awaits with a fresh bakery, butcher, mini market and 'Chateau Rhubarbe', our local café, with local wines and excellent cuisine. All the ingredients for a relaxing stay.

Bedrooms	Qty
Double	1
Twin	1
Single	1
Bed Size	**Qty**
King	
Queen	1
Double	
Single	3
Bathrooms	**Qty**
Ensuite	
Private	
Family Share	1

SAMAKI LODGE

Totara View Road, RD 1 Wakefield, Nelson
Ph (03) 541 9064
Mobile 027-436 5018
e-mail: *stay@samakilodge.co.nz*
www.samakilodge.co.nz

Features & Attractions

- *Single-party bookings assured*
- *3 national parks within 1 hr*
- *Walks, golf, beach, heated pool*
- *Dinner on request*
- *Small weddings venue*
- *Guided trips in the outdoors*

$	Double	$150-200
	Single	$100-150
	Child	Neg.

Stylish Country Suite

Bedrooms	Qty
Double	1
Twin/King	1
Single	
Bed Size	**Qty**
King	
Queen	1
Double	
Single	2
Bathrooms	**Qty**
Ensuite	
Private	1
Guest Share	

DIRECTIONS:
From Nelson take SH 6, just south of Wakefield turn left onto 88 Valley Rd. After 1.5km, turn 2nd left onto Totara View Rd. 1.5km to top of hill, on left – Woodward/**Samaki Lodge**.

Escape the hustle and bustle, relax and be pampered in our new, totally private quality accommodation at **Samaki Lodge**, situated in the hills 3km behind Wakefield, a quiet country village a half hour drive south of Nelson. Enjoy stunning uninterrupted views to Mount Arthur, stroll in our peaceful 3 acre garden or through the woodland area to the gazebo – a great place to have your glass of wine before dinner, or even your special breakfast. **Samaki Lodge** has a private guest suite with two bedrooms, luxury bathroom and lounge with all the "comfort extras". Our interests, boating, fishing, hiking, gardens and crafts, may entice you to stay awhile and let us take you to some of the spots only some of the locals know about. Make your stay more than just Bed & Breakfast. Our friendly cat and dog complete our warm hospitality – see you soon!

WESTLEIGH

Waimea West Road, RD, Brightwater, Nelson
Ph (03) 542 3654
email: *westleigh@paradise.net.nz*

Features & Attractions

- *Secluded park-like setting*
- *Close to good beach*
- *Great dinner available*
- *Near 3 good golf courses*
- *On wine & craft trail*
- *Relax & smell the roses*

$	Double	$125
	Single	$100
	Child	

Countrystay Bed & Breakfast

Bedrooms	Qty
Double	2
Twin	
Single	
Bed Size	**Qty**
King	
Queen	1
Double	
Single	2
Bathrooms	**Qty**
Ensuite	1
Private	
Guest Share	

Westleigh is a relaxing home set on 27 acres. An ideal base to explore all that the Nelson province has to offer. The house has evolved from an old farmhouse and is now surrounded by a woodland garden visited by many birds including wild ducks taking advantage of the large pond. We are a short drive from two good golf courses and an uncrowded safe beach.

There is a selection of good restaurants nearby, or you can enjoy a home cooked meal by arrangement.

Nelson has much to offer including on average seven hours of sunshine a day. Share our corner of paradise.

Our email address is accurate!

IDESIA

14 Idesia Grove, Richmond, 7002, Nelson
Ph (03) 544 0409, Fax (03) 544 0402
Mobile 027-632 7869
email: *idesian@xtra.co.nz*
www.idesia.co.nz

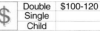

Features & Attractions
- *Dinner by arrangement*
- *Ample off-street parking*
- *Quiet location*
- *Central to Nelson/Tasman region*
- *Broadband Internet/wireless network*
- *Abel Tasman Park booking agent*

Bed & Breakfast

Double	$100-120
Single	
Child	

J enny & Barry offer you warm hospitality and quality service. Easily accessible from SH6, our modern home, in a quiet grove, is elevated to catch sun and views. **Idesia B&B** centrally located and only 20 minutes drive from Nelson, affords easy access to National Parks, beaches, vineyards and art/crafts. Upon arrival, enjoy a relaxing drink and home baking on our charming patio area. Guest rooms offer comfortable quality beds and ensuite/private bathroom with coffee/tea available. Breakfast, served with fresh seasonal fruits and your choice from a sizzling cooked selection. With our Broadband Internet and wireless network, you may use our laptop or yours. Come and let us make your stay a memorable one.

Bedrooms	Qty
Double	2
Twin	
Single	
Bed Size	**Qty**
S King/ Twin	1
Queen	1
Double	
Single	
Bathrooms	**Qty**
Ensuite	1
Private	1
Guest Share	

Sea kayaking - Abel Tasman National Park

Photo Ian Trafford

STAFFORD PLACE

61 Redwood Road, Appleby, Richmond, Nelson
Ph (03) 544 6103, Mobile 027-232 5121
email: *staffordplace@xtra.co.nz*
www.staffordplace.co.nz

Tariff : N.Z. Dollars	
Double	$250
Single	$150
Child	

Bedrooms	Qty
Double	1
Twin	
Single	1
Bed Size	Qty
Super King	
King	1
Queen	
Double	1
Single	
Bathrooms	Qty
Ensuite	1
Private	
Guest Share	1

    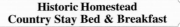

**Historic Homestead
Country Stay Bed & Breakfast**

Features & Attractions

- *Award winning homestead*
- *Secluded and quiet*
- *Mature English garden*
- *To Richmond in 10 minutes*
- *Clean, safe beach 4 km*
- *Single party bookings*
- *Email, fax and laundry available*
- *Abel Tasman National Park 1 hr*

Stafford Place, an historic homestead with great charm, built in 1866, half a km off the road, surrounded by 100 year old oaks, blue gums, an olive grove and apple orchards. Mature English garden, huge lawn, peace, quiet, space, seclusion, native birds, great breakfasts, complimentary drinks, spectacular ensuite, great weather and friendly hosts.

No swimming pool, but we don't need one with Rabbit Island beach at the end of our road – clean, safe, deserted, sandy and 10 km long. Jumping-off place for Abel Tasman, Kahurangi and Nelson Lakes National Parks, golf courses, vineyards, potteries, restaurants and other nice places. Single-party bookings only, so you have the place to yourselves. Come and go as

you please. Tea and coffee always on tap and your own fridge to keep your wine and beer cool. NEXT Magazine's appraisal of **Stafford Place** –
"To describe such luxury as a 'Bed & Breakfast' seems misleading, though literally true".

ARAPIKI

21 Arapiki Road, Stoke, Nelson
Ph (03) 547 3741
email: *wisechoice@nelsonparadise.co.nz*
www.nelsonparadise.co.nz

Features & Attractions

- *Centrally located in Nelson area*
- *Fully self-contained units*
- *Continental breakfast $7.50 pp*
- *Attractive garden setting*
- *Private deck or balcony*
- *Off-street parking*

Self-contained Homestay Units in Attractive Garden Setting

Double	$85-120
Single	$70-90
Child	

DIRECTIONS:
From the Stoke Shopping Centre Arapiki Road is on the right approx. 1 km north along the Main Road Stoke. It is approx. 6 km from Central Nelson.

Enjoy a relaxing holiday in the midst of your trip. The two self-contained smokefree units in our large home offer you comfort and privacy and are also very suitable for longer stays. These quality units in an attractive garden setting are centrally located in the Nelson area which has NZ's highest sunshine hours. Unit 1, which is larger, is in a pleasant and private garden setting. A ranchslider opens out to a deck with outdoor furniture for your use. It contains an electric stove, microwave, television, auto washing machine, phone and outdoors barbeque.

Unit 2 has a balcony setting with seating to enjoy sea and mountain views. It contains a television, microwave and phone. At present our affordable prices offer excellent value for money for the 'home away from home' accommodation provided.

Bedrooms	Qty
Double	2
Twin	
Single	
Bed Size	**Qty**
King	
Queen/Double	2
Double	
Single	1
Bathrooms	**Qty**
Ensuite	2
Private	
Guest Share	

SAKURA BED & BREAKFAST

604 Main Road, Stoke, Nelson
Ph (03) 547 0229, Fax (03) 547 0229
Mobile 021-0226 2632
email: *fumio.noguchi@xtra.co.nz*
www.sakura-nelson.co.nz

Features & Attractions

- *Special Japanaese breakfast*
- *Quiet, peaceful location*
- *Ample off-street parking*
- *Airport pick-up*
- *Warm, friendly hospitality*
- *Bone-carving artist's home*

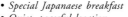

Bed & Breakfast

Double	$160
Single	$90-120
Child	neg

Come and enjoy our tasty, hearty, wholesome breakfast, choose either special Japanese or cooked European-style! We are friendly Japanese hosts and have been accommodating since 2000. **Sakura Bed & Breakfast** is situated in a quiet cul-de-sac off the main road with ample off-street car parking. Restaurants, cafés and supermarkets are all within walking distance. We are 5 min. from the Airport, 10 min. from central Nelson. The house is modern, clean and sunny with a peaceful garden and deck. Complimentary tea/coffee, Japanese green tea and cookies. The double room with ensuite has fridge, TV, microwave. We follow the Japanese custom of no shoes in the house (sorry). Fumio is a bone-carving artist and Sayuri is a Japanese calligrapher.

Bedrooms	Qty
Double	1
Twin	1
Single	1
Bed Size	**Qty**
King	1
Queen	
Double	
Single	3
Bathrooms	**Qty**
Ensuite	1
Guest Share	1
Family Share	1

AMBLESIDE LUXURY BED & BREAKFAST

237 Annesbrook Drive, Tahunanui, Nelson
Ph (03) 548 5067, Fax (03) 548 5067
Mobile 021-147 0898
email: *ambleside@paradise.net.nz*
www.amblesidenelson.co.nz

Tariff : N.Z. Dollars	
Double	$140-170
Single	$140-170
Child	

Bedrooms	Qty
Double	2
Twin	2
Single	

Bed Size	Qty
Super King	
King	
Queen	2
King/Single	2
Single	2

Bathrooms	Qty
Ensuite	4
Private	
Guest Share	

     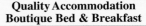

**Quality Accommodation
Boutique Bed & Breakfast**

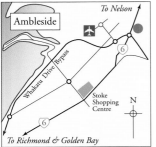

Features & Attractions

- *Purpose-built guest wing*
- *Off-street parking*
- *Gourmet breakfasts*
- *Gateway Abel Tasman Park*
- *Tea/coffee, refreshments*
- *Laundry facilities*
- *Email/Internet*
- *5 minutes to airport*

Ambleside, like its namesake in England, has a typical 'olde worlde' charm. The single-storey, purpose-built guest wing is luxuriously appointed, exuding comfort, style and ambience that belie the 'little cottage' frontage. Guests have own private entrance off the deck, separate lounge and each room, tastefully decorated, has its own ensuite. Breakfasts, according to our guests, are *"second to none"*, served on the deck, sunny courtyard or dining room. Choose from the extensive menu and dine at the time of your choice. Settle in with a cuppa and yummy home-made baking. Complimentary refreshments are served throughout your stay. A spirit of gracious hospitality sets **Ambleside** apart and you are assured of warm and friendly, (in guest's words) *"six-star service!"* In addition to our extensive brochure display, we are happy to help you make the most of your stay in the Nelson Region. Our central location affords you close proximity to Nelson City, beaches, world-class restaurants and beautiful Abel Tasman Park.

ANNICK HOUSE
29 Cleveland Terrace, Nelson
Ph (03) 548 0554, Fax (03) 548 0505
Mobile 021-1342 808

 email: *nick.james@xtra.co.nz*
home
NEW ZEALAND
www.annickhouse.co.nz

 VISA
MasterCard

Features & Attractions

* *5 min. easy walk to city*
* *Self-contained/off street parking*
* *Breakfast essentials included*
* *Quiet and peaceful area*
* *Internet/laundry facilities*
* *Free use of bicycles*

BB **Quality and Affordable Self-contained** **SC** **$**

	Double	$135-165
	Single	$120-150
	Child	neg

A nnick House offers two private self-contained studio units in a quiet and secluded garden setting five minutes walk to the city centre. Our **Out of Africa** and **A Touch Oriental** studios are tastefully furnished and have a private entrance and bathrooms. Both are fully equipped with kitchen facilities, cooking essentials and BBQ. We offer an optional breakfast tray including fresh fruits in season. Weekly rates are available. Our central location allows you to explore the region's many attractions. Walk the nearby tracks or ride bicycles to the beach. With our local knowledge we are happy to assist with your travel plans. You can be sure of a warm, friendly welcome from our two Tokinese cats and a comfortable stay.

Bedrooms	Qty
Double	2
Twin	
Single	
Bed Size	**Qty**
S King/Twin	2
Queen	
Double	
Single	
Bathrooms	**Qty**
Ensuite	
Private	2
Guest Share	

SHAKESPEARE COTTAGE
5 Shakespeare Walk, Nelson
Ph (03) 546 9913, Fax (03) 546 9913
Mobile 021-215 6950
www.shakespearecottage.co.nz

Features & Attractions

* *5 min. walk to city*
* *Riverside location*
* *Golf course, beach*
* *Fully self-contained*
* *Close to bus, info centre*
* *Off-street parking*

BA **Inner City Self-contained & Self-catering Accommodation** **SC** **$**

	Double	$120-150
	Single	$100-150
	Child	$10

Shakespeare Cottage and **Villa Apartment** are situated by the Maitai River, only a few minutes walk from the city centre with its wonderful variety of restaurants and cafés, galleries and gardens, the centre of New Zealand, river and bush walks plus a heated swimming pool just a stroll away. The cottage and apartment are completely self-contained and can sleep up to four people each.

The apartment is situated in a character villa, circa 1890. There is one spacious bedroom with large bay window area, bathroom with underfloor heating and washing machine, separate lounge with kitchenette, river views, private entrance and OSP. The cottage is situated in a private garden setting at the rear of villa. It is completely self-contained, fridge/freezer, dishwasher, underfloor heating, private sunny and fenced. Both the **Apartment** and **Cottage** are equipped with wireless internet and telephone access. Tea, real coffee and basic breakfast essentials are included.

Bedrooms	Qty
Double	2
Twin	
Single	
Bed Size	**Qty**
SuperKing/Twin	4
Queen	
Double-sofabed	1
Single	
Bathrooms	**Qty**
Ensuite	2
Private	2
Guest Share	

WARWICK HOUSE

64 Brougham Street, Nelson City
Ph (03) 548 3164, Fax (03) 548 3215
Mobile 021-688 243
email: *info@warwickhouse.co.nz*
www.warwickhouse.co.nz

Tariff : N.Z. Dollars	
$195-395	Double
$155-355	Single
$30-45	Child

Qty	Bedrooms
4	Double
1	Twin
	Single

Qty	Bed Size
3	Super King
	King
2	Queen
	Double
	Single

Qty	Bathrooms
5	Ensuite
	Private
	Guest Share

**Boutique Hotel, B&B
Self-Contained**

Features & Attractions

DIRECTIONS:
Please refer to our website for directions.

Advanced booking
recommended.

- *5 min. walk to central Nelson*
- *Views over the city to the sea*
- *Large ballroom for guest use*
- *4 storey octagonal 'fairytale' tower*
- *Inhouse aromatherapy/massage*
- *Winter rates*
- *Abel Tasman national park*
- *Wine and art trails*

Warwick House, built in 1854 is truly one of the countrys' most amazing heritage mansions. Home of important early Nelson residents, the Fells' and the Edwards, it provides a chance for guests to experience the true opulence and grandeur of the early Victorian era. Jenny and Nick and our black labrador 'Vicky' are experienced hosts who thoroughly enjoy ensuring that your stay will be a very memorable one.

The Nelson region offers so many great attractions from the countrys' highest sunshine hours, beautiful outdoors to the vibrant arts, crafts and wine scene. Cooked breakfasts are served to classical music in the grand ballroom. Self-catering is available to family groups of up to 6 persons.

Many great riverside and hilltop walks start within minutes of the property. In-house aromatherapy and massage are available if prebooked. Baby grand piano available for guest use. Ballroom for private functions.

'Make your stay in Nelson a special one'

SUNSET WATERFRONT B&B
455 Rock Road, Nelson
Ph (03) 548 3431 , Fax(03) 548 3743
Mobile 027-436 3500
e-mail: *waterfrontnelson@xtra.co.nz*

Features & Attractions
- *Quiet, secluded location*
- *Off-street parking*
- *Beautiful sunsets*
- *Walk to seafood restaurants*
- *Self-catering Cottage $180*
- *Sea and mountain views*

 Bed & Breakfast and Separate Suite   **VISA** **MasterCard** $

Double	$140-150
Single	$110-120
Child	

Bedrooms	Qty
Double	1
Twin	1
Single	
Bed Size	**Qty**
King	
Queen	2
Double	
Single	3
Bathrooms	**Qty**
Ensuite	2
Private	
Guest Share	

Sunset Waterfront B&B provides wonderful panoramic sea and mountain views of Tasman Bay. Ideally situated to walk to quality seafood restaurants. Stroll along the promenade to enjoy the sunset or take an evening walk along the beach. We are 10 minutes drive from Nelson Airport and the central bus station. Sunset Waterfront B&B is situated in a quiet and secluded location. Freshly brewed coffee and local fresh produce is provided for your breakfast. Also freshly picked raspberries and strawberries when in season. No children under 12. Come enjoy our paradise! Parking right up to the house. Cottage available next door.

SUSSEX HOUSE BED & BREAKFAST
238 Bridge Street, Nelson
Ph (03) 548 9972, Fax (03) 548 9975
Mobile 027-478 4846

 email: *reservations@sussex.co.nz*
www.sussex.co.nz

Features & Attractions
- *5 min. walk to city*
- *130-year-old residence*
- *Overlooking botan. gardens*
- *Riverside location*
- *Off-street parking*
- *Fluent French spoken*

 Quality Bed & Breakfast G $

Double	$140-170
Single	$110-140
Child	$20

 **VISA** **MasterCard** **AMERICAN EXPRESS**

Bedrooms	Qty
Double	3
Twin	2
Single	
Bed Size	**Qty**
King	
Queen	5
Double	
Single	2
Bathrooms	**Qty**
Ensuite	4
Private	1
Guest Share	

Situated beside the beautiful Maitai River, our charming Victorian family home has retained its original character and ambience. It is only minutes walk from central Nelson's award-winning restaurants and cafés, the Queen's Gardens, Suter Art Gallery, Botanical Hill (The Centre of New Zealand) and numerous river and bush walks. The five sunny bedrooms all have TV and are spacious and tastefully decorated. All rooms have access to the verandah and complimentary tea and coffee facilities are provided. Breakfast includes fresh and preserved fruits, home-made bread, hot croissants, home-made yoghurt, cheeses and a large variety of cereals. Our facilities include: a wheelchair suite, free email/Internet station, fax, laundry and complimentary port. We speak French, having lived for 25 years in New Caledonia.

HAVENVIEW HOMESTAY

10 Davies Drive, Walters Bluff, Nelson
Ph (03) 546 6045, Mobile 027-420 0737
email: *havenview@paradise.net.nz*

www.havenview.co.nz

Features & Attractions

- *New outdoor spa*
- *Dinner available*
- *Panoramic sea views*
- *Wireless internet & Sky TV*
- *Overlook Miyazu Gardens*
- *3 min drive to city centre*

$	Double	$130-155
	Single	$90
	Child	

Homestay
Bed & Breakfast

Bedrooms	Qty
Double	2
Twin	
Single	1
Bed Size	**Qty**
King	
Queen	2
Double	
King Single	1
Bathrooms	**Qty**
Ensuite	1
Private	1
Guest Share	

Welcome to our sunny, modern home, only three minutes from the centre of Nelson.
Relax on our deck sipping a complimentary local wine and nibbles each evening while enjoying the panoramic views across the bay to Able Tasman Park (see photo). Join us for an evening meal or dine at one of Nelson's fine restaurants. We serve a light cooked breakfast at a time to suit you; and then during the day visit the National Park; do a wine tour; or have a game of golf. We both play golf and can recommend various courses.
Our large queen ensuite has sea views, while our second queen room has a view of our garden. Come and let us make your stay a friendly, pampered experience.

DIRECTIONS: Exit motorway at Founders Park sign, 700 m turn left up Walters Bluff, right into Davies Drive, look for homestay sign after 3rd house on right. (We are down right of way).

ATAWHAI HOMESTAY
MIKE'S BED & BREAKFAST

4 Seaton Street, Atawhai, Nelson
Ph (03) 545 1671
email: *mikecooper@actrix.co.nz*

Features & Attractions

- *Easy access to Nelson City*
- *Gateway to West Coast*
- *Gateway to National Parks*
- *Ferries less than 2 hours*
- *Access to the BoulderBank*
- *Only 200m from the sea*

$	Double	$80
	Single	$80
	Child	neg

Homestay
Bed & Breakfast

Bedrooms	Qty
Double	2
Twin	
Single	
Bed Size	**Qty**
King	
Queen	2
Double	
Single	
Bathrooms	**Qty**
Ensuite	2
Private	
Guest Share	

Only five minutes by car from Nelson city centre, we give you a warm welcome to our comfortable home in a safe, quiet neighbourhood with superb views over Tasman Bay and out to the mountains beyond.
Our guest accommodation is almost self-contained and is well equipped with two ensuite bedrooms, a small kitchenette with fridge/freezer, microwave and complimentary tea and coffee making facilities; a lounge, holding some of our large book collection, which you are welcome to use, and a TV. Complimentary laundry facilities are available. Besides books and our rose garden, our main interests include travel, education, sea fishing and our beautiful Schnauzer dog.

A CULINARY EXPERIENCE
71 Tresillian Ave, Atawhai, Nelson
Ph (03) 545 1886, Fax (03) 545 1869
Free Ph: 0800-891 886
email: *aculinaryexperience@xtra.co.nz*
www.a-culinary-experience.com

Tariff : N.Z. Dollars	
Double	$175-225
Single	$160-210
Child	

Bedrooms	Qty
Double	2
Twin	
Single	

Bed Size	Qty
Super King/Twin	2
King	
Queen	
Double	
King Single	2

Bathrooms	Qty
Ensuite	2
Private	
Guest Share	

Luxury B&B Homestay
A Culinary Experience

Features & Attractions

- *Pampered holiday package*
- *Sea and mountain views*
- *Therapeutic massage and spa*
- *Gourmet breakfasts & dinners*
- *Boutique cheese maker*
- *Sculpture & herb garden*
- *Beautiful guest lounge*
- *Friendly hosts*

Welcome to our lovely home, filled with original art, laughter and fabulous food. Your caring hosts have created a unique boutique accommodation. Naturopath, Joe, provides therapeutic massage. Kay, cookbook author and former cooking school owner, provides delightful dinners or cooking classes. Let us pamper you.

Enjoy gourmet breakfasts: blueberry pancakes with glazed bananas, eggs benedict, crêpes. After exploring Nelson wineries, galleries, restaurants, golfing or hiking/kayaking in Abel Tasman Park, indulge in a massage or spa.

Choose the quiet, sun-drenched garden or a peaceful patio, sipping a complimentary wine served with yummy appetizers to celebrate sensational sunsets, exquisite bay and mountain views. Read in the sculpture garden and quaff the aroma of fresh herbs, fruit, and produce that we grow. Sit and chat about boats, art, Rotary, The Red Hat Society, travels and beautiful New Zealand.

Book a luxurious room: king-size beds, imported linens, heated tile ensuites (bathrooms). Homemade pastries, 24-hour tea facilities, laundry and broadband are next to the guest lounge. With so much to do in the region, three or more nights are recommended. Arrive as guests – leave as friends.

PARAUTANE LODGE
137 Parautane Way, Wakapuaka, RD 1 Nelson
Ph (03) 545 2959, Fax (03) 545 2958
Mobile 021-052 6842
email: *parautaneinfo@paradise.net.nz*
www.nelsonlodge.co.nz

Tariff : N.Z. Dollars	
Double	$180-340
Single	
Child	

Bedrooms	Qty
Double	4
Twin	
Single	
Bed Size	Qty
Super King	
King	1
Queen	3
Double	1
Single	1
Bathrooms	Qty
Ensuite	4
Private	
Guest Share	

**Country
Luxury Lodge**

Features & Attractions

- *Stylish Luxury Lodge*
- *10 acres lifestyle block*
- *180° sea and mountain views*
- *Ocean view from spa & rooms*
- *Art, craft & wine trails*
- *Beaches & town 12 min.*
- *Abel Tasman Nat. Park 1hour*
- *Hike, kayak, hunt, fish*

Parautane Lodge is an exquisite Bed & Breakfast in an idyllic country setting – the uttermost combination of peace and tranquillity while still catering to your every need. Situated just 12 minutes drive from Nelson City, Candace and Alan provide luxurious rooms, breathtaking views and generous breakfasts. It is the perfect retreat for a weekend away from the stresses of life or for a taste of New Zealand culture. From the comfort of your bed the rooms offer beautiful sea and mountain views. Each room accesses expansive decking from where you can wander down to the garden gazebo for a spa. Our 10-acre section allows you the opportunity to stroll about enjoying the tranquillity of the country. Lounge around the house or experience all the wonderful things Nelson has to offer, be it arts/festivals, beaches, sporting activities or wonderous cafés and eateries. Close to Abel Tasman and Kahurangi National Parks it is the perfect location to spend a week or two exploring the Nelson/Marlborough Region. Offering amazing comfort, romance and seclusion, the **Lodge** is also ideal for honeymooners and those seeking a retreat.

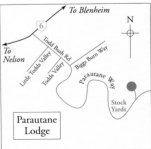

DIRECTIONS: Leave Nelson towards Blenheim on SH 6. After 10 km turn right into Todd Bush Rd. Landmark: Church on sweeping corner. We are 2 km from here. Follow off the end of Todd Bush Rd. onto Parautane Way, climb uphill until you see our sign on the left.

AVAREST BED & BREAKFAST

1 Kerr Bay Road, PO Box 25, St Arnaud, Nelson Lakes 7053
Ph (03) 521 1864, Fax (03) 521 1865
Mobile (027) 430 5036
e-mail: *avarestbnb@xtra.co.nz*
www.avarestbnb.co.nz

DIRECTIONS:
Enter Kerr Bay Road from
SH63, travel past the Dept of
Conservation HQ towards the
lake. We are the last driveway
on the left.

Tariff : N.Z. Dollars	
Double	$220-260
Single	$195-235
Child	

Bedrooms	Qty
Double	2
Twin	
Single	

Bed Size	Qty
Super King	
King	
Queen	1
Double	1
Single	1

Bathrooms	Qty
Ensuite	
Private	1
Guest Share	

VISA   MasterCard

**Boutique Accommodation
Bed & Breakfast**

Features & Attractions

- *1 min. walk to lake edge*
- *Single party bookings*
- *Comfortable and private*
- *Rhododendron gardens*
- *Overlooking Lake Rotoiti*
- *Bush walks, fishing, hunting*
- *Among mature native forest*
- *Relaxed atmosphere*

Situated in the heart of Nelson Lakes National Park, **Avarest** is the perfect luxury mountain retreat for people who wish to relax in style and comfort. Overlooking Lake Rotoiti, we are nestled among mature native forest filled with the sound of bellbirds and tuis.

Underneath the beech canopy are over 130 rhododendrons which flower progressively from September to January.

Guest rooms are comfortable and tastefully decorated with private luxury amenities, including separate toilet, shower and ladies' vanity room. A separate lounge with television, music, books and art is available for guests. Breakfast at **Avarest** can be as simple or elaborate as your appetite requires.

We are 70km from Nelson on SH 6, 80km from Blenheim on SH 63, 300km from Christchurch on SH 7. The National Park has world renowned tramps and walks available for all levels of fitness. You will be welcomed by our cat Kiri.

TRIPLE TUI

2454 Dry Weather Road, Glenhope, RD 2, Nelson
Ph (03) 548 4481, Fax (03) 548 4491
Mobile 027-517 1923
email: *stay@tripletui.co.nz*
www.tripletui.co.nz

Features & Attractions

- *Bush & river walks*
- *Peaceful & private*
- *Log fire in cabins*
- *Great trout fishing nearby*
- *Hunt, ski & white water raft*
- *Backs onto Kahurangi N Park*

$		
	Double	$160-180
	Single	$160-180
	Extra pp	$40-60

Self-contained Log Cabins

Bedrooms	Qty
Double	2
Twin	
Single	
Bed Size	**Qty**
King	
Queen	2
Double	2
Single	
Bathrooms	**Qty**
Ensuite	
Private	2
Guest Share	

Triple Tui's log cabins provide a central base from which many varied outdoor activities are on your doorstep. World class fly fishing is but a short cast away with rivers including the Buller, Wairau, Gowan, Owen and Motueka, lakes include Rotoiti and Rotoroa. If getting wet is an option, there is white water rafting and kayaking available in nearby Murchison. In the winter season skiing at St Arnaud and Rainbow ski fields might attract, with feet up on your return and a glass of wine in front of a roaring manuka fire. Our 50 acres, with the Hope Range behind us, allows plenty of privacy and tranquility. An ample breakfast basket, with tea and coffee, awaits in your log cabin, enough for every day of your stay. Visit our website.

DIRECTIONS: SH6 1hr south of Nelson, 30min north of Murchison. Dry Weather Rd (Glenhope-Tadmore Rd) is at the bottom of Hope Saddle. We are 4.5 km up road on left.

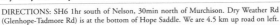

MURCHISON LODGE

15 Grey Street, Murchison
Ph (03) 523 9196, Fax (03) 523 9197
Free Ph: 0800 523 9196
email: *info@murchisonlodge.co.nz*
www.murchisonlodge.co.nz

Tariff : N.Z. Dollars	
Double	$140-180
Single	$115-160
Child	

Bedrooms	Qty
Double	3
Twin	1
Single	
Bed Size	**Qty**
Super King	
King	1
Queen	2
Double	
King/Single	2
Bathrooms	**Qty**
Ensuite	3
Private	1
Guest Share	

Quality B&B Lodge with Character

Features & Attractions

- *Peaceful setting*
- *Free wireless broadband*
- *Free use of bicycles*
- *Hosts in own cottage*
- *Easy walk to pubs & cafés*
- *Fishing, rafting, golf*
- *Children over 12 welcome*
- *Dinner platters available*

DIRECTIONS:
To find Grey Street when entering town:
From south & west take 2nd left.
From north & east take 1st right.

Tired of frantic bag packing every morning? Relax for a few days at this warm timber lodge, where you'll find comfortable beds and awake to the smell of fresh bread, and the prospect of fresh juice and breakfast cooked on the BBQ. Set on four acres, we have various animals and a friendly puppy. The Buller River provides swimming holes and fishing access; trees and mountains surround us, yet Murchison's pubs and cafés are within 5 mins walk. The area is renowned for its fly-fishing and white-water activities. Have free use of our bicycles or walk the local trails. Play golf or try gold panning at NZ's longest swingbridge. Alternatively, just 'chill' in a garden hammock or have a 'good old read' in the large and comfortable guest lounge, enjoying tea and home baking. Use our free wireless broadband to write home whilst sipping a cold beer on the verandah or a wine in front of the log fire.

MUDBRICK LODGE

150 Rimu Gully Rd, PO Box 92, Rai Valley, Marlborough
Ph (03) 571 6147, Fax (03) 571 6147
Mobile 027-251 3867
email: *tania@mudbricklodge.co.nz*
www.mudbricklodge.co.nz

Tariff : N.Z. Dollars	
Double	$200-260
Single	$190-210
Child	

Bedrooms	Qty
Double	2
Twin	
Single	

Bed Size	Qty
Super King	2
King	
Queen	
Double	
Single	

Bathrooms	Qty
Ensuite	2
Private	
Guest Share	

      **Self-contained Luxury**

DIRECTIONS:
Take French Pass turn-off from Rai Valley
on SH 6 halfway between Blenheim and
Nelson. We are 5 km from this turn-off,
signposted on each turn. Take 1st right
across Carluke Bridge, next right.
Then 1st left up Rimu Gully.

Features & Attractions

- *Blissful country retreat*
- *Spa pool in garden*
- *Self-contained suites*
- *Open fire, luxury lounge*

- *40 minutes to Nelson*
- *40 minutes to Marlborough*
- *Art, craft & wine trails*
- *Great base to explore*

Your host Tania searched the whole of New Zealand for a setting that would enable her to create a lifestyle she could share with others. **Mudbrick Lodge**, with its two luxury guest rooms, is the result. Tania's background as a professional chef with a passion for fine wines, along with her local Marlborough and Nelson connections, make her the ideal host for your exploration of this, one of New Zealand's most beautiful regions. Starting each day with a superb home-cooked breakfast, you decide just how energetic or relaxing your day will be by choosing from the endless array of activities the area provides. Whether you wish to tour the famous Marlborough vineyards, fish for the notoriously cunning trout in one of the local streams, horse ride through stunning scenery, hunt for deer and wild pig, kayak the beautiful Tennyson Inlet accompanied by dolphins, picnic on your own 'desert island' in the Sounds, bush walk to the crystal clear waters of the Emerald Pools, cast a line into one of the secret salt water fishing spots or just wish to relax on the patio with a good book and a crisp Chardonnay, **Mudbrick Lodge** is perfectly equipped to make each day a memorable one.

Pelorus Bridge - Marlborough ▷ YOUR HOSTS: Roz and Jack   Ph (03) 574 2841

PELORUS RIVER HORSES
5677 SH6, Pelorus Bridge, Marlborough
Ph (03) 574 2841, Fax (03) 574 2842
email: *riverhorses@xnet.co.nz*
www.pelorusriverhorses.co.nz

Features & Attractions

- *Stunning scenery*
- *Baths with a view*
- *Lots to do and see*
- *Comprehensive complimentary comforts*
- *Memorable magical horserides*
- *Really rather relaxing*

 Genuine Kiwi Flavour

	Double	$180
	Single	per
	Child	night

Ideal for long term stays in serious comfort and stunning scenery. Situated in the heart of a working equestrian facility with a river front within easy walking distance. Perfectly located as a base for enjoying Marlborough wineries, Nelson arts and crafts, the beauties of the Sounds and Kaikoura whales. The Ranch House complex contains everything you could wish for plus a few unusual attractions like an exclusive gift shop, a his 'n hers bath house and an extensive outside living complete with a BBQ. There is a tariff reduction for stays of more than one night and even better, half price for stays of eight nights or more. A breakfast is available on the first morning only, at extra charge.

Bedrooms	Qty
Double	1
Twin	
Single	1
Bed Size	**Qty**
King	
Queen	1
Double	
Single	3
Bathrooms	**Qty**
Ensuite	1
Private	1
Guest Share	1

Kenepuru Sound ▷ YOUR HOSTS: Alison and Robin Bowron   Ph: (03) 573 4432

THE NIKAUS
86 Manaroa Road, Waitaria Bay,
Kenepuru Sound, RD 2, Picton 7372
Ph/Fax (03) 573 4432, Mobile 027-454 4712
email: *info@thenikaus.co.nz*
www.thenikaus.co.nz

Features & Attractions

- *Genuine NZ farm experience*
- *Central location in Kenepuru and Pelorus Sounds*
- *Evening meal $30 pp*
- *Golf, fishing, water taxi*
- *Large country garden*

 Farmstay Bed & Breakfast

	Double	$120
	Single	$60
	Child	

The Nikaus sheep and cattle farm in Waitaria Bay, Kenepuru Sound, is 2.5 hours drive from Blenheim via Picton or Havelock. We offer friendly, personal service in our comfortable, spacious home. The large gardens contain many rhododendrons, roses, camellias, lilies and perennials with big sloping lawns and views out to sea.

We are interested in farming, boating, fishing and gardening and have pet cats, Minnie (Jack Russell) and farm dogs, donkeys, pet wild pigs, turkeys, hens, peacocks, sheep and cattle. We offer good, hearty country meals using home-grown produce. Local operators are available for fishing trips and water taxis. Tariff for full farmstay with Dinner, Bed & Breakfast is $90.00 per person per day. Prior booking essential.

Bedrooms	Qty
Double	1
Twin	2
Single	
Bed Size	**Qty**
King	
Queen	1
Double	
Single	4
Bathrooms	**Qty**
Ensuite	
Private	
Guest Share	1

NGAIO BAY ECO-HOMESTAY AND B&B

Ngaio Bay, French Pass Road, RD 3, Rai Valley,
Marlborough Sounds
Ph (03) 576 5287 Fax (03) 576 5287
email: *homestay@ngaiobay.co.nz*
www.ngaiobay.co.nz

Tariff : N.Z. Dollars	
Double	$240
Single	$160
Child	$80

Bedrooms	Qty
Double	2
Twin	
Single	

Bed Size	Qty
Super King	
King	2
Queen	
Double	
Single	3

Bathrooms	Qty
Ensuite	
Private	2
Guest Share	

 Remote Marlborough Sounds
Eco-homestay and Bed & Breakfast

Ngaio Bay
Homestay

N

Okiwi Bay

To
Nelson   Rai Valley
(6)
Havelock   To
Picton
To Blenheim & Picton ↓

DIRECTIONS:
Please phone for easy directions.

Features & Attractions

- *Sandy private beach*
- *Outdoor fire-heated bath*
- *Dinghies*
- *Dolphins & seabirds abound*
- *Bush & farm walks nearby*
- *Charter boats available*
- *Organic garden & orchard*
- *Stunning sunsets*

Experience something special at **Ngaio Bay**, with its own private beach, situated in a truly remote part of the Marlborough Sounds. Breathtaking wilderness and physical beauty, warm, welcoming hosts, scrumptious food, peace and tranquility, fresh seafood, own homegrown organic veggies and fruit when available, beautiful garden, stunning sunsets,

comfortable, private, separate accommodation. Views of the awesome waters of French Pass. Ideal for a romantic honeymoon, relaxing holiday, family get-together or wilderness adventure. Your stay at **Ngaio Bay** will be an authentic Kiwi experience. The 'Garden Cottage', with small private deck, is hidden in the garden and overlooks the beach. The loft-style 'Rose and Dolphin' is sunny and spacious. A small verandah overlooks a stream, bush and beach. A favourite speciality is our private outdoor bath enjoyed at sunset, or under sun, rain or stars, prepared by your hosts. Dinner is included in tariff. Three loveable labradors. *Arrive as strangers, leave as friends.*

FERNRIDGE

Double Cove, Queen Charlotte Sound, PO Box 545, Picton
Ph (03) 573 4471, Fax (03) 573 4472
Mobile 021-156 3836
email: *fernridge.homestay@clear.net.nz*
www.fernridgehomestay.co.nz

Tariff : N.Z. Dollars	
$250	Double
$180	Single
	Child

Qty	Bedrooms
1	Double
1	Twin
	Single

Qty	Bed Size
	Super King
1	King
1	Queen
	Double
1	King/Single

Qty	Bathrooms
2	Ensuite
	Private
	Guest Share

Waterfront Retreat
Tranquil Sounds Homestay

Features & Attractions

- *Warm friendly hospitality*
- *10 min Interisland ferry*
- *Water taxi arranged*
- *Queen Charlotte Track*
- *Incl dinner, bed & breakfast*
- *Ensuites & private decks*
- *Native bush, birds & glow worms*
- *Complimentary kayaks*

[Map of Queen Charlotte Sound showing FernRidge, Nopera Airfield, Te Mahia, Kenepuru Sound, Queen Charlotte Sound, Picton, Linkwater, with N compass]

Rest awhile in comfort in our unique environment of native bush, stunning waterfront views and boat-only access just ten minutes from Picton. We can advise on car storage in Picton, book your water taxi transfers and offer suggestions on activities and walks. Our facilities include very comfortable double or twin ensuite rooms with stunning water views and private decks. An adjoining shared guest lounge offers tea/coffee making facilities, television and reading material. Enjoy delicious meals with complimentary wine.

Activities include kayaking, swimming, bush walks, glow worms, a half or full day walk on the Queen Charlotte Track, or just relax with a book and enjoy the view! Running our home-based publishing business from **FernRidge** allows us to be flexible and we invite you to share in our relaxed "Sounds lifestyle".

"A warm welcome awaits you."

TIRIMOANA HOUSE
257 Anakiwa Road, Tirimoana, RD 1, Picton
Ph (03) 574 2627, Fax (03) 574 2647
Mobile 021-167 2342
email: *bookings@tirimoanahouse.com*
www.tirimoanahouse.com

Tariff : N.Z. Dollars	
Double	$160-260
Single	–
Child	enqurie

Bedrooms	Qty
Double	4
Twin	
Single	

Bed Size	Qty
Super King	
King	
Queen	4
Double	
Single	

Bathrooms	Qty
Ensuite	4
Private	
Guest Share	

This Is Our View!
Luxury Waterfront Accommodation

Features & Attractions

- *Swimming pool*
- *Local walks & boat trips*
- *Stunning sea views*
- *Wine trails arranged*
- *Great home cooking*
- *Queen Charlotte Track*
- *Outdoor spa pool*

Enjoying superb sea views of the Marlborough Sounds, **Tirimoana House** is located a convenient 30 min. drive from both Picton and the Marlborough wineries. Our two-storey home sits on an elevated waterfront site once occupied by the historic Tirimoana Hotel. Our 4 sumptuous bedrooms are all ensuite, all have antique French queensize beds (one has a 1789 four poster), antique bedside cabinets and chandeliers. Our home has antique furniture throughout and many works of art both local and international, collected by your hosts on their NZ & international travels (John and Michelle are both artists). Close by is the renowned Queen Charlotte Track (walk out - water taxi back), kayaking, mountain biking and famous wineries. Relax afterwards in our swimming pool or in front of the log fire in winter before enjoying a gourmet dinner of local fare and wines. Michelle is an international chef. We serve the finest espresso coffee. Minimum 2 night stay from Dec 1st – Feb 28th. Winter rates May 1st – Sept 30th: less 20%. We have a lovely poodle called Shug.

St Omer House

Kenepuru Road, Kenepuru Sound, RD 2, Picton
Ph (03) 573 4086, Fax (03) 573 4586
email: *stomer.house@xtra.co.nz*
www.stomerhouse.co.nz

Features & Attractions

- *Mussel farm & nature cruises*
- *Photographer's dream*
- *Crafts, books & paintings for sale*
- *Bird watcher's paradise*
- *9 hole golf course*
- *Shipwreck, glow worms*

**Historic Guest House
Cottage & New Motels**

Double	$140
Single	$70
Child	$35

We welcome you to our peaceful bay where the lawns run down to the shelly beach, surrounded by native bush. Sun-bathe, swim, kayak or go boating and catch a fish. Ramble through our large Victorian garden or take a bush walk and listen to the birdsong. Tennis court, games room, nine hole golf course and shipwreck to explore. Fishing trips and Pelorus Sound cruises arranged. Shop and licensed restaurant. Enjoy our homecooked meals including wild game, seafood and delectable sweets and local wines in our historic dining room. Take the scenic 2½ hour drive from Picton or Havelock, fly with Sounds Air to Nopera Airfield, float plane from Picton or Porirua, or arrive by water taxi. Ask for particulars.

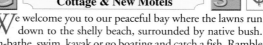

Bedrooms	Qty
Double	7
Twin	6
Single	2
Bed Size	Qty
King	1
Queen	3
Double	3
Single	7
Bathrooms	Qty
Ensuite	6
Private	1
Guest Share	2

Queensview B&B

259G Anakiwa Road, Anakiwa, Picton 7281
Phone (03) 574 2363, Mobile 021-0229 2864
e-mail: queensview@xtra.co.nz

Features & Attractions

- *Mountain biking*
- *Boat mooring available*
- *Art, craft & wine trails*
- *Kayaking & boat cruises*
- *Stunning scenery & sunsets*
- *Queen Charlotte Track 5min.*

**Quality B&B &
Self-contained Accommodation**

Double	$120-180
Single	$90-120
Child	neg.

Queensview B&B has arguably some of the best views of the Queen Charlotte Sound and with Picton only 30 min. and Havelock a mere 20 min., it's the ideal central location to enjoy the "Top of the South". Our home has 3 tastefully decorated guest rooms, beautiful gardens, where you can enjoy that evening glass of wine and a BBQ. The self-contained facilities include a fully equipped kitchen, TV/DVD, modest library, internet access and private boat mooring. From the house it's a mere 6-minute drive to the local Country Inn. Note: evening meals can be arranged, if sufficient notice given. Activities are plentiful, be it water sports, golf, mountain bikes, walks or the attraction of the wineries. All are within easy reach from **Queensview B&B**.

Bedrooms	Qty
Double	2
Twin	1
Single	
Bed Size	Qty
King	
Queen	1
Double	1
Single	2
Bathrooms	Qty
Ensuite	1
Private	1
Guest Share	1

SENNEN HOUSE LUXURY HISTORIC ACCOMMODATION

9 Oxford Street, Picton, Marlborough
Ph (03) 573 5216, Fax (03) 573 5216
Mobile 021-035 9956
email: *enquiries@sennenhouse.co.nz*
www.sennenhouse.co.nz

Tariff : N.Z. Dollars	
Double	$295-445
Single	$250-400
Child	$45

Bedrooms	Qty
Double	5
Twin	2
Single	

Bed Size	Qty
Super King	1
King	2
Queen	2
Double	
Single	

Bathrooms	Qty
Ensuite	5
Private	
Guest Share	

**Magnificent Heritage Colonial Villa
Unique and Luxurious**

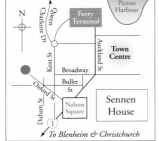

Features & Attractions

- *Five acre private setting*
- *Short stroll to Picton's amenities*
- *Marlborough wine tours*
- *National Trust protected grounds*
- *Luxurious character apartments*
- *Queen Charlotte Track & cruises*
- *Courtesy transfers/internet/phone*
- *Generous breakfast provisions*

Experience the timeless elegance, luxurious comforts and Victorian charm of **Sennen House**, a magnificent 1886 Heritage-registered 2-storey colonial villa, restored in keeping with its gracious style and era, to offer superior accommodation in 5 acres of mature gardens and native bush, only a short stroll to Picton's restaurants, ferries and foreshore. Three elegant apartments and two luxurious suites, three with private lounge and all with ensuite, kitchen facilities and private entrance, offer individual character, historic features, luxury linens, satellite TV, DVD, robes, telephone and wireless internet. Sumptuous daily provisions for leisurely breakfasts on sunny verandahs with views, seclusion, tranquillity and romantic timeless grandeur. Courtesy transfers, pre-dinner drinks, guest office and luggage storage. Superbly situated to explore the magnificent Marlborough Region.

TANGLEWOOD

1744 Queen Charlotte Dve, The Grove, RD 1, Picton
Ph (03) 574 2080, Fax (03) 574 2044
Mobile 027-481 4388
email: *tanglewood.hearn@xtra.co.nz*

  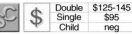

Features & Attractions

- 5km to Queen Charlotte Walkway
- Fifth generation Kiwi hospitality
- Self-contained accommodation
- Glo worms
- Four person spa/jacuzzi
- Dinner by arrangement $40pp

Bed & Breakfast
Self-contained Accommodation

	Double	$125-145
	Single	$95
	Child	neg

Our modern architectural home is nestled amongst the native ferns and overlooks the stunning Queen Charlotte Sounds. Enjoy one of our brand new luxury super king/twin ensuite rooms each with balcony and views; or our self-contained private guest wing which includes a queen and two single beds (each with ensuite), lounge, kitchen and sunny balcony/BBQ area. After a busy day you can relax in our spa/Jacuzzi surrounded by our beautiful native garden and birds, or take an evening stroll to view our glow worms. Substantial breakfasts are provided and dinners are available by arrangement. Make **Tanglewood** your base for Marlborough wineries, swimming, fishing, cycling, kayaking or walking the Queen Charlotte Walkway. Kiwi hospitality at its best!

Bedrooms	Qty
Double	3
Twin	1
Single	
Bed Size	**Qty**
Super King	2
Queen	1
King/Single	2
Single	2
Bathrooms	**Qty**
Ensuite	4
Private	
Guest Share	

RIVENHALL

118 Wellington Street, Picton
Ph (03) 573 7692, Fax (03) 573 7692
email: *rivenhall.picton@xtra.co.nz*

Features & Attractions

- *Town centre 4 min walk*
- *Full breakfast*
- *Ferry & bus pick-up*
- *Easy walk to restaurants*
- *Gracious home*
- *Laundry*

Homestay
Bed & Breakfast

  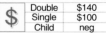

	Double	$140
	Single	$100
	Child	neg

Rivenhall, a gracious home with all the warmth and comfort of a bygone era, is up the rise on the left at the top of Wellington Street.

Picton, a small town with many cafés and restaurants is within easy walking distance from **Rivenhall**. Not just a stopover at the beginning or end of your South Island tour, Picton can be a destination of its own.

With Sound's activities and tours all running from the bottom of our street, suggested one day activities, wine tours, kayaking, return trip to Kaikoura for whale or dolphin watching (own transport), day trip to Nelson (two hour drive each way) or walking the Queen Charlotte track (one to four days) plus walks and shopping around town.

Bedrooms	Qty
Double	2
Twin	
Single	
Bed Size	**Qty**
King	
Queen	1
Double	1
Single	1
Bathrooms	**Qty**
Ensuite	
Private	2
Guest Share	

A SEA VIEW

424 Port Underwood Road, Whatamonga Bay,
RD 1, Picton 7281
Ph/Fax (03) 573 8815, Mobile 021-155 1890
email: *info@aseaview.co.nz*
www.aseaview.co.nz

Tariff : N.Z. Dollars	
Double	$149-199
Single	$140-160
Child	

Bedrooms	Qty
Double	3
Twin	
Single	

Bed Size	Qty
Super King	
King	2
Queen	1
Double	
Single	

Bathrooms	Qty
Ensuite	3
Private	
Guest Share	

**Self-contained
Bed & Breakfast**

Features & Attractions

- *Breathtaking views*
- *Secluded terraced garden*
- *Self-catering units*
- *2 tonne mooring*
- *Courtesy pick-up from Picton*
- *Outdoor activities & wine tours*
- *Delicious full breakfast*
- *Private entrance to rooms*

'A Sea View'

To Blenheim

You will feel welcome and relaxed at **A Sea View** which is nestled among the trees and just above the water of the Sounds. It offers unsurpassed, awe-inspiring views of the water and mountains from all guest rooms. Here you will experience the ever changing moods of the Queen Charlotte Sound and the peaceful tranquillity of the large garden with its great variety of plant and bird life. While enjoying the view from the deck, partake of a generous cooked breakfast which includes home made jams, yoghurt, muesli and bread. We also offer dinner and lunch by request. All rooms are warm with large comfortable beds, ensuites and tea and coffee facilities. Two rooms have kitchenettes. We would be pleased to help you discover the many activities that Marlborough is famous for: wine tasting, kayaking, boating, fishing, diving and trekking the Queen Charlotte Walkway, or a gentle cruise on the Sounds visiting the many beautiful bays.

DIRECTIONS: From High St in Picton take Waikawa Bay Rd for 9km, continue for 1km past Karaka Point until you see **Sea View** sign on your right (12-15 min Picton)

CHARLOTTE HOUSE

432 Port Underwood Road, Picton
Ph (03) 573 8969, Fax (03) 573 8969
Mobile 027-444 8011
e-mail: *charlothouse@kol.co.nz*
www.charlottehousemarlboroughsounds.co.nz

Features & Attractions

- *Magnificent seaviews*
- *Own private entrance*
- *Self-contained suite*
- *Continental breakfast*
- *Art, craft and wine trails*
- *Courtesy pick-up from Picton*

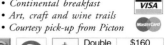

Self-contained Bed & Breakfast				Double	$160
				Single	$90
				Child	N/A

Visit us and enjoy the magnificence of the Queen Charlotte Sounds, where a uniquely tranquil and restful environment awaits you. **Charlotte House** is unique in the fact that it only takes one couple at a time, in its own private suite, called the Tui suite, which is airconditioned for your comfort, has a queen size bed, electric blankets and a magnetic wool underlay. The Tui suite consists of a bedroom, bathroom, sitting room and a kitchenette (with tea and coffee making facilities)– all with amazing uninterupted seaviews. The suite has a small freezer with a selection of frozen meals for purchase. It is equipped with LCD TV, DVD and CD players with selections of DVDs and CDs.

Bedrooms	Qty
Double	1
Twin	
Single	
Bed Size	**Qty**
King	
Queen	1
Double	
Single	
Bathrooms	**Qty**
Ensuite	1
Private	
Guest Share	

FINLAY GROVE HOUSE

6 Finlay Grove, Waikawa Bay, Picton 7220
Ph (03) 573 6113
e-mail: *holiday@finlaygrovehouse.co.nz*
www.finlaygrovehouse.co.nz

Features & Attractions

- *Magical water views*
- *Short walk to beach*
- *Private entrances*
- *5 min. drive from Picton*
- *Scenic boating trips*
- *Winery tours*

   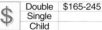

Bed & Breakfast Self-contained				Double	$165-245
				Single	
				Child	

Finlay Grove House is nestled into the lower slopes of Waikawa Bay. You will love holidaying in these luxurious suites with their fantastic views of the marina and bay below. The two beautifully appointed private guest suites are adjacent to, but separate from your hosts dwelling.

Perfect for honeymooners or that special break away!

Each morning your hosts, Diane and Brian, serve a delicious breakfast, either in your guest lounge or alfresco on the patio deck. A **warm welcome** together with a complimentary basket and a bottle of **world famous** Sauvignon Blanc wine awaits you on arrival.

DIRECTIONS:
Only 5 min. easy drive from Picton. Take Waikawa Road to Waikawa Bay.
Finlay Grove Road
is on your right.

Bedrooms	Qty
Double	4
Twin	
Single	
Bed Size	**Qty**
King	1
Queen	2
Double	
Single	2
Bathrooms	**Qty**
Ensuite	4
Private	
Guest Share	

VUE POINTE

PO Box 12, Waikawa Bay, Picton
Ph (03) 573 7621, Fax (03) 573 7621
Mobile 027-205 1664 / 021-041 1740
email: *j_roberts@xtra.co.nz*

Tariff : N.Z. Dollars	
Double	$275
Single	$275
Child	n/a

Bedrooms	Qty
Double	1
Twin	
Single	
Bed Size	**Qty**
Super King	
King	1
Queen	
Double	
Single	
Bathrooms	**Qty**
Ensuite	1
Private	
Guest Share	

Luxury Self-contained Accommodation

DIRECTIONS:
Accessed via private road 7 km from Picton.
Please phone for easy directions.

BOOKINGS ESSENTIAL

Features & Attractions

- *Magical views*
- *Very private and peaceful*
- *15 min drive from Ferry Terminal*
- *Golf, boating, vineyards, plus, plus*
- *Air conditioning & heating*
- *Continental breakfast basket*
- *Discounts for second and subsequent nights*

Vue Pointe is in an elevated position, private and set in native bush. 180° panoramic views of the Marlborough Sounds (Waikawa Bay, Marina and Queen Charlotte Sound). Relax on your private deck area, watch the boat traffic from on high and generally enjoy this special vantage point with its delightful views. This is a great base from which to explore and enjoy the region's attractions – excellent vineyards (cellar doors/restaurants), the mail boat on its delivery run around the sounds, a dolphin watching trip and/or a day's skippered sailing charter. Alternatively, sea-kayaking or a day long combined walk and boat trip can be as challenging or gentle as you wish! Luxury acommodation is provided in a modern self-contained suite with private entrance, consisting of a large double bedroom opening onto a private deck area, an ensuite, partially tiled open-plan bathroom with shower, bidet and undertile heating, and a large lounge and dining/kitchen area offering end to end views with access to your private deck area from one end and to a patio area at the other. A generous continental breakfast basket is provided, at your leisure and in the privacy of your own suite.

WHATAMONGA HOMESTAY AT WATERS EDGE
425 Port Underwood Road, RD 1, Picton
Ph (03) 573 7192, Fax (04) 472 4085
email: *info@whsl.co.nz*
www.whsl.co.nz

Tariff : N.Z. Dollars	
Unit	$240-300
Room	$200-250
Minimum	2 nights

Bedrooms	Qty
Units	2
Double	2
Single	

Bed Size	Qty
Super King	2
King	1
Queen	
Double	
Single	2

Bathrooms	Qty
Ensuite	2
Private	2
Guest Share	

Luxury Homestay Accommodation

Features & Attractions

- *Magnificent views*
- *Set in native bush*
- *Direct access to water*
- *Self-contained seclusion*
- *Dinner by arrangement*
- *20 minutes to ferry terminal*
- *Minimum 2 night stay*
- *Bookings are essential*

Your hosts at **Whatamonga Homestay at Waters Edge** are Alex and Colette Wilson. The homestay offers accommodation in secluded units, or in two separate bedrooms with own bathroom and deck under the main house. The homestay has been specifically designed by one of Marlborough's leading designers to face north for best sun and allowing guests to enjoy the view and their seclusion, or enjoy the interaction with the sea offered by accommodation with direct access to the water. Evening meals are served in the main house as are cooked breakfasts. Continental breakfasts can be delivered to the units or downstairs bedrooms by prior arrangement. Bookings are essential, especially during the summer months of October to May.

DIRECTIONS:
From Picton take Waikawa Rd. From Waikawa shop take Port Underwood Rd past Karaka Pt. After 2 km **Whatamonga Homestay at Waters Edge** sign is on the left.

OYSTER BAY LODGE

1474 Port Underwood Rd, Port Underwood, Picton
Ph (03) 579 9644, Fax (03) 579 9645
Mobile 0274-363 363
email: *enquiries@oysterbaylodge.co.nz*
www.oysterbaylodge.co.nz

Tariff : N.Z. Dollars	
Double	$180
Single	$150
Child	

Bedrooms	Qty
Double	3
Twin	2
Single	

Bed Size	Qty
Super King	
King	1
Queen	2
Double	
Single	3

Bathrooms	Qty
Ensuite	1
Private	2
Guest Share	

**Bed & Breakfast
Homestay**

Features & Attractions

- *Fishing/diving - compressor available*
- *Wonderful views*
- *Bush walks & native birds*
- *Direct water access*
- *Dinner by arrangement*
- *Outdoor activities available*
- *Spa & games room*
- *2 ton mooring available*

Waikawa

Picton

Oyster Bay
Lodge

To
Blenheim

DIRECTIONS:
14 km from Waikawa Bay, Picton on the
Port Underwood Road. Keep following the
road to the right. Sign posted in the bay.

Our lodge is set in picturesque Oyster Bay. We have an uninterrupted view over the bay in a charming and historical part of the Marlborough Sounds. Your hosts share an enjoyment of the outdoors and marine environment. Our 8metre boat can offer access to a full range of marine activities in comfort and safety. Personally guided tours and activities of your choosing available at the lodge. Relax in comfort and tranquility on expansive decks or be massaged in the luxury spa and enjoy the amazing array of wildlife and native birds in the garden. 3 course meals are $60 per person, local wines and beer included. Multiple night discount available. We welcome you to enjoy with us at **Oyster Bay Lodge** our unique lifestyle and opportunity.

  A two bedroom self-contained unit is now also available. Tariff: $160 - 1 room, $190 - 2 rooms

KOROMIKO VALLEY HOMESTEAD

30 Freeths Road, Koromiko, Picton
Ph (03) 573 7518, Fax (03) 573 7538
email: *info@koromikohomestead.co.nz*
www.koromikohomestead.co.nz

Tariff : N.Z. Dollars	
Double	$145-185
Single	
Child	

Bedrooms	Qty
Double	2
Twin	
Single	

Bed Size	Qty
Super King	
King	
Queen	2
Double	
Single	

Bathrooms	Qty
Ensuite	
Private	2
Guest Share	

**Bed & Breakfast
Self-contained Accommodation**

Features & Attractions

- *5 km south of Picton*
- *Close to Marlborough Sounds*
- *Wine & sightseeing tours*
- *Classic-style sports car hire*
- *20 mins to Blenheim*
- *Vineyards & restaurants*
- *Scenic flights & golf nearby*
- *Picton ferry/plane pickup*

DIRECTIONS:
From Picton travel south 5km along State Highway 1 to Koromiko. Turn left 100m past the golf club into Freeths Road. Koromiko Homestead is the first property on right hand side.

Take a break between Picton and Blenheim in the picturesque Koromiko valley. A warm welcome awaits you at our rural homestead and ten-acre farmlet. Relax in the quality self-contained, well-equipped guest accommodation which includes a comfortable lounge, small kitchen, and separate dining room, enabling you to be totally self-contained if you wish. The two queen-size bedrooms are both north-facing and have private bathrooms. Unwind with a stroll through the extensive gardens, smell the roses and watch the native birdlife. Enjoy breakfast served in your suite, or alfresco on the sun-warmed garden deck. Join Pat and Ian for a pre-dinner aperitif before dining out at one of the extensive choice of excellent restaurants within 30mins radius. Hire one of our specialised two-seater classic-style sports cars and tour the world-renowned Marlborough vineyards, go sightseeing westward up into the majestic St Arnaud range and the scenic Nelson Lakes, or visit the historic settlement of Havelock on the edge of the Marlborough Sounds. We offer you several one or two-day pre-selected tours. Picnic lunches are available on request.

BLUE RIDGE ESTATE

50 O'Dwyers Road, Rapaura, RD 3, Blenheim
Ph (03) 570 2198, Fax (03) 570 2199
email: *stay@blueridge.co.nz*
www.blueridge.co.nz

Tariff : N.Z. Dollars	
Double	$175-215
Single	$160-200
Child	

Bedrooms	Qty
Double	2
Twin	1
Single	

Bed Size	Qty
Super King	
King	
Queen	2
Double	
Single	2

Bathrooms	Qty
Ensuite	1
Private	2
Guest Share	

**Boutique Vineyard
Homestay**

Features & Attractions

- *Quiet and peaceful*
- *Stunning rural views*
- *Warm, friendly hospitality*
- *Excellent restaurants nearby*
- *Award winning home*
- *Comfort and privacy*
- *Tastefully furnished*
- *Heart of the wine region*

Set on a twenty acre purpose-designed homestay property, **Blue Ridge Estate**, 2002 Master Builders' House of the Year, enjoys a rural setting with stunning views across vineyards to the Richmond Range. Close to many of Marlborough's fine wineries, restaurants, gardens; only twenty five minutes from Picton, and seven minutes to the airport or Blenheim. Bedrooms and bathrooms are tastefully furnished – electric blankets, tea and coffee facilities, high quality linen, hair dryer, heated towel rail. Spend a winter evening in front of our open fire. Our home has proven popular with both international and New Zealand visitors. Come and share our home, where comfort and privacy will ensure your Marlborough visit is indeed a memorable one.

Reservations essential.

BAXTER BED & BREAKFAST

28 Elisha Drive, Blenheim, Marlborough
Ph (03) 578 3753, Fax (03) 578 3796
Mobile 021-129 2062
email: *baxterart@xtra.co.nz*
www.baxterhomestay.com

Features & Attractions

- *Panoramic views*
- *Private, peaceful, quiet*
- *Handy to wineries*
- *4 min from town centre*
- *Attractive gardens*
- *Brian Baxter Art Studio*

**Bed & Breakfast
Self-contained & Homestay**

$	Double	$130-200
	Single	
	Child	

Bedrooms	Qty
Double	4
Twin	
Single	
Bed Size	**Qty**
Super King	2
Queen	1
Double	
Single	1
Bathrooms	**Qty**
Ensuite	3
Private	
Guest Share	

Brian, a well known New Zealand artist, and Kathy welcome you to their spacious, sunny, modern home and art gallery. You will enjoy magnificent panoramic views over Blenheim and nearby vineyards or enjoy a wander through our prizewinning garden. Guests are welcome to relax in our spacious lounge with large screen TV, with Sky, or play our Yamaha piano. We are happy to help with NZ travel plans, arrange visits to wineries, restaurants, gardens, golf courses, art tours, Marlborough Sounds tours, etc. Our interests include gardening, music, travel, golf, tennis, fishing, art, skiing, video production and making people welcome in our home. Original art and tea/coffee making facilities in all suites. Guests may use our attractive barbeque area and facilities. Laundry available. Two new self-contained units. The luxury one with fully equipped kitchen, large screen TV and library (2 nights min).

TROTTERS REST

27 Dillons Point Road, Blenheim
Ph (03) 578 2764, Fax (03) 578 2764
email: *trotters-rest@xtra.co.nz*

Features & Attractions

- *Tranquil surroundings*
- *Art, craft & wine trails*
- *Close to town centre*
- *Dinner by arrangement*
- *Warm & welcoming*
- *Borders onto Opawa River*

**Homestay
Bed & Breakfast**

$	Double	$95
	Single	$70
	Child	neg

Welcome, come share with us a slice of tranquility only moments from town. Our adobe block and timber home is warm in winter and cool in summer. Enjoy the garden, take time out to rest in a shady spot at the river's edge, in the gazebo or under a leafy tree.

Marlborough has plenty to offer you and we are happy to advise on activities and make bookings for you. We offer tea/coffee making facilities, facsimile, internet and laundry facilities. Dinner is by prior arrangement, breakfast is bountiful with a choice of continental or English, served with homemade preserves and home grown fruit. We love to meet new people and can't wait to meet you.

Bedrooms	Qty
Double	3
Twin	1
Single	
Bed Size	**Qty**
King	
Queen	3
Double	
Single	2
Bathrooms	**Qty**
Ensuite	
Private	1
Guest Share	1

ARTLEE HOUSE BED & BREAKFAST
76B Lakings Road, Blenheim
Ph/Fax (03) 579 2225, Mobile 027-431 4117
email: *leona@artleehouse.co.nz*
www.artleehouse.co.nz

Features & Attractions

- *Comfortable, modern home*
- *Between airport and town*
- *Aviation Heritage Centre*
- *Close to wineries*
- *Peaceful garden setting*
- *Art and crafts*

Double	$150-195
Single	$100-150
Child	N/A

**Central Bed & Breakfast
in a Tranquil Setting**

Bedrooms	Qty
Double	1
Twin	1
Single	1
Bed Size	**Qty**
King	1
Queen	
Double	
Single	3
Bathrooms	**Qty**
Ensuite	
Private	1
Guest Share	1

Artlee House welcomes you. You will enjoy a central location just minutes from the town centre and airport, just off SH6. Wineries, restaurants, Omaka Heritage Centre and galleries are close by. Relax and feel at home in a peaceful garden setting with bird life and featuring mature trees and a natural spring-fed creek. Pure New Zealand bodycare by 'Linden Leaves' along with robes, CD radio/clocks, hairdryers, electric blankets, etc. are all available. A complimentary glass of wine or beer is available on your arrival. With home-made treats, tea and coffee there for 24 hours you're sure to enjoy your stay. **Artlee House** has been described by some guests as "a great find". Leona enjoys arts and crafts, walking and meeting people.

GREEN GABLES
St Andrews, 3011 SH 1, R D 4, Blenheim
Ph (03) 577 9205, Fax (03) 577 9205
Mobile 021-078 2142
email: *relax@greengablesbedandbreakfast.co.nz*
www.greengablesbedandbreakfast.co.nz

Features & Attractions

- *Close to town centre*
- *Wine tasting*
- *Walks & river fishing*
- *Wireless connection*
- *Email & fax facilities*
- *Variety of restaurants*

Double	$180-200
Single	$120-130
Child	

  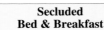

**Secluded
Bed & Breakfast**

Bedrooms	Qty
Double	3
Twin	1
Single	
Bed Size	**Qty**
Super King	1
Queen	
Double	3
Single	1
Bathrooms	**Qty**
Ensuite	3
Private	
Guest Share	1

Green Gables is set back from the road, nestled amongst 3.5 acres of Olive Groves and landscaped gardens. The Opawa River borders the northern section of the private garden which is host to winding paths and secret areas. Three guest rooms with ensuite; two queen and one super king (also a twin) dominate the upstairs along with a guest lounge. Downstairs the queen Garden room has shared bathroom facilities. All rooms have seating, TV, tea/coffee making facilities, robes, hairdryers and complimentary toiletries. Breakfast is served around our large dining table and boasts fresh fruits and yoghurts, homemade jams, marmalade, muesli, muffins, waffles and various combinations of cooked dishes. We will discuss with you what options are available and customise a breakfast served at a time to suit you. Evening meals available by prior arrangement and special diets can be catered for. A wireless connection, complimentary internet, computer and facsimile are available.

319

OMAKA HEIGHTS
BED & BREAKFAST COUNTRYSTAY

199 Brookby Road, Omaka Valley, RD 2, Blenheim 7272
Ph (03) 572 7402, Fax (03) 572 7403
email: *omakaheights@ts.co.nz*
www.omakaheights.co.nz

Tariff : N.Z. Dollars	
Double	$160-195
Single	$120-150
Child	neg

Bedrooms	Qty
Double	1
Twin	1
Single	
Bed Size	**Qty**
Super King	
King	
Queen	1
Double	
Single	2
Bathrooms	**Qty**
Ensuite	2
Private	
Guest Share	

  Countrystay Bed & Breakfast

Features & Attractions

- *Outstanding views*
- *Wine & sightseeing tours*
- *Art and craft visits*
- *Scenic flights*
- *Golf, fishing, boating*
- *Whale & dolphin watching*
- *Skiing and tramping*
- *Excellent dining nearby*

DIRECTIONS:
From Blenheim take Middle Renwick Rd, after passing the airport take 1st left into Godfrey Rd. Then take 1st right into Dog Point Road and first left into Brookby Rd.

Positioned in the picturesque Omaka Valley, just 12 km from Blenheim, our purpose-built hilltop Countrystay offers out-standing panoramic views over vineyards and farmland through to the Richmond Range in the distance. We are within a few minutes drive of over thirty wineries. There are numerous restaurants and cafés, offering world class cuisine, located within Blenheim town and the surrounding vineyard area. Our self-contained Countrystay wing offers two guest rooms with private ensuite facilities and private decks plus a guest lounge. The twin room/ensuite is completely wheelchair accessible. The lounge provides tea/coffee making facilities, refrigerator and television. The bedrooms are fully equipped with hairdryer and electric blankets. Guests are offered a hearty breakfast and complimentary pre-dinner beverages. Evening meals are available by arrangement. You may enjoy a stroll around our eight hectare property on which we farm alpacas.

CREEKSIDE
774 Rapaura Road, RD 3, Blenheim
Ph (03) 579 8018, Fax (03) 579 8218
On-site Ph (03) 570 5338
email: *janhood@xtra.co.nz*
www.creekside.co.nz

Features & Attractions

- *Wine & olive oil tasting*
- *All rooms with ensuite*
- *Beside Tennis Club*
- *Expansive, mature gardens*
- *Just minutes to Blenheim*
- *Close to Marlborough Airport*

$		
	Double	$160-200
	Single	
	Child	

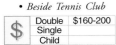

In the Heart of Blenheim's Wine and Olive Oil Country

Bedrooms	Qty
Double	3
Twin	
Single	
Bed Size	**Qty**
King	1
Queen	2
Double	
Single	2
Bathrooms	**Qty**
Ensuite	3
Private	
Guest Share	

This property adjoins both, the spring-fed stream and the popular Rapaura Tennis Club with access off both Rapaura Road and Giffords Creek Lane and is set back from the road, centrally located, not far from Marlborough's Airport and amidst the wine and olive oil industry of Blenheim. The 8 ha property comprises 6 ha of producing vineyard and 1ha of producing olive trees. Residence and Bed & Breakfast are set on the remaining land with its stream boundary, expansive mature garden with wildlife aplenty and numerous plantings of fruit and specimen tree. The main house consists of 3 bedrooms with ensuite facilities, a large garden, terrace and breakfast room. The 100sqm Olive Room is used for entertaining. Recover, rest and enjoy nature. Be in downtown Blenheim for shopping in only a few minutes. Take the car to the Marlborough Sounds or just be on the property to enjoy wine and olive tasting. The original owner was the pioneer of Marlborough's olive industry, owning one of the best olive plantations in the world.

TAMAR VINEYARD
67 Rapaura Road, RD 3, Rapaura, Blenheim
Ph (03) 572 8408, Fax (03) 572 8405
email: *tamar.vineyard@xtra.co.nz*
www.tamarvineyard.co.nz

 VISA
 MasterCard

Features & Attractions

- *A romantic retreat*
- *Four poster bed*
- *Sumptuous breakfast*
- *Heart of the wine trail*
- *15 min to Blenheim*
- *30 min to Picton*

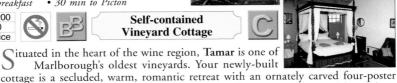

$		
	Double	$175-200
	Single	$150
	Child	half price

  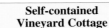

Self-contained Vineyard Cottage

Bedrooms	Qty
Double	1
Twin	
Single	
Bed Size	**Qty**
King	
Queen	1
Double	
Single	1
Bathrooms	**Qty**
Ensuite	
Private	1
Guest Share	

Situated in the heart of the wine region, **Tamar** is one of Marlborough's oldest vineyards. Your newly-built cottage is a secluded, warm, romantic retreat with an ornately carved four-poster bed, featherdown duvet and classic leather couch. From the wide verandah you have breathtaking views through the vines to the Richmond Ranges. Our sumptuous three-course breakfasts feature homegrown produce and preserves. As we are an easy stroll from several wineries and restaurants you may choose to lunch or dine out, or cater for yourself in your fully equipped kitchenette. Clive and Yvonne enjoy showing you round the vineyard and we can help arrange winery tours or trips to the Marlborough Sounds (30 min drive) and Rainbow Skifield (60 min drive). We look forward to welcoming you for a memorable stay.

REDWOOD HEIGHTS

245 Redwood Street, Blenheim
Ph/Fax (03) 578 0143, Mobile 027-680 3125
email: *k.besley@xtra.co.nz*
www.redwoodheights.co.nz

Tariff : N.Z. Dollars	
Double	$110-175
Single	$80
Child	

Bedrooms	Qty
Double	2
Twin	1
Single	
Bed Size	**Qty**
Super King	
King	1
Queen	1
Double	
Single	2
Bathrooms	**Qty**
Ensuite	1
Private	1
Guest Share	

Quality
Bed & Breakfast

Features & Attractions

- *Comfort and privacy*
- *4 min. from town centre*
- *25 min. from Picton Ferry*
- *Wireless, email & fax available*
- *Easy to find*
- *Close to wineries*
- *Spectacular views*
- *Laundry facilities*

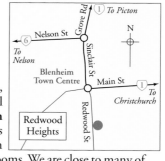

A warm welcome awaits you at **Redwood Heights**. Relax in private, modern, quality accommodation. Enjoy our quiet, peaceful country atmosphere and extensive views from our spacious **Steam Reserve** king bedroom with ensuite, refreshment-making facilities and fridge. All guest accommodation is upstairs and separate from hosts, with a guest lounge and balcony for your use and TV in all rooms. We are close to many of Marlborough's fine wineries and restaurants and we can help arrange winery tours or bicycle tours

through the vineyards, with pick-up from and return to **Redwood Heights**. We are adjacent to the Marlborough Wither Hills walkways, bike tracks and farm park and close to the Aviation Heritage Centre and golf courses. We are ideally situated to be a perfect base for day trips to Picton, Marlborough Sounds, Nelson or Kaikoura. Enjoy a full breakfast, warm hospitality and personal service. We look forward to meeting you.

STONEHAVEN VINEYARD HOMESTAY

414 Rapaura Road, Blenheim
Ph (03) 572 9730, Fax (03) 572 9730
Mobile 027-682 1120
email: *stay@stonehavenhomestay.co.nz*
www.stonehavenhomestay.co.nz

Tariff : N.Z. Dollars	
Double	$165-250
Single	$145-230
Child	

Bedrooms	Qty
Double	2
Twin	1
Single	

Bed Size	Qty
Super King	
King	1
Queen	1
Double	
King/Single	2

Bathrooms	Qty
Ensuite	2
Private	1
Guest Share	

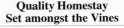

**Quality Homestay
Set amongst the Vines**

Features & Attractions

- *Dinner by arrangement*
- *Heart of the wine region*
- *Comfortable & welcoming*
- *Mountain & vineyard views*
- *Guest bikes for hire*
- *Swimming pool on site*
- *Children over 10 welcome*
- *Laundry & internet available*

Paulette and John welcome you to **Stonehaven Vineyard Homestay**, a beautifully constructed stone and cedar home set amongst 20 acres of Sauvignon Blanc vines, surrounded by stunning gardens and within walking or cycling distance of Marlborough's outstanding wineries and restaurants.

Stonehaven offers peaceful luxury accommodation with rooms boasting magnificent mountain and vineyard views. Bedrooms come equipped with crisp bed linens, electric blankets, tea & coffee making facilities, complimentary port and sherry, TVs and the the King Room with air conditioning and balcony. The ensuites have heated towel rails, and all have underfloor heating, robes, hair dryers and toiletries. A sumptuous 'white linen' breakfast is served in the summerhouse overlooking the swimming pool to set you up for your day of wine tasting, trout fishing, Marlborough Sounds cruising or hiking. Evening dining is by arrangement, consisting of a three course gourmet dinner of local fresh and homegrown produce. We are situated 5 minutes from Blenheim airport and 30 minutes from the Picton ferry.

THE STREAM ESTATE COTTAGE

856 Rapaura Road, Rapaura, PO Box 772, Blenheim
Ph (03) 570 5593 Mobile 0274-365 554
email: *cozzy@xtra.co.nz*
www.thestreamestate.co.nz

Features & Attractions

- *Self-contained privacy*
- *Located in vineyard*
- *Set beside natural spring*
- *Trout fishing at cottage door*
- *Town and airport 10 min*
- *Heart of wine trail region*

**Self-contained
Vineyard Cottage**

	Double	$200-250
	Single	
	Child	

DIRECTIONS: From Picton (SH 1), take Rapaura Road towards Nelson. From Nelson (SH 6) turn left into Rapaura Road, immediately after Main Wairau River Bridge.

Bedrooms	Qty
Double	1
Twin	1
Single	
Bed Size	**Qty**
King	
Queen	1
Double	
King/Single	2
Bathrooms	**Qty**
Ensuite	
Private	1
Guest Share	

Set beside a natural spring creek, renowned for its fantastic trout fishing, **The Stream Estate Cottage** offers total privacy within the vineyard. From the front patio, surrounded by vines and the natural fast flowing spring, the views are breathtaking. The Stream Estate Cottage is self-contained and well appointed with separate lounge, dining and kitchen area, featuring a large open fire and double doors which open onto the front patio from the lounge and main bedroom. Two double bedrooms, plus a shared ensuite complete the cottage. Being very centrally located on the Rapaura Road, the 'Golden Mile' of the Marlborough wine industry, **The Stream Estate Cottage** is within ten minutes of most wineries, restaurants and the town centre of Blenheim.

BEACHFRONT FARMSTAY

Karamea, State Highway 67
Ph/Fax (03) 782 6762, Mobile 021-782 676
email: *farmstay@xtra.co.nz*
www.westcoastbeachaccommodation.co.nz

Features & Attractions

- *Peaceful rural setting*
- *Special full breakfast*
- *Gourmet evening meal*
- *Trout fishing*
- *Elegant rooms*
- *Wild sea, grand beach*

$	Double	$150-170
	Single	$120
	Child	Neg.

**Farmstay
Bed & Breakfast**

Bedrooms	Qty
Double	2
Twin	
Single	1
Bed Size	**Qty**
King	1
Queen	1
Double	
Single	1
Bathrooms	**Qty**
Ensuite	2
Private	
Family Share	1

Our farm includes 2.5km of coastline overlooking the wild Tasman Sea. A 2 minute walk will take you to a sandy beach, which usually you have all to yourself. We are a working farm, milking 460 Friesian cows. Relax in elegant rooms with every convenience and privacy; enjoy our spacious home and garden. Our special farmhouse breakfasts are generous, including home-made preserves. For dinner enjoy delicious country cuisine with farm-grown beef, lamb and venison, organic vegetables from the garden and home-made desserts served with New Zealand wine. Karamea is surrounded by Kahurangi National Park, with lots of day walks available. There's also a 9-hole golf course, unique limestone caves and arches, and great spots for trout fishing.

[Map: Karamea Beachfront Farmstay]

DIRECTIONS:
Karamea Beachfront Farmstay
is 84 km north of Westport
and 3 km north of Little
Wanganui.

CHARMING CREEK BED & BREAKFAST

24 Main Road, Ngakawau, Westport
Phone (03) 782 8007, Fax (03) 782 8008
Mobile 027-481 6736
e-mail: *info@bullerbeachstay.co.nz*
www.bullerbeachstay.co.nz

Features & Attractions

- *Wild sealife & rare dolphins*
- *2 bedroom suite: $280, $70pp*
- *Walkway across park, beach 50m*
- *Beach cafés & art galleries*
- *River kayak, jetboat, jetski*
- *Fish, bike & rock climb*

$	Double	$150
	Single	
	Child	

**Best Breakfast on the
Planet - 'Planet West Coast'**

Bedrooms	Qty
Double	3
Twin	1
Single	
Bed Size	**Qty**
Super King	1
Queen	2
Double	
Single	2
Bathrooms	**Qty**
Ensuite	2
Private	
Guest Share	

"*We aim to give you the best breakfast on the planet – Planet West Coast!*" New in 2007, Charming Creek B&B is built for sun, sea and relaxation. Above tower the bush-clad cliffs of the high plateau – across the road, the Tasman Sea. Behind is the spectacular Charming Creek Walkway, and all the activities you could want from relaxed to extreme. All suites have massage showers, private sundecks, quality bedding, electric blankets, clock radios and hairdryers. Electric and gas heating throughout. The sun lounge has an automated Swiss Espresso machine, fridge/freezer, MP3/CD music system, and satellite TV. Broadband internet, phone and laundry services available. A full breakfast featuring home grown eggs and produce is included in your room rate. Bikes and free airport pickup with two night stays. Longer stay discounts!
Unmissable: The Heritage Coal Trail, the Denniston Incline, Millerton; and the natural wonders of Karamea and the Kahurangi National Park.

RIVER VIEW LODGE

SH 6 Lower Buller Gorge, PO Box 229, Westport
Ph/Fax (03) 789 6037, Mobile 027-405 5359
email: *info@rurallodge.co.nz*
www.rurallodge.co.nz

Tariff : N.Z. Dollars	
Double	$220
Single	$180
Child	n/a

Bedrooms	Qty
Double	4
Twin	
Single	

Bed Size	Qty
Super King	
King	3
Queen	1
Double	
Single	

Bathrooms	Qty
Ensuite	4
Private	
Guest Share	

  Luxury Rural Bed & Breakfast

Features & Attractions

- *Quiet peaceful surroundings*
- *Spacious comfortable rooms*
- *Dinner by arrangement extra*
- *Off season rates May-August*
- *Wonderful large garden*
- *Rooms with garden and river views*
- *Friendly NZ born host*
- *Discount for over 2 nights stay*

Situated above the Buller River, purpose-built **Riverview Lodge** is seven kilometres from Westport. Off the main road with picturesque views of the Buller River and country, overlooking a large garden for you to wander in and relax, or play a game of tennis on the grass court.

The four rooms are comfortable and tastefully decorated, all with ensuites and three open onto a large deck overlooking the river and garden.

Tariff includes a full breakfast in the dining room. Dinner is by arrangement only. Laundry is available. Discount for more than two nights and off-season rates available. We offer helpful, friendly advice on local activities and can recommend restaurants in the town.

HAVENLEE HOMESTAY

76 Queen Street, Westport
Ph (03) 789 8543, Fax (03) 789 8502
email: *info@havenlee.co.nz*
www.havenlee.co.nz

Features & Attractions

- *Warm friendly welcome*
- *'At home' atmosphere*
- *Peace and tranquility*
- *A garden oasis*
- *Local area information*
- *300m from Town Centre*

$	Double	$100-150
	Single	$90
	Child	neg

Bedrooms	Qty
Double	2
Twin	
Single	

Bed Size	Qty
King	
Queen	2
Double	
Single	

Bathrooms	Qty
Ensuite	
Private	1
Guest Share	1

**Best Choice for
First Class Hospitality**

DIRECTIONS: Along Palmerston Street turn right at Wakefield Street, left at Queen Street, 1st home on left.

Peace in Paradise - this is **Havenlee**. From the moment you arrive you will feel at home right away. A warm, welcoming greeting at our relaxed, spacious, quality homestay will introduce you to the fine hospitality you will receive during your stay with us. We were born and bred in the Westport area and are very proud of our West Coast heritage. Havenlee is centrally located: an idyllic base from which to explore the environmental wonderland, share local knowledge or just take time out. Check out the numerous adventure experiences and local attractions. Soak up the nature to rest and restore body and soul. As our guest you will enjoy a healthy, nutritous continental-plus breakfast. What a way to start the day! A well appointed private bathroom or guest share facilities. Shower room, toilet and bathroom (with large tub) each separate. Laundry facilities available. Treat yourself - stay a while and feel exhilarated.

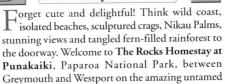

THE ROCKS HOMESTAY

Hartmount Place, Community Box 16, Punakaiki
Ph (03) 731 1141, Fax (03) 731 1142
email: *stay@therockshomestay.com*
www.therockshomestay.com

Features & Attractions

- *Pancake Rocks, Blowholes*
- *Adjoins National Park*
- *Spectacular panoramas*
- *Relaxed and friendly*
- *Dinner by arrangement*
- *Bush walking & beaches*

$	Double	$155-210
	Single	$120-130
	Child	

Bedrooms	Qty
Double	2
Twin	1
Single	

Bed Size	Qty
King	
Queen	2
Double	
Single	2

Bathrooms	Qty
Ensuite	3
Private	
Guest Share	

**Wilderness Homestay
Luxury Isolation**

Forget cute and delightful! Think wild coast, isolated beaches, sculptured crags, Nikau Palms, stunning views and tangled fern-filled rainforest to the doorway. Welcome to **The Rocks Homestay at Punakaiki**, Paparoa National Park, between Greymouth and Westport on the amazing untamed West Coast. Forget cellphones. Enjoy ensuite rooms, heated towel rails, hairdryers, minibars, electric blankets, conservatories, air/con and an extensive library of New Zealand books. Forget street lamps and traffic. Experience forest tracks and river walks, Pancake Rocks and Blowholes, beach rambles and memorable sunsets, environmental care and sustainable impact. Relish healthy breakfasts, fruit, muesli, yoghurt, home baking. Evening meals negotiable. Forget confusion! Accept our warm invitation to share our environmentally sensitive home nestled in the wilderness.

BIRDS FERRY LODGE & FERRY MAN'S COTTAGE

Birds Ferry Rd, 8 km north of Charleston, Westport
Ph (09) 958 3517, Free Ph 0800 212 207
Mobile 021-337 217
email: *info@birdsferrylodge.co.nz*
www.birdsferrylodge.co.nz

Tariff : N.Z. Dollars	
Double	$160-250
Single	$160-250
Child	neg

Bedrooms	Qty
Double	6
Twin	2
Single	

Bed Size	Qty
Super King	1
King	
Queen	4
Double	1
King/Single	2

Bathrooms	Qty
Ensuite	3
Private	
Guest Share	

**Luxury Bed & Breakfast
or Self-contained Cottage**

Features & Attractions

- Lodge dinners our speciality
- Cottage in its own garden
- Mountain & ocean views
- Spa enjoys ocean views
- Internet, laundry, refreshments incl.
- 2 km from highway - very quiet
- Local guiding service available
- 2 delightful friendly terriers

Take time out from your journey for a few days to relax and unwind at **Birds Ferry Lodge**. We are located 4-5 hrs from The Glaciers, Nelson, Picton and Abel Tasman. **Lodge** guests enjoy sunsets from the heated spa, guest lounge and log fire. Privately accessed

accommodation is ensuite with baths. Dinner is available by arrangement and includes wine from our selection of quality New Zealand Wines. Our own home-produced vegetables and

free-range eggs are used wherever possible. Homeopathic Massage Therapy also available. **Ferry Man's Cottage** is 300m from the **Lodge** and enjoys the same views. Complete privacy, garden bath and all the comforts of **Birds Ferry Lodge** with your own kitchen and laundry facility. Close by are numerous coastal and forest walks or you can visit an exhibition gold mine or take the Charleston Nile River Forest Train. 30 min. away is Punakaiki. A day trip distance north of us you can visit Heaphy Track, Karamea, Oparara Arches and historic Denniston.

DIRECTIONS:
17km south of Westport on SH 6. – 8km north of Charleston on SH6. Turn off the highway at our sign and drive for 1.7km.

KALLY HOUSE

13 Cargill Road, Barrytown, Runanga, RD 1, Westland
Ph (03) 731 1006, Fax (03) 731 1106
email: *kallyhouse@xtra.co.nz*
www.travelwise.co.nz

Features & Attractions

- *Sea views & sunsets*
- *Two licensed restaurants*
- *Pancake Rocks close by*
- *Fishing, walking, tramping*
- *Paparoa Adventure Park*
- *Lapidary stone beach*

$	Double	$115-130
	Single	$75
	Child	

Bed & Breakfast Homestay

Bedrooms	Qty
Double	3
Twin	1
Single	
Bed Size	**Qty**
King	
Queen	3
Double	
Single	2
Bathrooms	**Qty**
Ensuite	
Private	1
Guest Share	2

Our unique elevated location reveals a multitude of exciting adventure activities. Pancake Rocks in the national park just fifteen minutes north. Fishing, walks, tramping, canoeing, restaurants, lapidary stone beach are all close by. Our spacious home is six years old, centrally heated, well appointed, quiet and with views of the sea and bush. We have two queen bedrooms upstairs with television. Guest share bathroom. Family share lounge with widescreen television. Continental breakfast with hosts. We also have a self-contained apartment downstairs. It has a queen bedroom with twin beds in a spacious living area. Full kitchen, washing and drying facilities. Parking and separate entrance. We have a frost-free micro climate to enjoy.

YOUR HOST: **Jan Macdonald**   Free Ph: 0800 350 590 ◁   ***Greymouth***

BREAKERS

Nine Mile Beach, Coast Road, SH 6,
PO Box 188, Greymouth
Ph (03) 762 7743, Fax (03) 762 7733
email: *stay@breakers.co.nz*
www.breakers.co.nz

Features & Attractions

- *Fabulous sea views*
- *Incredible sunsets*
- *Beach access*
- *National Park close by*
- *Great hospitality*
- *Dinner by arrangement*

Seaside Bed & Breakfast

$	Double	$190-285
	Single	
	Child	n/a

Spectacular location is one of the comments made about **Breakers**. Overlooking the Tasman Sea, at Nine Mile Beach on the Coast Road (SH 6), **Breakers** is located 14 km north of Greymouth and 30 km south of the Pancake Rocks at Punakaiki. **Breakers** is nestled on the edge of the Paparoa National Park amongst two acres of native bush and garden, with all rooms overlooking the sea.

Wander down the track to the beach, collect driftwood, stones and sometimes find pounamu (jade) pebbles. Or just sit on your verandah/deck, and watch the waves, enjoy the view, you may never want to leave. A good range of eating places within a short drive or enjoy our hospitality with pre-arranged gourmet dinners.

Bedrooms	Qty
Double	2
Twin	2
Single	
Bed Size	**Qty**
King	2
Queen	2
Double	
Single	2
Bathrooms	**Qty**
Ensuite	4
Private	
Guest Share	

WESTWAY

58 Herd Street, Dunollie, Greymouth
Ph (03) 762 7077, Fax (03) 762 7377
Mobile 027-495 2844
email: *westway@xtra.co.nz*
www.westway.co.nz

home
NEW ZEALAND

Tariff : N.Z. Dollars	
Double	$110-120
Single	$85-95
Child	neg

Bedrooms	Qty
Double	2
Twin	1
Single	

Bed Size	Qty
Super King	
King	
Queen	2
Double	
Single	2

Bathrooms	Qty
Ensuite	1
Private	1
Guest Share	1

**Rural Homestay
Bed & Breakfast and Dining**

Features & Attractions

- *Tranquil & private places*
- *Glow worms - Native bush*
- *Bush walking from Westway*
- *Mountains, rivers & lakes*

- *Evening meals from Wayne's kitchen*
- *Powered site for Camp-a-van*
- *The Homestay for all seasons*
- *Winter wonderland - group bookings*

[Map showing Tasman Sea, To Westport, Punakaiki - (Pancake Rocks), Rapahoe, Dunollie, Runanga, To Reefton, Greymouth, To Glaciers, Westway]

Just minutes from Greymouth, Westway is situated in a native forest clad valley. An historic tunnel on the property dates from 1902 when New Zealand's first state-owned coalmine operated further up the valley – glow worms live around the entrance. There are private places in the garden where you can experience nature and the tranquility of **Westway.**

We're only five minutes drive from the sandy swimming beach at Point Elizabeth, the start of the famous Coastal Road.
We have a friendly and relaxing lifestyle; take pleasure in sharing our local knowledge and in creating an environment that visitors can enjoy.
There's space for your leisure equipment. Evening meals are available. Complimentary transport when appropriate.

"Come and let us spoil you."

OAK LODGE

Coal Creek, State Highway 6, Greymouth
(3 km north of Greymouth)

Ph (03) 768 6832, Fax (03) 768 4362
email: *relax@oaklodge.co.nz*
www.oaklodge.co.nz

Tariff : N.Z. Dollars	
Double	$160-280
Single	$140
Child	

Bedrooms	Qty
Double	4
Twin	3
Single	

Bed Size	Qty
Super King	2
King	
Queen	2
Double	
Single	3

Bathrooms	Qty
Ensuite	4
Private	1
Guest Share	

**Homestay
Bed & Breakfast**

Features & Attractions

- *Rural setting*
- *Spa/jacuzzi*
- *Sauna*
- *Swimming pool*
- *Extensive gardens*
- *Tennis court*
- *Billiards room*
- *Black sheep, hens, donkey*

DIRECTIONS:
3 km north of Greymouth
State Highway 6.
Oak Lodge is on the right,
an elevated section.

This 100 year old farmhouse is full of character, and only three minutes drive from Greymouth. It is surrounded by extensive gardens containing over 400 rhododendrons and azaleas. Pathways are interlaced throughout the garden for wandering and exploring.

The guest accommodation is upstairs and includes a spacious guest lounge with television and tea & coffee making facilities. You can sit on the balcony sipping your drink and gaze over the surrounding farmland and mountains; or rejuvenate yourself in the spa pool or sauna. For the more energetic there is a tennis court, swimming pool, or stroll over the eighteen acre farmlet. Our donkey, Finias, welcomes any snack and some patting, as does our black ram called Pete - he will always come to the sound of sheep nuts being rattled in the tin! We also have a collection of multi coloured sheep on the property, and a few hens to provide eggs for your farmhouse breakfast. Colette and Brian, who have travelled themselves, extend a very warm welcome to you. Guest comment: *"We came as guests and leave as friends"*

331

JIVANA RETREAT

8 Leith Crescent, PO Box 143, Greymouth
Ph (03) 768 6102, Fax (03) 768 6108
email: *sandie@jivanaretreat.co.nz*
www.jivanaretreat.co.nz

Tariff : N.Z. Dollars	
Double	$120-160
Single	$110
Child	$20

Bedrooms	Qty
Double	3
Twin	1
Single	

Bed Size	Qty
Super King	1
King	
Queen	2
Double	
Single	2

Bathrooms	Qty
Ensuite	1
Private	1
Guest Share	1

 Organic Bed & Breakfast / Boutique Self-contained

Features & Attractions

- Free infrared sauna
- Massage & yoga
- Pamper packages
- Purification/Detox Programs
- Candlelight dinners
- Spacious, yet cosy
- Mountains, lakes & rivers
- Haven for all seasons

Jivana is a serene, affordable, quality haven. Sandie spoils you with a home-made organic breakfast menu of your choice, served indoors in the sunny conservatory, or lush outdoors. Special diets catered for. You may enjoy a spacious, comfortable super king, or cosy queen ensuite, guest share, or private chalet. The fully equipped yoga / pilates studio is available for guests, meditation, fitness, or simply just a tranquil place to relax, listen to CDs or quietly read. Take the time to relax in a herbal outdoor bush bath under the stars, or allow yourself to be pampered with an aromatherapy herbal massage / reflexology session, or a beneficial health program.

Sandie is a certified health practitioner, and yoga tutor with a passionate love for the outdoors. Brent is a local trades contractor, with a keenness for boating, and fishing.

*"**Jivana Retreat** has been a wonderful experience of nurturing and nourishment. I definitely got what I came for – rest and rejuvenation."* T Williams.

MARYGLEN HOMESTAY

20 Weenink Road, Karoro, Greymouth
Ph (03) 768 0706, Fax (03) 768 0599
Mobile 027-438 0479
email: *seaview@bandb.co.nz*
www.bandb.co.nz

Features & Attractions

- *Seaview in bush setting*
- *Off main road*
- *Dinner available*
- *Own entrance off deck*
- *Relaxed and friendly*
- *Internetaccess available*

$	Double	$110-140
	Single	$85-125
	Child	neg

**Homestay
Bed & Breakfast**

Bedrooms	Qty
Double/Twin	2
Double	1
Single	
Bed Size	**Qty**
King/Twin	2
Queen	1
Double	
Single	1
Bathrooms	**Qty**
Ensuite	3
Private	
Guest Share	

Picture relaxing on our seaview deck amidst native bush - an oasis after your travels. Our homestay is on a hillside off the main road. Two rooms open to the deck and have their own entrance. Amazing sunsets can be enjoyed from the deck. Dinner is often served outside where the native bird sounds serenade us while we dine. Having lived on the West Coast for over twenty years now, we have some delightful spots, bush walks and drives to share – Punakaiki Pancake Rocks, Lake Brunner, Glaciers, Trans Alpine Train (complimentary pick up). Bridge players welcome – a game is a possibility.

Guests always comment – "Amazing location"

DIRECTIONS: Approximately 3 km south of town centre. Weenink Road - is on the east side of main road.

KIA ORA HOMESTAY

15 Keith Road, Paroa, Greymouth
Ph (03) 762 6770, Fax (03) 762 5850
Mobile 027-3918218
email: *stay@kiaora-homestay.co.nz*
www.kiaora-homestay.co.nz

Features & Attractions

- *Tranquil setting*
- *Sea view & sunsets*
- *Gold panning*
- *Off-street parking*
- *Coastal & bush walks*
- *Dinner by arrangement*

$	Double	$90-100
	Single	$65-70
	Child	neg

**Bed & Breakfast
Homestay**

Bedrooms	Qty
Double	1
Twin	1
Single	1
Bed Size	**Qty**
King	
Queen	1
Double	
Single	3
Bathrooms	**Qty**
Ensuite	
Private	
Guest Share	1

Kia Ora means "greetings", "welcome". We are set in a very quiet area off the main road, where the sound of the sea and bird song predominate. A place to relax and unwind. Guest rooms are quiet and peaceful. The large lounge opens out onto the deck, where you can relax with a complimentary beer enjoying the sea view and stunning sunsets. We are within 5minutes of town centre and the historic village of Shantytown. There are many attractions nearby. Having travelled the South Island extensively, we are able to help with forward planning. Laundry facilities, hairdryer, off-street parking and a delicious cooked or continental breakfast. Guest comments: *"Really beautiful and relaxing"; "Excellent accommodation – would like to have stayed longer".* We offer you a warm welcome.

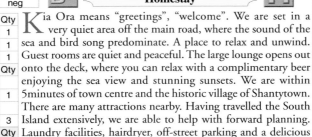

PAROA HOMESTAY

345 Main South Road, Paroa, Greymouth
Ph (03) 762 6769, Fax (03) 762 6765
Mobile 027-323 3118
email: *paroahomestay@xtra.co.nz*

Features & Attractions

- *Home away from home*
- *Off street parking*
- *Superb breakfast*
- *Seaview and mountain views*
- *Three minutes walk to beach*
- *Will organise tours (fishing etc)*

Homestay Bed & Breakfast

	Double	$110-140
	Single	$100
	Child	neg

Bedrooms	Qty
Double	2
Twin	
Single	1
Bed Size	**Qty**
Super King	1
King	1
Double	1
Single	
Bathrooms	**Qty**
Ensuite	1
Private	1
Guest Share	1

Imagine relaxing on twin terraces, overlooking Tasman Sea, enjoying incredible sunsets and mountain views. Just three minutes walk to the beach. Listen to chorus of native birds nesting amongst towering trees and native shrubs. Relax in the luxurious and spacious guest lounge in classic style home. Excellent restaurants are between three to six minutes drive.

Pam enjoys people, collects antiques and china, loves organic gardening and bush walking. Experience superb continental breakfast. Baking and cooking are Pam's forté (previously owning Greymouth's busiest cafés/bar). Pam has NZQA food hygiene qualifications. Being West Coast-born, Pam's vast local knowledge is invaluable. On arrival and for supper enjoy home-made cakes/biscuits.

Pam has welcomed guests for 13 years. Off-street parking.

Guests comments *"incredible breakfast (best in New Zealand)", "Beautiful home away from home - did not want to leave."* Looking forward to sharing my lovely home with you.

SUNSETVIEW HOMESTAY

335 Main South Road, Greymouth, Westland
Ph (03) 762 6616, Fax (03) 762 6616
email: *sunsetview@xtra.co.nz*

Features & Attractions

- *Sea & mountain views*
- *Short walk to beach*
- *Swimming pool/barbeque*
- *Relaxed & friendly*
- *Children welcome*
- *Generous breakfasts*

Homestay Bed & Breakfast

	Double	$100-140
	Single	$90-100
	Child	neg

Bedrooms	Qty
Double	4
Twin	
Single	
Bed Size	**Qty**
Super King	1
King	2
Queen	1
King/Single	2
Bathrooms	**Qty**
Ensuite	2
Private	1
Guest Share	

Welcome to our sunny home with amazing sea and mountain views. We offer well appointed queen and king bedrooms with Sky TV.

Full continental and cooked breakfasts, other home cooked meals available by prior arrangement. Our home is centrally heated. Internet, laundry/dryer facilities available. We have for your use an indoor pool which is heated from November till April. Beach is a 3min walk.

DIRECTIONS:
Approx 5km South of town centre

Downstairs we offer an apartment with its private entrance and two bedrooms, ensuite, kitchen/ dining/ lounge area. It can sleep up to 5 and can be enjoyed either as a regular B&B facility or as a self-catered basis. Fishing trips can be arranged. Courtesy car service to and from local restaurants and travel centres. Plenty of off-street parking.

ROSEWOOD BED & BREAKFAST

20 High Street, Greymouth
Ph (03) 768 4674, Fax (03) 768 4694
Mobile 027-242 7080
email: *stay@rosewoodnz.co.nz*
www.rosewoodnz.co.nz

Tariff : N.Z. Dollars	
Double	$150-200
Single	$125-160
Child	$25

Bedrooms	Qty
Double	4
Twin	2
Single	1
Bed Size	**Qty**
Super King	1
King	
Queen	4
Double	
Single	1
Bathrooms	**Qty**
Ensuite	3
Private	1
Guest Share	

Superior Bed & Breakfast

Features & Attractions

- *Character home*
- *Spacious rooms*
- *Separate guest lounge*
- *Courtesy pick-ups*
- *10-15 min walk to restaurants*
- *Ensuite or private facilities*
- *German spoken*
- *Off-street parking*

Whether you've just got off the Trans Alpine or are travelling through Greymouth between Christchurch, Nelson or the Glaciers, or just want a few days away, **Rosewood Bed & Breakfast** is the ideal place to stop and recover from your journey and the activities of the day. Rhonda and Stephan await you with a warm friendly welcome in their restored 1920's character home that has retained its grand features of wood panelling and leadlight windows. You will enjoy relaxing in the window seat in the guest lounge/dining room with a cup of tea or coffee and some of Rhonda's home-made biscuits before taking a wander into town for dinner in one of the cafés or restaurants. Spacious, well equipped bedrooms with private facilities will let you have a great night's sleep in a very comfortable bed. Full continental and cooked breakfast awaits you next morning to give you that perfect start to the day. Rhonda and Stephan appreciate all that the West Coast region has to offer, and would love to make your stay a memorable one for you!

PINERS HOMESTAY

75 Main South Road, Karoro,
Greymouth
Ph (03) 768 5397, Fax (03) 768 5396
email: *tpiner@paradise.net.nz*

Tariff : N.Z. Dollars	
Double	$85-95
Single	$60-65
Child	neg

Bedrooms	Qty
Double	1
Twin	1
Single	
Bed Size	**Qty**
Super King	
King	
Queen	
Double	1
Single	2
Bathrooms	**Qty**
Ensuite	
Private	
Guest Share	1

**Homestay
Bed & Breakfast**

Features & Attractions

- *Tariff includes full breakfast*
- *Special diets no problem*
- *Knowledgeable & friendly hosts*
- *Beautiful sunsets & mountain views*
- *5 minutes walk to seaside*
- *Very comfortable beds*
- *Off-street parking*
- *Rental Cars arranged*

We have been welcoming guests to our home for over fifteen years now and would love to share it with you. You will be very comfortable with a warm bed and a cosy fire in the winter. You will be able to enjoy delicious food made from our home grown and local produce. Dinner available with complimentary wine and pre-dinner drinks. Tea, coffee and home baking available at any time. Laundry facilities available for a small charge. We only take a maximum of four guests so you will have our total attention to making your stay in our lovely district everything you would wish for. As well as lots of local knowledge, we can also help you plan your activities when you journey to your next destination. You will be near the seaside and will see beautiful sunsets and mountain views. There is off-street parking. Courtesy pick up from Trans Alpine or bus. We are four kilometres south of the town centre. There is a second toilet adjacent to the bedrooms. We have two spoilt cats.

There is much more we could say but space does not allow. Why not come and see for yourself? See you soon!

NEW RIVER BLUEGUMS B&B

985 Main South Road, New River, Greymouth
Ph (03) 762 6678, Fax (03) 762 6678
Mobile 027-438 5324
email: *mail@bluegumsnz.com*
www.bluegumsnz.com

home
NEW ZEALAND

Features & Attractions

- *Owner-built log & stone home*
- *Two self-contained log cottages*
- *Floodlit tennis court*
- *10 min. walk to beach*
- *Feed farm animals*
- *Away from main highway*

$	Double	$135-180
	Single	$95-125
	Child	$25

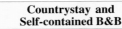

**Countrystay and
Self-contained B&B**

Bedrooms	Qty
Double	3
Twin	
Single	
Bed Size	**Qty**
King	1
Queen	2
Double	2
Single	1
Bathrooms	**Qty**
Ensuite	1
Private	2
Guest Share	

Sharon, Michael & Harry welcome you to the warmth and comfort of their log and stone home on a small farm. The homestead offers a king room with balcony. Two luxurious self-contained log cottages are superbly appointed, cosy, (double-glazing, heat pumps) and secluded, overlooking paddocks and the tennis court.

Wake to morning birdlife, stroll around paddocks with the cattle, feed the sheep or Piggy (Kunekune) and Coco (chocolate labrador).

"Beautiful setting! Delightful home! Your relaxed and welcome manner made us feel like we were somewhere special and we certainly were - thank you!" G&K – Guestbook.

AWATUNA BEACHSIDE BED & BREAKFAST

State Highway 6, Awatuna, RD 2, Hokitika
Ph (03) 755 6060, Mobile 027-404 6658
email: *awatuna-beachside@xtra.co.nz*
www.westcoast.net.nz

home
NEW ZEALAND

Features & Attractions

- *Scenic coastal views*
- *Historic gold trail walks*
- *Adventure activities arranged*
- *A taste of the country*
- *10 min from town*
- *Beach walks*

$	Double	$125-145
	Single	$75-125
	Child	Neg.

**Bed & Breakfast
Homestay**

Bedrooms	Qty
Double	2
Twin	1
Single	
Bed Size	**Qty**
King	1
Queen	1
Double	
Single	2
Bathrooms	**Qty**
Ensuite	3
Private	
Guest Share	

Awatuna Beachside Bed & Breakfast is nestled between the highway and the beach, in park-like grounds and with splendid views of the coastline and the Alps. We offer indoor and outdoor relaxation and ease. Walk along a lonely beach, or just soak up the views from our veranda, while enjoying a quiet drink. For the more active there is tramping, exploring the gold field trails, or a spot of fishing. A host of activities can be arranged.

The best of country living within minutes of town. Our house has been purpose-built – mixing modern living with traditional West Coast hospitality. Meet our two cats, Miranda and Sam. Complimentary transport offered when appropriate.

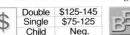

AWATUNA HOMESTEAD

9 Stafford Road, Awatuna, RD 2
Hokitika, Westland
Ph (03) 755 6834, Fax (03) 755 6876
email: *rest@awatunahomestead.co.nz*
www.awatunahomestead.co.nz

Tariff : N.Z. Dollars	
Double	$240-350
Single	$230
Child	neg

Bedrooms	Qty
Double	3
Twin	2
Single	
Bed Size	**Qty**
Super King	1
King	
Queen	2
King Single	2
Single	2
Bathrooms	**Qty**
Ensuite	3
Private	1
Guest Share	

Classic Country Accommodation & Self-contained

Features & Attractions

- *Cultural talks & story telling*
- *Vintage Morris 8 cars*
- *Private hot tub in bush setting*
- *Guest Internet/WiFi*
- *Dinner by request*
- *Extensive wine list*
- *Continental or special Breakfast*
- *Garden walks & beach fossicking*

Awatuna Homestead offers old-fashioned New Zealand hospitality with classic country accommodation, set in extensive park-like gardens, featuring native trees and shrubs. Elegant native timber interiors and an open fire in the guest lounge complement the beautifully appointed, superior guest rooms, which have French doors opening into wide verandahs. Pauline, Hemi, Eleanor and Peter welcome you to experience wood-stove warmth, country cooking, continental or special breakfasts and time spent sharing your hosts' traditional cultural knowledge of Polynesia and the West Coast. Take a walk on the wild West Coast beach, fossick for precious stones and driftwood treasures or enjoy the other activities offered. Masie and Poppy, our 2 small dogs, 2 horses, 2 cats and some sheep complete the family welcome. The Piper's Flat self-catering apartment (queen bedroom, twin bedroom and sofa-bed) has private access, exclusive deck with views to the mountains, the sea and gardens. Apartment tariff: $200-240 double, $35 each extra person. Breakfast $20pp extra by request. Recommend two nights stay.

HOKITIKA HERITAGE LODGE

46 Alpine View, PO Box 176, Hokitika
Ph (03) 755 7357, Fax (03) 755 8760
Mobile 027-437 1254
email: *info@hokitikaheritagelodge.co.nz*
www.hokitikaheritagelodge.co.nz

Tariff : N.Z. Dollars	
Double	$210-250
Single	$185
Child	

Bedrooms	Qty
Double	5
Twin	
Single	
Bed Size	**Qty**
Super King	
King	2
Queen	3
Double	
Single	1
Bathrooms	**Qty**
Ensuite	3
Private	1
Guest Share	

Luxury Accommodation

Features & Attractions

- *Heritage character Home*
- *Replica Heritage Cottage*
- *Bush setting hot tub*
- *Dinner by arrangement*
- *Magnificent sea vistas*
- *Spectacular mountain views*
- *Restaurants/glowworms close*
- *Beach & bush walks close*

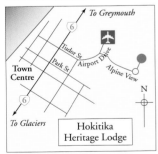

Hokitika Heritage Lodge

Enjoy amazing NZ hospitality in our Boutique Lodge, set on 1½ acres, overlooking extensive views of Tasman Sea, Hokitika Town and Southern Alps, including Mount Cook. The Lodge incorporates **Bank House** providing 3 spacious rooms with ensuites and full B&B. **Gatehouse Cottage**, completed in 2007, is self-catering and provides 2 beautiful bedrooms and private bathroom (breakfast available on request). Historic and stylish décor with attention to detail reflects NZ, West Coast and family history. Dianne, Literacy Teacher and Chris, Property Consultant and Rotarian, enjoy chatting with guests over a welcoming drink, home-baking or canapés. Enjoy a bush-setting spa or relax in one of the outside seating areas. Broadband Internet, wireless network, TV

and dinners are available. Stay a night or 2 or more. 2007 comments: *"A delightful stay with great NZ hospitality...fun, laughter and superb accommodation... wonderful hosts...cherished memories of our too short stay".accommodation... Wonderful hosts... Cherished memories of our too short a stay".*

339

BUSHLINE RETREAT BED & BREAKFAST
Bluespur Rd, RD2, Hokitika
Ph. (03) 755 6603
email: *bushlinebnb@xtra.co.nz*
www.bushline.co.nz

Features & Attractions
- *Great fishing & bush walks*
- *Private spa bathroom*
- *Pancake Rocks 75 min*
- *Families welcome*
- *Restaurant 5 min drive*
- *1¾ hours to Glaciers*

Bed & Breakfast Hosted Accommodation		$	Double	$125-150
			Single	$80-125
			Child	$25

Bedrooms	Qty
Double	4
Twin	
Single	
Bed Size	**Qty**
King	1
Queen	3
Double	
Single	3
Bathrooms	**Qty**
Ensuite	2
Private	1
Guest Share	1

Bushline Retreat is just a ten minutes scenic drive from Hokitika, in the heart of greenstone country 'Blue Spur'. Experience the true feeling of retreat with our peaceful surroundings, native birds and native bush setting.

Enjoy a relaxing breakfast taking in the views down the valley to the Tasman Sea. Unwind in our outdoor spa under a blanket of stars, after a short walk to our glow worm dell. Discount for multi night stays, families very welcome. With so much to do in the area why not stay an extra day or two. Handfeed the native Weka birds or try your hand at goldpanning.

At **bushline** we are more than happy to help with all your forward bookings. Award winning restaurant 5 minutes drive.

340

TEICHELMANN'S BED & BREAKFAST

20 Hamilton Street, PO Box 156, Hokitika
Ph (03) 755 8232, Fax (03) 755 8239
email: *teichel@xtra.co.nz*
www.teichelmanns.co.nz

Tariff : N.Z. Dollars	
Double	$195-240
Single	$165-185
Child	

Bedrooms	Qty
Double	5
Twin	2
Single	1
Bed Size	**Qty**
Super King	3
King	2
Queen	
Double	1
King/Single	1
Bathrooms	**Qty**
Ensuite	5
Private	1
Guest Share	

Bed & Breakfast

DIRECTIONS:
Turn left at Town Clock,
then first right.
Booking in advance is
recommended.

Features & Attractions

- *Quiet, central location*
- *Close to restaurants/cafés*
- *Heritage, character house*
- *Warm, friendly service*

- *Walk to beach & shops*
- *Interesting craft galleries*
- *Walks, golf and fishing*
- *Craft & heritage trails*

Frances and Brian pride themselves in offering friendly, informal hospitality within the comforts of a warm character home. It gives guests the opportunity to 'Catch Your Breath and Breakfast' after a long day travelling. **Teichelmann's**, located in the heritage area of Hokitika, is a large home built for Dr Ebenezer Teichelmann in 1897.

Its layout gives our guests privacy if they wish or to relax in the comfort of a separate guest's lounge. The house has been refurbished to include very comfortable beds, quality furnishings and excellent ensuite bathroom facilities. Join other guests for a substantial continental or cooked breakfast at our elegant table which seats ten and enjoy swapping experiences and stories with people from all parts of the world.

Children over ten years of age are welcome.
Our home is smoke free.

| **Hokitika** | YOUR HOSTS: **Anne and Spencer Routhan** | Ph: (03) 755 7615 |

STOPFORTH DYNASTY HOMESTAY
105 Weld Street, Hokitika,
Ph (03) 755 7615, Fax (03) 755 5262
email: *info@vacationnewzealand.co.nz*
www.vacationnewzealand.co.nz

Features & Attractions

- *Close to town centre*
- *Underfloor heating in bathrooms*
- *Punakaiki/Glaciers 1½ hours*
- *Lake Kaniere & Hokitika Gorge 20 minutes*

 Bed & Breakfast Homestay

Double	$120
Single	$65
Child	$10

A nne and Spencer welcome you to their slice of Heaven. This is where visitors from all over New Zealand and the world come to experience the "Hokitika Food Festival" held opposite, at the park. Spencer has been a goldminer and can show you a nugget or two.

An easy five minute walk to the town centre where you will find a choice of top restaurants. Our guests enjoy a continental breakfast with extras (homemade bread), comfortable beds and underfloor heating in the bathrooms. Children are welcome. Make our home your place away from home and stay more than one night.

Motor-cycle friendly.

Bedrooms	Qty
Double	1
Twin	1
Single	1
Bed Size	**Qty**
King	
Queen	2
Double	1
Single	
Bathrooms	**Qty**
Ensuite	2
Private	1
Guest Share	

| **Ruatapu - Hokitika** | YOUR HOSTS: **Eileen and Roger Berwick** | Ph: (03) 755 7876 |

BERWICKS HILL COUNTRYSTAY
106 Ruatapu Ross Rd, SH 6,
RD 3, Hokitika
Ph (03) 755 7876, Fax (03) 755 7870
email: *berwicks@xtra.co.nz*
www.berwicks.co.nz

Features & Attractions

- *Lake Mahinapua*
- *Beach walks*
- *Bush walks*
- *Sea and mountain views*
- *Breakfast from our menu*
- *Dinner by arrangement*

 Countrystay Bed & Breakfast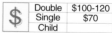

Double	$100-120
Single	$70
Child	

W e offer you a warm and friendly welcome to our comfortable home situated on the property that was settled by the Berwick family in 1907. The Tasman Sea and Southern Alps are seen from the living areas, the sunrises and sunsets are uniquely beautiful. We have sheep, cattle, and hens on our hobby farm, with one farm dog, a cat and a house dog. Beautiful Lake Mahinapua is only minutes away with many interesting bush walks. We are only a short distance from the beach and golf course. Hokitika is a ten minute drive with its jade (pounamu) carvers and many other arts, crafts and walks. We look forward to spending time with you and sharing our love of the West Coast.

Bedrooms	Qty
Double	1
Twin	1
Single	
Bed Size	**Qty**
King	
Queen	1
King/Single	2
Single	
Bathrooms	**Qty**
Ensuite	1
Private	1
Guest Share	

DIRECTIONS: Travel over the Hokitika Bridge on State Highway 6 for 12 km, on the right just past the southern Ruatapu turnoff.

WOODLAND GLEN LODGE

96 Hau Hau Rd, Blue Spur, Hokitika
Ph/Fax (03) 755 5063, Mobile 027-201 6126
email: *l.anderson@xtra.co.nz*
www.hokitika.net.nz

home
NEW ZEALAND

Tariff : N.Z. Dollars	
Double	$140-250
Single	$130-180
Child	——

Bedrooms	Qty
Double	5
Twin	2
Single	

Bed Size	Qty
Super King	
King	
Queen	5
Double	
Single	2

Bathrooms	Qty
Ensuite	3
Private	
Guest Share	1

AMERICAN EXPRESS
VISA
MasterCard
eftpos
JCB

Luxury Bed & Breakfast

DIRECTIONS:
From Main St into Hokitika
turn east into Hampden St.
Proceed straight for
approximately 2km
until sign on right.

Advance booking
recommended.

Features & Attractions

- *Quiet private surroundings*
- *Only 2 km to Hokitika*
- *Lake Kauiere & Hokitika Gorge*
- *Courtesy car to local restaurants for dinner*

- *Wonderful gardens*
- *Helicopter scenic tours*
- *Heli fishing & hunting*
- *Honeymoon packages*

Laurie and Janette welcome you to **Woodland Glen Lodge**, located on the outskirts of Hokitika. The gateway to Franz Joseph and Fox Glaciers, **Woodland Glen** is more than a home away from home. Our 6,500 square foot lodge is located on 21 acres and is surrounded in native Kahikatea trees which provide complete quiet and privacy. A great place for a retreat or just time out. We specialise in honeymoon package deals. Laurie is a fourth generation West Coaster, a retired 30 year police veteran with an aviation background as a commercial pilot on both helicopters and aeroplanes. Laurie has a wealth of knowledge of the region and its people. Janette is originally from Edinburgh Scotland and is presently employed as a health professional. She is actively involved in a local quilting group and has an interest in most crafts. **Woodland Glen Lodge** is an excellent base for local and regional tourist attractions so allow for at least 2 nights stay. From the lodge we provide helicopter scenic tours, guided heli fishing and hunting.

PARAMATA LODGE

554 Bold Head Road, RD1, Ross, West Coast
Mobile 027-367 2699
Skype: Paramatalodge
email: *stay@paramatalodge.co.nz*
www.paramatalodge.co.nz

Tariff : N.Z. Dollars	
Double	$200-350
Single	$180-250
Child	n/a

Bedrooms	Qty
Double	3
Twin	
Single	

Bed Size	Qty
Super King	2
King	1
Queen	
Double	
Single	

Bathrooms	Qty
Ensuite	3
Private	
Guest Share	

**Ecological Sanctuary
Warm and Friendly**

Features & Attractions

- *Complimentary tours*
- *Free canoes & walks*
- *3 fishing rivers 5km*
- *Remote sandy beach*
- *Free wireless internet*
- *Dinner & wine available*
- *30 minutes to Hokitika*
- *Mountain to sea views*

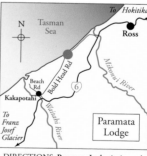

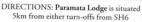

DIRECTIONS: **Paramata Lodge** is situated 5km from either turn-offs from SH6

Set in a spectacular landscape of indigenous forest stretching from the Southern Alps to the Tasman Sea, **Paramata Lodge** offers accommodation, dinner and guided tours at a brand new character home that has luxurious features at a secluded location. Spacious private rooms and shared lounges look out onto primeval forest, protected wetlands and coastal scenes with a mountain backdrop. Your hosts offer exclusive wilderness experiences for guests beginning with a complimentary tour. More in-depth interpretation of the ecology and history or special interest options is available by boat or walking. All rooms have unique features reflecting the local history and your host's artistic eye. In the kitchen food is prepared with Central European influences and fresh Pacific flavours, ingredients being picked from the garden on the day. The choice of Bed & Breakfast, dinner and tours is entirely yours. **Paramata Lodge** is 30 min. drive to Hokitika and just over an hour to Franz Josef Glacier.

344

WAPITI PARK HOMESTEAD

SH 6, Harihari, South Westland
Ph (03) 753 3074, Fax (03) 753 3024
email: *wapitipark@xtra.co.nz*
www.wapitipark.co.nz

Tariff : N.Z. Dollars	
Double	$375-545
Single	$300-475
Exclusive Use $1200	

Bedrooms	Qty
Double	3
Twin	3
Single	
Bed Size	**Qty**
Super King	3
King	1
Queen	
Double	
Single	2
Bathrooms	**Qty**
Ensuite	3
Private	
Guest Share	

**Boutique Country Lodge
Luxury Farmstay**

Features & Attractions

- *Quiet, peaceful surroundings*
- *Superior comfort beds*
- *5 course dinner by arrangement*
- *Evening glow worm tour*
- *Large, spacious rooms & lounges*
- *Traditional hospitality*
- *Morning elk farm tour*
- *Guided hunting/fishing available*

Nestled under the foothills of the Southern Alps at the northern gateway to the Glacier region, **Wapiti Park Homestead** stands on the site of the original Hari Hari Post Office and Accommodation house. Owner hosts, Grant and Bev, invite you to discover the special experience of a stay at their newly re-furbished luxurious colonial-style Boutique Country Lodge, which offers guests a unique blend of ambience and traditional West Coast hospitality. Relax in complete comfort, enjoying either the Rose or Fern suites with their private sitting rooms and hydro-spa ensuites, or the antique furnished 4-poster Oak room, or the total privacy of an "exclusive use" single party reservation. Extensive indoor/outdoor areas provide ample opportunity to enjoy the tranquility of the rural location. Wander

DIRECTIONS:
On the west side of State Highway 6 at southern approach to Harihari. Look for the sign.

award winning gardens, relax on the deck, catch up on some sleep, sample the legendary 5 course dinner, experience the in-house activities. **Wapiti Park** is now a destination so allow 2-3 days to experience and explore the area. The Lodge is non-smoking and unsuitable for young children, unless as part of an "exclusive use" reservation.

Mount Adam Lodge

State Highway 6, RD 1, Whataroa, South Westland
Ph (03) 753 4030, Mobile 021-170 2502
email: *mtadamlodge@paradise.net.nz*
www.mountadamlodge.co.nz

Tariff : N.Z. Dollars	
Double	$115-140
Single	$90-110
Child	

Bedrooms	Qty
Double	3
Twin	2
Single	2
Bed Size	**Qty**
Super King	
King	
Queen	2
Double	1
Single	6
Bathrooms	**Qty**
Ensuite	5
Private	
Guest Share	1

**Quality Lodge
Majestic Scenery**

Features & Attractions

- *Quiet, peaceful surroundings*
- *White Heron Bird Sanctuary*
- *35 min north of Franz Josef*
- *Licensed restaurant with home cooking*
- *Stay on a real farm*
- *Friendly hosts*
- *Farm and river walks*
- *Stunning location*

[Map showing Tasman Sea, To Hokitika, Whataroa, Mount Adam Lodge, To Franz Josef & Fox Glacier, State Highway 6]

If you are wanting to escape the crowds in the busy tourist centres, then we are the ideal place for you to stay. Just a short thirty-five minute drive north of Franz Josef Glacier. We are situated on our farm at the foot of Mount Adam, surrounded by farmland and beautiful native bush with breathtaking mountain views. Our lodge offers comfortable accommodation and a fully licensed restaurant with tasty home cooked meals. You can stroll along our farm tracks and river bank meeting our variety of farm animals on the way. We will be happy to provide details or make reservations for helicopter flights, walks, or helihikes at the glaciers and also the White Heron Bird Sanctuary at Whataroa. Elsa and Mac look forward to meeting you. You will find us on State Highway 6, half way between Harihari and Whataroa. Seventy minutes south of Hokitika, thirty-five minutes north of Franz Josef.

Molloy Farmstay

La Fontaine Rd, Harihari, South Westland
Ph (03) 753 3082 , Fax (03) 753 3082
e-mail: *chaos1@xtra.co.nz*

Features & Attractions

- *Awesome mountain views*
- *Quiet streamside, new house*
- *Native bush and birds*
- *Cows, pukekos, hens*
- *Dogs, cats & Appaloosa horses*
- *Fishing, hunting, walks*

$	Double	$150
	Single	$75
	Child	1/2 Price

A Real New Zealand Farm Experience

Bedrooms	Qty
Double	2
Twin	
Single	

Bed Size	Qty
Super King	
Queen	1
Double	1
Single	1

Bathrooms	Qty
Ensuite	
Private	
Guest Share	1

Centred in a tranquil river valley and surrounded by bush-clad hills and snow-topped mountains, we have 360° views, extensive lawns and flower gardens and a spring creek. Our homestay is on a working dairy farm. La Fontaine Stream, world famous for fly and nymph trout fishing, runs through the property. There are remnant Totara and Kahikatea stands on the farm. Many native birds. Mary and Lindsay, New Zealanders, have been living on the property for 30 years. With their extensive knowledge they would like to help you find bush and beach walks. Only 5 min. away are the 'Wanganui Coastal Walkway' and the landing site of Guy Menzies, the first aviator to cross the Tasman Sea in a single-engined bi-plane. 45 min. to the Glaciers. Share with us our quiet, spacious, new home. Generous, complimentary breakfasts included.

DIRECTIONS: From Harihari, half way between Hokitika and Franz Josef, turn down Wanganui Flat Rd. After 5km turn left onto la Fontaine Rd, then ½km to house with blue and yellow letterbox.

Te Taho Deer Park & Country Stay

1925 State Highway 6, Te Taho, Whataroa
Ph (03) 753 4263,
Mobile 021-328 197
e-mail: *pinney@xtra.co.nz*

Features & Attractions

- *Spacious rooms with ensuite*
- *Spectacular alpine & river views*
- *Guided hunting & fishing avail.*
- *Purpose-built 2007*
- *Own entrance to units*
- *30 min. north Franz Josef*

$	Double	$110-250
	Single	$90-180
	Child	

VISA MasterCard

Luxury Bed & Breakfast Farmstay

Bedrooms	Qty
Double	2
Twin	
Single	

Bed Size	Qty
Super King	2
Queen	
Double	
Single	

Bathrooms	Qty
Ensuite	2
Private	
Guest Share	

Te Taho Deer Park & Country Stay is set on 300 acres of pristine farmland covered in mature native trees. Nestled at the foot of the Southern Alps this provides you with stunning views west over Mount Adam and east as the sun sets down the Whataroa River. We are located just a short 30 minute scenic drive north of Franz Josef Glacier.

If it's peace and quiet you are looking for after your action filled day on the glaciers and are wanting to unwind in a truly beautiful part of the region, then **Te Taho Deer Park & Country Stay** is for you.

Our guest wing is separate from the main house allowing you a peaceful and private stay so you can sit back and relax in your luxurious, spacious, ensuite rooms and enjoy our friendly deer, who will greet you over your balcony.

MATAI LODGE

Whataroa, South Westland, South Island
Ph/Fax (03) 753 4156, Mobile 021-395 068
email: *jpurcell@xtra.co.nz*

Tariff : N.Z. Dollars	
Double	$150-180
Single	$120
Child	half price

Bedrooms	Qty
Double	2
Twin	1
Single	
Bed Size	**Qty**
Super King	1
King	1
Queen	
Double	
King/Single	2
Bathrooms	**Qty**
Ensuite	1
Private	1
Guest Share	

Farmstay
Bed & Breakfast

Features & Attractions

- *Glacier flights*
- *Forest & glacier walks*
- *3-course dinner $40 pp*
- *Stunning location*
- *Fishing - salmon and trout*
- ***White heron** bird sanctuary*
- *Golf, kayaking, horse riding*
- *Peaceful farm setting*

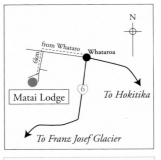

DIRECTIONS:
Whataroa is 20 minutes north of Franz
Josef Glacier. 3km west of SH 6:
Blue B & B sign.

If you are coming to see the Glaciers, walk in the World Heritage Park, the coastal track at Okarito or visit the White Heron Bird Sanctuary in Whataroa, you are warmly welcome to share with us our tranquil, rural retreat in our modern, spacious home on a 400 acre farm of sheep, cows and a farm dog.

Upstairs is a suite of two bedrooms, conservatory and private bathroom and downstairs a king size ensuite.

You are welcome to join us for a home-cooked dinner with New Zealand wine ($40 per person).

Our motto is: *"A stranger is a friend we have yet to meet"*.

Glenice speaks Japanese and has taught felting, spinning and weaving in Japan. Glenice also plays golf.

HOLLY HOMESTEAD B&B

State Highway 6, PO Box 35, Franz Josef Glacier
Ph (03) 752 0299, Fax (03) 752 0298
email: *stay@hollyhomestead.co.nz*
www.hollyhomestead.co.nz

Tariff : N.Z. Dollars	
Double	$200-320
Single	$170-290
Child	n/a

Bedrooms	Qty
Double	2
Twin	2
Single	

Bed Size	Qty
Super King/Twin	2
King	
Queen	2
Double	
Single	

Bathrooms	Qty
Ensuite	4
Private	
Guest Share	

Quality Bed & Breakfast
Fine Accommodation

Features & Attractions

- Friendly NZ-born hosts
- Central heating & log fire
- Glacier carpark 10 min.
- Restaurants 2 min. drive

- Character home
- Generous breakfast
- Off-street parking
- Year round activities

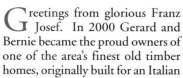

Greetings from glorious Franz Josef. In 2000 Gerard and Bernie became the proud owners of one of the area's finest old timber homes, originally built for an Italian family in 1926. We invite you to share the charm and ambience of this impressive colonial homestead. Recent renovations and extensions have carried on the warm timber theme. Relax in our cosy guest lounge after your adventures. Spend a restful night in comfortable beds with quality linen, wool duvets and electric blankets. All guest rooms have ensuite bathrooms, hairdryers and toiletries – and the comfort of wooden toilet seats! Socialise with other guests while enjoying a hearty continental and cooked breakfast. Enjoy a spectacular alpine view from the large breakfast table – clouds permitting! We offer helpful, friendly advice on local activities and are happy to assist you with bookings. Courtesy transport for guests travelling by coach. Children over twelve welcome. Allow yourself time to unwind in this magnificent region. We recommend a two night minimum. Don't be disappointed, book early.

FRANZ JOSEF GLACIER COUNTRY RETREAT

State Highway 6, Lake Mapourika, PO Box 11, Franz Josef
Ph (03) 752 0012, Fax (03) 752 0021
Mobile 027-545 1198
email: *stay@glacier-retreat.co.nz*
www.glacier-retreat.co.nz

Tariff : N.Z. Dollars	
Double	$195-295
Single	$175-275
Child	

Bedrooms	Qty
Double	10
Twin	2
Single	

Bed Size	Qty
Super King	5
King	
Queen	5
Double	
King/Single	4

Bathrooms	Qty
Ensuite	11
Private	2
Guest Share	

 Boutique Bed & Breakfast Luxury Lodge

Features & Attractions

- *Hosts 4th generation locals*
- *Mountain & lake views*
- *The quietest accommodation*
- *Free activity booking service*
- *Guest lounge with open fire*
- *Rooms all centrally heated*
- *DVD players, Sky TV in all rooms*
- *Guest laundry facilities*

DIRECTIONS: On State Highway 6, located 5 minutes drive north of the village, near Lake Mapourika.

We are delighted to welcome you to **Franz Josef Glacier Country Retreat**. Our retreat is set in 200 acres of peaceful farmland where our pioneer family has resided for over 100 years. Our building's design was inspired by a historical West Coast homestead. This unique accommodation offers traditional hospitality in luxurious surroundings, looking towards picturesque Lake Mapourika, 5 minutes drive north of Franz Josef

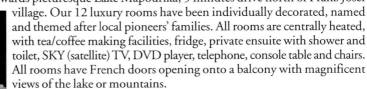

village. Our 12 luxury rooms have been individually decorated, named and themed after local pioneers' families. All rooms are centrally heated, with tea/coffee making facilities, fridge, private ensuite with shower and toilet, SKY (satellite) TV, DVD player, telephone, console table and chairs. All rooms have French doors opening onto a balcony with magnificent views of the lake or mountains.

We also have a special honeymoon suite with a four poster bed and an old fashioned claw-foot bath. Relax in the guest lounge with large gas open fire or in our spa-bathroom. Also have guest laundry and outdoor open fire/BBQ for all guests to use.

We look forward to sharing with you our special place.

KNIGHTSWOOD LODGE BED & BREAKFAST

State Highway 6, PO Box 70, Franz Josef Glacier
Ph (03) 752 0059, Fax (03) 752 0061
Mobile 027-433 0312
email: *info@knightswoodlodge.com*
www.knightswoodlodge.com

Tariff : N.Z. Dollars	
Double	$160-210
Single	$130-170
Child age dependent	

Bedrooms	Qty
Double	3
Twin	2
Single	

Bed Size	Qty
Super King	
King	2
Queen	1
Double	
Single	1

Bathrooms	Qty
Ensuite	2
Private	
Family Share	1

Bed & Breakfast Countrystay

DIRECTIONS:
On main SH 6, 3 km south of Franz Josef.
Travelling from the north we are on the
right, from the south on the left side.

Features & Attractions

- *Spectacular alpine views*
- *Peaceful rural setting*
- *Private native bush*
- *Many native birds*
- *Own entrance to ensuite rooms*
- *Comfortable beds*
- *Children welcome*
- *Glacial flights/hikes*

Enjoy this modern home alongside a forest and alpine splendor. Although **Knightswood Lodge** is located only minutes from town and Franz Josef Glacier, be assured peace and tranquility. Gerry, a former helicopter pilot and wildlife ranger, welcomes good conversation. Enjoy an interpretive guided walk within a private native forest or venture further toward the grand alpine expanse. Explore glaciers, the forest and perhaps the wilderness coast, or kayak and fish amongst lake and estuary.

Guest rooms have private entrance / outside verandah space. Be welcomed upstairs with evening / afternoon drinks – breakfast to suit.

FRANZ JOSEF ALPINE LODGE

117 Greens Road, Franz Josef, South Westland
Ph (03) 752 0688, Fax (03) 752 0688
Mobile 021-767 024
email: *jacque@franzlodge.com*
www.franzlodge.com

Features & Attractions

- *Franz Josef Glacier*
- *Guided walks*
- *Hunting & fishing*
- *Kayak Lake Mapourika*
- *Private ensuites*
- *Helicopter scenic flights*

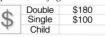

**Homestay
Bed & Breakfast**

Double	$180
Single	$100
Child	

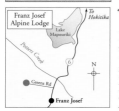

Jacque and Brian invite you to their home which adjoins 13 acres of rural land surrounded by Westland National Park. We are situated 1km off State Highway 6, just 7km north of the Franz Josef township. If you are looking for a peaceful setting to unwind, then this is the place for you. Brian is a helicopter pilot and you can do your scenic flight from your doorstep at your leisure. We also offer guided hunting and fishing tours. We enjoy meeting people and look forward to sharing our West Coast hospitality with you. **Franz Josef Alpine Lodge** is home to amazing native birdlife and in close proximity to Lake Mapourika and Lake Pratt.

Bedrooms	Qty
Double	3
Twin	1
Single	
Bed Size	**Qty**
Super King	1
King	1
Queen	1
Single	
Bathrooms	**Qty**
Ensuite	3
Private	
Guest Share	1

RIBBONWOOD RETREAT

26 Greens Road, PO Box 30, Franz Josef
Ph (03) 752 0072, Fax (03) 752 0272
email: *ribbon.wood@xtra.co.nz*
www.ribbonwood.net.nz

B&B

@home
NEW ZEALAND

qualmark
★★★★
guest & hosted

Tariff : N.Z. Dollars	
Double	$180-275
Single	
Child	

Bedrooms	Qty
Double	3
Twin	
Single	
Bed Size	**Qty**
Super King	
King	1
Queen	2
Double	
Single	1
Bathrooms	**Qty**
Ensuite	1
Private	2
Family Share	1

**Bed & Breakfast
Homestay**

Features & Attractions

- *Glacier views*
- *5 min to Franz Josef & restaurants*
- *Spectacular mountain scenery*
- *Self-contained cottage*
- *Contemporary home*
- *Relaxing rural outlook*
- *Modern bathrooms*
- *Scenic flights, glacier walks*

To
Hokitika

Greens Rd

N

Tatare River

Waiho River

6

Ribbonwood
Retreat

To
Fox Glacier

Franz Josef

To Franz Josef Glacier

DIRECTIONS: 5 km north of Franz
Josef (towards Hokitika), **Ribbonwood**
is situated on the corner of Greens Rd
and SH 6. Look for 2-storey house
with blue roof set back 100 m from
the highway, surrounded by trees.

Guests commented: *"Superb hospitality, food, facilities and local advice. Thank you so much."* Angela and Steve, Kent, UK. We are both Kiwis – Julie is a local schoolteacher and Jo has been a conservation ranger for nearly 30 years. As keen travellers and walkers, we know the local environment intimately. We cater for just a few guests at **Ribbonwood** because we want you to feel completely at home. We pride ourselves on our knowledge of the region and offer friendly, personalised advice. You will be warmly welcomed into our clean and sunny, modern home. Our home has two guest rooms with comfortable new beds with electric blankets and luxury bathrooms. The new, private, self-contained cottage has timber-panelled walls and a large deck looking out to the surrounding mountains and farmland. Breakfast includes fresh fruit crêpes, freshly ground coffee and delicious home-made bread. With its stunning views of mountains, glaciers and forests of Westland National Park, **Ribbonwood** is only five min. drive from glacier walks, scenic flights and restaurants of Franz Josef village. Off-road parking, spacious grounds and extensive replanting afford complete privacy.

Fox Glacier Lodge

Sullivan Road, PO Box 22, Fox Glacier 7859
Ph (03) 751 0888, Fax (03) 751 0888
email: *foxglacierlodge@xtra.co.nz*
www.foxglacierlodge.co.nz

Tariff : N.Z. Dollars	
Double	$240
Single	$90-180
Child	$40

Bedrooms	Qty
Double or Twin	8
Twin	
Single	
Bed Size	**Qty**
Super King	
King	1
Queen	7
Double	
Single	6
Bathrooms	**Qty**
Ensuite	8
Private	
Guest Share	

**Alpine Chalet Lodge
Bed & Breakfast**

Features & Attractions

- *Warm & friendly hospitality*
- *Magestic mountain views*
- *Tranquil rainforest setting*
- *Guided walks*
- *Double spa bath units available*
- *Mountain bikes available*
- *Central to cafés, restaurants & shops*
- *Scenic helicopter flights arranged*

DIRECTIONS: Sullivan Road is off SH 6, opp BP Petrol Station.

Experience our warm hospitality, mountain views and awake to the smell of freshly made bread and filter coffee. Our modern, solid timber, purpose-built lodge is in the heart of Fox Glacier Village. We are the closest accommodation to the glacier and only a one minute stroll to all cafés, restaurants and shops. Enjoy our tranquil setting, surrounded by unique temperate rainforest with majestic mountain views. Close by glow worm forest walk. We would be more than happy to offer our local knowledge in helping you book any local activities like glacier walks and scenic helicopter/fixed wing flights. Laundry facilities and mountain bikes are available for your use. We have 3 new apartment-style units, completed late 2005, all fully self-contained with spa bath. We will endeavour to make your stay a comfortable and memorable experience. We look forward to meeting you and sharing our little slice of heaven.

ROPATINI'S HOMESTAY B&B

81 Cook Flat Road, Box 15, Fox Glacier
Ph (03) 751 0779, Fax (03) 751 0789
email: *ropatinis@xtra.co.nz*

Tariff : N.Z. Dollars	
Double	$130-230
Single	
Child	

Bedrooms	Qty
Double	4
Twin	1
Single	

Bed Size	Qty
Super King	3
King	
Queen	1
Double	
Single	2

Bathrooms	Qty
Ensuite	3
Private	
Guest Share	1

**Quality Bed & Breakfast
Self-contained & Cottages**

Ropatini's

- *Ensuite or guest share*
- *Unique dining room table*
- *Great views of Mt Cook*
- *Dinner by arrangement*

- *Large gardens*
- *Free wireless broadband*
- *Free email access*
- *Glacier & Lake Matheson nearby*

Haere mai and welcome to our warm, comfortable home. We enjoy our large peaceful gardens and the spectacular views of the Southern Alps and Mount Cook. Travellers are always welcome here and we try to make them feel as comfortable as we do. The separate garden studios, with mountain views are ideal for those who like a little space of their own, and have super king beds, cosy bedding, turbo showers, heater, TV, fridge, tea and cofffee facilities. In the main house choose either an ensuite room or one of the two rooms which share a bathroom. Our dining room has this view of Mt Cook and a special unforgettable table. Refreshments and home baking are always available. We can help plan your day with local attractions and activities – from a peaceful fifteen minute walk to the thrill of ice climbing. Join us for pre dinner drinks served with genuine Kiwi hospitality and chat about your travels – stay for dinner or restaurants nearby. You are welcome to stay for a night or longer .

REFLECTION LODGE

Cook Flat Road, PO Box 46, Fox Glacier
Ph (03) 751 0707, Fax (03) 751 0707
email: *raelene@reflectionlodge.co.nz*
www.reflectionlodge.co.nz

Tariff : N.Z. Dollars	
Double	$150-190
Single	$130-150
Child	$45

Bedrooms	Qty
Double	2
Twin	1
Single	

Bed Size	Qty
Super King	
King	
Queen	2
Double	
Single	3

Bathrooms	Qty
Ensuite	1
Private	1
Family Share	

**Homestay
Bed & Breakfast**

Features & Attractions

- *Spectacular views*
- *Peaceful and tranquil*
- *Lake Matheson nearby*
- *Stunning scenic walks*
- *We arrange helicopter flights & heli-hikes*
- *Breakfast with lake views*

Welcome to the 'Glacier Region'. **Reflection Lodge** offers panoramic views of Mount Cook and Mount Tasman. New Zealand's two highest peaks reflecting in our very own private lake. Colin, a local helicopter pilot, and Raelene are fourth generation 'West Coasters' and have lived and worked in the glacier region for over 15 years. We invite you to share the comfort of our home and gardens. We are more than happy to assist you with any activities in our picturesque region. We enjoy meeting people and look forward to sharing our wonderful piece of paradise with you.

"Leave everything the way it is. You cannot improve the perfect."
Wolfgang Hebs, Wipperfuerth, Germany

"I feel comfortable. Just like I'm staying in my home." Yuko Sekiguchi, Nagoya, Japan

"Wonderful – we'll come again!" Peter & Billy Constable, Cincinnatti Ohio, USA

THE HOMESTEAD

Cook Flat Road, PO Box 25, Fox Glacier
Ph (03) 751 0835, Fax (03) 751 0805
email: *foxhomestead@slingshot.co.nz*

Tariff : N.Z. Dollars	
Double	$140-175
Single	
Child	

Bedrooms	Qty
Double	2
Twin	1
Single	
Bed Size	Qty
Super King	
King	1
Queen	1
Double	
King/Single	2
Bathrooms	Qty
Ensuite	2
Private	1
Guest Share	

Farm Retreat Amidst Stunning Scenery

Features & Attractions

- *Stained glass windows*
- *Stunning mountain views*
- *Delicious breakfast*
- *Peaceful rural retreat*
- *Guest lounge*
- *A place to unwind*
- *Children 7+ welcome*
- *Close to village facilities*

Kevin and Noeleen Williams welcome you to our 2200 acre sheep, beef-cattle farm. Beautiful native bush clad mountains surround our paradise, and we enjoy a view of Mount Cook. Our spacious 100-year-old character home, built for Kevin's grandparents, has fine stained glass windows. The breakfast room overlooks the house paddocks, and you are served homemade jams, marmalade, yoghurt, hot scones etc. Our guest lounge has a beautiful timbered ceiling, with an open fire for cooler nights. A variety of teas and coffees are provided.

The Homestead is a rural retreat within walking distance of village facilities. Famous Lake Matheson (Mirror Lake) and glacier are nearby.
It is our pleasure to help you with your helicopter flights, glacier walks and onward reservations.

THE WHITE FOX

4 State Highway 6, PO Box 82, Fox Glacier
Ph (03) 751 0717, Fax (03) 751 0717
Mobile 027-306 6759
email: *thewhitefox@slingshot.co.nz*
www.thewhitefoxbandb.co.nz

Tariff : N.Z. Dollars	
Double	$140-170
Single	$120-150
Child	neg by age

Bedrooms	Qty
Double	1
Twin	
Single	
Bed Size	**Qty**
Super King	
King	
Queen	1
Double	
Single	1
Bathrooms	**Qty**
Ensuite	1
Private	
Guest Share	

**Genuine NZ Family
Quality Homestay B&B**

Features & Attractions

- *Native bush & birdlife*
- *Local hosts, local knowledge*
- *Itinerary planning/booking*
- *Warm, friendly, relaxed*
- *Tea/coffee/home-baking*
- *Email - internet available*
- *Stroll to restaurants and shops*
- *5 km to Fox Glacier & Lake Matheson*

The White Fox offers you the convenience of a central location where you can relax and enjoy the genuine hospitality of a real New Zealand family home. Our property combines the peaceful outlook of Westland National Park bush and birdlife with an easy to find location on the Main Road. Your room has a superior comfort bed, quality linen, electric blankets and TV. The modern ensuite includes toiletries and hairdryer. Our house is sunny and warm and heated by a wood burner on the

occasional rainy West Coast day! Wake to the aroma of freshly baked bread and enjoy a generous continental breakfast with a choice of cereals, fresh and tinned fruits, yoghurts, spreads, selections of teas and quality Caffe

L'affare coffee. We share our warm and sunny home with 2 young daughters Meghan (4), Isla (2) and Jess the Border Collie dog.
"An excellent homestay, lovely family, lovely food, good advice on what to do and where to go" - David and Janet Martin, Yorks, UK.

MAHITAHI LODGE

SH 6, P O Box 130, Bruce Bay, South Westland
Ph (03) 751 0095, Fax (03) 751 0195
email: *stay@mahitahilodge.co.nz*
www.mahitahilodge.co.nz

Features & Attractions

- *Genuine West Coast hospitality*
- *Within walking distance of beach*
- *Dinner available*
- *Short drive to glaciers*
- *Veranda from each bedroom*
- *Activities available*

	Double	$245-295
$	Single	$195-245
	Child	

Boutique Accommodation

Bedrooms	Qty
Double	3
Twin	2
Single	
Bed Size	**Qty**
Super King	2
Queen	1
Double	
Single	2
Bathrooms	**Qty**
Ensuite	3
Private	
Guest Share	

Situated only 30 min. south of Fox Glacier and 50 min. north of Haast, and surrounded by the magnificent South Westland landscape, this Boutique Eco-Lodge, featuring various West Coast native timbers, provides an intimate atmosphere, where guests are treated to the utmost hospitality. All guest rooms have ensuite bathrooms complete with heated floors and mirrors, bathrobes, hairdryers and toiletries. There is also a fully self-contained suite available as a family unit. Enjoy our selection of local cuisine, freshly picked vegetables from our garden, fine NZ wines and John's complimentary interpretation tour of the area. It's all here: fishing, hunting, bush walking, the beach and wonderful photographic opportunities – and it's peaceful as well.

DIRECTIONS:
Bruce Bay is approx. 35 min. south of Fox Glacier and 50 min. north of Haast. **Mahitahi Lodge** is situated directly opposite the historic Bruce Bay Hall.

OKURU BEACH

Okuru, Haast, South Westland
Ph (03) 750 0719, Fax (03) 750 0722
email: *okurubeach@xtra.co.nz*
www.okurubeach.co.nz

Features & Attractions

- *Walking distance to beach*
- *Fiordland Crested Penguins*
- *Enjoyable forest walks*
- *Good trout fishing*
- *Craft shop for guests*
- *Friendly and relaxed*

	Double	$95
$	Single	$60
	Child	$25

Self-contained: $95-110 per night
Extra person: $15-25

Homestay Bed & Breakfast

Bedrooms	Qty
Double	4
Twin	3
Single	
Bed Size	**Qty**
Twin	6
Queen	
Double	4
Single	4
Bathrooms	**Qty**
Ensuite	1
Private	2
Guest Share	1

Okuru Beach gives you the opportunity to stay in a unique part of our country where time moves slowly. Enjoy the coastal beaches with interesting driftwood and shells. On a walk in the rainforest a variety of native birds can be viewed. In the season, Fiordland Crested Penguins can be seen within walking distance along a rocky beach, near Jackson's Bay, a 30-minute drive away. We and our friendly labrador dogs enjoy sharing our comfortable home and local knowledge of the area. With prior notice we can serve dinner at $25 per person, BYO, vegetarian is available. Our interests are handcrafts, coin collecting, fishing and tramping. We enjoy the chance to meet new people from New Zealand and overseas. Complimentary tea or coffee on arrival.

COLLYER HOUSE

Jackson Bay Road, PO Box 63, Haast
Ph (03) 750 0022, Fax (03) 750 0023
email: *neroli@collyerhouse.co.nz*
www.collyerhouse.co.nz

Tariff : N.Z. Dollars	
Double	$250-280
Single	$200
Child	

Bedrooms	Qty
Double	3
Twin	1
Single	

Bed Size	Qty
Super King	1
King	
Queen	1
Double	1
Single	2

Bathrooms	Qty
Ensuite	4
Private	
Guest Share	

 Bed & Breakfast Luxury Accommodation

Features & Attractions

- *Genuine hospitality*
- *Peace & quiet*
- *Stunning sea views*
- *Dinner by arrangement*
- *Scenic flights*
- *Jet boating*
- *World heritage area*
- *Antiques & quality fittings*

Collyer House has been purpose built on this isolated coastline, to offer comfort along with peace and quiet to travellers. It has been tastefully furnished, using antiques and quality fittings, and the spacious living areas are dominated by a large open fire made from local stone, a perfect place to relax. The well appointed bedrooms all have French doors leading to the verandah and the ensuites all have baths, bathrobes, heated towel rails, hair dryers and toiletries.

Every room in the house has a magnificent view of the river estuary and the Tasman Sea. I am the fourth generation of a pioneering family and enjoy sharing my knowledge and the history of this special place. After 28 years of travel and working in the city I have returned here to carry on a family tradition of great hospitality.

AWATEA COUNTRY BED & BREAKFAST

29 Skevingtons Road, RD 1, Kaikoura
Ph (03) 319 7075, Fax (03) 319 7075
Mobile 021-318 759
email: *info@awatea.co.nz*
www.awatea.co.nz

Features & Attractions

- *Amazing mountain & sea views*
- *Minutes to town, Whale Watch etc*
- *Spacious guest lounge*
- *Close to good restaurants*
- *Tranquil, quiet, private*
- *Walking distance to beach*

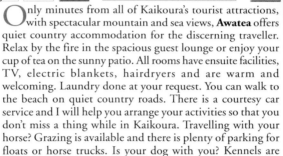

$	Double	$160
	Single	$100
	Child	neg

Bed & Breakfast

Bedrooms	Qty
Double	3
Twin	1
Single	
Bed Size	Qty
King	
Queen	3
Double	
King/Single	2
Bathrooms	Qty
Ensuite	4
Private	
Guest Share	

Only minutes from all of Kaikoura's tourist attractions, with spectacular mountain and sea views, **Awatea** offers quiet country accommodation for the discerning traveller. Relax by the fire in the spacious guest lounge or enjoy your cup of tea on the sunny patio. All rooms have ensuite facilities, TV, electric blankets, hairdryers and are warm and welcoming. Laundry done at your request. You can walk to the beach on quiet country roads. There is a courtesy car service and I will help you arrange your activities so that you don't miss a thing while in Kaikoura. Travelling with your horse? Grazing is available and there is plenty of parking for floats or horse trucks. Is your dog with you? Kennels are available. **Awatea** is a pet friendly place to stay.

CARRICKFIN LODGE B & B LODGE

Mill Road, Kaikoura
Ph (03) 319 5165, Fax (03) 319 5162
Mobile 025- 315 076
email: *rogerboyd@xtra.co.nz*
www.carrickfinlodge.co.nz

Features & Attractions

- *Stunning view of Kaikoura Mts.*
- *Whale watch*
- *Dolphin swimming*
- *Bird-watching trip*
- *Horse trekking*
- *Peninsula walks*

$	Double	$120-130
	Single	$120
	Child	

Bed & Big Irish Breakfast
Self-Contained Cottage

Bedrooms	Qty
Double	5
Twin	
Single	1
Bed Size	Qty
King	
Queen	5
Double	
Single	1
Bathrooms	Qty
Ensuite	6
Private	
Guest Share	

Welcome to Kaikoura. My name is Roger and I am the 4th generation 'Boyd' to live and farm **Carrickfin** which has been home of the Boyds since 1867. My great grandfather bought and settled on this land in 1867 for 100 gold sovereigns. The **Lodge** is built on 100 acres adjoining Kaikoura township. It was built well back from the road

DIRECTIONS: Mill Rd is 3km north of the township on No1 Highway. Easy to find and hard to leave! **Carrickfin Cottage** is located 90m from the **Lodge**.

amidst 2 acres of lawn, shrubs and trees, making it private and peaceful. Most rooms have stunning views of Kaikoura Mountains which are home to a unique variety of wildlife. Two large lounges with open fire, guest bar (BYO) and 24 hour coffee/tea making facilities make it most welcoming. The main feature of the **Lodge** is the '**Big Irish Breakfast**', which is legendary. We are 3km from the Whale Watch, Dolphin Encounter and some of the best restaurants. To view the **Lodge** and **Carrickfin Cottage** (great for families) go to the website and you will love it!

ARDARA LODGE

233 Schoolhouse Road, Kaikoura
Ph (03) 319 5736, Fax (03) 319 5732
email: *ardara@xtra.co.nz*
www.ardaralodge.com

Tariff : N.Z. Dollars	
Double	$135-150
Single	$120-140
Cottage	$165-265

Bedrooms	Qty
Double	6
Twin	2
Single	2
Bed Size	**Qty**
Super King	
King	
Queen	7
Double	
Single	4
Bathrooms	**Qty**
Ensuite	6
Private	
Guest Share	

 **Bed & Breakfast
Self-contained Accommodation**

Features & Attractions

- *Spectacular mountain view*
- *Whalewatch/dolphins 5min*
- *Quiet & tranquil*
- *Hot-tub / Spa*

- *Walk to 'Donegal House',
  Irish restaurant and bar*
- *Guest lounge with Sky TV*
- *Off-street parking*

DIRECTIONS:
Driving North, 4kms from Kaikoura on
SH 1, turn left into Schoolhouse Rd and
continue 1.5kms until our sign.

You will enjoy a relaxed and peaceful stay in a beautiful rural setting near the magnificent Kaikoura Mountains. Relax on our deck, view the Mountain panorama and enjoy Winnie's colourful garden. Enjoy the outdoor hot tub (spa), read in the guest lounge. Cottage: Upstairs bedroom, queen bed/two single beds. Downstairs, queen bed, bathroom with shower, lounge and kitchen. Private deck with Mountain view. House: Five ensuite rooms, queen beds, two triple rooms, one two bedroom unit. All units have television, fridge, settee, coffee/tea facilities and private entrance. Come and go as you please. Guest Lounge, laundry facilities, off street parking. Donegal House, an Irish bar and restaurant, is within walking distance. Phil's hobbies are fishing, diving and motor racing. Winnie's include gardening, lace making, embroidery and fishing. We look forward to your company.

AUSTIN HEIGHTS

19 Austin Street, Kaikoura
Ph (03) 319 5836, Fax (03) 319 6836
email: *austinheights@xtra.co.nz*
www.austinheights.co.nz

Tariff : N.Z. Dollars	
Double	$150-250
Single	$150-250
Child 12 and under $25	

Bedrooms	Qty
Double	
Twin	1
Single	

Bed Size	Qty
Super King	1
King	
Queen	1
Double	
Single	2

Bathrooms	Qty
Ensuite	2
Private	1
Guest Share	

 Boutique Bed & Breakfast on the Peninsula

Features & Attractions

- *Panoramic sea & mountain views*
- *Beautiful coastal walks/ bike hire*
- *Courtesy bus/train transfer*
- *Cot & high chair available*
- *Luxury outdoor spa*
- *Balconies & guest entrance*
- *Self-cont. family apartment*
- *Prize winning gardens*

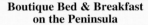

DIRECTIONS: From the south turn right before town centre into Scarborough St. 2 km Austin St is 2nd on left. From north by-pass town centre & turn left into Scarborough St.

Lynne, John and Oscar our friendly Ragdoll cat welcome you to **Austin Heights.** Situated on a prime elevated site on the Kaikoura peninsula with stunning views of the sea and Kaikoura ranges capped with snow most of the year. You will be central to whalewatch, dolphin encounters, the seal colony, local winery, town centre and the beach is only a short walk away. You have a choice of a super-king or a queen bed in the apartments. The rooms are sunny and have great views. Each opens out directly onto a balcony where you can relax. Each apartment has a flat screen TV, DVD, movies, stereo, CD player, local books, refrigerator, microwave, tea/coffee facilities, biscuits, chocolates, kitchenette, heating, hair-dryer , toiletries, bathrobes and heated towel rails. The most comfortable beds, (our guests always say) with quality bedding, electric blankets and woolrests. We serve a generous continental breakfast in the privacy of your room or with hosts in dining area. A cooked breakfast is available on request.

BENDAMERE HOUSE BED & BREAKFAST

37 Adelphi Terrace, Kaikoura 8280
Ph (03) 319 5830, Fax (03) 319 7337
Mobile 027-543 2559

home
NEW ZEALAND

email: *bendamerehouse@xtra.co.nz*
www.bendamere.co.nz

qualmark
★★★★
guest & hosted

Tariff : N.Z. Dollars	
Double	$130-190
Single	$100-140
Child	$20

Bedrooms	Qty
Double	5
Twin	3
Single	

Bed Size	Qty
Super King	
King	
Queen	5
Double	
Single	3

Bathrooms	Qty
Ensuite	5
Private	
Guest Share	

**Luxury Accommodation
Breathtaking Views**

Features & Attractions

- *5 ensuite rooms enjoy sea views*
- *Quiet, private & peaceful*
- *5 min. walk to township*
- *Expansive gardens & lawns*
- *Whalewatch/Dolphin Swimming*
- *Courtesy bus/train transfer*
- *Communal breakfast/dining room*
- *Ample, secure off-street parking*

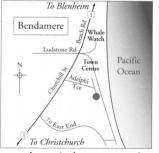

Kerry and Julie Howden welcome you to **Bendamere House** which boasts 5 luxury rooms all with private balconies and breathtaking views of Mountain Ranges and the Pacific Ocean. Watch the dolphins perform for you! Enjoy

our expansive lawns and rose gardens and unwind on our garden furniture. All rooms have first class facilities with large ensuites, quality sleepyhead beds, TV, tea/coffee, home-baked cookies, silent fridge, bathrobes, heatpump and electric blankets. Private, secure off-street parking directly behind your room. Courtesy pick up/drop off to train/buses. Within 5 min. walk to Kaikoura township. A delicious full continental breakfast, served in our communal dining room, includes fresh fruit salad, yoghurt, cereals, toast, spreads and home-baked muffins. Cooked breakfast at extra cost. Guest comments: R. Gaslan, USA *"The most amazing place I've been in in NZ. Best views in the world and the greatest hosts!"* Tania & Claudia, Germany *"Wonderful Hosts! Exquisite Views! Great Accommodation! Beautiful Garden! Thanks!"*

BUSH & SEA BOUTIQUE BED & BREAKFAST

14 Takahanga Terrace, Kaikoura
Ph (03) 319 6789, Fax (03) 319 6709
Mobile 027-4813150
email: *info@bushandsea.co.nz*
www.bushandsea.co.nz

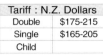

Tariff : N.Z. Dollars	
Double	$175-215
Single	$165-205
Child	

Bedrooms	Qty
Double	2
Twin	
Single	

Bed Size	Qty
Super King	1
King	
Queen	1
Double	
Single	

Bathrooms	Qty
Ensuite	2
Private	
Guest Share	

Panoramic Sea Views
Central Location

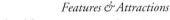

Features & Attractions

- *Delicious breakfast menu*
- *Package deals available*
- *5 min. walk to town, cafés, etc*
- *On-site massage therapy*
- *Stunning sea views over bush reserve*
- *Intimate B&B with just 2 suites*
- *Whale watch & dolphin swimming*
- *Guest decks and outdoor furniture*

Our home is nestled above a bush reserve with fabulous sea views yet is only minutes walk into Kaikoura's township with its busy café scene. We are well travelled Kiwi hosts, who enjoy the outdoors, music, family and friends and our Bed & Breakfast! Hence we have only two suites, so we can offer great service to our guests.

Our suites are purpose built with tiled ensuites and underfloor heating. They are sound insulated and have CD/DVD players (with disks to watch & listen to), silent fridges, tea/coffee, hair dryers, electric blankets, private access and decks with outdoor furniture. The wonderful comfort of our beds is always mentioned by our guests!

J. and D. Mellows, UK: "One of the highlights of our trip was undoubtedly our stay with you, in particular the wonderful crayfish, which Scott prepared for us."

C. Fisher, Paris: "Beautiful room, spectacular views from the deck and great welcome from a lovely couple!"

Bush & Sea Bed & Breakfast is an excellent base for local and regional tourist attractions, so allow for two nights stay. (Check our website for current package deals).

CHURCHILL PARK LODGE
34 Churchill Street, Kaikoura
Ph (03) 319 5526
email: *cplodge@ihug.co.nz*
www.churchillparklodge.co.nz

Features & Attractions
- *Awesome views*
- *Central location*
- *Friendly hospitality*
- *Quality accommodation*
- *Smoke-free rooms*
- *Private guest balcony*

Superb Bed & Breakfast Accommodation

Double	$120
Single	$95
Child	$20

Our Kaikoura Bed & Breakfast is purpose built, affordable, comfortable and highly recommended, offering fantastic views of the Kaikoura mountains and coastline from your room. We are centrally located on State Highway 1 on the hill capturing the views and only 5 minutes walk across Churchill Park to the town centre. The rooms are fully self-contained with ensuite bathrooms and a private guest entrance. We offer a continental breakfast served to your room for you to enjoy at your leisure. Enjoy **Churchill Park Lodge's** 'genuine Kiwi hospitality'. Your hosts are 4th generation New Zealanders, who are friendly, down to earth and also keen fishermen. You are welcome to join us on any trips we have planned during your stay, checking the lobster pots, catching a fish by boat or surfcasting from the beach. We also offer courtesy pick-up from the bus or train.

Bedrooms	Qty
Double	1
Twin	1
Single	
Bed Size	**Qty**
King	
Queen	1
Double	1
Single	1
Bathrooms	**Qty**
Ensuite	2
Private	
Guest Share	

LEMON TREE LODGE
31 Adelphi Terrace, Kaikoura
Ph (03) 319 7464, Fax (03) 319 7467
Mobile 027-648 0670
email: *info@lemontree.co.nz*
www.lemontree.co.nz

Features & Attractions
- *Spectacular views*
- *Whale-watch & dolphins*
- *Relaxed atmosphere*
- *Cafés, restaurants, shops nearby*
- *Luxury hot tub*
- *All rooms with ensuite*

Boutique Bed & Breakfast

Double	$150-290
Single	$144-200
Child	

Overlooking Kaikoura with spectacular ocean and mountain views. We are centrally situated and in easy walking distance of all the major activities, cafés and shops. Our four classic contemporary designed non-smoking rooms have shower ensuite facilities, TV, hair dryers, iron and ironing boards, bathrobes, mini fridges, beverage facilities, heating, and complimentary fruit and chocolate. Two of the rooms have their own private balconies, with elevated sea and mountain views. The other two are set in a relaxing garden environment with their own private deck. To the front of the building is a luxury 5/6-person hot tub and viewing deck where our guests can relax and soak up the views and atmosphere. A freshly made continental breakfast can be included, or you can book in on a room only basis. We cater for singles, couples and small groups. Not suitable for children.

Bedrooms	Qty
Double	4
Twin	
Single	
Bed Size	**Qty**
King	1
Queen	3
Double	
Single	
Bathrooms	**Qty**
Ensuite	4
Private	
Guest Share	

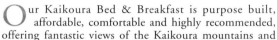

ENDEAVOUR HEIGHTS BED & BREAKFAST

1 Endeavour Place, Kaikoura
Phone (03) 319 5333, Fax (03) 319 5333
Mobile 027-224 0549
email: *dreavers@xtra.co.nz*
www.endeavourheights.co.nz

Tariff : N.Z. Dollars	
Double	$160-220
Single	$150
Child	neg

Bedrooms	Qty
Double	2
Twin	
Single	

Bed Size	Qty
Super King	
King	2
Queen	
Double	
Single	

Bathrooms	Qty
Ensuite	1
Private	1
Guest Share	

**Boutique
Bed & Breakfast**

Features & Attractions

- *Stunning sea & mountain view*
- *Elevated views*
- *Luxury bathrooms with baths*
- *Cafés, restaurants & shops nearby*
- *Private balconies – outdoor living*
- *Overlooking Peninsula Walkway*
- *Private and peaceful*
- *Warm kiwi hosts*

Endeavour Heights truly portrays excellence in hospitality, quality accommodation and scenic views. Nestled within the Kaikoura Peninsula, guests will experience a warm welcome from their kiwi hosts, Janice and Grant. **Endeavour Heights** is centrally located amidst Kaikoura's major tourist attractions, such as the popular Seal Colony, Peninsula Walkway and the Kaikoura township, all of which are accessible by foot. Guests may choose between the **Te Moana** suite, a luxury private apartment, or the **Te Maunga** suite with a large private bathroom and separate level living. Both rooms offer king beds, luxury bed linen, deep baths and comfortable surroundings.

Embrace the magnificence of the breathtaking views of *"Kaikoura, where the mountains meet the sea"* from your room and own private balcony. We welcome you to **Endeavour Heights,** warm, relaxing and peaceful. Easy to find but hard to leave.

PACIFIC ALLURE HEIGHTS

278 Scarborough St, Kaikoura
Ph/Fax (03) 319 5669, Mobile 021-319 735
email: *accommodation@pacificallure.co.nz*
www.pacificallure.co.nz

Tariff : N.Z. Dollars	
Double	$160-240
Single	$120-180
Child	$15

Bedrooms	Qty
Double	1
Twin	1
Single	

Bed Size	Qty
Super King	
King	2
Queen	
Double	
Single	

Bathrooms	Qty
Ensuite	2
Private	
Guest Share	

**Boutique Accommodation
with Stunning Views**

Features & Attractions

- *Spectacular ocean & mountain views*
- *15 min. walk from renowned Peninsula walkway*
- *Close to town*
- *Contemporary design and furnishings*
- *All rooms have private courtyard and gardens*
- *All rooms are self-contained with bathroom and kitchen*
- *Private entrance to each room*

Stunning inside and out! Relax in comfort in modern, self-contained apartments which open onto private courtyards with sweeping views of the Pacific Ocean and the Seaward Kaikoura Ranges.

Pacific Allure Heights is located on the Kaikoura Peninsula, nestled amongst beautiful gardens just a short walk from both the Kaikoura township and the popular Peninsula Walkway.

We offer king rooms with private ensuites, TV, tea/coffee making facilities, microwave, double glazing and off-street parking. Tariff includes continental breakfast.

Bookings can be arranged for popular local activities such as whale watching, dolphin, bird and seal swimming.

Your hosts, Judy and Alan, care about your comfort and are committed to making your stay a memorable one.

OLD CONVENT BED & BREAKFAST

Mt Fyffe Road, Kaikoura
Ph (03) 319 6603, Fax (03) 319 6690
Free Ph: 0800 365 603
email: *o.convent@xtra.co.nz*
www.theoldconvent.co.nz

Tariff : N.Z. Dollars	
Double	$120-195
Single	$100
Child	Neg.

Bedrooms	Qty
Double	15
Twin	7
Single	15
Bed Size	**Qty**
Super King	4
King	
Queen	5
Double	5
Single	11
Bathrooms	**Qty**
Ensuite	15
Private	
Guest Share	

Bed & Breakfast
"Where the Whales Are"

Features & Attractions

- *Glorious garden setting*
- *Peaceful, tranquil*
- *Divine food*
- *4 min. to town/whales*
- *Cooked breakfast*
- *Indoor/outdoor dining*
- *Great dawn chorus*
- *Family friendly*

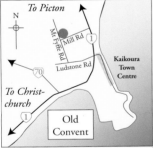

DIRECTIONS: Turn off SH1 at Mill Rd
or take Ludstone Rd, then Mt Fyffe Rd.

To Picton
To Christchurch
Mt Fyffe Rd
Mill Rd
Ludstone Rd
Kaikoura Town Centre
Old Convent

The **Old Convent** is reminiscent of a warm, lively country inn, where there is top-class food, including Kaikoura crayfish, venison and lamb and the famous chocolate cake, good conversation and a friendly atmosphere. The Chapel, now the lounge, the sunny deck and the travellers' bar are lovely places to sit and read or chat.

The owners, with backgrounds in journalism, human rights, aid work and heritage building restoration, have a wealth of knowledge of New Zealand. Their families settled in the Kaikoura and Otago areas in the 1850s.

"Before Gordon handed us the keys we knew we wanted to stay another night." – Guest 2006.

369

MIRA MONTE

324 Woodbank Road, Hanmer Springs
Ph (03) 315 7604, Fax (03) 315 7604
Mobile 021-129 9339
e-mail: *relax@miramonte.co.nz*
www.miramonte.co.nz

Features & Attractions

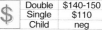

- *Village centre 5min drive*
- *Swimming pool*
- *Quiet and peaceful*
- *Large garden with mountain views*
- *Grand piano, selection CD's*
- *Golf course nearby*

**Delightful Countrystay
Bed & Breakfast**

Double	$140-150
Single	$110
Child	neg

Bedrooms	Qty
Double	2
Twin	
Single	
Bed Size	**Qty**
King	2
Queen	
Double	
Single	1
Bathrooms	**Qty**
Ensuite	2
Private	
Guest Share	

Tastefully peaceful – the ideal place to relax and enjoy a unique part of New Zealand. Near Hanmer Springs, a popular sub-alpine tourist resort, we offer delightful, warm, affordable accommodation. Lovely country garden setting. Relax in our swimming pool and enjoy the mountain outlook. We have it all! Our rooms are attractively decorated with your comfort in mind. Withdraw to your own sittingroom or join us for a coffee, wine or chat. After 20 years in the hospitality trade we know how to pamper you.

We have travelled widely and have many interests. Music, tramping and golf are some of our hobbies. We speak Dutch and German. Mindy, our Jack Russell, is part of our family. We'd love you to stay with us!

BELL BIRD HAVEN

20 Lulu's Lane, Mt Lyford, RD Waiau
Ph (03) 315 6411, Fax (03) 315 6442
Mobile 021-931 990
email: *info@mt-lyford.com*
www.mt-lyford.com

Tariff : N.Z. Dollars	
Double	$225
Single	$190
Child	

Bedrooms	Qty
Double	2
Twin	
Single	

Bed Size	Qty
Super King	
King	
Queen	2
Double	
Single	

Bathrooms	Qty
Ensuite	2
Private	
Guest Share	

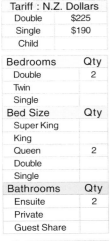

**Bed & Breakfast
Homestay**

Features & Attractions

- *Stunning views/spectacular location*
- *Newly built post & beam log home*
- *Underfloor heating/double glazing*
- *Two guest rooms with ensuite*
- *Back country 4WD tours*
- *Golf, fishing*
- *Skiing/snow boarding*
- *Horse treks, hiking, walking*

You are assured of the warmest of welcomes. Imagine sitting on the deck with a glass of wine surrounded by spectacular vistas in every direction. This is just the place to relax and unwind. Or if it's adventure you crave, there is plenty on offer in the surrounding area.

Our guests tell us the beds are so comfortable and we regularly get comments like "staying here is the highlight of our trip". Our log house has every creature comfort and has the **wow!** factor in the building and its setting. Dinner (home-cooked Kiwi style) is available, advance notice appreciated.

Make sure you include us on your itinerary and find out why our guests rave about the place and the hospitality they experience.

ALBERGO HANMER LODGE & ALPINE VILLAS

88 Rippingale Road, Hanmer Springs,
PO Box 79, North Canterbury
Ph (03) 315 7428, Fax (03) 315 7428
email: *albergo@paradise.net.nz*
www.albergohanmer.com

Tariff : N.Z. Dollars	
Double	$150-250
Single	from $120
S/C Villa	$250-525

Bedrooms	Qty
Double	4
Twin	
Single	

Bed Size	Qty
Amer.King/Twin	1
Super King/Twin	3
Queen	1
Double	
Single	

Bathrooms	Qty
Ensuite + Spa	2
Ensuite + Bidet	1
Ensuite	1

   Albergo Alpine Villas & Eclectic B&B Lodge

Features & Attractions

- *All day sun, views from all windows*
- *3-course breakfast, over 10 choices*
- *Perfect fusion of NZ & Swiss cuisine*
- *Hot pools, cafes & shops 2 min.*
- *S/C villas with cinema & hot tub*
- *Underfloor heat & aircon*
- *Swiss cheese fondue nights*
- *A place where magic happens*

The Wellness & Cuisine Haven in Hanmer Springs

Arrive to dramatic alpine views, blitz your senses in fresh n' fun eclectic interiors with whimsical touches. Stretch out on super-king beds in main lodge rooms, with TV/fridge/teas and spacious ensuites – choose the spa one for that bubble bath delight! Relax in cosy corners or Feng Shui courtyard with soothing waterfall. Your

DIRECTIONS:
At junction before main village, 300m past Caltex Garage, take Argelins Rd (centre branch), take 2nd left Rippingale Rd Albergo Hanmer is 800m down on left (sign at drive).

dedicated hosts have spent 8 years refining this accommodation experience by creating the stylish Alpine Villa, with 'wow' views from the high panorama window, while you shower. Slip on a fluffy bathrobe and wander out to the private jacuzzi and soak up Hanmer's starry night skies. Awesome cinema (great DVD library), American king bed and kitchen/lounge. **Served at a time to suit you, Albergo's** breakfast features: Designer fruit platters or Swiss Birchermuesli, French fluffy omelettes, wafer-thin crepes, 'Albergo Egg Nests', all with crunchy Swiss bread and Italian coffee! *"Albergo is the most warmest, adorable and fun place I have ever visited. Your kindness and spirit shine through in everything"* Marcia & Paul, Colorado, USA

CHARWELL LODGE

Medway Road, PO Box 227, Hanmer Springs
Ph (03) 315 5070, Fax (03) 315 5071
Mobile 021-347 905
email: *charwell.countrystay@xtra.co.nz*
www.charwell.co.nz

Tariff : N.Z. Dollars	
Double	$210-260
Single	$190
Child	n/a

Bedrooms	Qty
Double	3
Twin	
Single	

Bed Size	Qty
Super King	1
King	1
Queen	1
Double	
Single	

Bathrooms	Qty
Ensuite	3
Private	
Guest Share	

Homestay & Countrystay

Features & Attractions

- *A view from every room*
- *Tasty home cooking*
- *Large open fire*
- *8 mins to hot pools*
- *Private & peaceful*
- *Sheep dog demo avail*
- *Well travelled delightful hosts*
- *Magical alpine retreat*

To Hanmer Springs
Waiau River, Hanmer River, Medway Rd, 7A, 7, Ferry Bridge (Bungy), Charwell, N

DIRECTIONS: Cross historic ferry bridge over Waiau River. 1km turn right before Hanmer River bridge, signposted to Charwell Lodge. 100m from campground take steep drive on right. Keep left on drive at fork, we are 1st turn-off on right.

A little off the beaten track, on a sunny, private hillside in the Hanmer Basin, **Charwell Lodge** offers the perfect place to relax and enjoy a little luxury. Situated 1½ hours from Christchurch Garden City and International Airport, 8 minutes from Hanmer Springs Village and Thermal Resort, 1½ hours from Kaikoura Whale Watch activities on the Alpine Pacific Triangle and 40 minutes from the Waipara wine-growing region. Ours is the perfect

place to base yourselves for your visit to the South Island, be it holiday or honeymoon. The views from your ensuite room are awesome. On warm evenings you may sit on your private patio and soak in the scenery. In the winter months you can sit in front of our large open log fire and enjoy a complimentary glass of wine before sampling an evening meal at one of the many excellent restaurants in Hanmer Springs. A visit to our website www.charwell.co.nz will explain all the services we provide to make your stay an enjoyable experience.

CHELTENHAM HOUSE

13 Cheltenham Street, Hanmer Springs
Ph (03) 315 7545, Fax (03) 315 7645
email: *enquiries@cheltenham.co.nz*
www.cheltenham.co.nz

Tariff : N.Z. Dollars	
Double	$190-230
Single	$160-200
Child	neg

Bedrooms	Qty
Double	4
Twin	2-4
Single	
Bed Size	**Qty**
Super King/Twin	2
King	
Queen	5
Double	
Single	1
Bathrooms	**Qty**
Ensuite	5
Private	1
Guest Share	

**Boutique Heritage
Bed & Breakfast**

Features & Attractions

- 200m to pools, restaurants, etc.
- Tranquil setting on park-like grounds
- NZ hosts in Heritage Home
- Evening wine in Billiard Room
- Breakfast in your own suite
- Extensive breakfast menu
- Centrally heated throughout
- Outdoor spa

DIRECTIONS: Take Highway 7a into Hanmer Springs Village, on to Amuri Ave, Cheltenham Street is third to your right. **Cheltenham House** is the 4th property on the right hand side.

Relax in the warmth and tranquillity of our romantic 1930s character home. **Cheltenham House** is situated on extensive grounds, just 200 metres from thermal pools, forest walks, restaurants and shops in this picturesque alpine resort. We renovated this gracious home with our guests' comfort paramount. There are four spacious, sunny suites in the house and two cottages situated in the garden. All are centrally heated and provide comfortable seating and dining areas, quality bedding, fridge, television and tea/coffee making facilities. An open fire enhances the atmosphere in the billiard room, where we share a local wine with our guests in the evening. Awake to a delicious cooked breakfast in the privacy of your own suite. **Cheltenham House** has received widespread acclaim for its comfort and genuine NZ hospitality: *"This B&B is superb"* Lonely Planet. *"Best B&B in town"* Rough Guide to NZ. *"Great style at an unbelievably good price"* Frommer's NZ.

CHESHIRE HOUSE

164C Hanmer Springs Road, Highway 7A
Hanmer Springs
Ph (03) 315 5100
Mobile 021-269 2737
email: *janandchris@xtra.co.nz*

Tariff : N.Z. Dollars	
Double	$140-170
Single	$110-130
Child	neg

Bedrooms	Qty
Double	2
Twin	1
Single	

Bed Size	Qty
Super King	
King	
Queen	2
Double	
Single	2

Bathrooms	Qty
Ensuite	3
Private	
Guest Share	

Bed & Breakfast Luxury Accommodation

Features & Attractions

- *Hot thermal pools*
- *Relaxing forest walks*
- *Tranquil setting*
- *Lovely mountain views*
- *English hospitality*
- *Continental & English breakfast*
- *English breakfast, gluten free on request*
- *Superb restaurants nearby*

DIRECTIONS: Cheshire House is located just after the Welome sign to Hanmer Springs opposite the Highway B&B sign.

Cheshire House is conveniently situated a one minute drive from Hanmer Springs township. Come and experience a memorable stay here with outstanding English hospitality and relax to your heart's content in one of our three beautifully furnished ensuite bedrooms. Our bedrooms have stunning mountain views and you also have your private guest entrance with an outdoor decking area for relaxing 'al fresco' if you wish. For a great start to your day enjoy our continental and freshly cooked English breakfast, which is truly 'mouthwatering' and then, if you wish, choose from various activities which Hanmer has to offer, including horse-trekking, gorgeous forest walks, hiking, 'Thrillseekers' and much more! Jan and Chris take pride in everything they have to offer and will ensure that your stay is perfect in every way and quite unforgettable!

HANMER VIEW BED & BREAKFAST

8 Oregon Heights, Hanmer Springs
Mobile 021-040 6609
Ph (03) 315 7947
email: *hanmerview@xtra.co.nz*
www.hanmerview.co.nz

Tariff : N.Z. Dollars	
Double	$170-185
Single	$140-150
Child	n/a

Bedrooms	Qty
Double	2
Twin	1
Single	
Bed Size	**Qty**
Super King	1
King	
Queen	2
Double	
Single	2
Bathrooms	**Qty**
Ensuite	3
Private	
Guest Share	

'Hanmer View'

 Bed & Breakfast Boutique Accommodation

Features & Attractions

- *Panoramic views of forest' village & mountains beyond*
- *Tasteful, warm, spacious rooms*
- *Warm, friendly hospitality*
- *Delicious homemade breakfasts*
- *Walk to hot pools, restaurants etc*
- *Enjoy Hanmers forest walks*
- *Short drive to 2 ski fields*

Come and relax in the ambience of our purpose-built Bed & Breakfast. Enjoy the privacy of your own studio room, designed with television, ensuite and tastefully decorated with your comfort in mind. Laze on the deck

or in our guest lounge absorbing the fantastic views while watching the native birds that are frequent visitors to our garden.

Your needs are well provided for at **Hanmer View Bed & Breakfast**. Tea, coffee and home baking are always available.

Our generous breakfasts set you up for the day.

The Village Centre and Hot Thermal Pools are a short walk away. Jet boating, rafting, mountain biking, horse trekking, bungy jumping and skiing in winter are for the energetic.

You may just wish to walk in the forest or play a round of golf at our picturesque 18-hole course or simply soak in the hot pools.

- Wireless Internet and DVD player available

TARUNA

230 Taruna Road, Hawarden, North Canterbury
Ph (03) 314 4221, Fax (03) 314 4670
Mobile 027-0222 3214
email: *taruna@amuri.net*

Features & Attractions

- *Excellent local fishing*
- *Mountain bike trails*
- *Golf, hiking, horse treks*
- *Boutique wineries & wine trail*
- *Peace, space, privacy*
- *Gateway to Hurunui Lakes*

$	Double	$120
	Single	$70
	Child	POA

Farmstay Bed & Breakfast

Bedrooms	Qty
Double	1
Twin	1
Single	
Bed Size	**Qty**
Super King	1
Queen	
Double	
Single	2
Bathrooms	**Qty**
Ensuite	1
Private	
Family Share	1

Hawarden is a rural village 1¼ hours drive from Christchurch Airport and ¾ hours drive from Hanmer Springs. **Taruna** is a sheep and beef hill country farm situated 12km west of Hawarden in the foothills of the Southern Alps. The separate guest accommodation adjoins the house with doors opening to a private garden patio. It has an ensuite bathroom with heated towel rail and hair dryer. Fresh home-baking is included with the tea and coffee making facilities. We encourage guests to relax in our sunny home and enjoy panoramic mountain views. Laundry and internet access available. A farmstyle evening meal with garden fresh vegetables and New Zealand wines is available by prior arrangement, $30pp. As well as a background in farming we have an interest in classic cars and home-built aircraft. We have one affectionate terrier called Biggles.

Please phone, fax or email for reservations and easy directions.

BALLINDALLOCH

95 Long Plantation Road, Culverden,
RD 2, North Canterbury
Ph (03) 315 8220
Mobile 027-437 3184
email: *dianedougal@xtra.co.nz*

Features & Attractions

- *Quiet, peaceful surroundings*
- *Dinner by arrangement, $35pp*
- *Excellent trout/salmon fishing*
- *Magnificent mountain views*
- *Complimentary farm tour*
- *30 min to Hanmer Springs*

$	Double	$130
	Single	$80
	Child	$35

Farmstay Bed & Breakfast

Bedrooms	Qty
Double	1
Twin	1
Single	
Bed Size	**Qty**
King	
Queen	1
Double	
Single	2
Bathrooms	**Qty**
Ensuite	
Private	
Guest Share	1

Welcome to **Ballindalloch**, a 2090 acre irrigated farm 3 km south of Culverden. We milk 1500 cows in a floating rotary and a new 70 bale rotary dairy. We also have a 400 head Corriedale sheep stud. Our home is set amongst lawns and gardens with a swimming pool. Panoramic views of the hills and mountains surround us. Our home is centrally heated in winter and has a log fire. Culverden is situated between two excellent fishing rivers. We are 100 km north of Christchurch, ½ hour to Hanmer Springs thermal pools and 1½ hours to Kaikoura Whale Watch. We have travelled extensively overseas and appreciate relaxing in a homely atmosphere and extend this to all our guests. Complimentary farm tour. Please ring or fax for reservations. We have one cat Thomas, and guests are welcome to smoke outdoors.

Culverden

YOUR HOST: **Richard Boyle**

Ph: (03) 315 8224

PAHAU DOWNS

RD 2, Culverden, North Canterbury
Ph (03) 315 8224, Fax (03) 315 8224
Mobile 021-227 0040
email: *pahaudowns@xtra.co.nz*
www.pahaudowns.co.nz

Features & Attractions

- *Self-contained private cottage*
- *Excellent local fishing*
- *Sheep & beef farm, walks & tours*
- *Heated swimming pool*
- *High quality furnishings*
- *Dinner by arrangement*

**High Quality Farmstay
Self-contained Cottage**

	Double	$240
	Single	PA
	Child	PA

This romantic self-contained cottage is superbly furnished and available for your exclusive use as a base for fishing, walking and trips to local attractions such as Hanmer Springs, Mount Lyford Ski Centre and Kaikora. **Pahau Downs** is a tranquil hill farm set amidst stunning scenery between the Hurunui and Waiau rivers, famous for their excellent trout and salmon fishing (guides can be arranged). The cottage is superbly equipped with two large bedrooms, a shower and bathroom and a sunny sitting/dining room with woodburner. Enjoy the mountain views from the heated outdoor swimming pool, walk over the 6,000 acre farm or tour the working sheep and beef station with the owner.

Bedrooms	Qty
Double	1
Twin	1
Single	
Bed Size	**Qty**
King	
Queen	1
Double	
Single	2
Bathrooms	**Qty**
Ensuite	
Private	1
Guest Share	

DIRECTIONS: In Culverden turn past school till you reach a T-junction; turn right and follow the road till you reach a sign 'Pahau Downs Road', follow unsealed road till you reach the farm. (30 min from Hanmer Springs)

Amberley - North Canterbury

YOUR HOSTS: **Veronica and Bob Lucy**

Ph: (03) 314 9356

BREDON DOWNS

Bredon Downs, Amberley, RD 1, North Canterbury
Ph (03) 314 9356, Fax (03) 314 9357
Mobile 027-290 3067
email: *lucy.lucy@xtra.co.nz*
www.bredondownshomestay.co.nz

Features & Attractions

- *Amidst English-style garden*
- *Dinners by arrangement*
- *Delicious & filling breakfast*
- *Donkeys, peacocks, kune kune pigs*
- *Start of Waipara wine trail*
- *Less than 2 hr to whales at Kaikoura*

**Homestay
Bed & Breakfast**

	Double	$120-140
	Single	$75
	Child	$30

Our drive leads off State Highway One, so we are conveniently located en route to and from the Inter-Island ferry, and just forty minutes north of Christchurch - very easy to find.

The house is a very comfortable 100-year-old farmhouse, extensively renovated and restored, and surrounded by an English-style garden with swimming pool which guests are welcome to use. Amberley has a good choice of places to eat, and we are close to the Waipara Wine Trail, the beach and an attractive golf course. The hot thermal pools at Hanmer Springs, and whale-watching at Kaikoura are both an easy drive. We have traveled extensively and lived in Africa before coming from England to live here in New Zealand thirty-five years ago and enjoy welcoming local and overseas visitors into our home. We share our lives with a Newfoundland dog, three geriatric donkeys and Barney the cat.

Bedrooms	Qty
Double	1
Twin	1
Single	1
Bed Size	**Qty**
King	
Queen	1
Double	
Single	3
Bathrooms	**Qty**
Ensuite	1
Private	1
Guest Share	

ROSSBURN

Spark Lane, Rangiora
Ph (03) 313 7427, Fax (03) 313 7421
Mobile 027-430 0420
email: *sparkfarm@xtra.co.nz*
www.northbrookmuseum.co.nz

Features & Attractions

- *Working dairy farm*
- *Children very welcome*
- *Country hospitality*
- *Extensive colonial museum*
- *Rangiora 1 kilometre*
- *Christchurch & airport 25 min.*

$	Double	$110
	Single	$75
	Child	$25

**Farm and Museum
Bed & Breakfast**   F

Bedrooms	Qty
Double	3
Twin	
Single	1
Bed Size	**Qty**
King	
Queen	2
Double	1
Single	3
Bathrooms	**Qty**
Ensuite	1
Private	
Guest Share	1

Our home, **Rossburn**, is a large 102 year-old homestead, surrounded by park-like gardens and mature trees. Richard and Dawn, ex dairy farmer and kindergarten teacher, operate a function centre in conjunction with their extensive colonial museum, possibly NZ's largest private museum. This could be your trip highlight, you'll be amazed at the collections. Entry included in tariff. We enjoy entertaining people from all walks of life and sharing travel experiences. Our interests include our family of six adult children, grandchildren, farm and church life, pets and collecting NZ's social history. Beaches, wineries, and a superb lakeside walk are nearby (conservation winner). Please share a 3-course evening meal with us at $25.00pp (advise when booking). Welcome to **Rossburn**.

HIELAN HOUSE COUNTRYSTAY B&B

74 Bush Road, Oxford
Ph (03) 312 4382, Fax (03) 312 4382
Free Ph 0800 279 382
email: *hielanhouse@ihug.co.nz*
www.hielanhouse.co.nz

Features & Attractions

- *Quiet, private, rural setting*
- *A view from every room*
- *Tasty dinners & breakfasts*
- *Free e-mail, internet, fax*
- *Laundry, spa, sauna*
- *Gateway to everywhere!*

$	Double	$130-150
	Single	$110
	Child	$0-35

**Countrystay
Bed & Breakfast**   C

Bedrooms	Qty
Double	2
Twin	1
Single	
Bed Size	**Qty**
Super King	1
Queen	1
Double	
Single	2
Bathrooms	**Qty**
Ensuite	1
Private	1
Guest Share	

Shirley and John offer quiet quality accommodation just 3 minutes away from Main Street, Oxford. Elevated above the township, our home enjoys beautiful views. Come, relax and enjoy a peaceful night's sleep in comfortable beds and delicious continental and/or cooked breakfasts from our menu. Two well appointed upstairs guest areas include relaxing areas, ensuites, TV's, tea/coffee making facilities, fridges, hair dryers etc. Our grounds are yours to relax in. Dinners available (even at short notice) with home-grown meat/vegetables in season. Special diets catered for. Complimentary laundry, internet, sauna, spa, inground swimming pool(summer), cot available. Ladies' and men's golf clubs available for your use. Check out the farm animals. Welcome to **Hielan House**, we enjoy meeting guests and would love to host you.

CHIRBURY MANOR COUNTRYSTAY B&B

2 Somerset Drive, RD, Oxford
Ph (03) 312 1360, Fax (03) 312 1361
Mobile 027-220 4053
email: *jill@chirburymanor.co.nz*
www.chirburymanor.co.nz

@home
NEW ZEALAND

Tariff : N.Z. Dollars	
Double	$120-140
Single	$100-120
Child	$35

Bedrooms	Qty
Double	2
Twin	1
Single	

Bed Size	Qty
Super King	1
King	
Queen	1
Double	1
King Single	

Bathrooms	Qty
Ensuite	2
Private	1
Guest Share	

**Superb Countrystay
with Magnificent Views**

Features & Attractions

- *Superior rooms, fantastic views*
- *Great Kiwi hospitality*
- *Warm, sunny, modern home*
- *Beautiful, tranquil gardens*
- *Dinner by arrangement*
- *Guest media room / lounge*
- *Honeymoon suite, own balcony*
- *Fishing and bushwalks nearby*

[Map showing Chirbury Manor, Somerset Drive, Ashley Gorge Rd, Queen St, Church St, Weld St, Main St, Oxford Rd, High St, To Ashley Gorge, To Waimakariri Gorge, Arthurs Pass & Tekapo, To Christchurch, Rangiora & Kaikoura]

DIRECTIONS:
Situated on the corner of
Somerset Dr. and Ashley Gorge Road.

Welcome to our country home. Come, relax and refresh yourself while you take in the magnificent views of our wonderful country and farm scenes round our home. Stretch out on our extremely comfortable superking or queen bed and enjoy the best sleep you have ever had. Relax and make yourself a coffee or tea and enjoy the comforts of our large leather lounge chairs, open the private balcony doors and take in the spectacular, wonderful views from the executive **Bellbird Room**.

Wander through our gardens and say 'Hello' to Sophie, our pet deer and sheep – they just love attention. Enjoy our wonderful cooked/continental breakfasts and great 'Kiwi' hospitality.

Be Refreshed. Be Inspired. Be Relaxed.

THE OAKS HISTORIC HOMESTEAD

Corner SH 73 & Clintons Road,
Darfield, RD 1, Canterbury
Ph (03) 318 7232, Fax (03) 318 7236
Mobile 027-241 3999
email: *theoaks@quicksilver.net.nz*
www.theoakshomestead.co.nz

Tariff : N.Z. Dollars	
Double	$150-275
Single	$140
Child	FOC

Bedrooms	Qty
Double	3
Twin	
Single	1

Bed Size	Qty
Super King	
King	
Queen	3
Double	
Single	1

Bathrooms	Qty
Ensuite	1
Private	2
Guest Share	

home
NEW ZEALAND

VISA

MasterCard

eftpos

**Boutique Bed & Breakfast
Historic Homestay**

Features & Attractions

- *Boutique accommodation*
- *Open fires*
- *Home-baked meals*
- *35 minutes to Airport*
- *Private/ensuite bathrooms*
- *Ski fields & golf courses nearby*
- *Large garden/sunny verandahs*
- *Stunning Southern Alps scenery*

The Oaks Historic Homestead is surrounded by the stunning scenery of the Southern Alps on State Highway 73 to the West Coast.

Nestled between the Waimakariri and Rakaia River Gorges, it has all major Canterbury ski fields, golf courses and tourist attractions on its doorstep and is only a leisurely 35 min drive from Christchurch and the airport.

The homestead features four guest rooms (3 queen size and 1 single including a cot) with ensuite and private bathrooms. The separate guest dining room and stunning living room, complete with an inviting open fire, make your stay a memorable one. Relax on our beautiful verandas with a book, entertain some close friends, or simply take deep breaths of fresh, clean air amidst the beautiful tranquil setting.

Our traditional large homestead kitchen is heated by the original Atlas coal range. Enjoy a delicious freshly baked breakfast in the kitchen, in the elegant dining room or in the sun on the veranda. There is ample parking with large grounds for the children.

Dinner reservations can be made at point of booking.

St James Bed & Breakfast

125 Waimakariri Road, Harewood, Christchurch
Ph (03) 359 6259, Fax (03) 359 6299
Mobile 027-432 0996
email: *dj.frankish@xtra.co.nz*

www.stjamesbnb.com

Features & Attractions

- *Warm Kiwi hospitality*
- *Golf, equestrian centre*
- *Antarctic Centre*
- *Restaurants, shopping, wineries*
- *Delicious homemade breakfast*
- *Laundry facilities available*

Boutique Accommodation
Bed & Breakfast

Double	$110-140
Single	$80
Child	$30

Welcome to our small country estate in the city. Located five minutes from Christchurch Airport, ten minutes from city centre.

Begin/end your South Island trip in our warm, modern home with its tranquil garden setting, and meet our horses. Relax in the comfort of the queen-size bed in the '**Magnolia Room**' with its private lounge and ensuite bathroom, or choose the '**Pewter Loft**' with its super king-size, or three single beds. The '**Pewter Loft**' is a wonderful family room which accommodates extra children if necessary and boasts a lounge, entertainment centre and private spa-bathroom. Tea/coffee, TV and internet access are all available. Meet our friendly pups and family cat.

Bedrooms	Qty
Double	1
Twin	1
Single	
Bed Size	**Qty**
Super King	1
Queen	1
Double	
Single	3
Bathrooms	**Qty**
Ensuite	1
Private	1
Guest Share	

Stableford Airport Bed & Breakfast

2 Stableford Green, Burnside, Christchurch
Ph (03) 358 3264
Mobile 027-415 0834
email: *stableford@xtra.co.nz*
www.stableford.co.nz

Features & Attractions

- *Closest B&B to airport*
- *Off-street parking*
- *Good restaurants nearby*
- *Courtesy airport transfers*
- *Friendly, relaxed, comfortable*
- *Adjacent Russley Golf Course*

Airport Accommodation
Bed & Breakfast

Double	$140
Single	$130
Child	

Welcome to **Stableford**, the closest Bed & Breakfast to Christchurch Airport, making it ideal for arriving or departing visitors. City bus-stop at door.

We are situated adjacent to the prestigious Russley Golf Club. Let us know if you require a tee booking at the Russley Golf Course.

Stableford is new, clean and comfortable with a separate guest lounge. Airport transfer available. Full breakfast, continental and cooked.

Good restaurants nearby or dinner by arrangement.

Our interests are travel, sport, music, and antiques.

Bedrooms	Qty
Double	2
Twin	1
Single	
Bed Size	**Qty**
King	
Queen	2
Double	
Single	2
Bathrooms	**Qty**
Ensuite	2
Private	1
Guest Share	

BELMONT ON HAREWOOD

37 Harewood Road, Papanui, Christchurch
Ph (03) 354 6890, Fax (03) 354 6895
Mobile 021-388 670
email: *janalltd@paradise.net.nz*

Tariff : N.Z. Dollars	
Double	$95-140
Single	$70-115
Child	$25

Bedrooms	Qty
Double	3
Twin	
Single	

Bed Size	Qty
Super King	
King	
Queen	3
Double	
Single	

Bathrooms	Qty
Ensuite	1
Private	
Guest Share	2

  Bed & Breakfast

Features & Attractions

- *Edwardian Villa*
- *Central heating*
- *Quality bedding, generous rooms*
- *Disabled facilities*
- *Family cat , 'Possum'*
- *Email,internet and fax facilities*
- *Walk to restaurants, cafés, mall*
- *Excellent bus routes*

Jan and Alan welcome you to **Belmont on Harewood**. Our home has the beauty of yesteryear with ornate plaster cornices, ceiling roses, and beautiful rimu timber work. Enjoy the three metre high ceilings, crystal chandeliers, central heating, rimu furniture and very comfortable queen beds. Television and hairdryer in all rooms. Full disabled facilities are available.

Our mature gardens have a wonderful array of camellias and rhododendrons. A large paved BBQ area and off-street parking are provided for guests.

A five minute stroll takes you to a magnificent choice of multi cultural restaurants, boutique bars and the South Island's largest shopping mall at 'Northlands' complete with cinema and Irish Pub. Across the road from our home, you can wander through St James Park or alternatively, enjoy the glorious award-winning Sanitarium show gardens.

A few doors from our gate, bus-stops link you to the city centre, the airport, and all the major shopping malls in Christchurch.

RUSSLEY 302

302 Russley Road, Avonhead, Christchurch
Ph (03) 358 6510, Fax (03) 358 6470
Mobile 021-662 016
email: *haduck@ducksonrussley.co.nz*
www.ducksonrussley.co.nz

Tariff : N.Z. Dollars	
Double	$120-150
Single	$80-120
Child	

Bedrooms	Qty
Double	2
Twin	1
Single	1

Bed Size	Qty
Super King	
King	1
Queen	1
Double	
Single	3

Bathrooms	Qty
Ensuite	1
Private	2
Guest Share	

**Boutique Accommodation
Bed & Breakfast**

Features & Attractions

- Christchurch Airport 3 min
- Central city 15 min
- Courtesy airport transfers
- Christchurch - the Garden City
- Private spacious bedrooms
- Fax & email facilities
- Golf courses/driving range
- Antarctic exhibition

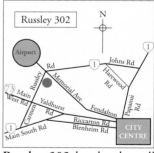

You are assured of a warm welcome and friendly hospitality at **Russley 302** - an ideal location for visitors to Christchurch. With abundant and secure off-street parking **Russley 302** has lovely well appointed guest rooms offering tea/coffee making facilities, fridge, TV and electric blankets. Laundry options are available upon request and you are welcome to use email and fax facilities. We are fortunate to be situated near the urban/rural boundary on a ten acre farmlet with sheep and chickens. Alfresco dining on summer evenings and a log fire in winter enhance a very relaxing atmosphere. Christchurch, the Garden City, has much to offer and is an ideal base for excursions to Canterbury's hinterland. Fishing, gardening, travel, vintage motor cars and convivial company are what we enjoy. Let us assist you with travel or sightseeing plans and further accommodation.

230C GLENVEAGH

230C Clyde Road, Fendalton, Christchurch
Ph (03) 351 4407, Fax (03) 351 4406
email: *boyd45@xtra.co.nz*
www.glenveagh.co.nz

Tariff : N.Z. Dollars	
$120-190	Double
$120-190	Single
$30	Child

Qty	Bedrooms
2	Double
1	Twin
	Single

Qty	Bed Size
1	Super King
	King
1	Queen
	Double
2	Single

Qty	Bathrooms
1	Ensuite
1	Private
	Guest Share

VISA   MasterCard   eftpos

**Bed & Breakfast
Homestay**

H

DIRECTIONS: Drive down Memorial Ave. towards city, turn left into Clyde Rd. We are 1km on right.

Features & Attractions

- *Email, laundry facilities*
- *Courtesy pickup airport, bus, train*
- *Located between airport & city*
- *Restaurants, shops, parks nearby*
- *Off-street parking*
- *On bus route to city*
- *Guest lounge, courtyard*
- *House w/floor heating*

Ian and Alison have sold Ardara Lodge B&B in Kaikoura and now have **Glenveagh B&B**. We have named our B&B, **Glenveagh**, which is a castle in Donegal, Ireland where Ian's ancestors came from. Our B&B is well designed for guests, with three upstairs bedrooms and downstairs a separate lounge and an outside courtyard. **Glenveagh** is just off the main road (Memorial Ave.) from the airport to the city. There are four

restaurants within walking distance. The central city is 5 minutes by car, alternatively there is a bus stop nearby. Off-street parking. Courtesy car available from bus, train and airport. Alison, ex-librarian, enjoys gardening, reading, tennis. Ian taught in secondary schools, designed and built houses, plays golf, tennis and both of us like to travel. Attractions: Cathedral Square, Art Centre, Art Gallery, Hagley Park, Botanical Gardens, Gondola, Antarctic Centre, Air Ballooning, Willowbank Wildlife Reserve. No smoking inside house please. We look forward to your company.

385

ANSELM HOUSE

34 Kahu Road, Fendalton, Christchurch
Ph (03) 343 4260, Fax (03) 343 4261
email: *anselm@paradise.net.nz*
www.anselmhouse.co.nz

Tariff : N.Z. Dollars	
Double	$150-190
Single	$130-150
Child	n/a

Bedrooms	Qty
Double	2
Twin	
Single	
Bed Size	Qty
Super King	
King	
Queen	2
Double	
Single	
Bathrooms	Qty
Ensuite	2
Private	
Guest Share	

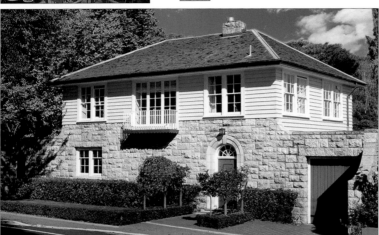

 Boutique Accommodation Bed & Breakfast

Features & Attractions

- *Secure off-street parking*
- *Outdoor tables by Avon River*
- *Free transport to/from airport*
- *Friendly family atmosphere*
- *Banks, mall, restaurants short walk*
- *Free Tranz Alpine transfer*
- *Handy to University and Mona Vale*
- *Walk to Hagley Park, Bot. Gardens*

"Kia ora!"

Anselm House is a landmark building beside the Avon River. Designed by the famous architect Heathcote Helmore, it is one of the few homes in Christchurch built of Hanmer Marble. Bay windows overlook the Avon River. Guests can relax in our peaceful riverside garden, or cross over the brick bridge to view historic Riccarton House and walk through Deans Forest. Remnants can be seen of the original kahikatea trees and native forest which once covered much of the Canterbury Plains. Delicious continental or cooked breakfasts are served in the formal dining room, in the family room or outside on the terrace by the Avon River. New Zealand wine and cheese are shared in the late afternoon. An evening meal is available by arrangement. We have wide experiences and interests including agriculture, horticulture, medicine, rugby, sport, education and travel. We are happy to share information and to help you plan your Canterbury, South Island or New Zealand experience.

AMBIENCE ON AVON

45 Totara Street, Fendalton, Christchurch
Ph (03) 348 4537, Fax (03) 348 4837
Mobile 027-433 3627
e-mail: *lawsonh@xtra.co.nz*
www.ambience-on-avon.co.nz

Tariff : N.Z. Dollars	
Double	$200-340
Single	$170-310
Child	

Bedrooms	Qty
Double	2
Twin	1
Single	

Bed Size	Qty
Super King	
King	
Queen	2
Double	
Single	2

Bathrooms	Qty
Ensuite	3
Private	
Guest Share	

**Luxury Boutique Hosted
Bed & Breakfast**

Features & Attractions

• *Luxury air-conditioned home*
• *Guest lounge, large fire*
• *Quiet, secluded street*
• *Tranquil Avon River garden*
• *Airport, city, rail 8 min.*
• *Courtesy transfers*
• *Special breakfast, home-baking*
• *Wireless LAN, email available*

Peace, tranquility and a warm welcome await you at **Ambience on Avon**, with park-like garden on 26 metres Avon River frontage in the heart of quiet, leafy suburb Fendalton. Helen and Lawson, your gracious hosts, look forward to welcoming you into their new architecturally designed, luxurious home with elegant, comfortable understated furnishings, guest lounge, large open fire and TV. Only 4 minutes walk to Riccarton Mall, banks, bus stop, university and easy walk to Hagley Park, botanical gardens and city centre. Guests may like to enjoy complimentary refreshments and home-baking in our peaceful garden and share a local wine before dining out. Art, comfortable beds, fine linen, electric blankets, air conditioning and all modern conveniences are here for a relaxing friendly-hosted stay. Close to city centre, airport, Tranz Alpine. Off-street parking. High speed broadband internet, laundry available. Lawson and Helen enjoy art, walking, garden, fine food, wine, singing around the vintage pianola. – Travel home and abroad, holiday planning, accommodation and travel bookings available.

387

GREATSTAY BED & BREAKFAST
33 Kilmarnock Street, Riccarton, Christchurch 8011
Ph (03) 343 1377, Fax (03) 343 1357
Mobile 027-622 0788
email: *ruske.greatstay@xtra.co.nz*
www.greatstay.co.nz

@home
NEW ZEALAND

Tariff : N.Z. Dollars	
Double	$230-250
Single	$150-180
Child	$50

Bedrooms	Qty
Double	2
Twin/King	1
Single	

Bed Size	Qty
Super King	
King	
Queen	2
Double	
King/Single	1

Bathrooms	Qty
Ensuite	3
Private	
Guest Share	

 'Top rated' Bed & Breakfast

Features & Attractions

- *Courtesy pick-up*
- *No smoking policy*
- *Quiet, restful environment*
- *Close large shopping complex*
- *Close to city centre*
- *Variety top restaurants*
- *Wireless - broadband*
- *Easy walk to town*

A wonderful home to begin your holiday. Courtesy transport on your arrival. Luxury, spacious, clean, quiet ensuited accommodation. Indulge yourself with a cooked/continental breakfast. Guest lounge for a quiet social time before going out for dinner. Our home is quiet and restful, and an easy picturesque walk to all attractions through Hagley Park and Botanic Gardens.

A car is not a necessity while staying with us, as public transport is at the gate. See our website for more details. We're a 'Top' rated accommodation on tripadvisor.com We would be pleased to assist planning your holiday.

"Come as a guest, leave as a friend".
Comments: *"Warm, vibrant people"* Sally & Ward (USA), *"Perfect host and hostess"* Don & Andrea (Canada), *"Don't change anything – spot on – 5 stars"* Bob & Frieda (UK).

LEINSTER BED & BREAKFAST

34b Leinster Road, Merivale, Christchurch
Ph (03) 355 6176, Fax (03) 355 6176
Mobile 027-433 0771
email: *brian.kay@xtra.co.nz*

Tariff : N.Z. Dollars	
Double	$150-175
Single	$120
Child	neg

Bedrooms	Qty
Double	2
Twin	1
Single	1

Bed Size	Qty
Super King	
King	
Queen	1
Double	1
Single	1

Bathrooms	Qty
Ensuite	1
Private	1
Guest Share	

**Bed & Breakfast
Homestay**

To Main North Rd
Leinster B&B
Papanui Rd
Innes Rd
N
Heaton St
Leinster Rd
Papanui Rd
Glandovey Rd
To Airport
Rossall St
Fendalton Rd
Bealey Ave
Park Tce
To City

- *Centrally located*
- *Easy to find*
- *Quiet comfortable rooms*
- *Excellent local restaurants*
- *Courtesy transfers*
- *Off-street parking*
- *Laundry & email facilities*
- *Gluten-free food on request*

A t **Leinster Bed & Breakfast** we offer a friendly, hospitable stay in our modern, sunny home. We pride ourselves on creating a relaxed, friendly atmosphere. Comfortable quiet rooms with television, tea & coffee, electric

blankets and heaters. Having travelled to many countries and most places in New Zealand, we enjoy meeting like-minded travellers and helping with their ongoing travel plans. This can be done around the breakfast table or in the evening whilst enjoying a good wine (or two). By car we are only five minutes to all the city attractions and ten minutes from the airport. For evening dining convenience there are excellent restaurants and wine bars at Merivale Village which is a leisurely stroll to the end of the street. So why not come and stay and see if you can agree with Jim and Jo from Colorado, who wrote and said: "Kay and Brian are a big #10. I hope we get to visit them again. We stayed longer than intended because of them and because of the beauty of Christchurch".

40 THORNYCROFT STREET BED & BREAKFAST
40 Thornycroft Street, Fendalton, Christchurch
Ph (03) 351 8228, Fax (03) 351 8820
Mobile 027-431 3348
e-mail: *bbthornycroft@clear.net.nz*
www.thornycroft.co.nz

Features & Attractions

- *Airport 5min, city 10min*
- *Delicious cooked breakfast*
- *Extremely quiet*
- *Walk to restaurants, shops*
- *Close to university, park*
- *Fax and email facilities*

**Boutique Accommodation
Bed & Breakfast**

	Double	$140-180
$	Single	$130-170
	Child	

DIRECTIONS: From the airport drive down Memorial Ave. Continue into Fendalton Road. Turn 2ⁿᵈ left into Glandovey Road, then 1ˢᵗ left into Thornycroft Street.

4 0 Thornycroft Street Bed & Breakfast is located in a peaceful cul-de-sac in the suburb of Fendalton, one of Christchurch's most appealing areas. It is a very sunny, modern house with double-glazed windows and underfloor heating (necessary in winter!) and is set in an attractive established garden with an enticing courtyard to relax in at any time of the day. The guest bedrooms are attractively and comfortably appointed. Each has its own private bathroom, TV, tea and coffee making facilities and many extra touches. A private reading/sitting room is provided for those requiring time out, and fine New Zealand wine before dinner is always popular. A delicious gourmet cooked breakfast caters for all tastes and if the weather is perfect, you may choose to enjoy this in the courtyard. Knowledgeable assistance with travel plans is offered.

Bedrooms	Qty
Double	2
Twin	
Single	
Bed Size	**Qty**
Super King/Twin	1
Queen	1
Double	
Single	
Bathrooms	**Qty**
Ensuite	1
Private	1
Guest Share	

ROWAN HOUSE
89ᴬ Aorangi Road, Bryndwr, Christchurch
Ph (03) 351 6092, Fax (03) 351 6092
Mobile 027- 666 2006
email: *wclancey@xtra.co.nz*
www.geocities.com/w_clancey/

Features & Attractions

- *Airport 10min, city 10min.*
- *Courtesy transfers*
- *On city bus route*
- *Warm, friendly hospitality*
- *Quiet, peaceful surroundings*
- *4 local restaurants*

**Quality Homestay
Bed & Breakfast**

	Double	$130-140
$	Single	$90-100
	Child	

DIRECTIONS:
Take SH 1, by-passing Christchurch, (Russley Rd). At Wairakei Rd roundabout (close to airport) drive towards Bryndwr, east along Wairakei Rd. At second group of shops, turn right along Aorangi Rd. 89A is soon on the left.

W e offer warm, friendly hospitality in our sunny, spacious, comfortable home on a very quiet back section.
There are two guest rooms, each with ensuite bathroom. One room opens to a balcony overlooking a swimming pool and the other opens into secluded gardens. Each room has TV, electric heating, and tea/coffee making facilities. A comfortable sunroom is available as a private lounge. Breakfasts are delicious and home-baking is always available. Four excellent restaurants are only ten minutes walk away.
We have both travelled, have a wide range of interests and are happy to help you plan your New Zealand trip.
Courtesy airport pick-up, laundry facilities and off-street parking are available.

Bedrooms	Qty
Double	2
Twin	
Single	
Bed Size	**Qty**
King	
Queen	2
Double	
Single	
Bathrooms	**Qty**
Ensuite	2
Private	
Guest Share	

THE CLOSE

home
NEW ZEALAND

10 Jane Deans Close, Christchurch
Ph (03) 343 5907, Fax (03) 343 5907
Mobile 021-402 427
email: *pandkmurray@xtra.co.nz*
www.theclose.co.nz

Tariff : N.Z. Dollars	
Double	$170
Single	$120
Child	–

Bedrooms	Qty
Double	2
Twin	
Single	

Bed Size	Qty
Super King	
King	1
Queen	1
Double	
Single	

Bathrooms	Qty
Ensuite	1
Private	1
Guest Share	

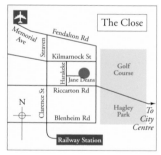

Boutique Homestay Accommodation

Features & Attractions

- *Courtesy pick-up*
- *Close to city centre*
- *Many top restaurants*
- *Close to golf course*
- *Email facility*
- *Safe parking*
- *Great food*
- *Tennis courts nearby*

The **Close**, as its name suggests, is situated in a leafy secluded close, within a 5 minute bus ride into the city centre. Alternatively you could walk through our beautiful Hagley Park via the botanic gardens, past the popular Art Centre into the city, a 25 minute walk. We are also near two historic homesteads, Mona Vale and Deans Bush, and within walking distance of a golf course and tennis courts. Also within 5 min walk are a large shopping complex and a huge variety of restaurants. We offer a courtesy pick-up as we are close to the airport and train station.

Paul and I are 50+ with two grown daughters, one in San Francisco and one in Melbourne. We have travelled extensively and always enjoy meeting new people. Our aim is to make your stay as comfortable as possible, indulge you with good food and hopefully good conversation, should you wish it.

SPRINGFIELD COTTAGES

137 Springfield Road, St. Albans, Christchurch
Ph (03) 377 1368
email: *relax@springfieldcottage.co.nz*
www.springfieldcottage.co.nz

Tariff : N.Z. Dollars	
Double	$190
Single	$190
Child	

Bedrooms	Qty
Double	1
Twin	
Single	
Bed Size	**Qty**
Super King	
King	
Queen	1
Double	
Single	
Bathrooms	**Qty**
Ensuite	
Private	1
Guest Share	

Self-contained
Boutique Accommodation

Features & Attractions

- *Self-contained and private*
- *2 km to city centre*
- *Heritage cottage*
- *All modern comforts*
- *Romantic hideaway*
- *Private garden with BBQ*
- *Quality bed linen*
- *Breakfast hamper available*

If you are looking for Boutique Accommodation in central Christchurch, **Springfield Cottages** offer a uniquely different experience with self-contained heritage cottages designed to be romantic, peaceful, private hideaways within two kilometres of the city centre.

All the cottages have been recently refurbished to a very high standard offering a delightful combination of classic colonial charm and modern comforts. They include a full, modern kitchen, (if you like to do a bit of home-cooking, supermarket and shops are close by), washing machine/dryer (to catch up on the laundry), and a home theatre system to watch the DVD's and listen to CD's. The bedroom has fresh flowers and a queen-size bed with fine linen. The bathroom has a shower and heated towel rail. Outside you can enjoy the tranquility of the cottage garden complete with a courtyard barbeque and garden furniture. You can order a breakfast hamper of provisions for continental and cooked breakfasts. Minimum stay two nights, bookings essential.

RIVERVIEW LODGE

361 Cambridge Terrace, Christchurch Central
Ph (03) 365 2860, Fax (03) 365 2845
email: *riverview.lodge@xtra.co.nz*
www.riverview.net.nz

Tariff : N.Z. Dollars	
Double	$170-210
Single	$100-150
Child	neg

Bedrooms	Qty
Double	3
Twin	
Single	1

Bed Size	Qty
Super King	
King	
Queen	3
Double	
King/Single	1

Bathrooms	Qty
Ensuite	3
Private	1
Guest Share	

Christchurch Central

Features & Attractions

- *10 min. river walk into Central Business District*
- *Romantic river setting*
- *Historic residence*
- *Swimming pool 10 min. walk*
- *Bicycles, kayaks, golf clubs for guests to use*
- *Fine dining 8 min. walk*

Riverview Lodge is a restored Edwardian residence that reflects the grace and style of the period with some fine carved Kauri and Rimu features. It is ideally situated on the banks of the Avon River in the tranquil setting surrounded by an old English garden with mature trees. Guest rooms are elegant combining modern facilities with colonial furnishings. All rooms have ensuite/private facilities, TV and heating. Balconies provide superb river views. Breakfast is a house speciality with a choice of cooked and continental fare. Your hosts, Mark and Andera, have international hospitality backgrounds and pride themselves on the ultimate service with a smile. Mark is a Canterbury Lad with a wealth of knowledge of the Canterbury province and can help guests with their queries of this region. Andrea, from Wigan Lancashire UK, also has extensive NZ travel experience.

The van Dooren family welcome all guests to **Riverview Lodge** and hope they leave with fond memories of this Edwardian Experience.

HOME LEA BED & BREAKFAST

195 Bealey Avenue, Christchurch
Ph (03) 379 9977, Fax (03) 379 4099
email: *homelea@xtra.co.nz*
www.homelea.co.nz

Tariff : N.Z. Dollars	
Double	$145-190
Single	$95-135
Child	neg

Bedrooms	Qty
Double	1
Twin	3
Single	1
Bed Size	**Qty**
Super King	
King	1
Queen	2
Double	
Single	4
Bathrooms	**Qty**
Ensuite	2
Private	2
Guest Share	

H   Bed & Breakfast
Homestay   **BB**

Features & Attractions

- *Central location*
- *Easy to find*
- *Warm & friendly atmosphere*
- *Special diets catered for*
- *Walk to city attractions*
- *Off-street parking*
- *Children welcome*
- *Grand piano for musicians*

Home Lea
To Airport
Bealey Ave
Hagley Park
Colombo St
Manchester St
Town Hall
Cathedral Square
Worcester St
N

DIRECTIONS:
Please phone for easy direct
route from airport.
Advance reservation recommended.

Home Lea offers the traveller a comfortable and enjoyable stay. Built in the early 1900's, **Home Lea** has the charm and character of a large New Zealand home of that era: Rimu panelling, leadlight windows, and a large lounge with a log fire.
Home Lea Bed & Breakfast is centrally located within walking distance of Cathedral Square, Art Gallery, Botanic Gardens and a large variety of restaurants. We are easy to find arriving from any direction into Christchurch, situated on the north side of Bealey Avenue near Colombo Street, Christchurch's main street.
Off street parking, and wireless internet facilities available for guests. Pauline and Gerald are happy to share their knowledge of local attractions and their special interests are travel, sailing and music.

DEVON BED & BREAKFAST HOTEL

69 Armagh Street, Christchurch
Ph (03) 366 0398, Fax (03) 366 0392
email: *stay@thedevon.co.nz*
www.thedevon.co.nz

Tariff : N.Z. Dollars	
Double	$128-180
Single	$89-145
Child	$35

Bedrooms	Qty
Double	6
Twin	3
Single	2

Bed Size	Qty
Super King	
King	
Queen	6
King/Single	1
Single	14

Bathrooms	Qty
Ensuite	6
Private	1
Guest Share	4

      **Bed & Breakfast Guest House**

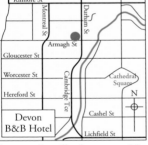

Features & Attractions

- *Central City*
- *Olde Worlde English Manor*
- *Edwardian architecture*
- *Elegant & comfortable*
- *Close to Hagley Park*
- *Hearty breakfasts*
- *Spacious guest lounge*
- *On historic tram route*

Located in the heart of beautiful Christchurch City, The **Devon** offers elegance and comfort in the style of an Olde Worlde English Manor. The historic Christchurch Tramway, re-established in 1994, runs past the front door. A short walk will take you to Hagley Park where you can relax, enjoy the frequent outdoor entertainment or just stroll through the beautiful Botanical Gardens. The **Devon** has retained its grace and dignified appearance for almost a century. The beautiful panelled entrance hall and dining room have a warm ambience that evokes the feel of a bygone era. Nowadays you can luxuriate in a comfortable queen-sized bed. Enjoy a hearty breakfast before venturing forth to take in the many attractions of our delightful garden city with its truly English atmosphere. The Christchurch Cathedral, Town Hall, Arts Centre, Christchurch Art Gallery, live theatre, movie theatres, the Casino, Museum, Hospital and excellent shopping are all within easy walking distance. Wireless Internet access/ + Internet access available.

We look forward to welcoming you!

HAMILTON'S

307 Cambridge Terrace, Christchurch 8001
Ph (03) 366 9993
Mobile 021-150 1228
email: *camb307@xtra.co.nz*

Tariff : N.Z. Dollars	
Double	$135-160
Single	$110-125
Child	

Bedrooms	Qty
Double	1
Twin	
Single	

Bed Size	Qty
Super King	
King	
Queen	1
Double	
Single	1

Bathrooms	Qty
Ensuite	
Private	1
Guest Share	

City
Bed & Breakfast

Features & Attractions

- *Architectural design*
- *Avon River views*
- *5 minutes to cafés etc.*
- *Guest sitting room*
- *A great place to stay*
- *A central city site*
- *Private guest facilities*
- *Underfloor heating*

This much admired architecturally designed home offers guests prime comfort and convenience. The home is situated in a quiet cul-de-sac yet it is just a short walk to the city through our unique poplar-tree lined river walk; a delight in any season and an absolute gem in autumn. The fireman's memorial is nearby. Conveniently located to many amenities and attractions the city offers. A delicious breakfast is served at a time to suit. In summer guests may enjoy breakfast alfresco on the spacious balcony overlooking the Avon River or in the private, sunny courtyard. In winter, you may decide to have your breakfast, tea or coffee beside the log fire. Tea and coffee facilities. Parking available. Garage and laundry facilities available at a small charge. I aim to provide that special Christchurch accommodation experience. Reservations recommended; please phone, email or write.

CENTRAL CITY B&B

31 Peacock Street, Christchurch
Ph (03) 377 8750, Fax (03) 377 8760
Mobile 021-134 4122
email: *trish.barry@actrix.co.nz*

Features & Attractions

- *Friendly hosts*
- *Delicious breakfasts*
- *Spa pool*
- *Very central location – walk to city, gardens, Hagley park*
- *Dinner by arrangement*

$	Double	$130
	Single	$100
	Child	neg

Homestay
Bed & Breakfast

Bedrooms	Qty
Double	2
Twin	
Single	

Bed Size	Qty
King/Twin	1
Queen	1
Double	
Single	

Bathrooms	Qty
Ensuite	
Private	1
Family Share	1

We are well travelled, fun loving and really enjoy meeting people. We provide a relaxing atmosphere and look forward to making your stay a happy and memorable one. We welcome you to our modern home, right in the city. It is tastefully and stylishly decorated and opens to a lovely lawn surrounded by olive trees and native grasses. Walk to all the inner city attractions.

Delicious continental and/or cooked breakfast is available at a time to suit you. Complimentary tea, coffee and home-baking is available at any time. We are keen sportspeople and love especially tennis, golf, and skiing. We are happy to help you organise your sporting activities. Relax in the garden in summer and by the fire in the winter.

DIRECTIONS:
Peacock Street is parallel to
Bealey Ave and runs between the
two one-way streets - Durham
and Montreal Streets.

DESIGNER COTTAGE

53 Hastings Street W., Sydenham, Christchurch
Ph (03) 377 8088, Fax (03) 377 8099
Mobile 021-210 5282, Free Ph: 0800 161 619
e-mail: *stay@designercottage.co.nz*
www.designercottage.co.nz

Features & Attractions

- *Excellent bus routes*
- *Peaceful surroundings*
- *Short walk to city centre*
- *Internet & wireless access available*
- *Private garden and courtyards*
- *10 min. walk to Jade Stadium*

VISA
MasterCard

$	Double	$60-90
	Single	$45-55
	Cottage	$100-250

Designer Retreat &
Self-contained B&B Cottage

Bedrooms	Qty
Double	5
Twin	1
Single	1

Bed Size	Qty
Queen	4
Double	1
King/Single	1
Single	1

Bathrooms	Qty
Ensuite	3
Private	1
Guest Share	2

Designer Cottage was a sailors' retreat in the 70s and is located in peaceful surroundings just off Colombo Street, near the shops and opposite Sydenham Park. The walk to the city centre from the cottage will give you the chance to admire many listed heritage buildings on Colombo Street. We offer a variety of tastefully decorated rooms with either shared facilities, a private room with ensuite and a self-contained cottage. Your friendly host, Chet, has an honours degree in Landscape Architecture and is passionate about traditional buildings and his landscaping ideas. **Designer Cottage** is one of his finest collections of the charms of yesterday and all guests are welcome to view the 'Designer Village' and hear his stories about the cottage.

Designer Cottage — Moorhouse Ave — Colombo St — Casson St — Brougham Rd — Hastings St West

ELIZA'S MANOR ON BEALEY

82 Bealey Avenue, Christchurch
Ph (03) 366 8584, Fax (03) 366 4946
e-mail: *info@elizas.co.nz*
www.elizas.co.nz

Features & Attractions

- *Listed heritage home*
- *Secluded courtyard*
- *Restaurants close*
- *Flat walk to Cathedral Square*
- *Day trip to Akaroa/Hanmer*
- *Smoke-free environment*

Classic Heritage Boutique Accommodation

Double	$185-295
Single	$165-275
Child	

Eliza's Manor on Bealey offers quality Bed & Breakfast accommodation in a beautifully restored 1860's homestead. Each of the eight rooms combines historic ambience with modern ensuite conveniences. A sumptuous breakfast is served as part of the room rate and includes a selection of fruits, cereals, yoghurts, breads as well as a choice of cooked breakfasts. Enjoy personal service as you unwind at a 'home away from home', where service and attention to detail are a priority. A guest computer on the ground floor provides free high-speed access to the internet. Wireless internet access is also available. Free off-street parking is available. **Eliza's Manor on Bealey** is a totally smoke-free environment. Situated in Bealey Avenue on the northern boundary of the Christchurch CBD, 15 minutes by taxi from the airport and the railway station, a 15 minute walk to the downtown city centre, arts activities and botanical gardens.

Bedrooms	Qty
Double	8
Twin	
Single	
Bed Size	**Qty**
Super King	4
Queen	4
Double	
Single	
Bathrooms	**Qty**
Ensuite	8
Private	
Guest Share	

THE CHESTER

Apt. 3, 173 Chester Street East, Christchurch
Ph (03) 366 5777, Fax (03) 365 6314
Mobile 021-365 495
e-mail: *thechester@clear.net.nz*
www.thechester.com

Features & Attractions

- *Spacious & private*
- *Large comfortable suite*
- *1km from City Center*
- *Quiet location*
- *Historic building*
- *Ample parking*

Boutique Accommodation Bed & Breakfast

Double	$95-120
Single	$65-75
Child	

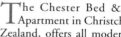 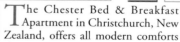

The Chester Bed & Breakfast Apartment in Christchurch, New Zealand, offers all modern comforts and amenities. It is within close walking distance of the city centre, restaurants, banks, town hall, Arts Centre, Casino and Convention Centre. Perfect for holiday or business. Your hosts, Jan and Jennifer van den Berg, will ensure your stay is comfortable and memorable.

Airport transfers, theatre and concert bookings can be arranged on request.

The Chester is situated in the historic Old Wards Brewery Building. This heritage building, which dates back to the 1850's, has now converted into elegant apartments.

Bedrooms	Qty
Double	1
Twin	
Single	1
Bed Size	**Qty**
Super King	1
Queen	
Double	
King/Single	1
Bathrooms	**Qty**
Ensuite	2
Private	
Guest Share	

THE CLASSIC VILLA

17 Worcester Boulevard, The Cultural Precinct, Christchurch
Ph (03) 377 7905, Fax (03) 377 0210
Mobile 027-434 0568
email: *frontdesk@theclassicvilla.co.nz*
www.theclassicvilla.co.nz

Tariff : N.Z. Dollars	
Room Rates from $189 to $449	
–	–

Qty	Bedrooms
8	Double
4	Twin
	Single
Qty	Bed Size
	Super King
	King
11	Queen
1	Double
	Single
Qty	Bathrooms
12	Ensuite
	Private
	Guest Share

 Boutique Hotel

Features & Attractions

- *Private ensuites in all rooms*
- *Mediterranean breakfast incl.*
- *Guest lounge with gas fire*
- *Inner city tram stops opposite*
- *Christchurch airport 20 min.*
- *Opposite Christchurch Art Centre*
- *Sky Sport, CNN and satellite TV*
- *In-room phone, broadband, WiFi*

The Classic Villa has a unique location in Christchurch city centre, on a very quiet and relaxed one-way pedestrian boulevard directly opposite the Christchurch Arts Centre and only minutes from Christchurch city-centre's major attractions. The property is a late 1800s Victorian Townhouse that has been extensively renovated and tastefully refurbished with the new owner's flair.

Only steps away for an early morning stroll through the park are the Christchurch Botanic Gardens. Breakfast can be taken in the luxury dining room or alfresco in the private paved courtyard with open gas fire. A shared lounge and outdoor barbecue area are available for guests to share their experiences over a glass of wine, coffee or tea.

DIRECTIONS:
From airport, take main route to city.
Follow Park Tce into Rolleston Ave.
Turn left into Worcester Boulevard
to the **Classic Villa** on the left.

399

DEVON ON THE PARK

13 B Devon Street, Beckenham, Christchurch
Ph (03) 337 1518, Fax (03) 962 5998
Mobile 021-743 814

home
NEW ZEALAND

email: *claire@devononthepark.co.nz*
www.devononthepark.co.nz

Tariff : N.Z. Dollars	
Double	$150-165
Single	$115
Child	

Bedrooms	Qty
Double	1
Twin	1
Single	

Bed Size	Qty
Super King	
King	
Queen	1
Double	
Single	2

Bathrooms	Qty
Ensuite	
Private	
Guest Share	1

**Quality Bed & Breakfast
on the Park**

Features & Attractions

- *Walk to cafés and shops*
- *Select breakfast menu*
- *Quiet park setting*
- *Off-street parking*
- *Private rooms with a view*
- *Warm hospitality-smoke free*
- *Courtesy transfer-air/rail/bus*
- *City & Botanic Gardens 5min*

DIRECTIONS:
From Cathedral Square travel south
on Colombo St towards the
'Port Hills' for about 2.5km.
Turn right into Devon St. at
Countdown Supermarket.
Please phone for directions if required.

DEVON
ON THE
PARK

Picture a typical English summer in the park. The clear, mellow sound of the Song Thrush as the occasional butterfly flits by. The lads all in white playing cricket on a Saturday afternoon. This is the scene from **Devon on the Park.** A modern 'terrace style' townhouse with two spacious upstairs bedrooms furnished with your home comforts in mind. A choice of continental or sumptuous cooked breakfast awaits you each morning. Frequent bus services take you to or around the city and suburban malls, arts and crafts, botanic gardens, museum, art gallery, Ferrymead Historic Park, many golf courses and wineries. A short drive to the foot of Mt Cavendish and a brief 'Gondola' ride to the top gives a spectacular 360 degree view of Christchurch City, Banks Peninsula, Pegasus Bay and the fascinating little port town of Lyttelton. Ross and Claire have a special interest in flowers and things horticultural and would welcome the opportunity to share with you or to assist you to organise as much or as little of your interests as you desire.

COASTAL CLIFFS

11 Balmoral Lane, Redcliffs, Christchurch 8
Ph (03) 384 2247, Fax (03) 384 2205
Mobile 021-1082977
email: *coastalcliffs@xtra.co.nz*
www.coastalcliffs.co.nz

Tariff : N.Z. Dollars	
Double	$150
Single	$80
Child	

Bedrooms	Qty
Double	2
Twin	1
Single	

Bed Size	Qty
Super King	
King	
Queen	1
Double	
King Single	2

Bathrooms	Qty
Ensuite	2
Private	1
Guest Share	

DIRECTIONS:
Drive towards Sumner and after causeway turn right into McCormacks Bay Road and Balmoral Lane is on your left immediately after 1ˢᵗ house.
Advance booking is recommended

Redcliffs
Christchurch

Features & Attractions

- *Warm, sunny Beach House*
- *Estuary bird sanctuary*
- *Yachting, wind-surfing, kayaks*
- *Unique interior design*
- *Close to beach, cafés, cinema*
- *Walk down woodland garden track to McCormacks Bay & walking tracks*
- *Fantails, kingfishers, bellbirds*

Coastal Cliffs provides a quiet hideaway – coastal living in an easy, relaxed and casual atmosphere. A large solar-heated swimming pool is surrounded by sheltered timber decks. Upstairs, the decks from the house offer uninterrupted views of the city and Southern Alps.

Nelly, our chocolate Labrador and Molly and Stella, our beautiful cats, add extra warmth. Our four white doves seem to show off when they fly, as they look so dramatic!

Self-contained apartment provides Television with DVD, microwave, fridge, tea and coffee facilities. Delicious breakfast can be served in your own room or enjoyed in the sunroom or on the outside decks.

Coastal Cliffs is 15 minutes from the city centre. – Laundry facilities are available.

SEASIDE HAVEN
165F Rockinghorse Road, Southshore,
Christchurch
Ph (03) 388 2177, Fax (03) 388 2177
Mobile 021-136 2770
email: *irwmethven@hotmail.com*

Features & Attractions

* *Sea and mountain views*
* *Immediate access to beach*
* *Wave ski, swimming, surfing*
* *Friendly, hospitable hosts*
* *Breakfast on the deck*
* *Single-party bookings*

Seaside Boutique Bed & Breakfast		

Double	$130-150
Single	
Child	

The sea and sand is our front garden. Guests will enjoy a delicious al fresco breakfast as they take in the breathtaking views over the Pacific Ocean, extending from Kaikoura to Banks Peninsula. Relax on the deck with a coffee as you listen to the surf roll in. Step out of your room onto the soft sand, into the surf, or sit and watch the sun rise over the horizon. Sea kayak, wave ski, boogie board, fish, swim or just stroll along this beautiful coastline, and all of this is only 20 min. from Christchurch city centre. Friendly, hospitable hosts offer you comfortable accommodation with all amenities in their beach home. There is an indoor swimming pool for summer use. Reservations for this Boutique Accommodation are recommended. Plenty of parking available. Meals on request. We look forward to your stay with us.

Bedrooms	Qty
Double	2
Twin	
Single	1
Bed Size	**Qty**
King	
Queen	1
Double	1
Single	1
Bathrooms	**Qty**
Ensuite	
Private	1
Guest Share	

ONUKU BED & BREAKFAST
27 Harry Ell Drive, Cashmere, Christchurch
Ph (03) 332 7296
email: *bob.wilkinson@paradise.net.nz*
www.onukubedandbreakfast.co.nz

Features & Attractions

* *Families welcome*
* *Hill walks*
* *Hiking tours arranged*
* *Golf & bridge arranged*
* *Warm friendly hospitality*
* *Dinner by arrangement*

Luxury Bed & Breakfast		

Double	$150-175
Single	$100
Child	

Onuku Bed & Breakfast is a stunning, newly created upmarket home, specifically designed for the comfort of guests. It has panoramic views from Banks Peninsula over the city and plains to the sea and mountains. The ground floor (with two bedrooms, two bathrooms and living area) is most suitable for a family or group. Bob is involved in the tourism industry and can arrange and accompany guests on golf and hiking tours.

Jenny is a New Zealand bridge representative and is happy to arrange a friendly game of bridge either at home or in one of the local clubs. They have both travelled extensively and promise fellow travellers a warm and friendly welcome along with our labrador, Max and cat, Tao.

Bedrooms	Qty
Double	2
Twin	1
Single	
Bed Size	**Qty**
King	
Queen	2
Double	
Single	2
Bathrooms	**Qty**
Ensuite	2
Private	1
Guest Share	

MT PLEASANT HOMESTAY

106A Mt Pleasant Road, Mt Pleasant, Christchurch
Ph (03) 384 1940, Fax (03) 384 1940
email: *mtpleasantbnb@clear.net.nz*
email: *bnb@mtpleasanthomestay.co.nz*
www.mtpleasanthomestay.co.nz

Tariff : N.Z. Dollars	
Double	$130-140
Single	$100
Child	neg

Bedrooms	Qty
Double	1
Twin	1
Single	

Bed Size	Qty
Super King	
King/Twin	1
Queen	1
Double	
Single	

Bathrooms	Qty
Ensuite	
Private	2
Guest Share	

Bed & Breakfast Homestay
Panoramic Sea Views

Features & Attractions

- *Sea and mountain views*
- *Rest, comfort, peace*
- *Courtesy transfers*
- *Friendly, hospitable host*
- *Stylish, contemporary design*
- *Purpose-built guest accomm*
- *Guest lounge and kitchen*
- *Delicious breakfasts*

Jan welcomes you to **Mt Pleasant Homestay**. Simply park your car at the front door and then enjoy great hospitality plus the warmth and comfort of a new, modern, purpose-built home with breath-taking views of Pegasus Bay as far as the Kaikoura Mountain Range. All rooms open onto the patio and the garden, which is young but blooming! A guest lounge has full cooking facilities. Laundry, facsimile, internet available. Sumner, the most popular beach in Christchurch (5min. drive) and its wonderful cafés will delight you and draw you back. The Christchurch gondola is minutes away as is the Ferrymead Heritage Park. Scenic walks and historical sights abound. If you wish, your host will happily introduce you to information to make the most of your time here and help with plans for further travel. Christchurch City Centre with its many attractions is 10 min. by car. You can be sure of a friendly, comfortable stay, plus sumptuous breakfasts at **Mt Pleasant Homestay**. Private Suite available ($190 incl. breakfast), lounge, kitchen, queen bedroom and private bathroom.

Estuary

To City

Ferry Rd

Main Rd

Mt. Pleasant Rd

Main Rd

To Sumner

Mt. Pleasant Homestay

TIROMOANA

89 Richmond Hill Road, Sumner, Christchurch 8
Ph (03) 326 6209, Fax (03) 326 6208,
Mobile 021-070 3777
email: *relax@tiromoana.co.nz*
www.tiromoana.co.nz

Tariff : N.Z. Dollars	
Double	$130-150
Single	$95-135
Child	$25

Bedrooms	Qty
Double	2
Twin	
Single	1
Bed Size	**Qty**
Super King	
King	1
Queen	1
Double	1
King Singles	2
Bathrooms	**Qty**
Ensuite	1
Private	1
Guest Share	

Boutique Homestay
Bed & Breakfast

Features & Attractions

- *Sea and mountain views*
- *Garden setting*
- *Breakfast on the deck*
- *Close to restaurants & cafés*
- *Bath outside under the stars*
- *Only 15 min. to city*
- *Walk to the beach*
- *Friendly and relaxed*

DIRECTIONS:
Drive towards Sumner.
Turn right at Surf Club building
(on beach) to Nayland Street, 1st
right to Richmond Hill Road.
We are on second sharp corner
with flat access.

Tiromoana is one of the original homes of Sumner, built in 1904 in a spectacular position overlooking the beach. The atmosphere is friendly, relaxed and informal, providing guests' lounge with kitchen facilities.

A fresh and generous breakfast is included in the tariff – weather permitting it can be taken on the deck looking out towards the sea. Wander the garden, have a bath outside under the stars and sleep to the sound of the sea. Make yourself at home.

Tiromoana is within walking distance of the village cafés, movie theatres and beach. Sumner is only 15 minutes from the city, a perfect spot to relax. We're happy to share our local knowledge to help you maximise your stay. Laundry facilities are available.

We look forward to welcoming you.

BROAD OAKS VISTA

4 Swanton Drive, Broad Oaks, Cashmere, Christchurch
Ph (03) 332 5724, Fax (03) 332 5724
Mobile 027-224 6537
email: *brianmor@clear.net.nz*
www.christchurchbandb.co.nz

Tariff : N.Z. Dollars	
Double	$180
Single	$160
Child	$120

Bedrooms	Qty
Double	2
Twin	2
Single	2

Bed Size	Qty
Super King/Twin	2
King	
Queen	
Double	
Single	

Bathrooms	Qty
Ensuite	2
Private	
Guest Share	

**Bed & Breakfast
Fine Accommodation**

DIRECTIONS:
Proceed along Colombo Street to bottom of hill. Turn left at the roundabout into Centaurus Rd. Travel along Centaurus Rd 0.9 km and turn right into Major Aitken Drive. Carry on up the hill and turn right at Kenmure Reserve. Proceed along Kenmure Drive and turn right at Swanton Drive. Turn into first lane on right.

Features & Attractions

- *A warm & happy place to stay*
- *10 minutes to city centre*
- *Full or continental breakfast*
- *Private off-street parking*
- *Internet and laundry facilities*
- *Pre-evening drinks*
- *Stunning sunsets*
- *Outstanding views from every room*

Our unique new home, situated on the Cashmere Hills in Christchurch, offers something special to all our guests. Each guest room, with super king or twin beds, is ideally sited to give individual privacy and modern comforts. Satin-jet showers, heated mirrors, hair dryers and personal robes compliment your ensuite setting. Your luggage can be conveniently placed in your own walk-in wardrobe. Each guest room looks out through glass doors to amazing views over Christchurch and beyond. Relax on your own outdoor patio and seating. Val and Brian enjoyed staying in B & B's so much they decided to design their own. Val is the keen gardener while Brian does the spade work. Brian is also active in Rotary and International Fellowship. We offer pre-evening drinks and take pride in our New Zealand wines. Close by are a number of dining cafés and restaurants. Beaches, estuary, vineyards, golf courses and walking tracks are all close by. Your hosts will assist you in every way with travel planning and transport. We thoroughly recommend at least a 3-night stop over to really appreciate what the Garden City of Christchurch has to offer.

ANDAVIEW BED & BREAKFAST

18 Woodlau Rise, Huntsbury, Christchurch
Ph (03) 332 5522, Fax (03) 332 5592
Mobile 027-433 2769
email: *andaview@xtra.co.nz*
www.andaview.co.nz

@home
NEW ZEALAND

Tariff : N.Z. Dollars	
Double	$170-230
Single	$150-175
Child	n/a

Bedrooms	Qty
Double	2
Twin	1
Single	

Bed Size	Qty
Super King/Twin	1
King	1
Queen	
Double	
Single	

Bathrooms	Qty
Ensuite	1
Private	1
Guest Share	

**Bed & Breakfast
Absolute Ambience**

VISA MasterCard eftpos

Features & Attractions

- *Stunning views, day and night*
- *Purpose-built for guests*
- *Separate guest lounge, balcony*
- *Evening hospitality hour*
- *Super comfortable beds*
- *Luxurious double spa bath*
- *Scrumptuous breakfasts*
- *Complimentary hi-speed internet*

DIRECTIONS: Drive south along Colombo St to bottom of hill. Turn left at roundabout into Centaurus Rd, then 1.3 km to shopping area on left. Turn right into Woodlau Rise.

We invite you to **Andaview** to experience genuine Kiwi hospitality just 10 minutes from the city centre. Our beautifully decorated guest rooms offer TV/DVDs, feather duvéts, super comfy pillows and beds, electric blankets, hair dryers, large, fluffy towels, luxurious bathrobes, fresh flowers and a choice of coffees, teas and homemade treats.

Your breakfast can be served on a tray in your room, on your balcony or at the dining table – it's up to you.

We have a comprehensive knowledge of Christchurch, the South Island and its many attractions, for example, 15 golf courses within 30 minutes drive, five ski fields within 2 hours drive, Akaroa, our French village, 1¼ hours and Hanmer Springs thermal resort 1½ hrs.

In the evening relax in our guest lounge with a New Zealand wine and watch the sun set behind the mountains.

We have ample off-street parking and a guest laundry. Late flight arrivals happily catered for.

Also complimentary, airport or rail pick-up or drop-off.

PACIFIC VIEW PARADISE

17 Harry Ell Drive, Cashmere, Christchurch
Ph (03) 332 6992
Mobile 027-272 7794
email: *stay@pacificviewparadise.co.nz*
www.pacificviewparadise.co.nz

Tariff : N.Z. Dollars	
Double	$150-250
Single	
Child	

Bedrooms	Qty
Double	3
Twin	
Single	
Bed Size	**Qty**
Super King	
King	
Queen	2
Double	1
Single	
Bathrooms	**Qty**
Ensuite	2
Private	1
Guest Share	

**Luxury-style
Bed & Breakfast**

Features & Attractions

- *Warm, friendly hospitality*
- *12 minutes to city centre*
- *Dinner by arrangement*
- *Peaceful surroundings*
- *Hunting, fishing, sightseeing arranged*
- *Hill walks from the B&B garden*
- *Stunning views from every suite*
- *Local wine tours and tastings*

Dramatic vistas, yet so close to the city...

Pacific View Paradise B&B offers luxury-style B&B accommodation in one of the most breathtaking locations in the South Pacific, yet only 12 min. drive from Christchurch city centre. The million-dollar views are simply stunning, taking in the Pacific Ocean, the snow-capped mountains and the beautiful 'garden city'. By night the lights of Christchurch sparkle and twinkle below. Situated alongside this idyllic retreat, with tranquil gardens and private courtyards, is a wonderful scenic walking track with immediate access to the historic Port Hills. Guests will stay in their own private suites, all with beautiful views, complimentary flowers, fruits, chocolates and NZ wines. Breakfast is served in your suite or on the courtyard overlooking the Pacific Ocean. You will be offered fresh juices, homemade cereals, fresh fruit and a cooked breakfast to follow. Linda caters for all diets and allergies. She will be more than happy to help with any inquiries and recommendations. New Zealanders, Linda and Paul, look forward to your visit and the opportunity to introduce you to their beautiful city. Linda has spent many years living and working overseas but believes **Pacific View Paradise B&B** is 'the jewel in the crown' as far as locations go.

CEDAR PARK GARDENS

"Cedar Park", 101ᴮ Lowes Rd, Rolleston, Christchurch
Ph (03) 347 7605, Mobile 027-436 5156
email: *anne@cedarparkgardens.co.nz*

www.cedarparkgardens.co.nz

Features & Attractions

- *Secluded 1.5 acre garden*
- *Warm, friendly hosts*
- *Close to airport/scenic train/city*
- *Secure off-road parking*
- *Superb breakfast menu*
- *Dinner by arrangement*

Quality Bed & Breakfast
Relaxing Homestay

Double	$100-160
Single	$90-130
Child	

Bedrooms	Qty
Double/Triple	1
Twin	1
Single	
Bed Size	**Qty**
King	
Queen	1
King/Single	1
Single	2
Bathrooms	**Qty**
Ensuite	1
Private	
Family Share	1

DIRECTIONS: At Rolleston BP Station, turn from SH 1onto Tennyson St, continue 1.5 km through stop sign to roundabout, turn right onto Lowes Rd. We are 300m on left, at **end** of private lane.

Welcome to **Cedar Park Gardens**. Enjoy a relaxing stay in our modern, sunny home, set in beautiful, **prize-winning gardens**, a short drive from Christchurch and airport. We're conveniently located 2km off State Highway 1, and within easy reach of Canterbury ski-fields, Lincoln University, Akaroa, wineries, golf courses, Christchurch attractions, airport, TranzAlpine, yet away from the hustle and bustle of city life. Excellent restaurants only 10 min. walk away. Our main guest room has a private entrance, **no steps**, parking at door, park-like outlook, tea/coffee facilities, TV, ensuite, and many extras. A twin room also available. Breakfast inside, or in our lovely gardens or gazebo. Transport to/from airport and **TranzAlpine Scenic Train** available on request. Our hobbies include gardening, cooking, crafts, sailing, photography, and NZ travel. We can advise or book activities for you. Along with 'Tigger', or cat, we look forward to welcoming you.

HAZELVIEW

1153 Springs Road, Lincoln, Canterbury
Ph (03) 325 3362
email: *enquiry@hazelview.co.nz*
www.hazelview.co.nz

Features & Attractions

- *Secluded orchard setting*
- *City/airport 17 minutes*
- *Superb nearby restaurants*
- *Off-road covered parking*
- *1 km Lincoln University*
- *Courtesy pick-up*

Quality Bed & Breakfast
Orchardstay

Double	$130
Single	$110
Child	Neg.

Bedrooms	Qty
Double	1
Twin	
Single	
Bed Size	**Qty**
King	2
Queen	
Double	
Single	
Bathrooms	**Qty**
Ensuite	1
Private	
Guest Share	

Welcome to **Hazelview**. Experience the quiet of the country just a short drive from the airport and city. Your spacious self-contained and well-appointed apartment assures a great stay. Dine out at the excellent nearby restaurants and wineries or prepare your own evening meal in the apartment kitchen. Take a stroll around the nut orchard (walnuts, hazelnuts, almonds, chestnuts, plus many different fruits and herbs) or simply relax in front of the TV, watch a video or read a book from the guest library. The spacious king-size bedroom, spa bath, and fine linen assure a great night's rest. Enjoy either a continental breakfast or by arrangement have a full cooked breakfast. Complimentary coffee, teas and nibbles.

HUNTINGDON GRANGE

Shands Road, RD 6, Broadfield, Christchurch
Ph (03) 344 5899, Fax (03) 344 5599
Mobile 027-446 6144
email: *stay@huntingdongrange.co.nz*
www.huntingdongrange.co.nz

Features & Attractions

* Beautiful country estate
* Generous, stylish rooms
* Hearty breakfasts
* Swimming, boules, croquet
* Outside bath, tennis
* Wineries, golf, shopping

Bed & Breakfast Countrystay

Double	$120-200
Single	$90
Child	neg

Enjoy the ambience of our small country estate. Superb choices of rooms including 'The Smithy' – a delightful hideaway and 'The Stablecroft' – a fully self-contained, queen bedroom apartment. Full breakfast. Tea, coffee, milk, sugar and cookies also provided. Unwind in the stylish lounge around the open fire or on the covered barbeque terrace. Quality furnishings and tasteful décor enhance your relaxation. Enjoy tennis, pétanque or croquet, swim in our pool (summer) or relax in the expansive gardens. Close to golf courses, wineries, restaurants, shopping, Christchurch City (15 min.), airport (10 min.) and Lincoln University (5 min.). Ski or snowboard at a dozen Canterbury ski areas, or we'll transfer you to the Tranz Alpine train for 'one of the greatest train journeys in the world'. **Huntingdon Grange** also offers **stabling** and full size **all-weather dressage arena** as well as a seminar room for sales meetings or board meetings.

DIRECTIONS:
Driving south from Christchurch City on State Highway 1, at Hornby turn left over the railway line into Shands Road. At 6.5 km look to see **Huntingdon Grange** sign on the right.

Bedrooms	Qty
Double	4
Twin	1
Single	
Bed Size	**Qty**
King	1
Queen	3
Double	
King Single	2
Bathrooms	**Qty**
Ensuite	3
Private	
Guest Share	1

WILLERSLEY COTTAGE

85 Sutherlands Road, Halswell, Christchurch
Ph (03) 322 7225
Mobile 021-102 1775
email: *willersley@inet.net.nz*

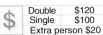

Features & Attractions

* Tranquil rural atmosphere
* Cottage exclusively yours
* Scenic drive to local wineries
* 8km to city centre
* 5 min to shopping centre
* Self catering

Double	$120
Single	$100
Extra person $20	

Self-contained Cottage in Unique Garden Setting

Bedrooms	Qty
Double	1
Twin	1
Single	
Bed Size	**Qty**
King	
Queen	1
Double	
Single	2
Bathrooms	**Qty**
Ensuite	
Private	1
Guest Share	

DIRECTIONS:
When you reach No 85 please drive through the brick entrance and along the tree-lined drive until you reach the house.

Willersley Cottage is situated in a peaceful secluded garden setting in a rural area on the outskirts of Christchurch. It has its own private entrance located well away from the main house on our 6 acre property. The sunny open-plan living area has french doors, which open on to the cottage graden. Washing machine and clothes line. All linen provided. Gardening is our passion and we invite guests to stroll through our slice of paradise. We have created an ornamental organic vegetable garden and adjacent apple orchard. Walk a little further and you will find an ornamental lake with visiting wild life.

The cottage is close to Christchurch City (12 min.), Lincoln University (10 min.) and airport (20 min.).

CEDARVIEW FARM BED & BREAKFAST
33 Barters Road, Templeton, Christchurch RD 5
Ph (03) 349 7491, Fax (03) 349 7755
Mobile 027-433 5335
email: *cedarviewfarm@xtra.co.nz*
www.cedarviewhomestay.com

Tariff : N.Z. Dollars	
Double	$125-170
Single	$100-120
Child	neg

Bedrooms	Qty
Double	2
Twin	1
Single	

Bed Size	Qty
Super King	
King	1
Queen	1
Double	
Single	2

Bathrooms	Qty
Ensuite	1
Private	1
Guest Share	1

Farmstay Bed & Breakfast
"Where town meets country"

Features & Attractions

- *Airport 10min, City Centre 15-20min*
- *Highways, north, south, west, nearby*
- *Relaxed, tranquil atmosphere*
- *Restaurants, wineries, golf*
- *Factory outlet shopping*
- *Modern smoke-free home*
- *Lovely garden setting*
- *Antarctic Centre*

Welcome to New Zealand. We moved here from the UK in 1986 and simply love our lifestyle. Our modern home is situated on a small farm close to central Christchurch. We keep beef cattle, hens and occasionally a lamb

or two. If animals interest you then an extra hand at feeding time is always appreciated. Especially when bottle feeding a baby calf! Take a trip to the ski fields (pick up at gate) then back home for a long hot soak in our spa pool.

Shopping, motor racing, golf, wineries and restaurants (enjoy a meal and see the kiwis at Willowbank Wildlife Reserve). Whatever your passion then we are close to it. Enjoy Carol's home-made bread, jams and preserves. Free-range eggs (providing the girls get busy and lay some of course) and even our own honey.

We look forward to getting to know you over a coffee, glass of wine or beer and helping you make the most of your stay in charming Christchurch.

BERGLI HILL FARM
265 Charteris Bay Rd, Teddington, Lyttelton Harbour, RD1
Ph(03) 329 9118, Fax (03) 329 9118
Mobile 027-482 9410
email: *bergli@ihug.co.nz*
www.vmacgill.net/bergli

Features & Attractions

- *Harbour views*
- *Friendly animals*
- *Interesting hosts*
- *Spa*
- *Self-built log house*
- *German & Japanese spoken*

$	Double	$125-150
	Single	$85-110
	Triple	$195-220

**Farmstay
Bed & Breakfast**

Bedrooms	Qty
Double	4
Twin	1
Single	
Bed Size	**Qty**
SuperKing/twin	1
Queen	1
Double	2
Single	4
Bathrooms	**Qty**
Ensuite	2
Private	
Guest Share	1

E njoy the panoramic views of the inner Lyttelton Harbour from the log house we built ourselves. We are both self-employed (wood worker and shadow puppeteer) and enjoy sharing the occasional sail on Max's yacht.

日本語出来ます

Our 100 acre farm has forests, sheep, cows and alpacas. Rowena also offers wool-fun and workshops. Golf, horse-trekking and walking tracks are nearby. **Bergli** is ideally situated for sightseeing in Christchurch (30 minutes), Akaroa (1 hour 10 minutes) and Banks Peninsula.

TINTAGEL HOUSE
22 Zephyr Terrace, Governors Bay, Christchurch
Ph (03) 329 9580,
Mobile 021-058 2075
e-mail: *tintagelhouse@xtra.co.nz*
www.tintagelhouse.co.nz

Features & Attractions

- *Walking and golf*
- *Quality accommodation*
- *Air conditioned bedrooms*
- *Dolphin watch*
- *Wow factor views*
- *Rest, comfort, peace*

$	Double	$140-180
	Single	$80-90
	Child	neg

**Superb
Bed & Breakfast**

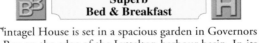

Bedrooms	Qty
Queen	1
Twin	1
Single	
Bed Size	**Qty**
Super King	1
Queen	1
Double	
Single	1
Bathrooms	**Qty**
Ensuite	1
Private	1
Guest Share	

T intagel House is set in a spacious garden in Governors Bay on the edge of the Lyttelton harbour basin. In its restful setting you may have breakfast on the terrace, to the sound of bellbirds with views across the water giving a relaxing start to the day. It is also an excellent starting point from which to explore Banks Peninsula and the city of Christchurch. Our village boasts a good pub and café to return to at the end of the day. Having run a busy B&B in Cornwall for four years a rest was needed. We came back to NZ to live here at the end of 2005 accompanied by our retriever Jolee and two cats Cinnamon and Pepper. With our batteries recharged, we are now looking forward to meeting new guests and making more friends. You will be very welcome to share our home and sense of humour, both of which we hope you will enjoy.
No credit cards accepted, payment by cash or cheque.

DECANTER BAY HOMESTEAD 1851

386 Decanter Bay Rd, Akaroa RD3
Ph (03) 304 8949, Fax (03) 304 8949
email: *rejuvenate@relaxnz.co.nz*
www.relaxnz.co.nz

Tariff : N.Z. Dollars	
Double	$175-220
Single	$140-175
Child	neg

Bedrooms	Qty
Double	2
Twin	
Single	1
Bed Size	**Qty**
Super King	
King	
Queen	1
Double	1
Single	1
Bathrooms	**Qty**
Ensuite	2
Private	
Guest Share	

 Secluded Beachside Retreat

Features & Attractions

- *Picturesque private bay*
- *Gas-heated outdoor bath*
- *Absolute beachfront/views*
- *Restored historic homestead*
- *Friendly dog*
- *Secluded gardens*
- *Swiss-German spoken*
- *Hill and valley walks*

DIRECTIONS:
80mins from Christchurch via Highway
75. At "Hilltop" take the Summit Rd to
Eastern Bays. Turn off at Little Akaloa
Bay Rd. Follow signs to Decanter Bay.

Relax awhile in our comfortable 1851 homestead, restored and stylishly decorated to reflect the past and the present. Our rural property extends to the foreshore of a picturesque private bay. The homestead has dramatic seascape and rural views from 2 private boutique guest suites. Each has a private entrance with sunny verandahs, ensuite and sitting room; one with a log fire. Tea/coffee making facilities and guest fridge. Enjoy fine music, interesting art, musical instruments and handcrafted antiques throughout the home of your well travelled hosts. Relax in our established secluded gardens; snooze to the sound of lapping waves; unwind on the beach, you may spot a **dolphin**. Try kayaking, swimming or tai chi instruction. Wholesome generous continental breakfast. The dinner menu (by arrangement) specialises in seafood, organic vegetarian dishes and special diets, served in a location of your choice... stay one night or several. Relaxing getaway weekends. Afternoon tea served on arrival and late checkout. Then take a scenic drive to explore the stunning Banks Peninsula landscape and the humming French village of Akaroa, just 30 minutes away.

ROSSLYN ESTATE

SH 75, Rapid #5797,
Main Christchurch - Akaroa Road,
Barry's Bay, RD 2, Akaroa

Ph (03) 304 5804, Fax (03) 304 5804
email: *Rosslyn@xtra.co.nz*

Tariff : N.Z. Dollars	
Double	$120-140
Single	$100
Child	neg

Bedrooms	Qty
Double	2
Twin	
Single	

Bed Size	Qty
Super King	
King	
Queen	2
Double	
Single	

Bathrooms	Qty
Ensuite	2
Private	
Guest Share	

Historic Farm Homestead
Bed & Breakfast

DIRECTIONS:
State Highway 75 **Rosslyn Estate** sign
behind picket fence (left travelling to
Akaroa) in Barry's Bay. The house
is 400m from the entrance.

Features & Attractions

- *Working dairy farm*
- *Situated in extinct volcano*
- *Bush-lined streams*
- *Abundant bird life*
- *Share NZ family table*
- *Refreshments on arrival*
- *3 km to winery & restaurants*
- *70 km to Christchurch*

Rosslyn is a large, historic homestead, built in the 1860's of native timbers milled on the property, set on a working dairy farm amid the rolling hills of Banks Peninsula overlooking the serene Akaroa Harbour. Our family home of four generations is situated within informal gardens and offers the tranquillity of farm life, while our entrance is conveniently situated on the main road between Christchurch and 12 km before Akaroa, allowing you to explore this intriguing volcanic peninsula with ease.

While with us, you will have a large ground floor bedroom, firm queen bed, ensuite bathroom, antiques, central heating and screened windows.

-A spa room, pool, and laundry are also available at no charge.
Breakfast ranges from fresh fruit to full cooked. We take pride in offering quality home-grown and prepared produce and preserves, served at the family table in the farm-style kitchen. We invite you to join us for dinner ($35 per person). We look forward to welcoming you with a refreshing tea, coffee or cool drink, served with home baking.

KAWATEA FARMSTAY

'Kawatea', Okains Bay,
Banks Peninsula 8161
Ph (03) 304 8621, Fax (03) 304 8621
email: *kawatea@xtra.co.nz*

Tariff : N.Z. Dollars	
Double	$115-155
Single	$75-95
Child	neg

Bedrooms	Qty
Double	1
Twin	2
Single	

Bed Size	Qty
Super King	
King	
Queen	3
King/Single	1
Single	1

Bathrooms	Qty
Ensuite	1
Private	1
Guest Share	1

**Historic Homestead
Quality Accommodation & Dinner**

Features & Attractions

- *1400 acre sheep & beef farm*
- *Creative dinners, NZ wine*
- *Warm country hospitality*
- *Peaceful romantic retreat*
- *Safe swimming beach*
- *Seals, dolphins, birdlife*
- *Coastal walks, kayaks, golf*
- *Akaroa Village 20 min*

DIRECTIONS:
Take Highway 75 from Christchurch
through Duvauchelle. Turn left at
signpost marked Okain's Bay. Kawatea is
11 km on right.

Escape to the beauty and tranquillity of the country. Enjoy a unique holiday experience in a gracious historic homestead set in beautiful mature gardens, and surrounded by land, farmed by our family for five generations. **Kawatea** is an elegant, carefully renovated home, built in 1900 from native timbers; it features stained glass windows, handcrafted furniture and much olde world charm. Enjoy a relaxing day with a book on the verandah, or participate in seasonal farm activities and feed the pet sheep. Wander our hillside farm enjoying the panoramic views of Banks Peninsula, or walk along the scenic coastline to secluded swimming beaches and a seal colony. Learn about Maori culture and the life of early settlers at the acclaimed Okain's Bay Museum or visit Akaroa with its French influence, cafés and craft shops. Join us for dinner savouring seafood from the bay and creative country fare from our garden, whilst sharing experiences with fellow travellers. We have been hosting since 1988 and pride ourselves on thoughtful, personal attention and friendly hospitality in a relaxed atmosphere.

BOSSU FARMSTAY

Wainui, Akaroa, RD 2, Banks Peninsula
Ph (03) 304 8421, Fax (03) 304 8421
Mobile 027-276 4900
email: *bossu@xtra.co.nz*
www.bossufarmstay.co.nz

Tariff : N.Z. Dollars	
Double	$165
Single	$110
Child	neg

Bedrooms	Qty
Double	1
Twin	1
Single	

Bed Size	Qty
Super King	
King	
Queen	1
Double	
Single	2

Bathrooms	Qty
Ensuite	
Guest Share	1
Family Share	1

DIRECTIONS:
First property on seaward side
after Wainui with a stone entrance.

**Farmstay
Bed & Breakfast**

Features & Attractions

- *Panoramic views of Akaroa Harbour*
- *Viewing dophins & sea birds*
- *French farm winery nearby*
- *Drinks, dinner & good company*
- *Farm tour & walks*
- *Hand feed pet sheep*
- *Golf course nearby*
- *Grass tennis court*

Our farm which has 2 km of coastline overlooks the beautiful harbour of Akaroa with panoramic views to the historic town of Akaroa. Our house is situated near this coastline with a large garden, and a well used grass tennis court surrounded by lovely mature trees. The property runs sheep, cattle, some forestry and two small vineyards. We have been hosting guests since 1977 so obviously, love having people to stay, and taking them, we think, on an interesting farm tour. From our motor boat we offer viewing of nesting sea birds, hector dolphins and penguins. There are lovely walks and interesting bays to visit on Banks Peninsula. Our interests include tennis, golf (Akaroa golf course is nearby) and bridge and many of our guests come with us to our local club. We have both travelled extensively so enjoy hearing about other countries. We have a small well behaved Jack Russell terrier. Most guests join us for dinner where we offer pre-dinner drinks and our locally grown wine for $35 per person. We look forward to your enquiry and hopefully meeting you.

415

AKA-VIEW
5 Langlois Lane, PO Box 100, Akaroa
Ph (03) 304 8008, Fax (03) 304 8008
Mobile 027-459 6042
email: *aka-view@xtra.co.nz*
www.aka-view.co.nz

Tariff : N.Z. Dollars	
Double	$160-185
Single	$125-150
Child	n/a

Bedrooms	Qty
Double	3
Twin	1
Single	
Bed Size	**Qty**
Super King	
King	
Queen	3
Double	
Single	2
Bathrooms	**Qty**
Ensuite	2
Private	1
Guest Share	

Luxury
Bed & Breakfast

Features & Attractions

- *Breathtaking view from all guest rooms*
- *Telephone, fax and email available*
- *10 min walk to shops & restaurants*
- *Scrumptious breakfast*
- *Quality bed linen*
- *Toiletries, hair dryers, robes*
- *Romantic Akaroa*
- *Relaxing atmosphere*

DIRECTIONS: On Rue Lavaud - main village street - turn left at BNZ corner into Rue Balguerie - then up to Langlois Lane, fifth on right.

Do you dream of a place "with a view"?
Elegant bedrooms, just made for two
Comfortable study - still "with a view"
Books, music, good coffee too -
A gourmet breakfast - sheer delight
Perfect - after a restful night
In a large country house
That's just all "brand new"
Fulfill your dreams at - Aka-View.

Aka-View is a purpose built Mediterranean styled Bed & Breakfast. The upper level features two queen suites, one twin, private guest study, separate tea/coffee facilites, all with unprecedented harbour views. In addition, guests may choose to use the formal lounge, with cosy fire, stylish but comfortable furnishings.
A romantic option is our lower level garden studio - private courtyard, sunny, queen with ensuite, lounge, television, full tea/coffee making facilities. Breakfast is a full gourmet surprise, either in the well appointed kitchen or a hamper delivered to your garden studio. For total relaxation enjoy our fine teas, superb coffee, tasty treats, CDs, in the guest study and garden studio.

CHEZ FLEURS

15 Smith Street, Akaroa, Banks Peninsula
Ph (03) 304 8674, Fax (03) 304 8974
Mobile 021- 155 7727
email: *chezfleurs@xtra.co.nz*
www.chezfleurs.co.nz

Tariff : N.Z. Dollars	
Double	$160
Single	$140
Child	n/a

Bedrooms	Qty
Double	2
Twin	1
Single	

Bed Size	Qty
Super King	
King	
Queen	2
Double	
King/Single	2

Bathrooms	Qty
Ensuite	2
Private	
Guest Share	

Homestay
Bed & Breakfast

Features & Attractions

- *Stunning waterfront views*
- *3 min walk to cafés & shops*
- *Beautiful, tranquil garden*
- *Laundry & BBQ available*
- *150 metres to beach*
- *Own private balcony*
- *Delicious breakfast*
- *Off-street parking*

DIRECTIONS:
Stay on Beach Rd, take Smith
St,opposite main beach, 2nd
street on left,past the BNZ.

Bonjour! Welcome to **Chez Fleurs**. We are situated 150 metres from the beach and 3 minutes walk from the cafés, galleries, restaurants and shops. Enjoy our stunning waterfront views and beautiful garden while relaxing on our guest balcony.

We offer superior accommodation with tea/coffee home-baking treats,fridge, TV, hairdryers and fresh flowers in your suite. Your delicious continental breakfast, using fresh home-grown produce, is served alfresco on your private balcony. Park up , relax and soak up the magic scenery, or take the short walk to explore our historic village.

Drive around our picturesque bays and beaches,learning of our colonial,French and Maori heritage on the way. Entertain yourself at our local wineries or cheese factory, or wander through our quaint, narrow streets. Our majestic harbour is a feast of scenic and wildlife encounters . Choose to cruise, fish, sail, kayak or swim with our famous hector dolphins, the smallest and rarest in the world.We also have salmon and paua pearl farms, penguins, fur seals and amazing birdlife. 'A Bientot' – See you soon.

PENLINGTON VIEWS B & B AKAROA

13 Penlington Place, Akaroa, Banks Peninsula
Ph (03) 304 8996, Mobile 027-699 9217
email: *penlingtonviews@xtra.co.nz*
www.penlingtonviews.co.nz

VISA
MasterCard

Features & Attractions

- *Stunning views*
- *Relaxing atmosphere*
- *Guest lounge*
- *Delightful garden*
- *Fresh flowers & chocolates*
- *BBQ & laundry available*

Bed & Breakfast
Self-contained Accommodation

Double	$140-170
Single	$80
Child	

Welcome to **Penlington Views** a great place to unwind and enjoy beautiful Akaroa. Admire the magical views and sunsets over the harbour from the sun-drenched balcony. On a warm summer's night enjoy the garden and BBQ area, or in winter cuddle up with a good book, or watch a movie in the lounge by the log burner. We offer Sky televison, continental or cooked breakfast. Enjoy our selection of teas or have a great coffee from our coffee machine.
Located within walking distance for all the major activites. Excellent restaurants and cafés, jewellery and beauty therapy facilities.
We hope we can make your stay a special one.

Bedrooms	Qty
Double	3
Twin	
Single	1
Bed Size	**Qty**
King	2
Queen	1
Double	1
Single	
Bathrooms	**Qty**
Ensuite	2
Private	1
Family Share	1

THE MAPLES

158 Rue Jolie, Akaroa, Banks Peninsula
Ph (03) 304 8767, Fax (03) 304 8767
email: *maplesakaroa@xtra.co.nz*
www.themaplesakaroa.co.nz

Features & Attractions

- *Historic house*
- *3 min walk to cafés*
- *Delightful garden*
- *Quiet and peaceful*
- *Guest lounge*
- *Relaxed & friendly*

VISA
MasterCard

Homestay
Bed & Breakfast

Double	$130-150
Single	$100
Child	

Built in 1877, **The Maples** is one of Akaroa's charming historic two-storey houses. We have tastefully decorated the interior and have combined modern comforts with yester-year charm. You can choose from our two queen rooms upstairs or our delightful separate garden room with a single and a queen bed. All our rooms are ensuited.
A delicious cooked and continental breakfast, which includes freshly baked croissants and home-made jams, is included in the tariff. We have a separate guest lounge, where complimentary tea and coffee is available. We also have a pretty cottage garden that you can sit and relax in. Centrally situated but quiet, it is only a three minute stroll to the water front and some of Akaroa's many excellent restaurants and cafés. We invite you to share our beautiful historic home and hope we can make your stay relaxed and special.

Bedrooms	Qty
Double	3
Twin	
Single	
Bed Size	**Qty**
King	
Queen	3
Double	
Single	1
Bathrooms	**Qty**
Ensuite	3
Private	
Guest Share	

GARTHOWEN

7 Beach Road, Akaroa 8161
Ph/Fax (03) 304 7419, Mobile 027-437 1096
email: *info@garthowen.co.nz*
www.garthowen.co.nz

Tariff : N.Z. Dollars	
Double	$260-280
Single	$240
Child	$100

Bedrooms	Qty
Double	3
Twin	1
Single	
Bed Size	**Qty**
Super King	4
King	
Queen	
Double	
Single	2
Bathrooms	**Qty**
Ensuite	4
Private	
Guest Share	

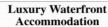
**Luxury Waterfront
Accommodation**

Guests comments:
"Wonderful, caring,
gracious hosts"
Jeremy & Wendy Lezin,
USA

Features & Attractions

• *Scrumptuous cooked breakfasts*
• *2 min. walk to shops & restaurants*
• *Guest computer, wireless Broadband*
• *Complimentary port, chocolates & min. water*

• *Purpose-built home*
• *Panoramic sea views*
• *Warm, friendly hospitality*
• *Finest linen, flowers, robes*

Sometimes you discover a very beautiful place. Akaroa is such a place. When you visit, **Garthowen** will provide you with the perfect setting in which to relax, unwind and feel pampered.
Situated right on the water front of Akaroa's main street, purposely built to the original 1890's Guest House, **Garthowen** opened in December '05 – an absolutely stunning home with harbour views. From your own dining room and lounge you can view the harbour or sit by the fire with a good book. Enjoy a delicious breakfast from our scrumptious menu served in the dining room or on the balcony while smelling the sea air. All rooms have TV, DVD's, air conditioning, underfloor heating, personalized gowns, tea/coffee, chocolates, quality linen, flowers and super-king beds.
Akaroa's fine restaurants – only a 2 minute stroll away.

We will make your stay a memorable one!
Bonnie and Jessie, our Jack Russells, love being spoiled by our guests.

Lake Coleridge

YOUR HOSTS: **Joanne and Kerry Munro**   Free Ph: 0800 525 326

LAKE COLERIDGE LODGE

Hummock Rd, P O Box 18, Lake Coleridge
Ph (03) 318 5002, Fax (03) 318 5004
email: *lakecoleridge@paradise.net.nz*
www.lakecoleridgelodge.co.nz

Tariff : N.Z. Dollars	
Double	$210-240
Single	$120-135
Child	neg

Bedrooms	Qty
Double	5
Twin	4
Single	

Bed Size	Qty
Super King	
King	
Queen	1
Double	4
Single	8

Bathrooms	Qty
Ensuite	2
Private	
Guest Share	3

**Alpine Retreat
Dinner Bed & Breakfast**

Features & Attractions

- *Cafe & bar on site*
- *9 hole chip & putt golf*
- *2-course Lodge dinner included*
- *Gas Heated outdoor baths*
- *Historic power station*
- *Fishing, hunting, skifields*
- *Quiet, peaceful village atmosphere*
- *5 skifields nearby*

DIRECTIONS: From Christchurch, drive out Yaldhurst Rd towards Darfield through West Melton. Turn off to **Hororata**. At Hororata round-about steer left to Lake Coleridge. At the Windwhistle stop sign go on to Lake Coleridge Township, don't turn off to Lake. Through township, around S-bend and up Hummocks Rd. The Lodge is situated on this corner.

Built in the early 1930's to accommodate workers on the nearby historic Power Station, **Lake Coleridge Lodge** has been refurbished to cater for visitors to the area. Nestled in a hidden alpine valley, surrounded by the majesty of New Zealand's Southern Alps, the Lodge welcomes travelers to a peaceful mountain village atmosphere. From the head of the valley, a 20 min. drive deep into the mountains alongside the crystal clear Rakaia River provides breathtaking views of our mountain region, with the main divide appearing directly ahead.

The Lodge also features a rich pictorial and written history, with many photographs of early life adorning the walls and hallways. The little known but extensive village Arboretum is a treat for tree lovers, and enhances the many walks in the area. Our licensed café is open seasonally, and packed lunches are available for those wishing to explore deeper into the valley.

420

RYTON STATION

Harper Road, RD 2, Darfield,
Lake Coleridge, Canterbury
Ph (03) 318 5818, Fax (03) 318 5819
email: *ryton@xtra.co.nz*
www.ryton.co.nz

Tariff : N.Z. Dollars	
Double	$290-350
Single	$155-180
Child	neg

Bedrooms	Qty
Double/Twin	7
Twin	
Single	
Bed Size	Qty
Super King	
King	
Queen	6
Double	1
Single	
Bathrooms	Qty
Ensuite	7
Private	
Guest Share	

**High Country Station Stay
Dinner, Bed & Breakfast**

DIRECTIONS: Follow Ryton signposts from either SH 72 at Windwhistle or SH 73 at Lake Lyndon, approximately ½ hour. On the north side of Lake Coleridge, 10 min once on Harper Road

Features & Attractions

- *High country merino sheep station*
- *37,000 acres (14,000 hectares)*
- *Superb views overlooking Lake Coleridge*
- *Sample high country life*
- *Trout, salmon fishing*
- *Walks and tramps*
- *Private ensuite chalets*
- *Horse trekking*

Adventure and hospitality in the South Island high country. **Ryton Station** is a wonderful place for a personal experience of home hospitality on a 37,000 acre high country merino sheep station. The scenery is magnificent, overlooking Lake Coleridge, the air and water crystal clear.

1½ hours inland from Christchurch, accessible all year round. Abundance of fishing, walks, tramping, station activities and 4X4 trips available. Skiing at Mt Hutt (60 minutes away), Porter Heights and Mt Olympus. Local golf courses nearby.

Relax and enjoy the native flora and fauna in the peacefulness of our environment. Office, Sky television and laundry facilities available at the homestead.

Ensuite chalet accommodation includes dinner with the family. Self-catering lodge accommodation also, next to the homestead.

421

Rakaia - Canterbury

YOUR HOSTS: **Miriam and Ken Cutforth**   Ph: (03) 302 7546

ST ITA'S GUESTHOUSE
11 Barrhill - Methven Road, Rakaia
Ph (03) 302 7546, Fax (03) 302 7564
Mobile 027-488 8673
email: *stitas@xtra.co.nz*
www.stitas.co.nz

Features & Attractions

- *40 minutes to Christchurch*
- *Historic convent school*
- *Salmon fishing*
- *Walk to shops, crafts & cafes*
- *Spacious grounds*
- *River walks*

 Bed & Breakfast Guesthouse

Double	$120
Single	$70
Child	$30

A warm welcome is assured at St Ita's Guesthouse. This former convent school was built in 1912, set in spacious grounds and is full of comfort and charm. Three guest rooms have ensuites and garden views: the fourth, the Chapel, has a private bathroom. Large lounge and games room for use. St Ita's is situated on the western fringe of Rakaia, opposite the domain, just past the Catholic church. Nearby: salmon fishing, golf, tennis, visiting local pubs and craft shops. Within 30 minutes drive, skiing, bushwalks, jetboating and more. Evening meal by prior arrangement or walk down to the local cafes. Full breakfast. Share the open fire with our two moggies.

Bedrooms	Qty
Double	3
Twin	1
Single	
Bed Size	**Qty**
King	
Queen	2
Double	1
Single	4
Bathrooms	**Qty**
Ensuite	3
Private	1
Guest Share	

Staveley - Mid Canterbury

YOUR HOSTS: **Caroline and John Lartice**   Ph (03) 303 0828

KOROBAHN LODGE
Burgess Road, Staveley, Mid Canterbury
Ph (03) 303 0828, Fax (03) 303 0826
e-mail: *carolinel@slingshot.co.nz*
www.korobahnlodge.co.nz

Features & Attractions

- *Mountain views*
- *Peaceful rural setting*
- *In room tea/coffee facilities*
- *On inland scenic highway 72*
- *Warm & friendly hospitality*
- *75 min. drive to Christchurch*

Countrystay Bed & Breakfast

Double	$130-160
Single	$100-120
Child	

DIRECTIONS: On inland Scenic Highway 72 in the village of Staveley. Visible from road and has prominent signs.

Welcome to **Korobahn Lodge**, a unique 'North American Barn'-style home, on the Inland Scenic Highway 72. **Korobahn Lodge** stands in two acres of gardens at the foot of Mount Somers, and is surrounded by farmland. Mount Hutt Ski Field is a short drive away. The property is furnished to a very high standard, and our three ensuite rooms offer accommodation of quality and comfort. We have a large sitting room for guest use, with a huge log fire, TV and pool table. Dinner is available by prior arrangement. This quiet corner of New Zealand offers many local activities, including hot air ballooning, fishing, golf, tramping, Lord of the Rings site, bird watching on glacial lakes and in season skiing, skating and curling.

Bedrooms	Qty
Double	2
Twin	1
Single	
Bed Size	**Qty**
King	
Queen	2
Double	
Single	2
Bathrooms	**Qty**
Ensuite	3
Private	
Guest Share	

TYRONE DEER FARM

Mt. Hutt Station Rd, Alternative Route
Methven to Rakaia Gorge
Ph (03) 302 8096, Fax (03) 302 8099
email: *tyronedeerfarm@xtra.co.nz*

Tariff : N.Z. Dollars	
Double	$150-160
Single	$105
Child	neg

Bedrooms	Qty
Double	3
Twin	1
Single	

Bed Size	Qty
Super King	1
King	
Queen	1
Double	1
Single	1

Bathrooms	Qty
Ensuite	2
Private	1
Guest Share	

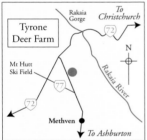

**Countrystay
Bed & Breakfast**

Features & Attractions

- *Centre of South Island*
- *Golf 18-hole courses, club hire*
- *Skiing MtHutt & heli-skiing*
- *Jet boating/hot air ballooning*
- *1 hour Christchurch Airport*
- *Tramping, alpine & bush walks*
- *Fishing, hunting guides available*
- *Mountain views*

Welcome to **Tyrone Deer Farm** centrally situated in the Mt.Hutt, Rakaia Gorge, Methven area, 5km from the Inland Tourist Route (SH72), an ideal stopover on the way to Queenstown and just 1hr from Christchurch International Airport. Enjoy beautiful views of Mt.Hutt and of our deer grazing just metres away. The ensuite bedrooms have electric blankets, wool underlays, duvets, heaters and hair dryers. The lounge has open fire, TV, tea/coffee making facilities and a guest fridge. Come and meet 'Gus' our pet deer, her daughter '$$s' and '10.30' our cat. Stay 2 or 3 nights, do some of our wonderful local walks, ski Mt.Hutt, laze in the garden, swim in the pool, but most of all **relax**! On arrival enjoy a cup of tea/coffee and home made muffins with your hosts. An evening meal, served with New Zealand wine, can be arranged.

Two further self-contained town house available on Main St. Methven (Mt Hutt Village). Tariff for 2 persons $140.00. Extra adult $20.00, child $10.00 (summer rates).

GREEN GABLES DEER FARM

185 Waimarama Road, Methven
Ph (03) 302 8308, Fax (03) 302 8309
email: *greengables@xtra.co.nz*
www.nzfarmstay.com

Tariff : N.Z. Dollars	
$140-180	Double
$110-140	Single
$55	Child

Qty	Bedrooms
2	Double
1	Twin
	Single

Qty	Bed Size
2	Super King
	King
	Queen
	Double
2	King/Single

Qty	Bathrooms
2	Ensuite
1	Private
	Guest Share

  Ensuites – Super King Beds
Sumptuous Breakfasts

Features & Attractions

- *International golf courses*
- *Fishing, jet boating, horse riding*
- *Trips to 'Lord of the Rings' film site*
- *Superb restaurants –4 km*
- *Sumptuous breakfasts*
- *Hot air ballooning*
- *Refreshments on arrival*
- *Skiing at Mt Hutt*

Set in tranquil surroundings at the foot of Mt Hutt, with many summer and winter activities close by, **Green Gables Deer Farm** is within easy reach of Christchurch (1 hr), Kaikoura for Whale Watching and Dolphins (3 hrs), Mt. Cook (3.5 hrs) and Queenstown (approx 5.5 hrs). Our stylish rooms have all the comforts you will require, with your own private entrance opening out

DIRECTIONS:
Situated on SH77, 4 km north-west of Methven. From Inland Scenic Route 72, turn into SH77 and travel 5 km, **Green Gables** is on the right.

onto the garden with a backdrop of graceful deer wandering in the paddocks and the ever changing colours of the mountain views. There is plenty of room to stroll, maybe feed the pet deer and meet our friendly dogs or just relax and unwind.

Dine in by arrangement and enjoy the fresh local produce used in our home-cooked meals and desserts, together with a complimentary pre-dinner drink.

CRICKLEWOOD HOUSE

120 Johnstone Street, Tinwald, RD 4, Ashburton
Ph (03) 3071980, Fax (03) 3071985
Mobile 027-2231939
email: *gdrobins@clear.net.nz*
www.cricklewoodhouse.co.nz

Tariff : N.Z. Dollars	
Double	$140-170
Single	$100
Child	

Bedrooms	Qty
Double	2
Twin	1
Single	

Bed Size	Qty
Super King	
King	1
Queen	1
Double	
Single	2

Bathrooms	Qty
Ensuite	1
Private	
Guest Share	1

Country Stay
Boutique Accommodation

Features & Attractions

- *Golf – two courses handy*
- *One hour south of Christchurch*
- *Three-course dinner available*
- *Email facilities*
- *Quiet, comfortable rooms*
- *Smoke-free inside*
- *Local restaurants nearby*
- *Friendly hosts*

Cricklewood House is a new house, purpose-built with guests' total comfort catered for. Formal dining room with period furniture makes our home very relaxing. We have one king-size bedroom with ensuite, one queen-size bed with shared guest bathroom, and one room with two single beds also with shared bathroom. There is also a separate sitting room for you to relax in.

When you arrive you will be greeted with a hot drink, and a very warm welcome. We will serve dinner with twenty four hour notice, alternatively you are only five to eight minutes to some fine Ashburton restaurants. We are situated just off Highway One, one hour south of Christchurch, well suited to travelling north or to Mount Cook, the Southern Lakes and Queenstown. We can also direct you to various activities in the district and further afield.

Our interests are gardening, sports, embroidery, and cooking. We are retired farmers who have been in the hosting business for over twenty years. We look forward to having your company at our place.

425

RIVERLANDS LODGE

232 Wrens Road, Coldstream, RD 3, Ashburton
Ph (03) 303 7058, Fax (03) 303 7054
Mobile 027-203 6791
e-mail: *TEEJAYRM1@xtra.co.nz*
www.riverlandslodge.com

Tariff : N.Z. Dollars	
$200	Double
$150	Single
	Child

Qty	Bedrooms
2	Double
	Twin
	Single
Qty	Bed Size
2	Super King
	King
	Queen
	Double
2	King/Single
Qty	Bathrooms
1	Ensuite
1	Private
	Guest Share

Bed & Breakfast
Luxury Accommodation

Features & Attractions

- *Peaceful country setting*
- *Office & internet facilities*
- *Outdoor spa*
- *Tarrif includes dinner & breakfast*
- *BBQ & outdoor fire*
- *Under floor heating*
- *Salmon & trout fishing*
- *Affordable luxury*

Located fifteen minutes drive from State Highway One, we're the perfect stop while you are exploring beautiful New Zealand. Come and join us amidst affordable luxury accommodation and experience a working farm with 1000 dairy cows and some Romney sheep.

You can truly relax in a warm and friendly atmosphere with the aroma of homecooked meals. Tariff includes three course evening meal and cooked breakfast. If you have any special dietary needs, we'll do our best to accommodate you.

Try fishing at the Rangitata River, one of the best salmon fishing rivers in the South Island. Snowsports, watersports, hot air ballooning, tramping activities and an historic theme park are all within easy access. At the end of your busy day, enjoy a spa under the canopy of the Southern Cross.

THE GARDENERS COTTAGE

Coniston, 30 Methven Highway, SH 77
Ph (03) 307 8189, Fax (03) 307 8179
Mobile 027-435 4705

e-mail: *coniston@xtra.co.nz*
www.coniston.co.nz

Features & Attractions

- 5.5 acres of garden
- Sheep, highland cattle and crops
- 1hr Christchurch, 3hrs Mt Cook
- Restaurants 3 min.
- Private and peaceful setting
- Breakfast extra charge

$	Double	$110
	Single	$80
	Child	$10

Historic Farm Cottage
Self-contained

DIRECTIONS:
Turn off SH1 onto SH77 to
Methven at McDonalds corner.
Coniston 3.1 km from SH1.

Bedrooms	Qty
Double	1
Twin	2
Single	1
Bed Size	**Qty**
King	
Queen	
Double	1
Single	5
Bathrooms	**Qty**
Ensuite	
Private	1
Guest Share	

The Gardeners Cottage, built in 1870, is situated on the edge of 5.5 acres of established gardens. **The Cottage** features 4 bedrooms including 1 double and 1 twin bedroom downstairs and 1 twin attic bedroom. There is also a small room with a single bed next to the double bedroom.
All beds have electric blankets. The kitchen/dining room has a log fire and is fully equipped. The lounge has an open fire, TV, video, CD player and board/card games for family entertainment. The bathroom features shower and original claw-foot bath. There is a separate laundry.
Outside you will find a barbecue area with gas barbecue and a tree swing and plenty of room for the children to play outdoor games. Portacot, highchair, stroller and bicycles provided. Continental and cooked breakfast provisions available (extra charge). Relax and enjoy the peace and quiet in this rural setting. A warm welcome awaits you.

VICTORIA VILLA

55 Cox Street, Geraldine, 7930
Ph (03) 693 8605, Fax (03) 693 8605
Mobile 027-482 1842
email: *jbasinger@xtra.co.nz*

Features & Attractions

- Ensuites or private bathroom
- Town & bush walks 7 min
- Modern heat & plumbing
- Private entrance & lounge
- Restored 100-year-old villa
- Molded ceilings & original wood

$	Double	$100-125
	Single	$80-100
	Child	neg

Boutique Accommodation
& Attached Studio

Bedrooms	Qty
Double	4
Twin	
Single	
Bed Size	**Qty**
King	
Queen	3
Double	2
Single	2
Bathrooms	**Qty**
Ensuite	3
Private	1
Guest Share	

We welcome you to our historic villa which was built in 1900 and has been completely refurbished. Each guest room has a television, tea and coffee facilities. A detached studio has three beds, ensuite, a light kitchen facility; ideal for family up to five people. We are only seven minutes stroll from Geraldine's main street which has boutique movie theatre, fine restaurants, cafés, sports pub, auto museum, antiques, world class glass blower, stained glass artists and boutique shops. Geraldine has two golf courses, only twenty minutes from Peel Forest, Rangitata River and 75 minutes from Mt Hutt and Dobson ski fields. Your hosts are well travelled and will assist to make your stay enjoyable. Continental or cooked breakfast provided.

To Christchurch
Victoria Villa
Talbot St
Cox St
N
To Fairlie,
Tekapo,
Mt Cook,
Wanaka &
Queenstown
To Timaru

427

THE DOWNS BED & BREAKFAST

5 Ribbonwood Road, The Downs, RD 21, Geraldine
Ph (03) 693 7388, Fax (03) 693 7388
Mobile 021-675 249
email:*info@thedowns.co.nz*
www.thedowns.co.nz

Tariff : N.Z. Dollars	
Double	$200
Single	$200
Child	

Bedrooms	Qty
Double	3
Twin	1
Single	
Bed Size	**Qty**
Super King	
King	
Queen	3
Double	
Single	2
Bathrooms	**Qty**
Ensuite	3
Private	1
Guest Share	

  Superior Bed & Breakfast Homestay Accommodation

Features & Attractions

- *Large garden setting*
- *Complimentary bar*
- *Free guest laundry*
- *Broadband Internet*

- *Tranquil surroundings*
- *Handy shops, restaurants*
- *Art studios*
- *High standard of facilities*

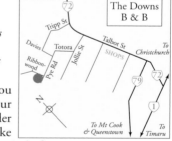

The Downs B&B offers you quality accommodation in our large, modern home. A wander round the beautiful park-like garden is a lovely way to unwind after your journey. Peace, tranquillity and bird song are part of the surroundings here. The guest rooms are spacious. Each has its own TV, comfortable armchairs and ensuites, all furnished to a very high standard. A full Kiwi and continental breakfast is served in the guest lounge or on the balcony overlooking the garden. There is also a complimentary self-service bar and tea and coffee making facilities and home-baked cookies are available at all times. The region of Geraldine has much to offer in the way of arts, crafts, dining experiences, golf, fishing, 4 WD tours and skiing. We are only too pleased to assist you with your further sightseeing plans and accommodation if necessary.

ASHFIELD HOUSE BED & BREAKFAST

71 Cass Street, Temuka, South Canterbury
Ph (03) 615 6157
email: *ashfield@paradise.net.nz*
www.ashfield.co.nz

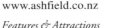

Features & Attractions

- *Spacious gardens*
- *Close to ski fields*
- *Trout & salmon fishing*
- *Warm hospitality*
- *Close to Timaru*
- *Email & internet access*

$		
Double	$110-150
Single	$90-100
Child	

**Victorian Boutique
Bed & Breakfast Homestay**

Bedrooms	Qty
Double	4
Twin	
Single	

Bed Size	Qty
King	
Queen	4
Double	
Single	

Bathrooms	Qty
Ensuite	1
Private	
Guest Share	1

Ashfield House, built in 1878, is set in four acres of gardens and woodland, which we share with our two Newfoundland dogs. You are assured of warm hospitality. We aim to make your stay enjoyable.

Temuka is only twenty minutes from Timaru and 1¾ hours from Christchurch. Close by is the Rangitata River, which is noted for its fly fishing, not to mention the salmon! No visit to Temuka would be complete without a visit to its famous pottery outlet. If you just want to relax, then **Ashfield** has lovely gardens and a stream, which is host to ducks and trout. Currently being assessed by NZ Historic Places Trust as a heritage building.

DIRECTIONS:
200m from SH 1

BLUEBERRY COTTAGE

72A High Street, Timaru
Ph (03) 684 3115, Fax (03) 684 3172
Mobile 027-636 4301
email: *relax@blueberrycottage.co.nz*
www.blueberrycottage.co.nz

Features & Attractions

- *Quiet sea-front setting*
- *Friendly home hospitality*
- *Sea to mountain views*
- *Gateway to Southern Alps*
- *Stroll to beach-walkways*
- *Relaxation at its best*

**Bed & Breakfast
Homestay**

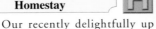

$		
Double	$95
Single	$70
Child	neg

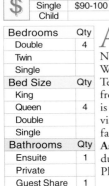

DIRECTIONS: Timaru South on SH 1. Turn into Queen Street. Pass hospital and right into High Street. **Blueberry Cottage** entrance on left.

Our recently delightfully up graded 1950s brick home exudes comfort with spectacular close-up views of the ocean and inland to Mt Cook. We feel it is a delight living here and would like to share this with others. The tastefully furnished rooms have television with access to separate outside patios. Handy to hospital and gardens. It is a comfortable walking distance to shops, cafés, bars, or eating place of your choice. Timaru is centrally situated on the east coast of the South Island, allowing easy access to many scenic spots, i.e. day trips to lakes, skiing in winter, Mount Cook, fishing rivers, bush walks, vineyards and other interesting towns. Shops display our high quality wool products and gifts of interest to overseas' visitors.

Bedrooms	Qty
Double	1
Double/Twin	1
Single	

Bed Size	Qty
Super King	1
S. King Single	2
Double	1
Single	

Bathrooms	Qty
Ensuite	
Private	
Guest Share	1

SEFTON HOMESTAY BED & BREAKFAST

32 Sefton Street, Seaview, Timaru
Ph (03) 688 0017, Fax (03) 688 0042
Mobile 027-473 7366

email: *trish@seftonhomestay.co.nz*
www.seftonhomestay.co.nz

Features & Attractions

* 2 hours from Christchurch
* Restaurants 5 min. easy walk
* Guest sitting room
* Email & internet access
* Quiet & peaceful bedrooms
* Full cooked breakfast

Homestay Bed & Breakfast

	$
Double	$120
Single	$100
Child	½ price

Conveniently located, just a few minutes walk from the Bay Hill restaurants, Caroline Bay and the Stafford Street shops. Once you arrive in Timaru, you can park your car off-street and explore the city on foot.

Relax in our superbly appointed and spacious two storey character brick home with sweeping views from the mountains to the sea. Refurbished with the feel of yesteryear, but with ambience and style you will love. There is a guest sitting room upstairs for you to unwind and enjoy a quiet read, hot drink or glass of complimentary sherry. Start or finish your holiday in New Zealand on a high note. We are just a couple of hours south of Christchurch Airport.

Bedrooms	Qty
Double	2
Twin	
Single	1
Bed Size	**Qty**
Super King/Twin	1
Queen	1
Double	1
Single	
Bathrooms	**Qty**
Ensuite	1
Private	1
Guest Share	

BERRILLO

32 Gladstone Road, RD 4, Timaru
Phone (03)686 1688, Fax (03)686 1678
Mobile 021-295 2451
e-mail: *oberrill@xtra.co.nz*
www.berrillo.co.nz

Tariff : N.Z. Dollars	
$145	Double
$100	Single
$45	Child

Qty	Bedrooms
1	Double
1	Twin
	Single

Qty	Bed Size
	Super King
	King
1	Queen
	Double
2	Single

Qty	Bathrooms
2	Ensuite
	Private
	Guest Share

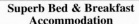

Superb Bed & Breakfast Accommodation

Features & Attractions

- *Stunning views*
- *Peaceful rural setting*
- *10 min. from city centre*
- *On working olive grove*
- *Warm hospitality*
- *Award winning home*
- *Complimentary wine*
- *Dinner by arrangement $40pp*

A touch of Tuscany in Timaru. A warm welcome awaits you and we offer a complimentary glass of wine on the terrace overlooking stunning views of Mt Cook. Our award winnning '*Home of the Year 2000*' is nestled in an olive grove.

We have a purpose-built guest wing with separate antique furnished lounge, Sky TV, tea/coffee making facilities. Sit and chat with us, or just relax and enjoy the peace. We enjoy golf, art and music. Golf courses nearby. With 24 hours notice we will serve a 3-course dinner with New Zealand wine.

We are situated on the west boundary of Timaru and are easy to find. Perfect stop-over from Christchurch, Dunedin or Mt Cook.

KINGSDOWN MANOR

10 Bristol Road, RD1 Kingsdown, Timaru
Phone (03) 684 9612, Fax (03) 684 9613
Mobile 027-2011316
e-mail: *info@kingsdownmanor.co.nz*
www.kingsdownmanor.co.nz

Tariff : N.Z. Dollars	
$180-250	Double
$135	Single
	Child

Qty	Bedrooms
3	Double
	Twin
1	Single
Qty	Bed Size
	Super King
1	King
2	Queen
	Double
1	Single
Qty	Bathrooms
2	Ensuite
1	Private
	Guest Share

 Luxury Accommodation Boutique Bed & Breakfast

Features & Attractions

- *Truly unique experience*
- *2hrs from Christchurch/Dunedin*
- *Extensive courtyard/ outdoor area*
- *Old country chapel onsite*
- *Fully licensed*
- *Private dining-room/guest-lounge*
- *Romantic, peaceful & private*
- *Dinner by arrangement*

DIRECTIONS: South from Timaru: Pass the 100km open road sign. After 6.5 km turn right onto Bristol Rd. Main entrance 100m from corner. Approaching Timaru from the South on SH1: Drive through the village of Pareroa. After 3km, turn left onto Bristol Rd.

Kingsdown Manor offers you exclusive Bed & Breakfast-style accommodation with a difference, a luxurious boutique lodge with its own turret, chapel, reception facilities, extensive gardens, and superb hospitality. Situated just a few kilometres from the Pacific Ocean and with stunning

views of the Southern Alps, but still only a few minutes drive from the city, you can experience the best of both worlds in a relaxed, rural setting. The large and spacious **Egyptian Room** with its theme of romance and tranquility, is overlooking the courtyard and beyond to the majestic Hunter Hills. In the **Captians Cabin**, marvel at the unique architecture and enjoy remnants of our past lives as mariners – full of interesting pieces, all with a maritime flair. Experience complete privacy and relaxation in the **Loft**, an elegant suite with stained-glass windows, an adjoining lounge and private bathroom. We also offer unique facilities for both weddings and other events, such as conferences, corporate or family functions, exhibitions and workshops.

Your hosts, Rochelle and Peter Young, are dedicated to providing you with the highest possible standard of service and look forward to meeting you soon.

RIVENDELL LODGE

15 Stanton Road, Kimbell, RD 17, Fairlie
Ph (03) 685 8833, Fax (03) 685 8825
Mobile 027-4819 189
email: *rivendell.lodge@xtra.co.nz*
www.fairlie.co.nz/rivendell

Tariff : N.Z. Dollars	
Double	$110-140
Single	$70-90
Child	neg

Bedrooms	Qty
Double	4
Twin	2
Single	

Bed Size	Qty
Super King	
King	
Queen	3
Double	1
Single	2

Bathrooms	Qty
Ensuite	2
Private	
Guest Share	2

 Country Homestay

Features & Attractions

- *Peaceful rural retreat*
- *Great home cooking*
- *Skifield 5 km*
- *Spa bath available*
- *Magnificent alpine scenery*
- *Guided walking & tramping*
- *Families welcome*
- *Ensuite rooms also have balconies*

"They stayed long in Rivendell and found it hard to leave. The house was perfect whether you liked sleep, or work, or storytelling, or singing, or just sitting and thinking best, or a pleasant mixture of them all. Everyone grew refreshed and strong in a few days there. Merely to be there was a cure for weariness, fear and sadness." - Tolkien.

To Lake Tekapo

N

Kimbell

Stanton Rd.

Garage ◆ ◆ Pub

(8)

Rivendell Lodge

To Fairlie

DIRECTIONS:
100m up Stanton Road at Kimbell on SH 8, 8km west of Fairlie.

Welcome to my one acre of paradise – a haven of peace and tranquility offering quality country comfort and hospitality.
As a well travelled writer I am passionate about mountains, literature and local history. I enjoy cooking and gardening, and delight in sharing home-grown produce. Take time out from the Christchurch-Queenstown route and enjoy our magnificent countryside. Fishing, walking, golf, watersports or skiing nearby.
Relax in the garden, complete with stream and cat, or come exploring with me. Complimentary refreshments on arrival. Laundry and email available. Dinner $40.00pp by arrangement.

BRAELEA ALPINEVIEW FARMSTAY
279 Highway 79, RD 17, Fairlie, South Canterbury
Ph (03) 685 8366, Fax (03) 685 8943
Mobile 021-070 9375
email: *braelea@xtra.co.nz*
www.alpineviewfarmstay.com

Features & Attractions

- *Complimentary farm tour at dusk*
- *Your own private guest wing*
- *Feed sheep, cattle, deer & hens*
- *Mt Cook 90 min, Chch 2 hrs*
- *Free email, laundry and BBQ*
- *Dinner often available*

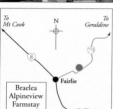

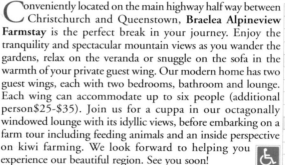

Farmstay Experience

	Double	$125-140
	Single	$100
	Child	$10+age

Conveniently located on the main highway half way between Christchurch and Queenstown, **Braelea Alpineview Farmstay** is the perfect break in your journey. Enjoy the tranquility and spectacular mountain views as you wander the gardens, relax on the veranda or snuggle on the sofa in the warmth of your private guest wing. Our modern home has two guest wings, each with two bedrooms, bathroom and lounge. Each wing can accommodate up to six people (additional person $25-$35). Join us for a cuppa in our octagonally windowed lounge with its idyllic views, before embarking on a farm tour including feeding animals and an inside perspective on kiwi farming. We look forward to helping you experience our beautiful region. See you soon!

Bedrooms	Qty
Double/Twin	4
Twin	
Single	
Bed Size	**Qty**
Super King/Twin	4
Queen	
Double	
Single	
Bathrooms	**Qty**
Ensuite	
Private	2
Family Share	1

ALLANDALE LODGE
555 SH 79, RD 17, Fairlie
Ph (03) 685 8722, Fax (03) 685 8722
email: *info@allandalehall.co.nz*
www.allandalehall.co.nz

Features & Attractions

- *Heritage style building*
- *Smoke house tastings*
- *Walking & biking tracks*
- *Great cafés/restaurants*
- *Ski fields, golf, lakes*
- *Mt. Cook 90min. drive*

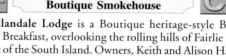

Heritage Style Bed & Breakfast
Boutique Smokehouse

	Double	$130
	Single	$80
	Child	neg

Allandale Lodge is a Boutique heritage-style Bed & Breakfast, overlooking the rolling hills of Fairlie in the heart of the South Island. Owners, Keith and Alison Hatton, exude true Kiwi hospitality in welcoming visitors to their home. Nestled on 5 acres of farmland, the historic Lodge has been lovingly renovated, offering 2 queen bedrooms and 1 single bedroom, both tastefully decorated to reflect the country colours of the Mackenzie region. The Lodge's living area, originally built as a school (1911), has polished New Zealand native timber floors and a log fire. Across the courtyard we operate a small, traditional Scottish smokehouse (**Fat Albert Smokehouse**), specialising in smoked venison, duck, salmon and other items.

Bedrooms	Qty
Double	2
Twin	
Single	1
Bed Size	**Qty**
King	
Queen	2
Double	
King/Single	1
Bathrooms	**Qty**
Ensuite	
Private	
Guest Share	1

DIRECTIONS: On SH79, 5km north of Fairlie ON main route Fairlie - Geraldine.

ASHGROVE B & B
Mt Cook Road, Fairlie, South Canterbury
Ph (03) 685 8797, Fax (03) 685 8795
Mobile 027-289 5323
email: *maria@ashgrove.co.nz*
www.ashgrove.co.nz

Features & Attractions
- *Restful stopover*
- *3 Ski fields close by*
- *Mt. Cook 90 mins drive*
- *Queenstown 3hrs drive*
- *Fishing and hunting guides*
- *Golf and walks*

Double	$125	
Single	$85	
Child	neg	

Countrystay Bed & Breakfast

Bedrooms	Qty
Double	2
Twin	
Single	

Bed Size	Qty
Super King	1
Queen	1
Double	
Single	

Bathrooms	Qty
Ensuite	1
Private	1
Guest Share	

DIRECTIONS: In the 80kph zone Tekapo end of Fairlie. The second Blue B&B sign leaving, and the first Blue B&B sign entering Fairlie.

Welcome to **Ashgrove**, your home away from home.
Our Guest Facilities for the Super king room include a spacious private sitting room with TV, fridge, tea and coffee making facilities, microwave, toaster and dishes etc and also a comfortable sofa bed to sleep 1 adult or 2 children in the separate sitting room. The super king may also be made into 2 singles.
The Queen bedroom with ensuite has a spacious sitting area with TV, fridge, tea and coffee making facilities, toaster and dishes etc and a comfortable sofa bed to sleep 1 adult or 2 children.
At an extra cost, I offer a cooked breakfast with eggs from our free-range chickens. We have sheep and lambs from October to March. Top quality restaurants 2 mins drive or 15 mins walk. We are two hours drive from Christchurch, one and a half from Mt. Cook and three hours to Queenstown.

CREEL HOUSE
36 Murray Place, PO Box39, Lake Tekapo
Ph (03) 680 6516, Fax (03) 680 6659
Mobile 021-137 9787
email: *creelhouse.l.tek@xtra.co.nz*
www.laketekapoflyfishing.co.nz

Features & Attractions
- *Church of the Good Shepherd*
- *Scenic flights glaciers/Mt. Cook*
- *Easy access to walking tracks*
- *Stargazing on clear evenings*
- *Skiing/ice-skating - winter*
- *Great outdoors*

Double	$150-160	
Single	$80	
Child		

Creel House Bed & Breakfast

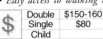

Bedrooms	Qty
Double	2
Twin	1
Single	

Bed Size	Qty
King	
Queen	2
Double	
Single	2

Bathrooms	Qty
Ensuite	1
Private	2
Guest Share	

"Welcome." Our home, built by Grant, has three storeys with panoramic views of Lake Tekapo, Mt. John, Southern Alps and surrounding mountains, and has a native garden. There is a separate guest lounge and guest entrance, and all rooms are spacious. Walking distance to shops and restaurants is 10-15 minutes. We have one secondary school daughter living at home and two cats. Our living quarters are on the ground floor with guest's accommodation on the middle and upper floor. Breakfast is a lavish, healthy continental with home-made produce.
Grant is a registered member of the NZ Fishing and Guides Association. He is available for guided fly fishing for day tours and packages are available. Details on website.

ALPINE VISTA BED & BREAKFAST

12 Hamilton Drive, Lake Tekapo
Ph (03) 680 6702, Fax (03) 680 6707
Mobile 027-599 6460
email: *info@alpinevista.co.nz*
www.alpinevista.co.nz

Tariff : N.Z. Dollars	
Double	$170-240
Single	$120-195
Child	

Bedrooms	Qty
Double	2
Twin	1
Single	

Bed Size	Qty
Super King	
King	2
Queen	
Double	
Single	2

Bathrooms	Qty
Ensuite	3
Private	
Guest Share	

**Delightful
Bed & Breakfast**

Features & Attractions

- *Warm hospitality*
- *Magnificent scenery*
- *Cooked breakfast*
- *Mount Cook 1 hour*
- *Restaurants 10 min walk*
- *Trout fishing*
- *Golf (clubs available)*
- *Christchurch/Queenstown 3 hrs*

Pete and Jill welcome you to **Alpine Vista**, our large, modern home offering amazing views of the Southern Alps, beautiful Lake Tekapo and the Richmond Range. Our home offers 3 guest bedrooms, each with an ensuite, tea/coffee making facilities, email and fax access. Our home is situated in a quiet location and being double glazed, a peaceful night's sleep is guaranteed. A full continental and English cooked breakfast is served in our large country-style kitchen. Each evening guests are invited to join us in the lounge for pre-dinner drinks. Lake Tekapo is halfway between Christchurch and Queenstown and is an ideal location to base yourself for a day trip to explore the Mt Cook National Park as it is only a one hour drive away. Lake Tekapo offers many attractions including golf, trout fishing, tramping, star gazing, snow skiing, (2 skifields within 40 minutes drive), scenic flights around Mt Cook – or just take in the peace and tranquillity.

FREDA DU FAUR HOUSE

1 Esther Hope Street, Lake Tekapo,
South Canterbury
Ph (03) 680 6513
email: *dawntek@xtra.co.nz*
www.fredadufaur.co.nz

Tariff : N.Z. Dollars	
Double	$140-160
Single	$99-110
Child	Full price

Bedrooms	Qty
Double	2
Twin	1
Single	

Bed Size	Qty
Super King	
King	
Queen	1
Double	1
Single	1

Bathrooms	Qty
Ensuite	2
Private	1
Guest Share	

**Bed & Breakfast
Homestay**

DIRECTIONS:
From SH 8 turn into Hamilton Drive
and then turn right into
Esther Hope Street where
you will see our sign.

Features & Attractions

- *Snowcapped mountains*
- *Crystal blue lakes*
- *Beautiful gardens & water feature*
- *Fishing and small game guide*
- *Handy to ski fields*
- *5 min to shops, restaurants*
- *1 hour from Mt. Cook*
- *Peaceful and quiet*

When you come to this area you will experience Tekapo's tranquility and a touch of mountain magic. Dawn and Barry extend to you a warm and friendly welcome. Our home with beautiful mountain and lake views is warm and comfortable. Rimu panelling, heart timber furniture and an attractive decor are blending in with the McKenzie Country.

All guest bedrooms in their private wing are overlooking the garden, two are opening onto a balcony.

Enjoy light refreshments on our patio surrounded by the scent of lavender and roses or view the ever-changing panorama from the lounge. In the morning you have the choice of either continental or special breakfast.

A five minute walk takes you to the centre with shops and restaurants. There are several lovely walkways nearby and Mount Cook is only a one hour scenic drive from Lake Tekapo.

TEKAPO HOUSE

8 O'Neill Place, Lakeview Heights, Lake Tekapo
Ph (03) 680 6607, Fax (03) 680 6691
Mobile 027-240 4974
email: *rayntek@xtra.co.nz*
www.tekapoholidayhomes.co.nz

Tariff : N.Z. Dollars	
Double	$140-160
Single	$80
Child	$35

Bedrooms	Qty
Double	2
Twin	1
Single	

Bed Size	Qty
Super King	1
King	
Queen	1
Double	
Single	

Bathrooms	Qty
Ensuite	1
Private	
Guest Share	1

Bed & Breakfast
Boutique Accommodation

Features & Attractions

- *Outstanding lake views*
- *Excellent walking tracks*
- *Excellent choice of restaurants*
- *Christchurch/Queenstown, 3 hr. drive*
- *Fishing*
- *Round hill ski field*
- *Amazing clear skies*
- *Generous cooked breakfast*

Treat yourself to Tekapo. Just three hours from Christchurch and three hours from Queenstown, Lake Tekapo is one of New Zealand's most celebrated beauty spots. The ever-changing colours of the lake with snow capped mountains beyond draw artists and photographers from around the world every season.

Take time to relax at **Tekapo House**, with stunning views from almost every room and hearty breakfasts to start your day. Enjoy warmth, comfort and home-style hospitality. Jenny and Peter used to run a farm and still have a small flock of sheep you can hand-feed. They know the area well and can advise on all local attractions. At Lake Tekapo you can fish, hike, bird-watch, horse-trek, take scenic flights over the Alps, and ski and skate in winter. Or simply take in the beauty of the environment. Treat yourself to memories at **Tekapo House**.

MOONLIGHT B&B

25 Murray Place, Lake Tekapo
Phone (03) 680 6514
e-mail: *info@tekapomoonlight.co.nz*
www.tekapomoonlight.co.nz

Tariff : N.Z. Dollars	
Double	$100-160
Single	$70-140
Child	

Bedrooms	Qty
Double	2
Twin	1
Single	

Bed Size	Qty
Super King	1
King	1
Queen	
Double	
King Single	2

Bathrooms	Qty
Ensuite	1
Private	1
Guest Share	1

 Life is what our thoughts make of it!

Features & Attractions

- *Million dollar lake views*
- *Warm, friendly hospitality*
- *Astrology birth horoscope*
- *Dutch & German fluent*
- *Hiking guide*
- *Stargazing guide*
- *Home made bread*
- *Well travelled hosts*

Marianne and René welcome you warmly to Moonlight: our European style Bed & Breakfast in a character home with high wooden beams, beautiful veranda outlook and lovely gardens. Enjoy unsurpassed views overlooking Lake Tekapo, the church of the Good Shepherd and the vast mountain ranges of the Mackenzie Country. Lake Tekapo is halfway between Christchurch and Queenstown and is amongst New Zealand's top 3 for sunshine hours. Marianne loves meeting people and preparing a healthy breakfast with home-made bread and fresh yoghurt. She has put a lot of effort in decorating Moonlight into a cosy house where you can be at ease and feel at home. René, a hiking and star-watching guide, is pleased to share his experience of the mountains, natural history, astronomy and astrology. He has spent 1yr of his life hiking in the Himalayas. All our beds have high quality mattresses and warm goose down duvets. Always remember: life is what our thoughts make of it!

439

LAKEVIEW BED & BREAKFAST & STUDIO UNIT
7 Hamilton Drive, PO Box 118, Lake Tekapo
Ph (03) 680 6673
Mobile 027-202 3419
email: *lakeviewlaketekapo@xtra.co.nz*
www.tekapolakeview.co.nz

Features & Attractions

- *Kiwi hospitality*
- *Picturesque lake views*
- *Fantastic night sky*
- *Tremendous walking tracks*
- *Close to lake & restaurants*
- *Mount Cook 1 hour*

**Bed & Breakfast Homestay
& Self-contained Studio Unit**

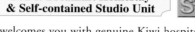

Double	$110-140	
Single	$80-90	
Child		

Bedrooms	Qty
Double	2
Twin	1
Single	
Bed Size	Qty
King	
Queen	2
Double	
Single	2
Bathrooms	Qty
Ensuite	1
Private	
Guest Share	1

Rayna welcomes you with genuine Kiwi hospitality to **Lakeview** and is happy to share her local knowledge with you. Enjoy the peace and tranquility at our unique location. From our elevated position you can look at beautiful Lake Tekapo, renowned for its aquamarine colour, and further up towards the surrounding mountain ranges. In the evening watch when the setting sun turns Mt. Edward into a glowing gold. Lake Tekapo is famous for its fantastic night sky. From our large balcony, which is ideal for stargazing, you may like to watch the Milkyway and the Southern Cross later in the evening .

You have the choice of staying as a Bed & Breakfast guest or enjoy your self-contained studio unit with private entrance. **Lakeview** is close to the lake and restaurants. Mount Cook is one hour's drive away.

ARTEMIS BED & BREAKFAST
33 North West Arch, PO Box 78, Twizel,
Mackenzie Country
Ph (03) 435 0388, Fax (03) 435 0377
email: *artemistwizel@paradise.net.nz*

Features & Attractions

- *Stunning alpine views*
- *Guest sitting room*
- *Private tea/coffee making*
- *Special continental breakfast*
- *3 minute drive to restaurants*
- *45 minutes to Mount Cook*

**Bed & Breakfast
Homestay**

Double	$130	
Single	$105	
Child		

Bedrooms	Qty
Double	2
Twin	1
Single	
Bed Size	Qty
King	
Queen	2
Double	
Single	1
Bathrooms	Qty
Ensuite	1
Private	1
Guest Share	

Jan and Bob welcome you to the magnificent Mackenzie Basin and the Mount Cook National Park. Our modern home, which is situated on a hectare of land, has stunning mountain views along with space and tranquility. We are a forty-five minute drive to Mount Cook and only three minutes drive to several restaurants.

There is a guest sitting room with a balcony and tea and coffee making facilities. We begin your day with a generous special continental breakfast. We look forward to sharing our home with you and are only too happy to discuss your New Zealand itineraries and sightseeing.

GLADSTONE COTTAGE AND HOMESTAY

32 North West Arch, PO Box 72, Twizel, 8773
Phone (03) 435 0527, Mobile 027-499 5572
e-mail: *info@gladstonecottage.co.nz*
www.gladstonecottage.co.nz

Features & Attractions

- *Tranquil country setting*
- *Mt Cook 45 minutes*
- *Fully self-contained*
- *Twizel 3 min. by car*
- *Breakfast available*
- *Extra person $30*

**Homestay
Bed & Breakfast**

		$
Double	$140	
Single		
Child	$15	

Bedrooms	Qty
Double	1
Twin	1
Single	
Bed Size	**Qty**
King	
Queen	1
Double	
Single	2
Bathrooms	**Qty**
Ensuite	
Private	
Family Share	1

Gladstone Cottage is situated in the beautiful MacKenzie Basin on the outskirts of Twizel, the closest town to Mt Cook. The town centre, with a good selection of restaurants and shops, is a leisurely 15 min. walk or 3 min. by car. **The Cottage** shares 6 arces (2.5 hectares) with Kharla, our Curly Coated Retriever, Paris, our Burmin Cat, and with our home, in a very tranquil setting with magnificent views of the Ben Ohau Ranges. Heated towel rails, washing machine, ironing, full kitchen facilities, underfloor heating, woodburner, Sky TV, video, telephone, Internet, BBQ and outdoor furniture. There are plenty of activities available in the beautiful MacKenzie and Aoraki, Mt Cook Region. We look forward to sharing our beautiful country lifestyle with you.

DIRECTIONS:
45 minutes from Aoraki, Mt Cook, and approximately half way between Christchurch and Queenstown on State Highway 8.

HEARTLAND LODGE

19 North West Arch, Twizel, South Canterbury
Ph (03) 435 0008, Fax (03) 435 0387
Mobile 025-688 6944
www.heartland-lodge.co.nz

Features & Attractions

- *Spectacular mountain views*
- *Sightseeing trips arranged*
- *Self-catering option*
- *Fly fishing guide*
- *Spa and sauna*
- *Peaceful rural setting*

**Homestay - Bed & Breakfast
and Self-Service 'Loft'**

		$
Double	$250	
Single	$180	
Child	neg	

Bedrooms	Qty
King/Twin	4
Twin	
Single	
Bed Size	**Qty**
Super King	
King	1
Queen	1
King/Single	2
Bathrooms	**Qty**
Ensuite	4
Private	
Guest Share	

Welcome to our lovely, large Homestay Lodge, only forty minutes from the Aoraki/Mt Cook World Heritage Park. Luxurious guest rooms feature ensuites with spa baths or therapeutic saunas. We are a short drive from the township of Twizel, which has all services including a bank and restaurants. Relax with your friendly Kiwi hosts. Kerry is of Maori descent and would love to share her culture and history with you, and Steve is a world renowned fly fishing guide.

HUNTERS HOUSE

58 Tekapo Drive, Twizel
Ph (03) 435 0038, Fax (03) 435 0038
email: *annehunter@xtra.co.nz*

Features & Attractions

- *Lovely peaceful views*
- *Close to Mt Cook*
- *Fishing opportunities*
- *Riverside walks*
- *6 min walk to town*
- *Sightseeing trips arranged*

  Bed & Breakfast Homestay & Self-contained Cottage

	Double	$150
	Single	$100
	Child	

"Cead mille fuilte".

Hunters House was built in 2003. It is architecturally designed for guests and features every comfort and a warm welcoming environment. It overlooks the native tussocks and trees of the green belt on the township boundary with the mountains as a backdrop. All rooms are tastefully decorated with all facilities and french doors opening to the peaceful outdoors sited for the sun and views. We also have a self-contained cottage, fully equiped with all home comforts and same views as **Hunters House,** situated on its own private setting. Available short or long term.

Bedrooms	Qty
Double	2
Twin	
Single	
Bed Size	**Qty**
Super King	2
Queen	
Double	
Single	
Bathrooms	**Qty**
Ensuite	2
Private	
Guest Share	

PINEGROVE COTTAGE

29 North West Arch, Twizel
Ph (03) 435 0430
Mobile 021-464 726
e-mail: *aljohpinegrove@hotmail.com*

Features & Attractions

- *Extensive garden & pond*
- *Mountain and tree views*
- *Fishing and -walks*
- *2 self-contained spacious units*
- *Relaxing outdoor & BBQ areas*
- *45 min. to Mt Cook / Aoraki*

  Bed & Breakfast Self-contained Cottage Units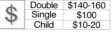

	Double	$140-160
	Single	$100
	Child	$10-20

Pinegrove Cottage, newly built, is situated in a sunny, tranquil location with alpine views.
In the evenings the local and native birds come down to the pond. You can also sit quietly by the water's edge to observe them. Feel free to wander through the garden and find a secluded spot to relax and contemplate.
We look forward to welcoming you and to make your stay enjoyable and relaxing. Each cottage unit has 2 bedrooms, fully equipped kitchen, laundry, bathroom, living area with heat pump and outdoor area with BBQ.
A continental hamper breakfast with home-made goodies is included in the tariff.

Bedrooms	Qty
Double	2
Twin	2
Single	
Bed Size	**Qty**
King	
Queen	2
Double	1
Single	1
Bathrooms	**Qty**
Ensuite	
Private	2
Guest Share	

BELLBIRD COTTAGE

121-125 Noema Terrace, Lake Hawea
Ph (03) 443 7056 or (03) 443 8676
Fax (03) 443 1807
email: *marge@xtra.co.nz*
www.bellbirdcottage.co.nz

Tariff : N.Z. Dollars	
Double	$130
Single	$130
Child	n/a

Bedrooms	Qty
Double/Twin	1
Twin	
Single	1
Bed Size	**Qty**
Super King	
King	
Queen	1
Double	
Single	1
Bathrooms	**Qty**
Ensuite	1
Private	
Guest Share	

Self-contained Luxury Accommodation

Features & Attractions

- *Cosy Log Fire*
- *Short walk to lake*
- *Full private laundry*
- *Television, DVD, stereo*

- *Attractive garden setting*
- *Seven day dining close by*
- *High speed wireless internet*
- *Fully equipped kitchen with dishwasher*

Our modern, self-contained cottage is situated in beautiful Lake Hawea village, surrounded by majestic mountains and extensive rural views. We are just 12 km from Lake Wanaka in the centre of the Lakes District of Central Otago. With Queenstown just an hour away, less than two hours to Mount Cook, you are close to all attractions. We are located about thirty minutes from two major ski fields – Treble Cone and Cadrona. Lake Hawea is renowned for fishing with guides available. Horse riding, nature walks, adventure trips, canoeing, paragliding are just some of the local attractions. The cottage construction is timber and rammed earth. The bedroom has a double and single bed and there is a double sofa sleeper in the lounge. If required on occasions we have a double self-contained bedroom adjacent complete with ensuite. A typical comment from our guest book is: "This is an outstanding cottage, cosy, tastefully decorated and thoughtfully well equipped. Together with warm hospitality this has perfected our holiday in New Zealand." Hosts are Marjorie Goodger, who has had a career in hotel management, and her sister Sheila McCaughan from a farming background. Should you wish, your log fire will be burning on your return from skiing. Dinner by arrangement hosted by Marjorie, Sheila and Brian McCaughan. Easy to find – Noema Terrace leads off the main road, Capell Avenue, where you are welcome at 121 & 125.

MATAGOURI COTTAGE

37 Elizabeth Street, Lake Hawea
Ph (03) 443 1987
email: *info@matagouricottage.co.nz*
www.matagouricottage.co.nz

Tariff : N.Z. Dollars	
Double	$130-160
Single	$95-120
Child	neg

Bedrooms	Qty
Double	1
Twin/Double	1
Single	

Bed Size	Qty
Super King	
King	
Queen	2
Double	
Single	1

Bathrooms	Qty
Ensuite	2
Private	
Guest Share	

**Bed & Breakfast
Homestay**

Features & Attractions

- *Purpose built cottage*
- *Secluded location*
- *Off-street parking*
- *5 min. walk to lake*
- *Relax on the verandah*
- *Dinner by arrangement*
- *Full breakfast*
- *17km to Wanaka*

Ian and Judith welcome you to charming **Matagouri Cottage**, which is nestled in trees in a tranquil part of Lake Hawea village.

Judith has come back to the district where she was raised on a sheep station, still in family hands and close by for visits. Ian trained as a quantity surveyor and has lived in Hong Kong and also in England, where he was involved in the running of a Bed & Breakfast. He's lived in New Zealand since 1987.

Matagouri Cottage, apart from the fact of its peaceful location, is the centre of an area famed for its diversity. Ski fields abound, mountains and lakes with their immense opportunities are a great attraction, a vibrant wine growing industry virtually on the doorstep and a world-renowned gliding centre nearby.

Matagouri Cottage has two charmingly appointed ensuite bedrooms and all the comforts of a New Zealand country home including an open fire in the sitting room and wood burner in the kitchen/dining room.

RIVERSONG

5 Wicklow Terrace Albert Town, No 2 RD, Wanaka
Ph (03) 443 8567, Fax (03) 443 8564
Mobile 021-113 6397
email: *info@happyhomestay.co.nz*
www.happyhomestay.co.nz

home
NEW ZEALAND

Tariff : N.Z. Dollars	
Double	$140-160
Single	$110
Child	$25

Bedrooms	Qty
Double	1
Twin	1
Single	1

Bed Size	Qty
Super King	1
King	
Queen	1
Double	
King/Single	1

Bathrooms	Qty
Ensuite	1
Private	1
Guest Share	

VISA   MasterCard

BB   **Homestay
Bed & Breakfast**   H

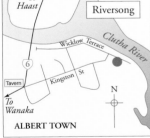

To Haast

Riversong

Wicklow Terrace

Clutha River

6

Kingston St

Tavern

N

To Wanaka

ALBERT TOWN

DIRECTIONS:
Kingston St joins SH6 opposite Albert Town Tavern. Travel the length of Kingston St to Wicklow Terrace, which runs parallel to the Clutha River. Turn right into Wicklow Terrace. **Riversong** is the 2nd last house.

Features & Attractions

- *Outstanding natural views*
- *Unique riverside setting*
- *Wireless/broadband facility*
- *Bedrooms with balconies*
- *Trout fishing opportunities abound*
- *Riverside walk to lake outlet*
- *Dinner by arrangement with hosts*
- *Book lovers and gardeners delight*

Riversong is an enchanting home in a stunning setting, and is one of Albert Town's most admired and historic homes. Situated on the banks of the Clutha River and a few minutes drive from Wanaka, it lies at the heart of Central Otago's unique scenic beauty, trout fishing, ski fields and entry to

Mount Aspiring National Park. The guestrooms all command stunning river, mountain and garden views. Privacy and full home comforts are assured and provided. Ann's background is in healthcare, Ian's law. Ian is happy to provide guests with the benefit of his local fishing knowledge and guidance services. Three ski fields are located within close distance. Otherwise just relax, walk or golf if you prefer, and take in the unsurpassed vista. All travellers are warmly welcome.

RIVERVIEW TERRACE

31 Matheson Crescent, Albert Town, Wanaka
Ph (03) 443 7377, Fax (03) 443 7378
Mobile 027-609 0650
email: *pphiggins@slingshot.co.nz*
www.riverviewterrace.co.nz

Tariff : N.Z. Dollars	
Double	$210-300
Single	
Child	

Bedrooms	Qty
Double	3
Twin	
Single	

Bed Size	Qty
Super King/Twin	1
King	2
Queen	
Double	
Single	

Bathrooms	Qty
Ensuite	3
Private	
Guest Share	

Bed & Breakfast
Luxury Accomodation

Features & Attractions

- *New luxury accommodation*
- *Stunning 360° views*
- *3 min. drive to Wanaka*
- *Courtesy car to restaurants*
- *Private guest lounge and patio*
- *Complimentary drinks and nibbles*
- *Close to ski fields*
- *Warm, friendly hospitality*

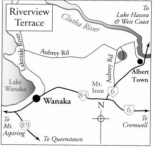

Wake up to amazing views and a generous cooked or continental breakfast, served in our dining room or on the patio. Your friendly hosts, Peter and Pam, can help to plan your kind of day at your pace. Choices include numerous walking and biking trails,  fishing (bikes and rods available), alpine sightseeing flights, boating, golfing, kayaking, horse trekking, skiing, wine tasting, day spa or enjoying a latté in the sun. These are some of the popular options in and around the Lake Wanaka area. **Riverview Terrace** is located above the picturesque Clutha River. It has a rural atmosphere and offers 3 large, spacious bedrooms with ensuites (one with a spa bath), all beautifully appointed and with electric blankets, hair dryers, mirror demisters, robes and writing desks. Our guests are welcome to enjoy watching sky TV, DVD, read from the library or relax in our 8 seater spa under the stars. Other facilities include ski storage, drying room, internet, laundry plus ample off-street parking.

FERRYMAN'S COTTAGE (CIRCA 1870)

4 Arklow St, Albert Town, Wanaka
Ph (03) 443 4147, Mobile 021-144 7513
email: *ferrymanscottage@xtra.co.nz*
www.ferrymanscottage.co.nz

Features & Attractions
- *Fragrant cottage garden*
- *Fisherman's paradise*
- *Fine food, crisp linen*
- *Scenic walks*
- *Stunning landscape*
- *Peace and tranquillity*

Double	$150-165
Single	$95-115
Child	

**Bed & Breakfast
Homestay**

Bedrooms	Qty
Double	2
Twin	
Single	
Bed Size	**Qty**
King	
Queen	2
Double	
Single	
Bathrooms	**Qty**
Ensuite	1
Private	
Guest Share	

Ferrymans is our recently renovated historic cottage, located 5 minutes from Wanaka, on the banks of the beautiful Clutha River (one of New Zealand's foremost fishing rivers). The warmth, peace and tranquillity of our home has been created for you and us to enjoy. A unique breakfast experience from Marie's kitchen awaits you. Following this you can either relax in our traditional cottage garden or partake of all the outdoor recreational activities that are available in our corner of paradise. We look forward to meeting you and ensuring that you have a memorable stay with us. Our cat 'Indy' left her previous home and adopted us. Let us pamper you in your 'home-away-from home'. – "Take time to smell the roses."

AVALANCHE BED & BREAKFAST

74 Bill's Way, Rippon Lea, Wanaka
Ph (03) 443 6665, Fax (03) 443 6701
Mobile 027-633 2364
e-mail: *davidpattison@xtra.co.nz*
www.wanakabedandbreakfast.com

Features & Attractions
- *Stunning mountain views*
- *Self-contained privacy*
- *Delicious home baking*
- *Close to 3 ski fields*
- *Short walk to lake*
- *Near Rippon vineyard*

Double	$135-165
Single	
Child	

**Bed & Breakfast
Self-contained**

Bedrooms	Qty
Double	1
Twin	
Single	
Bed Size	**Qty**
King	
Queen	1
Double	
Single	1
Bathrooms	**Qty**
Ensuite	1
Private	
Guest Share	

We offer a spacious, self-contained studio unit with independent access, ensuite, kitchen facilities and BBQ. Sliding doors open onto a private courtyard overlooking garden and farmland with stunning views of Mt. Avalanche. Just off Mt. Aspiring Road, Avalanche Bed & Breakfast gives skiers heading to Treble Cone a head start. We are only 8 minutes walk to the lake, near the Rippon Vineyard, and close to wonderful walking tracks, 2.5 km drive from town, or an easy scenic stroll around the lakefront. A quality restaurant is in walking distance. Delicious home-made continental breakfast supplies are provided. We have two cats, Fluffy and Ziggy, and a small, friendly dog, Roxy. Relax in this comfortable home away from home.

ALPINE VIEW LODGE

23 Studholme Road South, RD1, Wanaka
Ph (03) 443 7111
email: *stay@alpineviewlodge.co.nz*
www.alpineviewlodge.co.nz

Tariff : N.Z. Dollars	
Double	$110-250
Single	$90-225
Child	$20

Bedrooms	Qty
Double	6
Twin	4
Single	

Bed Size	Qty
King	
Queen	6
Double	
King/Single	2
Single	6

Bathrooms	Qty
Ensuite	6
Private	2
Guest Share	

**Bed & Breakfast and
Self-contained Accommodation**

Features & Attractions

- *3 minutes to lake & town*
- *Stunning mountain views*
- *Free Broadband Internet*
- *Cooking facilities, BBQs*
- *Laundry, bikes, spa pool*
- *Ski storage, drying room*
- *Secure locked storage*
- *Activity advice/booking*

Your holiday retreat... Set in four scenic acres, we offer the perfect destination for pleasure, business or special occasions. Our accommodation is spacious, private and ideal for singles, couples, families or a group of friends. **Sleep...** Our lodges are the perfect place to unwind after a day's travelling, sightseeing or thrill-seeking. Well equipped with a private deck or garden, your lodge becomes a peaceful retreat for a quiet break, or a base for an action-packed trip. **Eat...** Breakfast is an optional extra and our tempting menu allows you to indulge in delicious home-cooked food featuring the finest ingredients. **Relax...** Sit back and unwind while we arrange your day's activities. Keep in touch with home on our complimentary wireless internet. Sit under the star-filled night sky next to our outdoor fireplace. Lay in our constantly heated spa pool. **Refresh...** With fresh fruit, flowers and guest toiletries, we place your comfort foremost. "We enjoyed the setting, the scenery... that our one night stay turned into 4 nights!"

DIRECTIONS: From the centre of Wanaka, driving with the lake on your right, take a left turn into McDougall Street. Follow the road for approx. 3 minutes and turn right into Studholme Road. Alpine View Lodge is the second driveway on the left.

COLLINSONS COTTAGE
67 Manuka Crest, Wanaka
Ph (03) 443 7089, Fax (03) 443 7088
Mobile 027-443 0180
email: *stay@collinsonscottage.co.nz*
www.collinsonscottage.co.nz

Features & Attractions

- *Warm hospitality*
- *Relaxed location*
- *Off-street parking*
- *Garden setting*
- *Painting gallery*
- *Golf experience*

**Homestay Bed & Breakfast
SC. Studio & Apartment**

Double	$125
Single	$85
Studio	$135

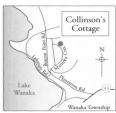

Collinson's Cottage

Y our hosts Brian and Susanne welcome you to our relaxing home and garden. Situated minutes from the town centre with thirty odd restaurants at your disposal. A quiet walk around our large garden will entice your camera and with a painting gallery to view local scenery. All the perks of home are enjoyed at the Collinsons - tea/coffee making facilities with filtered water on tap, plus television in your own lounge, and a secluded hideaway courtyard to enjoy in the summer evenings. Our interests are gardening, painting, sport and meeting people. Our passion is golf. The kids are gone and only our cat (Cambo) is in residence. You may arrive as a guest but hopefully you will leave as friends having enjoyed all that Wanaka has to offer.

Bedrooms	Qty
Double	1
Twin	1
Single	
Bed Size	Qty
King	
Queen	1
Double	
Single	2
Bathrooms	Qty
Ensuite	
Private	1
Guest Share	

HUNT'S HOMESTAY
56 Manuka Crescent, Wanaka
Ph (03) 443 1053, Fax (03) 443 1355
Mobile 027-427 2780
email:*relax@huntshomestay.co.nz*
www.huntshomestay.co.nz

Features & Attractions

- *New house in large garden*
- *Access to many activities*
- *Free laundry facilities*
- *Safe off-street parking*
- *Farm visits available*
- *Complimentary tea/coffee*

Double	$130-140
Single	$80-90
Child	neg

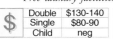
**Homestay
Bed & Breakfast**

Bedrooms	Qty
Double	1
Twin	1
Single	
Bed Size	Qty
King	
Queen	1
Double	
Single	2
Bathrooms	Qty
Ensuite	1
Private	1
Guest Share	

O nce settled in our roomy ground floor bedroom and lounge, our guests remark on the beauty of the lake and mountain views and how they change throughout the day. It was this aspect that drew us to this peaceful ½-acre section, when we left farming near Wanaka six years ago. Our architecturally designed house has two spacious bedrooms and 360° views of lake and mountains. By chance we became involved in homestay activities and have greatly enjoyed the experience. We realised we had a great wealth of information about the area that we could pass on to our guests.

DIRECTIONS: From town take Lakeside Road to Beacon Point Road, right to Manuka Crescent. We are opposite Manuka Crescent Motels.

Through our membership of "Lake Wanaka Tourism" we are kept informed of all tourist activities in the area. Whatever you want to do, we are happy to organise it. We look forward to enjoying your company in our beautiful area.

ATHERTON HOUSE

3 Atherton Place, Wanaka
Ph (03) 443 8343, Fax (03) 443 8343
Mobile 027-228 1982
email: *Roy.Kate@xtra.co.nz*
www.atherton.co.nz

Tariff : N.Z. Dollars	
Double	$200-275
Single	$180
Child	

Bedrooms	Qty
Double	2
Twin	
Single	
Bed Size	**Qty**
Super King	
King	
Queen	1
Double	
King Single	1
Bathrooms	**Qty**
Ensuite	2
Private	
Guest Share	

 Luxury Lakeside Bed & Breakfast

Features & Attractions

- *Stunning lake and mountain views*
- *Quiet and peaceful*
- *Lakeside walk to township*
- *Complimentry aperitifs*
- *Warm hospitality*
- *Free laundry facilities*
- *Generous breakfast incl.*
- *Dinner available with hosts*

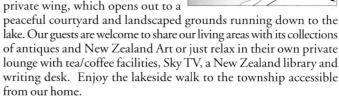

Welcome to our home offering luxurious comfort and warm Kiwi hospitality, set in an acre of lawns and gardens on the shores of beautiful Lake Wanaka. Visitors can unwind in their own spacious and tastefully appointed private wing, which opens out to a peaceful courtyard and landscaped grounds running down to the lake. Our guests are welcome to share our living areas with its collections of antiques and New Zealand Art or just relax in their own private lounge with tea/coffee facilities, Sky TV, a New Zealand library and writing desk. Enjoy the lakeside walk to the township accessible from our home.

After extensive experience hosting farm-stays we built **Atherton House** to provide tranquil and comfortable surroundings perfect for relaxing and enjoying the views. We enjoy art, antiques, travel, all sports especially golf, good food and wine, meeting and helping guests experience our wonderful part of the world.

BEACON LODGE

249 Beacon Point Road, Wanaka
Ph (03) 443 2200, Fax (03) 443 2277
Mobile 021-724 466
email: *info@beaconlodge.co.nz*
www.beaconlodge.co.nz

Tariff : N.Z. Dollars	
Double	$175-205
Single	$150
Child	

Bedrooms	Qty
Double	2
Twin	
Single	
Bed Size	**Qty**
Super King	
King	
Queen	2
Double	
Single	
Bathrooms	**Qty**
Ensuite	2
Private	
Guest Share	

  Bed & Breakfast
Luxury Accommodation

Features & Attractions

- *Drying room*
- *Off-street parking*
- *Delicious breakfasts*
- *Free laundry facilities*
- *Guests private entrance*
- *Wireless/broadband facility*
- *Courtyard with outdoor fire*
- *Open fires & underfloor heating*

Beacon Lodge is a new, architecturally designed home, set on an elevated one-acre site with stunning views of Lake Wanaka and the mountains.

Our spacious guest rooms are furnished with writing desks and flat screen TVs. Queen-sized beds are made up with fine linen and electric blankets. Robes are provided in the luxurious ensuite bathrooms and a fridge and tea/coffee making facilities are available in the dressing rooms. Both rooms open onto a private deck where you can relax and enjoy the lake and mountain views. Guests are welcome to use the spa pool, tennis court and peaceful garden.

Magnificent tracks around the lake are within walking distance and ski fields, golf courses, wine tasting and many other activities are within easy reach.

Steve's background is dentistry. He now enjoys fishing, tennis and skiing while Rosie is happy gardening, reading and walking. We look forward to sharing this special part of the world with you.

451

BLACK PEAK LODGE
38 Kings Drive, Wanaka
Ph (03) 443 4078, Fax (03) 443 4038
Mobile 027-457 3539
email: *blackpeaklodge@xtra.co.nz*
www.blackpeaklodge.co.nz

Tariff : N.Z. Dollars	
Double	$140- 200
Single	$120-140
Child	neg

Bedrooms	Qty
Double	2
Twin	1
Single	

Bed Size	Qty
Super King	
King	
Queen	2
Double	
King/Single	2

Bathrooms	Qty
Ensuite	1
Private	2
Guest Share	

**Boutique Lodge
Bed & Breakfast**

Features & Attractions

- *Mountain & lake views to die for*
- *Full business & internet facilities*
- *Decking and barbeque area*
- *Central Otago wineries close by*
- *Relaxing outdoor hot tub*
- *3 ski mountains within 30 min*
- *Architecturally designed*
- *Elegant furnishings*

B ed & Breakfast accommodation with a stunning mountain view – **Black Peak Lodge** is the place to stay. Enjoy warmth, comfort

and home-style hospitality, where our goal is to make your time with us as unforgettable and relaxing as possible. Soak up the ambience from the hot tub on the deck to the comfort of the guest rooms. The **Lodge** is fitted with elegant furnishings and three bedrooms. Each contains quality linen and electric blankets, TV, DVD and CD player along with lush spa robes. In winter curl up with complimentary aperitif in front of the feature fire place, while in warmer months the living room opens up onto decking, ideal for barbeques and admiring the sunset. Facilities include: computer, fax and internet connections for your use. Enjoy a delicious gourmet breakfast at a time that suits you while you plan your day around your needs. We welcome you to share the most beautiful part of the world.

BEACONFIELD B&B

251 Beacon Point Road, Wanaka
Ph (03) 443 2737,
Mobile 021- 150 5760
email: *mikerackley@xtra.co.nz*
www.beaconfieldbandb.co.nz

Tariff : N.Z. Dollars	
Double	$175-225
Single	$160
Child	

Bedrooms	Qty
Double	2
Twin	
Single	

Bed Size	Qty
Super King	
King	
Queen	2
Double	
Single	

Bathrooms	Qty
Ensuite	2
Private	
Guest Share	

  Bed & Breakfast Homestay

Features & Attractions

- *Breathtaking views*
- *New, architect designed home*
- *Warm, friendly hospitality*
- *Delicious, healthy breakfast*
- *Private and peaceful*
- *Well travelled hosts*
- *Complimentary refreshments*
- *Local knowledge*

Welcome to our lovely, brand new home set on one acre amidst a boutique vineyard and with breathtaking lake and mountain views. We invite you to share our Kiwi hospitality and local knowledge. Your guest room with ensuite has French doors opening to a sunny verandah with stunning views. You will never tire of the beauty and tranquility. Share our interests of food, wine, music, local art, antiques, travel and sports. Carla is a nurse and Michael was a lawyer and hospital manager. We are both widely travelled and have lived in the UK, USA and Australia. A delicious, healthy breakfast and refreshments are included. Laundry and email facilities are available as is the use of our home cinema.

453

DRUMMONDS ON WANAKA

137 Anderson Road, Wanaka
Ph (03) 443 1961, Fax (03) 443 1964
Mobile 027-244 8243
email: *stay@drummonds.co.nz*
www.drummonds.co.nz

Tariff : N.Z. Dollars	
Double	$265-325
Single	
Child	neg

Bedrooms	Qty
Double	5
Twin	
Single	
Bed Size	**Qty**
King/Twin	1
King	1
Queen	3
Double	
Single	
Bathrooms	**Qty**
Ensuite	4
Private	
Guest Share	1

     Fine Accommodation

Features & Attractions

- *Genuine Kiwi hospitality*
- *Luxurious, centrally heated*
- *Fine cuisine & wine available*
- *Skype & Broadband available*
- *Private guest lounge*
- *NZ gifts & artwork available to buy*
- *Fabulous mountain views*
- *Just minutes to town & ski fields*

DIRECTIONS: From SH 84 drive almost to the end of Anderson Rd at the T-junction with Aubrey Rd. Look for the B&B sign on the right before the T-junction.

Drummonds on Wanaka was purpose-built in 2003 as a luxury guest house. Just minutes from Lake Wanaka and the township, **Drummonds** is situated in a sunny position on a broad 2 acres. The alpine environment is well framed in the architectural design with

sweeping picture windows capturing the panoramic views of the lofty Harris Mountain Range and World Heritage Listed Mount Aspiring Park. When your hosts, Sally and Duncan Drummond conceived of **Drummonds on Wanaka**, their aim was to offer the very best in regional wine, home-cooked cuisine and fine accommodation. Sally, the highly-acclaimed **Drummonds** 'family chef', offers innovative, wholesome, home-cooked cuisine from fine dining to casual alfresco barbeques. You may choose meals and beverages in addition to your lodging. Duncan is the affable host, with an expansive character and passions for fishing, Bonsai, and photography. Jess and Hal, the Labradors, are always keen for extra company (or a walk). George, the cat, is always looking for a willing lap.

PEAK - SPORTCHALET
36 Hunter Crescent, Wanaka
Ph (03) 443 6990, Fax (03) 443 6971
email: *stay@peak-sportchalet.co.nz*
www.peak-sportchalet.co.nz

Features & Attractions

- *High quality standard*
- *Fully equipped kitchen*
- *Sun decks*
- *Cosy log fire*
- *Close to lake & walking tracks*
- *Drying room*

$		
Double	$110-155
Single	$90-100
Child	neg

Bedrooms	Qty
Double	2
Twin	1
Single	1
Bed Size	Qty
Super King	1
Queen	1
Double	
King/Single	2
Bathrooms	Qty
Ensuite	2
Private	1
Guest Share	

Experience our Hospitality and Ambience

Welcome to **Peak-Sportchalet**, your Qualmark 4 Star Accommodation in Wanaka. We would like to invite you to stay in our guest suites including our studio/double and self-contained Chalet. All are individually designed and appointed with fine furniture, ensuite or private bathrooms and also equipped with TV, DVD and sound system. Sliding doors open onto private sundecks. Awake refreshed after a relaxing night's sleep on our prime quality mattresses and duvets. Our luxury Chalet has 2 separate bedrooms, sleeping up to 5 guests, fully equipped kitchen and underfloor heating in the bathroom. The logfire provides an alpine ambience.

Start your day healthy with our memorable breakfast-buffet in front of an open fire. We also cater for special diets. Experience our hospitality and ambience.

STONEBROOK BED & BREAKFAST
18 Stonebrook Drive, Wanaka
Ph (03) 443 8150, Fax (03) 443 8154
Mobile 021- 341 460
email: *d.a.stretch@xtra.co.nz*

Features & Attractions

- *Friendly hospitality*
- *Mountain & lake views*
- *Off-street parking*
- *Internet & laundry facilities*
- *Ten minute walk to town*
- *Electric blankets, hair dryers*

$		
Double	$130-150
Single	
Child	neg

Homestay Bed & Breakfast

Bedrooms	Qty
Double	1
Twin	1
Single	
Bed Size	Qty
King	
Queen	1
Double	
Single	2
Bathrooms	Qty
Ensuite	1
Private	1
Guest Share	

Friendly hospitality awaits you on arrival at our new home, close to the lake. Drink-in the splendour of the mountains from your bedroom or the guests lounge. Walk to town in 10 minutes; longer if you study the history tiles along the millennium walkway. Our aim is to ensure your comfort, give friendly and helpful service and quality food, to make your stay a memorable experience. Food is our speciality, from home-baking, tea or coffee on arrival to delicious continental and or cooked breakfasts. Special diets catered for by arrangement. We'd like to share with you our enthusiasm for our natural environment and can offer suggestions of places to see and exciting things to do – in this idyllic corner of the globe.

DIRECTIONS:
From Helwick St. travel along Mt Aspiring Rd. for 1.2km, turn left into Meadowstone Dr. 1st left into Stonebrook Dr.

455

LAKE WANAKA HOME HOSTING

19 Bill's Way, Wanaka, Central Otago
Ph (03) 443 9060, Fax (03) 443 1626
Mobile 027-228 9160
email: *lex.joy@xtra.co.nz*
www.lakewanakahomehosting.co.nz

Tariff : N.Z. Dollars	
Double	$110-150
Single	$70
Child	$25

Bedrooms	Qty
Double	2
Twin	1
Single	

Bed Size	Qty
Super King	1
King	
Queen	1
Double	
Single	2

Bathrooms	Qty
Ensuite	
Private	2
Guest Share	

 Homestay - Bed & Breakfast

Features & Attractions

- *Peaceful lake walks*
- *A little luxury*
- *Meals on request*
- *Lovely patio garden*
- *Spacious, relaxing decor*
- *Mountain and lake views*
- *15-20 min. walk to shops*
- *Close to Rippon Vineyard*

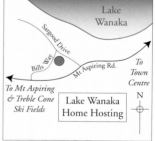

We welcome visitors to Lake Wanaka and enjoy sharing our natural surroundings with others. We have a large, peaceful home where our guests can experience not only the awesomeness of the lake and mountains around, but also experience the ambience of Wanaka itself. The picturesque twenty to thirty minute walk to Wanaka Town is very

worthwhile. Our guest room upstairs has the super king size bed with an adjoining lounge with tea and coffee making facilities, refrigerator, television and a private bathroom. Our double guestroom also has a private bathroom. We have smoke alarms, central heating and electric blankets in all beds. Good laundry facilities. We have no children living at home and no pets. Our interests are sport, gardening, boating, farming and good cuisine. Lex and I enjoy your company.

MINARET LODGE

34 Eely Point Road, PO Box 352, Wanaka
Ph (03) 443 1856, Fax (03) 443 1846
Mobile 021 - 644 406
e-mail: *relax@minaretlodge.co.nz*
www.minaretlodge.co.nz

Tariff : N.Z. Dollars	
Double	$395
Single	$375
Child	$60

Bedrooms	Qty
Double	5
Twin	5
Single	5
Bed Size	**Qty**
Super King	5
King	
Queen	
Double	
Single	
Bathrooms	**Qty**
Ensuite	5
Private	
Guest Share	

**Boutique Lodge
Luxury Bed & Breakfast**

Features & Attractions

- *Business facilities*
- *Spacious grounds*
- *Stunning mountain views*
- *Gourmet breakfast & aperitifs*
- *Sauna, spa, tennis*
- *Full activity service*
- *Fine furniture & linen*
- *10 minutes walk to town*

Wanaka's Luxury Boutique Retreat Bed & Breakfast Lodge, set in a park-like setting, located just 10 min walk from Wanaka town centre. Named after the spectacular Minaret Mountains, visible from the lodge, the lodge is just a short stroll away from the lake. With a backdrop of spectacular mountain scenery, set in landscaped grounds with its well established oak, silver birch and larch trees, this luxury retreat is a haven of tranquility. The lodge features a mud brick construction with plastered finish, incorporating local schist stone reflecting the traditional style of the Central Otago Region. The décor reflects casual elegance with a feel of refinement. Located behind the lodge are the guest rooms, constructed from local timbers and non toxic materials, tastefully furnished with unique décor and art in a setting of tranquil ambience. Each room has fine furniture, private ensuite with

heated tiled floor and deck. To begin the day, enjoy our special gourmet breakfast. Relax in our secluded sauna and spa, enjoy a game of tennis or petanque. Unwind with complimentary aperitifs in the lounge with its log fire. Your hosts, Gary and Fran Tate, welcome you to share the pleasures of this unique part of the world.

OAK TREE BED & BREAKFAST

4 Little Oak Common, Meadowstone, Wanaka
Ph (03) 443 9106, Fax (03) 443 9109
email: *r.s.mulqueen@xtra.co.nz*
www.oaktreewanaka.com

@ home
NEW ZEALAND

Tariff : N.Z. Dollars	
Double	$130-160
Single	
Child	

Bedrooms	Qty
Double	2
Twin	
Single	

Bed Size	Qty
Super King	1
King	1
Queen	
Double	
Single	

Bathrooms	Qty
Ensuite	1
Private	1
Guest Share	

 Bed & Breakfast Homestay

Features & Attractions

- *Warm & friendly hospitality*
- *Spectacular mountain views*
- *Modern spacious home*
- *Email & internet facilities*
- *Short walk to lake*
- *Peaceful setting*
- *Off-street parking*
- *Delicious breakfast*

DIRECTIONS: From town travel left along lakefront. Turn left into Meadowstone Drive. Little Oak Common is 3rd left

Oak Tree Bed & Breakfast ~ accommodation with friendly hospitality and stunning views of surrounding mountains and the magnificent Southern Alps. Within easy walking distance to lakefront and town centre, you will find a great range of restaurants, from casual to fine dining, cafés, bars, shops and the famous Cinema Paradiso. Our home is modern and spacious with comfortable beds, quality linen and electric blankets. A delicious continental breakfast is served in the dining area, at a time of your choice, whilst taking in the same superb views. Free laundry and email facilities available. Your hosts, Sharlene and Ray, invite you to take time to discover and experience the splendour of our alpine area in the heart of Mt Aspiring National Park. Ray works at the local 'Warbird Aircraft Collection' and for the renowned 'Warbirds over Wanaka' international air show. We are happy to advise or help you with either your plans in Wanaka or ongoing travel arrangements.

RENMORE HOUSE
44 Upton St, Wanaka
Ph (03) 443 6566, Fax (03) 443 6567
Mobile 027-434 2075
email: *renmorehouse@xtra.co.nz*
www.renmore-house.co.nz

Tariff : N.Z. Dollars	
Double	$185-210
Single	$150-170
Child	

Bedrooms	Qty
Double	3
Twin	
Single	
Bed Size	**Qty**
Super King Twin	3
King	
Queen	
Double	
Single	
Bathrooms	**Qty**
Ensuite	3
Private	
Guest Share	

**Bed & Breakfast
Homestay**

Features & Attractions
- *2 minutes walk to town*
- *Mountain bikes to explore*
- *Peaceful garden setting*
- *Spring-fed stream with trout*
- *Assistance with itinerary*
- *Laundry facilities*
- *Scrumptious breakfast*
- *Close to 3 skifields*

Blair, Rosie and Sophie, the cat, look forward to welcoming you to their home in Wanaka. **Renmore House** is situated in a quiet exclusive cul-de-sac 200 metres from Wanaka lakefront, cafés, restaurants, bars, shops and galleries. Enjoy panoramic views from our decks or relax in our garden beside springfed Bullock Creek. The entire ground floor, including a separate guest lounge and kitchenette, is devoted to guest use. Laundry facilities, the barbeque, tea/coffee making, home-baking, guest library and mountain bikes are all available for guests. Having been born in Otago and travelled extensively, we are very proud of our beautiful environment. An excellent golf course with superb views is within 5 minutes walk. There are fishing guides, kayaking, boating, canyoning, wonderful walking tracks, scenic flights, skiing and numerous other activities. We both love to take time to ensure you are getting the best value for time spent in our area and the rest of the South Island.

RIVERSIDE BED & BREAKFAST

home
NEW ZEALAND

11 Riverbank Rd, Wanaka
Ph (03) 443 1522, Fax (03) 443 1522
Mobile 027-464 0333
www.riversidewanaka.co.nz
email: *stay@riversidewanaka.co.nz*

Tariff : N.Z. Dollars	
Double	$140-180
Single	$90-100
Child	

Bedrooms	Qty
Double	2
Twin	1
Single	
Bed Size	**Qty**
Super King	
King	1
Queen	1
Double	
Single	2
Bathrooms	**Qty**
Ensuite	1
Private	1
Guest Share	1

 Bed & Breakfast Homestay **H**

 VISA   MasterCard

Features & Attractions

- *Quiet & private location*
- *Extensive garden & views*
- *Warm & friendly hospitality*
- *Generous breakfasts*
- *Many walking tracks*
- *Golf course nearby*
- *Ski fields*
- *Local vineyard*

We welcome guests to the quiet location of our home set on extensive grounds. Overlooking the Cardrona River we have superb mountain and rural views. We are located 100 metres off SH84, opposite SH6 and just 5 min. drive from the Lake and Wanaka's excellent restaurants. Well appointed rooms with quality linen, electric blankets, hairdryers and central heating ensures our guests a high level of comfort. There are 2 guest lounges, TV, DVD, with tea and coffee making facilities complete with home baking. Enjoy the open fire in winter or in summer relax on the terraced outdoor living areas. Our Luxury Mt Iron Suite with king bed has a private guest entrance and own sitting room with fridge, TV, DVD, tea and coffee making facilities as well. Delicious continental or home cooked breakfasts with your friendly hosts, ensures your stay will be enjoyable, sharing with you our beautiful area with ideas and suggestions that will make your holiday special.

VILLA VISTA

161 Stone Street, Wanaka
Ph (03) 443 7094, Mobile 021-1012941
email: *s.a.anderson@xtra.co.nz*

home
NEW ZEALAND

Tariff : N.Z. Dollars	
Double	$140-170
Twin	$140-170
Child	

Bedrooms	Qty
Double	1
Twin	1
Single	

Bed Size	Qty
Super King	
King	
Queen	1
Double	
Single	2

Bathrooms	Qty
Ensuite	
Private	1
Guest Share	

DIRECTIONS: Travel along the lakefront on Ardmore St. Turn left into McDougall St. (Queenstown, Cardrona - Highway 89) Travel 1.5km to turn right into Stone St. Travel 600m to 161 Stone St (on your left)

Bed & Breakfast
Homestay

Features & Attractions

- *Stunning lake & mountain views*
- *Warm, friendly hospitality*
- *Off-street parking*
- *Golf course 5min. drive*
- *Single party bookings only*
- *Free pick-up from coach, airport*
- *Private courtyard*
- *Laundry facilities*

Margaret and Stewart welcome you to **Villa Vista**.
"There are no strangers here – just friends we haven't met yet"
Share with us our modern home and garden in this most beautiful corner of New Zealand. Relax in the lounge or courtyard while taking in the breathtaking panoramic views of Lake Wanaka and surrounding mountains. Breakfast in the summer can be served in the courtyard, cooked or continental, at a time to suit our guests. Stroll to the lake, restaurants, cafés, bars, shops and art galleries.

We offer one queen room and one twin room, all with wool underlays and electric blankets. Single party bookings only. Central heating and a log fire make for cosy winter evenings. A short drive takes you to three internationally known ski fields for family, experienced or cross country skiing. There are many pleasant scenic walking tracks for all ages and fitness levels. Our interests include family, hospitality, golf, and Stewart also enjoys fly fishing.

461

Wanaka Jewel

7 Foxglove Heights, Far Horizon Park, Wanaka
Ph (03) 443 5636, Fax (03) 443 5637
Mobile 027-285 6234
email: *wanakajewel@xtra.co.nz*

Tariff : N.Z. Dollars	
Double	$185-225
Single	$170-210
Child	

Bedrooms	Qty
Double	2
Twin	
Single	

Bed Size	Qty
Super King	
King	
Queen	2
Double	
Single	

Bathrooms	Qty
Ensuite	1
Private	1
Guest Share	

**Bed & Breakfast
Homestay**

Features & Attractions

- *Peaceful park like setting*
- *Warm & friendly hospitality*
- *Spa, gym, pool, BBQ complex*
- *Tennis court, putting green*
- *Stunning lake & mountain views*
- *3 ski fields within 30 minutes*
- *Off street parking*
- *Walking tracks*

DIRECTIONS: 2.5 km west of
Wanaka central, off Mt Aspiring Rd.

Welcome to Wanaka Jewel – a stay in paradise.
Wanaka Jewel is a newly built, luxury home with a purpose-built Bed & Breakfast suite – set on one acre, surrounded by beautiful majestic mountains and superb lake views close to town. Your separate suite has private entrance and parking. Our beautifully appointed guest rooms have ensuite, quality linen, woolrest underlay, electric blanket, hairdryer, double glazing, radiator heating and a lovely patio to enjoy the view. Other facilities are fridge, microwave and TV. Complimentary tea, coffee and sweet treats available any time. The use of spa, pool, gymnasium, tennis court, BBQ, pitch and putting green is complimentary. Close to the famous Rippon vineyard and a 30 minute easy walk to town. Enjoy a sumptuous breakfast in our dining room. You can be assured of a warm welcome and a memorable stay. We have a friendly border collie who will also give you a big welcome. (Outside dog). We look forward to meeting you and sharing our paradise.

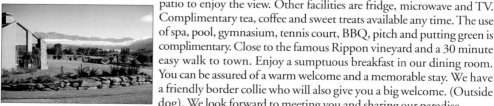

BURN COTTAGE RETREAT

168 Burn Cottage Road, Cromwell
Ph (03) 445 3050, Fax (03) 445 3050
Mobile 027-499 7177
email: *rosequedley@actrix.co.nz*

Tariff : N.Z. Dollars	
Double	$140175
Single	$125-140
Child	

Bedrooms	Qty
Double	1
Twin	1
Single	

Bed Size	Qty
Super King	
King	
Queen	1
Double	
King/Single	2

Bathrooms	Qty
Ensuite	
Private	1
Guest Share	

Boutique Bed & Breakfast and Self-contained Cottages

Features & Attractions

- *Peaceful, rural setting*
- *Self-contained cottages*
- *Hosta garden sales*
- *Cromwell / Lake Dunstan 3km*
- *Relaxed, informal atmosphere*
- *Queenstown/Wanaka 45min.*
- *Five ski fields within an hour*
- *Vineyards & orchards*

Welcome to **Burn Cottage Retreat**, a 24 acre rural oasis of peace and tranquillity and a haven from today's busy world. Relax and wander in our extensive woodland garden nestled amongst willow, poplar and walnut trees. An historic woolshed stands guard over the hosta garden – an absolute delight in summer with abundant bird life. Our spacious guest room (separate wing) ensures total privacy with luxurious bedding, quality décor, peaceful garden views and a private bathroom with a heavenly claw-foot bath, separate shower and undertile heating. Generous continental breakfast. Enquire about our boutique self-contained cottages currently under construction. Ideal for couples, these cottages will be beautifully appointed with natural gas fires, a king-size bed and a deck to enjoy the setting sun. Cromwell offers a fantastic climate, spectacular autumn scenery, blossoms in spring, wineries, orchards, golf, boating, fishing, historic gold diggings, walks and so much more. It is our pleasure to share our relaxed, informal atmosphere with you. 3km from town centre.

DUNES HOMESTAY ON THE 9TH

13 The Dunes, P O Box 219, Cromwell
Ph (03) 445 3184, Fax (03) 445 3184
Mobile 027-222 4284
www.duneshomestay.co.nz
email: *info@duneshomestay.co.nz*

Tariff : N.Z. Dollars	
Double	$125-135
Single	$110-125
Child	neg

Bedrooms	Qty
Double	2
Twin	
Single	

Bed Size	Qty
Super King	
King	
Queen	2
Double	
Single	1

Bathrooms	Qty
Ensuite	2
Private	
Guest Share	

 Homestay - Bed & Breakfast on the Golf Course

Features & Attractions

- *Golf from our front lawn*
- *Private residential community*
- *Purpose-built brand new home*
- *Wineries & restaurants nearby*
- *Cromwell - a sporting paradise*
- *Computer & internet access*

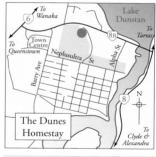

DIRECTIONS:
Please phone for easy directions.

Whether you desire privacy or our company, we will enjoy hosting you. Our new, sunny, purpose-built home is stylish, warm and quiet and is located in The Dunes, Cromwell's championship golf course.

Our home is ideally located for easy access to a large number of tourist attractions, including arts and crafts, orchards, vineyards, sporting facilities, heated indoor swimming pool, also great fishing (local guide available). Our comfortable non-smoking guest rooms have tea and coffee making facilities, fridge, Sky TV with teletext, free videos, clock/radio, electric blankets and hairdryers, private ensuites with showers.
Private entrances for your independence.
For further information see www.cromwell.org.nz

ANTRIM GUESTHOUSE

28 Antrim Street, Cromwell
Phone (03) 445 4099, Fax (03) 445 4099
Mobile 021-0225 0515
e-mail: jrsblancq@xtra.co.nz
www.antrimguesthouse.com

Features & Attractions

- *Walking distance to lake, golf course, central shopping area*
- *Quiet, comfortable & spacious*
- *Full roast dinner or Asian cuisine avail. on request*
- *Private garden with BBQ area*

$	Double	$120-140
	Single	$95-100
	Child	

Comfortable & Spacious
Beautiful Mountain Views

Bedrooms	Qty
Double	3
Twin	
Single	

Bed Size	Qty
King	
Queen	2
Double	
Single	2

Bathrooms	Qty
Ensuite	
Private	
Guest Share	1

Come stay with us! Enjoy warm hospitality in our comfortable, spacious home with beautiful mountain views. Easy walking distance to lake, golf course and central shopping area. We offer 2 double rooms with queen-size beds and one twin room. The spacious bathroom has two showers and a toilet and there's an additional separate toilet. All rooms have TV. Enjoy a substantial cooked or continental breakfast with fruit juice, cereals and fresh fruit from Central Otago orchards. Full roast dinner or exotic Asian cuisine is available by prior arrangement.

There are many interesting activities in and around Cromwell: winery tours, historic gold mining areas, quality golf course and fishing, to name just a few. We are only 45 minutes drive from Queenstown and Wanaka and an hour's drive from 4 top skifields. Your hospitable and friendly hosts, John and Rosa, look forward to welcoming you to **Antrim Guesthouse.**

LAKE DUNSTAN LODGE

Rapid No 485, Northburn, No 3 RD, Cromwell
Ph (03) 445 1107, Fax (03) 445 3062
Mobile 027-431 1415
email: *william.t@xtra.co.nz*
www.lakedunstanlodge.co.nz

Features & Attractions

- *Private, peaceful setting*
- *Trout fishing & golf course*
- *Wanaka/Queenstown 45 min*
- *Situated on lake edge*
- *Spectacular scenery*
- *Spa & laundry facilities*

Lakeside Stay
Bed & Breakfast

  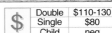

$	Double	$110-130
	Single	$80
	Child	neg

Bedrooms	Qty
Double	2
Twin	1
Single	

Bed Size	Qty
King	
Queen	2
Double	
Single	3

Bathrooms	Qty
Ensuite	1
Private	
Guest Share	1

Friendly hospitality awaits you at **Lake Dunstan Lodge.** Our spacious home is privately situated on the edge of Lake Dunstan, 6 km from Cromwell, 60 km from Queenstown. We previously farmed sheep and deer in Southland and have a cat "Ollie". Our interests include Lions, fishing, boating, gardening and crafts. The large sunny bedrooms have lake views and attached open balconies, refrigerator, tea and coffee-making facilities available at all times. Guests share our spacious living areas with television sets and make free use of our spa pool and laundry facilities. Local attractions include orchards, vineyards, gold diggings, golf course, fishing (local guide available), boating, walks, four ski fields nearby. We welcome you to have an evening meal with us, or just bed and continental/full breakfast. Come and fish or just relax in our peaceful surroundings.

DIRECTIONS:
5 km from Cromwell Bridge on
Tarras/Omarama Highway 8.
Sign at gate.

THE ORCHARD HOUSE

Rapid 90, Wanaka Rd, RD 2, Cromwell
Ph (03) 445 4484
Mobile 027-232 5149
email: *bookings@orchardhouse.co.nz*
www.orchardhouse.co.nz

Tariff : N.Z. Dollars	
Double	$200-250
Single	$180-230
Child	

Bedrooms	Qty
Double	2
Twin	
Single	

Bed Size	Qty
Super King	
King	2
Queen	
Double	
Single	

Bathrooms	Qty
Ensuite	2
Private	
Guest Share	

**Boutique Accommodation
Bed & Breakfast**

Features & Attractions

- *Luxury accommodation setting*
- *All season activities*
- *Hub of Central Otago wine district*
- *Complimentary local wine*
- *Set in a lovely orchard garden*
- *Short walk to Lake Dunstan*
- *Computer and internet access*
- *Complimentary fruit basket*

Trish, Fred and Bea, our friendly Australian terrier, invite you to stay with us in our private executive accommodation surrounded by our beautiful garden in an orchard setting. Cromwell and the Central Otago area is spectacular and inviting throughout all seasons – fishing all year, fresh summer fruit, water sports, wonderful golf courses, vineyard, restaurants, heritage gold mining sites, spectacular autumns colour, winter skiing, snow boarding. In spring – wonderful orchard blossom. Our location is on Main Highway 6, adjacent Jackson's Orchard, 2 min. from Cromwell and withing easy walking distance to Lake Dunstan and award winning vineyards, an hour's drive from Wanaka and Queenstown. Cooked and continental breakfast served in the dining room or in your room. Enjoy fresh fruit during the season from the house 'fruit salad patch'. Bedroom suites have private access, a balcony, ensuites, king-size beds, TV and wireless broadband. Shared tea making facilities. Laundry and barbeque facilities available. We look forward to meeting you and ensuring that you have a happy, relaxing and enjoyable time with us at **The Orchard House**.

VILLA AMO - *on Lake Dunstan*

9 Shine Lane, Pisa Moorings, No 3 RD, Cromwell
Ph (03) 445 0788, Fax (03) 445 0711
Mobile 027-286 8316
email: *VillaAmo@xtra.co.nz*
www.villaamo.co.nz

Tariff : N.Z. Dollars	
Double	$195
Single	$175
Child	n/a

Bedrooms	Qty
Double	2
Twin	
Single	

Bed Size	Qty
Super King	
King	
Queen	2
Double	
Single	

Bathrooms	Qty
Ensuite	
Private	1
Guest Share	

Homestay
Bed & Breakfast

Features & Attractions

- *Situated on Lake Dunstan*
- *Rugged mountain scenery*
- *Warm friendly hospitality*
- *5 skifields within an hour*
- *Peaceful, relaxing location*
- *Wireless broadband internet*
- *Vineyard and orchard tours*
- *7 minutes from Cromwell*

Welcome to **Villa Amo** in its tranquil lakeside setting on the shore of Lake Dunstan. Relax and enjoy warm friendly hospitality while taking in the breathtaking lake and rugged mountain views. Our private spacious guest room has a comfortable queen- size bed, quality cotton bed linen, tea/coffee making facilities, fridge, tv, dvd, film library and a well appointed full bathroom. To start the day enjoy a substantial breakfast, cooked and/or continental, at a time convenient to you. With superb fishing at our doorstep (summer and winter). If required, a professional fishing guide can be arranged. Cromwell has numerous attractions and historic walks or you may wish to visit our local wineries, orchards, craft shops or Old Cromwell Historic Precinct. Built in 1996, **Villa Amo** is the ideal base from which to explore the many delights of unique Central Otago or visit Queenstown or Wanaka. We are passionate about our region and would love to share with you our knowledge of this fascinating area, its history and its many attractions. A home away from home with that extra touch.

467

WALNUT GROVE

SH 6, Lowburn, RD 2, Cromwell
Ph (03) 445 1112, Fax (03) 445 1115
Mobile 027-477 4695
email: *walnut.grove@xtra.co.nz*
www.walnutgrove.co.nz

Tariff : N.Z. Dollars	
Double	$150
Single	$130
Child	n/a

Bedrooms	Qty
Double	2
Twin	
Single	
Bed Size	**Qty**
Super King	1
King	
Queen	1
Double	
Single	
Bathrooms	**Qty**
Ensuite	2
Private	
Guest Share	

 Countrystay - Bed & Breakfast

Features & Attractions

- *Valley & mountain views*
- *Set amid working orchards*
- *Cooked & continental breakfast*
- *Wireless internet access*
- *Restaurants & wineries handy*
- *Fishing, golf & walks*
- *Historic gold-mining area*
- *Relax away from crowds*

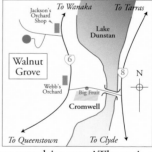

Relax! Enjoy our world! A place for all seasons! With dry climate, wonderful scenery and a slower pace of life, it is unforgettable.

Adventure activities of nearby Queenstown and Wanaka or the Central Otago Rail Trail from Clyde (bicycles for hire from Clyde) are all an easy drive away! The spring flowers and autumn colours are magical. Taste fresh cherries, apricots, peaches, nectarines in season, savour the fine local wines year round! Explore the rich history of Central. Our smoke-free home is on four acres with large garden and old shady walnut trees. Comfortable guest bedrooms have TV, clock/radio, coffee/tea making facilities and ensuite bathrooms. (The super king is also available as two single beds). Breakfast served at a time to suit you. A laundry is available. We have a Siamese cat and a friendly dog. We have travelled extensively, just love meeting people and would welcome you making our home your home for a night or more! Adrian is a member of Rotary. Reservations essential.

468

Stuarts Homestay

5 Mansor Court, Cromwell
Ph (03) 445 3636, Fax (03) 445 3617
Mobile 027-252 9823
email: *ian.elaine@xtra.co.nz*

Features & Attractions

- *Dinner by arrangement*
- *Golf, fishing, walks, boating*
- *Wanaka & Queenstown 45 min*
- *Off-street parking*
- *Wine & gold trails*
- *Quiet garden setting*

Double	$100-130	
Single	$70-80	
Child		

 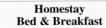

**Homestay
Bed & Breakfast**

Bedrooms	Qty
Double	2
Twin	1
Single	
Bed Size	Qty
King	
Queen	2
Double	
Single	2
Bathrooms	Qty
Ensuite	1
Private	
Guest Share	1

Welcome to **Stuarts Homestay** which is situated within walking distance of most of Cromwell's amenities. We are semi-retired Southland farmers who have hosted for over ten years. We enjoy sharing our modern sunny home and garden with visitors and a friendly stay is assured. Have tea, coffee and homemade baking available at all times. Share dinner with us (prior booking please) or just Bed & Breakfast (full or continental). We are also happy to transport you to and from buses.
Cromwell is a quiet and relaxed town which is known for historic gold diggings, vineyards, orchards, trout fishing, boating, walks and is close to major ski fields (forty-five minutes away).

Arrowtown Heights

6 May Lane, Arrowtown, Central Otago
Ph (03) 442 1726, Fax (03) 442 1726
Mobile 027-279 1552
email: *info@arrowtownheights.com*
www.arrowtownheights.com

Features & Attractions

- *Close to 4 ski fields*
- *Courtesy car from airport*
- *Peaceful, private setting*
- *Award wineries/restaurants nearby*
- *Southern Hospitality*
- *Well travelled hosts*

Double	$140-170	
Single	$120	
Child	neg	

**Luxury Accommodation
Bed & Breakfast**

Bedrooms	Qty
Double	2
Twin	
Single	
Bed Size	Qty
Super King	1
Queen	1
Double	
King/Single	2
Bathrooms	Qty
Ensuite	1
Private	1
Guest Share	

You are always sure of a welcome at **Arrowtown Heights**. Your spacious and luxurious accommodation is in a separate wing ensuring complete privacy at all times.
Step out of your bedroom to sit and relax in the garden, enjoy the surrounding panoramic views or the luxury of the outdoor spa. Choose to have breakfast inside or outside on the patio. Join us for coffee and a chat, we are happy to assist and direct you to a wide range of sights and activities. Email, fax, laundry and a barbeque are all available.
We look forward to your visit, sure in the knowledge that you will enjoy this special part of New Zealand.

BERNSLEIGH
21 Bracken Street, Arrowtown
Ph (03) 442 1550, Fax (03) 442 1540
Mobile 021-969 610
e-mail: *lindapeek@xtra.co.nz*

Features & Attractions

- *Peaceful private setting*
- *Southern hospitality*
- *Magnificent scenery*
- *Golf courses nearby*
- *Close to ski fields*
- *Near award winning wineries*

**Luxury Accommodation
Bed & Breakfast**

Double	$140-170
Single	$110-120
Child	Neg.

Bedrooms	Qty
Double	2
Twin	1
Single	
Bed Size	**Qty**
King	
Queen	2
Double	
Single	2
Bathrooms	**Qty**
Ensuite	1
Private	
Guest Share	1

Welcome to our modern, comfortable home situated in a peaceful location overlooking world-class golf courses. Enjoy the panoramic views of mountain and rural scenes. Private entry leads to your tastefully furnished rooms, which are equipped with all facilities including robes and hair-dryers. **Bernsleigh** offers a sunny, private courtyard and a cosy indoor atmosphere. Relax in the spa bath or admire the night sky in the outdoor spa. Email, fax, laundry -facilities and barbeque are available along with assistance with further activity/sightseeing planning. Take a short walk to a range of cafés and restaurants. A stay at **Bernsleigh** will be the highlight of your visit to historic Arrowtown, where you will enjoy the warm hospitality of David and Linda as they open their home to you.

WILLOWBY DOWNS
792 Malaghans Road, RD 1, Queenstown
Ph (03) 442 1714, Fax (03) 442 1887
Mobile 027-222 0964
email: *willowbydowns@xtra.co.nz*
www.willowbydowns.co.nz

Features & Attractions

- *Pick up airport or coaches*
- *Real southern hospitality.*
- *Limousine tours arranged*
- *Close to ski fields*
- *Golf Courses nearby*
- *15 min to Queenstown*

**Homestay
Bed & Breakfast**

Double	$130
Single	$100
Child	neg

Bedrooms	Qty
Double	2
Twin	1
Single	
Bed Size	**Qty**
King	
Queen	2
Double	
Single	3
Bathrooms	**Qty**
Ensuite	
Private	1
Guest Share	1

With Pam and David you are assured of a genuinely warm and friendly welcome, ex hoteliers they are passionate and practiced in the art of southern hospitality. Our home is off Malaghans Road, 500 metres down a driveway and approximately 5 km from the historic goldmining town of Arrowtown passing Millbrook Resort on the way. This B&B Homestay has features that will make you feel at home. With a coffee or tea on your arrival, you can relax in this warm and sunny home environment. **Willowby Downs** has lovely, well appointed guest rooms, electric blankets, TV, laundry options available, with the guests welcome to use the email, fax and telephone facilities. You have the choice of two master bedrooms with elevated views of Coronet Peak and the surrounding area. Pam and David are able to arrange any extra tours or special events you may require.

OLD VILLA HOMESTAY BED & BREAKFAST

13 Anglesea Street, PO Box 1, Arrowtown
Ph (03) 442 1682, Fax (03) 442 1682
Mobile 027-472 4543
email: *archie.june@xtra.co.nz*
www.arrowtownoldvilla.co.nz

Tariff : N.Z. Dollars	
Double	$130-150
Single	$110
Child	$20 u/13

Bedrooms	Qty
Double	2
Twin	1
Single	

Bed Size	Qty
Super King	
King	
Queen	2
Double	
Single	2

Bathrooms	Qty
Ensuite	2
Private	
Guest Share	

The Old Villa

**Homestay
Bed & Breakfast**

Features & Attractions

- *Home baking jellies & jam*
- *Wine trails, cafes, restaurants*
- *Peaceful town setting*
- *Real southern hospitality*
- *Fifteen minutes to Queenstown*
- *Inviting log fire during winter*
- *Laundry available*
- *Hiking trails*

DIRECTIONS:
Just two streets from Arrowtown's
main street. Please phone if you
require further directions.

Just 15 minutes from Queenstown, Arrowtown is an historic goldmining town that has retained much of it's olde world charm and offers travellers a peaceful and stylish alternative to the hustle and bustle of Queenstown. Stroll along the Arrow River or through the many tree-lined streets with cafés, restaurants, arts, cinema and a selection of shops. For the more active, there are many walking tracks in the surrounding hills, two local golf courses, or 4-wheel drive tours through the Arrow Gorge with Macetown and its goldmining ruins. In keeping with the history of the area, your hosts June and Arch Flint have built this lovely restored timber villa in classic settler style on a fabulous elevated site overlooking the main settlement just two minutes walk away. You have the choice of the master bedroom with ensuite, breakfast bar and your own private verandah overlooking a fabulous garden setting or the second spacious double bedroom with mountain views and an adjoining bathroom with a claw foot bath. Enjoy a coffee and homemade muffins on arrival and relax in the warm and welcoming home of your hosts who will happily assist you with any travel or administrative arrangements.

WILLOWBROOK
Malaghan Road, RD 1, Queenstown
(PO Box 118, Arrowtown) 9351
Ph (03) 442 1773, Fax (03) 442 1780
Mobile 027-451 6739
email: *info@willowbrook.net.nz*
www.willowbrook.net.nz

Tariff : N.Z. Dollars	
Double	$150-185
Single	$125-145
Child	

Bedrooms	Qty
Double	4
Twin	3
Single	

Bed Size	Qty
Super King	2
King	
Queen	2
Double	
Single	8

Bathrooms	Qty
Ensuite	5
Private	1
Guest Share	

 Rural Bed & Breakfast and Self-contained accommodation

Features & Attractions

- *Peaceful rural location*
- *Guest lounge, two open fires*
- *Large garden with tennis court*
- *Door to ski lift - 15 min*
- *Millbrook Resort - 3 min*
- *Luxurious outdoor spa*

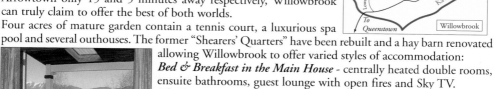

Willowbrook is a 1914 homestead at the foot of Coronet Peak in the beautiful Wakatipu Basin. The setting is rural, historical and distinctly peaceful, and with the attractions of Queenstown and Arrowtown only 15 and 5 minutes away respectively, Willowbrook can truly claim to offer the best of both worlds.

Four acres of mature garden contain a tennis court, a luxurious spa pool and several outhouses. The former "Shearers' Quarters" have been rebuilt and a hay barn renovated allowing Willowbrook to offer varied styles of accommodation:

Bed & Breakfast in the Main House - centrally heated double rooms, ensuite bathrooms, guest lounge with open fires and Sky TV.

The Barn – spacious accommodation with kitchenette, separate from the Main House. Super king bed, ensuite bathroom, lounge area with Sky TV and BBQ deck. Annex available for extra members of same party.

The Cottage – a delightfully cosy two bedroom cottage with full kitchen and laundry facilities. Ensuite bathrooms, underfloor heating throughout, Sky TV, spacious sundecks with BBQ and private lawn. Willowbrook is within easy reach of four skifields and three very picturesque golf courses. Trish and Tony are your hosts. Expect a warm welcome, friendly advice and traditional South Island hospitality.

Mt Rosa Lodge

Mt. Rosa Vineyard Estate, Gibbston Back Road,
RD 1, (PO Box 86), Arrowtown
Ph (03) 441 1484, Mobile 021-575 100
email: *info@mtrosalodge.co.nz*
www.mtrosalodge.co.nz

Tariff : N.Z. Dollars	
Double	$280-400
Single	
Child	

Bedrooms	Qty
Double	3
Twin	
Single	
Bed Size	Qty
Super King	1
King	2
Queen	
Double	
Single	
Bathrooms	Qty
Ensuite	3
Private	
Guest Share	

**Luxury Lodge,
Bed & Breakfast**

Features & Attractions

- *Mountain & vineyard views*
- *Wineries and cafés nearby*
- *Central to golf courses*
- *4 skiing mountains*
- *Vineyard walkways*
- *Open fire & outdoor fire*
- *Wine cellar dining*
- *Dinner by arrangement*

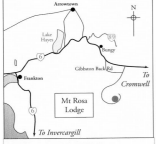

DIRECTIONS:
From SH6 turn into Gibbston back road,
continue straight up (500m) into Mt Rosa
Vineyard gates. Follow gravel road to lodge.

Mt Rosa Lodge is dramatically nestled high over the vineyards of Mt Rosa and Gibbston. The rooms are luxuriously appointed with private entrances and a guest fireplace is in one of the rooms for those cooler nights. Enjoy a glass of the region's Pinot Noir and local cheeses whilst sitting on your own private deck and view the sweeping vistas of vines and mountains. An array of wineries, cafés, golf courses, skiing mountains and walking tracks awaits your stay with us. Be spell-bound by the scenic wonders that Queenstown and the region has to offer you.

Relax in the evening in front of a huge open fire and as an option reserve your dining experience in our wine cellar. Brian has been in the wine industry for 30 years and Maureen is a Cordon Bleu graduate and is originally from Burma. An exciting blend of cuisines awaits you when dining at **Mt Rosa Lodge**.

RIVERBANK COTTAGE

Rapid 1350, SH 6, PO Box 1093, RD 1, Queenstown,
Ph (03) 442 1518, Fax (03) 442 1519
Mobile 021-347 804
email: *cottage@riverbank.co.nz*
www.riverbank.co.nz

Tariff : N.Z. Dollars	
Double	$215-265
Single	$195
Child	

Bedrooms	Qty
Double	3
Twin	
Single	

Bed Size	Qty
Super King	1
King	2
Queen	
Double	
Single	1

Bathrooms	Qty
Ensuite	3
Private	
Guest Share	

Boutique Accommodation
Bed & Breakfast

Features & Attractions

- *Four ski fields*
- *Golf courses nearby*
- *Fishing rods available*
- *Rafting and bungy jumping*
- *2 acre cottage garden*
- *Wineries*
- *Quilt gallery*
- *Restaurants 6 min.*

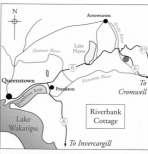

DIRECTIONS: From Cromwell drive 3½ km past Bungy sign, driveway on left. From Queenstown, 1½ km past 'Crown – Range' road sign, driveway on right.

Riverbank Cottage is situated above the banks of the Arrow River, and surrounded by deer farms, yet this beautiful secluded rural setting is only fifteen minutes from downtown Queenstown. The house is set in two acres of established cottage gardens with magnificent views of Coronet Peak, the Remarkables and surrounding mountains. **The Cottage:** Country style accommodation with full cooked breakfast included and each bedroom with ensuite. The guest lounge has beautiful views overlooking an extensive cottage garden, orchard and backdrop of mountains or relax in the shade of the courtyard in the height of summer.

If you are interested in quilting and patchwork, put a little time aside to look at the dozens of quilts on display in our gallery, or stroll out to the garages, where there is always an interesting car under restoration. If you require any help about what you should see or do during your visit, we would like to assist, as we have lived in the area for over 20 years. Our interests are quilting and patchwork, gardening, Ikebana, classic and antique cars.

MILESTONE

Ladies Mile, 1 RD, Queenstown
Ph (03) 441 4460, Fax (03) 441 4438
Mobile 027-541 4460
email: *jcturnbull@xtra.co.nz*
www.themilestone.co.nz

Tariff : N.Z. Dollars	
Double	$165-225
Single	$125-165
Child	Neg

Bedrooms	Qty
Double	4
Twin	
Single	

Bed Size	Qty
Super King	
King	1
Queen	3
Double	
Single	

Bathrooms	Qty
Ensuite	3
Private	
Guest Share	

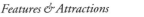

Stylish Accommodation with Warm Hospitality

Features & Attractions

- *Rose-covered stone cottage*
- *3 acres of garden*
- *Gourmet full breakfast*
- *Queenstown 10 min*
- *Marriage celebrant*
- *Guaranteed southern hospitality*
- *Romantic, peaceful & private*
- *Children & extra guests welcome*

Milestone is a modern, comfortable home. A working water wheel and waterfall are part of the three acres of peaceful and tranquil gardens. The surrounding mountains are a wonder to behold at all times of the year. The rose-covered stone schist cottage is self-contained and an ideal honeymoon hideaway, and as a marriage celebrant Betty can arrange and perform the ceremony to accompany the honeymoon.

The cottage has a four poster queen bed and a custom made queen divan in the living room for an extra guest. In the main house is a romantic ensuite with antique furniture and a private deck. Upstairs the 'Remarkable Suite' has a king and single bed, dressing room, lounge and ensuite. Another queen bedroom is available for extra guests in the party. Each room is spacious with TV, tea/coffee making facilities and spectacular views. Children are welcome – a port-a-cot is available. At **Milestone** we offer luxury, romance, privacy and tranquility along with warm southern hospitality.

THE TURRET

Rapid No 712, SH 6, Lake Hayes, Queenstown
Ph (03) 442 1107
Mobile 021-941 028
email: *theturret@xtra.co.nz*
www.theturret.co.nz

Tariff : N.Z. Dollars	
Double	$195-450
Single	$175-430
Child	$20

Bedrooms	Qty
Double	2
Twin	1
Single	

Bed Size	Qty
Super King	
King	1
Queen	2
Double	
Single	2

Bathrooms	Qty
Ensuite	2
Private	1
Guest Share	

Bed & Breakfast
Luxury Accommodation

Features & Attractions

- *Close to wineries & golf courses*
- *Close to four ski fields*
- *Opposite wildlife refuge & walkway*
- *Elegant cooked or continental breakfast*
- *Email & Internet access*
- *Award winning garden*
- *Stunning views*
- *Open log fire*

DIRECTIONS:
Overlooking Lake Hayes between Queenstown and Arrowtown on SH 6. Across the road from the Lake Hayes Pavillion.

This distinctive lakeside retreat, ideally situated between Queenstown and historic Arrowtown, offers luxury accommodation with stunning garden, lake and mountain views. Privacy, comfort and relaxation with warm hospitality will truly make your stay a memorable one.

Two of the guest rooms have french doors opening out onto the terrace, while the **Turret Suite** has its own balcony.

All rooms have fabulous views, tea and coffee making facilities and quality beds and linens. There is a separate dining room and a sitting room with a wood burning fire for guests' use.

Start your day with an elegant breakfast, served at a time convenient to you, then go out and experience all that Queenstown has to offer. Dinner is available upon request.

LARCH HILL B&B/HOMESTAY

16 Panners Way, Goldfields, Queenstown
Ph (03) 442 4811, Fax (03) 441 8882
email: *info@larchhill.com*
www.larchhill.com

Tariff : N.Z. Dollars	
Double	$130-180
Single	$110
Apartment	$195-275

Bedrooms	Qty
Double	2
Twin	1
Apartment	1

Bed Size	Qty
Super King	1
King	1
Queen	1
King/Single	2
Single	2

Bathrooms	Qty
Ensuite	2
Private	2
Guest Share	

**Homestay/Bed & Breakfast
Superb Accommodation**

Larch Hill
B & B

To
Cromwell
& Dunedin

Goldfield Heights
Panners Way

Sherwood
Manor

Queens-
town

Frankton

Lake
Wakatipu

N

6

To Te Anau &
Invercargill

DIRECTIONS:
From Frankton drive 2½ km on SH6A
(Frankton Rd) towards Queenstown. At
'Sherwood Manor' turn right into
Goldfield Heights. Panners Way is 2nd left.
We are No. 16 at end of accessway.

Features & Attractions

- *Magnificent scenery*
- *Tranquil setting*
- *Generous breakfast*
- *All rooms – own bathroom*
- *In-room tea/coffee making*
- *WiFi internet/email access*
- *Adventure/itinerary planning*
- *S/c apartment available*

Lesley and Chris offer you a warm welcome to **Larch Hill** in beautiful Queenstown. As featured in 'National Geographic Traveler Magazine' 2006 and Cathay Pacific's 'Discovery' Magazine 2004, **Larch Hill Homestay/B&B** is purpose-built on an elevated site with all rooms and sundeck overlooking Lake Wakatipu and the surrounding spectacular mountains. Our home provides a feeling of relaxation; a restful theme flows through the bedrooms into

the dining room with its library, opening onto a sunny courtyard surrounded by cottage gardens. We are only a 3 min. drive from the centre of Queenstown and within walking distance of the lake. Public transport passes our street every 20 min. Our self-contained apartment is ideal for families or groups of 4. Breakfasts are generous with home-made bread, freshly baked croissants and pastries, fresh fruit salad, yoghurt, and freshly ground, percolated coffee. We are booking agents for Queenstown tours and activities. Fax, email and wireless internet facilities available.

477

LAKE VISTA BED & BREAKFAST

62 Hensman Road, Queenstown
Ph (03) 441 8838, Fax (03) 441 8938
email: *graeme@lakevista.co.nz*
www.lakevista.co.nz

Tariff : N.Z. Dollars	
$160-220	Double
$110-175	Single
	Child

Qty	Bedrooms
2	Double
1	Twin
	Single
Qty	Bed Size
	Super King
1	King
2	Queen
1	King/Single
2	Single
Qty	Bathrooms
1	Ensuite
	Private
1	Guest Share

 Luxury Accommodation with Great Hospitality

VISA MasterCard eftpos

Features & Attractions

- *Panoramic lake & mountain views*
- *Gourmet breakfasts*
- *Wireless internet access*
- *5 minutes from airport*
- *Golf courses & skiing nearby*
- *Accredited tour booking agents*
- *Mini bars in all rooms*
- *Short walk to town*

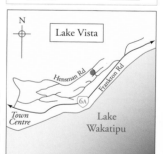

DIRECTIONS: From Frankton round-about take Highway 6A , after 4km turn right into Hensman Rd. Climb the hill, we are on left at 62 Hensman Rd.

Lake Vista , located on Queenstown Hill, 5 minutes from the airport and 2 minutes drive from downtown Queenstown. It is only a 20 minute, scenic walk into town and about $9.50 taxi ride home. Courtesy transport to/from airport or bus station is offered. Most guests gasp when they first look out at our magnificent all encompassing views over Lake Wakatipu to the Remarkables ranges from all rooms.You can even enjoy the views while lying in bed. The balcony outside all rooms is a great place to sit and have a drink after a hard day enjoying yourself. All rooms are individually decorated and have mini bars, refrigerators, beautiful duvets, under-floor heating, electric blankets, heated towel rails, colour TV, hair dryer, fresh flowers, bedside tables with side lamps and radio alarms. Being accredited booking agents we can even arrange your tours before you arrive to save disappointment at missing out on something during high season.

"FERRY HOTEL" B&B GUESTHOUSE (CIRCA 1872)

Spence Road, Lower Shotover, Queenstown
Ph (03) 442 2194, Fax (03) 442 2190
email: *info@ferry.co.nz*
www.ferry.co.nz

Tariff : N.Z. Dollars	
Double	$195-235
Single	
Child	Free u/12

Bedrooms	Qty
Double	2
Twin	1
Single	

Bed Size	Qty
Super King	
King	1
Queen	
Double	1
Single	2

Bathrooms	Qty
Ensuite	1
Private	1
Guest Share	

    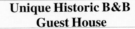

Unique Historic B&B Guest House

Features & Attractions

- *Ideal for families & small groups*
- *10 min. to Queenstown/Arrowtown*
- *Fishing advice & guide*
- *Central to ski fields/local attractions*
- *Genuine historic building*
- *Peaceful & relaxing location*
- *Photo display of Hotel's history*
- *Huge wood-burning fire*

DIRECTIONS:
From State Highway 6 turn into
Lower Shotover Road – Blue B & B Sign,
follow left turn into Spence Road.

Old World Elegance aptly describes this delightful Guest House – not just a place to stay, but a feature of your holiday. Formerly a popular hotel for over 100 years, the **Guest House** is a local landmark. Your hosts Kevin and Glenys have traced the hotel's history back to 1868 and in the process ascertained that they are the 25th owners of the Hotel. Hosts accommodation is separate but adjoining the Guest House. Glenys enjoys helping you to make the most of your stay in Queenstown offering advice and information and making bookings for local attractions. Kevin will advise, guide or teach Fly Fishing, Buckley our friendly English Springer likes to walk you along our beautiful track by the river. '**Ferry Hotel**' **Guest House** has 3 bedrooms, one of them with an antique brass bed and character ensuite bathroom. There is a kitchen that Granny would have been proud of and a charming lounge-dining room decked with historic photos, paintings and memorabilia, and kept warm by a roaring log wood-burner. Laundry facilities and a gas BBQ are available. Alfresco eating areas are situated in the English cottage garden.

KAHU RISE
455 Littles Road, RD 1, Queenstown
Ph (03) 441 2077, Fax (03) 441 2078
Mobile 021-104 0009
email: *info@kahurise.co.nz*
www.kahurise.co.nz

Tariff : N.Z. Dollars	
Double	$190-220
Single	$140-170
Child	—

Bedrooms	Qty
Double	2
Twin	
Single	
Bed Size	**Qty**
Super King	
King	
Queen	1
Double	
Single	2
Bathrooms	**Qty**
Ensuite	
Private	1
Guest Share	

   Bed & Breakfast

Features & Attractions

- Quiet rural location
- Beautiful mountain views
- Dinner by arrangement
- Skifields nearby
- Close to Queenstown
- Architecturally designed home
- Separate guest wing
- Delicious home baking

DIRECTIONS: From Queenstown, turn left off SH 6 onto Lower Shotover Road, just after crossing Shotover River bridge. Turn left onto Domain Road and left onto Littles Road. We are 1 km along on the right.

We warmly invite you to come and stay with us in our architecturally-designed home, set in 2½ acres of rolling countryside. From here you can easily access the nearby attractions of Queenstown, two skifields, golf courses, wineries, and historic Arrowtown. Your party will have exclusive use of our bed & breakfast accommodation wing. This comprises two double bedrooms, each with mountain views and opening directly onto the lawn and garden, plus your own full bathroom. There is an additional separate toilet and adjacent laundry. There is also a separate teenage sleepout. Tea and coffee making facilities, electric blankets, refrigerator and hair dryer are provided in the guest area. The house is centrally heated, covered parking is available. Each morning we serve freshly brewed tea and coffee and a delicious home-cooked breakfast at a time to suit. Dinner with complimentary wine by arrangement. Angela and Bill are well travelled, and together with their friendly family dog Tess, look forward to welcoming you at **Kahu Rise**.

CROWN VIEW B&B

457 Littles Road, Dalefield, Queenstown
Ph (03) 442 9411, Fax (03) 442 9411
Mobile 025-495 156
email: *info@crownview.co.nz*
www.crownview.co.nz

Tariff : N.Z. Dollars	
Double	$165-190
Single	$130-150
Child	

Bedrooms	Qty
Double	3
Twin	
Single	

Bed Size	Qty
Super King	2
King	1
Queen	
Double	
Single	

Bathrooms	Qty
Ensuite	1
Private	2
Guest Share	

DIRECTIONS:
From Queenstown/Frankton Airport cross over Shotover Bridge, turn left into Lower Shotover Road, left into Domain Road, left into Littles Road. 600m on the right.

Bed & Breakfast Farmstay

Features & Attractions

- *Quiet, peaceful rural location*
- *10 minutes to Queenstown and Arrowtown*
- *Separate guest lounge/open fire*
- *Four golf courses nearby*
- *Stunning mountain views*
- *Central to ski fields*
- *Warm hospitality*

Crown View is situated in rural Queenstown, just 15 min. drive from Queenstown and historical Arrowtown. Come, stay and enjoy the peace and tranquility of country life on our elevated rolling 8 acres. We have Suffolk sheep, 2 cows, 2 alpacas, chickens and our 2 friendly West Highland Dogs. All can be hand-fed. Just 10 minutes from Coronet Peak and close to 4 other ski fields. Also close by are jet-boating, sky diving, wineries, art galleries, 5 golf courses, walking tracks and gold panning. We have 3 large bedrooms with tea & coffee making facilities, TV hairdryers, toiletries and high quality linen. 2 rooms with super king/twin and 1 with a king bed. There is one ensuite and 2 private bathrooms. All rooms serviced daily. Hearty breakfast is served on the upstairs balcony, in the garden or in the guest lounge/dining room in front of the open fire. We have efficient radiators throughout. Reg and Caroll look forward to welcoming you.

481

TUSSOCK LODGE

293B Lower Shotover Road, RD 1, Queenstown
Ph (03) 442 0752, Fax (03) 442 0751
Mobile 021-808 018
email: *trevandjill@xtra.co.nz*
www.tussocklodge.co.nz

Tariff : N.Z. Dollars	
Double	$160-220
Single	$120
Child	–

Bedrooms	Qty
Double	2
Twin	
Single	

Bed Size	Qty
Super King	
King	1
Queen	1
Double	
Single	

Bathrooms	Qty
Ensuite	1
Private	
Family Share	1

 Stylish Accommodation with Great Hospitality

Features & Attractions

- *Peaceful private rural location*
- *Stunning 360° mountain views*
- *Physiotherapy aromatherapy massage*
- *Email, internet & laundry facilities*
- *All day sun, central heating*
- *Skiing, walking, golf*
- *Guided fishing trips*
- *Art galleries, wineries, restaurants*

Relax in the peace and tranquility of our home set on 30 acres of parkland in the beautiful Wakatipu Basin. Enjoy 360° views of the mountains and surrounding countryside. Courtesy vehicle for

pick-up/drop off at the airport. 10 minutes to Coronet Peak, 20 minutes to Remarkables. Enjoy local restaurants in Queenstown or quaint, historic Arrowtown. Child minding available in the evenings. Superb inhouse dining by arrangement featuring local produce and wines. Tennis court, mountain bikes, pétanque or take a quiet stroll in the grounds.

Luxury king size bedroom with private ensuite bathroom and spa bath. One king bed.

Queen bedroom with queen sized bed and shared bathroom.

Shared dining room, lounge and Sky TV.

Simple fresh breakfast, tea and coffee making facilities in your large bed sitting room. Cooked breakfast and/or dinner by request.

Jill and Trev offer you a warm welcome and pleasant stay.

THE CANYONS COUNTRY LODGE

13 Watties Track, Arthurs Point, Queenstown
Ph (03) 442 6108, Fax (03) 442 6208
Mobile 021-606 545

e-mail: *info@thecanyonslodge.com*
www.thecanyonslodge.com

Features & Attractions

- *Fabulous breakfasts*
- *Outdoor Jacuzzi spa*
- *Canapés & wine daily*
- *2 min. from town centre*
- *Guest lounge / open log fire*
- *Wireless email, skyTV, laundry*

$	Double	$285-549
	Single	
	Child	

Bed & Breakfast
Luxury Accommodation

Bedrooms	Qty
Double	4
Twin	4
Single	
Bed Size	**Qty**
King	2
Queen	2
Double	
Single	
Bathrooms	**Qty**
Ensuite	4
Private	1
Guest Share	

Welcome to **The Canyons Country Lodge**, a purpose-built luxury lodge set on a picture postcard site with spectacular views overlooking the celebrated Shotover River and Canyons. This large 2 hectare estate gives **The Canyons Country Lodge** a serenely peaceful and exclusively country feel and yet it is only minutes from the centre of Queenstown. The most outstanding and breathtaking mountain and river views can be enjoyed from every guest room in the lodge. The sun rises directly over the river valley in front of you each morning. Peregrine falcons circle effortlessly above. All the rooms have luxury linen, complementary flowers, bathrobes and kiwi toiletries. Afternoon teas, evening canapés and local wines. The ensuites comprise of Italian terracotta tiles with separate shower and claw foot bath.

THE PEONY GARDENS

231 Lake Hayes Rd, RD1, Queenstown
Ph (03) 442 1280, Fax (03) 442 1210
Mobile 027-436 1661
email: *ijchamberlain@xtra.co.nz*

Features & Attractions

- *Self-contained flat*
- *Close to 4 ski fields*
- *Restaurants 5 min.*
- *Peaceful rural location*
- *Golf courses nearby*
- *2 ha lovely garden setting*

$	Double	$130
	Single	$100
	Child	$20

Homestay
Bed & Breakfast

Bedrooms	Qty
Double	1
Twin	1
Single	1
Bed Size	**Qty**
King	
Queen	1
Double	1
Single	2
Bathrooms	**Qty**
Ensuite	
Private	1
Guest Share	

Ian and Margaret welcome you to **The Peony Gardens**, situated at Lake Hayes. Our garden was the original 'Peony Gardens' and during November and December our gardens are a delight to see. The self-contained flat has two bedrooms, full kitchen facilities, heat pump and opens onto a balcony which looks over to the Lake and our 4 acres of garden and woodlands. A short walk will take you to the edge of Lake Hayes with wonderful views of the local mountains. We are situated between Queenstown and historic Arrowtown. There is easy access to four of New Zealand's best ski fields and four very scenic golf courses. We enjoy meeting people and we will do all we can to make your time here memorable, including helping to plan your trips if you wish.

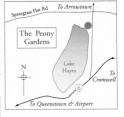

ANNA'S COTTAGE

67 Thompson Street, Queenstown
Ph (03) 442 8994, Fax (03) 441 8994
Mobile 027-693 3025
email: *annas.rose@xtra.co.nz*

Features & Attractions

- *Quality accommodation*
- *Very quiet location*
- *Tranquil garden setting*
- *Car parking at cottage*
- *Short walk to town centre*
- *Laundry facilities*

$	Double	$125
	Single	$95
	Cottage	$145

Self-contained Suites
Breakfast Available – Extra

Bedrooms	Qty
Double	3
Twin	
Single	
Bed Size	**Qty**
Super King	1
Queen	1
Double	
King/Single	1
Bathrooms	**Qty**
Ensuite	2
Private	
Guest Share	

DIRECTIONS: Take SH 6A into Queenstown, left at 2nd roundabout into Shotover St, through 2 more roundabouts. Turn at Waterfront Apartments into Brunswick Street, which goes into Thompson Street. **Anna's Cottage** is signposted.

A warm welcome to **Anna's Cottage** and **Rose Suite**. The **Cottage** has a fully equipped kitchen, living room, laundry, hairdryer, ensuite, quality linen and towels. The self-contained **Rose Suite**, which is attached to the end of our home, has a small kitchen, washing machine, queen bed with new ensuite, quality linen and towels. Both, **Cottage** and **Rose Suite**, are serviced daily.

Enjoy mountain views at this peaceful location. There is a private drive with parking at the **Cottage**. Thompson Street is just a few minutes from central Queenstown. Breakfast available at extra charge. We will help and offer advice on all Queenstown activities.

---

5 STAR LANE

5 Star Lane, Queenstown, Otago
Ph (03) 441 8118, Fax (03) 441 8116
email: *stay@5starlane.com*
www.5starlane.com

home
NEW ZEALAND

Features & Attractions

- *Lake and mountain views*
- *Finnish sauna*
- *Covered guest parking*
- *Delicious breakfast menu*
- *Air conditioning*
- *Email access and wireless LAN*

Luxury
Bed & Breakfast

$	Double	$185-265
	Single	$165-245
	Child	

E njoy the magnificent view from your own special corner of our home. Your luxurious bedroom has your choice of a super king or twin beds, spacious ensuite, individually controlled heating/cooling and private patio. Make yourself at home in the guest lounge/dining room with its cosy fire in winter and air conditioning in summer.

Take time to relax and unwind after a day enjoying the many activities Queenstown has to offer. Make the most of our personal attention and advice.

DIRECTIONS:
Take Highway 6a, Frankton Road, turn up the hill into Hensman Road, then 1st left into Panorama Terrace, then 1st right into Star Lane.

Bedrooms	Qty
Double	2
Twin	2
Single	
Bed Size	**Qty**
King	2
Queen	
Double	
King/Single	4
Bathrooms	**Qty**
Ensuite	2
Private	
Guest Share	

CORONET VIEW DELUXE BED & BREAKFAST
AND APARTMENTS

30 Huff Street, Queenstown
Ph (03) 442 6766, Fax (03) 442 6767
Mobile 027-432 0895
email: *stay@coronetview.com*
www.coronetview.com

Tariff : N.Z. Dollars	
Double	$165-250
Single	$150-230
Child	$30

Bedrooms	Qty
Double	7
Twin	3
Single	
Bed Size	**Qty**
Super King	6
King	
Queen	1
Double	
King/Single	3
Bathrooms	**Qty**
Ensuite	9
Private	1
Guest Share	

**Deluxe
Bed & Breakfast**

Features & Attractions

- *Wireless internet facilities*
- *Full laundry facilities*
- *Barbeque and spa area*
- *Self-catering apartments*
- *Close to town centre*
- *Web booking service*
- *Guiding service & tours*

Centrally located just ten minutes walk from town, Coronet View enjoys superb views of Coronet Peak, The Remarkables and Lake Wakatipu. Beautifully appointed rooms offer every comfort in either hosted accommodation or private apartments. Coronet View offers ten luxurious guest rooms plus three fully self-contained private apartments. Guest common areas occasionally shared with gorgeous persian cats include elevated and spacious dining and living areas, outdoor decks, a sunny conservatory, outdoor barbeque, pool and jacuzzi area and computers with internet access.

Bed & Breakfast - A home away from home with true kiwi hospitality. Most rooms feature super king beds with hand crafted fabric art quilts and all have sheepskin electric blankets. Your hosts are knowledgeable local people who can recommend and book your activities at no extra cost.

Apartments - 1-6 bedroom on site apartments. Most configurations feature ensuites, super king beds, generous living areas, fully equipped kitchens and laundries.

THE STABLE
17 Brisbane Street, Queenstown
Ph (03) 442 9251, Fax (03) 442 8293
email: *gimac@queenstown.co.nz*
www.thestablebb.co.nz

Features & Attractions

- *5 min. stroll to town*
- *100 metres to beach*
- *Historic building*
- *Quiet cul-de-sac*
- *Trees, gardens & birds*
- *No need for a car*

The Stable

DIRECTIONS: Follow SH 6A, **do not** veer right at the Millenium Hotel. Continue straight ahead. Brisbane St. (no exit) is 2nd on left. Phone if necessary.

**Historic Building
Bed & Breakfast**

Double	$180-200
Single	$150
Child	

A 130 year-old stone **stable**, converted for guest accommodation and listed by the New Zealand Historic Places Trust, shares a private courtyard with our home. The **Garden Room** is in the house. Both rooms are well heated with views of garden, lake or mountains. Tea / coffee making facilities are available at all times. Our home is in a quiet cul-de-sac and set in a garden abundant with rhododendrons and native birds. Less than 100 m from the beach. A small boat and canoe are available for guests' use. All tourist facilities are within easy walking distance. A courtesy car is available. Guests share our spacious living areas and make free use of our library and laundry. We can advise about and are booking agents for all sightseeing tours.

Bedrooms	Qty
Double	1
Twin	1
Single	
Bed Size	**Qty**
Super King	1
Queen	
Double	1
Single	2
Bathrooms	**Qty**
Ensuite	1
Private	1
Guest Share	

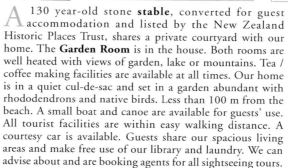

FINE ACCOMMODATION

5 Vancouver Drive, PO Box 1777, Queenstown
Ph (03) 441 8866, Fax (03) 442 9463
Mobile 027- 434 7209
email: *info@fineaccommodation.co.nz*
www.fineaccommodation.co.nz

Tariff : N.Z. Dollars	
Double	$220-260
Single	$200
Child	

Bedrooms	Qty
Double	3
Twin	
Single	

Bed Size	Qty
Super King	1
King	2
Queen	
Double	
Single	

Bathrooms	Qty
Ensuite	3
Private	
Guest Share	

**Quality Home
Bed & Breakfast**

Features & Attractions

- *Adventure capital of the world*
- *1km to downtown Queenstown*
- *Licensed tour operators*
- *Quality ensuites*
- *Quiet and private location*
- *Hosts been in tourism 22 years*
- *'Walter' marriage celebrant*
- *Views of lake & golf course*

You are assured of a warm welcome at **Fine Accommodation.** Your hosts Dale and Walter are semi retired after being in the tourism industry for over 22 years and are opening their home for Bed & Breakfast. We have three good-sized bedrooms with ensuite, one with a spa bath. We supply a continental breakfast of fresh fruits, cereals, yoghurt, toast, fruit juices, coffee and teas. On request dinners can also be provided. We are experienced in advising about the many activities and dining experiences around the Queenstown area. Walter is a Justice of the Peace and a very popular wedding celebrant. We are less than 5 minutes from downtown Queenstown. Recent guest's comments: *"Wonderful accommodation and what views, thank you for looking after us so well."* David & Pat U.K. *"Gracious hosts who have warmly welcomed Chris and I to their beautiful home with magnificent view from every aspect."* Chris & Sandra, Australia. *"Stunning spot, great room & delicious breakfast."* Nancy Viner, Toronto USA.

TRELAWN PLACE

35 Watties Track, off Gorge Rd, Arthurs Point,
PO Box 117, Queenstown
Ph (03) 442 9160 Fax (03) 442 9167
Mobile 021-101 5805
email: *trelawn@ihug.co.nz*
www.trelawnb-b.co.nz

Tariff : N.Z. Dollars	
Double	$350-395
Single	$275-350
Child	$60

Bedrooms	Qty
Double	5
Twin	3
Single	1
Bed Size	**Qty**
Super King	1
King	1
Queen	1
King/Single	2
Single	4
Bathrooms	**Qty**
Ensuite	3
Private	2
Guest Share	

**Luxury Bed & Breakfast
Self-contained Cottage**

Features & Attractions

- *Unique location beside the Shotover*
- *Fantastic mountain views*
- *Broadband wireless laptop*
- *Outdoor jacuzzi, spa, guest laundry*

- *5 min from town centre*
- *Large private garden*
- *Wedding venue*
- *Walkway to river*

Sited dramatically above the Shotover River with gardens and lawns sweeping to the cliff edge, **Trelawn Place** is a superior country lodge only four kilometres from busy Queenstown. We have five comfortably appointed ensuite rooms, furnished with country chintz and antique style furniture. Our guest sitting room has an open fire and a well stocked library. Outdoors you will find quiet sitting areas and shady vine-covered verandahs. Generous cooked breakfast features home-made and grown produce. If you are missing your pets, a cat and friendly corgis will make you feel at home. A forty-eight hour cancellation policy applies. Helpful information and bookings for all activities.

Two self-contained cottages, a honeymoon hideaway, with Juliet balconies, cosy fireside, roses framing the door.

CHARTLEA PARK

1 Chartlea Park Road, RD 1, Balfour
Ph/Fax (03) 201 6442, Mobile 027-285 5121
email: *ken.trish.mack@xtra.co.nz*
www.chartleaparkfarmstay.co.nz

home
NEW ZEALAND

Tariff : N.Z. Dollars	
Double	$140
Single	$85
Child u/12	$45

Bedrooms	Qty
Double	1
Twin	2
Single	

Bed Size	Qty
Super King	
King	
Queen	1
Double	
King/Single	4

Bathrooms	Qty
Private	2
Guest Share	1
Family Share	

**Historic Farm Homestead
Unique Farmstay Experience**

Features & Attractions

- *Farm experience*
- *Trout fishing rivers*
- *Vintage car/antique enthusiasts*
- *Beautiful garden setting*

- *Peaceful, rural retreat*
- *Relaxation at its best*
- *Home cooking a specialty*
- *Warm, friendly hospitality*

Chartlea Park Farmstay and the MacKenzie family welcomes you to a delightful corner of Northern Southland. Come and share a memorable experience on their 670 acre sheep, deer and beef farm. **Chartlea Park**, the original Balfour Homestead, dating back to 1896 and

once the hub of an 8559 acre estate, is perfectly positioned amidst some of the most beautiful New Zealand countryside. Our central position provides easy access to the delights of Invercargill, Te Anau and Queenstown (1 hour). Delight in wonderful home cooking, relax in our extensive garden setting, join us for a farm tour or assist with some farm activities. Or just enjoy the ambience of our home with its inviting range of antique treasures, reading material and music. We are committed to ensuring your time with us is **the** highlight of your holiday, from the welcoming refreshments on your arrival, through to your chance to meet and feed our pet animals to the tasty delights of your meals. For the keen fisherman we are minutes from some of the best fishing rivers around. Dinner on request at an extra charge.

ANTLER LODGE BED & BREAKFAST
44 Matai Street, Te Anau
Ph (03) 249 8188, Fax (03) 249 8188
Mobile 027-684 1385
email: *antler.lodge@xtra.co.nz*
www.antlerlodgeteanau.co.nz

Tariff : N.Z. Dollars	
Double	$120-155
Single	
Child	

Bedrooms	Qty
Double	3
Twin	
Single	
Bed Size	Qty
Super King	
King	1
Queen	2
Double	
Single	
Bathrooms	Qty
Ensuite	3
Private	
Guest Share	

Bed & Breakfast
Self-contained

Features & Attractions

- *Quality accommodation*
- *Close to restaurants & shops*
- *Trip bookings & pick-ups*
- *Mountain views*
- *2 fully self-contained units*
- *Continental breakfast*
- *Laundry facilities*
- *Off-street parking*

Helen and Chris warmly welcome you to Te Anau. We offer the privacy, independence and relaxation of self-contained units along with friendly helpful service. Our ground floor cottages have queen-size beds, full kitchen facilities and ensuite. While our upstairs unit has its own entrance to an attractive dining area that includes a refrigerator and microwave, the spacious bedroom, featuring warm timber and mountain views, has a king-size bed, a walk-in wardrobe and elegant ensuite.

All our rooms have relaxing, comfortable furnishings with efficient heating and electric blankets and of course complimentary tea and coffee. Breakfast is provided in the rooms for guests to enjoy at their leisure. We are looking forward to meeting you.

CAT'S WHISKERS BED & BREAKFAST
2 Lakefront Drive, Te Anau
Fax (03) 249 8112, Mobile 027-427 2624
e-mail: *book@catswhiskers.co.nz*
www.catswhiskers.co.nz

Features & Attractions

- *Lakefront location*
- *Fast Internet access*
- *10 min. walk to town*
- *Opposite Dep. of Conservation*
- *Cooked or continental breakfast*
- *Stunning mountain/lake views*

$		
Double	$165-195
Single	$130
Child	$40

Lakefront Bed & Breakfast

Bedrooms	Qty
Double	2
Twin	2
Single	
Bed Size	**Qty**
King	2
Queen	2
Double	
Single	
Bathrooms	**Qty**
Ensuite	4
Private	
Guest Share	

Stay for a few days and explore Fiordland National Park. Our home is a comfortable villa with 4 guest rooms, all with ensuite bathrooms. Our guests can enjoy the relaxing atmosphere and peaceful lakefront location with stunning views. Breakfast is usually a social occasion when you meet fellow guests around our dining table. You can enjoy a continental or cooked breakfast.
Lake Te Anau room has a kingsize bed. We have two rooms overlooking our garden courtyard with a queen and single beds. Our family room has a kingsize and 2 single beds.

COSY KIWI BED & BREAKFAST
186 Milford Road, Te Anau
Ph (03) 249 7475, Fax (03) 249 8471
email: *cosykiwi@xtra.co.nz* or *info@cosykiwi.com*
www.cosykiwi.com

Features & Attractions

- *Sumptuous breakfast buffet*
- *3 minute walk to centre*
- *Immaculately clean*
- *Trip booking and pick-up*
- *Email and fax facilities*
- *Off street parking*

$		
Triple	$175-190
Double	$140-160
Single	$130-140

Bed & Breakfast Guest House

Bedrooms	Qty
Double	7
Twin	4
Single	7
Bed Size	**Qty**
Super King	1
King	3
Queen	3
Single	7
Bathrooms	**Qty**
Ensuite	7
Private	
Guest Share	

Cosy truly describes how you will feel within our warm, architecturally designed, modern Bed & Breakfast home. We provide privacy with comfort. Our quiet bedrooms are spacious, ensuited with top quality beds, television, individual heating and double glazed windows. Enjoy a sumptuous buffet breakfast of homemade breads, topped with homemade jams, marmalade, fresh fruit salad, yoghurt, brewed coffee, special teas and our legendary pancakes sweet or savoury. We have a modern laundry, good off-street parking and luggage storage for track walkers. Our warm guest lounge provides excellent space to relax, chat and a computer to access emails.
Relax outside on our sun-terrace overlooking the ever-changing moods of the Murchison Mountains or stroll into the town centre to highly recommended restaurants (three minutes). We can recommend and book any sightseeing trips around Fiordland.

BLUE RIDGE BOUTIQUE BED&BREAKFAST

15 Melland Place, Te Anau, Fiordland
Ph (03) 249 7740, Fax (03) 249 7340
Mobile 027-258 9877
email: *info@blueridge.net.nz*
www.blueridge.net.nz

Tariff : N.Z. Dollars	
Double	$185-250
Single	$175-200
Child	neg.

Bedrooms	Qty
Double	4
Twin	2
Single	2
Bed Size	**Qty**
Super King	
King/Single	2
Queen	2
Double	
Single	2
Bathrooms	**Qty**
Ensuite	4
Private	
Guest Share	

Bed & Breakfast
Superior Accommodation

Features & Attractions

- Friendly, helpful hosts
- Peaceful, quiet setting
- 2 mins to town centre
- Delicious full breakfast
- Spa pool
- Complimentary port
- Home baking in rooms
- High speed internet & fax

Two types of accommodation are available at **Blue Ridge**. *The Kea Room:* A comfortable queen room with ensuite bathroom which also has a private sitting room where you can relax with a book, watch TV, or make a cup of tea or coffee.

Luxury Studio Units: *The Kaka, Bellbird, & Tui Rooms* – Each has a comfortable king/twin or queen bed. The décor is tasteful and modern in neutral tones with rich, warm accents. Beds have luxurious bed linen with sumptuous drapes and throws and there is strong use of hand-crafted native wood and wrought iron in the furniture. There is a sofa, dining table, chairs and a TV. All rooms have kitchenettes with microwave, fridge, kettle and toaster. The ensuite bathrooms are beautifully tiled with underfloor heating, heated towel rail, heater, hairdryer and bathrobes. All rooms are double glazed and have electric heating.

We are happy to make bookings for local attractions and excursions. Meet Latté and Meg, our very friendly Birman cats.

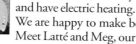

BLUE THISTLE COTTAGES

Rapid 168, Milford-Te Anau Highway, Te Anau
Ph (03) 249 8338
email: *info@bluethistlecottages.com*
www.bluethistlecottages.com

Tariff : N.Z. Dollars	
Double	$195-275
Single	
Child	

Bedrooms	Qty
Double	4
Twin	
Single	

Bed Size	Qty
Super King	
King	
Queen	4
Double	
Single	2

Bathrooms	Qty
Ensuite	4
Private	
Guest Share	

Luxury Cottages
Self-contained

DIRECTIONS:
Follow Milford-Te Anau
Highway 94 1½ km from town.

Features & Attractions

- *Magnificent views*
- *On road to Milford Sound*
- *Complimentary fastnet connection*
- *Large ensuite bedrooms*
- *Sky/cable television*
- *Friendly hosts*
- *Peaceful & quiet*
- *Smoke free*

Welcome to **Blue Thistle**. Our luxury self-contained cottages were opened for guests in January 2004. We are situated on ten acres of land just 1½ km from Te Anau on the road to Milford Sound. Each cottage is individually decorated and all have superb views. The bedroom has a queen slat bed with quality linen and electric blanket. The large ensuite bathroom has heated towel rails, heat lamps, hair dryer, fluffy robes and toiletries. The lounge has cable/Sky television, telephone, fastnet internet connection and CD/radio. The kitchen has a refrigerator, microwave and selection of teas and coffees.

We have been involved with tourism for the past sixteen years, previously in Franz Josef and also in Picton. You are likely to be met by Paris, a very friendly German shorthaired pointer. We also have three cats and several friendly Dexter cows. Allow yourself a couple of days to relax and enjoy all that Te Anau and **Blue Thistle** has to offer. Discount for two or more nights. Now available large two bedroom cottage – minimum two night stay. No meals included.

DUNLUCE BED & BREAKFAST

Aparima Drive, Te Anau, Fiordland
Ph (03) 249 7715, Fax (03) 249 7703
Mobile 027-330 2779
e-mail: *info@dunluce-fiordland.co.nz.*
www.dunluce-fiordland.co.nz.

Tariff : N.Z. Dollars	
Double	$195-250
Single	$170-220
Child	

Bedrooms	Qty
Double	4
Twin	
Single	

Bed Size	Qty
Super King	
King	4
Queen	
Double	
Single	

Bathrooms	Qty
Ensuite	4
Private	
Guest Share	

**Bed & Breakfast
Boutique Accommodation**

Features & Attractions

- *Gateway to Fiordland*
- *Lake & Mountain views*
- *Private guest wing*
- *Delicious full breakfast*
- *High standard guaranteed*
- *Warm & friendly hospitality*
- *Luxurious ensuite rooms*
- *Walking distance to town*

DIRECTIONS:
From Milford Rd turn left into
Howden Street and right into
Aparima Drive. We are 300
metres along Aparima Drive.

We welcome you to **Dunluce Bed & Breakfast** - a brand new architecturally designed home which has been purpose built with a guest wing offering you comfort, warmth, privacy and panoramic lake and mountain views. We are a 15 minute walk to the town centre or a 2 minute drive. All rooms have full-length glass doors that open to private decks facing the view. The rooms are modern and uncluttered in style with luxurious king size beds, quality bedding, electric blankets, heating, TV, DVD and broadband connection. The rooms have tiled ensuites with glass wall showers, underfloor heating, mirror demisters, pure lavender toiletries, hair dryers and luxurious towels. Our deluxe room has a deep double soaking/spa bath.

Guests have a private entrance and a lounge/dining room where an extensive homemade continental and cooked breakfast is served. We have tea and coffee making facilities, home baking, a guest fridge and a good selection of books, games and magazines. The lounge has air-conditioning, heating and a gas fire. We have ample parking space and offer locked storage and complimentary laundry facilities. We are able to give informed advice on local attractions and make bookings.

HOUSE OF WOOD

44 Moana Crescent, Te Anau
Ph (03) 249 8404, Fax (03) 249 7676
Mobile 021-158 6686
email: *houseofwood@xtra.co.nz*
www.houseofwood.co.nz

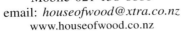

@ home
NEW ZEALAND

Tariff : N.Z. Dollars	
Double	$115-135
Single	$100-125
Child	Neg.

Bedrooms	Qty
Double	3
Twin	1
Single	

Bed Size	Qty
Super King	1
King	
Queen	3
Double	
King/Single	2

Bathrooms	Qty
Ensuite	3
Private	1
Guest Share	

Homestay Bed & Breakfast

Features & Attractions

- *Fishing, golf and tramping*
- *Friendly hosts*
- *Fiordland National Park*
- *Town centre 2 min. walk*
- *Hearty cooked breakfast*
- *Dinner by arrangement*
- *Views of the mountains*
- *Mountain bikes available*

We welcome you to our home, the **House of Wood**. Built of exotic timbers, it's conveniently located within two minutes' walk of our township with shops, restaurants, post office and cinema and a short walk to Lake Te Anau. Each room has comfortable beds, electric blanket, tea-making facilities, hairdryer, heater and outdoor table and chairs, so guests can admire the beautiful views from our balconies. We offer a delicious cooked breakfast and guests share a lounge. Dinner by arrangement. Our varied interests include golf, rowing, reading, gardening, fishing and boating. We can offer advice on tours available and can book them for you. For tourist trips you will be picked up from our gate. Two mountain bikes and luggage storage available. Laundromats nearby. We look forward to meeting you and sharing our slice of paradise.

CROWN LEA FARMSTAY

310 Gillespie Road, RD 1, Te Anau
Ph (03) 249 8598, Fax (03) 249 8598
Mobile 025-227 8366
email: *crownlea@xtra.co.nz*
www.crown-lea.com

Features & Attractions

- *Working sheep, cattle & deer farm*
- *Farmstyle dinners by arrangement*
- *Doubtful & Milford Sound day trips*
- *Farm tour available*
- *Local walking tracks*
- *Great fishing rivers*

Farmstay		Double	$140-160
		Single	$130-150
		Child	

Bedrooms	Qty
Double	2
Twin	1
Single	
Bed Size	**Qty**
Super King	1
Queen	1
Double	
Single	3
Bathrooms	**Qty**
Ensuite	1
Private	2
Guest Share	

DIRECTIONS: Please phone for simple directions.

We warmly welcome you to **Crown Lea**, our 900 acre sheep, cattle and deer working farm, offering an informative farm tour and sheep dogs working, after 6pm, with spectacular views of Lake Manapouri, the Fiordland Mountains and Te Anau Basin. Following the farm tour, a traditional farmstyle dinner (NZ $35 per person) of home grown produce is served. Our large, modern family home has three bedrooms for guests, electric blankets on all beds, heaters in each room, ensuite and private bathrooms. **Crown Lea** is within easy access of Doubtful and Milford Sounds, the glow worm caves, Milford and Kepler tracks or the superb fishing rivers in our area. We recommend at least two nights to enable relaxing days enjoying the Sounds, caves, tracks, sightseeing or fishing. Having travelled ourselves, we enjoy meeting guests from all parts of the world and we and Harriet, our cat, look forward to meeting you.

LYNWOOD PARK BED & BREAKFAST

State Highway 94, RD 2, Te Anau, Fiordland
Ph (03) 249 7990
Mobile 021-129 5626
e-mail: *lynwood.park@xtra.co.nz*

Features & Attractions

- *Country tranquility*
- *Home-like atmosphere*
- *Bird-filled garden & pets*
- *Pool table*
- *Laundry facilities, free*
- *'Laid back', friendly hosts*

Countrystay Bed & Breakfast		Double	$125
		Single	$100
		Child	$50

Bedrooms	Qty
Double	
Twin	
Single	
Bed Size	**Qty**
King	
Queen	4
Double	
Single	
Bathrooms	**Qty**
Ensuite	2
Private	
Guest Share	1

Kia Ora - Haere mai ki ta matou kainga. We are both of Nga Puhi/Irish descent, please expect to be greeted with the traditional 'hongi' on arrival. **Lynwood Park** is set amidst snow-capped mountains (Takitimu) and lovely green family farmland, just 5 min. drive to Te Anau and all of Fiordland's unique features. We are pleased to offer our guests a quiet relaxing stay during their visit to our beautiful country. **Lynwood Park** is the ideal honeymooners' retreat, self-catering continental breakfast provided, including fresh baked croissants, ham, cheeses, tomato and salami - delivered to you each morning. With 10 years experience and local knowledge we would like to help you book your ideal holiday attractions. All lifestyles welcome and catered for – Mauriora.

LOCHVISTA
454C State Highway 94, RD 1, Te Anau
Ph (03) 249 7273, Fax (03) 249 7278
Mobile 027-455 9949
email: *lochvista@xtra.co.nz*
www.lochvista.co.nz

Tariff : N.Z. Dollars	
Double	$140-170
Single	$140-150
Child	

Bedrooms	Qty
Double	2
Twin	
Single	

Bed Size	Qty
Super King	
King	1
Queen	1
Double	
Single	

Bathrooms	Qty
Ensuite	2
Private	
Guest Share	

  **Lakeside Bed & Breakfast**

Features & Attractions

- *Stunning mountain views*
- *Shops, cafés, bars - short drive*
- *Fishing & golfing*
- *Tramping & hiking*
- *On road to Milford Sound*
- *Overlooking Lake Te Anau*
- *Spectacular lake views*
- *Glowworm cave excursions*

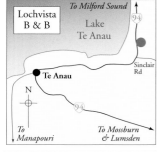

DIRECTIONS:
Travel along Milford Rd 4.6 km from the 80 km sign. Turn 1st right after Sinclair Rd and blue Lodge sign. Go 300m up road, turn right at the three letter boxes, following driveway down to house.

Welcome to magical Fiordland. **Lochvista** is situated on the Te Anau Milford highway just five kilometres from the town centre. **Lochvista** is ideally positioned, overlooking Lake Te Anau and the stunning Murchison Mountains. I have two rooms, one with king/twin bed and one with queen bed, both with ensuite, tea and coffee making facilities, refrigerator, television and hairdryer. French doors open onto the patio where you can sit and enjoy the spectacular views. Meet Mischief (my pet cat). Full cooked breakfast on request at $15 per person.

Fiordland has a great deal to offer and I am more than happy to help my guests with any bookings to make their stay more relaxing.

TE ANAU LODGE

52 Howden Street, Te Anau, Fiordland
Ph (03) 249 7477, Fax (03) 249 7487
Mobile 021-064 9354
email: *info@teanaulodge.co.nz*
www.teanaulodge.com

Tariff : N.Z. Dollars	
Double	$200-350
Single	$170-320
Child	

Bedrooms	Qty
Double	8
Twin	3
Single	8
Bed Size	**Qty**
Super King	3
King/Single	3
Queen	5
Double	
Single	4
Bathrooms	**Qty**
Ensuite	7
Private	1
Guest Share	

Luxury Bed & Breakfast
Historic Convent

Features & Attractions

- *Historic 'Sisters of Mercy' Convent*
- *Gateway to Fiordland Nat. Park*
- *Doubtful and Milford Sounds*
- *Hiking and walking*
- *Excellent trout fishing*
- *Kayaking*
- *Bird & nature watching*
- *Gardens & Stargazing*

DIRECTIONS:
Leaving the town towards
Milford, Howden Street is
the 2nd left off Milford Road.

Advance booking recommended.

We are delighted to offer you a unique opportunity to come and stay with us here at **Te Anau Lodge**, our lovingly restored former convent. At **Te Anau Lodge** we have endeavored to create an atmosphere which is homely, warm and inviting, where you can relax and unwind after a day of exploring stunning Fiordland.

Built in 1936, and more recently relocated to Te Anau from nearby Nightcaps, this former 'Sisters of Mercy' Convent still retains much of its original décor. **Te Anau Lodge** is positioned at the northern end of Te Anau township, surrounded by breathtaking lake and mountain views. The location of the lodge is quiet and tranquil, yet only 15 minutes walk to the town centre.

Enjoy our famous cooked breakfasts in the Chapel with plenty of home-made goodies, spend your evenings relaxing in our cosy guest library or having a drink in our sunny courtyard. Complimentary laundry facilities, luggage storage and high speed wireless internet access.
A unique and special accommodation experience.

Rob And Nancys Place

13 Fergus Square, Te Anau, Fiordland
Ph (03) 249 8241, Fax (03) 249 7397
email: *rob.nancy@xtra.co.nz*
www.homestays.net.nz/RobandNancys.htm

Features & Attractions

- *Warm, friendly atmosphere*
- *Quiet and peaceful*
- *Scrumptious breakfasts*
- *5 min. walk to town centre*
- *Off-street car parking*
- *Tour transfers to the door*

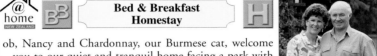

$	Double	$140-160
	Single	$130
	Child	n/a

Bed & Breakfast Homestay

Bedrooms	Qty
Double	2
Twin	
Single	
Bed Size	**Qty**
King	2
Queen	
Double	
Single	
Bathrooms	**Qty**
Ensuite	1
Private	1
Guest Share	

Rob, Nancy and Chardonnay, our Burmese cat, welcome you to our quiet and tranquil home facing a park with mountain views. It's just five minutes walk to the lake and town centre. We are a couple, retired from farming and enjoy meeting people and cooking generous breakfasts with homemade preserves and bread. Our modern home includes a courtyard barbeque and gardens.

Te Anau is a special place to visit, with the magnificent scenery of the Fiordland National Park, including Milford and Doubtful Sounds and walking tracks. All tours include pick-up and delivery to the door. Off-street parking and storage is available.

DIRECTIONS: Continue on around the lakefront to Matai Street, turn right, cross over Mokonui Street, first left into Fergus Square.

Rose'n'Reel

89 Ben Loch Lane, RD 2, Te Anau, Fiordland
Ph/Fax (03) 249 7582, Mobile 027-454 5723
email: *rosenreel@xtra.co.nz*
www.rosenreel.co.nz

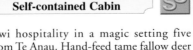

Features & Attractions

- *Lake & mountain views*
- *Extensive garden*
- *Peaceful farm location*
- *Guided fishing available*
- *Feed tame deer*
- *Warm country hospitality*

$	Double	$90-110
	Single	$65-80
	Child	neg

Deer Farm Bed & Breakfast Self-contained Cabin

Bedrooms	Qty
Double	2
Twin	
Single	1
Bed Size	**Qty**
King	
Queen	2
Double	1
King/Single	1
Bathrooms	**Qty**
Ensuite	
Private	1
Guest Share	1

Genuine Kiwi hospitality in a magic setting five minutes from Te Anau. Hand-feed tame fallow deer and meet our two friendly cats and Meg the dog. Relax on the verandah of our fully self-contained cabin and enjoy watching deer with a magnificent lake and mountain backdrop. The two-room cabin has cooking facilities, refrigerator, microwave, television, one queen and one double bed plus bathroom. Our modern smoke-free home is set in an extensive garden and has two downstairs guest bedrooms. Lex is a keen fly fisherman and guide and is available for guiding on our beautiful local rivers. Lyn loves to garden and enjoys sharing her garden with guests. Fiordland is a special place and we will do all we can to make your time here memorable, including helping to plan and book your trips if you so wish.

DIRECTIONS:
Please phone or email for bookings and easy directions

THE CROFT

Rapid 153, Milford Sound Road, RD 1, Te Anau
Ph (03) 249 7393, Fax (03) 249 7393
Mobile 027-682 0061
email: *jane@thecroft.co.nz*
www.thecroft.co.nz

Tariff : N.Z. Dollars	
Double	$150-175
Single	
Child	

Bedrooms	Qty
Double	2
Twin	
Single	
Bed Size	**Qty**
Super King	
King	
Queen	2
Double	
Single	1
Bathrooms	**Qty**
Ensuite	2
Private	
Guest Share	

 **Bed & Breakfast
Self-contained Accommodation**

Features & Attractions

- *Magnificent views*
- *Tranquil surroundings*
- *Modern private cottages*
- *Warm & friendly Kiwi hosts*
- *On the road to Milford Sound*
- *Small farm with pet sheep*
- *Walk across farm to lake*
- *Large private gardens*

DIRECTIONS:
Follow the Te Anau-Milford Highway 94
for 3 km from Te Anau town centre.
"The Croft" and "Bed & Breakfast" signs
are at the gate.
We are Rapid No. 153.

Warm hospitality and quality accommodation are guaranteed at The Croft, a lifestyle farm, just two minutes from Te Anau on the Milford Sound Road. Our two modern self-contained cottages enjoy magnificent lake and mountain views, are set in large tranquil gardens. Timber ceilings, window seats, large ensuite bathrooms, elegant furnishings are some of the highlights of our two spacious cottages. Both have microwaves, refrigerators, CD/mini systems,

DVDs and televisions. Enjoy a generous continental breakfast with Ross and Jane or have it served in your cottage at your leisure.

Pets include Dolly the sheep, Mac the Jack Russell, and Jerry and Kitty the cats. We have a small flock of sheep. Ross is a builder and Jane a past teacher. The Croft is an ideal base for all the many activities available in Fiordland.

Sign at gate.

SHAKESPEARE HOUSE

10 Dusky Street, PO Box 32, Te Anau
Ph (03) 249 7349, Fax (03) 249 7629
Mobile 021-101 1794
email: *marg.shakespeare.house@xtra.co.nz*
www.shakespearehouse.co.nz

Features & Attractions

- All ground floor units
- 10 min walk to town centre
- Courtesy car
- Trip bookings & pick-up
- Continental & cooked breakfast
- Internet & payphone on site

Double	$100-130
Single	$90-110
Child	$1-15

Guest House & Self-contained Accommodation

Bedrooms	Qty
Double	4
Twin/Triple	3
Quad	1
Bed Size	**Qty**
Super King	2
King	4
Double	
King/Single	2
Bathrooms	**Qty**
Ensuite	8
Private	
Guest Share	

Fiordland – the "Walking Capital" of the world – is right on your doorstep when you stay at **Shakespeare House**. Marg and Jeff extend a warm welcome to you and offer personal attention in a homely atmosphere. We are situated in a quiet residential area, yet are within walking distance of shops, lake, restaurants and attractions. Our units have their own private facilities, are warm and comfortable with tea/coffee, television and have the choice of king or twin beds. They open onto a sunny, relaxing conservatory where you may share your holiday experiences with other guests. We also have a two bedroom self-contained unit, which is popular with families or two couples travelling together. Our dining room catches the morning sun and has a lovely view of the mountains. Enjoy a substantial breakfast – either cooked from the menu or buffet-style continental. Good off-street parking, washing machine and dryers are available. We invite you to experience our hospitality.

DIRECTIONS: Drive north on Lake Front Drive, carry on along Te Anau Terrace. Dusky Street is the last right turn before the boat harbour.

"THE COTTAGE" HOMESTAY B & B

Waiau Street, Manapouri, Fiordland
Ph (03) 249 6838, Mobile 021-138 6110
email: *don.joymacduff@xtra.co.nz*
www.thecottagefiordland.co.nz

Features & Attractions

- Doubtful Sound boat, 2min walk
- Bush, mountain & water views
- Native bush walks and birdlife
- Genuine 'Kiwi' hospitality
- Yummy homemade breakfasts
- Peace and tranquility

Double	$120-150
Single	$100-120
Child	

Tranquil Cottage Homestay, Bed & Breakfast

Bedrooms	Qty
Double	2
Twin	1
Single	
Bed Size	**Qty**
King	
Queen	2
Double	
Single	2
Bathrooms	**Qty**
Ensuite	3
Private	
Guest Share	

Gateway to Doubtful Sound, an ideal base to explore the wonders of majestic Fiordland. Our spacious Homestay Bed & Breakfast in a tranquil country setting, offers old-world charm with loads of warm Kiwi hospitality. Enjoy a glass of wine or Southern Man beer before a pleasant evening stroll to one of our local cafés. Our cottage décor home has comfortable ensuite rooms and doors to cottage gardens where you may relax listening to the bird song, with bush, mountain and water views. A yummy homemade continental breakfast, which includes a boiled egg from Hamish's girls, is a good start to the day. May we, Don, Joy and Millie (our bearded collie), wish you a wonderful Fiordland holiday and safe travelling!

DIRECTIONS: Pass old churches, shop, garage on left, continue down hill towards Pearl Harbour. We are on the right.

CATHEDRAL PEAKS B&B

44 Cathedral Drive, Manapouri, Fiordland
Ph (03) 249 6640, Fax (03) 2496648
email: *cathedralpeaks@ihug.co.nz*
www.cathedralpeaks.com

Tariff : N.Z. Dollars	
Double	$150-250
Single	$130-200
Child	

Bedrooms	Qty
Double	3
Twin	
Single	

Bed Size	Qty
Super King/Twin	1
King	
Queen	1
Double	1
Single	

Bathrooms	Qty
Ensuite	3
Private	
Guest Share	

   Beautiful Lake Manapouri's Boutique Accommodation

Features & Attractions

- Smoke free
- Restaurant 3min. walk
- Spacious ensuite rooms
- Off-street parking
- Lake & mountain views
- Guest lounge/dining room
- Doubtful & Milford Sounds daytrips
- Fax, phone, email available

Janice and Neal, your friendly hosts, warmly welcome you to share their new and tastefully appointed home. Take advantage of our lakefront location to relax and enjoy the majestic and stunning

scenery from the comfort of your bedroom. Enjoy a continental or cooked breakfast in our exclusive self-contained guest lounge/dining room overlooking the lake. Rooms have tea/coffee making facilities, TV, heater, electric blanket, refrigerator and hairdryer. Looking towards the setting sun your view is rimmed with mountain peaks. Snow-capped in winter, unmarked by man's hand, their forested flanks lead your eyes to Lake Manapouri's edge. Forested islands blend into a silvered surface, which reflects mountain images, clouds, colours, stars, rainbows, the moon. Marvelous Manawapouri, even the name is shrouded in myth, mystery and mistakes. The mood ever changing, enchants – you may wish to never leave. 15 minutes drive to Lake Te Anau. 2 ½ hours drive to Milford Sound. 15 minutes walk to the Doubtful Sound departure point.

CORAL SEA COTTAGE &
OCEAN VIEW APARTMENTS
34 Harlech Street, Oamaru
Ph (03) 437 1422, Fax (03) 437 1427
Mobile 021-659 757 or 021-042 6997
email: *nmountain@xtra.co.nz*

Tariff : N.Z. Dollars	
Double	$90-145
Single	$40-90
Child	$0-25

Bedrooms	Qty
Double	2
Twin/Super King	4
Single	1

Bed Size	Qty
Super King/Twin	4
King	
Queen	2
Double	
Single	1

Bathrooms	Qty
Ensuite	2
Private	2
Guest Share	

**Magnificent Views
Rural Setting**

DIRECTIONS: From North: On right, after New World, Harlech St is 3rd road. From South: Drive through town centre, head north for approx 2km. 2nd on left after shops is Harlech St. Go to end and over cattle grid. Turn left to **Coral Sea Cottage**, straight ahead and up hill to **Ocean View**.

Features & Attractions

- *Secluded cosy cottage*
- *Bright & newly equipped*
- *Panoramic ocean views*
- *Quiet and peaceful*

- *Rural five acre location*
- *5 min. from town centre*
- *Famous blue penguins*
- *Historic stone buildings*

Come and relax at **Coral Sea Cottage** or **Ocean View** on a rural hillside with wonderful views of the ocean, town, harbour and surrounding countryside. Enjoy feeding our pet farm animals and visiting our son's art gallery. **Coral Sea Cottage** is a charming three-bedroomed holiday home, colourfully decorated with a fishy theme in its own grounds. **Ocean View**, our home at the top of the hill with magnificent panoramic views, has three bright new self-contained apartments – The Harbour, Penguin and Pacific Suites. Sky TV (except Pacific Suite). Toys, cot, breakfast basket available. We are near local shops and restaurants and five minutes drive to the historic town centre, art galleries and little blue penguin colony. Other attractions include yellow-eyed penguins, historic farm, surfing, golf and fishing. We look forward to welcoming you and are happy to offer help with planning your visit to our area.

"A touch of heaven in a busy world" (NZ guests).
"An absolute delight, the hosts, cottage and Oamaru" (UK guests).
"Great Beds", *"Very friendly and informative"* (Australian guests).
"Best stay we had" (German guests).

CHIMNEYS HOMESTAY BED & BREAKFAST

46 Reed Street, Oamaru, North Otago
Ph (03) 434 9824 Fax (03) 434 9824
Mobile 027-308 6369
email: *chimneys@xtra.co.nz*
www.chimneys-bnb.co.nz

Features & Attractions

- *Central city*
- *Clean, comfortable beds & rooms*
- *Dinner by arrangement*
- *Full cooked breakfast*
- *Historical Oamaru*
- *Blue & Yellow Penguins*

 **Early 1900's Character House
Oamaru Stone & Native Timber**

Double	$115-150
Single	$85-135
Extra pp	$5-35

Welcome to the 'Capital of Penguins'

Chimneys Homestay Bed & Breakfast was built in 1910 as a doctor's residence using Oamaru stone and native timber. Its unusual design is full of character – we love this house, and we hope you will too!! Since purchasing the house in March 2005 we have invested a great deal of time and effort carefully refurbishing our home to its former glory. This is an ongoing process which is not finished yet! While staying at **Chimneys Homestay Bed & Breakfast**, you will re-discover the prosperity of the city of Oamaru about 100 years ago. We are located in the central city, handy to shops, bus terminal, Oamaru historical precinct and penguin colonies. We are looking forward to seeing you here!!!

Bedrooms	Qty
Double	2
Twin	1
Single	1
Bed Size	**Qty**
King	
Queen	2
Double	
Single	5
Bathrooms	**Qty**
Ensuite	1
Private	1
Guest Share	1

EDEN LODGE

39 Eden St, Oamaru
Ph (03) 434 6524
e-mail: *ian@edenlodgeoamaru.co.nz*
www.edenlodgeoamaru.co.nz

Features & Attractions

- *Historic Oamaru stone house*
- *Off-street parking*
- *Walking tracks & gardens*
- *Historic precinct*
- *Penguin colony*
- *Restaurants*

$	Double	$100-120
	Single	$65
	Child	

Historic Homestay
Bed & Breakfast

Bedrooms	Qty
Double	3
Twin	1
Single	1
Bed Size	Qty
Queen	1
Double	2
King/Single	1
Single	2
Bathrooms	Qty
Ensuite	
Private	2
Guest Share	2

I invite you to stay in the lovingly renovated **Eden Lodge**, a central, yet peaceful Victorian Oamaru Stone House, one of Oamaru's earliest. My house retains the graciousness of a bygone era while offering all modern comforts. Enjoy the unique spacious bedrooms, filled with antique furniture and collectables. Relax in the garden, on the terrace or in the guest library and lounge. Linger over your tasty continental breakfast before exploring the wide range of activities available in Oamaru. Walking distance to shops, public gardens, walking tracks, museum, galleries, historic precinct, Janet Frame house and penguin colonies. I look forward to welcoming you with a refreshing tea or coffee whilst informing you of local sights.

HIGHWAY HOUSE

43 Lynn Street, Oamaru
Ph/Fax (03) 437 1066
email: *cns@ihug.co.nz*
www.highwayhouse.co.nz

VISA
MasterCard
AMERICAN EXPRESS

Features & Attractions

- *Historic Oamaru (stone)*
- *Harbour and blue penguins*
- *Idyllic rural scenery*
- *Free internet/email access*
- *English home/courtesy car*
- *French also spoken*

$	Double	$120-165
	Single	$100-130
	Child	neg

Boutique
Bed & Breakfast

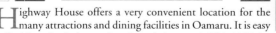

Bedrooms	Qty
Double	2
Twin	1
Single	
Bed Size	Qty
King	2
Queen	
Double	
Single	2
Bathrooms	Qty
Ensuite	1
Guest Share	1
Family Share	1

Highway House offers a very convenient location for the many attractions and dining facilities in Oamaru. It is easy to find from both the north and south (see map). This 1935 Arts and crafts character house and garden have been redeveloped with professional interior design and horticultural expertise for the tourists' pleasure, comfort and convenience. Attention has been given to top-quality beds, large showers, internet access, garden seating and off-street parking, together with tasteful extras. We provide a cooked and/or a light Kiwi breakfast using appetizing and sustaining wholesome ingredients. Stephanie and Norman wish you to make the most of your stay in Oamaru and can assist with your travel plans.

A recent comment: *"Great hospitality and breakfast. A credit to tourism in NZ, Thanks"* Auckland.

TOTARA PARK COUNTRY STAY

135 Maudes Road, PO Box 17, Oamaru
Ph (03) 434 8949
Mobile 027-228 5750
email: *totarapark@netspeed.net.nz*

Tariff : N.Z. Dollars	
Double	$120-160
Single	$80-110
Child	

Bedrooms	Qty
Double	1
Twin	
Single	

Bed Size	Qty
Super King	
King	
Queen	1
Double	
Single	

Bathrooms	Qty
Ensuite	1
Private	
Guest Share	

 Countrystay Bed & Breakfast

Features & Attractions

- *Country tranquility*
- *Separate, peaceful, private room*
- *Numerous animals*
- *3km to Oamaru*
- *Close to historic area*
- *Penguins*
- *Trout & salmon fishing*
- *Spa available*

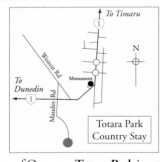

Just three kilometres from the centre of Oamaru, **Totara Park** is set amongst many beautiful trees, is very quiet and private. Bellbirds are frequent visitors. Domestic animals include Pogo, our pet rainbow lorikeet, who is most entertaining. Our guest room is large, separate and private with ensuite, refrigerator, television, stereo and snack facilities. The very comfy queen bed has quality linen and an electric blanket. Continental breakfast is substantial and includes homemade bread. A cooked breakfast is available and includes home grown and cured bacon. A spa and laundry facilities are also available.

Oamaru is close to the Waitaki River and within 2½ hours of Mt Cook. There are great climbing, tramping, boating and fishing opportunities this area.

The historic area and blue penguin viewing are just minutes away, as are the many restaurants and cafés in the town.

RANUI RETREAT

27 Woolshed Road, 8D RD, Totara, Oamaru
Ph (03) 439 5241
email: *happy1@actrix.gen.nz*
www.ranui-retreat.co.nz

Tariff : N.Z. Dollars	
Double	$125-160
Single	$100
Child	neg

Bedrooms	Qty
Double	2
Twin	
Single	

Bed Size	Qty
Super King	
King	
Queen	2
Double	
Single	

Bathrooms	Qty
Ensuite	1
Private	1
Guest Share	1

DIRECTIONS: Woolshed Road is off SH 1, second driveway on left.

**Bed & Breakfast
Homestay**

Features & Attractions

- *Quiet surroundings*
- *Friendly hospitality*
- *Comfortable, warm rooms*
- *1½ hours to skifield*
- *Arts & craft pursuits*
- *Dinner by arrangement*
- *Local & organic food*
- *Close to golf courses*

Welcome to **Ranui Retreat**. We are eight minutes south of historic Oamaru and 200m off the main highway to Dunedin. Views of Otago rural landscape stretching to the Kakanui Mountains enhance the rural sense of this five acre property of mature oak, elm and ash trees.

The land was originally part of the nearby Totara Estate. The garden is planted out in native and exotic trees, shrubs and a newly established olive grove. There is birdsong aplenty. Character bedrooms include rich, handmade patchwork quilts and throws of unique design, which add to the relaxed ambience. You are welcome to join the family for the evening or you may like to retire to other spaces with music and a good book from our library selection.

GLEN DENDRON FARMSTAY

284 Breakneck Rd, Waianakarua, RD Oamaru
Ph (03) 439 5288, Fax (03) 439 5288
Mobile 021-615 227
email: *anne.john.mackay@xtra.co.nz*
www.glenhomestays.co.nz

Features & Attractions

* 5 acres garden & views
* Feed sheep & alpacas
* Private golf course
* Bush walks, birds, waterfalls
* Penguin & seal colonies
* Moeraki Boulders nearby

**Award-winning Farmstay
With Spectacular Views**

Double	$120-160
Single	$100-120
Child	$45

DIRECTIONS:
Please phone for directions.

Our modern, award-winning homestay is spectacularly sited on a hilltop with panoramic river valley and ocean views. Enjoy tranquility and beauty when you stay in tastefully furnished bedrooms, two with ensuites. Explore the 5-acre garden and small farm. Feed sheep and alpacas, stroll through the forest or along the river, or play a round on our private 9-hole golf course. After a day of exploring the delights of the area, join us for a three-course dinner with wine. We are very keen gardeners.

After a lifetime in large-scale farming and forestry, before retiring to this 100 acre property, we now relish the opportunity to share our lifestyle with guests. Our adult family all live overseas so we travel frequently and have a great interest in other countries and cultures. An overnight stay is not enough to do justice to this area, so plan to stay a while! We don't mind short notice!

Bedrooms	Qty
Double	4
Twin	
Single	
Bed Size	**Qty**
SuperKing/Twin	2
Queen	2
Double	
Single	
Bathrooms	**Qty**
Ensuite	2
Private	
Guest Share	1

BOUTIQUE BED & BREAKFAST

107 Jefferis Road, Waikouaiti, East Otago
Ph (03) 465 7239, Fax (03) 465 7239
Mobile 027-224 8212
email: *info@boutiquebedandbreakfast.co.nz*
www.boutiquebedandbreakfast.co.nz

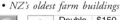

Features & Attractions

* Ideal setting to relax
* Situated on deer farm
* 30 min. north of Dunedin
* 4 hrs. to Christchurch
* Close to 2 golf courses
* NZ's oldest farm buildings

**Farmstay
Self-contained**

Double	$150-180
Single	$150
Child	

The uniqueness of **Boutique Bed & Breakfast** is its tranquil ambience, situated amongst picturesque Otago countryside where the beauty of nature blends with exceptional hospitality to offer you a truly memorable experience. This charming historic cottage with its completely rebuilt interior, contains 3 luxury units. Each room has private entrance, bathroom and kitchen facilities, quality furnishings, linen, fresh baking and coffee on arrival, fruit bowl, tennis court and BBQ. Enjoy a freshly baked breakfast, either in your room, on the verandah while watching deer graze, or in John and Barbara's homestead. Complimentary farm tour, beautiful beach, yellow-eyed penguins, seals and birds at Tavora Reserve. Visit historic buildings, local shops, cafés or the Moeraki Boulders. (Celebrity British chef, Rick Stein, was a recent guest.)

Bedrooms	Qty
Double	3
Twin	
Single	
Bed Size	**Qty**
King	
Queen	3
Double	
Single	
Bathrooms	**Qty**
Ensuite	3
Private	
Guest Share	

To Oamaru
Palmerston
Boutique
Bed &
Breakfast
Jefferis Rd
Waikouaiti
To Dunedin

ATANUI

378 Heywards Point, No 1 RD,
Port Chalmers, Dunedin
Ph (03) 482 1107
email: *atanui@callsouth.net.nz*

Tariff : N.Z. Dollars	
Double	$100-120
Single	$80-100
Child	$40

Bedrooms	Qty
Double	1
Twin	1
Single	

Bed Size	Qty
Super King Twin	1
King	
Queen	1
Double	
Single	

Bathrooms	Qty
Ensuite	1
Private	1
Guest Share	

     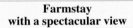

**Farmstay
with a spectacular view**

Features & Attractions

- *Walking tracks and beaches*
- *Pet animals and spa*
- *30 minutes from Dunedin*
- *Spa bath*
- *Spectacular views*
- *Quiet and relaxing*
- *Dinner by arrangement.*
  $30 per person

We welcome you to our spacious renovated stone house, in a peaceful rural setting only 30 minutes from Dunedin. From our home, which is heated throughout with radiators off the rayburn range, you can enjoy sweeping 220° views of the Otago Harbour, Otago Peninsula and the Pacific Ocean. Relax in the spa pool or feed our animals – emus, alpaccas, pig and pet sheep.

Walking tracks and beaches are close by. Morning and afternoon teas with home baking are complimentary. Three course farm style meals are available by prior arrangement. We invite you to experience our hospitality and meet our cats Honey and Penny. You will love the unique awe inspiring setting of our farm and take back home lovely memories of this truly special place.

DIRECTIONS:
From north turn left at Waitati, follow sign to Port Chalmers till crossroads. Turn left (No Exit) on to next junction take Heywards Point Road (metal road) 4km on right. From south down to Port Chalmers Highway 88, follow sign up the hill to Long Beach till Heyward Point Road (metal road) 4km on right.

LEITHVIEW
234 Malvern Street, Leith Valley, Dunedin
Ph (03) 467 9944
Mobile 027-490 7117
email: *lvconstruction@xtra.co.nz*
www.leithview.com

Tariff : N.Z. Dollars	
Double	$150-180
Single	neg.
Child	neg.

Bedrooms	Qty
Double	3
Twin	
Single	1
Bed Size	Qty
Super King	
King	1
Queen	2
Double	
Single	1
Bathrooms	Qty
Ensuite	1
Private	
Guest Share	1

 Country Living Close to Town

Features & Attractions

- *Private native bush walk*
- *Large rambling gardens*
- *Five min. from town*
- *Home fed by spring water*
- *Peaceful location*
- *Prolific birdlife*
- *Glow-worm grotto nearby*
- *Spa pool under the stars*

Marja and Peter would like to welcome you to **Leithview**, a forty acre lifestyle propery five minutes from the centre of Dunedin.

Our five year old home is nestled on the northerly slopes of the Leith Valley. All bedrooms have a northerly aspect and their own private decks looking out over extensive gardens and native bush, including 200 year old rimu and totara trees. Stroll around the propery with our retired sheep dog and the two cats, and then relax in our outdoor spa pool. The room rate includes a generous cooked or continental breakfast, and are subject to generous discounts during our off-peak season from April 1 to September 31st. Evening meals are available on request at an extra cost. Should you wish to renew contact with the hustle and bustle, we have the internet available and there is a bus stop at the bottom of our driveway.

DIRECTIONS: Once you reach our letterbox, follow the gravel drive for 500m past the **Leithview** sign up the hill.

HIGHLAND PEAKS

333 Chain Hills Road, RD 1, Dunedin
Ph (03) 489 6936, Fax (03) 489 6924
Mobile 027-351 0646
email: *info@highlandpeaks.com*
www.highlandpeaks.com

Tariff : N.Z. Dollars	
Double	$245-450
Single	$195-375
Child	

Bedrooms	Qty
Double	3
Twin	
Single	
Bed Size	Qty
Super King	2
King	1
Queen	
Double	
King/Single	4
Bathrooms	Qty
Ensuite	2
Private	1
Guest Share	

**Town & Country
Luxury Accommodation**

DIRECTIONS: From SH 1 take Mosgiel exit, then turn towards Kinmont. Travel along Quarry Road continue left along Morris Road towards Fairfield over motorway. Turn 1st left into Chain Hills Road and take left fork to **Highland Peaks** on left at road end.

Features & Attractions

- *Dunedin & Airport 15 min*
- *Panoramic vistas*
- *Luxury facilities*
- *Hydrotherapy spa pool*
- *Delightfully peaceful*
- *Albatross & penguin ecotours*
- *NZ cuisine & fine wine*
- *Handfeed friendly animals*

"Country beauty & peace, right next to the city..."

A newly completed luxury lodge, **Highland Peaks** specialises in warm hospitality, limited guest numbers and eco-tours. Centrally located between Dunedin and the airport, with panoramic mountain and sea views and twenty one acres of country grounds, you will enjoy privacy, tranquility, native birdsong and forest walks. **Highland Peaks is** purpose-built from natural stone to an eco-friendly, modern design. You'll stay in a private guest wing with three very comfortable suites. You can unwind in spacious guest lounges, in front of a large fire in winter, or on sundecks in summer. Alternatively enjoy the views while relaxing in our hydrotherapy spa pool. Dinner is served by arrangement, with quality home cuisine complemented by fine NZ wines. Peter, an ecologist and former director of New Zealand's National Trust, is happy to share his knowledge on New

Zealand's natural heritage. He also guides personal tours to see albatross, penguins, other wildlife and natural flora. We have a cat Jasper, dog Bud and friendly farm animals that you can hand-feed.

HARBOURSIDE BED & BREAKFAST
6 Kiwi Street, St Leonards, Dunedin
Ph (03) 471 0690, Fax (03) 471 0063
email: *harboursidebb@xtra.co.nz*

Features & Attractions
- *7 minutes to city centre*
- *Overlooking harbour*
- *Children welcome*
- *Complimentary tea on arrival*
- *Home baking*
- *Dinner by arrangement*

Double	$85-100
Single	$70-100
Child	$20

**Bed & Breakfast Homestay
Spectacular Harbour Views**

Wͤe are situated in a quiet suburb overlooking Otago Harbour and surrounding hills. Handy to all local attractions - Larnach Castle, Olveston, Royal Albatross and Yellow Eyed Penguin colonies, harbour cruises, Taieri Gorge Excursion train. Bookings can be arranged. There are many lovely bush walks close to the city. Children are very welcome (lots of preloved toys). We have a generous amount of living space for you to relax in after a busy day. Cooked breakfast is included and with a little notice, we can arrange a three course meal. Courtesy pick-up from bus or train.

Bedrooms	Qty
Double	3
Twin	
Single	
Bed Size	**Qty**
Super King	1
Queen	2
Double	
Single	3
Bathrooms	**Qty**
Ensuite	1
Private	
Guest Share	1

DIRECTIONS: On Northern Motorway turn left towards Port Chalmers (SH 88) from Anzac Avenue onto Ravensbourne Road. After 5km at St Leonards turn left into Moa Street, left into Kaka Rpad, straight ahead to Kiwi Street, turn left to No 6

CITY SANCTUARY BED & BREAKFAST
165 Maitland Street, Dunedin
Ph 03-474 5002, Fax 03-474 5006
email:*charmingenquiry@citysanctuary.co.nz*
www.citysanctuary.co.nz

Features & Attractions
- *Inner city location*
- *Elegant, spacious rooms*
- *Quiet and peaceful*
- *Personalised service*
- *Special breakfast*
- *Free email & video library*

**Inner City Oasis
Bed & Breakfast**

Double	$120-175
Single	$100-145
Child	neg

Wͤelcome to our attractive, restored villa in an oasis of cottage gardens and large trees, yet only 1km to the city centre and all its attractions. Three lovely, spacious bedrooms each have: queen bed with fleecy electric blanket, fresh flowers, oil heater, phone, TV and internet connection. One ensuite with spa bath and shower, and two private bathrooms. Relax in the guest living room with home theatre (a small library of CD's, DVD's and videos) and free email, or quietly unwind on the deck amidst the organic potager garden. Enjoy a special continental breakfast that includes home-made bread, smoked salmon and cheese. Paul's funky art abounds and a professional massage is available from Karen by appointment. 4 cats in residence.

Bedrooms	Qty
Double	3
Twin	
Single	
Bed Size	**Qty**
King	
Queen	3
Double	
Single	
Bathrooms	**Qty**
Ensuite	1
Private	2
Guest Share	

526 GEORGE STREET

526 George Street, PO Box 112, Dunedin
Free Ph: 0800 779 779
Phone (03) 477 1261, Fax (03) 477 1268
email: info@hotel526.co.nz
www.hotel526.co.nz

Tariff : N.Z. Dollars	
Double	$100-150
Single	$100-150
Child	

Bedrooms	Qty
Double	7
Twin/Double	7
Single	
Bed Size	Qty
Super King	
King	
Queen	14
Double	
Single	2
Bathrooms	Qty
Ensuite	14
Private	
Guest Share	

     **Guest House**

Features & Attractions

- *Downtown grand residence*
- *Adjacent university*
- *Adjacent museum*
- *Close to hospital*
- *Next to main shopping*
- *Disabled facilities*
- *Laundry, Internet access*
- *Full fire safety standard*

Welcome to **526 George Street**. This gracious residence was built in 1907 by Dunedin Hospital's surgeon Doctor Roberts as his grand family home. We are next to the City's retail shops and well over 50 restaurants and cafés on George Street. The property is on the flat, next to the National Archives Library, across the road from Otago Museum, across the Museum Reserve to the University of Otago and less than 400 metres from the hospital.

Our house is particularly suited for guests who have a link with any of the tertiary institutions and the hospital. The disabled access and facilities enable ease of use for a wheel chair around the spacious ground floor and lovely grounds. Suites range from doubles to large family rooms, enabling the house to cater for many accommodation needs. The house is a drop off/pick up point for sightseeing tours. Tours include wildlife - Albatross, Yellow Eyed Penguin, as well as Larnach's Castle and City Sights tours.

BELMONT HOUSE

227 York Place, Dunedin
Ph (03) 477 3713, Fax (03) 477 3712
Mobile 027-477 0165
email: *enquiries@belmonthouse.co.nz*
www.belmonthouse.co.nz

Tariff : N.Z. Dollars	
Double	$225-280
Single	$160-250
Child	

Bedrooms	Qty
Double	3
Twin	
Single	

Bed Size	Qty
Super King	
King	1
Queen	2
Double	
Single	

Bathrooms	Qty
Ensuite	2
Private	1
Guest Share	

 Luxury Accommodation Heritage House *Belmont House*

Features & Attractions

- *Centrally located*
- *Beautifully appointed rooms*
- *Full breakfast*
- *Quiet and peaceful*
- *Elegant guest lounge*
- *Great views & atmosphere*
- *Five minutes to Octagon*
- *Personalised service*

Advance booking recommended.

A short stroll from the city centre, **Belmont House** is situated on the city rise and affords grand views of the city, harbour and peninsula. Three spacious, well-appointed bedrooms, two ensuite and one private bathroom, are located on the upper floor. The rooms feature king or queen size beds, warm duvets, feather pillows, electric blankets, clock radios and heating. Fresh seasonal fruit, chocolates, magazines, books, fresh flowers, sparkling mineral water and bathrobes are also provided. Start the day with your choice of breakfast, served in the formal dining room. A selection of teas, fresh coffee and home-made biscuits are available anytime. The elegant guest lounge with city views is a relaxing and peaceful retreat at any time of the day. Curl up in a chair and relax with a selection of interesting books and magazines. A sound system, piano and television are at your disposal. **Belmont House** provides a quiet haven close to the vibrant city restaurants and attractions.

514

HERIOT HOUSE

26 Pitt Street, Dunedin
Ph (03) 477 7228,
Mobile 027-245 7719
email: *lcalvert@es.co.nz*

Tariff : N.Z. Dollars	
Double	$120-180
Single	
Child	neg

Bedrooms	Qty
Double	3
Twin	
Single	
Bed Size	**Qty**
Super King	
King	
Queen	3
Double	
Single	
Bathrooms	**Qty**
Ensuite	1
Private	1
Guest Share	1

**Elegant Bed & Breakfast
Accommodation**

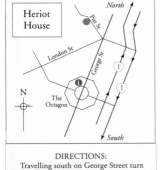

DIRECTIONS:
Travelling south on George Street turn
sharp right at Knox Church into Pitt Street

Features & Attractions

- *Centrally located*
- *3 minutes stroll to cafés, bars and restaurants*
- *Off-street parking*
- *Quaint cottage garden*
- *Gracious Edwardian home*
- *Friendly, helpful hostess*
- *Sumptuous breakfast*

Louise welcomes you to stay in her gracious old home situated right in the heart of Dunedin.
Only a casual stroll to shops and the local restaurants, bars and cafés. The quaint cottage garden has a pleasant charm that will draw you out of doors to inspect the treasures hidden from view.
All guest rooms are on the second floor with an area set aside in each room for those who prefer to relax in private. There is also a separate television room and a sitting room available for those who want a coffee and to chat.

You are sure of a warm, friendly and comfortable stay at **Heriot House**.

DEACONS COURT
342 High Street, Dunedin
Ph (03) 477 9053, Fax (03) 477 9058
email: *info@deaconscourt.com*
www.deaconscourt.com

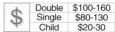

Features & Attractions

- *Spacious bedrooms*
- *Separate guest area*
- *Delicious cooked breakfast*
- *Close to city centre*
- *Large rose garden*
- *Historical home*

Bed & Breakfast Guesthouse	Double	$100-160
	Single	$80-130
	Child	$20-30

Deacons Court is a charming, spacious Victorian villa 1km walking distance from the city centre and is on the city's heritage building register. We are only 500m from cafés, restaurants, bars and some of Dunedin's unique attractions and offer you friendly but unobtrusive hospitality in a quiet, secure haven. Guests can relax in our delightful rose garden and conservatory.

Our bedrooms are large and have ensuite or private bathrooms, heaters, TV and electric blankets. Complimentary 24 hour tea or coffee, free parking and wireless broadband available.

Bedrooms	Qty
Double	3
Twin	
Single	
Bed Size	**Qty**
Super King	1
King	1
Queen	1
King/Single	2
Single	2
Bathrooms	**Qty**
Ensuite	2
Private	1

GRANDVIEW
360 High Street, Dunedin
Ph (03) 474 9472, Fax (03) 474 9473
Mobile 021-101 9857
email: *nzgrandview@msn.com*
www.grandview.co.nz

Features & Attractions

- *City & casino a short stroll!*
- *Free internet & video library*
- *Complimentary laundry use!*
- *Huge deck/viewing platform*
- *Hot spa tub - great view!*
- *Satelite television*

Bed & Breakfast Guest House	Double	$95-195
	Single	$75-140
	Child	$20

Grandview is centrally located yet offers some of Dunedin's grandest views! The casino, restaurants, shops, cafés and bars are only a short srtoll away! Relax in luxury in this charming 1901 heritage listed "Edwardian mansion". Featuring magnificent panoramic views from our viewing platforms and hot spa! Tourist information and holiday planning, **Big** screen movie lounge, videos, Satelite TV, **Fast** Internet, laundry facilities and scrumptious continental breakfasts are all a complementary part of the **Grandview** experience. Rooms to suit all budgets! From $75 (Single) to our luxury trendy spa suites for that "special escape" it's all here at **Grandview**. We strive to make your stay with us a time to remember and look forward to sharing our home with you!

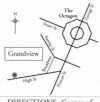

DIRECTIONS: Corner of High & Grant Sts - 400 mtrs up High St from the Casino on the right

Bedrooms	Qty
Double	7
Twin	3
Single	7
Bed Size	**Qty**
King	1
Queen	5
Double	1
Single	4
Bathrooms	**Qty**
Ensuite	2
Private	1
Guest Share	2

HULMES COURT BED & BREAKFAST

52 Tennyson Street, Dunedin, Otago
Ph (03) 477 5319, Fax (03) 477 5310
Mobile 027-435 1075
email: *reservations@hulmes.co.nz*
www.hulmes.co.nz

Tariff : N.Z. Dollars	
Double	$100-165
Single	$70-100
Child	enquire

Bedrooms	Qty
Double	8
Twin	4
Single	1
Bed Size	Qty
Super King	
King	3
Queen	10
Double	
Single	4
Bathrooms	Qty
Ensuite	8
Private	
Guest Share	3

Bed & Breakfast

Features & Attractions

- *Historic: built early 1860's*
- *Right in centre of Dunedin*
- *Off-street parking*
- *Complimentary laundry*
- *Young, friendly, intelligent staff*
- *Soltice, the cool cat*
- *Complimentary mountain bikes and Internet access*

Hulmes Court Bed & Breakfast is two beautiful homes only a few minutes walk from the heart of town and the Visitor Centre. Tennyson Street is quiet and we have private gardens, trees, decks and sitting areas. The **Victorian Hulmes Court** is one of the most historic homes in Dunedin. It was built in the 1860s by the first provincial surgeon Edward Hulme who helped found the Medical School. **Hulmes Too** is a large Edwardian home built next to **Hulmes Court** on the grounds of the original estate. **Hulmes Court** has a variety of rooms which cater for all tastes from the economical cute single Rose Room at $70 per night to our grand ensuite rooms in **Hulmes Too** at $165 per night. Your host Norman owns a variety of businesses and is interested in history, philosophy, geography and has stood for parliament twice. At the same time Norman at 41 and his staff are youthful, full of energy and travel widely. We provide complimentary laundry, internet and email, barbeque, mountain bikes and off-street parking.

DIRECTIONS: Leaving the Octagon by Upper Stuart Street, take the 2nd turning on the left into Smith Street, then just 50m left again into Tennyson Street.

517

THE TOWER HOUSE

9 City Road, Roslyn, Dunedin
Ph (03) 477 5678, Mobile 021-347 287
email: *bnb@thetowerhouse.co.nz*
www.thetowerhouse.co.nz

Tariff : N.Z. Dollars	
Double	$110-140
Single	$80
Child	

Bedrooms	Qty
Double	2
Twin	1
Single	1
Bed Size	**Qty**
Super King	
King	
Queen	2
King/Single	1
Single	2
Bathrooms	**Qty**
Ensuite	2
Private	
Guest Share	1

 Bed & Breakfast Guesthouse

Features & Attractions

- *Centrally located*
- *Restaurants nearby*
- *Smoke free inside*
- *Swimming pool nearby*
- *Wonderful views*
- *Friendly hospitality*
- *Delicious full breakfast*
- *Guest lounge & open fire*

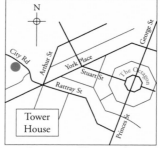

The Tower House offers visitors a magnificent panorama of Dunedin City and its beautiful natural harbour. It is ideally located, being close to the city and within walking distance of Roslyn Village and its pleasant restaurants. A ten minute down hill walk takes you to the city centre with its wide range of bars, cafés and restaurants. **The Tower House** has been designed for our guests to completely relax. Bedrooms are warm and comfortable with restful décor. The two double rooms have french doors opening onto a balcony where you can enjoy panoramic city views over a leisurely cup of tea or coffee. The morning newspaper is complimentary. All rooms have tea and coffee making facilities and televisions. Two rooms have ensuites and the others have a shared bathroom with an original claw footed bath. There is a guests' lounge with television and an interesting range of books and magazines. The lounge leads into a pleasant dining room where the full cooked breakfast, included in the tariff, is served.

TOP O' THE GLEN

9 Glen Road, Mornington, Dunedin
Phone (03) 453 3303
Mobile (021) 145 7411
e-mail: *top.o.theglen@xtra.co.nz*

Features & Attractions

- *Handy to City & Peninsula*
- *Gluten-free breakfast available*
- *Toy-poodle, cat & 2 cockatiels*
- *In-room tea & coffee*
- *BBQ for guests' use*
- *Children welcome*

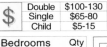

$	Double	$100-130
	Single	$65-80
	Child	$5-15

Travellers' Accommodation

Bedrooms	Qty
Double	2
Twin	1
Single	2
Bed Size	**Qty**
King	
Queen	1
Double	1
Single	3
Bathrooms	**Qty**
Ensuite	
Private	
Guest Share	1

Top o' the Glen is just a few minutes drive from Dunedin City and University and conveniently located on a bus route. A 20 min. drive takes you to the Otago Peninsula and its unique wildlife and scenic attractions. We enjoy helping guests to plan their tours, as we have spent many holidays travelling around Otago and Southland. Our comfortable rooms are equipped with heaters, bathrobes and hair driers. Beds are cosy with electric blankets and warm sheets. There is a guest lounge with books and TV. Toys and games for children are available. Breakfast, included in the tariff, may be taken in your room or with your hosts, Lynette and Neville. Gluten-free food can be arranged. Guests are assured of an enthusiastic welcome from Poppy, our toy poodle. Feebee, the cat, Dundee and Woody, the cockatiels, complete our household. There is a garden area for those who

---

YOUR HOSTS: **Kate Middleton and Robert Richardson**   Ph (03) 454 5475 ◁   *Dunedin*

RED FLAX B&B

7 Darnell Street, Shiel Hill, Dunedin
Ph (03) 454 5475, Fax (03) 454 5473
Mobile 021-118 8531
e-mail: *kate@redflax.biz*
www.redflax.biz

Features & Attractions

- *One party booking only*
- *Rural and sea vistas*
- *Memorable breakfasts*
- *Private courtyard entrance*
- *Close to city & restaurants*
- *Laundry and internet*

$	Double	$150-170
	Single	$100-110
	Child	Neg.

**Homestay
Bed & Breakfast**

Bedrooms	Qty
Double	2
Twin	
Single	
Bed Size	**Qty**
King	
Queen	1
Double	1
Single	
Bathrooms	**Qty**
Ensuite	
Private	1
Guest Share	

Red Flax B&B has tranquil rural and sea views and is situated at the entrance to the famous Otago Peninsula. The historic central city area of Dunedin is only 8 minutes drive away and has a splendid choice of restaurants and a casino. We are close to a regular bus route. **Red Flax** is situated in a private area of a modern, sunny home and has its own separate courtyard entrance. We only take one party bookings, which ensures that guests have exclusive use of the 2 bedrooms, bathroom, and a cosy lounge with tea making facilities, a refrigerator and TV. Caring hospitality and attention to detail throughout... cookies, bathrobes and toiletries, and a memorable breakfast. We have two small well behaved dogs in residence.

PATTONS HILL

Rapid No 974, Highcliff Rd, RD 2, Dunedin
Ph (03) 476 1007, Fax (03) 476 1007
Mobile 027-436 3663
email: *rbhall@es.co.nz*

Features & Attractions

- *Tranquil & relaxed surroundings*
- *Close to cafés & restaurants*
- *Magnificent harbour & ocean views*
- *Close to Dunedin City*
- *Walking tracks & stunning beaches*
- *Vintage car enthusiasts*

	Bed & Breakfast Homestay				
			Double	$100
			Single	$70
			Child	neg

Bedrooms	Qty
Double	1
Twin	1
Single	
Bed Size	**Qty**
King	
Queen	1
Double	
Single	2
Bathrooms	**Qty**
Ensuite	
Private	
Guest Share	1

We welcome you to come and stay with us in our modern family home situated on a 30 acre farm block originally settled in the 1800s, and share with us country living on the beautiful Otago Peninsula. Handy to all Peninsula attractions including Larnach Castle, albatross, penguin and seal colonies and Taiaroa Head and Marine Aquarium. Enjoy magnificent views of Otago Harbour and Pacific Ocean and the ever-changing panoramic views from around the property. Guest rooms are located upstairs, all equipped with heating and electric blankets. Join us in the evening or if you prefer a quiet time, relax upstairs where there is a TV in the double bedroom. We serve continental or cooked breakfast. Children are very welcome. We have a strong family link with the Otago Peninsula and are most happy to share our knowledge and advise on local attractions.

PORTERFIELDS BED & BREAKFAST

30 Porterfield Street, Macandrew Bay, Dunedin
Ph (03) 476 1360, Fax (03) 476 1362
Mobile 027-405 5868
e-mail: *bookings@porterfields.co.nz*
www.porterfields.co.nz

Features & Attractions

- *Convenient location*
- *Friendly & comfortable*
- *Quiet surroundings*
- *Modern facilities*
- *Spectacular views*
- *Top breakfasts*

	Quality Bed & Breakfast Spectacular Location				
			Double	$120-140
			Single	$90-110
			Child	Neg.

Bedrooms	Qty
Double	1
Twin	1
Single	
Bed Size	**Qty**
Super King	1
Queen	
Double	
King/Single	2
Bathrooms	**Qty**
Ensuite	1
Private	1
Guest Share	

Porterfields is spectacularly located in a mature garden setting with glorious views of Otago Harbour, Dunedin City and the Peninsula itself. Our modern, spacious and comfortable home offers two well-appointed downstairs lounges. The two guest rooms are located on the first floor, **Porterfields** king bedroom with private bathroom and Porterfields twin bedroom with ensuite. Our emphasis is on ensuring our guests' comfort, with each bedroom featuring high quality linen with electric blankets, cosy heating and TV. Continuous coffee and tea making facilities available on upstairs landing. **Porterfields** is located just 12 km from central Dunedin and within easy driving distance of all of the Peninsula's attractions. Susan and Neil Johnstone, themselves experienced travellers, believe they know what travellers appreciate when far from home and in unfamiliar territory.

BRYNYMOR HOUSE

6, St Ronans Rd, The Cove, Dunedin
Ph (03) 476 1110
email: *nzanneevans@yahoo.co.nz*
www.brynymorhouse.com

Tariff : N.Z. Dollars	
Double	$160-180
Single	$150-160
Child	

Bedrooms	Qty
Double	1
Twin	1
Single	
Bed Size	**Qty**
Super King	
King	
Queen	
Double	1
Single	2
Bathrooms	**Qty**
Ensuite	
Private	2
Guest Share	

Bed & Breakfast
Luxury Accommodation

Features & Attractions

- *Glorious 2.5 acre garden*
- *Panoramic harbour views*
- *Bellbirds and tuis*
- *Tranquil setting*
- *Private guest wing*
- *Sky TV and video library*
- *9 minutes to city centre*
- *Peninsula wildlife*

Brynymor House sits in a delightful 2½ acre garden in an idyllic harbourside setting. Whether on business or on holiday, treat yourself to a touch of luxury. You will enjoy relaxing on the verandah of our north facing colonial-style home overlooking the sea and mountains, or in the guest lounge or bedrooms, each of which enjoy panoramic marine views.

SKY TV, including all the sports channels, is available. The private bathrooms have heated floors and the bedrooms have electric blankets and individual heating. Coffee and tea making facilities, fresh fruit and snacks are provided and a choice of breakfast. The garden in our microclimate is yours to enjoy in all seasons of the year.

The Otago Peninsula attractions surround you and the city centre is only 9 minutes away. Take the sharp right turn before Glenfalloch Gardens into our pretty road, proceed to the top of the drive at the end where you will find our corner of paradise.

HARBOUR LIGHTS HOMESTAY B&B

1 Wharfdale Street, Macandrew Bay, Dunedin
Ph (03) 476 1019, Fax (03) 476 1019
email: *harbourlights@actrix.co.nz*

Tariff : N.Z. Dollars	
Double	$110-135
Single	$80-95
Child	neg.

Bedrooms	Qty
Double	2
Twin	1
Single	1
Bed Size	Qty
Super King	
King	
Queen	2
Double	
Single	2
Bathrooms	Qty
Ensuite	1
Private	1
Guest Share	1

Homestay
Bed & Breakfast

Features & Attractions

- *On beautiful Otago Peninsula*
- *Superb day & night harbour views*
- *Close to Dunedin City – 11km*
- *Taiaroa Head & Albatross Colony*
- *Yellow-eyed penguins & seals*
- *Armstrong Disappearing Gun*
- *Close to Glenfalloch Gardens*
- *Evening meals on request*

"What a view!" This is often the first remark of our guests upon arrival at **Harbour Lights Homestay,** but many have had a few pangs of regret at having to leave us. Many of our guests who have stayed here, now consider us as friends. We know how visitors feel upon arrival in unfamiliar surroundings, as our travels have taken us to many parts of the world. So please accept a warm Scottish welcome. The guest rooms are on the upper level to maintain our guests' privacy. All rooms are equipped with heating and electric blankets and include tea and coffee facilities.

In the morning choose either continental or full cooked breakfast. Libby and Alex are looking forward to welcoming you to **Harbour Lights Homestay.**

BROAD BAY WHITE HOUSE

11 Clearwater Street, Broad Bay, Dunedin
Ph (03) 478 1160, Fax (03) 478 1159
email: *broadbaywhitehouse@paradise.net.nz*
www.broadbaywhitehouse.co.nz

Tariff : N.Z. Dollars	
Double	$150-175
Single	$130
Child	

Bedrooms	Qty
Double	2
Twin	1
Single	

Bed Size	Qty
Super King	
King	
Queen	3
Double	
Single	1

Bathrooms	Qty
Ensuite	2
Private	1
Guest Share	

**Luxury Accommodation
Spectacular Harbour Views**

Features & Attractions

- *Tranquillity*
- *Spectacular harbour views*
- *'Superb food'*
- *Silver service*
- *Wildlife*
- *Penguins, seals, albatross*
- *Extensive gardens*
- *Friendly, knowledgeable*

G ive yourself a taste of luxury with "superb food and hospitality", peace and quiet, privacy and panoramic views over the harbour. You can relax after a busy day sightseeing, take time to wander through our extensive gardens and enjoy the abundant bird life. Have a fun game of petanque (botchee), no experience of physical fitness required. Your bedroom will be spacious and has

its own centrally heated bathroom. We use quality linen and bedding and also provide electric blankets. Wake to the morning song of native birds. All rooms have direct access to spacious decks with plenty of outside furniture for you to unwind with a glass of wine and complimentary cheese board or tea and coffee with cakes and biscuit.
Our semi-rural hideaway is located on the Otago Peninsula handy to the albatross, penguin and seal colonies, Larnach's Castle and other Peninsula attractions.

DIRECTIONS:
Follow the Peninsula signs from town along the south side of the harbour to Broad Bay. Take 1st turn right after the Broad Bay Boating Club. We are at the top of the street. Blue sign 'Broad Bay Whitehouse.'

CHY-AN-DOWR

687 Portobello Road, Broad Bay, Dunedin
Ph (03) 478 0306
Mobile 021-156 0715
email: *hermanvv@xtra.co.nz*
www.chy-an-dowr.co.nz

Tariff : N.Z. Dollars	
Double	$175-245
Single	
Child	

Bedrooms	Qty
Double	2
Twin	1
Single	

Bed Size	Qty
Super King	
King	1
Queen	1
King/Twin	1
Single	

Bathrooms	Qty
Ensuite	1
Private	1
Guest Share	

 Boutique Accommodation Bed & Breakfast

Features & Attractions

- *Panoramic harbour views*
- *Harbourside location*
- *Edwardian character home*
- *Wireless internet*
- *Albatross & penguins*
- *Great breakfast*
- *Dutch spoken*
- *Dunedin - 20 minutes*

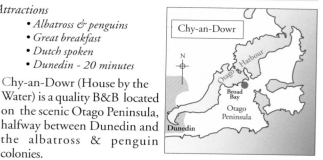

Chy-an-Dowr (House by the Water) is a quality B&B located on the scenic Otago Peninsula, halfway between Dunedin and the albatross & penguin colonies.

Our character 1920s home has panoramic harbour views and is situated opposite a small sandy beach. The upstairs guest area is

DIRECTIONS:
Follow signs to Peninsula. We are a 20 min drive along Portobello Road from Dunedin. We are on the corner of Portobello Road & Clearwater Street in Broad Bay.

spacious and private with comfortable rooms, bathrobes, tea/coffee, television, refrigerator, ensuite/private facilities and a sunroom with fabulous views. Enjoy a cooked/continental breakfast at your leisure.

Explore the Otago Peninsula with its many walkways and local arts and crafts. Originally from Holland, we enjoy welcoming people into our home and sharing our wonderful location with them.

ARTS CONTENT BED & BREAKFAST

1 Castlewood Road, Otago Peninsula
Ph (03) 476 0076, Fax (03) 476 0076
Mobile 021-152 3341
email: *artscontent@hotmail.com*
www.artscontentbnb.com

Features & Attractions

- *Absolute waterfront*
- *Panoramic harbour views*
- *Art Gallery on site*
- *Laundry facilities*
- *Secret garden with 80⁺ roses*
- *Larnach Castle 5min. drive*

$	Double	$125-150
	Single	$120-135
	Child	

B&B Self-contained
Absolute Waterfront

Bedrooms	Qty
Double	1
Twin	
Single	

Bed Size	Qty
King	
Queen	1
Double	
Single	

Bathrooms	Qty
Ensuite	1
Private	
Guest Share	

DIRECTIONS: From Dunedin follow signs to Peninsula. We are 15min. drive along Portobello Rd on the corner of Portobello Rd & Castlewood Rd in Company Bay. Look for **Arts Content** sign.

Arts Content is absolute waterfront, self-contained, cottage-style accommodation, ideal for a couple. Decorated in country style, it exudes charm and character. It adjoins our home and has private entrances and off-street parking. Enjoy sweeping, panoramic harbour views from the private deck. Leading off the spacious bedroom is your own ensuite. Upstairs is a lounge, dining, kitchen with comfortable seating including a sofa-bed. Heating is provided by a heatpump. Share our pleasure in our beautiful, 'secret' garden and take the time to stop and smell our 80⁺ roses. A generous basket breakfast is provided. Within easy reach of the city, we are ideally located to access all the attractions of the Peninsula. We also offer conducted Peninsula tours.

CRABAPPLE COTTAGE

346 Harington Point Rd, RD 2,
Lower Portobello, Dunedin
Ph (03) 4780103
email: *kay@crabapple.co.nz*
www.crabapple.co.nz

Features & Attractions

- *Close to wildlife attractions*
- *Pleasant, rural setting*
- *Private garden outlook*
- *5min. to restaurants & cafés*
- *25min. from Dunedin*
- *Restored settlers cottage*

$	Double	$115-130
	Single	
	Child	

Self-contained Cottage
Bed & Breakfast

Bedrooms	Qty
Double	1
Twin	
Single	

Bed Size	Qty
King	
Queen	1
Double	
Single	

Bathrooms	Qty
Ensuite	1
Private	
Guest Share	

Crabapple Cottage is a lovingly restored 1860s settlers cottage 25 minutes from Dunedin, on the beautiful Otago Peninsula. We are 10 minutes from the albatross colony, penguin beaches, Monarch Wildlife Cruises, off-road tours, the Portobello Aquarium, craft shops and beautiful beaches. Larnach's Castle is a 20 minutes scenic drive away. Our character cottage has a very comfortable queen-size bed, modern bathroom with all facilities, and a kitchen/lounge area equipped for basic self-catering. Enjoy a generous breakfast tray which includes eggs from our own hens and relax in an armchair or in the private herb garden with views of the hills and full afternoon sun. We are 5 minutes from restaurants, cafés and a general store with post facilities. We look forward to sharing our cosy cottage with you.

Fantail Lodge

682 Portobello Road, Broad Bay, Dunedin
Ph (03) 478 0110, Mobile 027-415 6222
email: *fantail.lodge@xtra.co.nz*
www.travelwise.co.nz

Tariff : N.Z. Dollars	
Double	$120-150
Single	
Extra pp	$25

Bedrooms	Qty
Double	2
Twin	
Single	
Bed Size	**Qty**
Super King	
King	
Queen	1
Double	1
Single	2
Bathrooms	**Qty**
Ensuite	2
Private	
Guest Share	

Harbourside
Self-contained Cottages

Features & Attractions

- *Harbourside cottages*
- *Exclusive spa pool*
- *Albatross, seals, penguins*
- *Larnach Castle*
- *Romantic hideaway*
- *Lush garden setting*
- *Free use of kayaks*
- *Breakfast opt. extra*

DIRECTIONS:

From Dunedin take Portobello Rd along harbour towards Taiaroa Head. After 15 km (20 min) you will see Broad Bay Boating Club and jetty. Turn next right into Clearwater St and turn again hard right in front of two storey B&B house on corner. Straight on to #682.

Fantail Lodge offers self-contained cottage accommodation set in a lush harbourside garden. We are situated centrally on the Otago Peninsula, within easy reach of unspoiled beaches, albatross, seals and penguins. Relax on the verandah and enjoy the company of native birds. Walk to the local castle or paddle a kayak on the harbour. With so much to explore we recommend you stay for at least two nights and we offer a discount for longer stays. We are five minutes drive to the local store and restaurants and twenty minutes from Dunedin. The cottages are equipped for self-catering with an optional continental breakfast hamper for busy travellers. There are two unique cottages for you to choose from:
'Fantail Cottage' offers double bed accommodation with two singles on a mezzanine floor. Ideal for two, but comfortably sleeps four people.
'Bellbird Cottage' offers queen bed accommodation. Relax and enjoy the exclusive use of a spa pool under the stars. Perfect for a couple.

THE COTTAGE
Broad Bay, Otago Peninsula, Dunedin
Mobile 027-228 3380, Fax (03) 476 1873
email: *thecottage@xtra.co.nz*

Tariff : N.Z. Dollars	
Double	$140-195
Single	
Child	

Bedrooms	Qty
Double	1
Twin	
Single	

Bed Size	Qty
Super King	
King	
Queen	1
Double	
Single	

Bathrooms	Qty
Ensuite	1
Private	
Guest Share	

**Coastal Cottage
Bed & Breakfast**

Features & Attractions

- *Olde-world charm*
- *Self-contained and private*
- *Optional hamper breakfast*
- *Sea views from verandah*
- *Close to wildlife*
- *Penguins, albatross & seals*
- *20 minutes from Dunedin*
- *Situated right by the water*

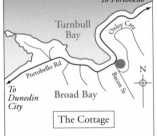

Whether you want to explore the wildlife of the Otago Peninsula with its great beaches and walkways, penguin, royal albatross and Seal colonies, harbour cruises and Larnach Castle or frequent the café scene, the galleries, the restaurants and city life of Dunedin, our **Cottage** is the ideal base for your adventures. Situated right by the water, this turn of the century fisherman's retreat is tucked among bush and trees with wonderful views of the harbour from the privacy of the verandah. **The Cottage** is full of old-world charm. It reflects the nostalgia of a bygone era whilst modern conveniences ensure a comfortable stay. The décor features the odd piece of original New Zealand art and numerous curiosities from yesteryear. Your hosts live nearby on the Peninsula. They are responsible for the scrumptious basket of ingredients for breakfast which is delivered to your cottage during the afternoon for the next morning (Needs to be ordered when booking). "If you spend only one night... you'll be sorry... A few days is best."(Grace Magazine).

THE LODGE - BROAD BAY

Broad Bay, Otago Peninsula, Dunedin
Fax (03) 476 1873
Mobile 027-228 3380
email: *julzandlutz@xtra.co.nz*

Tariff : N.Z. Dollars	
Double	$160-215
Single	
Child	

Bedrooms	Qty
Double	1
Twin	1
Single	
Bed Size	**Qty**
Super King	
King	
Queen	1
Double	
King/Single	2
Bathrooms	**Qty**
Ensuite	
Private	1
Guest Share	

Coastal Cottage
Bed & Breakfast

Features & Attractions

- *Modern with warm ambience*
- *Self-contained and private*
- *Optional hamper breakfast*
- *Magnificent sea views*
- *Close to wildlife*
- *Penguins, albatross and seals*
- *20 mins from Dunedin*
- *Situated right by the water*

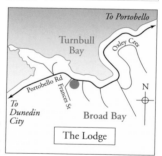

Explore the Otago Peninsula - royal albatross, penguin and seal colonies, great walkways and beaches, galleries and hidden gems, and a castle! Enjoy the city life of Dunedin with its cafés and galleries, shops and museums, its theatres and entertainment.

Then come home to this fully self-contained and private haven, relax and enjoy the breathtaking views of Otago Harbour.

The modern kitchen invites you to "cook up a storm", or you might choose to dine out at the nearby restaurants.

A scrumptious basket of ingredients for breakfast (optional) can be delivered by your hosts who live nearby on the Peninsula.

CAPTAIN EADY'S LOOKOUT

2 Moss Street, Portobello, Dunedin
Ph (03) 478 0537
Mobile 021- 478 785
email: *capteady@earthlight.co.nz*
www.capteady.co.nz

Tariff : N.Z. Dollars	
Double	$130-155
Single	$120-145
Child	neg

Bedrooms	Qty
Double	2
Twin	1
Single	

Bed Size	Qty
Super King	
King	
Queen	2
Double	
Single	

Bathrooms	Qty
Ensuite	2
Private	
Family Share	1

Bed & Breakfast
Homestay

Features & Attractions

- *Harbourside location*
- *Close to Albatross Colony*
- *Stunning Peninsula beaches*
- *Secluded garden*
- *Penguins, seals & native birdlife*
- *Special breakfasts, dinner available upon request*
- *Large character home, warm in winter*
- *Antiques, paintings by local artists*

Captain Eady's Lookout is a delightful Bed & Breakfast situated on the water's edge at Portobello on the Otago Peninsula, just twenty kilometres from Dunedin. This character house is set on a small bluff overlooking the Otago Harbour. It was built early last century by Captain Eady, a ferry master. The upstairs bedroom, with its own balcony, overlooks the water. The bedroom below opens onto a secluded garden.

You may have a special breakfast in the conservatory whilst taking in the splendid views of the harbour. The house has many antiques and on the walls are paintings by local artists. Feel free to enjoy our large jazz collection. **Captain Eady's Lookout** is an ideal base from which to explore the Royal Albatross Colony, Larnach's Castle, and ocean beaches deserted, save for penguins and seals.

CONEHENGE HOMESTEAD

Rapid 1589 Highcliff Road, PO Box 50,
Portobello, Dunedin
Ph (03) 478 0911, Fax (03) 478 0914
Mobile 027-202 0464
email: *kolig@ihug.co.nz*

Tariff : N.Z. Dollars	
Double	$145-165
Single	$145
Child	

Bedrooms	Qty
Double	1
Twin	
Single	
Bed Size	**Qty**
Super King	
King	1
Queen	
Double	
Single	
Bathrooms	**Qty**
Ensuite	1
Private	
Guest Share	

 Tranquil Rural Retreat
Boutique Bed & Breakfast

Features & Attractions

- *Magnificent harbour & sea views*
- *City & wildlife colonies 25 min*
- *Central & close to all attractions*
- *Single party accommodation*
- *Private native bush walk*
- *Meet donkeys & farm animals*
- *Ceramic artist*
- *German spoken*

DIRECTIONS:
1.2 km up the hill from Portobello
Village, on Highcliff Road.
Advance booking recommended.

Conehenge Homestead is an oasis for the discerning traveller who seeks tranquillity and privacy. Nestling on the slope of Harbour Cone the Homestead offers magnificent views over the open sea, the Otago Harbour, the bays and rolling hills of the Otago Peninsula. Equidistant to all wildlife attractions of the Peninsula and the city's cultural and architectural heritage makes **Conehenge** an ideal base for a longer stay. Enjoy a walk on our farm and in our private native bush reserve. Your room and patio have a fantastic view over harbour and sea. The double room has its own private entrance, king-size bed, electric blanket, ensuite, television. The studio facilities include a bar fridge, microwave, toaster, complimentary teas/coffee. Tiled low allergen room, no house pets. Room service breakfast (or

on your patio) features home-made continental specialty breads and other delectables. I am well travelled and am an established ceramic artist. Ich spreche deutsch. I invite you to view my unique art work and meet my favourites, Sheeba and Limpy the sheep, and Dolly and Henry, our utterly spoilt donkeys.

MCAULEY GLEN

13 McAuley Road, Portobello
Ph (03) 478 0724, Fax (03) 478 0724
Mobile 021-237 1919
email: *maryandpat@clear.net.nz*

Tariff : N.Z. Dollars	
Double	$155-195
Single	$135-185
Child	enquire

Bedrooms	Qty
Double	2
Twin	1
Single	

Bed Size	Qty
Super King	
King	
Queen	2
Double	
Single	2

Bathrooms	Qty
Ensuite	2
Private	
Guest Share	

**Bed & Breakfast
Homestay**

Features & Attractions

- *Superb food /home baking*
- *Stunning, private, peaceful garden*
- *Garden jacuzzi spa & sauna room*
- *Laundry service/off-road parking*
- *Personalised, guided sea kayak tours*
- *Short stroll to café & restaurant*
- *Close to albatross, seals, penguins*
- *Internet, email, fax*

Located on the magnificent Otago Peninsula, in a magical rural setting of beautiful gardens, **McAuley Glen** is an idyllic retreat. Mary and Pat invite you to indulge in their warm, friendly Kiwi hospitality. Delight in a generous hot gourmet breakfast, enjoy a real fresh fruit smoothie, delicious pancakes with wild berries and maple syrup. Relax in the hot spa pool, unwind in the sauna, join us for refreshments, nibbles and a chat. Happy to advise on/ book excursions. Evening meal/ BBQ available by prior arrangement. Our luxury bedroom suites, adjoining twin room, have an elegant, romantic ambience with private garden entrance, fine furnishings and linens, TV, DVD, CD, a service area with fridge, micro wave, toaster etc, fresh coffee/teas, home baking, chocolates and flowers. Spacious, tiled bathrooms feature: walk-in shower, heated floor, heated towel rails, hair dryer, quality bathrobes, and toiletries. **McAuley Glen** is also home to 'Peninsula Bike & Kayak'. Mary and Pat offer personal, fun filled, informative guided tours, or hire. Experience amazing wild life and fantastic scenery, visit *www.bike-kayak.com*

RUGOSA COTTAGE
1 Beaconsfield Rd, Portobello, Dunedin
Ph (03) 478 1076
Mobile 027-461 8422
email: *rugosa@xtra.co.nz*
www.rugosa.co.nz

Tariff : N.Z. Dollars	
Double	$155-175
Single	–
Child	–

Bedrooms	Qty
Double	2
Twin/Double	
Single	

Bed Size	Qty
Super King	
King	
Queen	1
Double	1
Single	

Bathrooms	Qty
Ensuite	2
Private	
Guest Share	

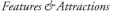
Bed & Breakfast Homestay and Self-contained

Features & Attractions
- *Relaxing, tranquil garden setting*
- *Harbourside location, seaviews*
- *Albatross, penguins, Larnach Castle*
- *Tours, excursions arranged*
- *Romantic hideaway*
- *Warm NZ hospitality*
- *Art and crafts*
- *Spa pool*

Welcome to **Rugosa Cottage and Seafarers Cottage.** Situated on the Otago Peninsula, our Bed & Breakfast overlooks the sea and is surrounded by beautiful gardens. Garden, book art lovers retreat. The cottages are decorated with panache, charm and a romantic ambience. Choose your accommodation, either our Rose Room with 4-poster queen-size bed, ensuite bathroom and French doors to rose gardens. Our **Seafarers Cottage** is self-contained with colonial bed, ensuite bathroom, small kitchenette – ideal for a couple who require a place of their own. French doors lead out to cottage-style gardens. A breakfast hamper is available. Alternatively you are welcome to join us for breakfast at **Rugosa Cottage**.

Rugosa Cottage

Otago Harbour

Portobello

Otago Peninsula

Dunedin

Guests' comment: "*Your hospitality was second to none and the food and accommodation first class*" Ralph and Cath Huggert - United Kingdom.

KAIMATA

297 Cape Saunders Road, RD2 Portobello, Dunedin
Phone (03) 456 3443, Fax (03) 456 3444
Mobile 021-062 4053
e-mail: info@kaimatanz.com
www.kaimatanz.com

Tariff : N.Z. Dollars	
Double	$265-350
Single	
Child	

Bedrooms	Qty
Double	3
Twin	
Single	
Bed Size	**Qty**
Super King	
King	1
Queen	2
Double	
Single	
Bathrooms	**Qty**
Ensuite	3
Private	
Guest Share	

Eco Retreat Self-contained with Continental Breakfast

Features & Attractions

- *Captivating location*
- *Nourishing breakfasts*
- *Private beach to enjoy*
- *Room rate or house rate*
- *Separate to hosts' dwelling*
- *Private eco-touring available*
- *Abundant birds and wildlife*
- *Central Otago fine wine selection*

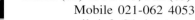

Encounter a uniquely New Zealand experience. Welcome to Kaimata, a secluded eco-retreat with sweeping views over Papanui Inlet and the back dunes of Victory beach at Cape Saunders, on the Otago Peninsula. Kaimata offers one king room with sitting area and private bathroom and two queen rooms with ensuites. Toiletry products contain only native New Zealand ingredients and fragrances. All rooms have water views with deck access. You can select rooms individually or house book. Generous open fire in lounge. Self-serve laundry and self-catering with basic kitchen stock. Fresh continental breakfast including seasonal fruit juices provided. We recommend you stop at a supermarket in Dunedin for additional foodstuffs. Try our boutique Central Otago wine selection and Dunedin speciality beer selection. Portobello Village 10 min. drive (amenities/restaurants). Pre-book therapeutic message and close to nature private eco-tours. Breathe fresh sea air and relax in seclusion at Kaimata.

ARGYLL FARMSTAY

Rapid No 246, Clutha River Rd, Clydevale, RD 4, Balclutha
Ph (03) 415 9268, Fax (03) 415 9268
Mobile 027-431 8241
email: *argyllfm@ihug.co.nz*
www.argyllfarmstay.co.nz

Tariff : N.Z. Dollars	
Double	$120-150
Single	$60-100
Child	neg

Bedrooms	Qty
Double	1
Twin	1
Single	1
Bed Size	Qty
Super King	
King	
Queen	1
Double	
Single	3
Bathrooms	Qty
Ensuite	1
Private	1
Guest Share	

**Farmstay
Bed & Breakfast**

Features & Attractions

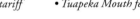

- *Superior accommodation*
- *Garden room has conservatory*
- *Tea/coffee making facilities*
- *Farm tour included in tariff*
- *Homestyle cuisine available*
- *Tranquil rural views*
- *Fisherman's paradise*
- *Tuapeka Mouth ferry*

DIRECTIONS:
Please phone for easy directions.

From the moment you step onto **Argyll Farm** you will experience the warmth, tranquillity and hospitality extended to you by Alan and Trish – third generation, sheep, deer and cattle farmers. **Argyll Farm** is situated on the banks of the Clutha River that provides guests with a unique opportunity to enjoy several recreational pastimes. We would like you to relax in our comfortable country home with a large garden, and beautiful views of green pasture and river flats. You can enjoy our day to day farm activities or enjoy quiet times. Go for walks, fish in the Clutha River bordering our property or explore. We will make your stay a memorable one, pampering you with exquisite accommodation and cuisine.

Our home is yours. Experience '**Argyll Farm**' for a magical stay.

LESMAHAGOW

Benhar Main Road, Benhar, Balclutha
Ph (03) 418 2507
Mobile 027- 457 8465
e-mail: *lesmahagow@xtra.co.nz*
www.lesmahagow.co.nz

Features & Attractions

- *Historic home & gardens*
- *Catlins scenic area*
- *Quality & comfort assured*
- *Evening dining*
- *Centrally heated*
- *Spacious bedrooms*

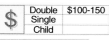

$	Double	$100-150
	Single	
	Child	

Boutique Bed & Breakfast

Bedrooms	Qty
Double	4
Twin	
Single	
Bed Size	**Qty**
King	
Queen	2
Double	2
Single	1
Bathrooms	**Qty**
Ensuite	
Private	2
Guest Share	1

Lesmahagow offers excellent accommodation in an historic homestead and garden setting. Centrally situated, discerning travellers can make Lesmahagow their base to explore the Catlins region, Dunedin and the Otago Peninsula or the historic goldfields of Lawrence. Centrally heated, with delightfully furnished bedrooms and gorgeous bathrooms, you can be sure of wonderful hospitality, and a truly memorable stay. Feel free to explore and relax in our gardens or take time out to enjoy the guest lounge with an extensive range of books magazines and music. We offer evening dining utilising fresh produce from the garden and locally grown meats. Our special breakfasts, at a time to suit you, with freshly squeezed fruit juices, fresh fruits, home made breads, muesli and home baking will satisfy all taste buds! We love to help plan your day's activities and can arrange a variety of local trips for you. Come as strangers, leave as friends.

CARDNO'S ACCOMMODATION

8 Marine Terrace, Kaka Point, The Catlins
Ph (03) 412 8181, Fax (03) 412 8101
email: *cardnos@xtra.co.nz*
www.cardnosaccommodation.co.nz

Features & Attractions

- *Great sunrises*
- *Native bush walks*
- *Yellow-eyed penguins*
- *Magnificent sea views*
- *Nugget Point Lighthouse*
- *Sea lions, seals, native birds*

 Modern Contemporary Accommodation

$	Double	$90-200
	Single	
	Child	n/a

45 minutes drive from Dunedin Airport, following the Southern Scenic Route, Kaka Point, a seaside destination with patrolled beaches in summer, is ideal to base yourself while exploring the spectacular Catlins - one of the last frontiers of tourist destinations in NZ, consisting of unique wildlife to spectacular outcrops. Or, simply relax, enjoying the spacious modern surrounding of your contemporary furnished accommodation. Each unit with its own entrance, is ensuited, has quality linen, wool rest electric blanket, woollen blankets, feather duvéts. TV, CD stereo, hairdryer, filtered water, BBQ area, and a 1 minute walk to the beach, restaurant/bar/shop. From your double glazed ranch sliders, enjoy amazing sunrises, wonderful views of the ocean and Nugget Point Lighthouse. An optional continental breakfast tray can be requested on arrival. These features and our hospitality will ensure your stay is comfortable and memorable.

Bedrooms	Qty
Double	3
Twin	
Single	
Bed Size	**Qty**
King	
Queen	3
Double	
Single	2
Bathrooms	**Qty**
Ensuite	3
Private	
Guest Share	

KEPPLESTONE-BY-THE-SEA

9 Surat Bay Road, Owaka, Newhaven, The Catlins
Ph (03) 415 8134, Fax (03) 415 8137
Mobile 027-242 4235
email: *kepplestone@xtra.co.nz*
www.travelwise.co.nz

Features & Attractions
- *Sandy beach & Hooker sealions*
- *Close to penguins and falls*
- *Southern scenic route*
- *Separate guest house*
- *Royal Spoonbills*
- *Native birdsong*

**Beachstay
Bed & Breakfast**

Double	$120
Single	$85
Child	$20

Bedrooms	Qty
Double	1
Twin	
Single	

Bed Size	Qty
Super King	1
Queen	
King/Single	
Single	

Bathrooms	Qty
Ensuite	2
Private	
Family Share	

There are no strangers here, only friends we have not met.

Kepplestone-by-the Sea is situated 100 metres from the beach, where Hooker sealions bask.
We are close to all Catlins scenery, waterfalls, walks, Royal Spoonbills. Enjoy private viewing of Yellow Eyed penguins. Spend a relaxing night in our separate guest house and watch tuis and bellbirds while having breakfast with our delicious homemade goodies.
Golf course nearby, clubs available.

DIRECTIONS:
Follow signs towards Pounawea, at golf course go across bridge and turn right to Newhaven and Surat Bay Road (3 km metal) first house on left

CURIO BAY BOUTIQUE ACCOMMODATION

501 Curio Bay Road, RD 1, Tokanui, Southland
Ph (03) 246 8797, Fax (03) 246 8334
email: *accommodation@curiobay.com*

Tariff : N.Z. Dollars	
Double	$160-220
Single	$160
Child	

Bedrooms	Qty
Double	2
Twin	
Single	
Bed Size	**Qty**
Super King	2
King	
Queen	
Double	
Single	
Bathrooms	**Qty**
Ensuite	2
Private	
Guest Share	

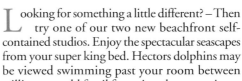

Absolute Beachfront Accommodation
Spectacular Seascape & Wildlife

Features & Attractions

- *Absolute beachfront*
- *Fossil forest*
- *Hectors dolphins*
- *Stunning sea views*
- *Yellow-eyed penguins*
- *Wildlife at your door*
- *Breakfast not included*
- *5 min. drive to local café*

L ooking for something a little different? – Then try one of our two new beachfront self-contained studios. Enjoy the spectacular seascapes from your super king bed. Hectors dolphins may be viewed swimming past your room between November and April. The 160 million year old fossil forest is only a ten minute walk along the beach. Yellow-eyed penguins also live at the fossil forest and may be viewed from the platform.

We offer a variety of music, freshly ground coffee and a place to put your feet up and relax. Our cell phone and television-free studios have solar heated water and floors, spacious bathrooms and sleep two to three people. Complimentary laundry facilities available on site. Local restaurant, café, art gallery and museum are only five minutes drive away.

Come and escape to Curio Bay!

Map:
To Invercargill
N
92
To Fortrose
To Balclutha
Waikawa
Curio Bay
Boutique Accommodation

GREENBUSH B&B AND FARMSTAY

298 Fortrose-Otara Road, No 5 RD, Invercargill
Ph (03) 246 9506, Fax (03) 246 9505
Mobile 021-395 196
email: *info@greenbush.co.nz*
www.greenbush.co.nz

Tariff : N.Z. Dollars	
Double	$150-200
Single	$120-150
Child	neg

Bedrooms	Qty
Double	2
Twin	1
Single	

Bed Size	Qty
Super King	
King	1
Queen	1
Double	
King/Single	2

Bathrooms	Qty
Ensuite	3
Private	
Guest Share	

 Bed & Breakfast Farmstay

Features & Attractions

- Stroll a wild beach
- Dinner by arrangement
- Enjoy the wildlife
- Comfortable guest lounge
- Enjoy golf by the sea
- Relax in the garden
- Delve into history
- Centrally heated home

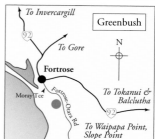

DIRECTIONS: At Fortrose on Southern Scenic Route turn into Moray Terrace, the Coastal Route. We are 4 km from that turn-off on the right hand side of Fortrose-Otara Road, Rapid No 298.

Ann and Donald McKenzie at **Greenbush Bed & Breakfast** are known for their wonderful southern hospitality. Greenbush is a 1000 acre family estate that dates back to 1865. A working sheep and cattle farm, guests at Greenbush have the opportunity to enjoy private beach access, the farm's lake and a farm tour. Nestled in two acres of garden, **Greenbush** is ideally situated five minutes from Fortrose off the Soutern Scenic Route. Within thirty minutes drive you can enjoy Curio Bay, Waipapa Point, Waipohatu and Slope Point, the southern most point in the South Island. **Greenbush** is forty minutes from Invercargill, an ideal stop-off either before or after visiting Stewart Island and Fiordland.

FORTROSE RETREAT

Southern Scenic Route, midway Fortrose and Tokanui
Ph (03) 246 9557, Fax (03) 246 9557
Free Ph: 0800 305 020
email: *info@fortroseretreat.co.nz*
www.fortroseretreat.co.nz

Features & Attractions

- *Secluded & private*
- *Outside double spa bath*
- *Native bush walk*
- *Farm & garden tour available*
- *Beach, fishing & golf nearby*
- *Continental breakfast*

$	Double	$175-200
	Single	neg
	Child	neg

Farmstay Cottage with Spectacular Views

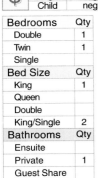

Bedrooms	Qty
Double	1
Twin	1
Single	
Bed Size	**Qty**
King	1
Queen	
Double	
King/Single	2
Bathrooms	**Qty**
Ensuite	
Private	1
Guest Share	

We offer you a warm welcome to this five star, fully self-contained cottage on the Southern Scenic Route. A private road through native bush will lead you to your own secluded "retreat" accommodation, which is set on a hillside of our 850 acre sheep farm. Be as busy as you like exploring the rugged Catlins coastline, join us on a tour around our farm and garden or just unwind in this tranquil setting.

Sliding glass doors from the living room and master bedroom open onto your covered deck, where you can enjoy the panoramic views over rolling farmland to the sea with views of Stewart Island and Bluff in the background.

When you are ready, relax in your outside double spa bath, soak in the ambience of the peaceful country atmosphere and watch the stunning sunsets.

WATERSIDE WAIKAWA

174 Progress Valley Road, Catlins
Ph (03) 246 8843
Fax (03) 246 8844
e-mail: *catlinsfarmstay@xtra.co.nz*
www.catlinsfarmstay.co.nz

Features & Attractions

- *Five minutes from Curio Bay, fossil forest, dolphins & penguins*
- *Good meals available locally*
- *Waterfront position*
- *Native birds abound, bush walks*
- *Waikawa Musuem*

$	Double	$180-250
	Extra person	–
	Child	–

Quality Self-contained Accommodation

Bedrooms	Qty
Double	1
Twin	
Single	
Bed Size	**Qty**
King	1
Queen	
Double	
King Singles	
Bathrooms	**Qty**
Ensuite	1
Private	
Guest Share	

Waterside Waikawa is situated in a quiet spot in the village of Waikawa, an old fishing settlement. Your accommodation is on the far left of the house picture, a separate studio unit with a little kitchen, microwave, cook top etc. The bathroom is of a good size with shower and toilet. The bedroom has a king bed, a sofa, a small table and slider doors to outside living and full laundry facilities.

Enjoy the wonderful view of ever changing waters of the Waikawa. No television or cell phone coverage, but look out the window and there i s the Discovery Channel! Email us for more info if needed. We would be happy to help you with your holiday plans.

SMITH'S FARMSTAY

365 Wyndham-Mokoreta Rd, No 2 RD, Wyndham, Southland
Ph (03) 206 4840, Fax (03) 206 4847
Mobile 027- 4286 6920
email: *beverly@smithsfarmstay.co.nz*
www.smithsfarmstay.co.nz

Tariff : N.Z. Dollars	
Double	$110-150
Single	$100-110
Child	neg

Bedrooms	Qty
Double	2
Twin	1
Single	

Bed Size	Qty
Super King	1
King	
Queen	1
Double	
King Single	1

Bathrooms	Qty
Ensuite	1
Private	1
Guest Share	1

 Fisherman's Retreat - Farmstay

Features & Attractions

- *Genuine sheep farm experience*
- *Close to 'Maple Glen' garden*
- *Hand knitted jerseys - pure NZ wool*
- *Beautiful 'Catlins' area close by*
- *Trout fishing 5 km,*
- *Comfortable, quality beds*
- *Quiet, peaceful surroundings*
- *Dinner by prior arrangement*

Beverly and Doug assure you of a warm welcome to their modern farm house and 260-hectare sheep farm. We are situated on the hills above **Wyndham, only 3.65 km,** set in quiet and peaceful surroundings. The **Mataura, Mimihau and Wyndham Rivers**, **renowned for Brown Trout** are only a short 5 km away. Doug, a

keen experienced fisherman, is only too happy to share his knowledge of these rivers with you. Beverly, a qualified nurse, enjoys cooking, floral art, gardening and hand knitting. Each bedroom has a view and is tastefully furnished to meet your needs. Genuine home cooking. Special diets available on request. You are most welcome to join us for the evening meal which is $40 per person. Children's rates negotiable. **Farm tour** and feeding of the animals when in season. We enjoy meeting people and both are of a friendly disposition with a sense of humor. Packed lunches, laundry facilities, fax and email also available.

DIRECTIONS:
Drive to Wyndham:
only 4 km from Wyndham
on the Wyndham Mokoreta Road.
Smith's Farmstay sign at gate.

THE MANOR

9 Drysdale Road, Myross Bush, Invercargill
Ph (03) 230 4788, Fax (03) 230 4788
Mobile 027-667 0904
email: *the.manor@xtra.co.nz*
www.manorbb.co.nz

Tariff : N.Z. Dollars	
Double	$100-140
Single	$70-85
Child	neg

Bedrooms	Qty
Double	3
Twin	
Single	

Bed Size	Qty
Super King	
King	
Queen	3
Double	
Single	2

Bathrooms	Qty
Ensuite	1
Private	1
Guest Share	1

Homestay
Bed & Breakfast

Features & Attractions

- *Quiet & peaceful*
- *Warm home*
- *City 5 minutes*
- *Email & fax facilities*
- *Golf courses close by*
- *Dinner by arrangement*
- *Near Southern Scenic Route*
- *2.5hrs to Te Anau/Queenstown*

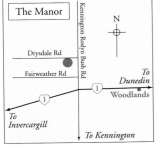

DIRECTIONS:
Signs on Highway One
at Kennington Corner.

Relax and enjoy our warm, comfortable home with under floor heating, situated in a sheltered garden setting on our ten acre farmlet.

There's a private guest area with television, refrigerator, tea/coffee making facilities. Alternatively you are welcome to join us in our lounge. We are retired farmers, keen golfers, enjoy gardening, harness racing, travel and meeting people.

We invite you to dine on meals of fresh homegrown produce and continental or cooked breakfasts.

Courtesy pickup from terminals. A stop on your way to Stewart Island, Southern Scenic Route, Queenstown or Te Anau.

We would enjoy having you stay with us.

541

84 ON KING

84 King Street, Invercargill
Ph (03) 217 3919, Fax (03) 217 3919
email: *84onking@xtra.co.nz*

Features & Attractions

- *Friendly hospitality*
- *Dinner by arrangement*
- *Email & fax available*
- *Close to city centre*
- *Walking distance to park*
- *Gateway to Fiordland/Queenstown*

**Homestay
Bed & Breakfast**

Double	$100-115
Single	$65-75
Child	

A warm welcome awaits you in our new home situated in the popular Windsor Shopping Centre adjacent to shops, restaurants and cafés and just a few minutes from the centre of Invercargill City. Our home is warm and inviting with underfloor heating and a sunny outlook. We are semi-retired farmers with interests in farming, golf, gardening, cooking, Lions and voluntary work in the community. Invercargill is a great place to spend a few days enjoying the green Southland farmland, bush walks, parks, golf courses and seashores on your way to Stewart Island, Fiordland or Queenstown. We have ample off-street parking or alternatively we will be happy to collect you from the airport or bus terminals.

Bedrooms	Qty
Double	1
Twin	1
Single	
Bed Size	**Qty**
King	1
Queen	
Double	
King/Single	2
Bathrooms	**Qty**
Ensuite	
Private	
Guest Share	1

GLENROY PARK HOMESTAY

23 Glenroy Park Drive, Invercargill
Ph (03) 215 8464, Fax (03) 215 8464
Mobile 027-376 2228
email: *home_hosp@actrix.co.nz*

Features & Attractions

- *Warm hospitality*
- *Home cooking*
- *Quiet retreat*
- *Gateway to Fiordland & Catlins*
- *Excellent golf courses*
- *Invercargill – a garden city*

$	Double	$110-120
	Single	$75-85
	Child	$12

Homestay
Bed & Breakfast

Bedrooms	Qty
Double	1
Twin	1
Single	1
Bed Size	**Qty**
King	
Queen	1
Twin	1
Single	1
Bathrooms	**Qty**
Ensuite	
Private	1
Guest Share	1

Exclusively yours in a quiet retreat, with parks, restaurants and shops only a short distance away. We enjoy meeting people and love to cook. We both garden, are enthusiastic golfers, with many courses nearby. Be our special guest and share an evening of relaxation and friendship. Dinner available. Invercargill, our garden city, has many historic buildings, lovely parks and gardens, and a unique museum with live tuatara lizards. Gateway to the pleasures of Fiordland, Queenstown, Catlins and Stewart Island.

DIRECTIONS: **From Queenstown:** Turn left at 2nd set of lights, Bainfield Road, travel 500m – we are 1st on left,Glenroy Park Drive, 3rd house on left.
From Dunedin: Along main street (Tay Street) turn right at War Memorial towards Queenstown, travel approx 5km, turn right at traffic lights into Bainfield Road, then as above.

VICTORIA RAILWAY HOTEL

3 Leven Street, PO Box 44, Invercargill
Ph (03) 218 1281, Fax (03) 218 1283
email: *vrhotel@xtra.co.nz*
www.vrhotel.info

Features & Attractions

- *Private boutique hotel*
- *An Invercargill icon*
- *Old world charm*
- *Historic Places Trust Class I*
- *Broadband internet access*
- *Breakfast optional extra*

$	Double	$125-160
	Single	$115-125
	Child	$15

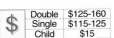

Boutique
Accommodation

Bedrooms	Qty
Double	4
Twin	3
Single	4
Bed Size	**Qty**
King	
Queen	5
Double	5
Single	3
Bathrooms	**Qty**
Ensuite	11
Private	
Guest Share	

Come and enjoy old-world charm, elegance and southern hospitality in a privately owned Boutique Hotel in the heart of Invercargill City. Built in 1896, the Hotel is a registered Class 1 New Zealand Historic Places Trust heritage building. We have completed significant refurbishment over the last three years: smoke detection, automatic fire sprinklers, CCTV, 24 hour PIR access, new bathrooms, broadband, etc. Internally we are now "modern" whilst retaining the building's atmosphere and character. In the evening come and relax in our Lounge Bar before dining and then enjoy traditional Asian Pacific Kiwi fare and a selection of local beers and fine New Zealand Wines. In the morning we offer both a continental and a full cooked "English" breakfast.

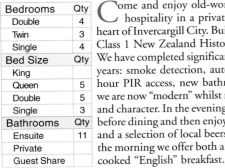

Sails Ashore & Kowhai Lane

11 View Street, PO Box 66, Stewart Island
Ph (03) 219 1151, Fax (03) 219 1151
email: *tait@sailsashore.co.nz*
www.sailsashore.co.nz

Tariff : N.Z. Dollars	
Double	$145-380
Single	
Child	

Bedrooms	Qty
Double/Twin	4
Twin	
Single	
Bed Size	Qty
Super King	
King/Single	3
Queen	1
Double	
Single	2
Bathrooms	Qty
Ensuite	6
Private	1
Guest Share	

 Luxury Boutique Accommodation or Self-catering House and SC Flat

Features & Attractions

- *Rakiura National Park*
- *Member NZ Birding Network*
- *Private central locations*
- *Courtesy Transfers*
- *Activities planning*
- *Specialist Natural History guides*
- *Ulva Island tours*
- *Scenic Road tours*

Iris, Anne and Peter welcome you to Stewart Island, **Sails Ashore Boutique Luxury Hosted Accommodation** (1st picture) and **Kowhai Lane Holiday Home** (2nd picture). Both overlook Halfmoon Bay and are about four minutes stroll from the waterfront. As well as delightful sea views both have private gardens for you to enjoy. Each house has a large sitting or sunroom, where you can enjoy our extensive library of books, photos and local interest DVD's. Telephone and internet is available, as is a guest laundry. For evening meals you have the option of eating out at one of the excellent local restaurants or alternatively have one delivered to you from their menu. An absolute 'must do' is a guided walk with us on Ulva Island, open sanctuary and

conservation showpiece. You may choose to extend this to include a leisurely exploration of Paterson Inlet aboard Talisker, or enjoy a scenic road tour with us. At **Sails Ashore** our border terrier will be absolutely delighted to take you for a walk. Guests may come as strangers, we hope they leave as friends.

 Sails Ashore Hosted Accommodation is $380 per room per night (2 king, king singles)
Kowhai Lane Holiday Home is $170 per room per night (2 king/king single, 1 queen)
Kowhai Lane Self-contained flat is $145 per night (2 single or extra double).

The
Translated Travellers' Pages

Herzlich Willkommen!

ようこそ！

歡迎！

"Lernen Sie das wahre Neuseeland kennen - die Neuseeländer selbst"

'Charming Places to Stay' in Neuseeland heißt Sie herzlich willkommen!

Eine überaus große Auswahl an Übernachtungsmöglichkeiten erwartet Sie in der Welt von "Bed & Breakfast" (private Übernachtung inclusive Frühstück) - vom einfachen Landhaus bis zum stattlichen Familiensitz. Überall werden Sie auf freundliche, aufgeschlossene Neuseeländer treffen. Manche von ihnen haben die Tradition des Gastgebens im Lauf der Jahre zu einer regelrechten Kunst entwickelt, auf die sie besonders stolz sind. Sogenannte "Homestays", "Farmstays", Gastehäuser oder "Boutique"-Unterkünfte - sie alle fallen unter den Begriff "Bed & Breakfast". Hier lernen Sie das wahre Neuseeland kennen: die Neuseeländer selbst.

- Ob Lehrer, Farmer oder ein pensionierter Angestellter, ob Künstler, Obstbauer, Heilpraktiker oder Schriftsteller, die Palette ist reichhaltig. Zum angenehmen Abenteuer kann die Übernachtung beispielsweise in einer Fischerlodge oder auf einer Schafsfarm im Hochland werden. Warum lernen Sie nicht nebenbei ein wenig reiten oder weben oder fühlen Sie sich einfach wie zu Hause in einem "Homestay" oder "Countrystay" in der Stadt oder auf dem Land. Die Neuseeländer sind bekannt als warmherzige Gastgeber, Sie werden sich überall willkommen fühlen und unvergeßliche Reiseerinnerungen mit nach Hause bringen.

Was Sie erwarten können

Bed & Breakfast in Neuseeland ist bekannt für guten Service. Die Unterkünfte sind sauber, verfügen über bequeme Betten und bieten ein gutes, reichliches Frühstück an. Natürlich steht Ihr Wohlbefinden an erster Stelle. Ihre Gastgeber werden Ihnen gerne bei der Planung Ihrer weiteren Reise behilflich sein. Die Gastgeber wissen am besten darüber Bescheid, was die jeweilige Region zu bieten hat. Nutzen Sie diese unbezahlbaren Informationen aus erster Hand.

Was man von Ihnen erwartet

Ihre Gastgeber werden alles versuchen, Ihnen den Aufenthalt so angenehm wie möglich zu machen. Vergessen Sie jedoch bitte nicht, daß Sie in den meisten Fällen in Privathäusern zu Gast sein werden. Bedenken Sie auch die scheinbar unwichtigen Dinge. Es empfiehlt sich beispielsweise, um einen Hausschlüssel zu bitten, bevor Sie abends länger ausbleiben. Falls Sie ein Ferngespräch führen wollen, ist es besser, zuerst den Tarif abzuklären. Sagen Sie bitte auch so bald wie möglich Bescheid, wenn sich Ihre Ankunft verspäten sollte. Ein wenig Rücksichtnahme Ihrerseits wird so dazu beitragen, daß alle Beteiligten die Zeit auf eine angenehme Weise verbringen.

Praktische Hinweise

Besonders während der Sommersaison können Sie unnötige Enttäuschungen vermeiden, wenn Sie Ihre Unterkunft im voraus buchen. Es empfiehlt sich auch, die Gastgeber einen Tag vor Ihrer Ankunft anzurufen, um die Buchung zu bestätigen und die ungefähre Ankunftszeit mitzuteilen. Einige Bed & Breakfast Häuser bieten einen Abholdienst von Bus, Bahn oder Flughafen an - dieser Service ist oft im Preis mit eingeschlossen. Sagen Sie auch bitte rechtzeitig Bescheid, wenn Sie bei Ihren Gastgebern zusätzlich zur Übernachtung gerne ein warmes Abendessen hätten.

Bed & Breakfast

Bed & Breakfast ist der Oberbegriff für alle Unterkunftsarten, die ein bequemes Bett, ein reichliches Frühstück und persönlichen Service im Preis einschließen. Während Ihres Aufenthalts werden Sie aufs Freundlichste von Ihren Gastgebern betreut.

Homestay

"Homestay" ist eine sehr beliebte Bed & Breakfast Variante. Sie wohnen in Privathäusern, die Gastgeber sind aufgeschlossen und freundlich und werden alles ihnen Mögliche tun, damit Sie sich "ganz wie zu Hause" fühlen nach dem Motto: "Sie kommen als Fremde und gehen als Freunde."

Countrystay

"Countrystays" sind Bed & Breakfast-Unterkünfte in ländlicher Umgebung. Sie wohnen meist in nächster Nähe von dem, was Sie am typischen Landleben so schätzen. Ob Sie wandern gehen wollen, angeln oder einfach nur die unbeschreibliche Natur pur genießen wollen, hier können Sie sich abseits vom Großstadtstreß in aller Ruhe erholen.

Farmstay

Wenn Sie echtes neuseeländisches Farmerleben hautnah genießen wollen, dann sind Sie im "Farmstay" gut aufgehoben. Üblicherweise können Sie bei der Farmtour mit auf die Weiden gehen und beim Füttern der Farmtiere mit dabei sein. Das Frühstück wird meistens mit der Familie zusammen eingenommen. Viele Farmstays bieten Vollverpflegung an.

Guesthouse/Inn

"Guest Houses" sind meistens Häuser, die eine größere Zahl von Gästen beherbergen, aber trotzdem eine persönliche Note aufweisen. Manche haben mehrere Aufenthaltsräume und einen speziellen Frühstücksraum. "Guest Houses" bieten im allgemeinen kein warmes Abendessen an.

Boutique Accommodation

Der Begriff "Boutique" soll Ihnen sagen, daß es sich hier um ganz besonders schöne Bed & Breakfast-Übernachtungsmöglichkeiten handelt: eine geschmackvolle Inneneinrichtung, stilvolle Architektur oder ein romantisches Ambiente. Die Gastgeber dieser Häuser legen größten Wert auf gepflegte Gastfreundschaft.

Luxury Accommodation

Die Luxusunterkünfte bieten eine hervorragende Ausstattung, exzellentes Essen und ganz besonderen Service. Oft sind diese Häuser architektonische Glanzstücke oder sie liegen in einzigartiger Umgebung. "Luxus" steht für außergewöhnliche Unterkunft und Gastfreundschaft.

Self-contained Accommodation

Unterkünfte für Selbstversorger sind oft komplette Einliegerwohnungen oder einzeln stehende Häuschen mit eigenem Badezimmer und eigener Toilette und meistens mit Küche, Waschmaschine und Wäschetrockner. In manchen Fällen nehmen Sie das Frühstück zusammen mit der Gastfamilie ein. Es wird aber auch oftmals an die Haustür gebracht, oder Sie finden die Zutaten bereits in der Küche.

"Auf einen Blick"

Kontaktaufnahme

Wer sind die Gastgeber und wo wohnen sie? Wie kommen Sie schnell mit ihnen in Kontakt?

"Auf einen Blick"

Übernachtungspreis

*Alle Preise gelten für eine Übernachtung. **Double** ist der Preis für zwei Personen in einem Zimmer, **Single** der Preis für eine Person in einem Zimmer. In einigen Fällen ist zusammen mit der Buchung eine Anzahlung erforderlich. Frühstück ist im Preis mit inbegriffen (falls nicht ausdrücklich anders erwähnt). **Alle Preise gelten in $ NZ**. Bitte lassen Sie sich die Preise von den Gastgebern bestätigen.*

"Auf einen Blick"

Symbole für Kategorien

Mit diesen einprägsamen Symbolen können Sie Ihre bevorzugte Unterkunftsmöglichkeit schnell ausfindig machen. Dieses System ist besonders hilfreich für Reisende, die die englische Sprache nicht fließend beherrschen.

"Auf einen Blick"

Kategoriestreifen

Die Gastgeber beschreiben ihre Kategorie in ihren eigenen Worten.

"Auf einen Blick"

Besondere Details

In Stichworten die attraktivsten Details der Unterkunft und der Sehenswürdigkeiten in der Umgebung.

"Auf einen Blick"

Kleine Straßenkarte

Im weißen Kästchen finden Sie den Namen des Hauses; der rote Punkt zeigt Ihnen die genaue Position. Im grünen Kästchen finden Sie die Wegbeschreibung.

Klar und übersichtlich

Schnell zu finden: Adresse, Telefon- und Faxnummer, E-Mail und Internetadresse.

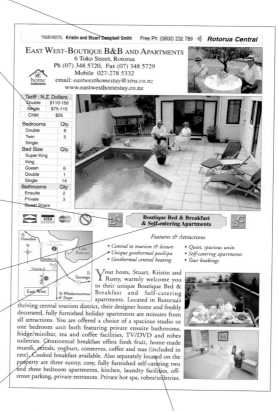

"Ein persönliches Willkommen"

Dieser Text, von den Gastgebern persönlich verfaßt, beschreibt deren Lebensstil und Interessen, die Art der Unterkunft und was Sie als Gast erwarten können.

 Nichtraucher

Abkürzungen

○SH – State Highway
h.p. – halber Preis
N.A. – nicht zutreffend
neg. – nach Vereinbarung
Qty – Anzahl
Tce – Terrace

Direkt buchen - Extrakosten vermeiden

Wenn Sie die Buchung selbst vornehmen, haben Sie von Anfang an persönlichen Kontakt mit Ihren Bed & Breakfast-Gastgebern in Neuseeland und vermeiden unnötige Kosten.

Wie wird dieser Reiseführer benützt – Zimmerdetails

Gästezimmer

Double = Zimmer mit Bett für 2 Personen
Twin = Zimmer mit 2 Betten für 2 Personen
Single = Zimmer mit Bett für eine Person

Bad/WC

Ensuite = Bad/WC mit Zimmer verbunden
Private = Eigenes Bad/WC, aber separat
Guest/Family Share = Bad/WC wird von Gästen oder der Gastfamilie mitbenutzt.

Bedrooms	Qty
Double	
Twin	
Single	
Bed Size	**Qty**
King	
Queen	
Double	
King/Single	
Bathrooms	**Qty**
Ensuite	
Private	
Guest Share	

Bettgrößen
Super King *180 x 200cm*
King *165 x 200cm*
Queen *150 x 200cm*
Double *135 x 190cm*
Single *90 x 190cm*
King Single *90 x 200cm*

Kategorie Symbole

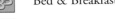 Bed & Breakfast

Boutique Accommodation

Countrystay

 Farmstay

 Guest House / Inn

Homestay

Luxury Accommodation

Self-contained Accom. & Cottages

Gängige Kreditkarten

 Amex – American Express

 Japanese Credit Card

 VISA

Diners

 Bankcard

 MasterCard

 Maestro

 Eftpos

Mitgliedschaft in folgenden Verbänden und Gesellschaften

 Kiwihost

 Qualmark NZ

 @home NEW ZEALAND.

 Historic Places Trust

The @home NEW ZEALAND logo represents the leading organisation of Hosted Accommodation providers in New Zealand. It assures you of a warm welcome from friendly, helpful hosts. Accommodations displaying this logo have been assessed and meet the quality standards laid down by the association.

ニュージーランドの家庭生活を実体験！

～ニュージーランド・B＆Bへのお誘い～

ニュージーランド人は、旅行者に対する心暖まる、フレンドリーなもてなしを誇りとする国民として知られています。この「ニュージーランド風のもてなし」をじかに体験できるのが、Bed & Breakfast（ベッド・アンド・ブレックファースト、B＆B）です。これは一般のホテルとは一味ちがった、アット・ホームなサービスを身上とする宿泊施設の総称で、その具体的な中身はいろいろです。宿泊の場所でいうと、町中の一軒家・コッテージ・釣り場のロッジ・高原の牧場・乗馬や機織りの学校・お城（！）といった具合に多岐にわたっています。実際の名称としては、 Guest House （ゲスト・ハウス）、 Inn（イン）、 Boutique Accommodation （ブティック・アコモデーション）、 Countrystay （カ

ントリーステイ）などがあります。また、安いものから高くて豪華なものまでありますので、予算に合わせて選ぶことが可能です。B&B のホスト(host, オーナー)は現役の教員・農家・芸術家・信仰療法家・作家、さらにはもと医師や弁護士など、実に多彩です。ホストの中には、単に話好き、という人から、専門的なサービスを提供する人まで、さまざまです。B&B は、「本物の」ニュージーランドを体験するのに恰好の機会といえます。ホストと、趣味や仕事の話などで盛り上がるのも楽しみのひとつではないでしょうか。

皆様の旅行が楽しく、思い出深いものとなりますように……

WHAT TO EXPECT

きれいな部屋、寝心地のよいベッド、おいしくて量もたっぷりの朝食、真心のこもったもてなし…ニュージーランドの Bed & Breakfast は、サービスの水準が高いことで知られています。さらに、ホストからは、その地域や周辺の見どころに関する詳しい「生の情報」を得ることができます。お客様の興味・関心をホストにお伝えください。ホストは皆様の旅行がすばらしいものとなる手助けができることを願っています。

— 宿泊者の心得

WHAT IS EXPECTED OF YOU

ホストは、お客様が楽しく思い出深いひとときを過ごすことができるよう、最大限の努力をしていますが、お客様の側にも配慮いただきたい点があります。それは、B＆Bは、基本的には「一般家庭」に泊まる、という形式をとっているという点です。ですから、ホストやその家族にたいする「ちょとした」気配りが大切です。たとえば、夜、帰りが遅くなる場合には、余裕をもって事前にその旨を伝えておき、「合鍵」を受け取っておくとか、電話を使用する際には、あらかじめ料金の確認をしておく、などです。こうした心遣いが、B＆Bでの滞在を成功させるカギなのです。

WHAT TO DO — HINTS

B&B 宿泊の貴重なチャンスを逃さないためには、予約するのが一番です。（特に真夏は込み合います。）予約されましたら、到着の前日にホストに予約の確認をし、到着予定時刻を伝えておくことをおすすめします。ホストの中には、coach（コーチ、長距離バス）・飛行機・列車の発着場からの無料送迎サービスを行っている人もいます。また、到着日の夕食を希望される場合には、前日または前前日に、その旨をホストに伝えておきましょう。

Bed & Breakfast Categories

ベッド・アンド・ブレックファースト

一泊・朝食付きの宿の総称です。快適なベッドと、たっぷりの朝食、それにホストの暖かいおもてなしを存分にお楽しみください。

ホームステイ

ごく一般の家庭で、ホストによる身近なもてなしを受けながら宿泊するものです。ホストは人と出会うのが好きで、宿泊客をまるで自分の家にいるような、和やかな雰囲気にしてくれます。宿泊客の皆様が、初めて会った時には「見知らぬ他人」でも、別れるときには「親しい友人」となることを、ホストは心得ているのです。

カントリーステイ

Homestay と同様、一般の家庭に滞在するものです。Countrystay の特徴は、場所が「いなか」にある点です。都会とはちがった、ニュージーランドの一面をじかに体験できます。

ファームステイ

ニュージーランドの農業について理解を深めたい、という人には理想的な機会です。動物たちと身近に接しながら、農場での生活を経験していきます。牧場内のツアーを行っているところもあります。通常、朝食はホストの家族とともにとります。場所柄、近所にレストランなどがないため、多くのFarmstay では昼食や夕食も出されます。

 ## ゲスト・ハウス

通常、規模が比較的大きく、他のB&B の施設に比べ、より多くの宿泊客を泊めることができる施設ですが、B&B ならではの、フレンドリーなもてなしは変わりません。複数のラウンジや、朝食室が用意されているところもあります。夕食は出されないのが普通です。

ブティック・アコモデーション

特色ある家屋を用いたB&B です。長い年月が醸し出す気品、優雅さ、ロマンス － Boutique Accommodation は、宿泊客の皆様をそうした雰囲気の中に包んでくれます。この雰囲気をいかに盛り上げるかが、ホストの腕のみせどころです。

ラクシャリー・アコモデーション

最高の立地条件のなかにある宿泊施設で、施設内外はさまざまな魅力でいっぱいです。豪華極まる設備や食事、それに群をぬいたハイ・クオリティーのサービスが特徴です。

セルフコンテインド・アコモデーション

宿泊者のための独立した入口・バスルーム・ラウンジを含むのが普通です。独立した台所や洗濯質室が用意されているところもあります。宿泊施設は、一軒家のなかの一区画として存在する場合と、別棟の建物として存在する場合とがあります。朝食はホストの家族とともにとる場合、宿泊施設まで届けられる場合、朝食の材料が宿泊所に用意されており、宿泊者が自分で用意する場合とさまざまです。

"at a glance"

イージー・コントロール・パネル
ホストの氏名・所在地・連絡先など。

"at a glance"

ここに表示されているのは、一泊あたりの
料金です。**Double**（ダブル）は、一部屋
を2名で使用した場合の料金です。**Single**
（シングル）は、一部屋を1名で使用した
場合の料金です。予約の際に deposit
（ディポジット、料金の一部前払い）が
必要なところもあります。特に明記のない
場合、料金には朝食代が含まれています。
料金の表記は、すべて「NZ ドル」です。
料金に関する詳しい内容は、直接ホスト
までおたずねください。

"at a glance"

カテゴリー・シンボル
おさがしの B&B のタイプがすぐに見つか
るよう工夫されたマークです。お役立て
ください。

"at a glance"

カテゴリー・パネル
該当する B&B のカテゴリーの、ホスト自
身による定義・説明。

"at a glance"

フィーチャーズ＆アトラクションズ
宿泊施設およびその周辺のみどころのご紹
介。

"at a glance"

ロケーション・マップ
宿泊施設の位置が赤丸で示されています。
白のかこみの中に施設の名称が記されてい
ます。行き方の説明が追加で示されている
場合もあります。

クリアー・アドレス・ディーテールズ
宿泊施設の所在地・電話番号・Fax 番号・
e-mail アドレス・インターネット・ホーム
ページのアドレスといった、大切な情報は
こちらをご覧ください。

YOUR HOSTS: Kristin and Stuart Campbell Smith   Free Ph: (0800) 232 789 ◀ *Rotorua Central*

EAST WEST-BOUTIQUE B&B AND APARTMENTS
6 Toko Street, Rotorua
Ph (07) 348 5720, Fax (07) 348 5729
Mobile 027-278 5332
email: *eastwesthomestay@xtra.co.nz*
www.eastwesthomestay.co.nz

Tariff : N.Z. Dollars	
Double	$110-150
Single	$75-110
Child	$25
Bedrooms	**Qty**
Double	8
Twin	5
Single	
Bed Size	**Qty**
Super King	
King	
Queen	6
Double	
Single	14
Bathrooms	**Qty**
Ensuite	7
Private	3
Guest Share	

Boutique Bed & Breakfast & Self-catering Apartments

Features & Attractions
- Central to tourism & leisure
- Unique geothermal pool/spa
- Geothermal central heating
- Quiet, spacious units
- Self-catering apartments
- Tour bookings

Your hosts, Stuart, Kristin and Rusty, warmly welcome you to their unique Boutique Bed & Breakfast and Self-catering apartments. Located in Rotorua's thriving central tourism district, their designer home and freshly decorated, fully furnished holiday apartments are minutes from all attractions. You are offered a choice of a spacious studio or one bedroom unit both featuring private ensuite bathrooms, fridge/minibar, tea and coffee facilities, TV/DVD and robes toiletries. Continental breakfast offers fresh fruit, home-made muesli, cereals, yoghurt, conserves, coffee and teas (included in rate). Cooked breakfast available. Also separately located on the property are three sunny, cosy, fully furnished self-catering two and three bedroom apartments, kitchen, laundry facilities, off-street parking, private entrances. Private hot spa, robes/toiletries.

パーソナル・ウォーム・ウェルカム
ホストから読者へのひとことです。宿泊
施設の特徴や、ホストの人柄・ライフ・ス
タイルといったものを垣間見ることができ
ます。

 No Smoking

Cnr – Corner: コーナー「角」
h.p. – half price: ハーフ・プライス「半額」
N.A. – not applicable: ノット・アプリカ
　　ブル「該当項目なし」
neg. – negotiable: ニゴーシャブル「交渉可」
Qty – Quantity: クウォンティティ「数量」
Tce – Terrace: テラス

宿泊予約申し込みは、B&B のホストに直接
なさいますと、ホストとそれだけ早くから
知り合うことができ、また中間業者を通し
た場合にかかる、さまざまな手数料を省く
ことができるので有利です。

ガイドのてびき － 客室・設備に関する記 述 について

Bedrooms

Double	=	二人用ベッドがある部屋
Twin	=	一人用ベッドが２つある部屋
Single	=	一人用ベッドが１つある部屋

Bathrooms

Ensuite	=	寝室に隣接
Private	=	各宿泊客専用
Guest Share/Family Share	=	他の宿泊客またはホストの家族と共用

Bedrooms	Qty
Double	
Twin	
Single	
Bed Size	**Qty**
King	
Queen	
Double	
King/Single	
Bathrooms	**Qty**
Ensuite	
Private	
Guest Share	

Bed Size

Super King	*180 x 200cm*
King	*165 x 200cm*
Queen	*150 x 200cm*
Double	*135 x 190cm*
Single	*90 x 190cm*
King Single	*90 x 200cm*

ガイドのてびき － カテゴリー・シンボル

 Bed & Breakfast

 Boutique Accommodation

 Countrystay

 Farmstay

 Guest House / Inn

 Homestay

 Luxury Accommodation

 Self-contained Accom. & Cottages

ガイドのてびき － お支払可能なクレジット・カード について

 Amex – American Express

 Japanese Credit Card

 VISA

Diners

 Bankcard

 MasterCard

 Maestro

 Eftpos

ガイドのてびき － B&B が提携している協会・団体について

 Kiwihost

 Qualmark NZ

 @home NEW ZEALAND.

 Historic Places Trust

 このマークは、ニュージーランド流の暖かく、フレンドリーで、質の高いサービスを保証するものです。Kiwi Host (キウ イ・ホ ス ト) は、我が国をリードする顧客サービス・トレーニング・プログラムです。

介　紹

"體驗真正的紐西蘭──它的民族"

歡迎來到紐西蘭多樣化的旅店住宿簡介

紐西蘭的住宿，由小屋到別墅，從經濟單位到豪華大宅，您都會享受到在一個親切友善且好客的環境中居住。有多種不同的住宿方式：家庭住宿、農莊住宿、旅客之家、小客店、豪華旅店、鄉村住宿等等，他們一律提供給您一張溫暖的床以及香噴噴的西式早餐。這些都能讓您親身感受到紐西蘭的生活，認識居住在這裡的居民。您更可選擇嗜好與自己相似的家庭住

宿，例如：老師、農夫、退休的專業人士、園藝專家、畫家、作家等等，住宿在他們的家，彼此交換心得，同時可享受獨特真誠的招待，體驗在漁村、郊外綿羊、海外之家的生活。不管是旅館或多樣化的家庭住宿，除了種類多之外，還充滿了紐西蘭獨特的友善及好客，不論您選擇那一種住宿，您將都是一位貴賓，盡情享受生活，讓日後有個難忘的回憶。

介　紹

期望什麼？

在紐西蘭床鋪及早餐享有標準服務的聲譽，住客會有最清潔、舒適的床，多種選擇熱烘烘早餐，及主人樂意友善的招待。除此之外，主人也會給於您居住地區的詳細資料。他們樂意幫您安排您在本地的旅遊計劃。他們豐富的經驗能增添您居住的樂趣。

對您的期望？

主人家會為您做任何的事，讓您享受一個難忘的停留。可是，請記得無論如何您只是一個客人。所以，請您注意一些事，例如，如果您晚歸的話，要向主人索取大門鎖匙，或當您要打長途、國內、本地電話時，應先詢問主人才可使用電話。請讓主人家知道您將夜歸。您處身置地的設想，會使您及主人都感到滿意。

給予您的建議

事先訂好一間房間，以避免屆時沒房間的失望，尤其在夏天時。除外，在您出發的前一天致電到主人家確定您訂好的房間及讓他們曉得您幾時會抵達。有些主人提供接送服務，如果您有需要的話。如果您需要他為您準備午餐的話，也請您早一、兩天前通知主人。

床鋪及早餐系列

床 鋪 及 早 餐

床鋪及早餐是所有不同種類住所的代稱，供您選擇。除外，在您居住時間，主人更會給予您親切友善的招待，讓您有賓至如歸之感。

古 典 大 屋

在床鋪及早餐系列中，古典大屋的建築物具有古典氣息、整齊美觀、寧靜浪漫，是適合喜歡這類型的您來居住，主人將這些建築物的特質保持得非常好，確保您最佳的享受。

鄉 村 居 住

鄉村居住類似家庭住宿。您將居住於私人家庭中，慢慢地認識及接觸鄉村迷人的風景。許多鄉村住宿都靠近著名的旅遊風景區，能讓您最方便認識這些地方。

農 場 住 宿

如果您選擇在農場居住，通常會由農場主人一家人接待您。如有需要，可為您安排參觀農場的行程，好讓您更加了解農場，您將跟農場主人一家人共同享用早餐；晚餐必須在事先通知，農場也將會為您準備，因為農場附近沒有餐館。

床鋪及早餐系列

旅客之家

旅客之家通常能容納較多的旅客。雖然如此，主人仍會給您友善親切的招待。旅客之家可能會有數間的客廳及餐廳。旅客之家不常提供晚餐給住客。

家庭住宿

家庭住宿是最普遍的住宿方式，居住在溫暖、友善、好客的家庭中。主人喜歡認識不同的人，且樂意讓您有"家"的感覺，讓您曉得，您剛來的時候雖是一個陌生人，當您要離開時卻是以朋友的身份離開。

豪華大宅

豪華大宅代表了一流的設備，上等的餐飲和超水準的服務，許多此類住宿都有各自的特色，給予您額外一流的享受，它們代表了優越的住宿。

私人住宿

此居住方式，通常包括了，私人的走道、浴室及客廳。它可以是一個家庭中隔出來的一部份或是一整間小屋。早餐可在主人家享用，也可送到您的門口或餐室。

容易聯絡的範圍

您的旅店老闆；無論是何人，
身在何處，都能迅速與他們取
得聯絡。

明確的地址

明確的地址，應包括住宿的地址，電話
和傳真號碼，電子郵件地址與網址。

價目表

價目表上的金額，表示住宿一晚的住宿
費。雙人（Double）表示兩人合用一間
房間的價錢。當您預定房間時，您可能要
預付訂金。價目表上的價錢通常包括早
餐，除非有特別註明不提供早餐。全部價
錢都以紐幣計算。請與旅店老闆確定住宿
明細資料。

各種住宿的代表符號

設計這些容易辨認的符號，是為了方便您
預約訂房，對於不太熟悉英文的遊客們，
這是絕對有幫助的。

住宿種類

旅店老闆會為您詳細介紹住宿種類。

地區特色及焦點

您住宿的四周環境以及您住宿區域的特
色與焦點，都會為您列出。

區域地圖

您所住宿的地點，在地圖上將以
紅點標示。旅店的店名，也會在
地圖上刊出。通常為配合找尋，
也都有方向圖來確認正確方向。

YOUR HOSTS: **Kristin and Stuart Campbell Smith**　Free Ph: (0800) 232 789　◀ *Rotorua Central*

EAST WEST-BOUTIQUE B&B AND APARTMENTS
6 Toko Street, Rotorua
Ph (07) 348 5720, Fax (07) 348 5729
Mobile 027-278 5332
email: *eastwesthomestay@xtra.co.nz*
www.eastwesthomestay.co.nz

Tariff : N.Z. Dollars	
Double	$110-150
Single	$75-110
Child	$25

Bedrooms	Qty
Double	8
Twin	5
Single	

Bed Size	Qty
Super King	
King	
Queen	6
Double	2
Single	14

Bathrooms	Qty
Ensuite	2
Private	3
Guest Share	

Boutique Bed & Breakfast
& Self-catering Apartments

Features & Attractions

* Central to tourism & leisure
* Unique geothermal pool/spa
* Geothermal central heating
* Quiet, spacious units
* Self-catering apartments
* Tour bookings

Your hosts, Stuart, Kristin and
Rusty, warmly welcome you
to their unique Boutique Bed &
Breakfast and Self-catering
apartments. Located in Rotorua's
thriving central tourism district, their designer home and freshly
decorated, fully furnished holiday apartments are minutes from
all attractions. You are offered a choice of a spacious studio or
one bedroom unit both featuring private ensuite bathrooms,
fridge/minibar, tea and coffee facilities, TV/DVD and robes
toiletries. Continental breakfast offers fresh fruit, home-made
muesli, cereals, yoghurt, conserves, coffee and teas (included in
rate). Cooked breakfast available. Also separately located on the
property are three sunny, cosy, fully furnished self-catering two
and three bedroom apartments, kitchen, laundry facilities, off-
street parking, private entrances. Private hot spa, robes/toiletries.

"一項特別及溫暖的歡迎"

通常歡迎詞是由旅店老闆親自設計。有關
店內設備以及獨特的住宿方式，都會有清
楚的説明。

 No Smoking

縮寫

Cnr—角落
h.p.—半價
N.A. —無此設備
Qty—可磋商
Tce—陽台

直接預約—省錢

與紐西蘭"床與早餐"
旅店系列的老闆直接預約住宿，
您從一開始就會省了許多
不必要的附加費用。

如何使用這本指南 — 客房資料

房　間

Double = 一或二張床提供兩人住宿的房間
Twin　 = 提供二張床給兩人住宿的雙人房
Single = 提供一張床給單人住宿的單人房

浴　室

Ensuite =浴室在您的房間內
Private = 提供您個人專用的浴室
Guest Share/Family Share =公共浴室，必須與
　其他家庭或住客共同使用。

Bedrooms	Qty
Double	
Twin	
Single	
Bed Size	**Qty**
King	
Queen	
Double	
King/Single	
Bathrooms	**Qty**
Ensuite	
Private	
Guest Share	

床的尺寸

Super King
180 x 200cm

King
165 x 200cm

Queen
150 x 200cm

Double
135 x 190cm

Single
90 x 190cm

King Single
90 x 200cm

如何使用這本指南 — 代號種類

BB	Bed & Breakfast	G	Guest House / Inn
BA	Boutique Accommodation	H	Homestay
C	Countrystay	LA	Luxury Accommodation
F	Farmstay	SC	Self-contained Accom. & Cottages

如何使用這本指南 — 旅店老闆接受信用卡付款

AMERICAN EXPRESS — Amex – American Express

Bankcard

JCB — Japanese Credit Card

MasterCard

VISA — VISA

Maestro

Diners — Diners

Eftpos — Eftpos

如何使用這本指南 — 協會

 Kiwihost

 @home NEW ZEALAND.

 Qualmark NZ

 Historic Places Trust

 這個商標就是保證您是受本地人所歡迎的，以及獲得親切友善的服務。Kiwi
Host 是紐西蘭顧客服務訓練計畫的得獎者，我們確信我們對於您的重視，與
您對於我們的肯定。

Special thanks to all of these friends who gave help and reassurance when deadlines loomed and spirits were low:

Lola Gloger, brilliant graphic artist.
Louise Davidson, next generation graphic designer
Joshua, Jamie, and Matthew Newman, photographers.
Karen Costello, proof reader extraordinaire.
Tim Cornelius, famous Dunedin map designer.

Translations

German translation by *Uli Newman.*
Japanese translation by *Yoshi Isoyama at Transla NZ, PO Box 8069
Dunedin, New Zealand. isoyama@xtra.co.nz*
Mandarin (Chinese) translation by *Stephen Liu at Asian Communication Company Ltd
Dunedin, New Zealand.*

Photographs:

Front Door. *Pg 3; copyright Ruslan Gilmanshin*
Destination Northland. *Pgs 4, 21, 24; E-Mail: northland@xtra.co.nz*
New Zealand Post. *Pg 17 (envelopes), E-Mail: cschelp@nzpost.co.nz*
Tourism Rotorua. *Fly Leaf, E-Mail: marketing@tourism.rdc.govt.nz*
Tourism Wairarapa. *Pg 19; E-Mail: tourwai@xtra.co.nz*
West Coast Tourism. *Pg 21, E-Mail: tourismwc@minidata.co.nz*
Tourism Nelson. *Pg 312, E-mail: info@tourism-nelson.co.nz*

NORTHLAND – BAY OF ISLANDS –
WHANGAREI

Houhora Lodge & Homestay,
   Houhora 24
Plane Tree Lodge, *Kaitaia* 25
Beachfront Ahipara, *Ahipara* 26
Shipwreck Lodge, *Kaitaia* 27
Siesta Guest Lodge and Villa Apartments,
   Kaitaia 28
Beach Abode Beachfront Lodge,
   Ahipara 29
Tasman Overlook, *Ahipara* 29
Sails Beachfront Apartment, *Mangonui* ... 30
114 on Waipapa Bed & Breakfast,
   Kerikeri 31
88 Lodge, *Kerikeri* 31
Birchwood, *Kerikeri* 32
Landing Cottage, *Kerikeri* 32
Matariki Homestay, *Kerikeri* 33
Waitui Lodge, *Kerikeri* 33
Palm View, *Kerikeri* 34
Pau Hana Lodge, *Kerikeri* 35
Rainbow Falls Lodge, *Kerikeri* 36
The Maples Bed & Breakfast,
   Kerikeri 37
Tea Tree Cottage, *Kerikeri* 38
Appledore Lodge, *Paihia* 39
Crisdon Castle, *Paihia* 40
Chalet Romantica, *Paihia* 41
Allegra House, *Paihia* 42
Bay View Suite, *Paihia* 43
Abri Apartments, *Paihia* 44
The Totaras, *Paihia* 44
Bay of Islands Beach House, *Paihia* 45
Swallow's Nest, *Paihia* 46
Windermere, *Paihia* 46
Decks of Paihia, *Paihia* 47

Marlin House, *Paihia* 48
Harbour House Villa, *Opua* 49
Mako Lodge, *Opua* 50
Pt. Veronica Lodge, *Opua* 51
Tinamara, *Te Haumi* 52
Waterview Lodge, *Opua* 53
Arcadia Historic Bed & Breakfast,
   Russell 54
Arapohue House, *Russell* 54
Aomotu Lodge, *Russell* 55
Belvedere Lodge, *Russell-Okiato* 56
Hardings' Aotearoa Lodge, *Russell* 56
Bay of Islands Cottages, *Russell* 57
La Veduta, *Russell* 58
Ounuwhao "Harding House" B&B
   Homestead, *Russell* 59
The White House Russell, *Russell* 60
Villa Russell, *Russell* 60
Russell Bay Lodge, *Russell* 61
Ten on One Country/Homestay,
   Kaikohe 62
Lupton Lodge, *Whangarei* 63
Parkhill Fine Accommodation,
   Whangarei 64
Channel Vista, *Whangarei* 65
Top Storey Bed & Breakfast,
   Tamaterau 65
Tide Song, *Whangarei* 66
Appin Cottage, *Whangarei Heads* 66
Parua House, *Whangarei* 67
Juniper House, *Maungatapere* 68
Owaitokamotu, *Maungatapere* 68
Kauri House Lodge, *Dargaville* 69
Awakino Point Boutique Motel,
   Dargaville 70
Tangowahine Farmstay, *Dargaville* 70

Index of Listings (by Regions)

Flower Haven, *Waipu Cove* 71
Zany's Haven B&B, *Waipu* 71
Mangawhai Lodge "A Room With A View",
   Mangawhai Heads 72
Zenford Lodge, *Waipu Cove* 73
Palm House, *Paparoa* 74
Petite Provence, *Matakohe* 74

AUCKLAND REGION

Kawau Island Experience, *Kawau Island* . 75
Belvedere Homestay, *Warkworth* 76
Alegria Beautyfarm, *Warkworth* 77
Warkworth Country House,
   Warkworth 78
Our Farm Park, *Puhoi* 79
Bayview Bed & Breakfast,
   Whangaparaoa 80
Gulf Harbour Views, *Whangaparaoa* 81
Peone Place Bed & Breakfast,
   Whangaparaoa 82
The Palms on Tindalls,
   Whangaparaoa 83
Waters Edge Manly, *Whangaparaoa* 84
Waiari Bed & Breakfast,
   Whangaparaoa 85
The Sheep and Shag, *Whangaparaoa* 86
Ormond House, *Silverdale* 86
Whitehills, *Kaukapakapa* 87
Kaipara House Bed & Breakfast,
   Helensville 88
Warblers Retreat, *Albany* 89
St Clair Bed & Breakfast, *Browns Bay* 90
Auckland Number One House,
   North Cote Point 91
Birdwood House, *Hillcrest* 92
Calico Lodge, *Kumeu* 93
Eastview, *Hobsonville* 94
Panorama Heights, *Swanson* 95

Hastings Hall, *Western Spring* 96
The Big Blue House, *Westmere* 97
Chalet Chevron - A Great Little Hotel,
   Parnell 97
Ponsonby Studio Loft, *Ponsonby* 98
Akarana's Nautical Nook – Sailing,
   Okahu Bay 98
Art Hotel - The Great Ponsonby,
   Ponsonby 99
Sunderland House Bed & Breakfast,
   Herne Bay 100
Moana Vista, *Herne Bay - Ponsonby* 101
Braemar on Parliament Street,
   Central Auckland 102
Ascot Parnell, *Parnell* 103
Amerissit Luxury Accommodation,
   Remuera 104
Laurel Cottage, *Epsom* 105
Woodlands, *Remuera* 106
Omahu Lodge, *Remuera* 107
Martini House, *Howick* 108
Cockle Bay Homestay, *Howick* 109
Brookwood Lodge, *Beachlands* 110
Totara Lodge, *Airport* 111
Hillpark Homestay, *Airport* 112
Airport Bed & Breakfast, *Airport* 113
Drury Homestead, *Drury* 113
Thistledown Lodge, *Ramarama* 114
Ngodevwa, *Waiuku* 114
Hunua Gorge Country House,
   Papakura 115
Brookfield Lodge, *Bombay* 116

COROMANDEL PENINSULA

Westwind Homestay, *Mangatarata* 117
Bonniebrae Farmstay, *Mangatarata* 117
Wharfedale Farmstay, *Thames* 118
Cotswold Cottage, *Thames* 118

Index of Listings (by Regions)

The Heights Bed & Breakfast,
Thames 119
Kauaeranga Country, *Thames* 120
Te Puru Coast Bed & Breakfast,
Te Puru 121
The Green House Bed & Breakfast,
Coromandel Town 121
Driving Creek Villas,
Coromandel Town 122
Driving Creek Cottage, *Coromandel* 123
Kaeppeli's, *Kuaotunu* 124
Kuaotunu Bay Lodge, *Kuaotunu* 125
Leighton Lodge, *Opito Bay* 126
Within the Bays, *Whitianga* 127
At Parkland Place, *Whitianga* 127
Centennial Heights Bed & Breakfast,
Whitianga 128
Flaxhaven Lodge, *Flaxmill Bay* 129
Cosy Cat Cottage, *Whitianga* 130
Glenvin Bed & Breakfast, *Whitianga* 130
The Mussel Bed, *Whitianga* 131
Ferry Landing Lodge, *Whitianga* 131
Mercury Orchard, *Whitianga* 132
Hahei Horizon, *Hahei* 133
Halcyon Heights Country Retreat,
Whitianga 133
Hot Water Beach Bed & Breakfast,
Whitianga 134
Kotuku, *Whangamata* 134
Colonial Homestay, *Tairua* 135
Copsefield Bed & Breakfast,
Whangamata 136
Waihi Beach Lodge, *Waihi* 137
Trout and Chicken B&B Countrystay,
Waihi 138
Waihi Waterlily Gardens, *Waihi* 138

HAMILTON – WAIKATO

Herb Garden B & B, *Te Kauwhata* 139
Herons Ridge Farmstay, *Te Kauwhata* 139
Parnassus Farm & Garden, *Huntly* 140
Las Palmas B&B Homestay, *Hamilton* ... 141
Matangi Oaks, *Hamilton* 142
Arbor Lodge, *Hamilton* 143
Saxon Lodge - The Organic Place,
Hamilton 143
Kua Makona, *Hamilton* 144
Abseil Breakfast Inn, *Waitomo Village* 145
Mt Heslington, *Otorohanga* 146
Redwood Lodge, *Otorohanga* 146
Tapanui Country Home, *Te Kuiti* 147
Park House, *Cambridge* 148
Glenelg, *Cambridge* 149
Riversong Bed & Breakfast Countrystay,
Lake Karapiro 149
Oaklane Lodge, *Morrinsville* 150

BAY OF PLENTY

Tranquility Lodge, *Katikati* 150
Cotswold Lodge, *Katikati* 151
Panorama Country Lodge, *Katikati* 152
Sagewood Lodge, *Tauranga* 153
Burr-wood Countrystay, *Katikati* 154
Tau Tau Lodge, *Tauranga* 155
Villa Collini, *Tauranga* 156
Sandtoft, *Papamoa* 156
Boatshed Motel Apartments,
Mt Maunganui 157
Hesford House, *Tauranga* 158
Fothergills on Mimiha, *Matata* 158
Pohutukawa Beach B&B and Cottage,
Matata 159
Beightons, *Whakatane* 160
Oceanspray Homestay, *Whakatane* 161

Index of Listings (by Regions)

ROTORUA

Panorama Country Homestay, *Rotorua* .. 162
Kotare Lodge, *Hamurana* 163
Springwaters Lodge, *Rotorua* 164
Te Ngae Lodge, *Rotorua* 165
Rotokawa Lodge, *Rotorua* 166
Aroden, *Lynmore* 166
Maple House, *Lynmore* 167
Appledale Cottage Bed & Breakfast,
   Rotorua Town 168
Ferntree Cottage, *Rotorua* 168
Tresco Classical Oasis B&B and Cottage,
   Rotorua 169
Innes Cottage, *Rotorua* 170
Moana Rose Lakeside Bed & Breakfast,
   Rotorua 171
Robertson House, *Rotorua Town* 171
East West, *Rotorua Town* 172
Koura Lodge Rotorua, *Rotorua* 173
Affordable Westminster Lodge and
   Cottage, *Rotorua* 174
Tirohanga-nui, *Kawaha Pt.* 175
Ariki Lodge, *Ngongotaha* 176
Bayadere Lodge, *Ngongotaha* 177
Clover Downs Estate, *Ngongotaha* 178
Country Villa, *Ngongotaha* 179
Deer Pine Lodge, *Rotorua* 180
Ngongotaha Lakeside Lodge,
   Ngongotaha 181
Ashpit Place, *Rerewhakaaitu* 182
Te Ana Farmstay, *Ngakuru* 183

TAUPO – TURANGI

Kinara Country Homestay, *Wairakei* 184
South Claragh Farm and Bird Cottage,
   Mangakino 185
Brackenhurst, *Oruanui* 185

Minarapa, *Oruanui* 186
Kinloch Lodge, *Kinloch* 187
Twynham at Kinloch, *Kinloch* 188
Acacia Bay Lakefront, *Acacia Bay* 189
Fourwinds Bed & Breakfast, *Taupo* 190
Highland Cottage, *Taupo* 191
Te Moenga, *Acacia Bay* 192
Magnifique, *Taupo* 193
Above the Lake at Windsor Charters,
   Taupo 194
The Pillars, *Taupo* 195
Fairviews, *Taupo* 196
Ambleside, *Taupo* 197
Moselle, *Taupo* 198
Pataka House, *Taupo* 198
Tui Lodge, *Turangi* 199
Pukatea Homestay, *Turangi-Motuoapa* ... 200
Founders at Turangi, *Turangi* 200
Southern Comfort Homestay,
   Turangi 201
The Birches, *Turangi* 202
Omori Lake House, *Omori* 202
Willsplace, *Omori* 203
Rangimarie Beachstay, *Anaura Bay* 203
Cedar House, *Gisborne* 204
Best Beach View, *Gisborne* 205

TARANAKI

Cottage by the Sea, *New Plymouth* 206
93 By the Sea, *New Plymouth* 207
Glen Almond House,
   New Plymouth 208
Hideaway Cottage,
   New Plymouth 209
Avocado Abodes, *New Plymouth* 210
Te Popo Gardens, *Stratford* 210
Villa Heights, *New Plymouth* 211

Index of Listings (by Regions)

TONGARIRO

Fernleaf Bed & Breakfast,
  Taumarunui 212
Cairnbrae House, *Ohakune* 213
Tussock Grove Bouitque Hotel,
  Ohakune 213
Mountain Heights Lodge,
  National Park 214
Spiral Gardens, *Raurimu* 215
Tarata Fishaway, *Taihape* 216
Mt Huia, *Mangaweka* 217

HAWKES BAY

Reomoana, *Nuhaka* 217
A Room With A View, *Napier* 218
Cobden Garden Homestay,
  Napier 218
Bay Bach, *Napier* 219
Broughton House, *Napier* 219
Maison Béarnaise, *Napier* 220
Mon Logis, *Napier* 220
Kerry Lodge, *Napier* 221
Oceans 63, *Napier* 222
Seaview Lodge, *Napier* 222
Spence Bed & Breakfast, *Napier* 223
The Green House On The Hill,
  Napier 223
Villa Vista – Napier, *Napier* 224
Mission Vista, *Taradale* 225
Touch Th' Tide, *Napier* 226
279 Church Road, *Taradale* 226
Ashcroft Garden Homestay,
  Taradale 227
Greenswood on the Park, *Napier* 228
Omarunui Homestay, *Waiohiki* 228
Waiwhenua Farmstay, *Hastings* 229
Whinfield, *Taradale* 230
The Loft Homestay, *Havelock North* 230

Options, *Havelock North* 231
The Brow, *Waipawa* 232
Otawa Lodge, *Kumeroa-Woodville* 232
Abbotsford Oaks, *Waipawa* 233

WANGANUI

Ashley Park, *Wanganui* 234
Arles Bed & Breakfast, *Wanganui* 234
Kembali, *Wanganui* 235
Misty Valley Farmstay, *Wanganui* 235
Anndion Lodge, *Wanganui* 236
Rothesay, *Hunterville* 237
@Riverhills, *Palmerston North* 238
Larkhall, *Palmerston North* 238
Serendipity Bed & Breakfast, *Levin* 239
Fantails Accommodation, *Levin* 240

WELLINGTON - WAIRARAPA

Driftwood, *Te Horo* 240
Country Patch, *Waikanae* 241
Awatea Lodge, *Waikanae* 242
Helen's Waikanae Beach
  B&B Homestay, *Waikanae* 243
Reikorangi Country Cottage,
  Waikanae 244
Riverstone Lodge, *Waikanae* 244
Ocean Retreat, *Paraparaumu* 245
The Martinborough Connection,
  Martinborough 246
The Vicarage, *Martinborough* 247
Martinborough Experience B & B,
  Martinborough 248
Beach Haven, *Pukerua Bay* 248
Dreamwaters, *Plimmerton* 249
Boating Club Point B&B,
  Plimmerton 250
Aquavilla Seaside Bed & Breakfast,
  Plimmerton 250

Index of Listings (by Regions)

Eirené Retreat, *Upper Hutt* 251

Brentwood Manor, *Upper Hutt* 252

Dungarvin, *Lower Hutt* 253

Paparangi Homestay, *Johnsonville* 254

Devenport Estate, *Korokoro* 254

At the Bay, *Eastbourne* 255

Ngaio Homestay, *Ngaio* 256

Harbour Vista, *Wellington Central* 257

Karori Cottage, *Wellington* 257

Mount Victoria Homestay,
Wellington Central 258

Harbour Lodge Wellington,
Wellington Central 259

Villa Vittorio, *Wellington Central* 260

Lambton Heights Boutique Bed
& Breakfast, *Wellington Central* 261

Homestay at Evans Bay, *Evans Bay* 262

Austinvilla Bed & Breakfast,
Wellington Central 263

Top O' T'ill, *Hataitai* 263

Buckley Homestay, *Melrose* 264

Ma Maison, *Island Bay* 265

Nature's Touch Guest House,
Owhiro Bay 266

GOLDEN BAY – NELSON

Clemmiec Bed & Breakfast,
Collingwood 269

Heron's Rest Bed & Breakfast,
Collingwood 270

Bay Vista House, *Takaka* 271

Beautiful Patons Rock Seaview
Homestay, *Takaka* 272

Garden Retreat Bed & Breakfast,
Takaka 273

Split Ridge, *Abel Tasman Nat. Park* 273

Bayview Bed & Breakfast, *Kaiteriteri* 274

Fraser Highlands, *Abel T. Nat. Park* 274

Bell Bird Lodge, *Kaiteriteri* 275

Kairuru Farmstay, *Takaka Hill* 276

The Resurgence, *Motueka* 277

Centre Ridge Farmstay, *Upper Moutere* .. 278

Lemonade Farm, *Upper Moutere* 278

Larchwood House, *Tasman* 279

Harakeke Lodge, *Upper Moutere* 280

Four Acre Park Accommodation,
Tasman 280

Olives@Mariri Bed & Breakfast,
Tasman 281

Mahana Escape, *Mahana* 282

Wharetutu, *Tasman* 283

Neudorfs Gingerbread House,
Upper Moutere 284

Mapua "Seaview" Bed & Breakfast,
Mapua 284

Accent House, *Mapua* 285

Clayridge House and Cottages,
Ruby Bay 286

Kimeret Place, *Mapua* 287

Tuivale Bed & Breakfast, *Mapua* 288

Felbridge, *Wakefield* 288

Samaki Lodge, *Wakefield* 289

Westleigh, *Brightwater* 289

Idesia, *Richmond* 290

Stafford Place, *Richmond* 291

Arapiki, *Stoke* 292

Sakura Bed & Breakfast, *Stoke* 292

Ambleside Luxury Bed & Breakfast,
Tahunanui 293

Annick House, *Nelson* 294

Shakespeare Cottage, *Nelson* 294

Warwick House, *Nelson Central* 295

Sunset Waterfront Bed & Breakfast,
Nelson Central 296

Sussex House, *Nelson Central* 296

Havenview Homestay, *Nelson* 297

Index of Listings (by Regions)

Atawhai Homestay, *Atawhai* 297

A Culinary Experience, *Atawhai* 298

Parautane Lodge, *Whakapuaka* 299

Avarest Bed & Breakfast, *St. Arnaud* 300

Triple Tui, *Glenhope* 301

Murchison Lodge, *Murchison* 302

MARLBOROUGH

Mudbrick Lodge, *Rai Valley* 303

Pelorus River Horses, *Pelorus Bridge* 304

The Nikaus, *Kenepuru Sound* 304

Ngaio Bay Eco-Homestay & B&B,
Pelorus Sound 305

FernRidge Homestay,
Queen Charlotte Sound 306

Tirimoana House,
Queen Charlotte Sound 307

St Omer House, *Kenepuru Sound* 308

Queensview BnB, *Anakiwa* 308

Sennen House, *Picton* 309

Tanglewood, *Queen Charlotte Sound* 310

Rivenhall, *Picton* 310

A Sea View, *Picton* 311

Charlotte House Bed & Breakfast,
Queen Charlotte Sound, Picton 312

Finlay Grove House, *Waikawa Bay* 312

Vue Pointe, *Picton* 313

Whatamonga Homestay at
Waters Edge, *Picton* 314

Oyster Bay Lodge, *Port Underwood* 315

Koromiko Valley Homestead,
Picton-Blenheim 316

Blue Ridge Estate, *Blenheim* 317

Baxter Bed & Breakfast, *Blenheim* 318

Trotter's Rest, *Blenheim* 318

Artlee House Bed & Breakfast,
Blenheim 319

Green Gables, *Blenheim* 319

Omaka Heights B & B Countrystay,
Blenheim 320

Creekside, *Blenheim* 321

Tamar Vineyard, *Blenheim* 321

Redwood Heights, *Blenheim* 322

Stonehaven Vineyard Homestay,
Blenheim 323

The Stream Estate Cottage,
Blenheim 324

WEST COAST

Beachfront Farmstay, *Karamea* 325

Charming Creek Bed & Breakfast,
Westport 325

River View Lodge, *Westport* 326

Havenlee, *Westport* 327

The Rocks Homestay, *Punakaiki* 327

Birds Ferry Lodge & Ferry Man's
Cottage, *Charleston* 328

Kally House, *Barrytown* 329

Breakers Seaside Bed & Breakfast,
Greymouth 329

Westway Homestay, *Greymouth* 330

Oak Lodge, *Greymouth* 331

Jivana Retreat, *Greymouth* 332

Maryglen Homestay, *Greymouth* 333

Kia Ora Homestay, *Greymouth* 333

Paroa Homestay, *Greymouth* 334

Sunsetview, *Greymouth* 334

Rosewood, *Greymouth* 335

Piners Homestay, *Greymouth* 336

New River Bluegums, *New River* 337

Awatuna Beachside Bed & Breakfast,
Awatuna 337

Awatuna Homestead, *Awatuna* 338

Hokitika Heritage Lodge,
Hokitika 339

Bushline Retreat, Hokitika 340

Teichelmann's Bed & Breakfast,
Hokitika 341

Stopforth Dynasty Homestay,
Hokitika 342

Berwick's Hill, *Ruatapu* 342

Woodland Glen Lodge, *Hokitika* 343

Paramata Lodge, *Ross* 344

Wapiti Park Homestead, *Harihari* 345

Mt Adam Lodge, *Whataroa* 346

Molloy Farmstay, *Harihari* 347

Te Taho Deer Park & Country Stay,
Whataroa 347

Matai Lodge, *Whataroa* 348

Holly Homestead, *Franz Josef* 349

Franz Josef Glacier Country Retreat,
Franz Josef 350

Knightswood Bed & Breakfast,
Franz Josef 351

Franz Josef Alpine Lodge,
Franz Josef 352

Ribbonwood Retreat, *Franz Josef* 353

Fox Glacier Lodge, *Fox Glacier* 354

Ropatini's Homestay B&B,
Fox Glacier 355

Reflection Lodge, *Fox Glacier* 356

The Homestead, *Fox Glacier* 357

The White Fox, *Fox Glacier* 358

Mahitahi Lodge, *Bruce Bay* 359

Okuru Beach Bed & Breakfast,
Haast 359

Collyer House, *Haast* 360

CANTERBURY – CHRISTCHURCH
Awatea Country Bed & Breakfast,
Kaikoura 361

Carrickfin Lodge, *Kaikoura* 361

Ardara Lodge, *Kaikoura* 362

Austin Heights, *Kaikoura* 363

Bendamere House Bed & Breakfast and
Homestay, *Kaikoura* 364

Bush and Sea B&B, *Kaikoura* 365

Churchill Park Lodge, *Kaikoura* 366

Lemon Tree Lodge, *Kaikoura* 366

Endeavour Heights Bed & Breakfast,
Kaikoura 367

Pacific Allure Heights, *Kaikoura* 368

Old Convent Bed & Breakfast,
Kaikoura 369

Mira Monte, *Hanmer Springs* 370

Bellbird Haven, *Waiau* 371

Albergo Hanmer, *Hanmer Springs* 372

Charwell Lodge, *Hanmer Springs* 373

Cheltenham House, *Hanmer Springs* 374

Cheshire House, *Hanmer Springs* 375

Hanmer View Bed & Breakfast,
Hanmer Springs 376

Ballindalloch, *Culverden* 377

Taruna, *Hawarden* 377

Pahau Downs, *Culverden* 378

Bredon Downs, *Amberley* 378

Rossburn, *Rangiora* 379

Hielan House Countrystay Bed &
Breakfast, *Oxford* 379

Chirbury Manor, *Oxford* 380

The Oaks Historic Homestead,
Darfield 381

St James Bed & Breakfast,
Harewood 382

Stableford Airport Bed & Breakfast,
Burnside 382

Belmont on Harewood,
Papanui 383

Russley 302, *Avonhead* 384

230C Glenveagh, *Fendalton* 385

Anselm House, *Fendalton* 386

Ambience on Avon, *Fendalton* 387

Index of Listings (by Regions)

Greatstay, *Riccarton* 388

Leinster Bed & Breakfast, *Merivale* 389

40 Thornycroft Street Bed & Breakfast,
Fendalton 390

Rowan House, *Bryndwr* 390

The Close, *Riccarton* 391

Springfield Cottages, *Central City* 392

Riverview Lodge, *Central City* 393

Home Lea Bed & Breakfast,
Central City 394

Devon Bed & Breakfast Hotel,
Christchurch 395

Hamilton's, *Central City* 396

Central City Bed & Breakfast,
Central City 397

Designer Cottage,
Christchurch Central 397

Eliza's Manor on Bealey, *Christchurch
Central* 398

The Chester, *Central City* 398

The Classic Villa, *Christchurch
Central* 399

Devon on the Park, *Beckenham* 400

Coastal Cliffs Bed & Breakfast,
Redcliffs 401

Seaside Haven, *Southshore* 402

Onuku Bed & Breakfast, *Cashmere* 402

Mt Pleasant Homestay, *Mt Pleasant* 403

Tiromoana, *Sumner* 404

Broad Oaks Vista, *Cashmere* 405

Andaview, *Huntsbury* 406

Pacific View Paradise, *Cashmere* 407

Cedar Park Gardens, *Rolleston* 408

Hazelview, *Lincoln* 408

Huntingdon Grange, *Broadfield* 409

Willersley Cottage, *Halswell* 409

Cedarview Farm B&B, *Templeton* 410

Bergli Hill Farmstay, *Lyttelton* 411

Tintagel House, *Governors Bay* 411

Decanter Bay Homestead 1851,
Banks Peninsula 412

Rosslyn Estate, *Banks Peninsula* 413

Kawatea Farmstay, *Banks Peninsula* 414

Bossu, *Banks Peninsula* 415

Aka-View, *Akaroa* 416

Chez Fleurs, *Akaroa* 417

Penlington Views B&B Akaroa,
Akaroa 418

The Maples, *Akaroa* 418

Garthowen Bed & Breakfast,
Akaroa 419

Lake Coleridge Lodge,
Lake Coleridge 420

Ryton Station, *Lake Coleridge* 421

St Ita's Guest House, *Rakaia* 422

Korobahn Lodge, *Methven-Steveley* 422

Tyrone Deer Farm, *Methven* 423

Green Gables Deer Farm, *Methven* 424

Cricklewood House, *Ashburton* 425

Riverlands Lodge, *Ashburton* 426

The Gardeners Cottage, *Ashburton* 427

Victoria Villa, *Geraldine* 427

The Downs Bed & Breakfast,
Geraldine 428

Ashfield House Bed & Breakfast,
Temuka 429

Blueberry Cottage, *Timaru* 429

Sefton Homestay, *Timaru* 430

Berrillo, *Timaru* 431

Kingsdown Manor, *Timaru* 432

Rivendell Lodge, *Fairlie* 433

Braelea Alpineview Farmstay,
Fairlie 434

Allandale Lodge Bed & Breakfast,
Fairlie 434

Ashgrove, *Fairlie* 435

Index of Listings (by Regions)

SOUTHERN LAKES DISTRICT

Creel House, *Lake Tekapo* 435

Alpine Vista Bed & Breakfast,
 Lake Tekapo 436

Freda Du Faur House, *Lake Tekapo* 437

Tekapo House, *Lake Tekapo* 438

Moonlight Bed & Breakfast,
 Lake Tekapo 439

Lakeview Bed & Breakfast,
 Lake Tekapo 440

Artemis Bed & Breakfast, *Twizel* 440

Gladstone Cottage, *Twizel* 441

Heartland Lodge, *Twizel* 441

Hunters House, *Twizel* 442

Pinegrove Cottage, *Twizel* 442

Bellbird Cottage, *Lake Hawea* 443

Matagouri Cottage, *Lake Hawea* 444

Riversong, *Albert Town* 445

Riverview Terrace, *Albert Town* 446

Ferryman's Cottage (ca. 1870),
 Albert Town 447

Avalanche Bed & Breakfast,
 Wanaka 447

Alpine View Lodge, *Wanaka* 448

Collinsons Cottage, *Wanaka* 449

Hunt's Homestay, *Wanaka* 449

Atherton House, *Wanaka* 450

Beacon Lodge, *Wanaka* 451

Black Peak Lodge, *Wanaka* 452

Beaconfield Bed & Breakfast,
 Wanaka 453

Drummonds on Wanaka, *Wanaka* 454

Peak-Sportchalet, *Wanaka* 455

Stonebrook Bed & Breakfast,
 Wanaka 455

Lake Wanaka Home Hosting,
 Wanaka 456

Minaret Lodge, *Wanaka* 457

Oak Tree Bed & Breakfast, *Wanaka* 458

Renmore House, *Wanaka* 459

Riverside Bed & Breakfast, *Wanaka* 460

Villa Vista – Wanaka, *Wanaka* 461

Wanaka Jewel, *Wanaka* 462

Burn Cottage Retreat, *Cromwell* 463

Dunes Homestay on the 9th,
 Cromwell 464

Antrim Guesthouse, *Cromwell* 465

Lake Dunstan Lodge, *Cromwell* 465

The Orchard House Bed & Breakfast,
 Cromwell 466

Villa Amo on Lake Dunstan,
 Cromwell 467

Walnut Grove, *Cromwell* 468

Stuarts Homestay, *Cromwell* 469

Arrowtown Heights, *Arrowtown* 469

Bernsleigh, *Arrowtown* 470

Willowby Downs, *Queenstown* 470

Old Villa Homestay B&B,
 Arrowtown 471

Willowbrook, *Arrowtown-
 Queenstown* 472

Mt Rosa Lodge, *Queenstown* 473

Riverbank Cottage, *Queenstown* 474

Milestone, *Queenstown* 475

The Turret, *Queenstown* 476

Larch Hill B&B/Homestay,
 Queenstown 477

Lake Vista Bed & Breakfast,
 Queenstown 478

Ferry Hotel B & B Guesthouse,
 Queenstown 479

Kahu Rise, *Queenstown* 480

Crown View, *Queenstown* 481

Tussock Lodge, *Queenstown* 482

The Canyons Country Lodge,
 Queenstown 483

Index of Listings (by Regions)

The Peony Gardens, *Lake Hayes* 483
Anna's Cottage Rose Suite,
    Queenstown 484
5 Star Lane, *Queenstown* 484
Coronet View Deluxe B&B,
    Queenstown 485
The Stable, *Queenstown* 486
Fine Accommodation Queenstown,
    Queenstown 487
Trelawn Place, *Queenstown* 488
Chartlea Park, *Lumsden* 489
Antler Lodge Bed & Breakfast,
    Te Anau 490
Cats Whiskers, *Te Anau* 491
Cosy Kiwi Bed & Breakfast,
    Te Anau 491
Blue Ridge Boutique Bed & Breakfast,
    Te Anau 492
Blue Thistle, *Te Anau* 493
Dunluce Bed & Breakfast, *Te Anau* 494
House of Wood, *Te Anau* 495
Crown Lea Farmstay, *Te Anau* 496
Lynwood Park, *Te Anau* 496
Lochvista, *Te Anau* 497
Te Anau Lodge, *Te Anau* 498
Rob and Nancy's Place, *Te Anau* 499
Rose 'n' Reel Farmstay, *Te Anau* 499
The Croft, *Te Anau* 500
Shakespeare House, *Te Anau* 501
The Cottage – Manapouri,
    Manapouri 501
Cathedral Peaks Bed & Breakfast,
    Manapouri 502

SOUTHERN SOUTH ISLAND
Coral Sea Cottage & Ocean View
    Apartments, *Oamaru* 503
Chimneys Homestay B&B, *Oamaru* 504

Eden Lodge Oamaru, *Oamaru* 505
Highway House, *Oamaru* 505
Totara Park Country Stay, *Oamaru* 506
Ranui Retreat, *Totara* 507
Glen Dendron Farmstay,
    Waianakarua 508
Boutique Bed & Breakfast,
    Waikouaiti 508
Atanui, *Port Chalmers* 509
Leithview, *Dunedin* 510
Highland Peaks, *Chain Hills* 511
Harbourside Bed & Breakfast,
    Dunedin 512
City Sanctuary Bed & Breakfast,
    Dunedin 512
526 George Street Boutique Hotel,
    Dunedin 513
Belmont House, *Dunedin* 514
Heriot House B&B, *Dunedin* 515
Deacons Court, *Dunedin* 516
Grand View, *Dunedin* 516
Hulmes Court, *Dunedin* 517
The Tower House, *Dunedin* 518
Top o' the Glen, *Dunedin* 519
Red Flax B&B, *Dunedin* 519
Porterfields Bed & Breakfast,
    Macandrew Bay 520
Pattons Hill, *Otago Peninsula* 520
Brynymor House, *Otago Peninsula* 521
Harbour Lights Bed & Breakfast,
    Macandrew Bay 522
Broad Bay White House, *Broad Bay* 523
Chy-an-Dowr, *Broad Bay* 524
Arts Content B&B, *Company Bay* 525
Crabapple Cottage, *Portobello* 525
Fantail Lodge, *Broad Bay* 526
The Cottage - Broad Bay,
    Broad Bay 527

Index of Listings (by Regions)

The Lodge - Broad Bay, *Broad Bay* 528

Captain Eady's Lookout, *Portobello* 529

Conehenge Homestead, *Portobello* 530

McAuley Glen Bed & Breakfast,

    Portobello 531

Rugosa Cottage, *Portobello* 532

Kaimata Retreat,

    Portobello-Cape Saunders 533

Argyll Farmstay, *Balclutha* 534

Lesmahagow, *Balclutha* 535

Cardno's Accommodation, *Catlins* 535

Kepplestone by the Sea, *Catlins* 536

Curio Bay Boutique Accommodation,

    Tokanui 537

Greenbush Bed & Breakfast, *Catlins* 538

Fortrose Retreat, *Fortrose* 539

Waterside Waikawa, *Waikawa* 539

Smith's Farmstay, *Wyndham* 540

The Manor, *Invercargill* 541

84 on King, *Invercargill* 542

Glenroy Park Homestay, *Invercargill* 543

Victoria Railway Hotel, *Invercargill* 543

Sails Ashore, *Stewart Island* 544

www.phototrips.info

Index of Locations

A
	PAGE
Abel Tasman Nat. Park	273-274
Acacia Bay	189, 192
Ahipara	26, 29
Akaroa	416-419
Albany	89
Albert Town	445-447
Amberley	378
Anaura Bay	203
Arrowtown	469-472
Ashburton	425-427
Atawhai	297-298
AUCKLAND	80-116
Awatuna	337-338

B
	PAGE
Balclutha	534-535
Banks Peninsula	412-415
Bay of Islands	31-61
Barrytown	329
Blenheim	316-324
Bombay	116
Broad Bay	523-528
Browns Bay	90
Bruce Bay	359

C
	PAGE
Cambridge	148-150
Cape Foulwind	325-327
Cashmere	402, 405, 407
Catlins	535-539
Chain Hills	511
Charleston	328
CHRISTCHURCH	382-411
Coromandel Town	121-123
Cromwell	463-469
Culverden	377-378

D
	PAGE
Darfield	381
Dargaville	69-70
Drury	113
DUNEDIN	509-533

E
	PAGE
Eastbourne	255
Epsom	105
Evans Bay	262

F
	PAGE
Fairlie	433-435
Fendalton	385-387, 390
Fortrose	537-539
Fox Glacier	354-358
Franz Josef Glacier	349-353

G
	PAGE
Geraldine	427-428
Gisborne	204-205
Glenhope	301
Greymouth	329-337

H
	PAGE
Haast	359-360
Hahei	133
Half Moon Bay	544
Hamilton	141-144
Hanmer Springs	370-376
Harihari	345-348
Hastings	229
Havelock North	230-231
Hawarden	377
Helensville	88
Hillcrest	92
Hobsonville	94
Hokitika	339-343
Houhora	24
Howick	108-109
Hunterville	237
Huntly	140

I
	PAGE
Invercargill	541-543

J
	PAGE
Johnsonville	254

Index of Locations

K

	PAGE
Kaikohe	62
Kaikoura	362-369
Kaitaia	25, 27-28
Kaiteriteri	274-275
Kapiti Coast	240-244
Karamea	325
Katikati	150-152, 154
Kaukapakapa	86-87
Kawau Island	75
Kerikeri	31-38
Kuaotunu	124-125
Kumeroa-Woodville	232
Kumeu	93

L

Lake Coleridge	420-421
Lake Hawea	443-444
Lake Hayes	483
Lake Karapiro	149
Lake Tekapo	435-440
Levin	239-240
Lincoln	408
Lower Hutt	253
Lumsden	489
Lyttelton	411

M

Mahana	282
Mahia Peninsula	217
Manapouri	501-502
Mangatarata	117
Mangawhai Heads	72
Manukau	110-115
Mapua	287-288
Martinborough	246-248
Matakohe	74
Methven	422-424
Mosgiel	511
Motueka	273-277
Mt Cook	440-442
Mt Lyford	371

	PAGE
Mt Maunganui	153-158
Murchison	302

N

Napier	218-228
National Park	214-215
Nelson	289-299
Nelson Lakes	300
New Plymouth	206-211
Ngongotaha	176-181
Northcote Point	91
Nuhaka	217

O

Oamaru	503-507
Omori	202-203
Ohakune	213
Opua	49-53
Orakei	98
Otago Peninsula	519-528
Otorohanga	146
Owaka	535-536
Oxford	379-380

P

Paihia	39-48
Palmerston North	238
Papamoa	156
Paraparaumu	245
Parnell	97, 103
Pelorus Bridge	304-305
Picton	304-316
Plimmerton	249-250
Ponsonby	98-100
Port Chalmers	509
Port Underwood	315
Portobello	525, 529-533
Puhoi	79
Pukerua Bay	248
Punakaiki	327

Index of Locations

Q

	PAGE
Queenstown	470-488

R

	PAGE
Rai Valley	303
Rakaia	422
Ramarama	114
Rangiora	379
Raukapakapa	87
Remuera	104-107
Riccarton	388, 391
Ross	344
Rotorua	162-183
Ruby Bay	286
Russell	54-61

S

Silverdale	86
Southshore	402
St Arnaud	300
Staveley	422
Stewart Island	544
Stoke	292
Stratford	212
Swanson	95

T

Tahunanui	293
Taihape	216-217
Takaka	269-273, 276
Taradale	225-227, 230
Tasman	279-283
Taumarunui	212
Tamaterau	65
Taupo	184-198
Tauranga	153-158
Te Anau	490-501
Te Awamutu	144
Te Haumi	52
Te Horo	240
Te Kauwhata	139
Te Kuiti	147
Te Puru	121

	PAGE
Temuka	429
Thames	118-120
Timaru	429-432
Turangi	199-202
Twizel	440-442

U

Upper Hutt	251-252
Upper Moutere	278-280, 284

W

Waianakarua	508
Waiau	371
Waihi	137-138
Waikanae	241-244
Waikawa	537, 539
Waikawa Bay	312
Waikouaiti	508
Waipawa	232-233
Waipu	71
Waipu Cove	71, 73
Waitomo Caves	145
Waiuku	114
Wakefield	288-289
Wanaka	447-462
Wanganui	234-236
Warkworth	76-78
WELLINGTON	245-266
Western Spring	96-97
Westport	325-327
Whakatane	158-161
Whangamata	135-136
Whangaparaoa	80-86
Whangarei	63-68
Whitianga	126-134
Woodville	232
Wyndham	540

Comments

Uli and Brian Newman at TRAVELwise would appreciate
your comments, favourable or otherwise.
Your ideas and suggestions will be used to further develop
the Charming Places to Stay guide.
So please, don't hesitate to send us your ideas, suggestions,
complaints or compliments.

_____

_____

_____

_____

_____

_____

_____

_____

_____

_____

_____

_____

_____

_____

TRAVELwise Ltd.